THE ART OF DARKNESS –

THE ART OF DARKNESS - THE HISTORY OF GOTH

JOHN ROBB

Editors: Kate Cherrell, Naomi Dryden-Smith, Jennifer Barber. Paul Woods

Additional content: Paul Woods

Back Cover Illustration: Iman Kazai-Hazell from a photograph by John Middleham

Cover Design: Richard Baldwin

Photos Courtesy of: Mick Mercer - mickmercer.com

Transcriptions: Nadine Large

Thanks to Maria Cosgrove

JOHN ROBB is a multi-faceted creature of the night and day. He runs the Louder Than War website, is the founder and bassist of UK post-punk band Membranes, has written the best selling book, 'Punk Rock - An Oral History', has created the eco-education scheme Green Britain Academy and runs the Louder Than Words literary festival..

Website: johnrobbofficial.com
Twitter: johnrobb77
Instagram: johnrobb77
Facebook: johnrobbofficial

CONTENTS

Introduction

THE DOORS ARE OPEN...

Mad, bad and dangerous to know, The art of darkness has been with us for centuries because every generation has got to deal with its blues. What was once expressed in art, architecture, Romantic literature and painting was, in the post-punk wars, a cimmerian alternative culture creating its own dark narrative whilst accelerating away from the Big Bang of punk. It was a thrilling time when music soundtracked the style, and a culture coalesced from a bricolage of black.

What was then called 'goth', after the fact, was defined by those unholy twin trinities of British pop culture: music, clothes and the dance floor with an added twist of stygian sex, style and subversion.

Of course, none of the bands were 'goth', and of course, everyone hated the term because it compressed a nuanced and fascinating journey full of groundbreaking musical and stylistic ideas into a simple cliché that this book will unpack.

Yet, there was a definable culture with a shadowy sartorial style, and a soundtrack to match that was reacting to those dystopian post industrial times. The disparate bands that were painting it black had a melancholy, a sense of theatre, and an artful sensuality to their styles. They somehow married those moods to a post-punk skreegh and to the pulsating dance floor, embracing funk, disco and dub. They were the true answer to punk's questions, and many have become 21st century legends whilst others are highly influential footnotes. We celebrate them all, here, in their own chapters like they are a playlist from a trad goth club dance floor from the scene's glorious tenebrous birth.

The book also goes further back, starting with the fall of Rome which was sacked by the original Goths. Then it threads its way through shadowy folk tales, ghost stories, Gothic architecture and the literature of 'turn the centuries turn' and finally settles down, deep in the dark heart of the forest of pop culture, with the first band to be called gothic, The Doors.

It then cavorts like Pan and his wild eyed followers to the life-changing adventures of glam and punk's culture war, and arrives at the crucial post-punk period in a scene that was loosely called 'alternative' and was then retrospectively termed 'goth' which annoyed everyone.

What was once underground is now mainstream. In the 21st century, culture/dystopia is everywhere, from the news to Instagram influencers, goth gaming, goth-influenced novels, films and music. TV series *Wednesday* is just the latest populist cathode ray incarnation of all things goth, opening up the doors, yet again, to the attractive melancholy lurking all around us.

The book looks at why goth happened, and where, and when, and how, before dancing the dystopian dance with a soundtrack to an idiosyncratic and crucial culture that risked life and limb to dress to thrill and then somehow becoming all-pervading in the modern world.

Join me for a deep dive into the dark matter. Let me take you down to the gothic hinterland where we can submerge ourselves in the delicious dark energy and take a walk on the dark side, and dance, dance, dance to the diablo darkness...

Chapter 1

FLOORSHOW: A NIGHT OUT

In a forgotten town on a long-lost evening of melancholic weather, pointed shoe heels and combat boots clacked the damp pavement as the cobbles were transformed into catwalks. Defiant hair was piled high above the fifty shades of black gothic garments covered by huge coats hiding the exotic, erotic, clothes beneath. Sheltered from the damp night time cold and the scavenging beer-stained bullies, the goth couple clattered through the post-industrial backdrop. Fortified by the pre-club ritual of bedsit booze and their empowering sartorial armour, they jangled with jewellery and expectation.

Arriving at their subterranean lair, they descended the stairs and submerged into the dark decibels. A couple of beauteous freaks sat behind a table and collected the 50p door tax from them before they entered the smoky, pulsating labyrinth. The club's name was daubed in cheap red and black paint on a wall that was stained with nicotine and an encroaching damp. There were dole office strip lights on the ceiling, and a pulsating death disco was cranked through the PA enveloping a room full of walking works of art, sex beat cadavers and goth pioneers.

It was the late seventies/early eighties, in what was then called an 'alternative club'[1] and across Britain's towns and cities, a murder of gothic crows would flock to these interzones for the weekend adventure.

The room stank of snakebite[2], stale cigarettes and mould, and the hatchet-faced bar staff looked as though they would rather be anywhere else. Punters sipped vodka, or Pernod and black (black for goth!) and the stench of poppers hung in the air and set the heart racing.[3] There was also some speed, which made you drink twice as much as usual, and dance even more. It also drove spittle-flecked conversations about music, clothes, post-punk politics, the occult or sex.

The atmosphere was dusky, dark, dangerous and fun.

The boys were in the girls' toilets doing their hair, while the girls were in the boys' toilets trying to avoid the cubicle queue. The air was thick with the acrid scent of singed hair, crimper-burnt at the root, sticky with the toxic support of Elnett, Aqua Net and Insette hairspray (extra hold, of course) or, simpler still, just soap rubbed in over layers of black hair dye and coaxed sky-high with frantic follicle-splitting backcombing.

---

1 The term 'goth' had yet to be coined, either in cultural salute or mockery.

2 Snakebite was almost de rigueur. It was a mixture of lager and cider, sometimes dashed off with blackcurrant cordial for sweetness or even a shot of Pernod. It was a quixotic mix that tasted sweet and quickly degraded the senses, and because of its potency was often rumoured to be illegal.

3 'Poppers' is a slang term for amyl nitrate. When sniffed, it induces a throbbing rush of dizziness, warm sensations and, if you're lucky, euphoria. The drug also has a relaxing effect on the smooth muscles of the throat and anus, making it a popular sexual enhancer, particularly in gay clubs.

Once truly ready, they then exploded onto the dance floor in a monochromatic blur of black clothes and pallid flesh. The pre-club bedsit ritual had already prepared the gothic gladiators well with a loud crowd crammed into the small flat, exchanging styles and clothes along to a cranked Dansette of post-punk and alternative music crackling through the cheap speakers. This was the weekly warm up of swigging vodka and teasing hair whilst swapping tops, makeup and catty catwalk comments as they stained fingers and towels with hair dye and hope.

The preparations were wild and noisy. Hair and hair gunge products were burned onto crimpers that were then cooled down and pushed back into black handbags. The sides of skulls were shaved with Bic razors or handheld hair clippers as post-punk Mohicans and Mohawks prepared to dance the tribal dance.

As Shakespeare had once observed, the soul of a person comes in their clothes, and the apparel often proclaims that person whilst the appurtenance of welcome is fashion and ceremony - of course, the proto-goths knew this. Instinctively. The sartorial code of trad goth[4] was set to 'dress to kill/dressed to thrill' with a dark sensibility spectacular.

Once in the club, the parliament of gothic rooks resonated and flapped in the smoky room in their trench coats, long macs, paisley shirts, leather jackets and the tangled layers of black clothing that hung over pointed winkle-pickers, ubiquitous Dr. Martens, army boots, pixie boots, multi buckled pike boots, all manner of army and navy store footwear, and even some clogs.

In the cheap dry ice and the gender blur, there was a mix of DIY clothes tailored and personalised that combined with accessorises. Detail was everything, with multiple chains, intricate jewels, layered clothing, chunky rings, heavy studded belts and wristbands and sometimes even ornate Indian jewellery.

There were fingerless gloves, army pants, fishnet tights and fishnet tops that were often carefully ripped. There was velvet, satin, leather, abundant lace and a hint of PVC and latex, in a nod to the overlap with punk and BDSM styles.

This was all topped off with a smattering of bleached hair, dyed hair, occasional tattoos, foundation-enhanced white skin with an elaborate makeup of delicious dark lips smeared with purple or black lipstick. There was thick eyeliner and lurid blusher to highlight and sharpen cheekbones, Siouxsie/Cleopatra-kohl eyes and, everywhere, the rattle of crucifixes, beads, and bone necklaces could be heard. There were many variations on many themes - sub-genres within genres, styles within styles. There were punks, goths and even a few of the long Mac/raincoat brigade still looking for their alternative fix, and a furtive clutch of Oxfam second-hand suits crowned with Eraserhead hair. Some wore black skinny jeans, if they could be found in the all too rare alternative clothes shops.

At a time when jewellers often refused to pierce men's ears, earlobes were self-punctured with a compass 'sterilised' in boiling water and pushed through the lobe onto a piece of waiting cork. This was typical of the element of DIY or die of the

---

4 21st century term for the goth pioneers.

style, as the goth shops, like the X Clothes chain across the north of England, were yet to open, and trips to London's exotic markets were rare.

Clothes mattered, with sartorial styles as extreme as the music. This was androgyny and angst on the dole with an added walk on the dark side. A new aesthetic was being forged that married the sensuality of the dance floor to an embrace of sex and death - the twin peaks of goth fascination.

Voluptuous, voluminous and vibrant in black the vampires were vamping it up. Dressed up or dressed down, there was a confusion of styles from road warrior chicken dancers to the frozen Ice Queens with their antique, mystery wardrobes and exotica hair... It could be dressed up or dressed down, unisex, polysex or middlesex, as anything goes in the sex and death show. It was sometimes genderless, sometimes gender-full and sometimes the gender was pumped to the max and always with the borders as blurred as their mascara.

All this black peacocking was now exposed, finally free from the enormous coats now clogging up the cloakroom. Coats that provided protection against the non-stop rain and the cold last bus journey home. They were also armour and a disguise from the accompanying catcalls, beatings and abuse from disbelieving strangers or the fist-clenching Tetley Bittermen on those journeys in and out of town.

After punk's amphetamine psychosis, sex was now back on the agenda. The speed-driven squelch of punk sex was now far more erotic. Taking its lead from the more fetish-clad punks, goth took sex out of the closet and into the suburbs. More overtly, it paraded its fetishism in the clubs and took it back home to the boudoir for a shivering bedsit shag next to the whirring fan heater. Gothic sexuality was fluid by definition and also in practice. The borders were often as blurred as the genders, and visual fetishes were a staple. Rubber wear was normalised, with some costumes handmade and others obtained from backstreet London shops or niche mail-order catalogues.

Goth introduced new alternatives to traditional propriety. Parts of the new scene became a celebration of non-traditional sex and gender blur, both in look and in practice, with S&M and fetish aesthetics becoming another strand.

Goth, the scene that 'oft dare not speak its name', was not only defined by the music but also by its style and there were many disparate elements in that volatile mix: The 'wham bam thank you, ma'am', of prime time glam, B movies, kitsch and camp art; the trash aesthetic; sixties psychedelia; the Romantic poets of the early 19th century; the decadent iconoclasts of the *fin de siecle*. There were artful takes on Dada, fine art and period *haute couture*; a fascination with Neo-Victorianism and funerals, decadent 1920s Berlin and the contemporary urban hell of New York – and, of course, a large dose of punk aesthetic and the dandyish androgyny inspired by Bowie, Bolan and the whole glam rock canon.

Early role models like Siouxsie Sioux – with her teased hair, fishnets and fiercely indomitable spirit – influenced a whole generation of Medusa-like young women and some more daring men. Other early sartorial inspirations would soon include The Cramps' freakishly exotic guitar player Bryan Gregory, with his animal-bone necklaces, Dave Vanian's gravedigger cool, Southern Death Cult's homespun ethnic exotica, Bauhaus' dark glam and the raggedy *Struwwelpeter* bohemian Byron that was Nick Cave of The Birthday Party plus a whole plethora of individual looks.

There was a power to the dressing.

The women could be voluptuous but very much in control, giving off the powerful aura of look but don't touch.

> Most goth women's experiences suggest that they derived a sense of empowerment from their clothing, and it isn't for me to suggest otherwise. I think it's really complex. There's an article in *Goth: Undead Subculture*, by Joshua Gunn, which looks at how androgyny is often practised by men, but seldom by women, on the scene. This also intersects with the LGBTQ+ scene. But if we are talking gender-bending, the models of womanhood aren't always that challenging – fetish wear (PVC, latex, big dom boots etc) equals the stereotype of the femme fatale – sexualised, objectified, male fantasy etc. The evolution of the Victorian-influenced goth – big skirts, long hair, narrow waist, big bust, is often a very passive image. I think the challenging aspect was always how far these stereotypes could be adapted and reconfigured.[5]

Perhaps it's the corsets dotted around the club that somehow defined all the inherent yet thrilling contradictions in the style.

The corset was always an unstable signifier and meant different things at different times. Historically, it was all about regulating women's unruly bodies, and yes, men wore corsets too, but this was less common, and the most prominent examples relate to fetish. The adverts from the 19th century for corsetry are hilarious – they have a rhetoric of 'health' attached to them. But they were basically about constricting women's bodies and shaping them for the male gaze. That said, Victorian women also used them in challenging ways – they had been used to induce miscarriage for unwanted pregnancies, and performers, like the British Blondes burlesque troupe, used corsets on stage – which meant they were exposing in public what would only be conventionally for the sight of one's husband in the marital bedroom. Similarly, the fetish/punk appropriation of corsets does something slightly different to its original history – underwear as outerwear, and constriction as a fetish experience. However, this can also be co-opted back around to normative ideas of femininity.[6]

Whilst the women were playing with style and giving off their own complex messages and codes, the men were also blurring their own borders.

> I suppose it always depended on the type of male goth – there were always loads of different sartorial styles. Certainly, the scene always espoused non-normative ideas about masculinity – the eyeliner and nail polish, the long hair, the ability to wear skirts as club wear, There was always an element of gender-bending, but there was also the model of the edgy Byronic hero who is actually quite masculine, despite his obvious emotional sensitivity – dark, moody, mysterious, a man with a secret, a bit dangerous, liable to break your heart or turn into a vampire! Obviously, this has a long tradition in literature (Heathcliff, Byron, Shelley, Werther, Manfred),

---

5 Prof Claire Nally (Northumbria University) to John Robb.

6 Prof Claire Nally (Northumbria University) to John Robb.

but it also maps onto a sartorial code of excess – the frilly shirts and frock coats, the impracticality of this as everyday wear. It's also interesting in class terms – historically, these are the clothes of the *gentleman,* although in this case, it's clearly more of the *dark gentleman* than anything else! I think Anne Rice has a lot to answer for here! Dave Vanian would be a good example on the scene of this look. Then there's Eldritch and his biker jacket, or Carl McCoy with the cowboy hat and the rock n roll scene.[7]

*****

Wardrobe/drink/drugs sorted?

To the dance floor! The music was pounding. The new bands embraced by the scene were moving beyond punk, all armed with strangely saturnine names like Southern Death Cult, Sex Gang Children, Bauhaus, and The Sisters of Mercy. The goth sound was truly a mix of dark aesthetics, early electronica, new tech, post-punk experimentalism and a dark disco with an industrial groove. The incoming tech was moving music beyond punk's obsession with the rudimentary and the Year Zero. It was time to fast forward to the future, and new production techniques, new guitar pedals, drum machines[8] and keyboards were added to the palette of possibilities.

Black music was a key influence as goth embraced the rhythms and the nuance of the sensuality and space of black dance music. Soul and disco had been seen by some punks as an antithesis to 'real music', but many goth musicians assimilated disco's feline, flexible beat and funk's groin exchange groove into their music. Scene forerunners such as Siouxsie Sioux were fans of disco, while The Sisters of Mercy would cover Hot Chocolate's mournful soul-pop ballad 'Emma' in a deadpan celebration. Black music was entwined with a dark energy that filled the dance floor with a curious mixture of darkness and delight, feeling the beat and the bite[9].

There was a funk and disco undercarriage to Killing Joke, whose tribal beat was inflected with occultic lyrics and intense warnings about the end of times. Their 'Follow the Leaders' was an avalanche of sound, a punk disco anthem and electro-chant that mashed Donna Summer with the apocalypse. The Sisters of Mercy's glacial 'Alice' was a regular addition to a great dance floor soundtrack that shackled the clipped neo-disco grooves of the drum machine with a melancholic surge.

Bauhaus were scene favourites who had appropriated a dark form of dub on their genre-defining debut single, 'Bela Lugosi's Dead.' Adam and the Ants' 'Kings of the Wild Frontier', with its Burundi drumming, was a gateway release for many future goths with those tribal beats and glam rock dark thunder. The track was already a club favourite after a rogue pressing was played weeks before it was commercially released. Everyone had heard that Adam had 'gone pop', but no one had expected

---

7 Prof Claire Nally (Northumbria University) to John Robb.

8 Drum machines had been around since 1930 in one form or another. The first pop hit to use one was Robin Gibb's 'Saved By The Bell' and also Sly and the Family Stone's 'There's a Riot Goin' On' in 1971.

9 From The Sisters of Mercy's classic track 'Floorshow' - musically and lyrically the perfect summation of dancing to the new dark beats.

this: a magnificently mad mesh of tribal drums and glam rock power chords. The early Adam had been a music press untouchable with baffled writers backing off from his black and white face paint intensity, acting out his darkly decadent fantasies. The original 'Ant music for sex people' was made up of catchy songs of pain and perversion, set to clanging punk guitar shackled to the off-kilter disco drumming of a young Dave Barbe.

As the night progressed, a speaker oozed out the proto-techno goth of Alien Sex Fiend's 12-inch 'Ignore the Machine', a devilish slice of pre-techno electronica disco wonk throb that went on to become an influence on future goth and alternative artists. There was also an eclectic bunch of sounds that embraced Spear of Destiny's 'Liberator', a thrilling post-punk anthem that encouraged chicken-dancing flat-top boys to thrash their elbows into each other.[10] It would be swiftly followed by a cascade of dirty feedback and primitive drums from rockabilly grave keepers The Cramps and their spooked 'Human Fly'.

'A Forest' by The Cure was a hypnotic journey into the shadows that felt like it could last forever whilst The Birthday Party's 'Release the Bats', with its florid poetry and kinetic guitar skreegh, sounded so perfect for this brave new world that it seemed like it had been written for these very dance floors, while the imperious Siouxsie swooned and preened like the ice queen of the scene with one of her many anthems of post-psychedelic kaleidoscope sound. Next up was Southern Death Cult's 'Fatman', a mystical pounding, Native American-inspired mantra from a new northern band.

Added to the mix were non-gothic curveballs like the odd Fall track or Donna Summer's 'I Feel Love'. Bolan, Bowie, Iggy and Roxy were perennially popular, an unspoken nod to the glam gods that were precursors to goth, whilst Gary Numan, the Bowie replica in black, went down well with the couple of Numanoids in the room.

For the more daring, there were also the outré left-field sounds from exotic names like Laibach, an industrial band from Slovenia, who later layered their harshness with neoclassical passages and a controversial thought-provoking artfulness.[11] Then there was Virgin Prunes, a brilliant auditory freak show from Dublin, challenging the stuffy morality of their home country with material ranging from the French *chansonnier* tradition to sequenced drones. A daring DJ could triumph by adding maverick tracks like Grace Jones' icy pop pioneering *sprechgesang* over her dub funk minimalist take on Iggy Pop's 'Nightclubbing' – or, at the other end of the spectrum, Xmal Deutschland's 'Incubus Succubus', if the mood was right.

If German industrialists Einstürzende Neubauten or Australian mavericks SPK didn't quite fill the floor, they induced head-nodding with their metal percussion and clattering, claustrophobic sound. Neubauten took the found sound metallic

---

10 'Chicken dancing' was flapping your elbows up and down like chicken wings. It inevitably led to the occasional fight.

11 Were they serious? Who knew? Their intellectual incitement played with images and fire to make their anti-totalitarian statements. A series of Laibach covers, starting with the Stones' 'Sympathy for the Devil', made them into paradoxically unique *pasticheurs*.

textures and added human elements like Blixa Bargeld's sinister baritone whisper and terrifying inward scream.

The music was intense, powerful, and sometimes melancholic but never dour. Most importantly, you could move to it. Amid the dole culture of Thatcher's Britain and the broken post-industrial cityscapes, the clubs and the dressing up black enabled good times on a shoestring budget with an attractive dark aesthetic.

*****

Defying the broken heartland of the post-industrial cities, the semi-forgotten satellite towns and the grim real politic of the Thatcher years, there was a network of clubs full of the dark dance, a brand new beat spreading across the country with their late-night floorshows. Nightclubbing was the beating heart of goth. It defied its graveyard ethos of being a darkly subversive strand of pop culture by dancing.

The audience was now the dark star!

In the post-Warhol age, flamboyance could make anyone a player, and in this alternative future, everyone would be famous for 15 minutes[12] or, at least, four songs in a goth club, dancing in the 'violent hour to the violent sound'.

Post-war pop culture had always had an enticing cimmerian[13] flavour, and goth seemed to arrive by symbiosis as a logical escape from punk. North v South. Leeds v London. It was a convergent evolution. Much of the scene, as we know it, evolved in places like Bradford, Northampton, Wakefield or Crawley: satellite towns, mill towns, dead towns. It was in these unlikely landscapes that the goth aesthetic began to thrive.

These towns took their cues from the patchwork of mid-seventies Bowie/Roxy nights in the big cities and the pioneering alternative/goth clubs like the Phono in Leeds and The Batcave in London[14]. Soon everywhere would have its own goth night. Every town and city would have at least one 'alternative' club years before they were called 'goth' clubs. Safe havens where the freaks could come out to play. All over the UK, in the most unlikely nooks and crannies, a whole new network of clubs emerged, driving the culture forward.

Liverpool's sartorial scene flamboyance was initially celebrated in Eric's and in gay clubs such as Jody's, providing a safe space for the proto-goth scene. The city then had its own goth club, the legendary Planet X, which was named by Paul Rutherford from Frankie Goes to Hollywood, and was opened in 1993 by the indefatigable Doreen Allen, who'd been a central player in Liverpool's alternative culture since the '60s. 'Planet X was truly subterranean – you went downstairs into this lair which played dark, electronic, cold music,' remembers DJ Marc Jones, adding, 'It was

---

12 Andy Warhol's original quotation was 'In the future, everyone will be world-famous for 15 minutes.'

13 'Cimmerian' not in any geohistorical sense, but in the sense of those mythical people dwelled in fog and shadow.

14 The first goth club in London was Beasts, opening Feb 14th, 1981 on Carnaby Street.

mixing the hard edge attitude of punk but with the key technology of electronica, early synthesisers and also tribal drum beats to create a whole new atmosphere.'

Manchester already had Pips, which was open from 1972 to 1978, with its most influential DJ being the late Dave Booth.

> It was a subterranean set of cellars, where each scene had its own room. Before punk, in the mid-'70s, the Roxy room played Bowie and Roxy Music and those nights were where it all started. By post-punk, it had become the main alternative club in town that birthed the local goth culture. Unfortunately, Pips closed just before all these other clubs opened, but it was where all the early bands that influenced the goth scene played. Joy Division did their debut gig there[15]. They were actually billed as Warsaw, but they changed their name on the night. There should be a blue plaque for that gig alone!'[16]

Post-punk Manchester was full of new nights. Across town, Devilles was filled with big hair that twitched along to the likes of The Cure's 'A Forest', while Cloud 9's post-punk fusion mixed early psychobilly with Adam and the Ants before they became pirates. The 1980-85 period saw The Berlin Club, famed for its camo netting, dry ice and constant playing of The Sisters, Sex Gang Children, The Birthday Party and Southern Death Cult. There was also Placemate 7, Blood Club, Monday night at The Ritz, Legend - with its alternative Thursday nights. The Playpen, The Banshee – all were key to the new cultural frontier.

---

15 January 25th, 1978.

16 Dave Booth to John Robb.

At eighteen years old, future Smiths guitarist Johnny Marr was a junior freak experiencing the power of these new club nights in Manchester – Legend in particular. As well as being a lifelong expert on music culture, Johnny used to manage Aladdin's Cave, a goth/alternative clothes shop in Manchester, from 1981-82 until The Smiths got signed. [17]

Legend was a good place to go and to derail your senses. They had the most amazing lights and a great sound system. Thursday nights was the new music night and after drinking vodka and orange, and loads of beer – by half one in the morning, you would dance to Iggy Pop's 'The Passenger' and then sing along to The Cure, PiL and Adam Ant.

And there was always Bowie.

No Bowie – no scene.

In the clubs, we were free of the music press, and it was amazing. The music was under the radar and out of the understanding of a lot of the rock writers at the time. Music journalists like Nick Kent would have had no idea about what these kids were dancing to. It was not just goth but the new pop in the clubs. For me and my friends, this new club world was not just personally throwing off the shackles of classic rock but also punk rock, which had been rammed down your throat by an older generation.[18]

As ever, it was in the United Kingdom, driven by its innate dandy nature and the vacuum of post-industrial cities, that a powerhouse of post-punk culture tribes had

---

17 If The Phono in Leeds and The Batcave in London were the instigators (more on this in Chapter 19) then they had willing displays across the nation. In Blackpool, The 007 Club (owned by ex-boxer Brian London, who fought Muhammad Ali in 1966) had a goth and post-punk Saturday night, until it moved to the grotty but much-loved Your Father's Moustache club near the bus station. Deeper into Lancashire there was Colne Franks, where floor-fillers ranged from The Velvet Underground to Bauhaus' 'Lagartija Nick' – which, according to locals, went down a storm after a massive sniff of poppers. Preston had its famous Warehouse, with regular alternative club nights at weekends, where Joy Division had played a legendary early gig. There was also a goth night at Clouds and at Park Hall on Sundays. Further up the road was The Sugar House in Lancaster and The Peppermint Lounge in Warrington. Blackburn had The Castle, Oldham had The Hurricane Club, while Wigan Pier went goth on Wednesdays and Southport Sandbaggers likewise on Fridays. Burnley had goth nights at Angels and Whiskers and there was even one in Accrington at The Miners WMC.

Back in Yorkshire which had started the whole thing with Le Phono in Leeds, it was now in the satellite towns with the arrival of Huddersfield's Charlies, Keighley's Funhouse, and Wakefield's Raffles and Xlusiv. In Hull, there was Spiders and Silhouette; York had The Roxy; in Sheffield, there was The Limit on Thursdays, the monthly SinBin at Turnups, Astral Flight Embassy club, Batfink and Romeo And Juliet's (where New Order had played a very early gig).

Further north there was the small room at the Mayfair in Newcastle and Blaises in Middlesbrough. Even a place like Redcar could boast two goth nights, at The Sandpiper and The Bulldog. Also in Carlisle, there was the gothically damp and dingy Twisted Wheel.

In Birmingham, there was Steptoes, Zigzag and The Tin Can, where Southern Death Cult, Play Dead, Alien Sex Fiend, Shakin' Pyramids, Xmal Deutschland, Balaam and the Angel, Theatre of Hate and The March Violets all played live. Chesterfield had Gotham City; downstairs at The Garage in Nottingham with noisier left-field sounds like Big Black. Just up the road was the Retford Porterhouse, while Stoke had Chicos and Cannock had Stamps. Further south was Juicy Lucies in Corby, while nearby Luton had The Switch Club – named after the Banshees song.

The deep south had The Crypt in Hastings, The Basement and Sister Ray in Brighton and Weston-Super-Mare had the legendary Hobbits. The Underground/Nightline rolled along in Bath, while Bristol boasted The Whip and Cardiff, The Square Club.

Post-Batcave, London had seen the dawn of many new goth nights, including The Kit-Kat Club in Westbourne Grove, Full Tilt at The Electric Ballroom, Catacombs at Manor House, The Underground in Croydon and eventually Slimelight in Islington. They all operated in a city where, at one time, you could find a goth night seven nights a week.

Beyond England, there was The Bistro in Rhyl, North Wales; in Scotland, Nightmoves ran in Glasgow from 1980 to 1984, while Madisons and The Banshee thrived amid the Gothic atmosphere of Edinburgh.

Thanks to a pre-internet spider's web of information, the culture was everywhere. Every small town had its goth outpost, its subterranean lair, and its safe house for outsiders.

18 Johnny Marr to John Robb.

emerged, including a distinctly dark subculture. The British streets had always been a breeding ground for international style creating an English civil style war that saw the other youth tribes – Teddy Boys, skinheads, punks, metal heads, rockabillies and psychobillies – fighting pitched battles. Goths though, preferred to dress up, read, think, fuck and dance; these new creatures of the night came alive on the dance floor.

And yet this was no modern dance.

The embrace of the dark and the gothic had been with us for millennia.

For an eternity, humans have loved the dark, shivery tales, melancholic music and a walk on the dark side. Over the centuries, gothic had meant so many different things to so many different people. From the mad, bad and dangerous to know poets to visionary painters and medieval architects bucking the classical trend.

Goth had imbued dark art, music and ideas for an eternity, from when the original goths - a fierce Germanic tribe had sacked Rome in 410…and this is where our story starts.

Chapter 2

THE FALL OF ROME

On August 24, 410 AD, the heart of the Roman Empire was fatally breached. On that late summer night, the eastern Germanic tribes massed outside Rome, the self-styled eternal citadel of 800,000 people. Their mighty leader, Alaric – an imposing, fierce and dark-clad overlord – led his Visigoth army into the breaches.

The Goths had arrived.[19]

The collapse of the Empire's most iconic city was met with unbridled horror. 'In one city,' wrote theologian and Catholic priest St. Jerome, 'the whole world perished.'[20] By the end of the 5th century, the Roman Empire in the west was no more. The Goths had brought down Europe's largest bloc. They had destroyed the indestructible – and indelibly etched their name into the continental consciousness.

*****

Ever since then, the term 'gothic' has been associated with that walk on the dark side.

The Gothic cathedrals of the late medieval era from the 12th to 16th centuries defied the highbrow longing for the classical[21]. The controversial new style with the flying buttress, the ribbed vault and the immediately recognisable pointed arch and stained glass windows was seen by those still in thrall to the classical as distasteful and Germanic in style. The move away from classical lines was seen as, at best gauche, and at worst, sacrilegious. These were imposing edifices that pointed towards the heavens, bedecked with stone gargoyles – close cousins of the hellions seen in paintings of the infernal pit. The most celebrated of these structures, Notre Dame de Paris, was a devotional world of darkness flooded by pits of light from its huge stained glass windows.[22]

The term 'Gothic' was first applied to bricks and mortar in the 16th century in a 1518 letter from Raphael to Pope Leo X. The Italian painter and architect derisively claimed the pointed arches of the new churches looked like the primitive huts of the Rome-sacking Goths of yore. Florentine Renaissance master Giorgio Vasari then described the 'barbarous German style' in his *Lives Of The Artists* and

---

19 Not quite Germanic - the original Gothic tribes were perhaps the Gutones of South Scandinavia or Poland and their traces are celebrated in city names like Gothenburg. Like the later Vikings, they moved from their colder climes and across Europe, coming into conflict with the Romans whom they eventually defeated. In time the Visigothic Empire was defeated by first the Eastern Roman Empire in the 6th century, and then the Umayyad Caliphate in the 8th Century, leaving only an isolated community of Crimean Goths to eke out the centuries until they too died out.

20 St. Jerome translated the Old Testament of the Bible from Hebrew to Latin in 382 AD.

21 Like an ancient ELO to The Beatles, perhaps it's more fitting to use the term Romanesque rather than Classical as Gothic's precursor. As in Romanesque relating to a style of architecture which prevailed in Europe c. 900–1200, although sometimes dated back to the end of the Roman Empire (5th century).

22 It was also the fictional setting for Victor Hugo's Quasimodo, a lovelorn gargoyle made flesh.

attributed the new architectural features to the Goths, who he held responsible for destroying the ancient buildings after they had conquered Rome, and erecting new ones in this style. He labelled this new style a 'Gothic art' and 'monstrous and barbarous', signalling the debut of the G-word as a pejorative.

Later appropriated in the Gothic revival of the 18th and 19th centuries, the term then described a crudity of style in architecture. Its in your face ornamentation, redolent of medieval fortresses, created a kind of sub-classical vulgarity much pooh-poohed by the sophisticates of the time. Of course, what invites the disdain of culture's arbiters is sure to create its own appreciative cliques and a new style that harked to a north European rather than a classical aesthetic emerged.[23] Despite this, many of Europe's new landmark Gothic edifices like Amiens Cathedral - the tallest completed cathedral in France, Notre-Dame de Reims, Basilica of Saint-Denis, Chartres Cathedral in France, Santa Maria del Fiore and Milan Cathedral in Italy, Westminster Abbey and Canterbury cathedral in the UK, are now celebrated.

In the eyes of the critics, 'Gothic' was seen as the uncultured realm of a barbaric tribe and yet the styles of the later Gothic revival also became an inspiration to a whole host of architects and artists much despised by sophisticates that would slowly spread across Europe. So it was with Gothic literature. The 'romances'[24] that valued atmosphere above plot or dialogue came with what we now think of as the trappings of the Gothic: windswept moors, old dark mansions or ruined castles. Charlotte and Emily Bronte's respective 1847 novels of doomed love, *Jane Eyre* and *Wuthering Heights*, in hindsight, seem to share a strange kinship with Mary Shelley's *Frankenstein*, which recounts an altogether more demonic form of loneliness.

Folklore was already filled with myths, bogeymen and strange creatures, but the Gothic imagination placed its central focus on the alienated or inhuman outsider. After such imaginings came to the silver screen in the early 20th century, the form was further vulgarised (or made more exciting, according to your taste) by the 1930s coining of the term 'horror movie'.

In a sudden retrospective shift, the classic Gothic romances of the 19th century – *The Monk*, *The Strange Case Of Dr Jekyll And Mr Hyde*, *Dracula*, to name a few of the most obvious – were rechristened 'Gothic horror', often in response to their Hollywood adaptations. To many, it was the most wonderfully ugly flowering of the Gothic imagination; as the debauched Romantic poet Baudelaire had once written, the flowers of evil were in bloom. It gave rise to an aesthetic that would extend all the way to the 'monster culture' of 1950s adolescents (exemplified by

---

23 Centuries later, the goth bands being sniffed at by serious music critics, in the same way, is an interesting cultural parallel!

24 Imaginative fiction – the term didn't denote (though neither did it exclude) sentimental love stories.

Stephen King, who'd bring Gothic to Small Town USA[25]) and, later, to the so-called 'elevated horror' of the 21st century.

In the late 20th century, the electricity of pop culture galvanised a new Frankenstein's Monster that became known as goth. While few performers or bands accepted the backhanded term, the darker aesthetics that had infiltrated rock music for years began to coalesce.

---

25 Kate Cherrell, PhD in Nineteenth Century Gothic: 'Terror is mainly attributed to Victorian Gothic works as a creeping, unseen, uncertain threat. Horror is a graphic, visual threat and its consequences.' Stephen King, horror fiction's most successful exponent said 'Horror: the unnatural, spiders the size of bears, the dead waking up and walking around, it's when the lights go out and something with claws grabs you by the arm… Terror, when you come home and notice everything you own has been taken away and replaced by an exact substitute. It's when the lights go out and you feel something behind you, you hear it, you feel its breath against your ear, but when you turn around, there's nothing there…'

Chapter 3

DEEP IN THE FOREST

Europe's Gothic History

From prehistory to the 21st century, frissons of fear provided inspiration for artists and storytellers alike. Cultural taboos have infected literature and art for centuries – even the Bible is full of visions of apocalyptic violence; folk tales are filled with horror; classical music chimes with crepuscular scales. The Gothic has always been with us.

Pre-Christianity, the ancient Greeks presented theatrical tragedies where bloody events and the fateful interplay of humans and gods, were commented on by a chorus[26] rather than shown in their full gory glory. They were full of the dark stuff. In the 5th century BC, the playwright Aeschylus fashioned *The Oresteia*, a trilogy which recounted the atrocities begat by King Agamemnon, including sacrificing his daughter to the gods in return for victory in the Trojan War. Sophocles' *Oedipus Tyrannus* would provide Freud, the father of psychoanalysis, with a namesake syndrome after its hero, the King of Thebes unwittingly killed his estranged father and bedded his mother – before gouging his own eyes out. All the horrors in the world were turned loose, albeit as theatrical artifice rather than explicit images.

Sometimes lasting up to a day in their presentation, some historians believe Greek tragedies were an extension of the ancient rites carried out in honour of Dionysus.[27] In Greek mythology, Dionysus was the God of the grape harvest and its intoxicating offspring, as well as ritual madness, the wilderness, vegetation, fertility and religious ecstasy. Portrayed as an outsider, a beautiful foreigner and the last of the gods to arrive, a version of Dionysus is thought to have been first mentioned way back in Minoan Crete.

Always placed beyond the borders of the known world, he would arrive dancing in his chariot drawn by exotic beasts and his drunken attendant with his procession of wild female followers[28] and bearded satyrs with erect penises. Dionysus was also the protector of those who do not belong to conventional society and symbolised everything that is chaotic, dangerous and unexpected, which escapes human reason and can only be attributed to the unforeseeable action of the gods.

Dionysus's wine, music, and ecstatic dance freed his followers from self-conscious fear and care and subverted the oppressive restraints of the powerful. Those who partook of his mysteries were possessed and empowered by the God himself, whose

---

26 What would you give to hear this chorus now? The chorus consisted of between 12 and 50 players, who variously danced, sang or spoke their lines in unison, and sometimes wore masks. It would be a splendid piece of unnerving theatre.

27 Otherwise known as Pan or Bacchus.

28 Maenads.

mystical role was a divine communicant between the living and the dead - surely the aim of any high-decibel modern dancer?

The first rock star!

A hero for the suppressed for his anti-authoritarian stance and his free and easy lifestyle, he was the Robin Hood of the gods and has remained an inspiration to artists, philosophers and writers into the modern era. It's for these reasons that Friedrich Nietzsche, the 19th century's iconoclastic philosopher, appropriated Dionysus in much the same way as he did the ancient Iranian keeper of the flame, Zoroaster.[29] 'He who is richest in the abundance of life, the Dionysian God and man,' he wrote in *The Gay Science*, 'can allow himself, not only the sight of the fearsome and questionable but even the fearsome deed and every luxury of destruction, disintegration, denial…'

For Nietzsche, the self-styled Antichrist, the sensuous Dionysus was the God of the dance, mocking Christianity's piety and restraint – as well as its charity and compassion. 'Have I been understood? – *Dionysus against the crucified*,' wrote the iconoclast, as much Romantic poet as a philosopher, in his final work *Ecce Homo*, before suffering a complete mental collapse in 1889.

Jim Morrison understood all right.

By far the most erudite personage on LA's 1960s psychedelic rock scene, Nietzsche was a major influence[30] – to the extent that Doors guitarist Robbie Krieger could claim, 'Nietzsche killed Jim,'[31] rather than his frontman's recklessness with drugs and booze.

Jimbo provided the template for the modern goth rock star, emulating the Nietzschean conception of Dionysus on and off stage. The self-styled Lizard King drowned himself in alcohol, eroticism and the ecstatic experiences of a Greek God who, as articulated by another literary influence, William Blake, believed that 'the road of excess leads to the palace of wisdom.'

The Doors' own Dionysian parade moved riotously, dancing to ancient melodies.

The recorded version of 'The End' erupts into a non-verbal scream.

'Father?'

'Yes, son?'

'I want to kill you. Mother, I want to…'

Legend has it that in the live version performed at LA's Whisky A Go Go, in 1967, Jim would scream out, 'I want to fuck you!' And via the Dionysian aesthetic and LSD, he was transported back to the original Oedipal tragedy.

Little wonder that when Jim Morrison died in 1971, his self-destructive disciple, Iggy Pop, dyed his hair dark in anticipation of leaving his disintegrating garage band, The Stooges, to replace Jim in The Doors. It never happened, but a big part of Morrison's chaotic ethic stayed with Iggy.

---

29 Who became the Nietzschean *ubermensch*, Zarathustra.

30 Morrison's 1968 improvisation 'Ode To Friedrich Nietzsche' can be found on YouTube. Accompanying himself on staccato piano, he celebrates the German philosopher's sudden descent into insanity.

31 In his memoir of The Doors, *Set The Night On Fire*, co-written with Jeff Alulis (Little, Brown, 2021).

'Dionysiac' in Greek times was when a bunch of people would get together, and they would erect a paper phallus 50 feet long and carry it around and chant to some God they believed in, right? It ushers in the creation of an event, it's an eventful art. 'Apollonian' is when you make a statue, it's there forever, and it's set out very clearly. There's a Dionysiac element to my art, therefore, I suppose a lot of people might be quite frightened to be me, but I'm quite happy to be that.[32]

In some ways, Dionysus was a shaman. A shapeshifting magician who indulged in mind-altering substances and assumed animal form, bringing back word from the gods whilst wearing animal furs and taking psychedelic soups to shift into this transitory state.[33] Jim Morrison again toyed with this - a Sunset Strip shamanistic presence – entering the beyond via lab-produced Owsley acid, rather than natural psychotropics.

Of all The Doors-influenced performers that followed, it was goth icon Ian Curtis of Joy Division who like the title character in Dostoyevsky's *The Idiot*, seemed to glimpse infinity during his seizures.[34] As for drug-induced transmogrification, Britain's mystical pagan past seemed to just add another layer to the creative imagination and the embrace of timeless ritual for Jaz Coleman of Killing Joke.

> I think that if you look at the old stone circles in Great Britain, and indeed some of the burial mounds, they have a line of stones, which is a line to the circle of burial mounds, there is a line to the autumn equinox, which is, of course, All Hallows Eve. This is when they would call on their ancestors to help them through the difficulties of the coming winter – and of course, if you listen to the old Anglican prayer book of the Church of England, on this same day, we say a prayer for the deceased, this old pagan tradition that has survived in modern prayer, to this day.[35]

The imperial interlopers of Rome who suppressed the pagan also understood stadium spectacle and gore as entertainment, the Colosseum making latter-day shock-rock-figures Alice Cooper and Marilyn Manson seem lightweight. Aside from the slaughter of humans and beasts in amphitheatres, the Romans also held a deep fascination with ghost stories and dark fables. Ironically perhaps, many such tales were preserved by the Goths, Visigoths and Vandals, who, after sacking Rome, disseminated its tales, along with Christianity, across Europe.

The fall of Rome heralded the Dark Ages of superstition, witchcraft and strange imagined beasts. The European continent cultivated a rich culture of sinister tales and mythical creatures: from French werewolves to Norwegian gjenganger (ghosts) and trolls, from Irish banshees to the Romanian Strigoi (undead) and the Portuguese

---

32 Interview with Tom Snyder, *The Tomorrow Show*, 12-02-81.

33 Shamanism in its original form is an Asian tradition. However, the equivalent among indigenous peoples of the Americas also consumed psychedelic substances like peyote, a cactus containing natural mescaline, and ayahuasca, derived from a root found in the Amazonian basin.

34 For Curtis, unlike the innocent Prince Myshkin, infinity seemed to confirm only the bleakness of existence.

35 Jaz Coleman to The Quietus.

Bicho-papão (a bogeyman or Krampus-type figure) Europe was full of fertile figures of fear.

The ensuing Middle Ages was full of the dread of the lingering terror of what lay in the great beyond, enflamed by biblical warnings, and aggravated by the horrors of ergot poisoning.[36] In the theatre, Shakespeare and his Elizabethan or Jacobean contemporaries created their own darkly imagined vistas.

In *Doctor Faustus*, Christopher Marlowe pre-dated Goethe by warning of the dangers of a pact with the Devil; Thomas Middleton made bloody revenge synonymous with Jacobean tragedy; in *The Duchess Of Malfi*, John Webster introduced what we'd now recognise as Gothic horror (complete with a character who believes himself a werewolf). The Bard himself left a Gothic imprint with the bloody occult tragedy *Macbeth*; ghosts also appeared in his *Hamlet* and history plays – while *Titus Andronicus* was like a Roman splatter movie, its atrocities including cannibalism.

Europe was full of macabre and shamanic dread.

No wonder the more modern poets would have so much to draw from in the Gothic and dark.

---

36 Caused by infected rye in bread, Ergot Rye led to nightmarish hallucinations, the painfully compulsive St Vitus Dance and gangrenous limbs. It's surmised that ergot may have produced the apocalyptic visions of St John the Divine in the Book of Revelations. When the psychoactive ingredient was separated and synthesised in the 20th century, it became known as LSD-25.

Chapter 4

'MAD, BAD AND DANGEROUS TO KNOW'

The Romantics and the Gothic Imagination

Comprised of a loose coalition of poets, painters, authors and thinkers who earnestly and perhaps beautifully felt that creativity could change the world, the Romantic era believed in the intensity of emotions played out in art. They were lyrical alchemists making gold from lead and a Gothic magic from language, sound or vision. Perhaps sparked by the initial idealism that drove the 1789 French Revolution and the violent chaos that resulted from it, the Romantic movement produced its own century-long artistic revolution[37].

Often fuelled by alcohol or laudanum,[38] wild visions were accompanied by radical political ideas and a reinvigorated sense of connection with pre-industrial times. It ranged from Wordsworth, invoking a gentle nature mysticism, and a warm glow of nostalgia, to more hardcore Romantics like John Keats, William Blake, and Percy Bysshe Shelley, invoking the pre-industrial revolution and critiquing child labour, industry and the destruction of nature and the green and ghostly land. They embraced the power of nature in all its forms and the endless cycle of life and death.

Their poems fought back against the clank and grind of the new industry, whilst the more rakish Romantics introduced elements of irrationality and horror in their work. As the Industrial Revolution gave rise to machinery and mass production, Venetian artist Giovanni Battista Piranesi, who initially found fame etching classical ruins and palaces in the late 18th Century, was drawing scenes of dystopian factories and prisons. It had an influence on the landscape and psyche, with London's Newgate Prison renovated in the style of Piranesi's utilitarian nightmare. This, to the Romantics, was the shape of an undesirable future.

They were idealists.

Romantics.

Proto-goths.

The immediate precursors to the Romantics were the 18th century 'Graveyard Poets' like Thomas Gray, who instilled a sense of the unearthly and supernatural into his poems, while Thomas Parnell was more stoically religious: 'Death's but a path that must be trod / If man would ever pass to God.' Robert Blair wrote of ghosts, while Edward Young was existentially fixated on the isolation of the departed soul. All had a fascination with the physical finality of death and their elegiac meditations on mortality – all within the backdrop of the churchyard – were perfectly Gothic in essence.

---

37 There were 3 phases - the first emerged in the 1790s and 1800s, the second in the 1820s, and the third later in the century.

38 A solution of opium, dissolved in an alcoholic drink.

They were, like much early Gothic fiction, often dismissed by contemporary critics, but they cast their shadow over both the incoming Romantics and the future Gothic novelists. As did Thomas Chatterton. Born in 1752, his prodigious talent and brief life ended in suicide at the age of seventeen. A precocious polymath whose leanings extended beyond poetry to music, radical politics and the occult, he was an undisputed influence on the big four Romantic poets - Shelley, Keats, Wordsworth and Coleridge who were awed by his brief journey and wrote poems in his honour.

The German *Sturm und Drang*[39] movement was of equal resonance in its attempts to reset the modern world through art. The polymath Goethe's 1774 novel, *The Sorrows of Young Werther*, became a key text via its protagonist's lovelorn and ultimately despairing musings – its influence would extend to the classic Gothic novel, *Frankenstein,* by Mary Shelley.[40] Goethe's defining work is felt by many to be the two-part play *Faust*, written over several decades in the late 18th and early 19th centuries. An update of the classic Faustian pact with the Devil, it deals with a distinctly Frankensteinian form of forbidden knowledge.

Like their British counterparts, German Romantics redrew their past to create a new literary psyche. The tragic and troubling author Heinrich von Kleist has been called an antecedent of Kafka, but his 1811 story *Earthquake In Chile'* foreshadows the 20th-century group hysteria of Shirley Jackson's *The Lottery*[41]. By the time of his death in 1822, the prolific ETA Hoffmann was synonymous with what Freud later called the *unheimlich*[42]. Short masterworks like 'Der Sandmann' epitomised the German 'fantastic', much as his disciple Poe would do in the USA.

Central to this new myth-making was the ideal of childhood innocence, which sparked a wider fascination with folk tales and children's stories. Significant literary figures Clemens Brentano and Achim von Arnim together published *Des Knaben Wunderhorn*, a collection of versified folk tales, in 1806-08. Five years later, the first collection of *Grimms' Fairy Tales* by brothers Jacob and Wilhelm Grimm was published, a collection of edited folklore from the German hinterland.

The Brothers Grimms had partially simplified the original folklore into these strange and baroque stories filled with headless corpses and strange magic, set in a haze between fantasy and reality. Filled with violence and slightly skewed moral undertones, they still make for compelling reading: love and greed battle it out in a gnarled old forest, with axes close to hand; a strange old man, who may be the Devil in disguise, appears from behind bushes and cuts off someone's foot.

Lewis Carroll's 1856 *Alice's Adventures in Wonderland* and its sequel, *Alice Through the Looking Glass*, are both laced with a genuine childlike strangeness and sinister undertow that has made them standalone classics that have infused pop culture.

---

39 'Storm and stress.' It would become associated in the 19th century with Richard Wagner and his proto-nationalist operatic fantasies.

40 *Werther* is one of the contemporary texts read by the novel's alienated monster. This creature is a very different character to the 'poor dumb brute' of the classic monster movies.

41 1948 dystopian short story in which a member of the community is selected by chance and stoned.

42 'The unfamiliar'.

Siouxsie Sioux was fascinated by Carroll's works[43] and once made a 50-minute TV special where she and The Banshees– then including Robert Smith, moonlighting frontman of The Cure – dressed up as characters from the *Alice* novels.[44]

Just before the golden age of the Romantic poets, there was the key influence of the towering genius of William Blake, born in 1757 and who saw little recognition in his own lifetime. A visionary who claimed to have glimpsed 'a tree of angels' in south London's Peckham as a child, his visual art and poetry attested to a strange divinity that we might nowadays call schizophrenia. As the poet who paralleled 'Jerusalem' with 'England's green and pleasant land', his dualistic form of Christianity has been much misunderstood. Blake saw existence in the form of conflicting 'contraries'. This reconciliation of spirit and instinct was given voice in his book *The Marriage Of Heaven And Hell*, which today seems closer to Gnosticism[45] than to organised Christianity. Its imaginative and philosophical themes were more recently taken up by Norwegian dark electronica band Ulver, on their 1998 album *Themes From William Blake's The Marriage Of Heaven And Hell.*[46]

Born in Manchester in 1785, the political reactionary and Wordsworth fan Thomas De Quincey achieved an intensity of vision via the use of laudanum as recounted in his 1821 *Confessions Of An English Opium Eater.*[47] Haunted by bizarre sliding visions and strange creatures resulting from his use of the milk of paradise, it was the progenitor of the junkie chic that plagues rock culture to this day. De Quincey was also a precursor to the 1890s Decadent authors, such as JK Huysmans, via his macabre satirical essay *On Murder Considered As One Of The Fine Arts*, which focused in large part on the East End's Ratcliffe Highway murders of 1811.

Birthed at the tail end of the 18th Century, Romanticism itself had reached its climactic peak in the *fin de siècle* of the 1890s. The impact on the arts was irrefutable, but the lives of its flamboyant stars like George Gordon, aka Lord Byron, and his friend Percy Bysshe Shelley, who, like many key Romantic figures, lived fast and died young, were extinguished long before the movement passed into history.

---

43 Lewis Carroll was a pen name. The Reverend Charles Dodgson was a Maths prodigy and ground breaking photographer who had a very Victorian fascination with children and wrote the books for Alice Liddell, daughter of the Dean of Christ Church, Oxford, who he also photographed many times.

44 Siouxsie later titled the Banshees' 1987 covers album *Through the Looking Glass*. In some ways she was a forerunner to Marilyn Manson, who, in 2010, began prepping a feature film titled *Phantasmagoria: The Visions Of Lewis Carroll*. The project remains seemingly forever in stasis. An intriguing promo showreel, featuring surrealistic juxtapositions of sex and blood, is said to have nixed its funding. Despite the presence of nymph-like model/actress Lily Cole, it contains nothing suggestive of any child-sex taboos.

45 1st century AD belief that emphasised personal spiritual knowledge above the orthodox teachings.

46 Their Blakean concept album marks Ulver's branching out from the Scandinavian black-metal scene into computerised electro sonics. These recording methods bring a low-budget soundtrack quality to the great visionary's dualistic musings. Still, the presence of members of reputedly satanic Norwegian bands Emperor and Darkthrone remind us that Ulver are 'of the Devil's party' – as Blake said of John Milton, author of Luciferian epic poem *Paradise Lost*.
In the Gothic rock canon, Blake is most widely recognised for lending The Doors their name via his quote: 'If the doors of perception were cleansed every thing would appear to man as it is, Infinite.' It comes from *The Marriage Of Heaven And Hell*, but Jim Morrison cribbed it from Aldous Huxley's book-length essays *The Doors Of Perception/Heaven And Hell*. Huxley, who would write alarmingly in the 1930s of a drug-sedated future in *Brave New World*, realised late in life that not all drugs are narcotic. In his final days he became an evangelist for psychedelics.

47 De Quincey's near-contemporary Coleridge also attributed the visionary dream that inspired his epic poem, *Kubla Khan*, to opium use. In his case it was taken as a remedy to dysentery rather than as an addictive routine.

The Romantic era also saw the emergence of painters such as Caspar David Friedrich, who created wild mountainscapes of his native Germany, equal to JMW Turner in their depiction of nature as mystical and untamed.[48] The Frenchman Eugene Delacroix shared Byron's vision of conflict as inherently romantic, though his *Medea About To Kill Her Children* draws upon the classical horrors of mythology. The Parisian-based composer Frederic Chopin died young, and it's grimly ironic that the piano virtuoso's most instantly recognisable work is the now traditional 'Funeral March'. Similarly, the manic depressive Robert Schumann's last completed work was the *Geistervariationen* ('Ghost Variations'), before his death in the 1850s.

But it's the Romantic poets whose lineage can best be traced to the more modern gothic music scene. Samuel Taylor Coleridge's narrative ballads were filled with haunting supernatural imagery; his *The Rime Of The Ancient Mariner* gave us a classic image of death personified,[49] while his unfinished *Christabel* possesses similar sublimated lesbian vampire imagery to J. Sheridan Le Fanu's novella of the same period, *Carmilla*.

Lord Byron was the most celebrated Romantic; a veritable dark lord Dionysian 'live fast, die young' rock star over a century before the rock n roll era. 'Mad, bad, and dangerous to know,' as Lady Caroline Lamb said of her lover,[50] he rampaged through his life and culture before dying in the Greek War Of Independence in 1824 with scant regard for any modern moral code. There is an abundance of grotesque war imagery in his novels and poems, while his satyr-like nature gave rise to rumours that his half-sister, Augusta Leigh, was among his conquests. Byron was a legendary vagabond and pleasure-seeker, the prototype for the immoral rock star poet. Reputedly bisexual, bacchanalian and debt-ridden, Byron was also a lifelong vegetarian and champion of the poor who wrestled with his own demons whilst bombarding his senses with whatever came to hand like a template for a Nick Cave/ Blixa Bargeld type figure of the post-punk period.

His friend Percy Bysshe Shelley, who died similarly young in July 1822, was a radical atheist, vegetarian, philosophical anarchist, feminist, anti-monarchist and republican whose values foreshadowed the most radical of modern pop culture and whose work would accommodate images of the Devil and witchcraft. His greatest work *Ozymandias* explored the ravages of time and the impermanence of life and empire, with all legacies fated to decay into oblivion. His *Prometheus Unbound* told of the Titan sentenced to eternal torture by the Greek gods for stealing the fiery source of life itself.

---

48 Friedrich's *Wanderer Above The Sea Of Fog* was adopted by Penguin Classics to adorn its edition of Nietzsche's final work, *Ecce Homo*. Its image of a cane-bearing gentleman looking down upon the mountains evokes Nietzsche's years of wandering and aloofness from the rest of humanity.

49 *The Rime Of The Ancient Mariner* has also seen modern musical interpretations by acts as far apart as heavy-metal band Iron Maiden and 'punk cabaret' trio Tiger Lillies. The latter self-consciously style themselves after the decadence of Weimar Berlin.

50 Cave's own acknowledged literary influence from the Romantic era is Charles Baudelaire, dissolute visionary.

Before they both died, they created a legacy that perhaps peaked on a remarkable Geneva weekend in June 1816[51]. In those few days, Romanticism took on a pronounced Gothic hue after the famous ghost-story contest proposed by Lord Byron, which took place at the rented Villa Diodati[52] near Lake Geneva in Switzerland.

That summer, Byron hosted Mary Shelley and Percy Shelley, Byron's personal physician (and rumoured occasional homosexual partner), Dr John Polidori, who was keeping a diary of the entire event.

The challenge began, according to Polidori, with a group reading of *Fantasmagoriana*[53] before the guests were invited to tell their own tales. Those three rain-saturated days saw the young poets shouting stories at one another, their imaginations running wild. It has subsequently been suggested that they were also drenched in a miasma of alcohol and laudanum. The Gothic aesthetic of drawing an emotional response from the reader was now titillated with supernatural monstrosities and threats to a female protagonist's virtue. Byron himself straddled both sensibilities in life as well as art. He was often the tortured soul at the centre of the action – like the alienated titular figure in his 1817 *Manfred* – perhaps autobiographical? O, so very goth…

Inspired, Mary sketched out the bare bones of what would eventually become her novel, *Frankenstein*, while Polidori plotted out *The Vampyre*. The latter tells the story of the dashing and manipulative Lord Ruthven, a handsome man with a rich wardrobe and sulphurous sexuality who happens to be a poorly-concealed creature of the night. The name *Ruthven* was taken from Lady Caroline Lamb's historical novel *Glenarvon,* where the mythic archetype was, in turn, an acerbic parody of Byron's character, which makes Dracula a Byronic antihero by default.

Polidori took the name, but in later rewrites of *The Vampyre*[54], he intended to change 'Ruthven' to 'Strongmore'. There's long been conjecture over who the model was for Count Dracula's darkly domineering persona. Candidates include Sir Henry Irving - Bram Stoker's employer, an imperious and demanding knight of the stage.

The Vampyre is widely regarded – along with Le Fanu's *Carmilla* – as the archetypal vampire story. It was seminal in interpreting vampiric folklore and influenced Bram Stoker's 1897 *Dracula*. They were not the first, of course. The first Western literary representation of the phenomenon was Heinrich August Ossenfelder's 1748 poem, *The Vampire*, which set the template for the erotic undertones of sex and death – a Gothic staple beloved by generations.

All are variations on a theme with roots in Serbia in the 1720s, via the legends that sprang up around the exhumation of bodies that seemingly tried to claw their way out of the casket. In hindsight, we may see them as unfortunates buried prematurely,

---

51 Perhaps the non-summer of 1816 caused by long volcanic eruption of Mount Tambora is another unseen influence on goth and the creative dark clouds!

52 Controversial French artist Balthus lived there as well in 1945. His son Prince Stash was close friends with The Rolling Stones in the 60s.

53 An 1812 French anthology of German ghost stories.

54 Initially published without his permission and assumed to be Byron's work at one point.

possibly as sufferers of catalepsy. In their time, they were suspected vampires, to be despatched with a stake through the heart.

The most recognisably monstrous child of the Diodati nights, *Frankenstein*, is often seen as an early work of science fiction, but its science is vaguely glimpsed and unspecific. Victor Frankenstein creates life from corpses in the manner of a legendary black magician or alchemist. In this sense, it's not far removed from a supernatural novel like *Dracula*.

It's interesting that at the time when short Gothic fiction was pretty ubiquitous in periodicals and newspapers, there was a similar growing field in popular science and theological periodicals. I think the changing roles of man and God were similarly played out through scientific, pseudo-scientific and theological publications.

The literate public, often inclusive of middle class women, could openly and frequently discuss theories and personal reflections via an instant format that required little editing and had little to no qualification requirements. Namely, sectors of the public could voice their thoughts on biblical theory alongside clergy; this hadn't been especially possible before.

I wouldn't say that Victorian Gothic was created in reaction to scientific discoveries, but it definitely sculpted the fixations of the age. As the popular literature of the time, you could say that the people were able to explore their place in an increasingly secular world via this fiction, but without the fear of serious ramifications. In being forced to question and confront God, and, subsequently, the afterlife, it left huge holes in people's understanding of their purpose. I personally believe this yearning for a mysterious past seemed to ease the uncertainty about their own futures. There are plenty of Gothic stories that are blanketed in Anglican, Catholic or general non-conformist thought, but there are just as many who focus on creatures and acts that are not of God's creation. Just look at *Dracula* – the Count is not of God, nor Satan, but there are discussions of soullessness and immortality. Stoker, as with many other Gothic writers, offers no concrete answers, but a huge pool of uncertainty and opportunities for further discussion. Science, literature and religion are so interlinked in discussions of changing common thought in the Victorian era, it's really tricky to objectively separate them.[55]

But it was in the town of Whitby on the Yorkshire coast in 1890 that Bram Stoker was first informed by a friend of the history of an obscure Romanian warlord.[56] In the completed novel *Dracula*, the Count remarks: 'Who was it but one of my own race who crossed the Danube and beat the Turk on his own ground?' He is referring to Prince Vlad III of Wallachia, who infamy later commemorated as *Vlad Tepes* ('Vlad the Impaler') for his sadistic treatment of Turkic Ottoman invaders.[57]

---

55 Kate Cherrell, lecturer/speaker on 'Victorian Gothic, Mourning and the Spiritualist Movement'.

56 Or, more accurately, Wallachian – Wallachia being the East European principality that in the 1800s was absorbed into the newly established Romania.

57 According to pamphlets circulated in Saxony and Hungary, Vlad the Impaler also applied his extreme cruelty to those committing crimes or petty misdemeanours in his own principality. How much of this was true and how much was 'black ops' by the Voivode's distrustful near-neighbours is now lost to the mists of time.

Minor controversies still simmer over whether Stoker was identifying his character as a descendant of the Impaler or as Vlad Tepes himself, sustained over hundreds of years by fresh blood. But there can be no doubt as to where the title character's name originated: as the son of a fellow war hero known as 'Dracul' ('the Dragon'), Vlad III, therefore, became known as 'Dracula' ('Son of the Dragon').[58]

In *Dracula*, the Demeter docks in Whitby bay – its crew are all dead; the captain strapped to the helm, with two puncture marks in his throat. A huge black dog which leaps ashore is implied to be the Count in bestial form. When he returns to the narrative, the white-haired, moustached old man is growing younger thanks to fresh blood. His dark hair and elegant attire bring him closer to the caped seducer we know from pop culture.

Whitby has repaid the compliment by hosting a goth weekend at Halloween, every year since 1994. Many Goths have moved to the town, creating a gothic enclave by the seaside. Kate Cherrell gets her teeth into the neck of the subject.

When describing the relationship between Gothic literary aesthetics and the goth scene, the temptation to just hold up a picture of Dave Vanian[59] is enormous. I think that without a cultural idea of what is macabre, feared or threatening, there would have been nothing to subvert – not just in terms of appearance and clothing, but in terms of lyrical content too. Graveyards, social ideas of 'what we should leave alone', the threat of unseen, ancient curses and superstitions, and what is 'proper' and 'improper' for a woman is all very much interlinked with the written Gothic.

A lot of popular Gothic literature, while not actively consumed by early goth music 'pioneers', was already in the cultural pool surrounding them at a base level.

While it might just seem to be a bold and brazen background, I think Gothic literature firmly pumps through the heart of goth. When it comes to embracing an existing mythology, the Pre-Raphaelites did that better than anyone in the latter part of the 19th century. Their own works drew from – and fed into – the rise of interest in Arthurian mythology. However, even with the wealth of historical inspiration at hand, it was the fictional tragedies that proved to be the most successful, creatively speaking – i.e. *Ophelia* by Millais,[60] *The Lady Of Shalott* by Waterhouse and countless Arthurian works by Burne-Jones.

Obviously, not all authors were keen to create their own mythos, but there seems to be a keen sense of a realistic British past not being *enough*. I think this is due to the rise in Romanticism as a movement, the opening of the continent for wealthy holidaymakers, and overseas study for the wealthy.

---

58 The soubriquet can also be translated as 'Son of the Devil'.

59 Vampiric-styled frontman of The Damned.

60 Millais' most famous work, *Ophelia* (1851-52) has become Romantic shorthand for the broken-hearted heroine. Depicting the suicide by drowning of Ophelia from Shakespeare's *Hamlet, Prince Of Denmark*, its imagery has been recreated across contemporary Gothic culture. It's most recognisable in the music video for Nick Cave and the Bad Seeds' 'Where The Wild Roses Grow', with Kylie Minogue as both love object and murder victim.

In terms of romanticised Gothic landscapes, a good example is *Carmilla* (1871), by J. Sheridan Le Fanu.[61] The setting of Austria[62] affords Fanu the opportunity to take liberties with his landscape. Any sense of unfamiliarity helps to instantly heighten any sense of the 'uncanny'. This literary way of playing with landscapes was reflected in the Victorians' love of controlled nature: take the ornate public parks, garden cemeteries and landscaped gardens that sprung up across the new cities. These well-tended patches of grasses and shrubbery were preferred over Britain's wild forests, which – while occasionally appreciated by those in the arts – were viewed by many middle classes as of little interest to a cultured and refined society. While this mindset was not shared with Romantic artists, the country's keenness for horticulture and landscape gardening is undisputed.

Imagined landscapes opened up new realms of possibilities for the burgeoning Gothic audience of the UK. Many writers saw this as a licence to depict another country's history, or landscape through the lens of imagination, rather than through fact. In the 18th Century, Ann Radcliffe's *The Italian* was hailed for its wonderful descriptions of landscapes. All despite the fact she had never visited Italy![63]

Mrs Radcliffe was one of the most successful Gothic novelists of her time – albeit of an anaemically bloodless kind. In startling contrast to later controversial bestsellers like Matthew Gregory Lewis' *The Monk*, oft accused of blasphemy, her popular romances featured menaced, virginal heroines and only a semblance of supernatural phenomena. Ultimately explained away by some rational if unlikely pretext, they were precursors to the 1960s popularity of Gothic romances by authors like Victoria Holt.[64]

In the 19th century, many writers created their own landscapes and crumbling family piles. Few works were referenced at the best of times, so popular Gothic

---

61 Le Fanu's novella *Carmilla* may be considered a direct descendant of one the first literary representations of vampirism, Coleridge's unfinished 1797 poem 'Christabel' (not published until 1816). The heroine, Christabel, is seduced by a supernatural being called Geraldine, who tricks her way into the title character's residence – in the tradition of the vampire of legend, who may not cross a threshold without being invited.

Similarly, in Le Fanu's 1872 story (first run as a serial), Carmilla is revealed as an unholy immortal after seducing the heroine, Laura. The unambiguous, if restrained, depiction of lesbian love is remarkable, given that Le Fanu was writing in 19th century Ireland. *Carmilla*'s juxtaposition of bloodsucking and implicit eroticism was likely an influence on *Dracula* (1897), by expatriate Irishman Bram Stoker – once jovially described by author Colin Wilson as a novel about the fear of sex.

Carmilla herself has haunted the cinema screen in startlingly divergent forms. Carl Dreyer's *Vampyr* (1932) lifts key elements of the novella in a subtle expressionist work, albeit with a nightmarish scene of burial alive adapted from a story in the same Le Fanu anthology (*In A Glass Darkly*). *Blood And Roses* (1961) was directed by Roger Vadim, who made a sex symbol of Brigitte Bardot. (The film also lent its name to an 1980s British 'positive punk', or goth, band.) Casting his future wife Annette as Carmilla, Vadim's Gothic horror was more explicitly erotic.

But it was *The Vampire Lovers* (1970), the first in Hammer Films' Karnstein trilogy (the others being *Lust For A Vampire*, 1971, and *Twins Of Evil*, 1972) that launched the 'lesbian vampire' subgenre. Its sensationalism was soon outdone by Euro exploitation filmmakers like Jesus Franco with his *Vampyros Lesbos* (1971), where fanged nipples are more prominent than punctured jugular veins.

Elizabeth Harris' 'elevated horror' film *Carmilla* (2019) restores subtlety and sensitivity. But unlike Dreyer's *Vampyr*, here it's the supernatural which is sublimated and sexuality becomes overt. Very far from crude exploitation, *Carmilla* is a tragic story of love as a cultural taboo.

62 Specifically Styria.

63 Kate Cherrell to John Robb.

64 Or possibly even the deflating denouements of TV's *Scooby Doo, Where Are You?* – where crooks with hordes of treasure or cash would have got away with a pointless charade as a werewolf or Egyptian mummy, 'if not for you meddling kids.'

literature – intended for the enjoyment of a lower-class, non-academic audience – created a bit of a free-for-all.

If a writer creates a new space, a new fantastical situation, history or mythos, they don't have to adhere to the same social constraints as other contemporary writers. If one was to write a historical novel, it has a social and cultural grounding from the outset. Set it abroad or in unfamiliar territory, and creative constraints fade away.

The landscape of Victorian England, broadly speaking, was filled with far more abandoned castles, country houses, follies and ruins than today. These were also, essentially, crumbling domestic spaces. *Northanger Abbey* and *Villette*[65] are good examples of writers playing to these established clichés of the form. After all, the majority of Victorian Gothic was played out through widely distributed periodicals; Gothic was not high art. However, in most of these short-form Gothic stories, cathedrals and vast places of worship seem to only be mentioned in passing due to their inability to mimic a domestic space. Aside from Matthew Gregory Lewis' *The Monk*, obviously.[66]

If the Romantics had been harking back to a mythical notion of the preindustrial age, then Gothic authors embraced the physicality of the buildings themselves. These were atmospheric locations that already had their own stories, perfect backdrops for the imagination. It was a small step for a creative mind to fill these stories with supernatural creatures or events, themes of madness, lust and creeping death.

Romantic sensibilities naturally informed the birth of the Gothic novel, in the late 18th century. Horace Walpole was an early progenitor of the form, which merged its nightmare imagery with Gothic architecture. The English author's own fairytale home, Strawberry Hill House in Twickenham, is a fine example of the Gothic revival. Similarly, Gothic fiction as we know it grew from his 1764 novel, *The Castle of Otranto*, which in its second edition was subtitled 'A Gothic Story'. It's a strange tale of hauntings, with ghostly objects such as a giant knight's helmet dropped onto the castle's inhabitants like a Terry Gilliam animation from *Monty Python*. It drew much derision from literary critics of the time but acquired a sizeable cult audience.

'Twas ever thus with Gothic.

William Beckford was, like Walpole for a time, an English parliamentarian. He was also a keen restorer of neo-Gothic architectural styles, such as Fonthill Abbey in Wiltshire and Lansdown Tower ('Beckford's Tower') in Avon. His Gothic novel, *Vathek,* was first published in English in 1786. A 'grotesque and arabesque'[67] take on *The Arabian Nights*, its popularity would continue into the 20th century when it was reprinted with previously expurgated chapters.

---

65 *Northanger Abbey* is Jane Austen's parodic reworking of the popular Gothic romance. *Villette* sees Charlotte Bronte following in the now-established tradition of her earlier *Jane Eyre* – though satirising its psychological charge. Kate Cherrell: '*Villette* is the ultimate satire and insult to the consumer of the genre. While it's a great piece of work, exploring the psychology of isolation and gendered repression, it is, at its heart, mocking the overblown nature of Gothic.'

66 Kate Cherrell to John Robb.

67 As Edgar Allan Poe might have termed it.

Furthering the tradition of English MPs as Gothic novelists, Matthew Gregory Lewis' controversial 1796 *The Monk* pushed the same dark buttons as goth bands two centuries later. It moved Gothic lit into a more shocking and horrific space than Horace Walpole's almost comical hauntings. *The Monk* is full of spectral bleeding nuns, mob violence, murder, sorcery and incest. Telling of its title character's fall from the grace of God, it's an amoral romp full of satanic debauchery similar to the Marquis de Sade's two transgressive novels of the same era, *Justine* and *Juliette*.

De Sade was a fan of 'Monk' Lewis, writing favourably of his work in the essay 'Reflections On The Novel'. The major difference was that Lewis had his hero, Ambrosio, punished for his transgressions, whereas De Sade had no such moral qualms. His 1791 *Justine* (*or, The Misfortunes Of Virtue*) is a sordid tale of a young woman trying to live a virtuous life in a wicked world which ultimately destroys her.[68] It's a novel full of Gothic tropes but devoid of the supernatural, dwelling instead on the dark side of sex.

Its 1797 companion piece on Justine's depraved sister, *Juliette* (*or, The Prosperities Of Vice*), is filled with violently pornographic scenes intertwined with De Sade's philosophy and musings on the amorality of nature. The libertine himself was enjoying a period of freedom after a decade in prison via a *lettre de cachet* issued by his vengeful mother-in-law, for sexual deviations, both consensual (orgies with prostitutes, anal sex with a manservant) and cruel (flogging a beggar and filling her lacerations with wax).[69] His sibling novels were so controversial, though, that they resulted in De Sade spending the last thirteen years of his life in jails and mental asylums, on the orders of no less a personage than Napoleon Bonaparte.

Author of the sensual and morbid collection 157's *Les Fleurs Du Mal*[70] Parisian poet and translator of Edgar Allan Poe into French, Charles Baudelaire, was much pursued by the arbiters of Christian morality in the mid-19th century. His verse still carries a startling *frisson* today: an erotically-tinged ode to a vampire; a *memento mori* to his lover, which imagines her, with alarming necrophile overtones, as a rotting corpse.

If Baudelaire had any ideals at all, they manifested in shocking the bourgeois class he'd escaped from. His lifestyle was a template for both the end-of-century Decadent movement and the darkest exponents of goth – dissolute, bohemian, estranged from his family, bankrupt, and sexually experimental. He ate hashish and smoked opium, associated with artists and petty criminals rather than 'respectable' people, and wore funereal black before his death in his forties from the syphilis that had tormented him for years.

He was goth before goth!

---

68 After surviving rape, torture and almost every form of indignity, Justine is despatched by a lightning bolt. As Nick Cave remarked in an early 1980s interview, even God seems to hate her.

69 De Sade has bequeathed us the terms 'sadism' and 'sadistic'.

70 The Flowers Of Evil.

In the late twentieth century, Baudelaire's doomed vision is imprinted on the more esoteric side of modern music. Most remarkably, the operatic range of dissident Diamanda Galas was put to infernal effect on the title track of her 1982 *The Litanies Of Satan*, an aural evocation of the poem in *Les Fleurs Du Mal*. It's a frighteningly enticing sonic storm that combines the atonality of a Penderecki with the thud-and-crash of industrial music, at its centre is Galas' declamatory spitting of Baudelaire's verse: 'O Satan, prends pitié de ma longue misère!' ('Oh Satan, take pity on my sore distress!') she demands more than pleads.[71]

Baudelaire was also a profound influence on the Symbolist poets who sought to represent absolute truths symbolically through language and metaphorical images, mainly as a reaction against naturalism and realism and who coincided with the end of the century Decadents. His poetry became a key part of the DNA of key Symbolist poets like Paul Verlaine, and his younger lover, Arthur Rimbaud[72] - the teenage prodigy who abandoned a short literary career after his relationship with Verlaine ended violently. Before he bailed, he managed to produce *Une Saison En Enfer* ('A Season In Hell'), an epic multi-part poem whose hallucinatory themes would further influence the twentieth-century Surrealist movement.[73]

Published between 1868-69 in six separate *chants* (songs) or books, Isidore Ducasse's French poetic novel (or long prose-poem) *Les Chants de Maldoror* was another (albeit oft suppressed) influence on the *fin de siècle* and, in turn, influenced by such exponents of nineteenth century Gothic as Charles Maturin[74] it went far beyond that genre.

With its title character's name suggesting malign misanthropy, the young, doomed poet, publishing under the name of the Comte de Lautréamont,[75] created an amoral force of nature who embraced evil and opposed God. *Maldoror* would have its posthumous moment in the surrealist movement of the 1920s when its bizarre scenarios and unreliable narrator challenged the God-like authority of the conventional novelist.

---

71 Perhaps more surprisingly, The Cure's 1987 album of love songs, *Kiss Me Kiss Me Kiss Me*, features an elegantly jangly piece of regret called 'How Beautiful You Are'. Robert Smith's lyric is a faithful adaptation of Baudelaire's poem 'Les Yeux Des Pauvres' ('The Eyes Of The Poor'). Recalling a day in Paris with a woman he was smitten with, the narrator of poem and song recalls a bedraggled man and his malnourished children gazing on her with awe: inducing delight in him and fury in his love object. ('And this is why I hate you… No one ever knows or loves another,' laments Smith.).

72 Ville Valo, frontman of Finnish goth-rock band HIM, is a known devotee of Baudelaire and Rimbaud. He similarly chose to play his first solo shows under the pseudonym 'Rambo Rimbaud' as a nod to his favourite poet.

73 In terms of contemporary music, NY punk poet Patti Smith has been Rimbaud's most vocal advocate. On her raw but startlingly inventive 1975 debut, *Horses*, longer tracks like near-namesakes 'Birdland' and 'Land' carry the French debauchee's lyrical influence.

74 Author of the classic *Melmoth The Wanderer*.

75 The name Lautréamont is lifted from Eugene Sue, the French proto-pulp novelist whose chapterwork *The Mysteries Of Paris* was a sensation in its day.

'…It's because he, Isidore Ducasse, desired to be the Count of Lautréamont that he died,' opined surrealist playwright Antonin Artaud.[76] For the mysterious Isidore, of whom very little is known, was undoubtedly inhabiting a literary role.

In the late 1800s, fellow Parisian JK Huysmans would create the archetypal decadent aesthete, Des Esseintes, in his novel *A Rebours* ('Against Nature'). His *La-Bas* ('The Lower Depths') was a sensation, describing a Black Mass purportedly based on the rituals of 15th-century child murderer Gilles de Rais ('Bluebeard'). The ageing Huysmans averted scandal by embracing Catholic architecture as his subject in *The Cathedral* – in parallel, perhaps, to how the satanic Baudelaire never lost respect for the priesthood.

There was no such equivocating with Lautréamont, though. He was the vehicle via which Isidore Ducasse set *Maldoror* loose upon the world. Meanwhile, young Isidore could express more polite philosophical and religious sentiments in his *Poems*. Maybe Artaud was correct in his seeming belief that half-mad iconoclasts like himself were the *true* Maldoror.[77] Maybe less of a direct influence on the goth bands of the post-punk era unless you count a doom metal band called Des Essences or In the Nursery's song 'A Rebours', these poets created an ideal for living, a dark and dank place full of sex and death to play around in and helped to formulate the goth narrative and no self-respecting goth is without at least some knowledge of their poetic volumes

But the 19th century's darkest, most enduring Gothic icon remains Baudelaire's muse, the neurotic American, Edgar Allan Poe.[78] Enraged by the universal mortality he knew he could never escape, Poe developed a near-necrophilic fixation on dead and dying women that arose from his own fetid circumstances. As a toddler, he witnessed the early death of his mother; in his own sad marriage, he watched his child bride Virginia (his first cousin, whom he married when she was thirteen) succumb to consumption.

Several of his short stories fixate on recently dead women: 'Ligeia', 'Berenice', 'Morella', and 'The Fall Of The House Of Usher' where Madeline Usher's claustrophobic relationship with her brother implies incest. It was such dark tales

---

76 Artaud, self-styled founder of the Theatre of Pain, was also a heroin addict who spent much of his adult life in mental asylums. His school of psychodrama, chiefly notable for disturbing playlet *The Spurt Of Blood*, was acknowledged by Jim Morrison for its effect on his performance style.

77 The tricksy, nihilistic figure of Maldoror has also cast his shapeshifting shadow on modern music. Maldoror, the Italian black metal band of that name, were perhaps too traditionally Gothic for fans of Lautréamont's poem. Made-up in trad black and white corpse paint, Maldoror's 1998 album *Ars Magika* lays the Gregorian chant and 'Carmina Burana'-type atmospherics thickly onto an ambient backdrop.
She, the 1997 collaboration by Japanese noise musician Masami Akita and Mike Patton of Faith No More, also went out under the heading of Maldoror; more sonically unpredictable (and indeed more noisy), it seemed to better evoke a universe were neither morality nor reality are relevant.
As if to underline how millennial underground rock had finally seen the dark, the Italian goth band Chants of Maldoror combined similar elements to the above with much more conventional post-Cure indie pop on their 2000 album *Thy Hurting Heaven*.

78 Baudelaire became acquainted with Poe's fevered short stories and melodramatic poetry only shortly before the Bostonian man of letters' 1849 death, aged forty. Even the manner of his demise carries a Poe-like mystique: his death certificate read 'congestion of the brain': theories as to what this meant range from a fatal drinking binge, with Poe led around polling booths to vote multiple times by a corrupt political acolyte, to an outbreak of rabies in Baltimore, the city of his death.

that made Poe the undisputed master of the macabre – oft adapted for the screen in the 20th century, but rarely faithfully.

His literary reputation in the USA was cemented by his melancholy poem, 'The Raven', lamenting 'the lost Lenore'. But he began his career as a short story writer with 'Metzengerstein', which seems to be a parody of the Gothic form, while 'The Masque Of The Red Death' remains a compact masterpiece, embodying in human form the plagues that blighted medieval Europe. Supernatural overtones are ambiguous with Poe; instead, he brought a gripping psychological depth to Gothic lit, as had not been known before.

Poe also left his morbidly sensitive taint on music. Claude Debussy, born in 1862, is recognised as the composer who bridged the gap between Romanticism and Modernism. [79] Towards the end of his life, in the early 20th century, an ailing Debussy became obsessed with two of Poe's short stories, 'I have gotten into the way of thinking of nothing but Roderick Usher and "The Devil And The Belfry",' he admitted. An opera based on 'The Fall Of The House Of Usher' was to crown his life's work, until mortality intervened.

Only a twenty-five-minute section of Debussy's *La Chute De La Maison Usher* survives, but its cinematic string overture and tripartite libretto (representing the narrator and doomed siblings Roderick and Madeline) telegraph the power of what nearly was. Debussy, as his health faded, is said to have identified fully with the neurasthenic Roderick.

It would be almost sixty years from its 1917 semi-completion that part of Debussy's work was recorded. It's a tribute to how Poe cast a shadow over popular culture that the work was first heard not in a classical recital, but on a progressive rock album.

Tales Of Mystery And Imagination[80] by The Alan Parsons Project is named after the famous anthology of Poe's short stories, a labour of love by former recording engineer Parsons.[81] On the studio band's evocation of 'The Fall Of The House Of Usher', the opening overture from Debussy was strangely uncredited.[82] Still, Parsons, and the band got into a suitably tenebrous groove before the creaking collapse of the house that mirrors Roderick's mental state.

It's amusing how the most revered practitioners of prog rock, as with goth, baulk at having anything to do with the genre. So it is with Peter Hammill, co-founder of Van Der Graaf Generator in late 1960s Manchester, but they were truly on their own trajectory. Frontman Hammill's intense vocals, which could be shockingly sonorous, were cited as an influence by John Lydon back in peak Pistols/pre-Public

---

79 He is also credited as the first Impressionist composer, a term he personally hated.

80 The 1976 album also includes a wailing evocation of 'The Tell Tale Heart', one of Poe's tales of irrationally compulsive murder (see also 'The Imp Of The Perverse' and 'The Cask Of Amontillado'). The vocalist is early shock-rocker Arthur Brown and the track is goth rock in embryo – histrionic and homicidal.

81 Best known till then for his work on Pink Floyd's *The Dark Side Of The Moon*.

82 In a further macabre twist, a 1987 remix of the album featured a suitably morbid introduction by Orson Welles over Debussy's opening theme. Director/actor Welles had by this point been dead for two years.

Image days.[83] Mark E. Smith of The Fall recognised a fellow uncompromising soul and conducted a correspondence with Hammill. So when the vocalist reunited with fellow Van Der Graaf founder/songwriter Chris Judge Smith for an opera based on 'Usher', the foundations were sure to quake.

Rich in electronic keyboards and harpsichord, the libretto gave voice to Poe's decaying house as Hammill sang the characters of Roderick and the house as if intertwined. It's as gothic in atmosphere as any recording mentioned in this book with guests like Lene Lovich (in her gothic finery) and Erasure›s Andy Bell. Decadent dark cabaret crooner Marc Almond felt nonplussed by Bell's inclusion. A lifelong Hammill fan who'd covered two of his celebrated love songs,[84] Almond even facilitated *Usher*'s release on Some Bizzare, the label he recorded for throughout the 1980s/90s. 'I must admit I was very, very hurt, but I blamed myself for not pursuing the project more,'[85] he confessed. Hammill's interpretation of Poe's morbid vision made Marc reticent, backing off from his own imp of the perverse.[86]

A more agonisingly personal connection to Poe was felt again by Diamanda Galas. In 1988, the infernal operatics first heard on her Baudelaire-inspired *Litanies Of Satan* were developed further on the *Masque Of The Red Death* triple album. Titled after Poe's depiction of a masquerade ball where an embodied plague mingles with the guests, the theme was rendered contemporary by personal suffering.

Playwright Philip Dimitri-Galas died in 1986, consumed by the early years of the AIDS pandemic. His formidable sister conflated the two pestilences. The first of her discs, *The Divine Punishment*,[87] is a raw take on darkness, death and spirituality and AIDS. She showed the courage of her conviction in December 1989, when arrested with the ACT UP protest group at St Patrick's Cathedral, NYC. In 1992, Ms Galas tattooed the claim, 'We are all HIV positive,' on her hand.

In 1997, Hal Willner, the producer who'd lose his own life to the pandemic of 2020, added *Closed On Account Of Rabies* to his catalogue of themed tribute albums. The subject was Poe, its title referring to one of the theories about his death. To low-key musical atmospherics, vocalists including Diamanda Galas and Iggy Pop recited the great neurotic's prose and verse. Galas' pleasingly guttural tones delivered the salutary tale of 'The Black Cat', equating cruelty to animals with violence against women. It contains an aptly just vengeance, as recounted by one of the key subjects of RE/Search Publications' 1991 title, Angry Women.

Poe's celebrated obsessiveness has continued to cast a shadow over the new millennium. In 2001, playwright/theatrical director Robert Wilson and quintessential

---

83 On the young Johnny Rotten's celebrated July 1977 Capital Radio show, he played Hammill's 'The Institute Of Mental Health Is Burning' – from classic 'pre-punk' album *Nadir's Big Chance*.

84 'Vision' and 'Just Good Friends'.

85 Marc Almond to Jim Christopulos.

86 Almond embraced Baudelaire instead, on his Francophile *Absinthe* album. Two new translations of 'Abel And Cain' and 'Remorse Of The Dead' by Paul Buck were interpreted as songs.

87 The sister discs, *The Saint Of The Pit* and *You Must Be Certain Of The Devil*, further married her uniquely phonetic vocalese to the aesthetics of atonal music. A celebrated live performance of the cycle at the Church of St John the Divine, NYC, was issued as the *Plague Mass* album in 1991.

New York rock artist Lou Reed made their second collaboration: *POEtry*, performed at the Brooklyn Academy of Music in the fall. Reed, who'd provided a seminal influence to goth rock in The Velvet Underground, assimilated literary influences as naturally as he'd expanded the sonic templates of rock n roll. They ranged from Dostoyevsky to Hubert Selby Jr. – and, indeed, to Edgar Allan Poe.

'To me, it would slip right into my idea of what rock could be… with the real power of the language,'[88] Lou said of his inspiration. *POEtry* updated Poe's words into contemporary dialogue and lyrics, without any jarring anachronism. When Reed came to record the songs for an album, he hooked up with producer friend Hal Willner. On 2003's *The Raven*, an extended credit list of vocalists included David Bowie and Antony Hegarty[89], while actors Willem Dafoe, Steve Buscemi and Amanda Plummer truncated Poe's tales of spiralling self-destruction.

Reed lent his Brooklynite drawl to the voice of the narrator (Edgar, of course), who visits the house of Usher.[90] He also reinterpreted one of his earlier songs, 'The Bed', from the doomy romantic song cycle *Berlin*. Opening as a scratchy threnody, the reimagining places its suicidal heroine, Caroline, in the canon of Poe's mortal icons Madeline Usher and Ligeia.

*****

If Poe's neurosis was atypical of its era, then his familiarity with death was not. For death became an enormous industry in the first half of the 19th century in England, where he had attended public school as a boy. Victorian social mores, combined with the era's sense of decency, encouraged elaborate funereal rites to become grander than before. Families would feel beholden to spend every penny on horse-drawn hearses, mourning 'mutes'[91] and black mourning dress. To not provide the deceased with an appropriate funeral would be the ultimate affront; many grieving widows bankrupted themselves in the process, with most remaining in funerary wear for two years.

Mourning jewellery – particularly made from Whitby jet (fossilised black wood) – was a decorative necessity for the well-to-do. Similarly, Victorians appreciated the memento value of hair, taken both from the living – to signify love or friendship – and the dead. Locks were woven into jewellery, wreaths or placed into brooches, and the custom has since enjoyed a revival of interest with contemporary goths[92].

---

88 Lou Reed to Jon Pareles, New York Times, November 25, 2001.

89 Of Antony and the Johnsons.

90 In the age of goth rock, Poe's influence seems both ubiquitous and impossible to measure. It's most obvious in the name of a German band, The House of Usher, formed by Jorg Kleudgen in 1990 and active to this day. An exercise in atmospherics, their sound combines the sonic spaces of Joy Division's recorded output with more contemporary electronica and darkwave folk influences.

91 Silent 'professional mourners', often in pairs. It was rare for the mute to be actually incapable of speech.

92 Modern gothic culture romanticises elements of Victorian mourning wear. Its nostalgia for overt, almost theatrical presentations of grief can be seen in the donning of Victorian frock coats and top hats at goth festivals.

Neo-Victorianism is a more recent term but I think if we look at some versions of goth – the Victoriana element, the interest in the literary texts, the ways in which Victorian cultures of mourning (Whitby jet) are appropriated and reinterpreted, then it's a good place to start. Some goth borrows from the nineteenth century, but does so by pairing this with the conventions of the present like the short skirt and corset, or the full Victoriana but makeup which suggests a modern sensibility. I think goth is doing this quite self-consciously, juxtaposing the past and the present. [93]

Many Victorians were now able to afford the cost of a photographer, who could forever preserve the image of a lost loved one at far less than the price of a commissioned portrait. Public health was improving among the new middle classes, though the poor remained vulnerable to early death. But the high Victorian child mortality rate has bequeathed us images of ghostly children who appear alongside their brothers and sisters, or their favourite toys. This new business of *memento mori* photography created images of the dead in the midst of life. It has also been posited that it contributed to the atmosphere of the classic Victorian ghost story, where the dead are never too far removed from the world of the living.

Chief among its tellers was one Montague Rhodes James, provost of Eton – or MR James, as literary posterity remembers him. This gentle-mannered son of the establishment created some of the most atmospherically engaging ghost stories and horror tales ever told. Their chilling supernatural manifestations often appear in settings familiar to his contemporaries: from the quiet halls of academia to a children's Punch and Judy show. James himself claimed to be a sceptic, which made his uncanny denouements all the more effective. In *Casting The Runes*, one of the most effective of his short stories, an occultist named Karswell moves effortlessly from scaring kids with a 'magic lantern' (slide) show to raising a pagan demon to pursue a vendetta against a hapless academic. [94]

While MR James epitomises the Victorian ghost story, he outlived the era by a full thirty-five years. Like him, the Welsh author and London suburb dweller Arthur Machen straddled the Victorian, Edwardian and interwar years. His tales of 'rapture, beauty, adoration, wonder, awe, mystery, sense of the unknown, desire for the unknown', as he described them, reach back beyond the ghosts in the Christian belfry to an earlier pagan period when, claims Machen, nameless evils and unspeakable rituals ingrained themselves into the hillsides and monolithic stones of Britain.

Two signature Machen works, *The Great God Pan* (1894) and *The White People* (1899), still carry macabre revelatory undertones, as the scales of modern rationalism are ripped away from the reader's eyes, and all that remains are the mysteries with us since prehistory. *The Great God Pan* reawakens them via the mad-doctor shtick

93 Prof Claire Nally (Northumbria University) to John Robb.

94 'It's coming for me through the trees,' Kate Bush intones dreamily in her 1985 'Hounds Of Love'. It's a reference to the classic 1957 British horror movie *Night Of The Demon*, based on 'Casting The Runes'. The mid-80s also gave us The Fall's 'Spectre Vs. Rector', a much more visceral MR James-inspired rant which namechecks the man himself: 'I've waited since Caesar for this… I'll rip your fat body to pieces,' drawls Salfordian frontman Mark E. Smith.

of brain surgery, resulting in a *femme fatale* who carries all of the ancient obscenities inside her.[95]

Machen's contemporaries included William Hope Hodgson, whose *The House On The Borderland* (1908) is suffused with a similarly sweeping cosmological horror: amok time, subverted evolution, 'swine people'. But the closest parallel lies across the Atlantic, with the *Weird Tales* pulp author who venerated Machen in his 1927 essay, 'Superatural Horror In Literature'. H.P. Lovecraft was also influenced by Poe, but the mania of his own short stories and novellas manifested itself in a personal cosmos where malign, tentacular beings from another dimension sporadically break through into our own, bringing with them a 'crawling chaos'.[96]

Lovecraft's Cthulhu Mythos is, collectively, a masterpiece of weird fiction. After his 1937 death, it became generic, with additions to the mythos by writers extending from his friend August Derleth to Colin Wilson, author of *The Occult*, and Ramsey Campbell, the late 20th century's Liverpudlian master of the macabre.

But it's Aleister Crowley who is arguably the early 20th century writer most widely embraced by the goth scene. Only a Gothic author in the most dilettante-ish sense, his youthful membership of the Hermetic Order of the Golden Dawn – alternately seen as a philosophical or occultic society, its membership including poet, WB Yeats and *Dracula* author, Bram Stoker – was but the prelude to his self-aggrandising career. Developing a series of 'sex magick' rituals that the Ordo Templi Orientis (OTO) claimed he'd plagiarised, he styled himself the Great Beast 666 after the Bible's Book of Revelations. The Sunday tabloids preferred the more catchpenny 'Wickedest Man in the World', which probably suited his lust for attention just as well.

Since his death in 1947, Crowley's many and various personae have become immortalised: 'sex magickian' and founder of his own occult order;[97] erotic poet and painter; author of one Gothic novel;[98] libertine and seducer of women; bisexual enthusiast for sodomy (on the submissive end); international traveller and mountaineer; huge imbiber of cognac and cocaine; and in the end, a hopeless heroin addict.

Aleister Crowley enjoyed a wild life appreciated by many wishing to dip their toe into the occult. Epitomising an age of disobedience (in which was to be found

---

95 'Leave The Capitol', from The Fall's early *Slates* EP, contains the lines, 'You laughed at the Great God Pan / I didnae! I didnae!' While the track is oft interpreted as Smith's anti-London sentiment, it could equally be a description of Machen quitting his room in the suburb of Harlesden. The late MES was a member of the Friends of Arthur Machen appreciation society.

96 'Spectre Vs. Rector' also refers to Lovecraft's Yog-Sothoth, father of the xenophobic visionary's Outer Gods. The cantankerous Mark E. Smith would have spat on the idea that The Fall, his post-punk/post-psychedelic garage band, was in any way 'goth' – but he understood the internal reality of Gothic horror. Other bands have paid more overt homage: 1960s Chicago psych-folk outfit H.P. Lovecraft were obviously named after the author. Fields of the Nephilim, were named after a mythical lost race alluded to in the Bible; Lovecraft appropriated the name as another strand of Cthulhu's lineage.

97 Regarded as a chaos magician, Crowley was something of a mystical synthesist. He claimed *The Book Of The Law* – the foundation of Thelema, his post-Christian religion – was dictated to him by a mystical ancient entity called Aiwass. It holds faint echoes of how the altogether more pious Prophet Mohammed described the fundaments of *The Koran* as revealed to him by the Angel Jibril.

98 *Moonchild*, Crowley's supernatural novel (which gave its name to a Fields of the Nephilim song) was reprinted in the 1970s by the Dennis Wheatley Library of the Occult. It was an interesting choice: the stuffy but learned Wheatley believed himself to be at war with the forces of darkness, much like his hero the Duc de Richeliu in *The Devil Rides Out* – whose villain, Mocata, was based on Crowley. Dr Karswell in MR James' 'Casting The Runes' was similarly inspired by the Great Beast.

'the greatest joy'), Crowley is one of the iconic figures featured on the cover of The Beatles' *Sgt. Pepper's Lonely Hearts Club Band*.[99] The Great Beast (who made a religion out of the beast with two backs) was also a major personal influence on Led Zeppelin guitarist Jimmy Page, who went so far as to purchase Crowley's old house, Boleskine, on the shores of Loch Ness.

Page was at one point the soundtrack composer for Kenneth Anger's art film *Lucifer Rising*, until a falling out with the mercurial director left the compositions unreleased for decades.[100] Anger, a Crowleyite and early member of the USA's Church of Satan, claimed his celebrated *Magick Lantern Cycle* comprised not so much films as magick spells to usher in the Aeon of Lucifer.[101]

In the early 1970s, the young David Bowie flirted with the twilight zones between eastern mysticism and the occult. This was the period immediately before his adoption of character personae onstage. But he knew that music, like magick, has a transmuting power to transcend mere rationalism.

On his 1971 *Hunky Dory* album, the song 'Quicksand' references both the Great Beast and the occultic society where he cut his teeth. Bowie himself would begin a period of self-reinvention, culminating in his emergence as a major American star mid-decade. By this time, his persona was the Thin White Duke, sartorially similar to the cod-English alien portrayed in his feature-film debut, *The Man Who Fell To Earth*, but infused with a cold, coke-heightened mysticism.

It all seemed a little incongruous for an artist then recording 'plastic R&B' love songs. And yet Bowie's *Station To Station* album has Crowley as part of its DNA. 'My overriding interest was in Kabbalah and Crowleyism. That whole dark and rather fearsome never-world of the wrong side of the brain,' he said at the time of its release.

A year prior to the recording of *Station To Station*, Bowie had been photographed drawing the cabalistic Tree of Life – a symbol adopted by the Golden Dawn and by Crowley's new religion, Thelema.[102] The Kabbalah is the esoteric strand of Jewish mysticism, which, as with any profound occult doctrine, works as a symbolic discipline to enhance the latent powers of the mind. The title track of the album contains the line 'one magical moment from Kether to Malkuth' in its opening

---

99 Along with Poe.

100 *Lucifer Rising* was recut by Anger multiple times after its initial 1972 release. The 1980 version features an atmospheric soundtrack by Bobby Beausoleil – long-term US convict and onetime member of the Manson Family. Beausoleil wasn't involved in the infamous Tate-LaBianca massacre but remains in prison to this day, for the 1969 murder of an acid dealer. Ironically perhaps, it was his own arguments with Anger (who regarded Bobby as his muse) which aborted the original 1967 version of *Lucifer Rising*. Legend has it the completed print was buried in the desert by the Family.
What remained of the 1967 footage was refashioned by Anger into another Crowleyite spell, *Invocation Of My Demon Brother*, with a droning Moog synthesiser soundtrack by Mick Jagger. The Rolling Stones further enhanced their fallen-angel image with the majestic track 'Sympathy For The Devil', but, despite their association with Anger, its lyrical evocation of Lucifer through the ages was satirical. (Inspired by *The Master And Margarita*, Mikhail Bulgakov's Stalinist-era novel about the Devil coming to Moscow).
The Stones-Anger association gradually evaporated. But it lasted long enough for Jagger's ex, Marianne Faithfull, to portray a visibly smacked-out goddess, Lilith the Destroyer, in the completed 1970s cut of *Lucifer Rising*.

101 Lucifer, in Crowleyite terms, was the 'Light Bringer' – a symbol of individual consciousness and personal freedom. In Milton's epic poem *Paradise Lost*, Lucifer the fallen angel is punished by God for his independence; cast out of Heaven, he is transformed into Satan, ruler of Hell. But pious Christians make no distinction between the rebel angel and the Devil.

102 Reinforcing the point that Crowley was a mystic who drew from many and various sources – not merely a stereotypical Satanist.

section – that is, between the sublime and earthly realms in the Kabbalah's Sephirot, its levels of existence.

Bowie would tell *Q* magazine in 1997 that *Station To Station* was 'the nearest album to a magick treatise that I've written. I've never read a review that really sussed it. It's an extremely dark album.' For all his immersion in the esoteric,[103] in Bowie's paranoid coke fantasies, he seemed to see himself as an unorthodox Christian bulwark[104] fighting an occultic war against figures like Jimmy Page – an old friend with whom he'd had a trivial falling out.

In the late 1970s through the 1980s, more extreme strands of Crowleyana manifested in the UK's underground music scene. Genesis P-Orridge, a lifelong cultural provocateur, had a sympathetic relationship with the occult through the years of his seminal industrial noise band, Throbbing Gristle. This was cemented in his subsequent outfit, Psychic TV – more accessibly neo-psychedelic, but as much the cultural wing of an occult society as a band.

Thee Temple ov Psychick Youth wore their Crowleyite credentials in the magickal spelling of their name. Later ruptured by schisms, the Orridge-era TOPY was a lifestyle experiment encompassing sexuality, gender, altered consciousness and mind control. 'Gen' would front different versions of PTV up to his death in 2020, but in 1991 he and his family self-exiled from the UK after a Channel 4 *Dispatches* documentary[105] accused the Temple of 'satanic abuse' rituals.

Footage of consensual bloodletting (apparently staged) prefaced a few short moments from a Crowleyite ritual where, the programme's Christian fundamentalist presenter claimed, an abortion was forcibly performed. In fact, the supposed victim was Orridge's first wife, Paula, who had given birth to two healthy children; the scenes were taken from a PTV performance art video, *First Transmission*, which had been available since 1982.[106] Neither fact prevented the Obscene Publications Squad from raiding the Orridge family home prior to the show's broadcast.

Orridge's friend and former bandmate Peter 'Sleazy' Christopherson subsequently formed Coil with his boyfriend, John Balance.[107] More accessible than early industrial music, Coil were nonetheless at the darker end of 1980s electronica. Esotzerica, surrealism, Crowleyism and a strong dose of homoeroticism all tempered their sonic textures.

Christopherson had an aesthetic track record as a photographer, album cover designer[108] and, eventually, video maker that allowed space for occult symbolism. Even the video for their 1984 cover of Gloria Jones' northern soul classic, 'Tainted

---

103 Which included fascistic posturing, embodied in the coldness of the Thin White Duke 'throwing darts in lovers' eyes'.

104 Bowie's form of Christianity at the time may have been inspired by Gnostic dualism; like Crowley, he was a magpie of ideas. But in any case, the album track 'Word On A Wing' plays as a devotional love song by a believer who still questions everything in Heaven and Hell. It was a long way from the young man who decried 'bullshit faith' on 'Quicksand', five years earlier.

105 Fittingly titled 'Beyond Belief'.

106 At the time, *First Transmission* could easily be obtained via mail-order ads in New Musical Express.

107 The celebrated partnership of Sleazy and Balance has since departed this mortal coil, in 2020 and 2010 respectively.

108 For Hipgnosis, noted for the striking sleeves of Pink Floyd's *The Dark Side Of The Moon* and *Wish You Were Here*.

Love',[109] incorporated Crowley's Eye of Horus symbol and the line 'Love is the law, love under will.' (A completion of the philosophy expressed in the seemingly nihilistic 'Do what thou wilt shall be the whole of the law.')

Sleazy's early PTV bandmate, David Tibet, is perhaps one of the most distinctive figures in British underground pop culture.[110] His stage name, bestowed by Genesis P-Orridge, tips the nod to a fascination with Buddhism and eastern mysticism – though these are aligned with Christianity's more esoteric tenets and symbols. As a religious synthesist, it seems inevitable that Tibet should also be taken with the cultural significance of Crowley. The numerological title of his musical project, Current 93, is said to denote both Thelema and the Christian concept of Agape, or unconditional love – a cross-cultural synthesis embracing both the light and dark.

David Tibet's personal and spiritual obsessions have long provided context for Current 93, which began as abrasive electronics but latterly evolved into stark neofolk. But when the esoteric makes inroads into the mainstream, it becomes ripe for parody. Current 93 obliged by recording the *Crowleymass* EP in 1987, a collaboration with Icelandic experimentalist Hilmar Örn Hilmarsson: 'Don't give us no sass or we'll kick your ass / 'Cos we're the heralds of Crowleymass,' Tibet gleefully intones over electro rhythms infused with snatches of devotional chant. The exigencies and ecstasies of Thelema were becoming clichés, in need of a good old piss-take.

By this point, Crowley's hybrid philosophy of occult discipline and personal licentiousness had found some crude avenues of expression. In 1983, post-punk band Blood and Roses (fronted by Lisa Kirby, with a sound more 'punk' than 'post') recorded an EP entitled *Love Under Will*. It did its best to reduce the symbolism and ambiguities of Thelema to thrashy two-and-a-half minute songs, but is chiefly notable for Blood & Roses being among the first wave of bands labelled 'goth'.

In 1988, Fields of the Nephilim scored a UK chart hit with 'Moonchild', a portentously growling number titled after Crowley's neglected Gothic novel. In the evocative video, vocalist Carl McCoy hovers above a supine moonbride, ready to impregnate her like an incubus ('lower me down'). In its heavily stylised manner, it hints at how Crowley lionised himself in the book as the hero Simon Iff – seeking to move the human race forward via a young woman's conception of a supernatural being.[111]

On their 1994 debut album, *Portrait Of An American Family*, Marilyn Manson[112] would yowl out, 'We're gonna ride to the Abbey of Thelema' over metal riffs, with

---

109 'Tainted Love' is reinterpreted as a mournful lament, its melody line played slowly on pealing bells. It's also notable for being the first AIDS charity record, the 'tainted' of the title denoting the mortal threat faced by the gay community. 'Tainted Love is, of course, best known as a hit for electro duo Soft Cell whose vocalist, Marc Almond, appears in the Coil video as a callous ex-lover on a hospital visit – interpreted by some as the Angel of Death.

110 Tibet is also an archivist of neglected or forgotten popular culture, and can be credited with reviving the careers of both Shirley Collins and Tiny Tim late in life.

111 Crowley's romanticised version of himself in *Moonchild* is a white magician countering a cabal of black magicians – effectively the reverse of Wheatley's Crowleyite character in *The Devil Rides Out*.

112 Then a band with a namesake vocalist, as the early Alice Cooper had been.

a rock n roll reference to 'Highway 666'. The song was 'Misery Machine',[113] but here the misery is inherent in Middle America – not in the joyousness of the Great Beast's new religion. To the self-mythologising Crowley, all this attention would have signified we were entering the Age of Horus – or perhaps the Aeon of Lucifer.

It wasn't just the written word that was going through these many cycles of change as it came to grips and reacted with the then modern age.

Music, too, was reacting to the Romantics - especially on the continent.

---

113 'Misery Machine' opens with a sample of an evangelical preacher warning against three thousand Satanist groups active in the USA. It was the era of the 'satanic panic', which had caused Genesis P-Orridge to flee his British homeland. The tradition continues, manifest today in QANON with its online allegations that the liberal wing of US politics is composed of Devil worshippers who cannibalise children. The fact that genuine American occult groups like the Church of Satan have Nietzschean or libertarian right-wing inclinations has been leapfrogged. The tradition continues, manifest today in QANON with its online allegations that the liberal wing of US politics is composed of devil worshippers who cannibalise children.
The same slur was used to demonise early Christians (see Norman Cohn's Europe's Inner Demons, 1975).

Chapter 5

EURO VISIONS

Even if we leave aside the infernal fate of Don Giovanni in Mozart's remarkable 1788 opera, this was an era when composers turned their attention to darker feelings, exploring the beauty of that Gothic darkness. Of course, there had been echoes of a dark, mysterious beauty in music for centuries. One of the most pervasive forms is the Gregorian chant, with its sacred hymns originating from pre-existing Jewish and Byzantine traditions. Named after Pope Gregory I, who codified the form during the 6th century AD, it became universal throughout the Catholic Church in the West. To this day, the Gregorian chant remains among the most spiritually moving and haunting forms of devotional music; it also became the basis of so much melancholic melody.[114]

A requiem, as the musical setting of a mass for the dead, is similarly 'gothic'. Italian operatist Giuseppe Verdi's *Requiem* is the genre in its most epic form, running to an hour and a half. Despite this, it cannot be said to possess the power of Mozart's *Requiem Mass In D Minor*, written (and not quite completed) whilst the increasingly sick composer was on his deathbed in early 1791. '…Death's image is not only no longer terrifying to me, but is indeed very soothing and consoling,' he had previously insisted, yet he remained haunted by the idea that the commission he'd been anonymously granted for the *Requiem* was to mark his own passing.[115]

Of Mozart's near-contemporaries, perhaps the ultimate classical 'proto-goth' was the Hungarian composer Franz Liszt. His *Totentanz* ('Dance Of Death') is a Romantic update of the traditional Gregorian chant for the dead, whilst *Dies Irae* ('Day Of Wrath'), is noted for its daring stylistic innovations. It saw the composer, whose pounding and complex pieces made him famous for breaking piano strings at concerts, floridly encapsulating themes of death, divinity, heaven and hell.

Inspired by Goethe's epic poem, Liszt's bad-boy status was bolstered by his 1857 *Faust Symphony*. Beginning at fever pitch, it prefigured the melodramatics of Hammer horror movies' 20th century soundtrack composer James Bernard albeit, with much greater complexity. The satanic sentiments continued with the 1859-62 *Mephisto Waltzes*, marking him out as the gothic star of the 19th century.[116]

---

114 For a more contemporary variation, check 'The Seventh Seal' by Scott Walker. The late singer-songwriter once took a hiatus from 1960s hearthrobs The Walker Brothers to study Gregorian chant on the Isle of Wight. Its monastic tones echo through his lyrical retelling of Ingmar Bergman's 1957 film: via a Poe-like scenario of Europe under plague, both screen classic and song positing questions of the existence (or non-existence) of God.

115 Mozart's death, aged thirty-five, was first suggested to be the handiwork of his Austrian court rival Antonio Salieri in Alexander Pushkin's play *Mozart And Salieri*. In the 20th century, playwright Peter Shaffer ran with the idea in his popular *Amadeus*. It remains compelling but is pure speculation.

116 Ken Russell, vivid cine-biographer of the great composers, felt the same way. In his *Lisztomania* (1975), Roger Daltrey of The Who plays Franz Liszt as a 19th century rock star amid a plethora of wacky imagery including giant phalluses, spacesuits and Wagner portrayed as a vampire. To its credit, the film also has some oddly effective arrangements of Liszt by prog keyboard maestro Rick Wakeman.

Hector Berlioz's *Dreams of a Witches' Sabbath*,[117] from his 1830 *Symphonie Fantastique*, floats melodically in darkness and is described by Leonard Bernstein as the first piece of psychedelic music. This may be chiefly due to the influence of opium, although whether this reflects the composer's indulgence or the overriding theme of a jilted lover's opium dream of murdering his lost love under its influence is a moot point. But the sabbat movement is a terpsichorean fantasia, joyfully suggesting Satan's unholy denizens with a leavening of the funereal tones of Berlioz's holy *Te Deum*.[118]

Its chief competition in the field of jaunty macabre classicism is *Danse Macabre*, written in 1874 by the French composer Camille Saint-Saëns. Its dizzy waltz evokes Death calling the dead from their graves to dance to his fiddle. *Danse Macabre* is instantly recognisable in its upbeat ghoulishness, used widely in films and TV shows like the lightweight paranormal detective series *Jonathan Creek*.

Similarly, Carl Orff's more ominous *O Fortuna* from his *Carmina Burana* cantata has been called 'the most overused piece of music in film history'.[119] His 1935 adaptation of a thirteenth-century poem imploring a pagan goddess of fortune for some respite is so familiar from TV adverts and film trailers that its post-Wagnerian drama is almost overwhelmed by familiarity. Most uncomfortably, perhaps, it remains a universally recognised overture of unease by a composer of the Third Reich era.

Orff's strident *Sturm und Drang* has an obvious antecedent. 'Siegfried's Funeral', from Richard Wagner's 1876 opera *Götterdämmerung*, the climax of his *Ring Cycle*, captures the German composer's mastery of sorrow in an ominous piece of uber-brooding. Its lament for the legendary Norse warrior of old pagan Europe carries a genuinely ethnic sense of Gothic dread, punctuated by percussive explosions.

Götterdämmerung itself would become a byword for the fall of Hitler's Reich – fittingly, as Wagner was one of the sacred cultural touchstones for der Fuhrer's vision of a pan-European Germanic culture. Its title was a translation of the Norse Ragnarök, the mythical twilight of the gods, after the war in Odin's Asgard, it would bring further destruction on Earth.[120] 'Wagnerian', in its wider bombastic sense, is a term later applied to rock music from the most uncompromising black metal to the apocalyptic post-punk of Killing Joke.

While Wagner's operas – performed then, as now, annually at Bayreuth – were regarded by many as the apex of European culture, some of his contemporaries were not so fortunate. Modest Mussorgsky, the Russian nationalist composer who drew

117 It was the last wish of Ian Brady, the 'Moors Murderer' who took De Sade's lurid imaginings to heart, that 'Dreams Of A Witches' Sabbath' be played at his funeral rites. It was a mark of the sadist's delusion that he imagined the career criminals he was protected from (under the UK penal system's Rule 43) would celebrate his life. In the event, his ashes were dumped unceremoniously in the Atlantic in October 2017.

118 Inspired by the Latin funeral chants of medieval Gregorian monks.

119 Jeff Bond, 'Review of *Mission Impossible 2*', 8 January 2014, via 'Wayback Machine', *Film Score Monthly*, July 2000.

120 Nietzsche titled his penultimate work *Twilight Of The Gods* – though his personal war was against rationalism and what he saw as life-denying Christianity, rather than the old myths of Valhalla. As an avid Wagnerian, he had broken with the great composer over Wagner's antisemitism. Nietzsche, perhaps surprisingly, expressed a preference for the Jews over the stolid Germans of the late nineteenth century. But while his philosophy was crudely cherrypicked by the Nazis, if he'd somehow survived into the twentieth century then his anti-moralism would have precluded any objection to the Holocaust.

on folk as well as classical traditions, was derided in a way that might seem familiar to the later practitioners of goth rock. Musically self-taught and unschooled, a heavy drinker, depressive and morbid in his themes, he would not find much approval until decades after his early death in 1881.

Today, we know *Night On Bald Mountain*, Mussorgsky's wonderful 1867 piece of Russian baroque, from its animated sequence in Walt Disney's 1941 classic *Fantasia*: when the demon Chernabog casts his batwings over the mountain, heaping fire upon and plucking the souls of the dead from the village below. His 1874 *Pictures At An Exhibition*, a much reworked and rearranged collection of piano themes based on his late painter friend Victor Hartmann's works,[121] features 'Baba Yaga (The Fowl's Hut On Legs)' – a piece full of the fire and brimstone of gothic. Its title character is a hideous witch of Slavic folklore, sometimes featured in Euro horror or exploitation films. (Most recently, the 2020 Russian film *Baba Yaga: Terror Of The Dark Forest*.)

In the twentieth century, the late Polish composer Henryk Górecki's works included the brooding devotional beauty of his *Symphony Of Sorrowful Songs*. Their introspective religiosity shares something with the Estonian composer Arvo Part, whose work captures the atmospheric twilight of his home country in piano and choral pieces inflected with folk tradition and echoes of the atonality of Schoenberg.

In terms of folk balladry, melancholia has been at its heart since time immemorial. Outside of the church walls and concert halls of the past century and a half, the secular ballads of the French trouvères and troubadours flourished. From the haunting music of the Yiddish Klezmer to the Portuguese Fado that emerged in the 1820s and the Greek Rebetiko a century later,[122] each played an important role in the European patchwork of lyrical mournfulness.

Folk songs were an oral culture, meaning that few were transcribed, and most have been lost to time. Many long-lost British songs of sex and death were buried by the Industrial Revolution, and many more were edited from memory when the folk song's history was collated in the 1950s. Singer Shirley Collins knows differently because she is steeped in the folk tradition of this windswept isle, particularly as it relates to her native Southern English county of Sussex.

Born in 1935, Ms Collins hasn't flinched from the darker side of this tradition. Her austere yet commanding voice also brought to life antique murder ballads from a timeless catalogue. Her haunting 1971 rendition of 'Murder Of Maria Marten' reflects many of goth's perennially beloved themes, as nurtured in the deep dark heart of melancholic England. It tells the factual tale of a young rural Suffolk woman, murdered by her lover William Corder in the 1820s. His capture and hanging for the

---

121 In audaciously rearranged forms, *Pictures At An Exhibition* became a staple of 1970s prog rock and electronica. Emerson, Lake and Palmer's progged-out stage show featured some additional lyrics, wailing Moog synthesiser and Spanish guitar. Japanese electronicist Isao Tomita's arrangements of the same pieces sounded like Stockhausen having a good laugh.

122 Rebetiko has been termed 'the music of the Greek underground' – the culture of the socially subterranean, rather than any kind of intellectual demimonde. When it was first popularised in the 1920s, its natural habitat was said to be the hashish den and the jail.

crime is said to have been precipitated by her mother's dream that Maria lay buried in a place known as the 'Red Barn'.[123]

Shirley Collins retired from the folk scene in the late 1970s, in part due to an emotional trauma. Her gradual resurgence was largely due to her younger mentor, the aforementioned David Tibet of Current 93 – a cultural archivist of a darkly esoteric tint.[124]

*****

In the late 20th century, gothic music began to straddle the distance between classical forms and the vocal troubadour elements of rock. If post-punk was the rejection of punk rock's over-reliance on the Chuck Berry riff and recycled Americana, goth was European, neoclassical and introspective and pulling from a different tradition.

These hybrid sounds were spearheaded by Melbourne's Dead Can Dance and Sheffield's In the Nursery. Both released influential albums in the mid-Eighties which pioneered the darkwave genre. Delving into darker classical textures, in 1985, Dead Can Dance released their second album, *Spleen and Ideal*, an epic work drenched in the drama of neoclassicism, which initiated what music critic Ned Raggetty called the band's 'consciously medieval European sound'.

In 1987, In the Nursery released *Stormhorse*, a leap forward for the band that fused their post-industrial roots with a cinematically symphonic sweep. As co-founder Nigel Humberstone explains:

> Neoclassicism was more an aesthetic movement, a reaction to Romanticism, with Stravinsky as one of its most famous proponents. Personally, I now think of neoclassical as a term to describe modern electronic and alternative rock music that utilises classical elements, instrumentation and structure.
> All the best music (including classical) has melancholic undertones. You can't get away from the fact that the majority of musicians throughout history have been self-destructive, inspired by loss – how could the resulting music not be melancholic?
> Authors, artists, poets and musicians seem to create their best work whilst suffering depression, anxiety and loneliness.[125]

Known for creating soundtracks to already existing films, In the Nursery created their own soundtrack to the 1919 German film, *The Cabinet Of Dr Caligari*, an early expressionist/Gothic classic. It's an example of the classical filtered through the contemporary, like, more recently, Icelandic cellist Hildur Guðnadóttir's darkly sparse soundtrack for *Joker* (2019), which is stunningly gothic in essence. Ms Guðnadóttir had previously played with reformed industrial transgressives Throbbing Gristle and drone metallists Sunn O))). Her low-key, insinuating tones mark the final point

---

123 *The Murder In The Red Barn* was a staple of English melodrama for decades. Famously, in the 1935 film version, twenty something ladies' man Corder was played by Tod Slaughter – a corpulent veteran stage villain who was fifty at the time.

124 In 2016 Ms Collins recorded *Lodestar*, her first album in forty years, under the mentorship of Tibet. It was also marked by a compelling documentary film on her life, *The Ballad Of Shirley Collins*.

125 Nigel Humberstone to John Robb.

of reclaiming Batman's arch enemy from camp supervillain status. As reinterpreted here, he's closer to – though goes further than – the psychopathic Harlequin of Bob Kane and Bill Finger's original 1930s comic book character.

Aural melancholia is now long established as the main strand of the gothic musical aesthetic. In the 1980s, Frankfurt's Sopor Aeternus and The Ensemble of Shadows brought theatricality to the field in the shape of their transgender vocalist Anna-Varney Cantodea.[126] With a baroque take on the *chansonnier* tradition and a penchant for Poe, the ensemble were as self-consciously gothic as one can get without falling into self-parody. Les Secrets de Morphée, a Parisian ensemble, boasted a Romantic sensibility and feminine vocals orchestrated at a pitch between light opera and popular Euro balladry.

Such atmospherics were more soberly explored in the 1990s by French neoclassicists Elend ('Misery' in German), whose use of chamber orchestras lent a sublimity to sadness that was paradoxically uplifting. Fellow Parisians Dark Sanctuary brought a repetitively ethereal colouring to the ambient tones that had evolved from Scandinavian black metal.[127] Milan's Camerata Mediolanense, classical medievalists, boasted intricately arranged vocals pitched between the operatic tradition and the Renaissance madrigal.[128] Ferrara's Autunna et sa Rose combined chamber music with operatic vocals to dramatic effect. The new millennium saw Nox Arcana's distinctly gothic take on neoclassicism and trad European folk, the American outfit also drawing inspiration from the original 19th-century lit. In Norway, black metal band, Ulver, created a symphony that they performed with the Norwegian national orchestra. The Dutch lute player Josef Van Wissem plays a dark, hypnotic sound that is a mix of a gothic soundtrack and ancient melodies in a captivating whole.

Gothic themes and motifs have been entwined within the arts for centuries. So it was inevitable that post-war pop culture would follow suit, immersing itself in the darker influences of the past. Away from the classical tradition, when post-war pop culture added the elements of sex and electricity to the cordite mix, there would be explosive results.

---

126 Rather disarmingly, the 'Varney' in her stage name was derived from *Varney, The Vampire* (or; *The Feast Of Blood*) – the Victorian 'penny dreadful' serial that pre-dated *Dracula* by decades, albeit with far less literary elegance.

127 An antecedent can be heard in Virgin Prunes' 1981 'Red Nettle', an almost mantric piece of neoclassicism.

128 Incredibly, their musical aesthetic brought them under physical attack in 2008, at a performance in the Swiss town of Fribourg where their instruments were trashed. It seems some on the Left see neoclassicism as somehow 'fascist'.

Chapter 6(66)

THE DEVIL HAS THE BEST TUNES

Coinciding with the invention of the teenager, popular culture exploded in the post-war years. As the darkness and uncertainty of the late 1940s and the previous war years faded into a new decade, it was time to be alive. The USA was having an economic boom, and the post-war youth were having their own party. This new demographic's lifestyle was soundtracked by three-minute songs that succinctly celebrated the new electric *now*.

The raucous optimism of the 1950s, an otherwise conservative decade, placed sex, style and good times at the top of the agenda for its new young consumer generation. Elvis Aaron Presley was the über-symbol of the era, the truck driver turned worldwide phenomenon who now epitomised the American dream.

Yet even his sudden rise to fame was tinged with darkness and a Gothic shiver. His electrified breakthrough, 'Heartbreak Hotel', was composed by songwriter Mae Axton [129] after the song's co-writer guitarist Tommy Durden read a Florida newspaper story about a lovelorn guy who committed suicide in his hotel room, inspiring her to write the classic. But then, the drama of human tragedy has always been at the heart of great popular music

There was always a darkness at the edge of town.

Even if it was played for kooky laughs[130].

In the same era that Middle America got shocked by the rock, gothic horror ingratiated its way into the living room. In 1957, Universal Pictures licensed its classic 1930s/40s monster movies to TV under the lurid title *Shock Theater*. The ersatz European fantasies that once kept Americans awake at night now seemed disarmingly friendly: a new generation looked on Gothic demons like Count Dracula, the Frankenstein Monster and the Wolf Man as if they were older brothers.

It was the beginning of what's been termed 'monster culture': the adoption by American youth of vampires, werewolves, ghouls and ghosts as fantastic f(r)iends that carried them through adolescence, rather than haunting their nightmares. It opened up an untapped market for the terror of teratology.

Famous Monsters Of Filmland magazine was launched in 1958, with its archive of vintage and contemporary monster movie stills, and its pun-laden, juvenile-friendly tone. Then there was the horror-movie host, a kitschy TV character riffing on the classic Hollywood grotesques, staying just the right side of mockery. *Shock Theater* had the ghoulishly cadaverous Zacherley, but the archetype was a horror hostess.

---

129 The so-called 'Queen Mother Of Nashville' who wrote over 200 songs was best known for her Elvis song which was his first number one hit. She also introduced Elvis to his manager Colonel Tom Parker - so not all good!

130 Maybe as a reaction to the dark days of Senator McCarthy and his political paranoia that so dominated the discourse in the late 40s that must have had a knock on on 50s horror schlock.

The Vampira Show had run for one year, from April 1954, on Los Angeles ABC station KABC-TV. Its originator, Maila Nurmi, was an actress of Finnish descent with a svelte hourglass figure and a bohemian air. Her show didn't have *carte blanche* from the old Hollywood studios, so she often lent her pallid allure to B-pictures from a double bill. But still, in creating Vampira, Ms Nurmi coined an alternative glamour that's very recognisable today.

Vampira was briefly a pop-culture favourite, in the period when rock n roll was about to explode. She was even an icon before Elvis. In 1956, when performing in character for Las Vegas shows with Liberace, maestro of the camp candelabra, she met the young Elvis himself playing some shows without his three-man backing band. Things didn't go to the youthful singer's plans.

'*Life* Magazine are going to discover you and they will kiss your shoes,' she reassured him, when even the house orchestra baulked at his flamboyance. This wasn't the Memphis Flash who'd conquer Vegas with his comeback shows of the early 1970s. But Maila Nurmi surely wasn't wrong.

Elvis too was impressed by what he saw. A series of photos exist of him with Ms Nurmi, in all her starved elfin charm. This wasn't Vampira with her flaxen raven hair, but it sure wasn't the Hollywood glam blondes that the King of Rock'n'Roll would later date. Legend (and Ms Nurmi) has it that the gauche twenty-one-year-old came on to her: 'If you'd like to come back after the show, I'd be proud to take you back to my bungalow,' he purportedly told her, whilst noting her advanced age (mid-thirties).

Maila declined the offer. She was, after all, a married TV actress rather than a sex-kitten vampire.

But legend also tells that she'd already met the demimonde of 1950s youth culture, in the shape of posturing 'rebel without a cause' James Dean. When his star was still on the rise, they could be seen caffeinating together at a late-night coffee shop. Like her, Dean was a TV actor – till he hit pay dirt with the first of his iconic movie roles.

'I don't date cartoons,' the new Hollywood icon responded to an interviewer when asked if he and Vampira had been an item. He went into an almost goth like spiel about how he'd studied *The Golden Bough*[131] and De Sade, but was disappointed to find the TV vampiress was all makeup and no occult power.[132]

Morbid mythology insists she proved him wrong when Dean went for a last spin in his Porsche, on September 30, 1955. Ms Nurmi said the legend originated in her response to his putdown, when she sent a photo of herself at Forest Lawn Cemetery in Glendale, inscribed with, 'Having a wonderful time – wish you were here.'

---

131 James Frazer's classic anthropological study of religions and magic. *The Golden Bough* is best known for its influence on TS Eliot's epic poem, *The Waste Land*, but also resonates in Gothic culture: cited in pieces as diverse as 'The Call Of Cthulhu' by H.P. Lovecraft and Jim Morrison's lyric for The Doors' 'Not To Touch The Earth'.

132 It's hard to see why Jimmy Dean regarded the nihilistic marquis as a doyen of the occult, but rumours of his own sex life carry Sadean (or indeed masochistic) elements. Stories abound which he didn't live long enough to deny – like being burned by cigarettes in a gay S&M scenario.

Jimmy Dean never lived to see the rock'n'roll era he became implicitly linked with. But his slighted friend, Vampira, became an icon of proto-goth kitsch. Her influence could be seen weekly on network TV in the mid-sixties, by which time the old Hollywood monsters were figures of fun.

In *The Munsters*, Yvonne De Carlo was vampiric but buxom Lily, a devoted wife to Frankenstein-alike Herman. But the Vampira image came full circle in *The Addams Family*, with the svelte but ghoulish Morticia played by Carolyn Jones. This was the character Maila Nurmi cribbed from Charles Addams' *New Yorker* cartoons, adding details like talon fingernails to make it her own.

In the 1980s, actress Cassandra Petersen would become a Vampira for another era, with her horror hostess Elvira. She had the deathly pale vamp look,[133] but the big-haired brunette also had something of Priscilla Presley about her. It must have been a look that Elvis went for: when Ms Petersen was a Las Vegas showgirl, in the mid-sixties, she'd enjoyed (to evoke The Cramps) a date with Elvis.

But while her descendants became mainstays of pop culture, the original Vampira faded into black and white legend. A copyright dispute between Nurmi and ABC TV sucked the character into limbo. Vampira's startling last hurrah was *Plan 9 From Outer Space*,[134] the celebrated sci-fi/Gothic horror hybrid by sub-low-budget filmmaker Edward D. Wood, Jr.

Filmed in 1956, the movie wouldn't see a very limited release till 1959. Vampira's appearance is brief but effective, reaching forward with her intimidating nails like she's in a silent expressionist film. (Reputedly, she refused to speak Wood's quirkily stilted dialogue.) Her glorious ham acting was matched by Bela Lugosi's swansong: once Universal Pictures' imperious Count Dracula, now elderly, frail, and recently out of rehab for morphine addiction.

Lugosi's part in *Plan 9* was a poignant echo of his best known vampire role. After he died during production, the irrepressible Wood placed a stand-in who was much younger, taller and with lighter hair behind the Dracula cape.

Old Bela expired on August 16, 1956. It was the same date – albeit twenty-one years earlier – as when Vampira's would be beau, Elvis, would die, his heart stifled by prescription pills and hamburger grease.

*****

---

133 Horror hostesses, up to and including Elvira, also seem possessed by the sensual spirit of Betty Page. (Sometimes 'Bettie Page' – her preferred spelling.) The ravenite darling of 1950s soft porn, her bondage photos in *Bizarre* magazine still carry a charge. Ms Page left the glamour photography industry in the late 1950s to become a born-again Christian, seemingly leaving her unhappy and conflicted.

134 *Plan 9 From Outer Space*, Ed Wood's inept magnum opus, is variously described as 'the Worst Movie Ever Made' or a genuine auteur vision, depending on who's watching it. The Damned, the UK's early punk/proto-goth band, evoked the title in their 1979 track 'Plan 9, Channel 7'. The neo-psychedelic song is far more concerned with Vampira than with Wood's movie; the lines 'She lays a wreath of lilies on his grave / His flame gone along with the love he never gave,' allude to the love-that-never-was between her and James Dean.

When Elvis shook his pelvis on *The Ed Sullivan Show*, it terrified Middle America, and rock n roll genuinely seemed to be the Devil's music. Johnny Cash, the original Man in Black, was an early contemporary of the young Presley on the Sun Records label. He had a more traditional appeal as he fused traditional country and western, part of the bedrock of rock'n'roll, with its mutant offspring, rockabilly.

Still, despite his good-natured early hits, Cash could sing from the perspective of a psycho: 'I shot a man in Reno / Just to watch him die,' he intoned from the bottom of his boots in 'Folsom Prison Blues' and his resonating captivating baritone, and outlaw attitude would be part of the future goth DNA. Not far away from Cash's charcoal heart and soul there was the melancholia of Hank Williams and his heartbreak muse that saw him seemingly possessed by forces which kept pulling him down into the depths of darkness and shadows.

The late Jerry Lee Lewis provided a snapshot of the schizoid nature of early rock'n'roll, brawling with personal demons both in his private life and his music.[135] Lewis lived his life as a battle between God and the Devil. With the Devil mostly winning out. His Christian schooling in the Bible Belt told him his love for rock'n'roll was inherently sinful, and it was in the tension between the two that his greatest songs were created.

White Jerry Lee's piano-pounding Black counterpart, Little Richard, had his own battles with himself to fight. A similarly church-raised rock'n'roller who, like Lewis, would go on to record an album of gospel songs, his flamboyant pompadour and lightly applied makeup hinted at his hidden bisexuality. His eyeshadow foreshadowed glam rock, but back in the day, it could have cost him his career.

If the Bible Belt boys felt guilt over playing 'the Devil's music', it wasn't without foundation. Rock'n'roll was a joyously shrieking eagle that came out of the American South. It flew on parallel wings, one of which was country, and the other was the blues. Black America's own roots musicians were just as likely to have been dragged up in church as their white counterparts – but there was a demonic element in the legends that birthed the blues.

In the 1930s, the music of the Mississippi Delta had drawn on the griot chants of African-American slaves and the guitar ballads of European folk. Few lived the licks and the legend more authentically than Robert Johnson. Playing his battered acoustic, even today his slim catalogue of recordings sounds like two guitarists (or at least a twelve-string) at work.

Johnson's song about meeting the Devil down at the crossroads crystallised his legend as if striking a Faustian pact was what made him a Delta blues virtuoso. It can only have strengthened his appeal with posthumous fans like Led Zeppelin, who copped his licks as well as snatches of his lyrics. The last song Robert Johnson recorded plays like an occultic foretelling of his own demise. In 1938, aged twenty-seven, he

---

135 Like that wannabe Southern gentleman Edgar Allan Poe, Jerry Lee married his thirteen-year-old cousin. It cost him the cancellation of his 1958 British tour and, back home in the USA, a relegation from major concert halls to clubs and bars for a decade.

met an untimely death that even outdoes Poe's in its many interpretations. Syphilis; burst ulcer; poisoned by a jealous husband after a dancehall show. When there's no cause given on the death certificate and the deceased is buried in a homemade coffin, there's plenty of room for the imagination to get to work.

As the decades rolled on and the blues turned electric, the posthumously-discovered Johnson remained the archetypal bluesman; boasting of his sexual prowess, fearful of God and sometimes imploring to Jesus – but with one foot entrenched on the dark side, redolent of ancestral magic rituals in Africa or Haiti. Celebrating his hard life to a defiantly upbeat tempo.

It was in 1956, just as Elvis was about to make America scream, that one of a new generation of bluesmen played up the hoodoo to a theatrical level. But Screamin' Jay Hawkins wanted none of the poverty that went with the blues tradition. He wanted a hit record – and it was just as well he fashioned one out of his gleefully maniacal 'I Put A Spell On You'. The song has become a theatrical classic that sold a million without ever officially top of any chart.

At first, an insistent love ballad that Hawkins tapped out at the piano, its brass-driven riff became more compelling as he and his band got drunk in the studio. By the end, his cackling laughter added to the illusion that it was some kind of voodoo invocation.

It was the uniquely manic nature of 'I Put A Spell On You' that made it a bestseller, even though the same aspect kept it from white folks' radio stations. Over time it's become a much covered standard, best known in a smouldering interpretation by Nina Simone.[136] It also made Jay Hawkins into the first shock-rocker, albeit by default. Offered $300 by DJ Alan Freed, the man who coined the term 'rock'n'roll', to climb out of a coffin on stage, he demurred at first: 'No black dude gets in a coffin alive – they don't expect to get out!'

Then the showman instinct took over. Witchdoctor-style bones through the nose. A companion skull named Henry, who Jay would sometimes treat to a cigarette. All were components in the birth of horror rock and an influence on the more ghoulish performers in the goth era.

*****

Across the Atlantic, rock'n'roll fervour was biting hard. But British rock'n'roll, at least before the 1960s beat boom, held little of the authentic hysteria that alarmed conservative types back in the USA.

North London's David Sutch may have been emblematic of this. A seemingly irrepressible showman with a craving for attention, in his twenties, he refashioned himself into little Britain's answer to Screamin' Jay Hawkins. As Screaming Lord Sutch, his schlock-shock tactics somehow embedded him in the national psyche without his ever having a hit record. The nearest he came was with 'Jack The Ripper'

---

136 Post-Birthday Party, the nascent Bad Seeds – briefly known as Nick Cave and the Cavemen – performed a menacing live cover. The additional lines, 'You better kick it / Before it kicks you,' had their own chemical resonance.

in 1963. Purporting to tell the tale of Victorian London's infamous serial killer, it's a cover of an obscure US 45 by Clarence Stacy. Sutch's version is like those old Benny Hill sketches where the TV comedian parodied 1960s pop; it also fudges Stacy's menacing line, 'Is your name Mary Clark?', making it sound like 'Mary Blood'. But then the original stole the line from a British horror movie anyway.[137] (The closest name to Mark Clark in the Ripper's 'canonical five' is Mary Jane Kelly – the last known victim.)

Sutch's cover received a blanket ban by the then very stuffy BBC and never made the charts. But a rare early pop promo can be seen online: in saturated colours, Sutch plays the top-hatted Ripper as a gurning music hall villain. Though the murders are bloodless, there's a gleeful and unsettling savagery to the stabbings. Screaming Lord Sutch's pantomime rock'n'roll had its own unique place at the end of the British seaside pier. As the 1960s wore on, the stage presentation grew increasingly elaborate, featuring knives and swords as props, and (reputedly at one show) butcher-shop offal.[138]

A fixture of Brit pop culture who, paradoxically, never became a star, Sutch would migrate to the absurd shores of UK politics with his formation of the Monster Raving Looney Party.[139]

'Jack The Ripper' had been produced by the tragic genius of early British rock, Joe Meek. A West Country native with an ear for sonic innovation but no musical ability himself, Meek briefly turned out an intriguing string of disparate hits from his home studio above a shoe shop in north London's Holloway Road.

First among them was 'Johnny Remember Me', rendered by young actor John Leyton. The least cloying of a trend of 'death ditties' (like 'Tell Laura I Love Her', wherein a dying racer bids farewell to his girl from the wreckage of his hotrod), the sniffy BBC refused to play it because of an ambiguous line about 'the girl I loved and a lost a year ago'. Nonetheless, it hit number one in the charts – a tribute to the atmospherics of Meek's production, particularly the ghostly female voice that calls to her lover from the treetops.[140]

Success was short-lived for Joe Meek, despite the reel-to-reel recording techniques that find echo even in our digital age. He was legally barred from receiving royalties from his worldwide hit 'Telstar', due to a lawsuit by French soundtrack composer

---

137 The 'Mary Clark' line is a plot device in *Jack The Ripper* (1959), which runs with the fictional theory that the Ripper was a London gent seeking the prostitute who corrupted his son. Sutch may have fudged it as 'Mary Blood' to avoid copyright claims by London film/TV production team Baker-Berman, who made the movie.

138 If the anecdote about animal organs as stage effects is true, it places Sutch alongside the early US gore movies for Grand Guignol effect. It also puts him ahead of classic shock-rocker Alice Cooper for sloppy authenticity.

139 The Raving Loony Party, as they were truncatedly known, were a regular fixture of UK general elections for two-and-a-half decades – a seemingly harmless distraction for those who didn't mind throwing their vote away. Lord Sutch himself failed to get elected on forty-one occasions.
David Sutch finally took his own life by hanging on June 16, 1999. He'd been suffering from depression his entire life, according to his bereaved girlfriend.

140 Siouxsie Sioux – who compared being labelled 'the Queen of Goth' to being called 'the Prince Regent of Fools' – numbers 'Johnny Remember Me' among her earliest musical influences. (It topped a list of her favourite records on a BBC Radio 1 'My Top Ten' show in the 1980s.) In the early 1990s, Rose McDowall of Strawberry Switchblade teamed up with US cultural bogeyman Boyd Rice as the duo Spell, recording a suitably eerie cover on their album *Seasons In The Sun*.

Jean Ledrut who accused him of plagiarising the theme from the film *Austerlitz*. The suit would be settled in Meek's favour – but not till three weeks after his death.

As the hits dried up, so Joe's use of amphetamines and barbiturates accelerated. He reached a classic level of speed psychosis, believing poltergeists inhabited his cramped flat-cum-studio at 360 Holloway Road and alien beings were trying to control his mind. A possibly apocryphal story has Phil Spector, the US producer Meek is sometimes compared to, calling him in 1964 and suggesting they hook up when he visited the UK. Meek reputedly freaked and told Spector to stop stealing his ideas.[141] He also turned down Brian Epstein's overtures to produce The Beatles. Four times.

On February 3, 1967, Joe Meek's world finally imploded. After a petty argument about unpaid rent and noise with his landlady, Violet Shenton, he blew her away with a shotgun confiscated from his singing protégé, Heinz. Realising he had nowhere further to turn, Joe turned the gun on himself and completed the act of murder-suicide.[142]

Still, it's for his production methods, and his use of the studio as an instrument, that we remember Joe Meek. Two years before 'Telstar', he showcased his aural imagination in the four-track *I Hear A New World*, recorded with Ealing skiffle/ exotica band The Blue Men. Joe described his intention as creating a sonic 'picture of what could be up there in outer space'.

The EP was on a very limited edition and created few waves in 1960. A second EP was planned but aborted; incredibly, it wasn't till 1991 that we got to hear an album version. Its lo-tech/high-imagination evocation of other worlds – nay, other dimensions – and marks it out as a genuine precursor to Martin Hannett's work with Joy Division.[143]

The fifties were the harbinger and foundation of future pop culture. The stylised bequiffed romp through post-war culture threw up many reference points from ghoulish kitsch to the very notion of being a rock'n'roll star that would be so much part of the goth equation, but it was in the next decade with the youthquake becoming mainstream and revolutionary at the same time that the real dark energy stands would start to coalesce.

---

141 In the actuality, Spector's and Meek's techniques were far apart. Spector's 'Wall of Sound' was built up from mono-era overdubs, layering the instrumentation until pop music approached a Wagnerian level. Meek had his backing band playing live in sync, but was a master of compression and spatial separation.

142 It's in Meek's homicidal act that we find parallels with Spector. It's led to speculation about the 'edginess' of record producers, though there's little to suggest they're more unstable than any other creative workers.
The US Wall of Sound pioneer cut a slight figure, for which he overcompensated with a fixation on firearms. At various times, he threatened everyone from former wife Ronnie Spector to Leonard Cohen (during recording of 1977's *Death Of A Ladies' Man* album) with handguns.
On February 3, 2003, the semi-retired legend finally, perhaps inevitably, went too far. In a 911 call, his driver quoted Spector as saying, 'I think I killed somebody.' The victim was forty-year-old B movie actress Lana Clarkson, who expired at the producer's Californian mansion from a gunshot wound to the mouth.
Spector's defence team tried to spin it as suicide, but after six years and two trials the State of California handed him nineteen-years-to-life for murder. He spent much of the rest of his existence as a prison hospital patient, dying from Covid-19 complications in January 2021.

143 Think of Hannett absorbing the sound of smashing crockery into the sonics of *Unknown Pleasures* – literally throwing in the kitchen sink. Then consider that Meek recorded many of the sound effects for *I Hear A New World* in his kitchen, rather than creating them electronically.

Chapter 7

PAINT IT, BLACK

The Dark Heart of the Psychedelic Sixties

The '60s saw a pop culture explosion. Led by The Beatles, it put the UK at the centre of the youthquake and pop culture at the forefront of the generation gap. Initially, the battle lines were drawn over 'long hair', but the bright and breezy music of the early sixties was full of a joie de vivre optimism that believed it could change the world. As the decade progressed, things would hint at an innate and attractive darkness and a surly rebelliousness that was compounded by strange new drugs and a clutch of bands who would attempt to paint things very black.

The Swinging Sixties also embraced an increasingly serious flirtation with the dark side. When The Beatles turned pop fans on to acid and (perhaps more influentially) eight-track stereo recording with *Sgt Pepper's Lonely Hearts Club Band*, The Rolling Stones followed suit with *Their Satanic Majesties Request*. For some, it may have come over as more cod-psychedelic than satanic, but for your author, it's the Stones' singular greatest album, with its off-kilter trips and Brian Jones's spectral mellotron adding to the glacial space rock weirdness. From the off, the Stones - pushed by their visionary manager Andrew Loog Oldham - were walking on the dark side and exploiting a bad boy image that was a shadow-self of the perceived cuddlier Fab Four.

Their classic 1966 single, and proto-goth classic, 'Paint It, Black', has been described by hippie-era pop-culture historian Les Daniels as 'a minor key tribute to death and despair with a droning sitar accompaniment'.[144] The sitarist was the band's founder, Brian Jones, a leering 1890s-style dandy decadent with a suitably chaotic lifestyle.

Brian was the rebel from stuffy Cheltenham who hero-worshipped black bluesmen but never got credited with writing a single Stones song. In his regency pomp of 1966/67, draped in beads and layers of finery, topped off with the immortal and most perfect bowl-cut hairstyle, he and best friend 'Prince Stash'[145] lived out the Byronic cliché of being mad, bad and dangerous to know. Jones was not the only Stone to be caught up in media-fuelled drug busts by the police in 1967/8, but he had the most fragile personality and found the legal ordeals hard to withstand.[146] In his final days with the Stones, he was increasingly absent – even when he was in the same room.

---

144 Les Daniels, *Fear: A History Of Horror In The Mass Media*, Granada Publishing 1977. Cover versions of 'Paint It, Black' in what can be loosely termed 'gothic pop-culture' are innumerable: ranging from Marc Almond's orchestral dramatics to Ministry's noisy histrionics. Inkubus Sukkubus's darkwave version plays like a meshing of the two.

145 Stanislaus Klossowski De Rola, son of the French artist Balthus – one of the Twentieth century's great erotic aesthetes.

146 Stash, on the other hand, a fellow blues enthusiast who'd been caught up in Brian's drugs raids, has lived to be an octogenarian. Like a self-styled *fin de siècle* decadent, he went on to write studies of the classical alchemist's tradition.

Brian's use of drugs escalated with his mixing of barbiturates (downers) and booze – a potent combination often found in the bloodstreams of dead people. In art filmmaker Jean-Luc Godard's semi-documentary centred on the recording of 'Sympathy For The Devil',[147] for the 1968 album *Beggars Banquet*, bad boy Brian is barely an appendage whilst Jagger/Richards are visibly the dominant musical and psychological force..

Less than a month after he'd left The Rolling Stones, he was found dead at the bottom of his swimming pool at Cotchford Farm, Sussex, on 3 July 1969. The band were already scheduled to play a free festival at London's Hyde Park, two days later. It would become a memorial for their wayward founder. Jagger, made-up in the style of Turner, his character in the as-yet-unreleased film *Performance*, read aloud from Shelley's 'Adonais', his elegy on the death of the poet Keats: 'he is not dead, he doth not sleep, / He hath awaken'd from the dream of life…'

Brian's awakening from our mortal dream spawned its own legend over the years. Friends who were with him that night, including his girlfriend and his chauffeur, cried 'murder'. The band has always been dismissive of the murder theory.

'…I just don't know what happened to Brian that night,' said Richards. 'If anyone was going to kill Brian, it was going to be me.'[148] Indeed, it's been claimed that 'Keef', as he became popularly known, had pulled a knife on his ex-bandmate earlier that day – though this was a row over rights to the name 'The Rolling Stones' and went no further.

From that point and beyond, the visual icons of the band have been the undivorceable Jagger/Richards. But for a few, Brian the blond boy-brat, remains its 1960s 'Godstar' – to evoke Psychic TV's mid-'80s psychedelic tribute.[149]

There was plenty of iconography around the Stones which saw the band become the template for all rock'n'roll groups. There was Jagger's proto-glam androgyny of the late '60s and early '70s. But most enduring was Keef as the 'elegantly wasted', bone-earringed pirate. His ghostly pallor and crow's-nest hair would become an archetypal gothic image – even if the guitarist himself claimed to listen to nothing but black music, adding 1970s funk and reggae to his blues palate. Whether or not the Stones truly held any sympathy for the Devil, they would flirt with darkness for years. It reached its apogee with their festival at Altamont Speedway, northern California, on December 6, 1969. In *Gimme Shelter*, the startling documentary film of the Stones' activities in the dying days of the sixties, Hells Angels appointed as security guards are seen blithely beating fans with pool cues in front of the stage. To some, it seemed as if the satanic flirtations, the paean to Lucifer and the courting of

---

147 Godard's film was originally titled *One Plus One*, but has long been distributed as *Sympathy For The Devil*. It's a period piece, the non-musical sequences comprising political satire that extols Marx and equates right-wing conservatism with Nazism; redolent of a time when some people took the politically conservative Jagger as a genuinely radical figure.

148 Victor Bockris, *Keith Richards: The Unauthorised Biography, Revised and Updated Edition*, Omnibus Press, 2013.

149 It was a unique moment when Genesis P-Orridge, former Throbbing Gristle provocateur, turned psych-pop star. 'When I was at school, when I was a schoolboy, I actually met Brian Jones once…' he told Muriel Gray on *The Tube* in 1985. 'The strange thing that struck me then, and I didn't try and articulate, was that he seemed completely separate from the other people in the room the whole time. Like a phantom, like he was not real.'

Kenneth Anger,[150] had come home to roost. In any case, the innocence of the 1960s was now truly over. The Manson murders had terrified Hollywood in the summer, while meth and smack had long since eclipsed psychedelics in San Francisco.

As for The Rolling Stones, they had never really been members of the counterculture anyway – more akin to decadent nouveau aristocrats. And as we shall see, there were performers with greater claims to wiping out the sixties.

*****

The underbelly of the '60s saw all kinds of weird and wonderful bands that would be feeding into the future narrative. Many of the regional garage bands who sprang up in reaction to the 'British Invasion', headed by The Beatles and The Stones, saw an Americanisation of the Brit beat boom, which had plundered US rock'n'roll and R&B in the first place. These groups' musical psychedelia, with primitive fuzztone guitar and Farfisa organ, were cranked to max distorted garage anthems. The importance of these mostly one-hit wonders was celebrated in 1972, with the release of the compilation *Nuggets: Artyfacts From The First Psychedelic Era 1965-68*. Its sleeve notes, by *Creem* journalist and later Patti Smith Group guitarist Lenny Kaye, were among the first writings to coin the phrase 'punk rock'.

Fired up by the Stones' brooding cool, this generation of garage bands like The Standells' made a virtue of their grinding simplicity and produced a heartfelt blue-collar lament, 'Sometimes Good Guys Don't Wear White', later covered by psychobilly originators The Cramps.

The largely unsung cult bands of the time are legion. The Monks comprised US servicemen in Germany who dressed to match their name, complete with tonsure. They played with a raw, catchy repetitiveness on their only album, *Black Monk Time*, with seemingly improvised lyrics as socially angst-ridden as any of their long-haired brethren back home.[151]

Emerging from LA, The Seeds' hit 45 'Pushin' Too Hard' showcased a snotty, whining, stripped-down, Farfisa-inflected sound. The intensity of frontman Sky Saxon granted him cult status long after The Seeds disbanded (around the time *Nuggets* was released). Saxon later resurfaced in the prolific, tripped-out, psych-folk band Yo Ha Wha 13, led by Eastern-styled guru Father Yod (real name James Baker). It was a perfectly wacky, if benign, bookend to the psychedelic era.

Roky Erickson, lead singer of Seeds contemporaries the Thirteenth Floor Elevators, followed a darker trajectory. The Austin, Texas band's big hit was 'You're Gonna Miss Me', another resentful, Stones-influenced sneer that bridged the gap between garage punk and the full-blown psychedelia of a band like Arthur Lee's Love. But Roky had a heap of trouble coming his way. An advocate of hallucinogens, despite being treated for incipient schizophrenia, he was busted in his home state for possession of

---

150 See Chapter 4.

151 Play The Monks and The Fall back to back; hear why Mark E. Smith acknowledged them as an influence.

a single joint in 1969. Facing a draconian Texan prison sentence of up to ten years, he took a plea to enter a mental hospital instead. It led to three years of electroshock treatment and the chemical cosh of Thorazine.

When Roky came home from the hospital, he seemed a whole lot crazier than when he went in. The handsome young man with a full head of bouffant hair now had a Manson-esque beard and the air of a charismatic homeless person until his 2019 death. Still, he'd earned enough kudos to remain an eternal cult figure.[152]

*****

Rock music was first taken seriously by the intelligentsia in the mid-sixties when folkie poet Bob Dylan went electric. While some interpretations by the literati were a little absurd, staking out territory way beyond their neighbourhood, many of Dylan's songs of the time had a detectable darkness in their DNA.

Dylan's 'lyrics came closest of all to the standards of traditional poetry,' wrote Les Daniels in his very accessible study of macabre pop culture.[153] 'His middle and most powerful period (post-protest and pre-prettification) contained some shattering images of urban despair, complete with characters like Jack the Ripper… and the Phantom of the Opera.' Daniels is referring to Dylan's first fully electric album, *Highway 61 Revisited*. The surrealistic, *Wasteland*-inspired flamenco of 'Desolation Row' also features the Hunchback of Notre Dame.

All were figures in Bobby's amphetamine-crazed vision of the time, anachronisms dredged up from an unsleeping unconscious. As Daniels observed, the songs exhibit a 'sickness of the soul', before his re-emergence after a serious July 1966 motorcycle crash gave him a more earthly grounding.[154] This sickness haunts the vividly downbeat 'Just Like Tom Thumb's Blues', where the narrator on drunken Mexican wanderings warns the listener to watch out for the 'hungry women' 'down on Rue Morgue Avenue' – a reference to Poe's 'The Murders In The Rue Morgue'.

Latterly, Dylan is often linked with his near-contemporary Leonard Cohen. It's a lazy comparison, though both were folk singers of North American/Jewish heritage. The older Cohen was an established poet before he began his musical career, his central influence being the Spaniard Federico Garcia Lorca. Aligned with the Surrealists, Lorca's verse nonetheless displays a high Romantic sensibility which combines sensuality and religious faith. [155]

---

152 In the early 1980s, Roky Erickson & the Aliens would release 'Creature With The Atom Brain', its compulsive riff accompanying a retelling of a 1955 sci-fi horror movie: 'these crimes were being perpetrated by dead men charged with atom rays, which gives them superhuman strength and makes them impervious to bullets. Well, if you want to believe that story you can,' says the newsreader-style voiceover. 'I just like horror,' the amiably askew Roky told a BBC Radio1 interviewer in 1980.

153 Daniels, *Fear: A History Of Horror In The Mass Media*.

154 More than one Dylanologist contended that the motorbike wreck may have been an invention by manager Albert Grossman, to take his revered young icon out of the public eye. According to them, Dylan had developed a speed and smack habit that required some serious cleaning up.

155 A gay man of left-wing sympathies, the poet was murdered by Franco's nationalists in the early days of the Spanish Civil War. Much later, Leonard Cohen would pay the ultimate tribute by naming his daughter Lorca.

It was these aspects of sexual metaphor and religious iconography that Cohen brought to his own songs. Initially intending to cut a country and western album to solve his financial problems, his pairing with folk-country band Kaleidoscope created a lo-fi acoustic sound that was haunting in its contrasts.

On *Songs Of Leonard Cohen*, his 1967 debut, his gently lugubrious voice (deepened over subsequent decades by 'fifty thousand cigarettes and several swimming pools of whisky'[156]) and minimalist classical guitar chop come out of one speaker; a swirl of strings, bass, organ and minimal percussion inhabit the other. When some of those songs, notably 'Sisters Of Mercy' and 'Stranger Song', were beautifully placed on the soundtrack of Robert Altman's 1971 'anti-Western', *McCabe And Mrs. Miller*, the re-recordings sounded notably less primitive. The songs and the drama seem inextricable now. The 'Mrs. Miller' of the title is a cockney brothel keeper and opium smoker played by Julie Christie.[157] Cohen's 'Sisters Of Mercy' were, of course, hookers who he graced with the ecclesiastical dignity of nuns. It's a metaphor that echoes down the years. At the turning point of the 1970s/80s, Andrew Eldritch would co-opt it as the name of his band.[158]

In more recent years, the very loosely defined (but stylistically gothic folk-inspired experimental music that emerged from post-industrial circles) neofolk [159] genre wore the influence of early Cohen as an emblem. Commentators with loud mouths but one-dimensional opinions pinned him as a 'misrerabilist', but the late Leonard's oeuvre rarely descended into mournfulness.

Though when it did, the results could be devastating. On early 1970s album *Songs Of Love And Hate*, the foreboding 'Avalanche' was the only Cohen song to fully embrace gothic imagery. In 1984, Nick Cave[160] would cover 'Avalanche' on *From Her to Eternity*, the first Bad Seeds album. Everything is more overt on Cave's version: his vocal contortion reflects the psychologically deformed man's anger; Barry Adamson's bass line plays like a warning to stay away; the psychic avalanche itself is given shape by Mick Harvey's crashing drums.

Perhaps the unlikeliest shore of 1960s folk was inhabited by a band who, audaciously, cribbed their name from one of pop fiction's most revered/derided visionaries. H.P. Lovecraft came out of Chicago but, at the height of the 1967-68 psychedelic scene, were briefly a fixture at San Francisco clubs like the Filmore. Their self-titled debut album is a dated grab-bag of styles, but 'The White Ship' combines folk harmonies

---

156 Paul Zollo, *Songwriters On Songwriting*, Da Capo Press, 1997.

157 Siouxsie at one point numbered *McCabe And Mrs. Miller* among her favourite films, fond of quoting Constance Miller's emblematic line: 'I ain't no do-gooder.'

158 The early Sisters of Mercy sound had little in common with Cohen, cleaving to the post-punk template of Stooges/Joy Division. As with most early 'goth' bands, more subtle nuances crept in when the four-piece electric lineup was sometimes jettisoned.

159 Inspired by the poetic darkness of Cohen and the mournful late period Nico and flirted through the post-industrial quark originators like David Tibet (Current93, Douglas Pearce (Death In June) and Tony Wakeford (Sol Invictus) mixed a fascination with a music from the soil folk tradition and neo-pagan and occult sensibilities into a powerful dark take on more haunting traditional forms.

160 Cohen's lyrical influence on Cave seemed to grow as the Bad Seeds lineup changed and he grew away from the deconstructed blues of the early years. Certainly, both artists are mordant humorists – a quality that's often overlooked.

and flute to ethereal effect; evoking the fantasies of a dreamer, it avoids the downbeat ending of H.P. Lovecraft's short story.

Their second album (imaginatively titled *H.P. Lovecraft II*) is far more interesting – in terms of sonics rather than songs, as it was recorded while tripping on acid. 'At The Mountains Of Madness' is charmingly demented, with a passage of lysergic laughter, but lacks the vividness of the Lovecraft fantasy that provided the title. For his was a personal cosmology created by a vivid inner life (as well as his xenophobic fear of much of the human race), rather than a couple of hundred micrograms of a hallucinogen.

The leader of The Mothers of Invention, Frank Zappa, was an experimentalist inspired by Stravinsky and Varese, as well as an R&B and doo-wop fan. He was also a vicious satirist: *Absolutely Free*, the second Mothers album, was interspersed with skits parodying Middle America. It was such iconoclasm that would allow Zappa to endure the Year Zero ethos of punk, with credibility intact. Admirers included Mark E. Smith and Mark Perry.[161]

For a period in the late '60s, he was also a music-label mogul. On a distribution deal with Warner Bros Records, Bizarre Records issued records by the Mothers themselves and busking outsider Wild Man Fischer. When the label ran into trouble, it was supplanted by the counterintuitively titled Straight Records: home to groupie band The GTO's (Girls Together Outrageously) and the early Alice Cooper, then a chaotic psychedelic band.

Straight carved itself a niche in musical history when it issued *Trout Mask Replica* by Captain Beefheart and His Magic Band in 1969. The good captain's real name was Don Van Vliet, and he was an old high school friend of Zappa (who gave him his stage name). In varying lineups, the Magic Band recorded a couple of albums where blues rock headed into psychedelia.

But the Straight double set was a reductio ad absurdum which, heard only once, some listeners would never recover from. Beefheart's surrealist take on the blues had little to do with drug experimentation[162] and everything to do with a maniacal, ruthlessly imposed discipline. His hapless (but musically sharp as nails) Magic Band were subjected to a cult-like lockdown at a studio in Woodland Hills, California.

That *Trout Mask Replica* sounds like one of the only authentic rock albums ever recorded is due in part to how its influence filtered through,[163] long after it met with bemusement. The growling Van Vliet voice applied itself to expressionistic lyrics about wind and sex and railroads and animals. Its immediacy was due as much to sound as to meaning, meshed with blues licks broken down and re-syncopated.

---

161 Editor of the seminal Sniffin' Glue Xerox zine and founder of the band Alternative TV.

162 'I would say that it's an awfully overrated aspirin and very similar to the old people's Disneyland,' Van Vliet said of his brief use of acid. Quoted in Mike Barnes, *Captain Beefheart: The Biography*, Omnibus Press 2011.

163 The Birthday Party are oft cited as Beefheart descendants. Nick Cave denies listening to him at that point, but he was only one part of a devastating sum total: guitarist Rowland S. Howard, bassist Tracy Pew or drummer Mick Harvey mayhap have swallowed some of the Beefheart influence.

Beefheart would enjoy relatively more success in the 1970s, with his hip expressionism anchored to a more laidback style. His 1982 *Ice Cream For Crow* was a return to jagged form, but also his swansong. For the rest of his life, he worked as a painter in a house close to the Californian coast. His primitive art shared a David Lynch-like fascination with nature's little critters. Fittingly, cinematic visionary Lynch once named *Trout Mask Replica* as his favourite record of all time.

The voodoo swampland of New Orleans was a perfect backdrop for the late Dr John musical character created by local resident Mac Rebennack for for his swampy dark blues. After moving to LA to pursue his own music career, he created the Dr. John character as an African prince, conjure man, herb doctor, and spiritual healer who had come to New Orleans from Haiti and was embedded deeply in the local voodoo and Gris Gris culture. The 1968 Dr John *Gris Gris* debut album saw him fully immersed in his new characters and the swampy blues was as gothic as it gets, as goth icon and singer/poet Lydia Lunch recognises:

> Spooky, kooky, hoodoo voodoo (that) brings me back to a New Orleans that I was lucky enough to spend 2 glorious years in, long before the man-made disaster that was the aftermath of Hurricane Katrina, which ripped the soul right out of the place. New Orleans, just like Dr. John, once it's in your blood remains a low-grade infectious fever causing night sweats, palpitations and an overwhelming urge to grind your hips into the nearest thing.[164]

✶✶✶✶✶

Back in the UK, the late sixties were panning out in their own idiosyncratic direction. In the slipstream of the Brit beat boom, Pink Floyd arrived just after The Beatles and Stones had created a new world of flamboyance. Like their peers, the well-educated Floyd were inspired to form a band by black R&B players: their name was taken from Piedmont bluesmen Pink Anderson and Floyd Council. But the band's leading light, tousle-haired Syd Barrett from the university town of Cambridge, occupied his own space altogether.

An erudite reader of children's literature and Eastern mysticism, Syd's early songs like 'The Gnome' and 'The Scarecrow' struck bells for anyone who read the whimsical fantasy of Lewis Carroll or the nonsense verse of Edward Lear. He was also an enthusiast for psychedelics; a film exists of the young Syd having an ecstatic revelation on psilocybin mushrooms in the Gog Magog hills of Cambridgeshire[165] in the summer of 1966, when Pink Floyd had already formed and based themselves in London. Tripping out – which continued with some regularity, as LSD supplanted mushrooms – may have had an incalculable effect on the Floyd sound.

'Interstellar Overdrive', as performed at the UFO Club or the Roundhouse, could last for well over a quarter of an hour; it was the birth of 'space rock', the outward momentum of psychedelia which mapped out inner rather than outer space reshaping

---

164 Lydia Lunch to Louder Than War.

165 *Syd Barrett's First Trip* is an eleven-minute piece of 8mm footage taken by film student Nigel Gordon.

parts of the rock'n'roll landscape before Syd burned out so prematurely. The troubled genius's intense creative flow is still remembered by his former manager, Pete Jenner:

> The music seemed to pour out of him for a brief period, and then it stopped almost as soon as it had started. All the stuff on Floyd's first album he wrote in the autumn of 1966. In fact, nearly all the songs he ever wrote for the group or solo were in that six months. [166]

That first album, *The Piper At The Gates Of Dawn*,[167] initiated the tradition in 'progressive rock' of an album not containing the band's singles. Peter Jenner's management partner, Andrew King, later remembered the origin of Pink Floyd's unlikely debut:

> Syd told me it took him weeks to perfect the lyrics for "Arnold Layne". There was a lot of intellectual effort involved. I miss him every day of my life, really. He had everything. He was a songwriter, painter, actor, charmer. [168]

Tragically, that natural star quality proved finite. But 'Arnold Layne' is the quintessential 1967 psych-pop single, so startling in sound and vision that it made a youthful Captain Sensible stop on his walk home, to sit on a wall and listen.[169] With a throbbing bass line and an echoey refrain of the title character's name, it's an oh-so-English tale of a knicker-nicker fetishist whose collar is felt by the law.

It was followed quickly that spring by the sublime 'See Emily Play'. The lyric was hauntingly simple (with its ghostly image of the girl who floats 'on a river / Forever and ever'[170]), though the music was a neat encapsulation of avant-garde sound in a sub-three-minute pop single. It made the top ten, and the Floyd played it three times on UK TV's weekly *Top of the Pops*. But this, according to bandmates, is when Syd started to slip out of sync with them.

On Pink Floyd's debut tour of the USA in late 1967, he appeared on a TV show where he refused to mime to his own songs, staring motionless at the camera. In retrospect, it's seen as the start of a psychotic breakdown catalysed by too many trips.

Syd was certainly feeling the need to come down to the other side of the acid experience, as shown by his increasing use of Mandrax.[171] At one show, he poured a compound of Brylcreem and 'mandies' into his hair, which beneath the stage lights gave the impression of his face as a melting wax candle.

The autumn of 1967 attempt to get Syd to write another hit resulted in 'Vegetable Man', an extraordinary meld of whimsy and psyched-out R&B. But it was a little

---

166 Pete Jenner to John Robb.

167 The title came from a chapter of *The Wind In The Willows* by Kenneth Grahame, the book that introduced Toad of Toad Hall to children's lit. It signifies the English whimsy that was a part of Syd Barrett.

168 Andrew King to John Robb.

169 Ray Burns – the good captain, at various times bassist/lead guitarist/songwriter of The Damned – was then thirteen years old. Whilst one of the original UK punk rockers, his main influences were figures like Syd Barrett and Kevin Ayers who sprang from British psychedelia. He tried to recruit Syd as producer of The Damned's second album, but the sometime visionary had gone home to Cambridge for good. The captain's men ended up with Floyd drummer Nick Mason instead.

170 On *Pin Ups*, David Bowie's 1973 tribute to bands on the 1964-67 London scene, his version of 'See Emily Play' plays up the eeriness by using grotesque multi-speed vocals on the chorus – as on his own 'After All' and 'The Bewlay Brothers'.

171 A powerful British sleeping pill of the time, often used for recreational purposes. Its nearest transatlantic equivalent would be Quaaludes in the 1970s, with similar dangers if taken in high dosage.

more disturbing this time: the crazed nature of the lyric seemed authentic and in its refrain – 'Vegetable man, where are you?' – Syd appeared to be addressing himself.

The rest of the band felt it would be indecent to release it, given their friend's fragmenting state; it's a position surviving members have maintained, blocking its release on Pink Floyd retrospectives.[172] Another song, 'Scream Thy Last Scream' was also suppressed, and another abortive Floyd single deemed too enticingly suggestive of psychosis, with its changes of tempo and multi-speed backing vocal by Syd. (The original recording featured Nick Mason on lead vocal; as with 'Vegetable Man', bootleg copies can be found online.)

By early 1968, Syd Barrett was a stranger in his own band. On *A Saucerful Of Secrets*, the second Floyd album, he was supplanted by old Cambridge pal David Gilmour. On 'Jugband Blues', his only track on the album, the whimsy was overcome by melancholia, and it served as his departure note. Plans by the band to keep their songwriting genius on as a non-performing member came to nought.

But it wasn't the end. Syd stayed on in west London, sharing a flat with late pop artist Duggie Fields. Legends abounded in the following decade of how excessive use of acid and Mandrax tipped him further over the edge: of how a short stint living with a crazed couple had them spiking his morning coffee. Most disturbing were rumours of the formerly gentle young man inflicting cruelty on girlfriends, perhaps the depressive reaction of a man crazed by downers,

Dave Gilmour made the sensitive observation that his old friend had been deeply affected by the early death of his father. The childlike imagination, melancholia and fragility had all been there early on, before LSD did its work and fragmented his personality.

It was Gilmour, along with emergent Floyd songwriter Roger Waters (whose poetic pessimism supplanted Syd's surreal vision), who drew him back into the recording studio. *The Madcap Laughs* and *Barrett*, the resultant early seventies albums, held some extraordinary songs about the contents of the writer's private world which, like an English Beefheart, incorporated nature's little offshoots ('Rats', 'Terrapin').[173]

But the edginess of those recordings stems, in part, from how difficult they were to put together. Recollections by producers Gilmour, Waters and Malcolm Jones suggest that the fragments they had to work with were reflective of their writer's mood swings.

By the time Pink Floyd recorded their synth-inflected mid-seventies album, *Wish You Were Here*, with its 'Shine On You Crazy Diamond' tribute to Syd, they didn't recognise the man himself when he showed up in the studio. Reputedly, Waters was in tears when he realised the chubby guy with a shaven head and no eyebrows was his old pal.

Roger 'Syd' Barrett left London three years later, walking the whole fifty miles back to Cambridge. His sister, Rosemary, said he was never institutionalised, though

---

172 'Vegetable Man' is easily found on YouTube today. Back in 1984, when it could only be heard on a vinyl bootleg, The Jesus and Mary Chain recorded a punkish cover on the B-side of their debut 45, 'Upside Down'.

173 Unreleased tracks and rather crazed outtakes eventually found release in the 1990s, when EMI released the collection *Opel*.

records exist of psychiatric therapy as an outpatient. 'Perhaps the very vision that he had turned inwards on himself rather than being passed on to us,' reflected onetime manager Peter Jenner.[174]

A much quieter aspect of the Barrett legacy is the vividly coloured, impressionistic abstracts and nature studies he devoted much of the rest of his life to painting. It's to be hoped it brought him fulfilment, away from the music industry where such a singular genius could never fit in. His influence echoes through the decades, with both Bowie and Bolan turning his unique vision into the twin pillars of glam rock and onwards entwined into the punk and post-punk periods.

*****

Psychosis of a totally theatrical kind also made itself felt in the late 1960s. 'Fire', by the Crazy World of Arthur Brown, was a freak UK number one that arrived on cue for the late '60s occult craze. Vocalist Brown was a renegade from the British R&B/soul scene with a semi-operatic range. Born in the Yorkshire town of Whitby (now the locale for the annual goth weekend), he'd also trained as an actor in Paris. None of it went to waste.

Beginning his legendary black and white *Top of the Pops* performance in a fiery helmet[175], it was soon discarded in case it set his hair on fire. The act set a template for shock-rock that went somewhere darker than the Screamin' Jay Hawkins/Screaming Lord Sutch pantomime. 'Fire' was a transatlantic hit; the young man who'd rechristen himself 'Alice Cooper' saw the thin, wiry Arthur gyrating in skeletal body paint. It's an image that has endured down through black metal and Marilyn Manson, and the endless parade of dark overlords of showbiz hellfire.

Arthur Brown's eccentricity was of a wilfully British pedigree. He could have milked the shock-rocker image further, but never returned to the commercial overground. Instead, he created a second Crazy World album, *Strangelands*, that was too far out for release and didn't see daylight until 1988.[176]

To this day, even in his eighties, Brown is still a brilliant live performer and his music is a portal back in time. In the 1970s, his wild gigs drew the attention of a snotty teenager named John Lydon.[177] By the end of the 1960s, as the fashions got

---

174 *The Lyrics Of Syd Barrett*, Omnibus Press, 2021.

175 Brown was a protégé of songwriter/guitarist Pete Townshend, who got him signed to The Who's old label, Track Records. The west London foursome were vital 1960s iconoclasts. Described as a 'new form of crime' by manager Kit Lambert, their performances were influenced by the 'auto-destruction' of conceptual artist Gustav Metzger, who tutored Townshend at art school. Metzger fashioned new images out of the destruction of everyday objects or fabrics. Brought to Britain in the *Kindertransport* from Nazi Germany, he saw his art as somehow challenging authoritarian control. Townshend, Metzger's protégé, adopted the ritual smashing of his own instrument as aggressive showmanship, echoed by performers from Hendrix to The Jesus And Mary Chain. *Tommy*, the 1969 rock opera by The Who, has undergone numerous revivals. It's not macabre in itself but is certainly bizarre – a religious cult that emulates the sensory deprivation of a deaf, dumb and blind boy playing pinball.

176 Play it now and it's a curious mixture of musique concrete, soundscapes and psychedelia. It's also apparent that Arthur had copped a listen to *Trout Mask Replica*.

177 He's 'my mate,' the young Johnny Rotten boasted of old Arthur to his even younger friend, John Wardle (Jah Wobble) – later the subterranean-pitched bassist of PiL. Cherry Red Records, 'Jah Wobble – Meeting Johnny Rotten and Sid Vicious at college', YouTube.

hairier and the post-industrial malaise began to kick in, pop culture was brought back down to earth.

Quite literally by a band initially called Earth.

In the Midlands city of Birmingham, the industry was still grinding along – as teenage sheet-metal worker Tony Iommi found, when an accident severed the tips of the middle and ring fingers of his right hand. It's debated to this day as to how far it led the young guitarist to create a new genre of rock music. But there's little doubt the decreased sensitivity caused by protective thimbles added to his stripped-down, heavier interpretation of blues rock when his band Earth morphed into Black Sabbath.

It created a new sonic backdrop which came to be known as heavy metal.[178] The music, with its high decibels and hard riffing, remains anathema to more sensitive goth ears. But in their heyday, Black Sabbath were unique. Their eponymous 1969 debut has also been termed, along with The Doors, as the first 'gothic rock' album.

It all starts with the cover, where a black clad, witchy young woman seems to cross generational lines between hippy, punk and goth. Then there's the sub-Poe poem on the sleeve, describing 'a grey earth of severed bird wings', and the title track, 'Black Sabbath': opening with a rainstorm, it describes a Black Mass and demonic manifestation, with vocalist Ozzy Osbourne crying out like his ass really is on the sacrificial altar.

This gothic horror schtick was later honed by bass guitarist/lyricist Terry 'Geezer' Butler, whose lower-key detuning, alongside guitarist Iommi, created the doomy Sabbath sound. 'I liked the Hammer horror films in the 1960s and magazines such as *Man, Myth And Magic*,' he'd much later recall, 'but I had a few supernatural experiences as a child and dreams that came true. That, more than anything, shaped my interest in the occult.'[179]

Add to the mix a love of Dennis Wheatley's fiction, especially *The Devil Rides Out*, and a fascination with his opposite number Crowley, and the band became an exemplar of the late sixties occult craze. Their name seems to have been lifted from the great Italian horror-movie director Mario Bava. Under the English title *Black Sabbath*, his 1963 portmanteau work featured veteran actor Boris Karloff as a Balkan vampire compelled to victimise his own family.[180]

Anecdotes suggest the film was playing in re-release or on a midnight show at a local Odeon close to where the band were rehearsing – though the endearingly addled Ozzy seemed less clear on that.[181]

---

178 Black Sabbath never actually knew they were playing heavy metal in their earliest, most influential years. As with any band that coins a new style of rock music, the label came later – as with punk, or indeed goth. 'Heavy metal' was a rock critic's term that may (or may not) have derived from Uranian Willy, the Heavy Metal Kid, in William S. Burroughs' *Nova Express* trilogy of novels.

179 'Five Things Geezer Butler Wants To Do After Retiring From Black Sabbath', *Week.com*, Nathan Carson, September 6, 2016.

180 Based on *The Family Of The Vourdalak*, a Nineteenth century Russian Gothic novella by AK Tolstoy.

181 'There was the fucking *Monster From The Bottom Of The Bog* or something on, and there was a queue for this hideous stupid horror film,' Ozzy later told *Spin* magazine. 'And [Tony] said, "Why don't we do a band and make it horror rock – see how it goes?"' The title *Black Sabbath* seemed not to ring any bells by this point.

Black Sabbath rode on a wave of fascination with black magic that also informed theatrical Brit prog rockers Black Widow and US occultist folkies Coven. In the more obscure corner of UK psych-pop, Jason Crest, from Tonbridge in Kent, went for broke on the B-side of their final 45: 'Black Mass', with its tripped-out backwards guitar and horrified shrieks it sounds like a late-period Damned outtake.

As with the title track to *Black Sabbath*, 'Black Mass' describes a satanic invocation not with approval but with horror. (It also equates the great God Pan – to evoke Arthur Machen – with the Devil. It's a common Christian error, due to both entities' hybrid man-goat anatomy.)

On the third Sabbath album, *Master Of Reality*, on the proto-grunge 'Lord Of This World' the Devil chastises humanity for letting him become its master. It was this *Paradise Lost*-style imagery, along with Sabbath's iconic inverted crucifix, that led squeamish types to label them as Satanists. But listen to 'After Forever' on the same album. The oft-quoted 'Would you like to see the Pope on the end of a rope?' was intended not to provoke but to admonish – as lyricist Butler was a lifelong Roman Catholic, a faith he shared with Iommi.

Their fifth album, *Sabbath Bloody Sabbath*, has a celebrated evocative cover painting of a dying man receiving demonic visitations,[182] but the songs themselves are mostly lyrical cries of personal frustration. In this, Black Sabbath set the template for grunge more so than they did for metal.[183]

Sometimes mentioned in the same breath, Led Zeppelin have been miscast as the twin template of occult metal in the late sixties. But theirs was a more traditional sound, whether borrowing directly from the blues or mystically echoing the acoustic vibes of folkies like Fairport Convention and The Incredible String Band.

While half of Zeppelin (singer Robert Plant/drummer John Bonham) were Midlands compatriots of Sabbath, Greater London-born guitarist Jimmy Page had long been a name in the industry. As a teenage session man, he'd played on seminal records by The Who and The Kinks; he'd also played lead in the psychedelic era incarnation of The Yardbirds.[184]

But of course, it was Page's stated interest in Aleister Crowley that fed into the Zeppelin mystique. Unlike Black Sabbath, for whom the occult merely provided an image, one half of the Page-Plant partnership was attuned to the Great Beast's mystical synthesis and philosophy of personal freedom. It manifested in his soundtrack for cinema magus Kenneth Anger's *Lucifer Rising* (ultimately rejected – see Chapter 4),

---

182 It seems inspired by the great occult visionary Austin Osman Spare – but, disappointingly, artist Dale Struzan, who later designed the *Star Wars* franchise posters, said it was just another assignment to him.

183 Black Sabbath were the greatest articulators of working-class adolescent angst pre-punk. It seems odd how DJ John Peel, for decades the UK's great champion of underground music, always declined to play them. But then he had his pet dislikes, including The Doors – once describing Jim Morrison as 'a tosser' for wearing leather strides made from calves' hides.

184 Page's chequered early career also included a stint as a producer. Working for The Rolling Stones manager Andrew Loog Oldham's Immediate label, he helmed 'I'm Not Sayin'', the first recording by German model Nico. The B-side, the cod-mystical 'The Last Mile', was written by Page and had guitar accompaniment by Brian Jones. Oldham tried to shape Nico in a similar way to Stones muse Marianne Faithfull, with wistful acoustic folk songs, which only made her Teutonic accent stand out all the more.

and in the design of his personal occultic symbol: commonly pronounced 'Zoso', an astrological hybrid lifted from a medieval grimoire.

But there was nothing so obvious as occultic themes in Zeppelin's songs. As they headed into the 1970s – when they became one of the world's biggest live bands, along with the Stones and The Who – their fourth album, rather than following the previous title sequence of *Led Zeppelin 1-III*, printed the four musicians' personal symbols in lieu. (The record became known as 'Four Symbols' – though there are variations such as 'The Runes Album'.)

The nearest the record got to satanic visitation was a reference to 'the Dark Lord' on 'The Battle Of Evermore', a piece of fantasy medievalism where Page played mandolin and Plant duetted with Fairport folkie Sandy Denny. It wasn't Satan but Sauron, ruler of the hellish Mordor in JRR Tolkien's trilogy *The Lord Of The Rings*.

Led Zeppelin's most directly occultic song was on their 1973 album *Houses Of The Holy*, with its eerie purple-shaded cover image of mermaid-like children. But even here, 'No Quarter', a ballad by keyboard/bass player John Paul Jones,[185] sided with the snowbound heroes whose every step was mocked by the Devil. Reference to 'the winds of Thor' grounds it in Norse mythology, one of the folkloric elements that fed into Tolkien's epic fantasy. This wasn't black metal – it was Ragnarok and roll.

In 1976's *The Song Remains The Same*, Page's section is naturally imbued with mysticism, his visual image based on 'The Hermit' from the Waite/Coleman-Smith Tarot deck.[186] It's redolent of an age when rock stars had become distant, neo-pagan gods. An anachronism, perhaps, in a new era of punk rock which threatened to tear such hierarchies down.

The late '60s were full of these dark journeys, but the true darkness was embraced by three bands who have become the go to staples of any serious student of the dark side.

---

185 Later in his career, Jones recorded the 1994 album *This Sporting Life* with gothic chanteuse Diamanda Galas.

186 Mystic AE Waite and illustrator Pamela Coleman-Smith were members of the Hermetic Order of the Golden Dawn – as were Crowley and Arthur Machen.

Chapter 8

ALL THE CHILDREN ARE INSANE, OR PEOPLE ARE STRANGE.

The (un)holy Trinity. The Doors/Velvets/Stooges

The '60s dream didn't come to a sudden grinding halt with Charles Manson, Altamont or The Beatles splitting up. It was already wounded, and the bands that were driving the change were the (un)holy trinity of The Doors, The Velvet Underground and The Stooges banging high-decibel nihilistic nails into the coffin lid.

Bringing new darkness to the landscape, the true progenitors of goth first coalesced in 1965, in the sunshine state of California. That summer, four relatively affluent and well-educated dropouts from the American Dream formed The Doors, learning their licks from the blues[187] but subverting them with a baroque intensity. Keyboard wizard Ray Manzarek played bass pedal with his foot whilst making Wurlitzer-like organ runs on his Vox Continental combo organ with his hands that had something of the burlesque about them, as vocalist/lyricist Jim Morrison sang darkly erotic songs in a lascivious, neo-Sinatra croon with a plate reverb adding to the sonorous effect. Guitarist Robbie Krieger had absorbed influences like classical flamenco and jazz, while drummer John Densmore added a jazz player's lightness of touch and exotic swing.

The standard 4/4 rock band they were not. The Doors hinted at a musical future where all the shades of darkness were as integral as the flickering tones of light. This new mood was first described with the first mention of a band being 'gothic' by music critic John Stickney in an article entitled 'Four Doors To The Future: Gothic Rock Is Their Thing', printed in the student newspaper *The Williams College Record* on 24 October, 1967. Stickney reviewed their Forest Hills gig and details a meeting with the band at a press event in New York on 14 August.

The Doors are not pleasant, amusing hippies proffering a grin and a flower; they wield a knife with a cold and terrifying edge. The Doors are closely akin to the national taste for violence, and the power of their music forces each listener to realise what violence is in himself. The Doors met New York for better or for worse at a press conference in the gloomy vaulted wine cellar of the Delmonico hotel, the perfect room to honour the Gothic rock of The Doors.

Morrison is oft exalted as a modern Byronic figure, immersed in the Romantic canon that provided his tortured muse. But his literary influences – which, in his case, seem more integral than any musical forebears – went far beyond that canon.

---

187 'The men don't know but the little girls understand' – a line from Howlin' Wolf/Willie Dixon's 'Back Door Man', as covered on The Doors' eponymous first album, became a byline for the young, slender Jim Morrison's sexual magnetism. By the time of his final Doors album, *L.A. Woman*, when he was a bearded, burgeoning beer-gutted drunk, he could still ooze his way through the innuendo of John Lee Hooker's 'Crawlin' King Snake'.

There's a good case for Jimbo enduring not just as a rock n roll star but as the epitome of what came to be termed, in the late twentieth century, 'aesthetic nihilism'.

As a US Navy Admiral's son[188] who refused to follow in his father's footsteps, he found the call of hedonism far more compelling than that of service.[189] As a student, James Douglas Morrison was renowned for his erudition, able to quote from a plethora of classical works. He also immersed himself in the Nineteenth and Twentieth centuries' literary iconoclasts.

French surrealist playwright and essayist Antonin Artaud informed the 'killer awoke at dawn' performance segment of 'The End' via his *The Theatre And Its Double*, a manifesto for psychodrama. Friedrich Nietzsche, as we have seen, infused the young performer with the anti-Christian exuberance of the Dionysian, as first expressed in the poet-philosopher's *The Birth Of Tragedy*. Arthur Rimbaud extolled the extremes of consciousness, whether fever dream or hashish hallucination. Albert Camus challenged the superficialities of moral propriety in his novels *L'Etranger* (*The Outsider*) and *La Chute* (*The Fall*), while *La Peste* (*The Plague*) [190] examined human society under stress.

The visionary William Blake provided the band's name: 'If the doors of perception were cleansed everything would appear to man as it is, infinite.' It may have come second-hand, via Huxley's essays on the celestial/hellish extremes of mescaline and LSD, but it epitomised the age. The sublime influence of Baudelaire on a neo-decadent like Morrison can't be underestimated either.

Then there were the extremes of esoterica: Jimbo read extensively in the fields of 16th and 17th-century demonology. Informed by the superstitious agenda of the European witch craze[191], it encouraged later poseurs like Nineteenth century French occultist Eliphas Levi to claim forbidden knowledge. The fantastical triptychs of Fifteenth-century devotional painter Bosch provided, perhaps ironically, church-sanctioned images of hell to Morrison, and to the gothic generation that succeeded him.

His interest in experimental psychology extended to Sandor Ferenczi, a controversial disciple of Freud. Ferenczi insisted all allegations of childhood rape or sexual abuse should (in defiance of Freud) be treated literally. Freud's own interpretation of the original *Oedipus* tragedy was also played out onstage by the band. The Doors were his 'civilisation's discontents' writ large, dissatisfied with a life defined by American affluence and consumerism that ironically had bathed them in its wealth.

---

188 His father, George, had witnessed Pearl Harbour first-hand.

189 Morrison's father was a commander of US aircraft carriers during the Gulf of Tonkin incident of August 1964, which sparked an escalation of American involvement in Vietnam.

190 *The Outsider* provided the narrative for 'Killing An Arab', the vinyl 45 debut of goth-pop band The Cure; *The Fall*, the narrative of a lawyer seeing through the moral pretences which formerly guided his life, lent its title to the UK's perennial maverick garage band; *The Plague* is echoed in Scott Walker's classic psych-pop song of the same name, where 'anguish strikes me like a fist'.

191 The European witch craze of the 14th to 17th centuries was a unique historical combination of accusations against people, especially women, of whom the overwhelming majority were innocent.

Morrison would define himself as the Lizard King, via his neo-pagan poem 'Celebration of the Lizard',[192] a self-styled 'erotic politician' and Dionysian symbol of the counterculture, he became an iconic figure to the hippie generation whose personal apocalypse was the Vietnam war. It was something never directly addressed in his lyrics or poetry, but it was little wonder he claimed his militarist father was dead.

Musically, The Doors shackled themselves to the blues rock chassis that had become the rock'n'roll staple. However, their interpretation of that era's beat music had its own baroque sensibility, encompassing a jazz edge and, in one of their defining moments, tripped-out eastern drones as the leather black clad Morrison unconsciously set the gothic rock template with the closing track of the band's self-titled debut album. 'The End' was an eleven-minute carnival of funereal pop styles, in psychotic collision with each other with the guitar playing a chiming sitar line. Beginning as an ode to a lost love affair, it quickly expanded to encompass sex, death, the Oedipal tragedy, and ultimately the destruction of civilisation.

Its beating on the doors of Artaud's Theatre of Cruelty with its killer walking at dawn lines has inextricably linked 'The End', since 1979, with Francis Coppola's sprawling, psychedelic war film, *Apocalypse Now*. At the time, the film attracted much criticism; ostensibly anti-war in its sentiment, its location shoots were run like a military boot camp by director/co-writer Francis Coppola – who was safely ensconced in Hollywood when the Vietnam war was its most tumultuous.

Still, Coppola could claim *Apocalypse Now* wasn't really about Vietnam at all. Based on seafaring author Joseph Conrad's 1902 novella *Heart Of Darkness*, it follows a river journey to find a civilised Westerner who's embraced a neo-pagan savagery.[193] By the film's climax, when Marlon Brando's renegade colonel allows his Special Forces assassin to fulfil a savage destiny, the soundtrack returns to the quasi-mystical 'The End'.

As Morrison and the band reach their staccato peak of atavism, Colonel Kurtz's killing is intercut with the ritualised (and authentic) dismembering of a live water buffalo.

Death as a Dionysian celebration.

Apocalypse Now was apocryphally claimed to boost recruitment for the US Army, by portraying war as the most nihilistic LSD trip imaginable. It also sparked a posthumous revival of Doors fandom, cementing the band's influence on the then current post-punk scene and pushing it into a goth direction. The Doors were now

---

192 More a performance poem than a song, it was edited down to a melodic bite-size chunk to become 'Not To Touch the Earth' on The Doors' third album, *Waiting For the Sun*.

193 In *Heart Of Darkness* he's ivory trader Mr. Kurtz, worshipped as a God by Congolese natives; in *Apocalypse Now* he's Colonel Kurtz, a renegade Green Beret turned nihilist philosopher. Both exhibit their power as earthly deities by displaying human heads on pikes. In journalist Angus McKinnon's 1979 cover feature on Coppola's film for *New Musical Express* – probably the most potent piece of writing ever for the British music press – it's noted that the two Kurtzes exist in separate realities but may be aware of each other. In *Apocalypse Now*, Colonel Kurtz reads 'The Hollow Men' by TS Eliot as he awaits his own assassination; the poem is epigrammed by a line from *Heart Of Darkness* spoken by a local boy: 'Mistah Kurtz – he dead.'

part of a scene that they had instigated despite Jim Morrison having, by this stage, been dead for some eight years.

It was all quite fitting.

Rock stardom seemed to mean little to Jim. He continued poking his finger in the eye of authority, though in the end, it brought him nought but boredom. The singer-poet also changed from a psychedelic shaman to an increasingly out of control drunk. Like many who'd exploded their psyche with hallucinogens (or amphetamines), he needed to come down to a more earthbound vision. Booze fitted the bill.

By early 1971, the unravelling Morrison checked himself out of the band on what they claimed was a temporary leave of absence. He was reaching the end of a $50,000 bail period that kept him out of jail on a conviction for 'lewd behaviour' onstage in Miami. 'Take your fucking friend and love him,' the erotic politician had told the crowd. 'Do you want to see my cock?'[194] Big Jimbo was mostly so drunk by then that little Jim might have had trouble standing up. But the Florida cops claimed to have got a flash, which led to seven months of legal trouble.

By March 1971, Jim Morrison had had enough. He decamped to Paris with his on-off girlfriend, Pamela Courson, to pursue the literary life of a poet. It went well for a few months until she found his lifeless body in the bathtub on 3 July. He was buried with unseemly haste, without an autopsy but with a coroner's written description of 'heart failure' on the death certificate.

The mystery surrounding Jim's death led to vintage conspiracy theories: 'he hadn't died', 'the whole process had been faked to allow him to flee the pressures of rock stardom'; 'he'd predicted his own murder in a track on his final Doors album, 'Cars Hiss By My Window'.

These days it's accepted that a heroin overdose may have stamped out the Lizard King – it's the opinion stated (as fact) at the end of Oliver Stone's biopic, *The Doors*. Never a known smack user, Morrison may have fatally combined it with alcohol at the encouragement of Ms Courson. She did nothing to belie the theory when she made an opiated exit from life herself, three years later.

In death, Jim Morrison attained the literary status which evaded him in life. He lies in Père Lachaise cemetery, Paris, where near-neighbours include novelist Honore Balzac and Irish decadent-in-exile Oscar Wilde. In 1990, his father placed a new headstone with a Greek inscription translating as either 'True to his own spirit' or (more Dionysian perhaps) 'According to his own daemon.'[195]

Morrison's final album as lead vocalist, with The Doors *L.A. Woman*, was a menacingly understated return to blues rock, but it retained the residue of dark psychedelia. The insistently low-key 'Riders On The Storm' was based on an infamous case Jim heard about as a kid. Billy Cook, a Missourian drifter with 'HARD LUCK'

---

194 Jerry Hopkins and Danny Sugerman, *No One Here Gets Out Alive*, Plexus Publishing, 1980.

195 The grave has long been a pilgrimage site for goths. When this writer visited, he found a maudlin atmosphere of Christian mournfulness – surely Jimbo would have appreciated a Dionysian celebration of life's tragedy? In any case, someone had the good sense to leave an empty wine bottle as a tribute.

tattooed across his knuckles, lived out his animus by shooting a family of five dead whilst hitchhiking in California, in 1950.

In 1978, the surviving Doors would issue *An American Prayer*, an album of their music backing Morrison's spoken poetry. His brief dialogue 'The Hitchhiker', set to the storm-and-keyboard backing of 'Riders', continues this murderous travelogue theme which was played out further in the 1980s psycho-horror pic *The Hitcher*, which screenwriter Eric Red acknowledged was inspired by 'Riders On The Storm'. The progenitor for both the song and its pulp-cinema offspring was a 1969 experimental film (pitched somewhere between Warhol's blank *cinéma-vérité* and the French *nouvelle vague*) originated by Morrison himself.

In *HWY: An American Pastoral*, he took the role of a hitcher in the Mojave desert who makes vague allusions to having killed the driver of a car he's stolen. Salvaged scenes appear in Tom DeCillo's celebrated 2009 Doors documentary *When You're Strange*, and a rough time coded cut can be found online. (Doors geeks still hope for a fully remastered DVD print.)

In mainstream pop culture, echoes of The Doors were heard in the 1980s Brat Pack horror movie *The Lost Boys*. 'People Are Strange', the catchy ode to alienation from their second album, *Strange Days*, becomes an anthem for a town full of teen vampires. Fittingly for its era, it wasn't the original version but a cover (or tribute) by dreamily atmospheric post-punk band Echo & The Bunnymen.

The Doors were the true progenitors of goth rock.

Sex. Death. Psychodrama.

Their legacy foreshadowed the culture that would follow.

*****

On the East Coast, in gritty Gotham, an NYC band explored the dark side on a far more streetwise level. The Velvet Underground would also be equally important to the later goth template – though they never enjoyed anything like the same level of fame or success as The Doors did in the 1960s.

Their 1967 debut, *The Velvet Underground & Nico*,[196] album with its iconic Warhol banana cover, created a musical hybrid of claustrophobic droning and beautifully crystalline guitar pop. Originally called The Primitives, the band were renamed after a tawdry paperback exposé of sex in suburbia, and their lineup was as unlikely as their name.

Singer/songwriter/guitarist Lou Reed was an R&B fanatic and journalism graduate; he considered the gritty realism of novelists like Nelson Algren and Hubert Selby Jr. to provide perfect content for songs. Seeking to expand the lexicon of pop, Lou Reed consciously incorporated a literate gentle, introspective beauty or a dark, druggy, or

---

196 It was actually recorded in 1966. Verve, the Velvets' record label, delayed it in favour of releasing The Mothers of Invention's debut double, *Freak Out!* Only one set of musical and songwriting boundaries could get broken at a time.
While *The Velvet Underground & Nico* was ostensibly produced by Warhol, the man at the controls was Tom Wilson – also the Mothers' producer. Chief Mother Frank Zappa, whose abstemiousness belied his freak image, was openly critical of Lou Reed's hard-drug songs. He later took a conciliatory line, numbering 'All Tomorrow's Parties' among his favourite rock songs.

sexual narrative common to films, plays and novels into a pop song format. On their first two albums, that format also got blown wide open in a way that mirrored Reed's love of modern jazz artists like Ornette Coleman.

On the experimental side of his songwriting, Lou initially found the perfect foil in John Cale, a classically trained Welshman, who had performed at a Fluxus art movement event as a student at Goldsmiths College in London before arriving in New York on an art scholarship in 1963. In the Big Apple, he participated in a 'piano-playing marathon' with avant-garde composer John Cage. As a part of experimental musician La Monte Young's Theatre of Eternal Music, the young Cale played 'drones' – sustained notes played in unison, shifting on a glacially slow harmonic scale. It was this creative dissonance that Cale brought to the Velvets, adding droning viola as well as more conventional bass or keyboard accompaniments. The influences of free jazz and Indian music could be heard, but the music's ultimate destination can only be defined as 'somewhere else'.

> The whole idea of a European culture, at the end of the Second World War, was kind of fragmented, and you really had to search to find what was going on. Then there were these people like John Cage from New York doing interesting things. So when I read about John Cage handing over the baton over to La Monte Young, I said, right. I'm gonna go and see that. So I went to New York, and it was a real eye-opener. It was open 24 hours a day for a start and a really amazing spread of ideas.[197]

Added to the mix were Sterling Morrison, ostensibly the lead guitarist, whose lines snaked in and out of (and were sometimes inextricable from) Reed's. Then there was Maureen Tucker who replaced original drummer Angus MacLise, an erratic poet and occultist. Tucker may be one of the most underrated rock percussionists, with her repetitive mantric beats. She was also unable to play a roll on the drums, but her style was perfectly effective and highly influential.

> We didn't really have any respect for the boundaries. One of the powerful things about the Velvets was that you had to learn to respect the other people in the band and what they did and make it work. Initially, with Lou, we would just improvise. I would sit down with the viola, and he would have his guitar, and he could just spin these stories out. It kept pouring out, and I thought if we could get those chords to work with the drone, then we could give Bob Dylan a run for his money. [198]

The Velvets' amphetamine-driven New York cool was the antithesis of the West Coast counterculture of the time. They had no utopian vision of changing the world for the better; they just strove to evoke the modern urban world accurately, which they sometimes achieved with chilling precision. In the relatively short period that they were managed by pop-art entrepreneur Andy Warhol and his sidekick, underground filmmaker Paul Morrissey they were at the centre of pop culture.

---

197 John Cale to John Robb.
198 John Cale to John Robb,

That scene that he was putting together was driven by his acceptance of what you were prepared to contribute to the situation. He was very generous with his ideas and very generous to me. He was a fascinating character. If you asked him a stupid question, you would get a creative answer and something that would be odd and unusual. It was very exciting being part of his Factory set up, as there were so many things going on.[199]

Part of Warhol's tearing of the trad pop culture fabric was what was then perceived as the incongruous addition of Nico to the band (nee Christa Päffgen). An imposingly good-looking model and sometime actress, with an almost androgynous bone structure, her aloof tones graced but a few of Reed's songs.

Andy said, in his soft voice, 'hey, there's this girl who works with Bob Dylan. In Woodstock. And she's a real, really fascinating individual.' I wasn't so much aware of the competition between Andy and Woodstock. It was quite visceral. Nico was there and because she's a wanderer she had wandered to New York and Andy suggested her into the band.[200]

The most notable song with Nico, 'All Tomorrow's Parties', was retrospectively described by US rock critic Kurt Loder as a 'mesmerising Gothic rock masterpiece'. Certainly, the mournful sound of this droning masterpiece was going to have a big effect on many of the future architects of goth. Literary allusions at the time were more direct: 'The flowers of evil are in full bloom with the Exploding Plastic Inevitable,' praised the *Chicago Daily News* – evoking both Baudelaire and, more contemporarily, the Warhol Factory[201] revue that was showcasing the Velvets.

The hypnotic riffs and droning viola further enhanced 'Venus In Furs', an encapsulation of the novella by Leopold von Sacher-Masoch – the flagellant who gave the world the term 'masochism'. In the twilit Manhattan world of the Velvets, allusions to S&M were not a taboo.[202] Nor were the more traditional urban forms of drug use.

'Heroin' is no more a hippie-style paean to the supposed benefits of drugs than it is a moral admonition. Instead, it just *is*. '...Thank God that I'm as good as dead,' observes Lou of a drug he was intimately familiar with. (Though reputedly not, unlike the song's narrator, addicted to. His own near-nemesis came in the form of injectable methamphetamine.)

---

199 John Cale to John Robb.

200 John Cale to John Robb.

201 The Warhol Factory's 'Superstars' comprised a glorious freak show coterie of deviants, performance artists, drag queens and speed-or-smack abusers. But most of all, it was a screen-print production line where the savvy Warhol put everyone to work. The Velvet Underground's almost accidental rep as Factory house band ultimately disenchanted Reed, who found management elsewhere.
His defection earned the enmity of Paul Morrissey, director of the films credited (rather dubiously) as Andy Warhol's *Flesh*, *Trash* and *Heat*. With their retinue of Superstars, the movies depict tongue-in-cheek the lives of hustlers, hookers and junkies. Notoriously controversial at the time (1969-72), they share a moral undertone with one of Reed's great literary influences, Hubert Selby Jr. Many assumed that because the characters' lifestyles were given to you straight, it equated with approval; absolutely not, protested Catholic conservative Morrissey.

202 'Severin, down on your bended knee' is Reed's reference to the central character of *Venus In Furs*. In the 1970s, young Englishman Steven Bailey adopted the name when he co-founded seminal punk-era band Siouxsie & The Banshees.

The most gothic title on the band's March 1967 debut 'banana album' is 'The Black Angel's Death Song', but this too eschews any obviousness with lyrics that were chosen as much for their sound and rhythm, and carry the influence of Lou's literary mentor, Delmore Schwarz[203]. This was the birth of 'art rock'. Middle America would never take to it, but for a brief moment, there was no limit to what could be expressed in song.

After the Velvets left Warhol, they were just as uncompromising on their 1968 second album *White Light/White Heat*, its title a tribute to speed psychosis. Cale's ghoulish British tones could be heard intoning 'Lady Godiva's Operation', a scratchy account of an early gender realignment (Reed put its dispassionate morbidity down to electric shock treatment he'd had inflicted on him as a kid), and 'The Gift' – a spoken word piece about a suitor who mails himself to his love object. Inevitably, he comes to grief when she cuts open the package. It was like a twisted version of an O. Henry[204] short story, but the musical backing was pure freeform rhythm and blues.[205]

The form reached its apotheosis in 'Sister Ray', occupying most of side two on the vinyl edition. As far as the lyric can be followed (or heard, given the primitive production), it recounts the visit of some sailors to a drag queen which all goes murderously wrong. Images of shooting up and 'sucking on a ding-dong' outdo even the more sordid passages of Selby's *Last Exit To Brooklyn*. But the music, particularly Cale's staccato organ, goes so far out at times that it becomes pure noise.

It couldn't last. In late 1968, Reed decided he wanted some chance at commercial success. Cale, meanwhile, was indulging his avant-garde impulses, coming up with ideas like recording amplifiers underwater. Lou told him it was time to get melodic or leave – with emphasis on the latter. 'You're going back to folk,' John reputedly accused.[206] But then, so was much of the music industry in the late 1960s.

The third Velvets album, post-Cale, did at least include 'The Murder Mystery'. Pre-dating the nervy neo-funk of Talking Heads, its stream-of-consciousness lyric contained some grotesque imagery but it was basically poetry concrete – chosen for sound rather than meaning. Lou spent his last couple of years in the Velvets playing 'pretty songs' influenced by his and Cale's songwriting hero, Brian Wilson of the Beach Boys.

John Cale himself went 'back to folk' with his first solo album, *Vintage Violence*; so did Nico with hers, *Chelsea Girl* – which featured 'It Was A Pleasure Then', a collaboration with Lou and John which continued the Velvets' moody atonality.

Reed and Cale would re-emerge separately in the 1970s, a more cynical decade when they would be relatively more appreciated. But as for Nico, she began to plough a lonely, beautifully melancholic furrow that has yet to receive full recognition even today.

---

203 Delmore Schwarz who died in 1966 had taught Reed at Syracuse University and was short story writer and poet whose 'poker-faced satirical takes on the bohemians and outright failures of his generation were some of the best'.

204 Nineteenth century American short story writer who also wrote the novel Cabbages and Kings.

205 A phrase used to describe the early space rock of Pink Floyd – it seems to fit the original Velvets just as well, if not better.

206 John Cale interviewed on *HARDtalk*, BBC World News, April 11, 2016.

It's to John Cale's great credit that he acted as her producer and arranger – her enabler and facilitator, on *The Marble Index*, the first solo album of her own compositions. Recorded in late 1968, she was given the confidence to indulge its ghostly Teutonic muse by Jim Morrison, with whom she enjoyed an affair and a revelatory peyote trip in the desert.[207]

Resonant with an otherworldly melancholy, this was not a music of the modern world but of its own timeless dimension. It was orchestrated in a spare chamber-style arrangement of wheezing harmonium, Cale's droning viola and glockenspiel.

'Nico was like a European gargoyle. She certainly was unique,' Cale later acclaimed as a backhanded compliment. 'There was nobody doing that gothic folk stuff.'[208]

It's been termed 'the first goth album' – but it's certainly not gothic *rock*. In terms of bleak tonality, it has more in common with Mahler's orchestration of *Kindertotenlieder* ('Songs On The Death Of Children') – even though her own little boy was very much alive at that time.

It was the first of a sporadic trilogy that honed Nico's bleak neoclassicism to an emotionally desolate kind of accessibility. The second, *Desertshore* in 1970, was composed in part as the soundtrack to French filmmaker Philippe Garrel's *La cicatrice intérieure* ('The Inner Scar'). In a cover shot from the film, Nico is led on a horse through the desert.

In their ten-year relationship, she and Garrel would lead each other further and further into heroin addiction. It was the opposite to the psychedelic apocalypse she'd experienced with Morrison. But the human distance imposed by heroin is hauntingly mirrored in Nico's early seventies masterpieces.

Bauhaus frontman Peter Murphy would later perfectly describe Nico as 'Mary Shelley Gothic, while all the other bands were Hammer horror'. It was an ethos she stayed true to for the rest of her career, though her sound was occasionally compromised by rock instrumentation. For years after 1974's *The End*, rumours persisted that Nico had met with Ray Manzarek and the other surviving Doors with a view to briefly taking Jim's place in the lineup, possibly for a concert in Paris.

It's the perfect legend, though it may never have happened at all. For in her quietly menacing declamation of the title track, she found the release in nihilism and destruction that was beyond nice guys like The Doors.

In her later years, she would recall the 1945 fall of Berlin that she witnessed as a child: 'The buildings falling down around you... The streets full of dust, you

---

207 Nico's other legendary lovers, rumoured or otherwise, include Bob Dylan, Brian Jones, Reed, Cale, and French film star Alain Delon – purportedly the father of her son, Ari. (Delon denied it but, tellingly, his own mother played a central role in the child's upbringing.)

Then of course there was a wiry young rock n roll iconoclast called Iggy, the leader of The Stooges, to whom Cale introduced her when he was producing their debut album. Iggy spoke later of an 'older woman' who took his virginity when he was, startlingly, already twenty. He also appeared, uncredited, in an arty promo film for 'Evening Of Light', a track from *The Marble Index*.

208 Richard Witts, *Nico: The Life and Lies of an Icon*, Virgin Books 1993.

choked... At night you could see the city burning, the sky red as blood... The smell of burning buildings on the wind.'[209]

In the post-punk period, she had even moved to Manchester where, despite her ongoing addiction, she was still capable of delivering stark and spellbinding performances. At the 1982 Futurama Festival, she mesmerised with her distinctive German accent and rich voice, sustaining her influence on many of the bands within the alternative subculture.

*****

The third band in the unholy trinity were The Stooges, who reduced everything down to a raw primitivism and a dark nihilism that profoundly affected punk and goth. With frontman Iggy Pop's urgent Midwestern drawl and guitarist Ron Asheton's repetitive fuzz tones, which made the instrument sound like it was playing itself, The Stooges were the progenitors of punk rock and had a profound influence on what would follow in goth. But in their own time, they were rock'n'roll pariahs.

Bursting out of Ann Arbor, a college town near Detroit, Iggy was a wired-up early twenty something at nihilistic war with what he termed 'sick America'. For him, self-expression was of no use unless it went the whole way – and going the whole way always meant going too far.

Little Jimmy Osterberg first got fired up by seeing The Doors play the University of Michigan on 20 October 1967, on the back of their erotically enticing debut hit 'Light My Fire', to a surprisingly small crowd. The wide-eyed ex-drummer was transfixed by Morrison's dark theatrics, seeing for the first time just how far you could push a performance. It pre-dated The Stooges' first gig by only eleven days.

The former drummer of beat group The Iguanas professed how he was impressed by how The Doors' singer could turn on the girls and goad the guys with his confrontational Theatre of Cruelty-inspired performance. Iggy took himself down a similar route, but with a lot less theatre.

'I took two grams of biker speed, five trips of LSD and as much grass as could be inhaled before the gig,' he later recalled his pre-show prep. 'I found this concoction effective enough to completely lose my senses... we'd gather like a football team and hype ourselves up to a point where we'd scream "OK guys, what're we gonna do? Kill! Kill!! Kill!!!" Then we'd take the stage.'[210]

Smart but slightly unhinged, Iggy took live performance to new levels of danger and intensity. Just three years after The Beatles had played Shea Stadium in their collarless suits, he was flailing around on stage shirtless, his double-jointed body bent into impossible shapes.

But this was just the start of his physical contortions. The Stooge on the edge (of the stage and sanity) would launch himself into the crowd long before stage diving

209 Interview with Piccadilly Radio, Manchester – as described by James Young, *Nico: Songs They Never Play On The Radio*, Bloomsbury 1992.

210 Quoted by Nina Antonia, *Iggy Pop*, Virgin Modern Icons, 1997.

was 'a thing' He'd physically attack members of the audience, most often those he knew could beat him bloody. Toned but slight, the wired performer knew most of the violence would be turned back on him.

Back on stage, to complement his masochistic ritual with the audience, he might continue battering himself with the mic stand, and as Iggy ventured further into self-mutilation, the tendency to cut himself with instruments like splintered drumsticks would grow more extreme and more dangerous. Whatever personal exorcism he was enacting never seemed to rid him of his demons.

Iggy was so far removed from external reality by drugs that the resulting performance could consume him. The no-holds-barred insanity, combined with deceptively simple but wildly potent music, was the antithesis of the 1960s hippy love-in. This was the dark reality of America, coming out to play, and The Stooges wanted none of the flower children's starry-eyed pieties.

Hedonism and self-harm combined in Iggy's performances with The Stooges. It was no act. His art back then was an act of nihilistic self-sacrifice. As Mick Jagger's character, Turner, said in the 1970 cult movie *Performance*: 'the only performance... that makes it all the way, is the one that achieves madness.'

The extremity was matched by uncompromising music. Their eponymous 1969 debut album was rock music stripped-down to its most brutal and simplistic and all the more effective for it. It was garage rock in essence, but The Stooges' second album, 1970's *Fun House*, is oft credited with a free jazz style stemming in equal part from the addition of sax player Steve Mackay and the freeform closing track, 'LA Blues'.[211]

The albums bombed. The press famously hated them, and the band were totally out of sync with the time. Iggy would later boast that he had trashed the hippie ethos of the 1960s,[212] but it was the Woodstock generation who temporarily consigned The Stooges to the ashcan of obscurity.

Wanting to be everything at once, Iggy was always an absurdly contradictory Yin and Yang. He was the macrobiotic yoga disciple who also began consuming large amounts of heroin when The Stooges moved to LA. The communal Fun House lifestyle, which had begun in Michigan, was a moveable feast, but now the drugs were of a more destructive kind. Iggy was taking life to its extremes and seemed to be following Jim Morrison to an early grave.

By 1971, The Stooges were falling apart, and Iggy was washed up. He was trying to kick his smack addiction, taking methadone and living with his parents back in Michigan.

But he would soon crash-land into a whole new era that he had helped kick start and where he found salvation.

---

211 It seems less highfalutin to credit Stooges tracks like 'LA Blues', and the long-unreleased 'Asthma Attack', with pre-empting the 1980s guitar noise of Sonic Youth and Big Black – or even Lou Reed's 1975 *Metal Machine Music*.

212 'I think I helped wipe out the sixties' – Iggy Pop, interviewed in *Gimme Danger*, directed by Jim Jarmusch, 2016.

Chapter 9

WHAM BAM THANK YOU GLAM

The Dark Side of Glam Rock

Amid the denim dreariness of the post-hippie early 1970s music scene, the UK's *Top of the Pops* often presented a steady stream of forgettable bubblegum 45s and leftover 1960s crooners. However, on 6 July 1972, a performance was broadcast that was like an electric shock to a small coterie of watching teenage wildlife.

Mid-twenties industry veteran David Bowie was back in the charts with 'Starman' – his second hit after the similarly sci-fi-themed 'Space Oddity', three years earlier. This time around, the formerly tousle-haired singer-songwriter had reinvented himself as an exotically bright young thing: luminous orange hair; multi-coloured jumpsuit adapted from the look of the 'droogs' in *A Clockwork Orange*; and most outrageously, to mums and dads, he had an arm draped around the shoulders of platinum-blond guitarist Mick Ronson.

For all the young droogs, this was the wake up call, and something stirred both hormonally and artistically in most of the key players in what would become goth which arguably was glam 2.0 minus the glitter.

Bowie's recently released album, *The Rise And Fall Of Ziggy Stardust And The Spiders From Mars,* was now manna from the glam God. A manifesto. The single was perfect pop, a last-minute addition to the album that spliced together a lyric about a subversive alien[213] with the octave leap from Judy Garland's 'Somewhere Over the Rainbow' and the Morse-code pulse of The Supremes' 'You Keep Me Hangin' On'.

The *Ziggy Stardust* album was Bowie's great pop statement: a collection of his most tuneful songs that began with a darkly nihilistic view of humanity under threat of extinction, in 'Five Years'. That many people think there's a unifying concept to the album is due to the concluding songs about Ziggy himself, the 'leper messiah' rock star who whips his fans up to such an extent that he's (ambiguously) killed by them but then survives to wander London's night time streets in the doomy epic 'Rock'n'Roll Suicide'.

The character of Ziggy lent Bowie a mystique that was symbiotic, and a song like 'Lady Stardust' perhaps reacted to the ambiguous/androgynous sexuality that he discussed in the January 1972 interview with the *Melody Maker,* in that famous chat where he had revealed, 'I'm gay, and I always have been,' expressing surprise that anyone should think otherwise.[214]

---

213 Though the extraterrestrial's only apparent message was, 'Let all the children boogie.'

214 Roger Griffin, *David Bowie: The Golden Years, Omnibus Press*, 2016. All evidence suggests Bowie's period of bisexual experimentalism had been in the 1960s, as a young man. Certainly, his known 1970s history is of prolific heterosexuality. But this was an artist who was hungry for his moment and knew what would grab attention.

On the 1972 *Ziggy Stardust* tour, when Bowie performed 'Lady Stardust' at London's Rainbow Theatre, the face of his contemporary and friendly rival was projected on a screen: Marc Bolan.

Bowie didn't get to glam first. Teenagers had already headed into the glitter zone at the behest of hippie turned 'bopping elf' Marc. Bowie had merely upped the glitter ante. T. Rex's 'Ride A White Swan' had been released in autumn 1970, and its spritely upbeat images of druids, tall hats and tattered gowns had a supernatural resurgence in early 1971 that took it to the top ten.

In the 1960s, the young Bolan[215] had been a fixture on the London underground scene as half of Tyrannosaurus Rex. Their pseudo-folk stylings – influenced more by the hippie fad for Eastern music than affinity with the British folk scene – were offset by Marc's reverberating 'Larry the Lamb' vocals and a tendency to whimsical fantasy, heavily influenced by Tolkien.[216]

But Bolan became the first glam rock star[217] when he truncated the band name to T. Rex, reverted to his early love of rock'n'roll stars Eddie Cochran and Gene Vincent, and draped his diminutive figure in satin and tat. In March 1971, the number one 'Hot Love' began a run of hits that turned T. Rex into the UK teenage phenomenon of the early 1970s.

Having been fixated on his visual image since his days as a teenage mod in Hackney, Bolan was now vamping up his glam look. Evolving into androgyny, Marc was a modern Beau Brummell[218] played out through his performances on *Top of the Pops*. It started with 'Hot Love', which saw him dressed in tight satin and glitter makeup at the suggestion of his stylist, the exotic sixties it girl, PR Chelita Secunda. Bowie was watching. 'What was so great,' he explained, 'was that we both knew he hadn't got it quite right. It was sort of glam 1.0. We were straining in the wings with versions 1.01 and 1.02, while Marc was struggling with the satin. But boy, he really rocked. He did, y'know?'[219]

The fantasy imagery of Marc's songs also underwent a modern upgrade. Tolkien may have seemed just a little too quaint and hippie-esque by now. 1971's *Electric Warrior* album was Bolan's high watermark, and one of the greatest pop records ever made. The classic 'Cosmic Dancer' summed him up, while 'Mambo Sun' references Marvel Comics' occultic hero Dr Strange.

---

215 Nee Mark Feld – from a working-class family in the Stoke Newington neighbourhood of Hackney, northeast London. Bowie had similarly humble beginnings, born David Jones to lower middle-class parents in Brixton, Lambeth, in the southwest of the English capital.

216 As a songwriter, Bolan was heavily influenced by Syd Barrett – in fact his first wife, the former June Child, was one of Syd's girlfriends. In thematic terms, the Tolkien borrowings in the Tyrannosaurus Rex days were fairly obvious. Listen to DJ John Peel reading children's story 'Frowning Atahuallpa (My Inca Love)' on the debut album, *My People We Fair And Had Sky In Their Hair... But Now They're Content To Wear Stars On Their Brow*.

217 'Glam' was one of the most faddish and vaguely defined of generic rock terms. By the time it was widely recognised, it was almost retrospectively describing a phenomenon past its heyday. Rock journalists like NME's Nick Kent used it almost as a term of abuse but then, of course, it was a generation gap in pop.

218 Brummell was an iconic figure in Regency England, the archetypal 'dandy' for whom the cultivation of visual style and fashion was everything. As Mark Paytress notes in *Bolan: The Rise And Fall Of A 20th Century Superstar* (Omnibus 2002), he was also a figure of fascination for Marc, who had read one of the Brummell biographies.

219 David Bowie to Mick Rock.

1972's *The Slider* saw Bolan at the height of a fame and success he'd never quite recapture. It featured the iconic image of Marc in his celebrated leather bound top-hat. It's a classic rock'n'roll look that caught on quickly – passed down via Bolan's contemporary, Alice Cooper, to numerous Victorian-styled goths and even to Slash from Guns n' Roses. *The Slider* also featured fantasy imagery that was somewhat darker: 'Ballrooms Of Mars' features uniquely high-pitched Bolan-esque guitar and tells, in Lovecraftian style, of night time monsters.

But it was the colourful phenomenon of Marvel that held sway with Bolan. Down the other side of his peak as a star, he held a 1975 presenter slot on Thames TV's *Today* show. One of his interviewees was Marvel chief editor Stan Lee, creator of the immortal comics *The Amazing Spiderman* and *The Incredible Hulk*. Marc's own devotion to the Marvel universe was obvious, particularly his favourite strip: Lee's cosmic drifter, *The Silver Surfer*.

The Surfer makes an appearance in Bolan's 1974 hit, 'Teenage Dream'. It was also the recording where he incorporated the sound of black America[220], via the backing vocals of his new partner, soul singer Gloria Jones.[221] Apart from her fated relationship with Marc, she is best remembered today for her 1964 version of 'Tainted Love', a song by Standells producer Ed Cobb that she recorded as a B-side. (It later became a favourite at Northern Soul nights in England – prompting electro duo Soft Cell[222] to take a cover version to the top of the charts in 1981.)

The moment when Bolan fell off the podium on the last episode of his eponymous 1977 TV pop series, *Marc*, marked the end of an era. He'd just improvised an incomplete song with his old friend and rival David Bowie, called (a little obviously) 'Standing Next To You'. Ironically at the time, Marc had every reason to believe he'd truly come back.

The punks had embraced him. The Damned – in their punk peak before later transitioning towards the gothic neo-psychedelicists they'd become – had supported him on his *Dandy In The Underworld*[223] 1976 tour. Siouxsie Sioux, an ardent Bolanite, was photographed with her glam rock hero before the Banshees were even signed to a record label. 'I consider myself to be the elder statesman of punk,' Marc audaciously declared in January 1977. 'The Godfather of Punk if you like.'[224]

Few disputed his claim.

---

220 Marc adding soul to glam before Bowie.

221 The new sound – credited to Marc Bolan & T. Rex – pre-dated Bowie's assimilation of 1970s funk and Philadelphia soul on his *Young Americans* album by almost a year.

222 Soft Cell singer Peter Mark Almond restyled himself 'Marc' after Bolan.

223 *Dandy In The Underworld*, the album and the title-track single, was vintage Bolan despite barely scraping the charts. An upbeat confessional with a doo-wop break, the cleaned up Marc's description of himself as an 'exalted companion of cocaine nights' was censored on the 45 version.
It later lent its title to the 2007 autobiography of modern dandy Sebastian Horsley – self-deprecating artist, acidic memoirist and friend of Nick Cave. Horsley, an atheist who had himself crucified in the Philippines so that he could understand the experience, died several years later of an overdose.

224 In *Bolan: The Rise And Fall Of A 20th Century Superstar*, glam historian Paytress suggests the Siouxsie look of electrified dark hair and heavy eyeshadow originated with Marc's appearance on mid-seventies pop show *Supersonic*, singing 'Dreamy Lady'. There may be something to it, but it foreshadows her 1980s style rather than the more severe punk era.

And then, on 16 September 1977, whilst travelling back from a boozy session at a London restaurant in the Mini that Marc had never learned to drive, Gloria hit a fence post and then a tree on Barnes Common. She broke her arm and jaw. Marc was killed instantly.[225]

The teenage dream was truly over.

But the memory of Bolan would permeate both post-punk and goth, where he was a key influence.

*****

If Bolan had been glam's progenitor, Bowie was its more studied visionary. Both were the twin dark glam gods that goth would be built on, but Bowie's daydreams of urban madness began long before. In 1966-67, the young performer, only then entering his twenties, forsook the beat groups he'd fronted on the London club scene to try to be a kind of all-round entertainer.

It bore mixed results but drew on an interesting inspiration. Anthony Newley was a London-born[226] singer/songwriter/actor/scriptwriter. As crooner of the ballad 'What Kind Of Fool Am I?', he'd later be credited by Bowie as one of the first singers (along with Syd Barrett) he'd ever heard use an English accent.

As a songwriting partner of Leslie Bricusse, Newley had composed such instantly recognisable tunes as 'Goldfinger' and 'Feeling Good' (a hit for Nina Simone). And then there was the theatricality: even before the celebrated Newley-Bricusse West End musical, *Stop The World – I Want To Get Off*, there was the 1960 TV series *The Strange World Of Gurney Slade* – which bemused viewers with its title character (played by Newley) who wanted to break the fourth wall and escape the sitcom he was trapped in.

Newley's dilettante talents inspired young David Jones to transition to David Bowie – singer/songwriter/actor/mime artist/painter. It's most obvious on the 1967 debut album, *David Bowie*, where the chirpy music hall elements are offset by a darkness, particularly on 'Please Mr. Gravedigger'. This early soundscape – complete with piddling rain, tolling bell and shovel-into-mud sound effects – had the young man recite a rhyme to a ghoulish old sexton, who's purloined a locket filled with a dead little girl's hair.

The first take was recorded in October 1966, six months after the trial of 'Moors Murderers' Brady and Hindley at Chester Assizes. Excruciating detail was heard of the abuse, torture and murder of ten-year-old Lesley Anne Downey, which her tormentors had taped. Lesley Anne seems to have been Mary Anne in the young Bowie's imagination, making the chill of 'Gravedigger' undeniable.

---

225 It's not suggested that Gloria was in the same drunken state as Marc, but she fled Britain with their son, Rolan, before she could face trial for driving while unfit. She revisited in later years without charge, participating in a thirty-year commemoration concert with Marc Almond and others in 2007.

226 Newley was born in Hackney, the same borough as the young Marc Bolan. They attended the same primary school, though years apart. As was common to the neighbourhood at the time, both shared a Jewish heritage.

Bowie's influential visions of future dystopia first came to the fore in the Newley-ish 'We Are Hungry Men'. Young Bowie, as cockney demagogue, rouses a crowd of starving people in an overpopulated world, before (predictably) they swarm in to eat him. It might have attracted moral outrage if anyone had been listening.

But this was just one of a young dilettante's passing phases. One day David's muse might be Oscar Wilde, whose children's stories, 'The Happy Prince' and 'The Selfish Giant', he admired; the next day it was Mahayana Buddhism, from which he drew upon the idea that one's 'real' self was an illusion, merely a transient state of being. Eternal renewal, viewing oneself as an ever-changing creation, seemed to be one means of escaping the veil of unreality. The young Bowie claimed he'd come close to forsaking pop culture to live as a Buddhist monk. But true to form, he wrote two very catchy pop songs on the theme instead, 'Silly Boy Blue'[227] and 'Karma Man'.

With the failure of his first album, Bowie returned to the rock scene – or at least to folk rock, styling himself as a very anglicised counterpart to Dylan. His second album, yet again titled *David Bowie*, opened with the moon-landing exploitation of 'Space Oddity' – which, despite being released as a 45 one month before the Apollo 11 mission in August 1969, took four months to reach the top ten. Major Tom's stranding in space is seen now as more of a parable of alienation,[228] but darker themes followed.

The B-side, 'The Wild-Eyed Boy From Freecloud', is a haunting ballad: a young mystic is to be hanged in the morning by superstitious villagers, his crime being 'the madness in his eyes'. (It brings to mind the unsettling effect Syd Barrett's piercing stare is said to have had – or perhaps, closer to home for Bowie, the mental disintegration of his half-brother, Terry Burns.) But they face the wrath of the protective mountain as it rains its boulders down. Futuristic but Dylanesque, 'Cygnet Committee' points to the apocalyptic Bowie of the 1970s. In its nightmare of a 'love machine' it's a science fiction allegory of the revolution that devours its own.

When Bowie returned to the studio in 1970, he was a bona fide rock performer. *The Man Who Sold The World* wasn't 'glam rock' per se, but Marc Bolan (affectionately parodied on 'Black Country Rock') was on the verge of stardom. Most remarkably, Bowie talked his record label, Phillips/Mercury, into a cover shot of him reclining on a chaise longue in a 'man's dress' by British designer Michael Fish. The performer, ever the aesthete, said it was inspired by pre-Raphaelite painter Dante Gabriel Rossetti; others noted that, with his blond locks, he looked like Hollywood actress Lauren Bacall.

Mercury's US arm baulked at the British cover, running a cryptic comic book design by Michael J. Weller, a friend of Bowie, which showed a Western gunman

---

227 The first Bowie song to be covered by an established artist, 1960s pop star Billy Fury – immediately after his own long run of hit records had finally ceased.

228 Possibly even a metaphor for hard drug abuse, with Bowie later hinting at a period of heroin experimentation when he wrote the song. Certainly, by the time the character returned in 1980's 'Ashes To Ashes', Major Tom was a junkie.

afront a foreboding mansion 'cold and grey'.[229] The music was rock of the hardest kind, created largely by newly recruited guitarist 'Ronno' (Mick Ronson) and producer Tony Visconti, who also played a mean bass.[230]

Visconti talked about how Bowie was hardly present for the recording. The artist later blamed it on he and his wife Angie's copious intake of hashish at the time. His friends disputed it, but the way in which hash darkens the imagination of regular smokers (or eaters) may have contributed to the lyrics.

The opening track, 'The Width Of A Circle', plays like Black Sabbath if they were informed by the proto-psychedelic art of occultist Austin Osman Spare, rather than the crusty supernatural chillers of Dennis Wheatley. Bowie had played a folk version on John Peel's *Sunday Show*, but the addition of Ronson and later verses turned it into an infernal trip, where mantric riffing and chanted backing vocals deepened its depiction of meeting a doppelgänger monster and a sexual encounter with a demon. The song had a tragic, almost voyeuristic resonance. For Terry, the illegitimate elder son of Bowie's mother, had experienced it in hallucinatory form at Chislehurst Caves in Kent, when he fell into the frightening alternate reality of schizophrenia.[231] Terry was now the long-term inmate of a mental institution, a predicament his half-brother presented in lyrical form in 'All The Madmen'. As exploitative as it may seem, there's no doubting where Bowie's sympathies lay and he would later claim he lived in apprehension of a psychotic lineage.[232] While the band worked up the backing, David re-emerged intermittently with darkly fantastic lyrics.

The eerie ballad 'After All' depicts humankind as stunted children, seen through the divergent belief systems of Buddhism and Crowleyism: 'Running Gun Blues' celebrates the recently established American tradition of mass public shootings, seen through the eyes of an amok Vietnam veteran. 'Saviour Machine' is a breezy pop apocalypse, as a politician turns on a compliant public with the promise that he may kill them all.

The Man Who Sold The World, as a rock album, may be as gothic in tone as anything that has come before or since – with a certain effete but sinister Englishness to the vocal performance. It ends with two classic tracks. 'The Man Who Sold The World' which has a lyric inspired by the *fin de siècle* poem 'Antigonish' by William Hughes Mearns:

'Yesterday, upon the stair,
I met a man who wasn't there!'

---

229 It was an accurate depiction of Cane Hill mental hospital, in the south London suburb of Croydon, to which unfortunate half-brother Terry had been committed. His predicament inspired the album's classic 'All The Madmen'.

230 As well as producing T. Rex.

231 Peter and Leni Gillman, *Alias David Bowie*, Hodder and Stoughton 1986.

232 Ibid.

It may have been the reflexive state of a hash trance. Or maybe closer to Terry's personal dislocation. It fades out with Ronson's throbbing electric flamenco and the guitarist's sighing vocal coda, leaving all of us – narrator, listeners – as ghosts adrift.[233]

'The Supermen', a tuneful lament for an imagined ancient world, was self-deprecatingly dismissed by Bowie as coming from a period 'when I was pretending that I understood Nietzsche'.[234] Certainly, drummer Woody Woodmansey's pounding of a tympani evokes Strauss's 'Also Sprach Zarathustra'.[235] But the theme is how Superman tore 'his brother's flesh', desperate to die and escape immortality.[236] In this sense, the reading in a late seventies *NME* Bowie (by Charles Shaar Murray) was on the money: the Supermen were pre-history figures of dark fantasy, like Lovecraft's Elder Gods.

These days, Visconti plays in a band that recreates *The Man Who Sold The World*.[237] Back then, he was so disenchanted with what he saw as Bowie's disengagement that it ruptured their working relationship for a few years.

Enter producer Ken Scott, a former engineer for The Beatles. His production of 1971's *Hunky Dory* put a smooth, florid edge on some of Bowie's stranger lyrics. Audible influences included Lennon and McCartney, Dylan, The Velvet Underground, and singer-songwriter mavericks Biff Rose and Scott Walker.

The first Bowie album to even approach commercial success, some of its tracks are celebrated – like the beautifully arranged 'Life On Mars?', where 'the girl with the mousy hair' is lost in the alternate realities of the cinema screen. 'Oh! You Pretty Things' was even a chart hit for ex-Herman's Hermits vocalist Peter Noone, though its lyric required a little softening. On the refrain, 'gotta make way for the Homo Superior,' the songwriter was beating his Nietzschean drum again – even if he'd cribbed it from a kids' TV sci-fi show.[238]

Then there was 'The Bewlay Brothers', which has a claim to be Bowie's strangest song. Its styling was folkie, with Ronson's wailing guitar muted, but its surreal lyric was almost impenetrably personal. Bowie described it back then as '*Star Trek* in a leather jacket'[239] – the US sci-fi series having been only recently broadcast on the BBC. In the longer term, he was more explicit, recalling it as a 'vaguely anecdotal

233 Nirvana's celebrated cover of 'The Man Who Sold The World' is a fine evocation, but in replacing the haunting backing vocals with a guitar line it loses an exotic dimension.

234 David Buckley, *Strange Fascination: The Definitive Biography Of David Bowie*, Virgin Books 1999.

235 An orchestral evocation of one of Nietzsche's defining essays, *Thus Spoke Zarathustra*. Filmmaker Stanley Kubrick selected it for use on the soundtrack of *2001: A Space Odyssey* (1968), in its Nietzschean depiction of humanity as 'a rope stretched between the animal and the Superman'. BBC TV, perhaps unmindful of nuance, took it as a cue for use as accompaniment to their coverage of the 1969 moonshot.

236 'The Supermen' is surpassed only in its depiction of eternal life as existential hell by 'Still Life', Peter Hammill's title song for the 1976 Van der Graaf Generator album. Expansive and balladic, it's also more chilling, in that it's about human beings sinking into degradation rather than demigods.

237 Holy Holy, named after the non-album Bowie song in which he struggled with his Buddhist beliefs.

238 In the early 1970s, Bowie discussed one of his new songs with TV producer Roger Price – who suggested its theme chimed with a series he was developing about a young group of 'Homo Superior'. It's a measure of how quickly the songwriter absorbed ideas back then that 'Oh! You Pretty Things' saw release two years before *The Tomorrow People* debuted on ITV, in 1973. Cited in Griffin, *David Bowie: The Golden Years*.

239 Bowie's notes on the album, used in RCA Records' press release of the time.

piece about myself and my brother, or my other doppelganger. I was never quite sure what real position Terry had in my life…'[240]

As his younger brother became world famous, the tormented Terry Burns lost any one-on-one relationship with him at all. In 1971, however, David still regarded the big brother who taught him about beat literature and modern jazz as his shadow-self.

Hunky Dory is classic Bowie, but within a few weeks, the man himself had formulated the big one: a blueprint for his own stardom, founded on the creation of a mythical star.

Ziggy Stardust was the first post-modern pop star, assembled from the scraps of discarded pop culture. His diverse component parts included Britain's great lost rock'n'roll star, Vince Taylor. A charismatic leather-clad Gene Vincent wannabe from west London's Middlesex suburbs, Vince (formerly Brian Holden) never had a UK hit but was later seen as a seminal figure.[241]

Then LSD hit the culture, exploding his psychogeography. The pre-Bowie David Jones met Vince several times at London parties. He later caught up with him in the centre of town, in a memorable close encounter: 'I remember him opening a map outside Charing Cross tube station, putting it on the pavement and kneeling down with a magnifying glass. He pointed out all the sites where UFOs were going to land.'[242]

By the time Ziggy became a phenomenon, Vince Taylor had decamped to France where he had experienced some success as a leather-clad rock n roller. But then, as Bowie recalled: 'He came out on stage in white robes and said he was Jesus Christ. It was the end of Vince – his career and everything else.'[243] Like a leper messiah, indeed.

Ziggy's surname had its roots in the ultimate outsider musician, the Legendary Stardust Cowboy. His notorious 1968 psych-country[244] single, 'Paralyzed', resembles original psychobilly Hasil Adkins taken to ground zero, with nothing but whoopin' and a-hollerin'. The LSD Cowboy (initials a coincidence, he said) stormed off *Rowan & Martin's Laugh-In* TV show when they turned it into a comedy skit. Bowie was smitten by 'the idea' of the Cowboy, if not the caterwauling music, as soon as he heard of him.

Then there was Ziggy's, the name of a tailor's shop Bowie passed on a train through London's East End. 'As it was a tailor's shop, I thought, well, this whole thing is going be about clothes, so it was my own little joke,'[245] he later said, emphasising his creation as a visual shtick. Then of course there was the similarity to Iggy, who he had first met on a September '71 sojourn to New York…

240 Griffin, *David Bowie: The Golden Years.*

241 The Clash would cover Vince Taylor's 'Brand New Cadillac' on their 1979 *London Calling* double album.

242 *Juke Box Heroes*, BBC One, August 21, 2001.

243 Ibid.

244 That's 'psych' as in psychotic, rather than psychedelic.

245 Paul Du Noyer, 'Put your hands together for… Ziggy Stardust! The Thin White Duke! The Laughing Gnome!', Q, April 1990.

Bowie later claimed Ziggy's most direct influence was fictional: Nik Cohn, one of the first journalists to write seriously about rock'n'roll (and later disco), created a pulp-fiction antihero in his 1967 novel *I Am Still The Greatest Says Johnny Angelo*. His title character was inspired by Texan balladeer PJ Proby, who became a pop star in the UK,[246] but Johnny's antics went a lot further than splitting his strides like Proby. Ramping up to murder, he was gunned down by the cops like a true rock'n'roll suicide.[247]

In terms of self-reinvention, the Warhol Factory acolytes may have been inspirational in the contrivance of Ziggy. In August 1971, Bowie met the cast of *Andy Warhol's Pork* when they were performing at the Roundhouse. He and his wife, the charmingly bombastic Angie, were taken with the retinue of Superstar outsiders and drag queens – like Wayne County,[248] who, in the self-referential play, was portraying a character named Vulva based on Factory trannies like Holly Woodlawn, Candy Darling and Jackie Curtis.

Another part of the creative soup that congealed in Ziggy was Bowie's former mentor as a mime artist, Lindsey Kemp. Inspired by the movements and makeup of Japanese Kabuki, Kemp had influenced young David's performance in an obscure 1967 short horror film, *The Image*.[249]

His influence became more overt in the video for the post-'Starman' hit, 'John I'm Only Dancing', where his body-painted troupe's sexual ambiguity matched that of the song. It was a persona recreated by Kemp himself at the Rainbow in August 1972, in the performance of 'Starman'.[250]

Kubrick's take on Anthony Burgess's *A Clockwork Orange* visually created the nihilistic youth culture hinted at in his novel.[251] Bowie borrowed from the fashion sense and sexual animus of charismatic gang leader Alex, whilst discarding his ultraviolence.[252] In the following year, *A Clockwork Orange* was assured of the ultimate cult status when it was withdrawn from UK cinemas at the request of the director himself.[253]

---

246 Check his later recordings with Savoy Records in Manchester: everything from a cover of Joy Division's 'Love Will Tear Us Apart' to a recitation of Eliot's *The Waste Land*.

247 In 2017, crime-fiction publishers No Exit Press reprinted *I Am Still The Greatest Says Johnny Angelo* as a paperback double-header with Cohn's *King Death*.

248 Later Jayne County, the punk performer known for unsentimental come-on 45 'Fuck Off'. Reputedly the first transsexual rock star, Miss Jayne is believed to have kept her male equipment.

249 *The Image* was one of very few British shorts issued with an 'X' certificate. Director Michael Armstrong intended to cast Bowie in his first feature, *The Haunted House Of Horror* (1969), but ended up with future *Grease* co-star Frankie Avalon. Armstrong is chiefly known for witch-hunt 'video nasty' *Mark Of The Devil* (1970).

250 The gloriously theatrical Kemp claimed the young Bowie had been his lover, which was neither refuted nor confirmed. Folk-horror fans may recall him as the pub landlord in 1973 classic *The Wicker Man*.

251 A youth culture despised by both Burgess and Kubrick, as conservatively-inclined middle-aged men.

252 Alex's love of Beethoven echoed in Walter Carlos' electronic arrangement of the chorale from the Ninth Symphony ('Ode To Joy'), preluding the Ziggy show at the Rainbow and the final July 1973 Hammersmith Odeon performance.

253 *A Clockwork Orange* remained legally unviewable in Britain for twenty-six years, until Kubrick's death. He took no responsibility for a supposed copycat gang-rape and the murder of a tramp, but the zealots protesting outside his Hertfordshire home begged to differ.

Then there were the fashion designs of Freddie Burretti and Kansai Yamamoto, whose rainbow threads were androgynous yet cut to the bodily shape of a man. In their recreation of Bowie as Ziggy, he was neither masculine nor female; neither earthling nor alien. Ziggy was the third sex. By the time he arrived at the Rainbow, the further influence of Noh theatre on his makeup was very apparent.

Tony Defries, Bowie's manager of the time, recognised that Ziggy could make his charge more than a mere pop star. This was to be a full-blown phenomenon. The self-fulfilling profit prophecy was that if you acted like the biggest star in the world, people would believe it to be true. To be truly iconic, one had to redesign oneself as an icon.

Bowie's understanding of the advertising industry he'd briefly worked in (as a graphic designer) allowed to him grasp the importance of media theorist Marshall McLuhan's maxim: 'The medium is the message.' For Bowie, reborn as Ziggy, image and content were interchangeable. It would create a series of compelling identity crises that only ceased when he stopped playing characters and became ostensibly 'himself' again.

But the schizoid role-play was truly gothic, both visually and psychologically. Its peacocking and creation of elaborate personae would echo down the decades of popular culture that followed.

*****

1973's *Aladdin Sane* was the last album of original Bowie material to be produced by Ken Scott. Written and partly recorded on a trans-American tour, it's filled with the observations of a newly ordained star, sharpened by what he termed 'fast drugs'. Its vision is also more coldly apocalyptic at times than the softer *Ziggy*.

The top ten single 'Drive-In Saturday' was mutant doo-wop, where irradiated lovers got aroused by watching video films. 'Panic In Detroit' evoked the USA in the era of the Weathermen and the Patty Hearst kidnapping.

Even the European content carried an understated menace, like the portentous '1913-1938-197?' that accompanied the title track in parenthesis. Its image of 'passionate bright young things' taken away to war was inspired by reactionary satirist Evelyn Waugh's *Vile Bodies*, which Bowie read on the US jaunt; its piano accompaniment by New York jazzman Mike Garson suggested a musical panic attack. As for the *Aladdin Sane* cover, the red-and-blue lightning bolt on the singer's face was disturbingly redolent of the British Union of Fascists' flag in the 1930s.

Then there was 'Time': a nerve-jangling echo of the *Cabaret* music that evoked decadent Berlin in Bob Fosse's 1972 film – itself a pastiche of the politicised musicals of playwright Bertolt Brecht and composer Kurt Weill.[254] Time is an even more imposing MC than Joel Grey in Fosse's film: he can be found 'in Quaaludes and red wine / Demanding Billy Dolls and other friends of mine.'

---

254 The Doors covered 'Alabama Song' from *The Fall Of The State Of Mahagonny*, Brecht/Weill's satire of a corrupt and venal 'roaring twenties'. Bowie later did likewise, seemingly in tribute to Jim Morrison.

(This type of OD was typical of the 1970s drug culture. The bright young corpse was Billy Murcia, drummer of New York Dolls – the band that straddled the breach between glam and a whole new generation.)

By the following year, Bowie considered himself such a phenomenon that he dispensed with his forename for the next album.[255] He also ruthlessly discarded the band who'd become his own (rather than Ziggy's) Spiders From Mars – though he did still choose some of the content of Mick Ronson's 1974 solo set, *Slaughter On 10th Avenue*, albeit from a distance.[256]

Bowie's 1974 album, *Diamond Dogs*, was a vivid flowering of the evil promise inherent in earlier records. '[The] final nightmare of the glitter apocalypse,' acclaimed *NME* Bowie-ite Shaar Murray; Banshees founder Steven Severin later described it as Bowie's 'masterpiece';[257] biographer David Buckley termed it stylistically 'Gothic'.[258]

The grotesquerie began with the album cover: the increasingly skinny singer as mutant canine. It was based on recent promo shots taken of him in a Muchacho hat and neck scarf, with a Great Dane on a leash. In the painting by Guy Peellaert, who'd collaborated with Nik Cohn on the epochal *Rock Dreams*, the two became a carnivalesque hybrid. (Bowie's reputedly imposing genitalia were airbrushed out by RCA.)

The lyrics were phantasmagorical, with several dystopias flowing into one. The second half contained a song cycle based on George Orwell's *Nineteen Eighty-Four*, headed by the subtly menacing 'We Are The Dead', after the mutual pledge made by the novel's doomed lovers.[259]

It was a personal reading of authoritarianism, rather than the ultra-communist hegemony ('Ingsoc') that democratic socialist Orwell warned about. Bowie seethes about the personal nightmare of a young star who'd come home from his first US tour to find himself hugely in debt.

The glitter apocalypse itself took place as the album began. 'Future Legend' was a macabre scene-setter, a recited poem telling of the Great Disaster that is never specified, but the total catastrophe suggests the Big One has dropped. It was eerie but also celebratory. The mutant survivors had taken over Hunger City's skyscrapers and pillaged its once-luxurious furriers for leg warmers. These were the Diamond Dogs, mutant gangs likened at the time to William S. Burroughs' homo-nihilists in his novella *The Wild Boys*.

---

255 A young British fan named Steven Morrissey may possibly have taken note.

256 Bowie provided lyrics for 'Music Is Lethal', from the original 'Io vorrei... Non vorrei... Ma se vuoi' by Italian singer-songwriter Lucio Battisti. Unable to find a workable translation, he fashioned a blood and wine-soaked continental ballad like a jacked-up Brel, populated by 'mulatto hookers' and 'cocaine bookers'. Bowie's lyric to stomp-along glam ballad 'Hey Ma Get Papa' plays like an excised passage from Selby's *Last Exit To Brooklyn*, with a panicked young guy leaving a man he'd stabbed to die in the street. 'Slaughter On 10th Avenue' itself is Ronno's celebratedly histrionic arrangement of the theme from Richard Rodgers' modern ballet, about a waterfront crime of passion. It reflected Bowie's infatuation of the time with the Broadway composer, replayed in 'Future Legend' – the spoken opening track of *Diamond Dogs*, where 'Bewitched, Bothered And Bewildered' is played as a guitar line in the background.

257 John Robb, 'Steve Severin: His Top 10 Albums', Louder Than War, 2 November 2014.

258 Buckley, *Strange Fascination: The Definitive Biography Of David Bowie*.

259 'We are the dead,' say Winston and Julia resignedly, recognising they'll never see the overthrow of Big Brother in their lifetime. 'You are the dead!' blurt out the Thought Police, as they come crashing through the window.

Burroughs' post-modern science fiction had become a huge influence on Bowie. After the performer decamped from the suburbs to a Chelsea townhouse, Wild Bill visited several times when he was in London. He also demonstrated to the much younger man the literary cut-up technique[260] he'd adopted from his friend Brion Gysin, artist and occultist.

Burroughs used it to fracture his narratives, introducing stark juxtapositions and unconscious links. Bowie inserted it into his doomy romantic song of love in a doorway, 'Sweet Thing'.

Apart from being the '70s, stardust Bowie was also had a key role as a crash course for the ravers turning the glam kidz onto writers like Burroughs, as well as artists and a whole host of esoteric genius, and resurrecting the careers of Lou Reed, Iggy and Mott The Hoople, which saw him save the small town band from breaking up by giving them their classic hit and the anthem of glam, 'All The Young Dudes'. It was a generous proposition, given that, pre-'Starman', Bowie had yet to attain pop star status himself. It became the glitter anthem, with singer Ian Hunter's long ginger locks and shades and own songwriting brilliance adding to the band's platform boots (bassist Overend Watts was the first to wear them), acquiring a second-hand glam mystique.

'Diamond Dogs', the title track, is a gaudier piece of pop-gothic with Bowie drawling over a Stonesy riff. It evokes Johnny Eck, the 'Half-Boy' in *Freaks*, who hopped along on his hands.[261]

(In Bowie's lyric, this writer hears Harlan Ellison's 1969 dystopian SF novella, *A Boy And His Dog*, far clearer than Burroughs' homoeroticism. In Ellison's nihilistic fantasy, a teenage boy and his telepathic dog wander through a post-nuclear landscape – evading mutant gangs and looking for girls to rape.)

When Bowie promoted *Diamond Dogs* live in the USA, the looming Hunger City sets were based on Fritz Lang's futuristic classic *Metropolis* (1927). They became less prominent until they were dispensed with at the end of the tour, when Bowie transitioned from quintessential English outsider to inauthentic 'young American' soul man. But the role-play wasn't over yet.

In *The Man Who Fell To Earth* (1976), Nicolas Roeg's film of Walter Tevis' novel, Bowie took the role of disoriented Englishman TJ Newton – who is actually a displaced alien, beguiled (and ultimately defeated) by terrestrial culture and booze.[262] Hyper-thin, living on a diet of cocaine, milk and peppers, it was the performer's

---

260 Literally, cutting up a text and reassembling in random order. After using the technique for his breakthrough, the junk-sick nightmare of *The Naked Lunch* (1959), Burroughs enhanced it to the point that his *Nova* trilogy of novels (1961-64) were in part cut-ups of each other.

261 *Freaks* (1932) is the celebrated/excoriated exploitation movie by Browning, ex-carny/director of *Dracula*. While describing bodily disabled people as 'freaks' seems starkly cruel, there's no doubt where Browning's sympathies lay: the physically normal trapeze artist and strongman are the monsters, until the ranks of the deformed gang up for revenge. The movie was banned from British exhibition until 1963, whereafter young hipsters like Bowie could view it in London cinema clubs.

262 In a coda to his life and career, Bowie contributed four new songs and a range of his earlier work to *Lazarus* – a Broadway musical sequel to *The Man Who Fell To Earth*, starring Michael C. Hall as Newton. He attended the December 2015 opening night, his last public appearance before his death in January 2016.

unearthly state that got him hired, after Roeg and screenwriter Paul Mayersberg viewed him in the BBC *Arena* documentary *Cracked Actor*.

Newton's conservative style of dress and emotional detachment were retained for the Thin White Duke, the character who performed on 1976's *Station To Station* tour. But the Duke, 'throwing darts in lovers' eyes', exhibited few of Newton's vulnerabilities. As we have seen (in Chapter 4), he was an occult magus born of Crowleyan philosophy[263] and fascist aesthetics. The superstar as Übermensch.

In a frighteningly egocentric interview with LA rock kid Cameron Crowe,[264] Bowie lit a black candle to keep 'the neighbours' (malevolent entities) at bay. He also made a throwaway remark that defined him for a while: 'I think I might have been a bloody good Hitler. I'd be an excellent dictator. Very eccentric and quite mad.'

He was referring to how the British media took his messianic Ziggy character at face value: "This ain't rock music, this is bloody Hitler!' (A cute parallel to *Diamond Dogs*' 'This ain't rock'n'roll, this is genocide!')

But it coincided with a period when he was staying up for days, viewing holes that opened up into other dimensions, reading books on occultic theory and the Third Reich. It was his ambition, he said, to write and direct a film about Nazi propagandist Goebbels' early days.

For this was the 1970s and liberalism was decaying, as far as Bowie was concerned. The age of Aquarius, as he'd note a couple of years later, was predicted to have dark consequences rather than heralding a hippie aeon of peace and love.

Station To Station straddled eras, a tightrope between plastic rhythm and blues (to use Bowie's own term) and a more experimental European approach. The title track, with its electronic evocation of railway transit, pointed the way to a Neu Musik while the rest of the album was entrenched in soulful R&B.

By the time the Thin White Duke returned to the country of his birth, he'd told a Swedish press conference that Britain needed a fascist leader. It was a position he visualised for himself in ten years or so – though he drew the line at 'Nazi'. But when he arrived at Victoria Station in May 1976, a wave he gave from an open-topped Mercedes was interpreted by a suspicious *NME* in the headline 'Heil And Farewell'.

Yet this was the singer who'd recently become only the second white artist to appear on US TV's *Soul Train*. A sober Bowie would later claim his fascination with the Third Reich had no connection with racial supremacism, but everything to do with occult symbolism.

It was inherent in his reading matter. *The Morning Of The Magicians*, the cult 1960 text by French journalists Pauwels and Bergier, reinterpreted history by positing that the Nazis had been fighting a mystical evolutionary war. It was the most provocative form of conspiracy theory, as was *The Spear Of Destiny* (1972) by Trevor Ravenscroft

---

263 The seemingly obscure line 'making sure white stains', in 'Station To Station', is a reference to an early piece of Crowleyana – *White Stains*, his poems of erotic transgression.

264 Cameron Crowe, 'David Bowie: Ground Control to Davy Jones', Rolling Stone, February 12, 1976.

– depicting a spear that pierced the side of Christ as a supernatural artefact sought by the Third Reich.[265]

All was fantastical. All was symbolic. All was profoundly irrational.

Such terms have also been applied to Bowie's 1976 support act. While the early electro of Kraftwerk played over the speakers, the first visual presence was a silent film. *Un Chien Andalou*[266] (1929) was directed by Luis Bunuel and written by surrealist artist Salvador Dali. Created as a cinematic equivalent to automatic writing, with no rationality or unifying theme,[267] it presented startled Bowie fans at London's Wembley Empire Pool with the image of a passive young woman's eyeball razored open.

Bowie claimed the sparseness of the stage was based on Brechtian theatre, but the white light framing the Thin White Duke had something of Nazi architect Albert Speer's Cathedral of Light – a central feature of Nuremberg rallies.

They were grey days in the 1970s, but there were austere bursts of monochromatic colour at Bowie's 1976 performances. Gavin Friday, of Dublin's Virgin Prunes, was one of many who fell under Bowie's commanding spell and was inspired to create his own groundbreaking band in the post-punk period who played with androgyny and outrage that made them a key goth period band:

> As a kid, my only salvation was David Bowie and music. I had some idea in my head that you had to be a super genius to be in a band and that it was for other people and it was punk that changed that.
>
> I remember my first experience of punk was when I got the boat and train to see Bowie in 1976. It was the *Station To Station* tour. At the time I had long hair. I remember queuing up to get into the gig after I had slept on the station. At the Bowie gig, I saw all these fucked-up, post-apocalypse Ziggy fans and they looked like the Bromley Contingent we had read about and that was amazing. I went back to Dublin and we created an imaginary gang like that in our heads, we liked music and art, and spontaneously we became the Lypton village with what would become U2 and also Virgin Prunes. I saw this thing at the same time as *Lou Reed Live* came out and the photos of him at the time where he is wearing big shades and black and white makeup. Not long after it was punk and it was all shades, spiky hair, torn clothes, chains, pins, and it became like a religion and it was the biggest philosophy that connected with me.
>
> In many ways, New York was the city of punk, but it was different in England and Ireland. It was about the dole queue and a real horror of the term "no future" was so relevant if you were growing up in that era. You were told to fuck off or get

---

265 It fed into subsequent Holy Grail lore, as well as inspiring *The Spear* (1978) by horror author James Herbert. (Herbert opted to remove the part of his purely fictional work which ran closest to Ravenscroft's theory, rather than pay him legal damages.) *The Spear Of Destiny* would also provide the name of the post-punk band led by Kirk Brandon.

266 Bowieologists will recognise the similarity of the title – translating as 'An Andalusian Dog' – to the chant at the end of 'All The Madmen': 'Zane! Zane! Zane! Ouvre le chien!' ('Open the dog!' – 'Zane' is untranslatable.) Suffice to say, there are no canines in either film or song.

267 Devotees of Bunuel's subsequent films may take issue. In the scene where a besotted woman risks her life in traffic to retrieve a beloved, a severed hand begins his theme of the 'obscure object of desire'.

WHAM BAM THANK YOU GLAM

a dead-end job. Everywhere was grey and it felt like it was permanently raining. Bowie and then punk was the release from this.[268]

*****

Back in 1972, in the midst of Bowie's new found stardom, his hyper-kinetic swirl of activity engaged him with some of his main influences. He'd first heard *The Velvet Underground & Nico* on an acetate brought back from New York by his manager of the time, Ken Pitt. Within a month of the album's release, in spring 1967, he was already recording his own bluesy demo of junkie anthem 'I'm Waiting For The Man' with north London R&B band the Riot Squad.[269]

In his September 1971 visit to New York, Bowie first met Lou Reed, who expressed approval of *Hunky Dory*'s 'Queen Bitch'. ('Some VU. White light returned with thanks,' Bowie wrote of his tribute on the sleeve notes.)

As they were now on the same record label, RCA, and Lou was starting a solo career after a brief hiatus, Bowie inserted himself and Ronson as producers (and in Ronno's case, as musical arranger). It was a savvy move for Reed, as the combination of a tuneful set of songs and an association with Bowie at the height of glam gave him a commercial breakthrough.

Transformer, the late 1972 album, was marked by the times. The cover photo by Mick Rock was so overexposed that it looked like a negative, suggesting Lou was wearing heavy mascara. The glamorous woman and the macho man in the biker/ cap on the back cover were long rumoured to be the same person, dragged up, but it was pure myth. (The girl was a pro model; the macho was a friend of Lou's with, reputedly, a banana down his crotch to simulate a big hard-on.)

The songs were pop numbers which, with the exception of the almost plaintive 'Perfect Day', played up the singer's rep as a sometime acolyte of the Warhol scene. Indeed, 'Walk On The Wild Side' became an all-too-rare top ten hit, with its blatant references to transvestitism, giving head and speed psychosis – plus a cool jazz break from Bowie's old sax tutor. The title was cribbed from Nelson Algren's novel about a New Orleans bordello, but the lyric was ensconced in the Warhol Factory.[270]

The song's Warholian love of the shallow surface image struck a chord with a lot of Brit teenagers. The artfulness of the New York demimonde seemed hopelessly glamorous to a generation living amid the dinginess of the early 1970s, with the glitter of the glam racket as their only escape. Still, some old Velvets aficionados

---

268 Gavin Friday to John Robb.

269 It's a mark of the young Bowie's hunger for stardom that he'd shlep all the way from southeast London to rehearse at The Swan, a Tottenham pub, for a three-month period before recording his Newley-like *David Bowie* album. The Riot Squad had been recording with Joe Meek, but David joined them soon after the producer's suicide.
Their demos would eventually be released in 2012: the sax on 'I'm Waiting For The Man' sounded nicely sleazy, but it wasn't by Bowie, whose vocal was embarrassingly cod-American. A song called 'Little Toy Soldier' also plunders the 'I am tired' refrain of the Velvets' 'Venus In Furs'.

270 Reed was writing about figures like transsexual Warhol superstar Holly Woodlawn as characters, rather then people he knew intimately. Actor Joe Dallensandro complained that the hustler 'Little Joe' wasn't him, but the characters he played in Morrissey/ Warhol movies *Flesh* and *Heat*. (He later took the role of gangster Lucky Luciano in Coppola's *The Cotton Club*, 1984.)

were decidedly snobby about Lou's only hit thus far, with music writer Nick Kent claiming he'd fallen into self-parody.

He'd return to more uncompromising territory in 1973. A few years later, a belligerent Lou would boast to *NME*'s Paul Morley of aspirations to place his songs on the level of great literature: 'I'm talking about Shakespeare, Dostoyevsky. I want to do that rock'n'roll thing that's on the level of *The Brother Karamazov*.'[271]

But while there were *roman noir* elements to his 1973 album, it was helmed by a controlling producer, Bob Ezrin, who wanted to make a 'movie without pictures'[272] – just like he had for gothic glam shock-rocker Alice Cooper.

The opening title track of *Berlin* is a rearranged version of a love song from Lou's first solo album. This time the Germanic elements are played to the hilt, with a spine-tingling piano solo following sound effects suggestive of Marlene Dietrich taking the stage in *The Blue Angel* (1930).

But this was no period piece. When Lou answered Ezrin's call for a thematic song cycle, he focused on the mutually destructive relationship of Caroline – a sexually-promiscuous, speed-freak Billie Holliday wannabe, with likely masochistic tendencies – and Jim – an American drug dealer, violently antagonised by the overt sexuality he finds alluring at first.

'Berlin is a divided city, and a lot of potentially violent things go on there,'[273] the songwriter said of his central metaphor.[274] Back in those vinyl days, sides one and two of *Berlin* were a slide from tarnished romance to sadomasochism.

Two songs have the Velvets-like title 'Caroline Says': the first is an upbeat rock n roll number about a capricious lover; the second is a lament in which Caroline, raising herself from the floor, declares she doesn't care how much violence Jim inflicts on her anymore. With its haunting 'It's so cold in Alaska' coda, the song would enter the repertoires of Marc Almond (in his Marc & the Mambas period) and Lydia Lunch (performing with ex-Birthday Party guitarist Rowland S. Howard).

Reed and Ezrin admitted that the work took an emotional (and even physical[275]) toll. For the songwriter, it was autobiography through a magnifying lens. Lou's first wife, Bettye Kronstad, later confirmed that, while she suffered the rages of his speed and whisky days, they never locked into Caroline and Jim's dance of death: 'He gave me a black eye the second time he hit me. Then I gave him a black eye, too, and that stopped him from using his fists,'[276] she wrote, disarmingly.

271 Paul Morley, 'Lou Reed: I Love It When You Talk Dirty', New Musical Express, 21 April 1979.

272 Anthony DeCurtis, *Lou Reed: A Life*, John Murray, 2018.

273 Ibid.

274 Peter Doggett, *Lou Reed: Growing Up In Public*, Omnibus Press, 1991.
The tensions between Western and Eastern Europe infected Berlin, until the fall of the Berlin Wall in 1989. Mick Harvey of the Bad Seeds later opined that the potency of drugs – particularly speed – in the western sector may have been fuelled by the East German Stasi.
In any case, *Berlin*, the album, was actually recorded at Morgan Studios in Willesden, northwest London – as was *Transformer*.

275 Relatively naïve, Ezrin required hospitalisation after a period of indulging in Reed's hard drugs lifestyle.

276 DeCurtis, *Lou Reed: A Life*.

With a similar unapologetic eye for degradation as Sade or Selby, *Berlin* was one of the moments when Reed lived up (or down) to his literary aspirations. It was also produced and arranged by Bob Ezrin with the aplomb of a great cinematic director. Listen to the ghostly voices at the end of 'The Bed', after Caroline slashes her wrists, then compare and contrast with the use of composer Gyorgy Ligeti's *Lux Aeterna* in the moon exploration scene of *2001: A Space Odyssey*.

At the end, Ezrin subverts the 'Someday I'll wish upon a star' melody line of 'Somewhere Over The Rainbow' for 'Sad Song', where Jim has ceased caring about the tragedy ('Somebody else would have broken both of her arms'). And then of course there's 'The Kids' – when the authorities took Caroline's daughters away and their crying voices were provided by Ezrin's little sons.

Berlin was a unique narrative moment in the history of rock music. And of course, it took shit for it.

In the UK, where *Transformer* had granted Lou minor star status, it was briefly a top ten album. In the US it scraped into the lowest end of the *Billboard* chart. 'There are some records that are so patently offensive that one wishes to take some kind of physical vengeance on the artists that perpetrate them,'[277] wrote Stephen Davis in *Rolling Stone*. Even Lester Bangs, the *Creem* journalist and Velvets fan whose interviews with Lou were jousts between two speed-freaks, called it 'a gargantuan slab of maggoty rancour'.

In our era, *Berlin* is recognised as an unflinching masterpiece. From late 2006 through 2008, Reed toured the album across the world in its entirety, as arranged by Ezrin or conducted by fellow producer Hal Willner.[278] It finally got its dues, but it was typical of the revisionist approach to the artist who insisted rock'n'roll could plumb the lower depths just as profoundly as a novel, film or play.

In the mid-1970s, Reed paid his commercial dues by reverting to a parody of himself. Stick-thin from amphetamine use, he glammed up in black mascara and cropped bottle-blond hair. Guitarists Steve Hunter and Dick Wagner – who'd previously played on Alice Cooper albums – turned old Velvets classics into pristine heavy metal. Performing 'Heroin' live, Lou would go through the motions of jacking up onstage.

1974's *Sally Can't Dance* was another album of Lou Reed parodying his own reputation, albeit with stronger songs. ('Kill Your Sons', from the Velvets era, was a crashing deadpan recitation of the electroshock and psychiatric 'therapy' he'd received as a teenager – because, he claimed, his parents had discovered he was attracted to men.)

Then, in 1975, the reception to *Metal Machine Music* made that of *Berlin* seem like floral bouquets. Originally a double album with each side clocking in at 16:01 of guitar feedback, it made the on-off avant-garde experimentation of ex-Velvets

---

277 DeCurtis, *Lou Reed: A Life*.

278 It was commemorated by the performance documentary *Berlin: Live At St Ann's Warehouse* (2007), directed by Julian Schnabel.

compadre John Cale sound like folk. Fans of *Transformer* returned the album *en masse*, feeling they'd been victims of a massive put on.

There may have been something in that. Lou veered between conceding it was a fuck you to the music industry – and his new fans – and claiming it was '"real" rock about "real" things'.[279] It was certainly electric music taken down to its essence. The tolerant ear can find structure below its atonal howling; possibly even validation of the composer's claim he'd put a melodic reference to Beethoven's *Eroica* in there. But this was before such a thing as industrial music existed, so it played like career suicide.

Or amphetamine psychosis. The cover art carried the chemical symbol for Benzedrine ('Benny', back in the jazz era). 'My week beats your year,' Lou sneered in the sleeve notes, in a period when he stayed up for days at a time.[280]

Time has been kind to *Metal Machine Music*. Fans included Mark E. Smith of The Fall, who surviving band members say used to play the album after gigs. It underwent a renaissance in 2002, when German composer Ulrich Krieger created a touring arrangement for the ten-piece Berlin ensemble Zeitkratzer. Rather than relying on electronics, he amplified a traditional chamber quartet to the point where it resembled an industrial-classical hybrid.

Back in the mid-seventies, Lou Reed's constant seesawing between provocation and pop culture led him to de-glam himself: 'No more bullshit, dyed hair faggot junkie trip,'[281] he told journalist/Patti Smith Group member Lenny Kaye.

Lou sounded almost homophobically intolerant of his own bisexuality, but the truth was more interesting. He may have reverted to his natural dark hair for 1976's *Coney Island Baby*, and the melodic guitars may have sounded like a Dire Straits template – but the object of the title track's affection was Rachel,[282] a pre-op transexual who'd shared Lou's life for a couple of years.

Rachel's sudden disappearance from Lou's apartment (and his life) wasn't such a grotesque scenario. But a life spent turning tricks as a hustler frequently entailed violence[283]. She was last spotted working as an emaciated hooker in Greenwich Village, when the AIDS and crack epidemics had both taken hold. She'd die of the disease in 1990, aged thirty-seven.

If the 'faggot' element of Reed's life hadn't receded yet, then neither had the 'junkie' side.[284] In 1978, his most street level solo album, *Street Hassle*, made a virtue of it. Full of sardonic urban rock'n'roll, its title track was a three-part song suite that gave

---

279 DeCurtis, *Lou Reed: A Life*.

280 Reed often mused at this time about what it would like to stay up for a week. As a note to the curious, it's been observed to result in death.

281 DeCurtis, *Lou Reed: A Life*.

282 Believed to have been born Richard Humphreys.

283 Most often with Rachel as the victim, who reputedly suffered injuries to her face and male genitalia. She was also known to carry a switchblade herself.

284 'Junk' in the widest vernacular sense, as Lou was shooting speed rather than smack. He wouldn't get free of amphetamine – and the hard drinking that took the edge off it – till the early 1980s. Check 1982's 'Waves Of Fear', in which the lyrics and Robert Quine's guitar lines capture a speed and booze-inspired panic attack.

a precise description of urban horrors, worthy of Hubert Selby Jr. With a sha-la-la refrain harking back to the Shangri-Las, it told of an erotic encounter that ended with the female partner fatally OD'ing.[285]

It was a more accessible version of the musical and literary sensibilities that drove The Velvet Underground. But this was the punk era, and in the UK at least (which had first granted him star status) new orthodoxies had taken hold: one being that Lou Reed solo would never reach the greatness of the Velvets.[286]

In 1979, Lou flipped out in a Knightsbridge restaurant when a de-coked Bowie suggested producing his next album if he cleaned up. The former Thin White Duke – by then rid of his theatrical personae – was slapped around by Reed at the dinner table. The collaboration didn't happen, but the album did.

The Bells was one of old Lou's most uneven sets, but the title track was something else. With the addition of jazzmen Marty Fogel and Don Cherry (who'd played with Lou's bebop/free jazz idol Ornette Coleman), he'd sounded so noir-cinematic as on 'The Bells'. As submerged voices and cryptic narrative rose slowly to the fore, it became a more sophisticated counterpart to the Velvets' 'The Murder Mystery'. It also seems to echo one of Lou's literary inspirations, Poe,

Almost inevitably, sales of *The Bells* went through the floor. For Lou Reed was seen for most of his career as a creature of legend, rather than as a major recording artist. As we saw in Chapter Four, the muse of the doomed poet Edgar manifested in *The Raven*; in his last recorded album, *Lulu* in 2011, Lou returned to the metallic guitar sounds of his *Rock'n'roll Animal* period – this time with his most unlikely collaborators, thrash-metallists Metallica.

Like his Poe project, it was salvaged from a theatrical concept; in this case, it was based on German playwright Frank Wedekind's *fin de siècle Lulu* plays, which inspired GW Pabst's classic 1929 film *Pandora's Box*.[287] In truth, Reed's verse, enunciated against the band's onslaught, are an often opaque reading of Wedekind's themes. Both he and the band would earn probably the worst reviews and sales in their career.

Laurie Anderson, the performer's third wife and widow, said Bowie had told her, 'Listen, this is Lou's greatest work… it will be like *Berlin*. It will take everyone a while to catch up.'[288] The man who made rock darkly literate suffered the collapse of his much-challenged liver in autumn 2013. As with Poe, it may take the world a while to fully recognise his uniqueness.

---

285 The third part of the song ends with the sentiment 'Love has gone away / But oh how I miss him' – suggesting the deceased may have been a tranny like Rachel.

286 This writer saw Adam and the Ants at the Roundhouse in 1978, when they were an S&M glam-punk band – very much a prototype for goth rock. Their manager, late punk icon Jordan, sang a screeching rant called 'Lou', which ended on an accusatory refrain of 'An-dy WAR-HOL!' Remember that this was contemporary to *Street Hassle*, which is every bit as powerful as much of Reed's Velvets material.

287 *Pandora's Box*, now regarded as a classic of German cinema, starred American actress Louise Brooks as Lulu – who makes a fated descent from good time girl to streetwalker, dying at the hands of Jack the Ripper. As with most cinematic readings, the glamorous victim and her tragic killer are far removed from the lost souls of 1888 Whitechapel. Brooks, a 1920s 'flapper' with a dark bob hairstyle, originated an iconic look. It influenced goth styles, though not as much as Theda Bara – Hollywood's ersatz Egyptian femme fatale.

288 DeCurtis, *Lou Reed: A Life*.

*****

That same eventful September of 1971, when Bowie first met Reed at Max's Kansas City in New York, he also got acquainted with the World's Forgotten Boy.

Little Jimmy Osterberg was in a different state to Reed, who was about to re-enter the music industry after a post-Velvets stasis. The Stooges were loved by only a handful of rock'n'roll cognoscenti and now they were all washed up. Post-*Fun House*, Iggy wasn't doing much more than sofa-surfing at his friends' apartments; nodding on smack and watching the late show.

Iggy was thrown a lifeline by manager and publicist Danny Fields. It was he who brought him to meet his English fan in the backroom of Max's, after reading how David loved the 'brashness' of The Stooges in a recent interview.

'He appreciated oddballs – people who looked different and spoke in a certain way,' Iggy would recall of his friend (and later saviour). 'He had a very strong curiosity and had very absolute aesthetic values.'[289]

It was a pivotal time for Bowie. The Xerox machine of pop culture was feeding on his influences. He was also pumping them back out into the cultural ether: tributes to Lou and Andy on *Hunky Dory*; suggestions to Ken Scott that *Ziggy* should be rawer, more rock'n'roll, more like Iggy Pop (who the producer had never heard of).

The charismatic Stooges frontman may have been self-destructive, but he retained enough intelligence to know a meeting with a Brit superfan and his manager, Tony Defries, offered him something like a last chance. (Though Iggy would exhaust more last chances than any other performer in the 1970s.) For a brief period at least, the hurtling fast track to oblivion would be halted.

Bowie had been enthralled by Iggy's rock'n'roll madness since US rock critic John Mendelson introduced him to The Stooges' debut album. The star-fan would pay tribute on 'The Jean Genie', a Stones-ish 45 where Ronson's razor-sharp riffs accompanied shapeshifting lyrics about a simple-minded, feral creature who 'loves to be loved'.[290]

MainMan, Bowie's management team, stepped in to save Iggy from himself. Relocated to London, Bowie initially toyed with the idea of teaming him up with underground rockers Third World War.[291] This was soon dismissed, with Detroit hot shot guitarist James Williamson promoted from a second-stringer role to supplant the original Stooge, Ron Asheton.

His buddy Ron, who'd brought him to the band, complained he'd been sent to 'Schmuck City' when relegated to bass. But Williamson brought a demonic

---

289 Iggy Pop to Rolling Stone .

290 The title character was modelled on Iggy but the name was a pun on Jean Genet – the French vagabond novelist who led a life of vagrancy, theft, male prostitution and prison before flowering success as a writer (literally, with *Miracle Of The Rose* – a homoerotic fantasy associating the bodies of male prisoners with flowers.) The association between rock's wildman and the recidivist man of letters may not be obvious, but the latter was sanctified as *Saint Genet* by Jean-Paul Sartre – a martyr in opposition to bourgeois morality. Iggy seems to have played a similar role for Bowie.

291 Former by manager John Fenton, Third World War were a manufactured band. But they had a raw, working-class angst that plays as authentic (and unfairly neglected). A bridge between blues rock, prog and what became punk.

virtuosity to garage rock, a sulphurous style where every note cut into the listener. It was an aural parallel to Iggy's self-mutilation. 'Straight James', as he'd later jokingly call himself,[292] was now the Stooge with a delinquent air and a raven-haired, Keef-ish persona.

Ron and drummer brother Scott Asheton flew over to London too. It was the birth of Iggy & The Stooges – a new dynamic where the self-destructive frontman and his axeman provocateur were the twin focus. In the band's original lifetime, they only played one London gig, at the King's Cross Cinema[293] on north London's Pentonville Road.

It was Saturday, 15 July 1972 – the night after Lou Reed had played the same venue and Mick Rock took the panda-eyed pic that graced *Transformer*. The photographer would pull off a similar coup at the next night's after hours show, burning the post-midnight oil at 2am.

Just five weeks after the release of *Ziggy Stardust*, Iggy reinvented himself as a glammed up 'streetwalking cheetah with a heart full of napalm', to quote the 'Nam terminology of 'Search And Destroy'. Resplendent in silver hair, silver strides and black lipstick, his image was perfectly captured by Rock for the cover of what would become *Raw Power*. Iggy was now a tinfoil reptile, the ultimate incarnation of rock star as outsider.[294]

The set list is lost to legend, but the show was confrontational to an extent most early 1970s audiences couldn't handle. 'The total effect was more frightening than all the Alice Coopers and *Clockwork Orange*s put together, simply because these guys weren't joking,' wrote Nick Kent in *NME*.[295]

MainMan never pushed Iggy & The Stooges as a live act again, concentrating on their boy Bowie's new starman status instead. Amongst the bemused and nonplussed crowd was a sixteen-year-old boy, John Lydon from nearby Highbury. It could be argued that punk rock had its scowling, spitting birth that night.

In the late summer of 1972, *Raw Power* was recorded at CBS Records' London studios with a temporarily cleaned up Iggy in the unfamiliar role of producer. His original mixes[296] had a lo-fi rock'n'roll ferocity, as if laid down in the era of mono recording.

Bowie was called in to remix the tracks in LA that autumn, which remains a bone of contention to Stooges purists. They may be flawed, with the rhythm section playing in a different town to Iggy's vocals and Williamson's guitar. They may be

292 After Iggy's opening dialogue with himself on 'Dum Dum Boys': 'What about James? He's gone straight.'

293 It later became the Scala Cinema Club, venue for such events as Nick Cave reading to piano accompaniment from his debut novel, *And The Ass Saw The Angel*, in 1989, and an all-day show of Richard Kern's *Death Trip* films featuring Lydia Lunch, Sonic Youth and Henry Rollins, in 1991. In 1993, the cinema was put out of business when Warner Bros sued after a clandestine showing of *A Clockwork Orange*.

294 Williamson was the only band member who made the back cover. He'd overdone the white pan-stick to such a degree that he looked like a ghoulish freak.

295 Griffin, *David Bowie: The Golden Years*.

296 Released in 1989 by Bomp Records under the title *Rough Power*.

erratic, with guitar solos appearing out of thin air at incredibly high volume, making little technical sense. But they also sound thrilling and wild.

But sex – on 'Gimme Danger' and 'Penetration' – never sounded so forbidden. And rock'n'roll itself, as on 'Death Trip', was never so terminal. Self-mutilation sounded like something beyond onstage catharsis. Only broken bottles could cut as sharply as those guitar licks.

'It took Iggy with "Death Trip" to snap back a few heads and plunge us all into the abyss,' wrote Allan Jones in *Melody Maker* the following year. 'Spinning recklessly down the spine of [Charles] Manson's equation of death n sex being the final trip. The ultimate self-destruct orgasm.'[297] *Le petit mort* amped up to the power of eleven.

Everything on *Raw Power* was a nihilistic classic that made most rock music preceding it – and most that followed – sound prissy and posed. Maybe it's ironic that Iggy composed the lyrics in the genteel surroundings of a sunny Kensington Gardens. When the album was released in May 1973, it was a rarity to find a copy in London record stores. It followed a similar fast track to oblivion back in the USA.

So did Iggy and his three Stooges. They were kicked off their record label, CBS, for running up debts of $500,000 – much of it spent on drugs. While former mentor Bowie was becoming a world superstar, they played a chain of low-rent clubs and dives that eventually led back to their native Detroit.

On February 9, 1974, the crowd became as confrontational as the band after Iggy called out a biker gang, The Scorpions, on local radio. It's not known if it was actually they who went on the attack at the Michigan Palace, but a few nights previously, one of their number had responded to the frontman's goading by beating the shit out of him.

A bootleg tape of two performances at the same venue would be released on the French Skydog label as *Metallic KO*. Lester Bangs described it as 'the only rock album I know where you can actually hear hurled beer bottles breaking against guitar strings.' According to Iggy, they had everything from shovels to four-gallon jugs thrown at them. 'Who out there hates The Stooges?' he provoked at one point. '... Well, we don't hate you. We don't even care.'

His dismissiveness was no act. The Stooges fell apart after that night. The story wasn't over, but there was nowhere to go but down.

Iggy and James (not so straight in those days) still had the LA blues. They continued to live and, occasionally, play and record together, until heroin and quaaludes got the upper hand. Their demos from this period later appeared as the album *Kill City*,[298] but the original songs were never released in time to save their creative partnership.

In August 1974, Iggy performed an improvised psychodrama at Rodney Bingenheimer's English Disco on the Sunset Strip that he called 'Murder Of The Virgin'. It seems to have been a reaction to how his superfan, Alice Cooper, had

---

297 Nina Antonia, *Iggy Pop*, Virgin Modern Icons, 1997.

298 In the 21st century, when he and Iggy were the only surviving Stooges, James Williamson would re-record the songs from this period as *Re-Licked*, with various post-punk and indie-rock vocalists.

grabbed all the limelight whilst using horrorshow props.[299] But this was Iggy Pop on the downslide. He had no budget for a stage show. All he had was his own toned, muscular flesh that would (to cite his lyric of the time) open up and bleed.

'Do you want to see blood?'[300] he asked the club-sized crowd. It got the affirmative. True to masochistic form – for little Iggy was good at starting fights, in the knowledge it was him who'd suffer most – it's reputed that he once goaded someone in the audience, offering him a steak knife in provocation, but the abused patron wasn't taking the bait. He'd have to do the deed himself.

A nihilistic Iggy would attest he was ready to die just a few months later, having practised for years.[301] The English Disco night testified to it: while he may have threatened a young LA woman theatrically with the knife, full-colour photos that survive (though no sound recordings, sadly) show his torso smeared with its own gory redness.

Former Stooges guitarist Ron Asheton was an enthusiastic participant in the evening's Grand Guignol, dressed in the Nazi regalia he semi-fetishised. He whipped Iggy, stamped on him, subjugating him in a black-comic theatre of cruelty.

In October that same year, Iggy, Williamson and ex-Doors keyboardist Ray Manzarek supported New York Dolls at The Death Of Glitter, hosted by former psych-pop producer Kim Fowley at the Hollywood Palladium. The event's title heralded the end of glam rock and the Dolls, too, seemed to have had their last credible shot at stardom.

One of the defining TV moments of the decade had been when the Dolls played 'Jet Boy' and 'Looking for a Kiss' on the UK's *The Old Grey Whistle Test*, on 26 November 1973. The New York band took trash glam to its extreme (check the cover of their self-titled debut album), but they were a perfect parody of the swagger and surly cool of The Rolling Stones.[302] As David Johansen pouted and declaimed his way through the songs, he had twin Keefs in the shape of Johnny Thunders and Sylvain Sylvain.[303]

Presenter Bob Harris incredulously muttered 'mock rock' at the end of their flamboyant performance, but it became the second night of crystallisation for UK punk (the first being when Iggy & The Stooges terrified King's Cross.) The moment passed all too quickly, but on *New York Dolls* producer Todd Rundgren gave a sheen to their sleazy raunch, similarly to what Bob Ezrin had done for Alice Cooper. [304]

---

299 Iggy later commented on Detroit compatriots Alice (originally a band, not just a singer): 'They took our themes; articulated them well enough; threw all the crazy shit out; did very, very good songcraft and good vocals – good, strong, nasty, rock vocals. And they did the units.' *Motor City's Burning: From Motown To The Stooges*, BBC4, 2008.

300 Rolling Stone, '20 Wildest Iggy Pop Moments', 21 April 2016.

301 *Ready To Die* is, of course, the title of the second and last post-millennial Stooges reformation album. It followed the death of original lead guitarist Asheton; other members of the band would soon follow his mortal lead.

302 Jagger was reputedly underwhelmed, not taking it as a compliment.

303 Original drummer Billy Murcia had checked out in London one year previously, via 'Quaaludes and red wine' – as commemorated in Bowie's 'Time'.

304 On 'Frankenstein', the Dolls made the ultimate gothic monster into a byword for messed-up street kids – a rock'n'roll outsider, just like when Big Daddy Roth-style cartoon artists drew old Frank in a hotrod.

At the Hollywood Palladium, Iggy and his combo played support to New York Dolls with a set of blues/rock'n'roll covers, rather than current songs. It heralded an end rather than a new beginning. Any personal dream of replacing Morrison in a reformed Doors (as had been mooted), or having a solo album produced by Manzarek, was nixed when the piano man objected to Williamson's coruscating chord sequences.[305]

All that was left of his career had become a car crash. Iggy moved from surfing sofas to sleeping on the street. In 1975, when he was arrested by the LAPD in a downered-out state, sheltering beneath the counter of a burger joint, he was regarded as a two-time nutjob. (He'd previously been arrested for the intriguing offence of 'impersonating a female'. Specifics are unclear, but he'd been known to wear a dress in at least one early Stooges performance.)

Given a choice between county jail and psychiatric treatment, he opted to become an inmate at the UCLA Neuropsychiatric Institute.

It had been a long and colourful road down from the Fun House to the nuthouse.

*****

That other bastard son of Jim Morrison, the Detroit rocker who renamed himself Alice Cooper, drank with the Lizard King in the late sixties.[306] But the early days of Alice Cooper [307], playing LA clubs were not salubrious, they were likely to be drunk on cheap Ripple wine rather than experimenting with acid.

Frank Zappa signed them to his vinyl freak show, Straight Records, impressed by their reputation as the 'Worst Band in the World'.[308] Any act that could attract an audience that came along just to heckle held a certain morbid fascination. The ensuing albums, *Pretties For You* and *Easy Action*, are a kind of sub-psych noise-rock (the band were influenced by Barrett-era Pink Floyd, who they'd supported in California) that could sometimes fall apart.

But the second disc had tracks heralding the Alice Cooper of the early seventies: 'Mr. And Miss Demeanour' is a fake blues with dirty vocals, name checking Lucky Luciano; 'Refrigerator Heaven' had a spiky staccato riff and a lyric about a patient cryogenically frozen to survive cancer. It ripped its theme off an old Boris Karloff film, *The Man With Nine Lives*; inspiration came direct from the midnight movie on TV.

Though Vince as Alice could be reticent when he wasn't drunk, there was always a carnivalesque element to his schtick. When the band became a shock-rock phenomenon, the myths proliferated. The most infamous was that Alice (the singer)

305 Paul Trynka, *Iggy Pop: Open Up And Bleed*, Sphere, 2007.

306 Old Alice says The Doors line, 'Got up this morning and I got myself a beer,' was a verbatim quote from him. 'Jim Morrison Quoted Alice Cooper In "Roadhouse Blues"', *Uncut*, 10 July 2008.

307 a psychedelic garage-band rather than just a frontman (real name Vince Furnier)

308 Mark Paytress, *GLAM! When Superstars Rocked The World*, 1970-74, Omnibus Press 2022.

killed a live chicken on stage – like the geek who bit heads from chickens and slept, like a subhuman, in straw in the old American carny.

The truth was almost as startling: appearing at the Toronto Rock n Roll Revival Festival in 1969, Vince/Alice picked up a chicken that wandered onstage and tossed it into the audience, unmindful of how it couldn't fly. The first few rows ripped the luckless bird to pieces when it fell upon them.[309]

It made the papers, but the bemused frontman disclaimed responsibility to his label boss. 'Well, whatever you do, don't tell them you didn't do it,' admonished Zappa,[310] more than a little attuned to the value of outrage.

But it would be a while before shocks equalled bucks for Alice Cooper. Their label mates and sometime girlfriends, The GTO's, drawn from the premier league of groupies, made the band up in a way they thought looked androgynously cute. But Alice, who dyed his hair blond for a while, had other ideas. He'd later play up the grotesquerie of slap paint, aiming for a look akin to Bette Davis in *Whatever Happened To Baby Jane?* (1962).

The adoption of a female name seemed like a calculated affront to 1960s Middle America, but the band said it was chosen because it sounded so prim and schoolmarmish. Still, the later legend about a dead witch named Alice Cooper contacting them via an ouija board wouldn't hurt…

A commercial and critical failure in California, the five Arizonans went into retreat. They shacked up near a city where there was a down-and-dirty hard rock scene going on: Detroit, the place of Vince's birth.

Also in retreat in the early seventies were The Stooges, who'd briefly come home, bloodied but unbowed, from LA. Alice/Vince knew of the chaos that followed Iggy from stage to street and back again, but found him an inspiration. He was the ultimate flesh-and-blood incarnation of ferocity.

'It was like smearing peanut butter all over himself and jumping into the audience,' an elderly Alice would recall. 'He was a show unto himself. Musically, they weren't very theatrical. The band just kind of stood there and played, but Iggy did all the work. Whereas Alice Cooper, every single song was a theatrical bit.'[311]

The factor that solidified the ramshackle promise of the Alice Cooper band was the arrival of Bob Ezrin, a young Canadian producer. They were drinking at the Last Chance Saloon. Straight Records had ceased and parent company Warner Bros was deciding which of its acts was salvageable.

Toronto Bob did them the greatest favour of their careers, honing and editing their psych style into an accessible but menacing hard rock. Glen Buxton, a guitarist who played feedback like The Stooges' Ron Asheton, became a purveyor of memorable riffs.

---

309 As surreal cartoonist/underground journalist Savage Pencil (Edwin Pouncey) once told this writer: '*They* were the geeks. The audience were the geeks.'

310 *Super Duper Alice Cooper* (2010), directed by Scot McFadyen, Sam Dunn and Reginald Harkema.

311 *Motor City's Burning: From Motown To The Stooges*. Iggy: 'They did a gig with The Stooges and three months later they were neighbours.' (laughs) 'And all of a sudden it was "Under My Wheels"! And "Eighteen"! And they killed us.'

It got results: '(I'm) Eighteen', a downbeat youth anthem, got them into the US top forty for the first time. Where Ezrin gelled with Alice Cooper was in a shared cinematic sensibility, the 'movie for the ear' aesthetic he'd later bring to Lou Reed's *Berlin*.

Look at the inner sleeve of the mid-seventies *Alice Cooper's Greatest Hits* collection, and you'll see artwork of the band dressed up as gangsters at the St Valentine's Day Massacre. Their love of old movies is seen in line drawings of Humphrey Bogart and Edward G. Robinson; but look to the back of the garage setting, and you'll see the faces of Karloff and Lugosi, the demon princes of old Hollywood Gothic.

On *Love It To Death*, Alice's 1971 breakthrough, they embrace their *Shock Theater* roots on 'Ballad Of Dwight Fry', a melodramatic descent into psychosis. Alice gibbers, '*I want to get out of here!*' in the style of tragic character actor Fry[312] as Renfield, the incarcerated lunatic in *Dracula* (1931). 'Black Juju', as darkly magical as anything The Doors ever did, is a Voodoo or Macumba-style raising of the dead set to tribal drumming and a swirling organ. Dennis Dunaway, Alice's booming bassist, called his eerie composition 'desert music'.

When Alice, the band, first came to London, in November 1971, there were some attentive young droogs in the audience. David Bowie (still with Garbo-esque blond hair) brought along Mick Ronson, bassist Trevor Bolder and drummer Woody Woodmansey to viddy the mildly threatening androgynes from across the sea. Bowie's band thought Alice rocked, but their main-man left early, finding spectacles like Alice strapped into an electric chair for 'Black Juju' too 'premeditated'. Still, he promised the nascent Spiders From Mars a new visual image: 'Wait till you see what we can do.'[313]

Meanwhile, Alice Cooper ramped up the theatricality. The mock executions became more elaborate; *Killer*, the late 1971 album that followed *Love It To Death*, originally featured a fold-out 1972 calendar with Alice hanging, bedraggled and bloody, from a gallows.

It was established that Alice – Vince Furnier's Mr Hyde – would face gleefully retributive capital punishment from the band, though he'd return from beyond the grave. (At one point, the resurrected killer led the audience through a rendition of 'God Bless America.')

Killer ventured furthered into pop-cinema territory, with Western gunfighters ('Desperado') and international saboteurs ('Halo Of Flies'). But it also got sicker. 'Dead Babies', one of the songs that made Alice Cooper infamous, was a cruel satire of US society where a small child is left alone to poison herself.

On stage such nuances were lost, with Alice the killer hacking away at baby dolls. The visuals were crude but the symbolism was brutally potent – as Alice's old mentor, Frank Zappa, could have told him.

---

312 Or Frye, as he was billed.

313 Griffin, *David Bowie: The Golden Years*.

While Bowie and Lou Reed sneered at Alice (no longer seen as a band, even then) for his rocky horror showmanship, *Love It To Death* and *Killer* became totems for a transgressive generation yet to come of age. 'Eighteen', the anthem of chaotic youth, provided the perfect Sex Pistols audition for a young John Lydon. It was on the jukebox in Malcolm McLaren's shop, Sex, on Chelsea's King's Road,[314] and the soon-to-be rechristened Johnny Rotten threw himself into a charismatically contorted parody of Alice's vocal.

The snarky north London youth had an affinity with modern music's outsiders; Alice was as close as he got to a rock'n'roll idol. As a high school kid, he'd horrified an English teacher by ripping off 'Dead Babies' in a poem.[315] Having joined the Alice Cooper Fan Club at sixteen, he'd later opine that *Killer*, with its tuneful sleaze and morbid theatre, was the greatest rock album of all time.

For the post-punk figures who came out of New York's 'No Wave', *Love It To Death* was the unholy artefact. Lydia Lunch would record a cover of 'Black Juju' as darkly hypnotic as the original on *Shotgun Wedding*, her 1991 collaboration with Rowland S. Howard.[316] In a 1986 John Peel session, Sonic Youth covered 'Hallowed Be My Name', preacher's son Alice's sneering screed at pious hypocrisy.

After shock-rocking his way into the USA's pocketbooks, Alice turned himself into public enemy number one (and hit number one in the charts) in glam-era Britain. 'School's Out', with its lairy metal riff, was the 1972 summer-holiday anthem for kids just out of their crumbling comprehensive schools. On *Top of the Pops* they danced around their friendly uncle bogeyman, who made mock-threats with a rapier sword.

The *School's Out* album was more theatrical still. The sleeve design comprised a defaced school-desk, juvenile delinquent-style shots of the (mid-twenties) band and a pair of paper girlie knickers. The content was not so gothic, but still violent. 'Gutter Cats Vs. The Jets' subverted a song from *West Side Story*, jettisoning the dancing for a *Clockwork Orange*-style gang fight. 'Luney Tune' was the narrative of an institutionalised patient cutting his own throat.

In 1973, the Alice Cooper band's commercial magnum opus, *Billion Dollar Babies*, dished out all the shock, all the sleaze and all the showbiz at once. From the mock-snakeskin wallet cover to the inner sleeve showing Alice menacingly handling a (real) baby, sick America's superstars were going for broke.

Billion Dollar Babies was a media event. Recorded in the US and London, it reputedly featured Marc Bolan among the guests who showed up at the studio.[317]

---

314 When band Svengali McLaren was recruiting a vocalist, his partner, future *haute couturist* Vivienne Westwood, told him to look out for a young punk named John. It's been said that she meant John Ritchie (Sid Vicious), but a historic accident made the more interesting selection.

315 Fred and Judy Vermorel, *Sex Pistols: The Inside Story*, Omnibus Press, 1987.

316 For three brief days in the fall of 1983, the divine Lydia performed with Nick Cave, Jim Foetus and Marc Almond in The Immaculate Consumptive, an infernal cabaret lineup. Their brief roster of shows in New York City and Washington, DC featured her singing Alice Cooper's 'Blue Turk', a sensuously sleazy piece of ersatz bebop from the *School's Out* album.

317 Alice was too drunk on Budweiser in those days to recall which track Marc appeared on. This writer's ears hear Bolanesque guitar on the title track, but we'll never know now.

Housing three hit 45s, including the 1972 presidential campaign spoof 'Elected', it also ramped up the horror theatre.

'Billion Dollar Babies' featured a Dick Van Dyke accent intoning, 'I'm so scared your little 'ead will come off in my 'and';[318] on 'Sick Things', affable Vince's alter ego sang to his fans like they were death cult members;[319] 'I Love The Dead' was what its title suggests, leading UK MP Leo Abse to denounce Alice's 'anthems of necrophilia'.[320]

'I Love The Dead' was a s(l)ick piece of pop drama, but Abse (who joined Christian cleanup campaigner Mary Whitehouse in calling for Alice to be banned from the UK[321]) identified its transgressive appeal. Beneath Ezrin's orchestrated strings is heard the vocalist's panting, as he pretends to fuck a corpse.

'Sure, people keep getting sicker, so do we,' Alice shrugged provocatively.[322] It may have all been an act, but the *Billion Dollar Babies* tour turned up the theatrical gore. A guillotine became centrepiece of the execution climax, with headsman illusionist the Great Randi[323] retrieving Alice's splattered head from the basket.

It evoked the Grand Guignol theatre of Paris that ran for much of the twentieth century – pre-dating the splatter movie in its theatrical gore, whether it was presenting Jacobean tragedy or contemporary horror plays. Alice and the band were too young to witness it, but the Grand Guignol's influence was felt in American exploitation movies like *Blood Feast* (1963), where butcher's shop offal was used for special effects, or cinematic sick-joke *The Baby* (1973), where a man is kept in perpetual infancy.

By the mid-1970s, the name 'Alice Cooper' was synonymous with the man. In retrospect, the original band members may have been too trusting when he told them he was going to make a solo album – he was carrying the brand, after all.

Welcome To My Nightmare (1975) was the culmination of Bob Ezrin's penchant for movies on vinyl. Impeccably arranged by the producer, its string orchestrations complemented the pyrotechnics of former Lou Reed guitarists Hunter and Wagner. Ezrin had long since imbedded himself as Alice's main collaborator and was prominent in the songwriting.

Amid the metallic rock was the showbiz Gothic of 'Years Ago' and 'Steven', whose eponymous character was a tormented man in perpetual infancy. 'The Black Widow' was pure cheese, but introduced horror actor Vincent Price to pop music. As a museum curator, he ranted about how his precious venomous spider would take

---

318 Almost unbelievably, the 'cockney' voice was Scottish hippie folk-singer Donovan.

319 The following year, Alice camped it up on TV as a cult leader known as 'the Warlock Prince', on a 'tec series called *The Snoop Sisters* with veteran actress Helen Hayes. He sang 'Sick Things' in a skeletal bodysuit.

320 Paytress, *GLAM! When Superstars Rocked The World, 1970-1974.*

321 The *Billion Dollar Babies* tour's itinerary was fixated on the USA, so it wasn't an issue. But the Alice Cooper band sent cigars to Abse and flowers to Whitehouse for increasing their infamy.

322 Bob Greene, *Billion Dollar Babies*, Atheneum, 1974.

323 The late James Randi was, in the words of a doc film about him, 'an honest liar'. A pro stage magician and lifelong sceptic, the foundation set up in his name claimed to hold a cheque for $1m to anyone who proved paranormal powers. The money was never claimed – though occultist detractors accused Randi of setting the bar impossibly high.

over the world;[324] Alice gloated about the male of the species, and 'the virgins and the children he's deflowered'. But then, the 1970s was a different time…

Welcome To My Nightmare was the first 'solo' Alice album, and probably the best. It spawned a stage show that spotlighted the spectacle (giant spiders, a Cyclops monster) and downplayed the gore. The family-entertainment aspects suited a performer who'd guest on *The Muppet Show* a couple of years later.

The ever-opportunistic Alice has jumped on multiple bandwagons since then: soft rock, heavy metal, electronica. In the end it always came back to his core appeal of hard rock, Gothic imagery and gore – entailing an unlikely 2011 reunion with his original, casually discarded band.[325]

Ultimately, he'd pass the baton of shock-rock to the well-manicured hands of post-goth icon Marilyn Manson. 'He has a woman's name and wears makeup. How original,' Alice sneered when he first heard of the Antichrist Superstar. By 2013, with both artists past their prime, they'd pair up on the Masters of Madness tour.

It was an unlikely meeting of monsters. Alice had long since re-embraced the Christianity he was brought up on, dropping the seductively nasty 'I Love The Dead' from his set. Marilyn boasted he'd been ordained as a priest of the Church of Satan by its late founder, Anton Szandor LaVey. Long before then, the trash aesthetic of early Alice had been inherited by The Cramps.[326] In the late 1970s, when he was performing soft rock songs about people he'd met in the sanatorium,[327] they were reviving the sounds of rockabilly, garage rock and early psychedelia. All to a cathode ray backdrop of late-night horror movies on a black and white TV…

More outrageous than Alice was the symbiotic theatrical merging of 1950s rock'n'roll and 1950s monster culture first took place in Britain – with a subversive glam twist that would become a key goth influence. Opening in the small room above the Royal Court Theatre on the King's Road, in June 1973, *The Rocky Horror Show* picked up a cult audience. Bowie and Reed were said to have enjoyed it; even Vincent Price was reportedly amused.

Written by out-of-work actor Richard O'Brien, the sleazily flamboyant musical starred Tim Curry, an actor for whom subtlety was just an ugly rumour, as Dr. Frank-N-Furter. Frank is a 'sweet transvestite from transexual Transylvania' – not just a Carpathian backwoods, but an alien planet.

In its post-glam fetishisation of the 1950s, science fiction was paid as much lip service as Gothic horror. ('Science Fiction' was the show's opening theme song.)

---

324 Price was the velvet-voiced screen villain who gave bravura performances in such camp-Gothic classics as *The Tingler* (1959) and Roger Corman's Poe adaptations. To many, he's remembered for his odd voiceover in Michael Jackson's 'Thriller' – surely inspired by 'The Black Widow'. There's a lot to make a Gothic horror fan cringe in 'Thriller' (from the lame song itself to the generic title, suggestive of detective or spy films) – but the promo video by Jon Landis, coming off the back of *An American Werewolf In London* (1981), is visually brilliant.

325 Minus underrated guitarist Buxton, who'd long ago succumbed to hard living.

326 To hear a lineage between Alice Cooper and The Cramps, check his 'Slick Black Limousine'. Issued as a flexi-disc via *NME* in 1973, at the height of his UK popularity, it's rockabilly gone sleaze.

327 Alice dried out in the late 1970s. After adding a bottle of whisky to his daily intake of a crate of Budweiser, he'd started to vomit blood.

But the basic story of Frank creating human life – essentially so he can get laid by a muscleman – was a camp comedy riff on *Frankenstein*.

When clean-cut kids Brad and Janet arrived at his bizarre gothic mansion, after becoming trapped during a storm, they sang a song called 'Over At The Frankenstein Place'. When Frank was finally dispatched by hunchbacked servant Riff Raff (played by O'Brien), he and his sister Magenta were revealed as aliens. (Magenta had the hairstyle of *The Bride Of Frankenstein*, 1935.)

Along the way there was trashy sex comedy aplenty, plus gender fluidity, as Frank seduced both Brad *and* Janet. There was also audience participation, as patrons were prepped with written instructions on how to dance a rock n roll routine called the Time Warp.

And then something strange happened to *Rocky Horror* on the way to the big screen. It transferred successfully to both the King's Road Theatre and the Roxy in Los Angeles, before bombing badly in New York. It didn't augur well for *The Rocky Horror Picture Show*, which opened in 1975 to very small but enthusiastic audiences.

But then some bright young thing working for 20th Century Fox had the idea of emulating the midnight movie scene in New York: don't blow a promo budget on the opening weekend; rent theatres after dark and wait for the cult crowd to show up.

It worked like a wet dream. The same audiences came to the show weekend after weekend, with a greater sense of character identification due to increased familiarity. Knowing they couldn't disrupt an onscreen performance, they became a part of it. They would dress as the characters; answer them back with rehearsed lines; even throw props at the screen at key moments.

Umpteen Frank-N-Furters could be seen in every midnight crowd, both male and female. There were flurries of outrageously androgynous black dresses and suspenders. The craze worked its way back home, with midnight shows running at the Screen on Baker Street well into the 1980s. Today, the film's screenings are a thing of the past – but whenever the show runs in repertory theatre, all the transexual Transylvanians turn out for a nostalgic celebration of pre-AIDS camp.

Rocky Horror made its obvious mark on what would become the goth subculture. Along with *Cabaret* (1972) – with its Weimar decadence, Liza Minnelli in bowler hat and low cleavage, and Joel Grey as clownishly made-up MC – its characters were absorbed into the sartorial statements of a new generation.

Back in the day, Britain, birthplace of the Gothic novel, wallowed in its own disreputable taste. Hammer Films made a brief commercial glam resurgence[328] when the company made the implicit erotic element in Gothic horror more overt; Le Fanu's relatively subtle novella, *Carmilla*, was transformed into the softcore romps of *The Vampire Lovers*, *Lust For A Vampire* and *Twins Of Evil*. (See Chapter One.)

---

328 Hammer Films' popularity declined throughout the 1970s, as American movies like *The Exorcist* and *The Texas Chainsaw Massacre* brought audiences to new levels of shock. By late 1974, *The Rocky Horror Picture Show* could be filmed at Hammer's Bray Studios due to the low level of activity.

At the supposedly highbrow end of the cinematic spectrum, Ken Russell filmed Aldous Huxley's historical work, *The Devils Of Loudun*, in the iconoclastic style of his own classical composer biopics. *The Devils* (1971) starred Oliver Reed as doomed Father Urbain Grandier, a sexually permissive priest accused by French Catholic authorities in the 17th century of being in league with Satan.

Cue scenes of sexual hysteria, sadistic perversion, torture and ultimately death, set amid baroque production designs by Derek Jarman prior to his own directorial career. *The Devils* remained extreme even after cuts by the British censor; it was also one of the most successful films of its year at the UK box office.

In a more sedate (though also depressed) cultural atmosphere, in 1974 the ITV commercial channel celebrated the end of power cuts and mandated 10:30pm closedowns by broadcasting Bela Lugosi as *Dracula*. It marked a resurgence of interest in old Hollywood Gothic. The following year, BBC TV began a decade-long run of double bills pairing those old black and white horrors with gorier modern versions.

It was a cultural glut of glam and gothic, feeding into the psyches of suburban teenagers like young David Lett[329], Susan Ballion and Steven Bailey.[330]

*****

Taking their cues from Bowie and Bolan, a generation of performers who'd spent their youths on the UK touring circuit opted for a similar sparkly flamboyance. For all its posturing, most glam rock was anything but gay in its sensibility; it was meat-and-potatoes rock'n'roll, rolled in glitter.

The commercial peak of UK glam pop was in 1973; that January, The Sweet appeared on *Top of the Pops* with number one hit 'Blockbuster!' A dramatic stomp anthem about a super-criminal on the loose, it supposedly took its title from the blockbuster bombs the Royal Air Force dropped on Germany in World War II.

That may have been justification enough for bass guitarist Steve Priest to slap up in heavy makeup and a German army helmet[331] to deliver his ultra-camp line: 'We just haven't got a clue what to do!'

The song reused the same old blues riff as 'The Jean Genie', leading to a miffed claim by Bowie that he'd lifted it first. His disapproval, according to Priest, ran to the bassist's use of makeup: in the *TOTP* dressing rooms, David admonished Steve for laying it on thick, telling him to be more subtle; but Bowie, according to Priest, 'didn't get it'. This wasn't the Warhol Factory or off-Broadway theatre; it was in the tradition of drag queens at boozy workingmen's clubs.

The Sweet – led by vocalist Brian Connolly, a glam supayob take on Brian Jones – were all jobbing rock n rollers on the circuit before they signed up to be a bubblegum

---

329 Or David Letts.

330 Respectively, Dave Vanian, Siouxsie Sioux and Steven Severin.

331 It was a spiked officer's helmet, WWI vintage. On the *TOTP* Christmas show at end of year, Priest reputedly went the whole hog and dragged up as a camp Hitler complete with swastika armband. It was a staple of Brit light entertainment at the time, when comedians like Freddie Starr played der Fuhrer as a figure of fun. It remains a fading memory to 1970s pop kids, as contemporary accounts insist the show remains 'lost' – particularly as it features glam pop's biggest star, the deviant Gary Glitter.

band with songwriters Nicky Chinn and Mike Chapman. They weathered the 'brickies in drag' put-downs well, once 'Blockbuster' put a rocky edge on their hit 45s. They looked pretty cool in a deranged kind of way, as they released one teenage anthem after another penned by the Chinnichap partnership: 'Hellraiser' plays now like proto-pop-punk; 'The Ballroom Blitz' would be covered later by The Damned. Even less glam were Mud who also managed a series of great goofy stomp anthems whilst dressed as Butlins teddy boys on the piss.

Among their Chinnichap stablemates, they were friendliest with Suzi Quatro – a diminutive woman in leathers who migrated from the Detroit rock scene.[332] Playing a bass guitar almost as big as she was, she snarled like a ferocious femme through strangely-titled rockers like 'Can The Can' and '48 Crash'.

Suzi was taken as part of the androgynous glam scene as, while The Sweet laid on the Max Factor, 'I had no makeup on and wore a plain black jumpsuit while everyone else was glittered up.'[333] In those far-off days, it led to speculation on her sexuality, but she was as hetero as most glam rockers. Certainly, the pubescent boys who felt a strange awakening when they saw her on *TOTP* harboured few doubts. With her fierce vocals and mean bass style, she preceded the tougher girl bands of punk and beyond.

Seen in retrospect, the villain of the era was Gary Glitter. Take a look at the infamous 1974 footage of him on fellow sexual abuser Jimmy Savile's show, with both draping their arms lecherously around vulnerable underage girls. And try not to shudder.

But as well as personifying the predatory nature of the era, and the media's wilful blindness to it, Glitter was a true Brit superstar of the 1970s. A veteran of the industry, then in his late twenties, Paul Raven (as he was formerly known) was a no-hit wonder, a nearly man who never broke through. He was also a big fan of Elvis who, while he had none of his idol's vocal range, could belt out a rock'n'roll tune.

So it was that he became a lamé-and-sequins vehicle for a new sound. On *TOTP*, with hirsute chest and platform boots, he put his cheesy charisma to work before an adoring young audience. It was also a shopfront. What made those 45s so remarkable was writer and producer Mike Leander's vision and the 'Glitter beat'; played by his band, The Glittermen (formerly the Boston Showband). 'Rock & Roll Parts One & Two', the first Glitter hit in early '72, broke through largely on the strength of the B-side. Dropping the vocalist's jukebox lyric out, the instrumental version was left with thudding drums and a call-and-response 'Hey-ey! *Hey-ey!*', like a metallic form of dub.

The Glittermen would develop the sound further on their own hit 45s, as The Glitter Band, under the further tutelage of Mike Leander – as was pretty much the whole Gary Glitter package. Leander would die in 1996, aged fifty-five. Original

---

332 'No, that's not Suzi Quatro on guitar,' Bowie joked as he introduced Mick Ronson on Ziggy's 'retirement' night at Hammersmith Odeon, on 3 July 1973. See DA Pennebaker's documentary film, *Ziggy Stardust And The Spiders From Mars*.

333 Paytress, *GLAM! When Superstars Rocked The World, 1970-74*.

Glittermen/Glitter Band member John Rossall created the brass sounds (sax and trumpet) on the early singles; he also co-wrote 'Angel Face', the first Glitter Band hit.

> What people miss out on is the fact the whole Glitter thing comes from Mike Leander. The whole Glitter sound started on a Mike Leander instrumental. He was working on a David Essex session and when David had rung in sick with a cold, Mike started work on this instrumental. He was trying to do a John Kongos/ Osibisa type of thing and it developed from there. He then put this amazing droning guitar sound on it. He found an old guitar with a really bad action on it and put it through some really heavy Fender tube amps till it was jumping off the floor, and he got me in to provide the brass parts and that was how that sound came about.[334]

The deservedly maligned Gary Glitter has thankfully been consigned to the pop dustbin, but the sound of the records, which had little to do with him, were key in the goth playbook. From Killing Joke to Adam and the Ants to The Fall to Bow Wow Wow to Marilyn Manson, the so-called 'glitter beat' has been staple. Mike Leander's take on 1971's 'Burundi Black' saw him inspired by that single's pure cinematic atmosphere, with evocative piano and guitar lines embellished by the drumming and voices of the Ingoma tribe of Burundi.

The most extraordinary ethno-pop of that hit was also possibly the most exploitative. The cut-up composition was the work of French composer Michel Bernholc (under the credit 'Burundi Stephenson Black'); it was a top forty hit in the UK, with the Burundian musicians reportedly never seeing a penny from it. Added to Leander's inspiration was the Ghanaian expat fusion band Osibisa who made everything sound like a party and the added influence of John Kongos and his second hit, 'Tokoloshe Man'.[335] They all inspired the experimental recording session that produced 'Rock & Roll Parts One & Two'.

When Leander moonlighted from the production of David Essex's latest recording to create 'rock'n'roll', the young *Godspell* star had yet to hit. That changed with 1973's ghostly 'Rock On'. It's debatable how much of a glam star he was – but gypsy raven hair and a single earring[336] made him part of the era. 'Rock On', though, was something else. Producer Jeff Wayne[337] took the singing actor's stark tribute to 1950s pop culture and made it a minimalist dark doo-wop dub. Elements like backing vocals and strings would briefly appear and then disappear over the heartbeat shudder. The nostalgic vocal about the 'blue-jean baby queen' on the movie screen was somehow haunting, particularly when it evoked James Dean – the romantic icon of early death.

---

334 The late John Rossall from The Glitter Band to John Robb.

335 Released on the Fly label, like T. Rex's early chart hits.

336 To some belligerent pubgoers, a man with one small earring was proof positive of homosexuality and pretext for a pasting. The Dutch band who called themselves Golden Earring must have known it would earn a few column inches.

337 In 1978, Wayne wrote and produced a concept album based on HG Wells' *The War Of The Worlds*, with Essex in the singing role of the Artilleryman. The project, which has been revised and performed every decade or so, is the most commercially successful prog rock adaptation of fantastic literature – eclipsing The Alan Parsons Project's *Tales Of Mystery And Imagination* on a per-buck basis.

The sonic skeleton that carried it was a minimal bass line by Herbie Flowers, who'd performed a similar role for Lou Reed on 'Walk On The Wild Side'. Like dub reggae, the music was all about the space between the notes. Heard now, 'Rock On' plays like a third uncle to 'Bela Lugosi's Dead' by Bauhaus. But then, the Gothic aesthetic has always been found in the unlikeliest places...

*****

Glam rock was the moment that a grey world turned Day-Glo. Colour TV in the early 1970s was a luxury item seen in few UK households, but in retro, *Top of the Pops*, for all its lo-tech special effects, was a colourful part of the revolution begat by Bolan and Bowie.

It was a perfect medium for art school pop, as initiated by Roxy Music with the release of their first single, 'Virginia Plain', in the late summer of 1972. Singer Bryan Ferry had an outgrown 1950s quiff and wore glittery eyeshadow; sax player Andy Mackay looked like a futuristic dragon variant on the Teddy Boy; electronics bod Eno (then known only by his surname) had a camp exotic cool leopard-skin look like a hybrid of Bet Lynch in *Coronation Street* and Riff Raff in *The Rocky Horror Show*. The feather boa was optional, though he flaunted it on the gatefold of Roxy's eponymous debut.

Their music encompassed everything all at once – The Velvet Underground, Motown, Sinatra-esque ballads, avant-garde atonality – but steered clear of the boringly banal boogie of mainstream rock. In this sense, it better fitted a club scene that was either 'deviant' (gay clubs – still a subterranean world when gay sex had only been legal for five years) or still somewhere in the future now of the about to emerge Bowie/Roxy club nights.

Ferry's classic songwriting style had been filtered through his art school background. The startling 'Virginia Plain', with its oboe-driven riff and electro-noise interlude, was essentially cryptic lyrics referring to the band striking a record deal.

But its closing, 'What's your name, Virginia Plain?' alludes to an art school painting by the young Ferry, featuring a pack of Virginia Slims cigarettes adorned with the image of 1964's 'Girl Of The Year'. It was a Warholian concept that carried over to Roxy's music: style had become substance.[338]

So it was that Ferry – a Newcastle miner's son and former schoolteacher – would reinvent himself as his own stylistic creation. Even in the early days of sparkly sequinned jackets, he was cultivating a louche lounge-lizard style. He would even appropriate the line 'Here's looking at you, kid,' from Bogart's world-weary nightclub owner character, Rick, in the classic *Casablanca* (1942) on the centrepiece of the first Roxy album's tribute to Bogie, '2HB'. Even the title was another piece of Ferry wordplay, lifted from the insignia on an everyday pencil. In a matter of months, Ferry would discard the glitter garb, in favour of a white tuxedo and black bowtie.

---

338 Paytress, *GLAM! When Superstars Rocked The World, 1970-74.*

It was the look of Bogart as Rick Blaine.

Ferry would later tell of how he only enjoyed the classic cinema of the black and white era. But then 'Roxy' was a name redolent of both British high streets and screen dreams – the picture palaces of the 1930s-50s that, eventually, met the tawdry fate of down-marketing to bingo halls.

The imagery clashed brilliantly with Eno's quirky sonic improvisations. For here was a self-professed 'non-musician' who played sounds rather than notes. Like Ferry, Brian Peter George St John le Baptiste de la Salle Eno was schooled in fine art, before realising the possibilities inherent in the humble arena of popular music.

It also coincided with the popularisation of Dr Robert Moog's keyboard synthesiser. 'A complete beginner like me had as much right to say "I'm a synthesiser player" as anybody else did,' Eno would note. 'More so in a way.'[339]

He was no virtuoso progmeister. Watch the old TV clips of early Roxy now and you're more likely to see Eno twiddling knobs than playing the keys. But it lent depth to the sound and, increasingly, layers of atmosphere.

On the second Roxy album, *For Your Pleasure*, the title track was eerily evocative of the type of unnamable emotions we all know but don't have the earthly vocabulary to describe. 'You're rubbing shoulders with the stars at night… getting older,' Ferry intoned, his quavering baritone crackling slightly as he seems to age in a matter of moments. As the vocalist bids his listener (and perhaps his life?) 'Tara',[340] Eno distorts the layer of sound in which Phil Manzanera's guitar resides, as Ferry's farewell echoes.

This collage of concepts and sounds reached its apex on the same album's 'In Every Dream Home A Heartache'. Here it's positively sinister, a truly modern gothic. Set to a sinuously mantric backing, Ferry's neurotic narrator (a rare departure from his aloof Romanticism) sings of the 'perfect companion' to his 'penthouse perfection': a vinyl sex doll, comically absurd and yet descriptive of contemporary alienation.[341] The building nervous tension explodes into a guitar break and a premature fade… before coming back on waves of phased sound.

Ferry's lyric, in its depiction of the existential absurdity of modern living, echoes the more satirical work of his onetime art tutor, Richard Hamilton. Latterly known for his minimalist sleeve design of 1968 double album *The Beatles*,[342] Hamilton initially ignited controversy with his pop art collage for the 1956 *This Is Tomorrow* exhibition at London's Whitechapel Gallery.

Created for the exhibition's catalogue, *just what is it that makes today's homes so different, so appealing?* was considered shocking for its time. Its re-appropriated and juxtaposed advertising imagery depicts a naked woman on a sofa and a hyper masculine bodybuilder holding an oversized lollipop labelled 'Pop' over his genitals. Their own dream home incorporates domestic gadgetry and a page from a romance

---

339 Ibid.

340 It seems to be a measure of old Bryan's fondness for 'For Your Pleasure' that he named one of his sons Tara.

341 In our own era, late-night TV documentaries alert us to advances in artificial companionship – i.e. sex robots that offer a limited range of movements and verbal phrases. 'In Every Dream Home A Heartache' now seems quaintly old school.

342 Known as 'The White Album' for Hamilton's use of minimal typography on an otherwise blank white sleeve. As a record it's an uneven and at times inspiring artefact, influential in very different ways on figures ranging from Siouxsie to the Manson Family.

comic displayed as kitsch art. It was, effectively, the birth of British pop art, with a profound influence on conceptual graphics in the 1970s that lasted into the punk era.[343]

Hamilton had taught Bryan Ferry at art school in Newcastle in 1969, later describing him as his own 'greatest creation'. Ferry repaid the compliment in 2010, naming his former tutor as the living person he most admired,[344] saying, 'he greatly influenced my ways of seeing art and the world.'

This stylised aestheticism was absorbed into the early Roxy experience, with Eno creating an extra sonic dimension by putting instruments through sound filters. He made the mixing desk into an extramusical instrument, a technique he'd further explore in his extraordinary post-Roxy work.

By early 1973, however, 'the other Brian' was expressing dismay at how the glam element of Roxy Music's albums, the high-class cover models, was becoming a cliché.[345] Though he was consistently glammed up in Max Factor both on and offstage at that time, Eno was very much the John Cale figure in the band.[346] Reputedly, Ferry grew uncomfortable when his bandmate wanted to subject the frontman's voice to the same experimental filters that subverted the instrumentation.

As with Lou and John in the Velvets, there was only space for one creative ego to dominate. 'I was cramping Eno's style,' Ferry disarmingly claimed when the sonic innovator took his leave in July 1973. 'Two non-musicians in a band is one too many.'[347] Though of course, Bryan was no slouch as a piano man.

For his part, Eno was relieved to breathing his own air. He was complimentary about Roxy's third album, *Stranded*, released that autumn – which featured young Eddie Jobson, ex-Curved Air, effectively 'doing an Eno' on the glorious electro cacophony of hit single 'Street Life'.

But Roxy Music would remain Bryan Ferry's band now. His romantic balladeering reached its apotheosis in the album's 'A Song For Europe', where the Gothic cathedral of 'Notre Dame casts a long, lonely shadow' and the vocalist laments, 'Jamais!' as if he were Brel.

Eno, post-Roxy, was a wilder card both conceptually and musically. In an interview with *Melody Maker*, he'd describe 'insanity' as 'one of the most important elements of my musical life'.[348] He didn't fail to deliver on that count.

Solo Eno set about changing the very fabric of music. His first solo work, *Here Come The Warm Jets*, was adorned with a cover shot of Brian's apartment and his kitschy collection of *objet d'arts* – including framed photos of himself in full slap. He

---

343 Check Linder Sterling's hybrid collage of the naked female form and domestic objects for Buzzcocks' 'Orgasm Addict'.

344 Richard Hamilton would die in the following year.

345 The striking Amanda Lear was the model on *For Your Pleasure*, leading a black panther on a leash. A former muse of surrealist genius Salvador Dali, rumours (seemingly backed by documentary evidence) persist to this day that Ms. Lear was born a man. She has consistently denied all such reports.

346 Kindred spirits Cale and Eno have since worked creatively together on several occasions.

347 Paytress, *GLAM! How Superstars Rocked The World, 1970-1974.*

348 Ibid.

was backed by an impressive range of collaborators including his Roxy bandmates (sans Ferry), Robert Fripp of King Crimson, members of space rockers Hawkwind and Ladbroke Grove deviants Pink Fairies.

The lyrics were surreal, freely associative, making juxtapositions that were sometimes macabre, but always in the province of skilful wordplay that rhymed and scanned. On 'Baby's On Fire', the highbrowed one crisply enunciated his intoxicating lyrics set against short bursts of feedback guitar, the very Englishness of his tones was in itself startling.

1974's *Taking Tiger Mountain (By Strategy)* featured lyrics and music produced by an early version of the artist's Oblique Strategies – conceptual games of chance formulated by instruction cards. 'Third Uncle'[349], a rushing, jangling, clanging proto-punk lyric contained emotionless couplets like 'Burn my fingers, burn my toes / Burn my uncle, burn his books,' returning to the refrain of, 'Then there was you.' It was word association of the most evocative kind.

Between the two albums, there was the remarkable single 'Seven Deadly Finns'. Watch the YouTube clip from a Dutch TV pop show in 1974 and witness an Eno now lost in time: an androgynous glam pop star dolled up to the nines, who looks the part but has no theatrical moves; singer of a very literal (for him) song full of artful *double entendres* about erotic naughtiness in a European port; yodeller par excellence in the outro.[350]

It wouldn't make the pop charts – but then Eno never became a pop star. His 1975 album, *Another Green World*, was transitional. Less than half the tracks are songs; the predominating instrumentals are as much about the space between notes as the music itself; their non-linear composition was a further evolution of Eno's systems music. A little later it would come to be known as 'ambient'; in its own quiet way, it would change aspects of musical history.

But by 1974, Roxy Music had already made an indelible mark on British pop. Glam was officially passé, according to the press, but in its fallout came what some termed art rock. Cockney Rebel, led by mouthy former *East London Advertiser* reporter Steve Harley, were one of the EMI label's few signings of 1973.

The frontman boasted that the Rebel were playing 'third-generation rock'.[351] On the cover of their debut, *The Human Menagerie*, the band posed in lounge chairs wearing bowties, waist-coasts and floppy fringes. In the wake of Roxy, rock'n'roll attire was out; studied classicism supposedly equalled sophistication.

It certainly seemed to on 'Sebastian', the big production number released as a 45. With an orchestral backing augmenting the Rebel's own electric violinist, Jean-Paul Crocker, the strangely decadent love song alluded to 'Persian eyes' and 'Parisian

---

349 Covered later by Bauhaus - one of many goth era bands who proclaimed Roxy Music and Eno as a profound influence.

350 Yodelling being a rather underrated aspect of glam rock. As a lover of madness in pop, Eno likely shared his future friend Bowie's liking for novelty records like The Singing Postman's 'Have You Got A Light, Boy?'.

351 Ibid.

demands'. (It also referred mysteriously to being 'slagged in a Bowery saloon' – which gets the imagination working.)

It was enhanced by the fragility of Harley's delivery; some vocalists seem vulnerable but he sounded positively ill, as if singing in some fractured European patois. It took the song to the top five in Belgium, birthplace of Jacques Brel.

On sleeve notes for its parent album's CD release, the singer-songwriter later described 'Sebastian' as 'possibly a sort of gothic love song, possibly not'. On *The Human Menagerie*, it was outdone by 'Death Trip'[352] – another piece of over the top bombast.

'Sebastian' did nothing back home, where great things had been expected of it. Undeterred, Harley and his increasingly sidelined band released the brilliant 'Judy Teen', which grabbed the hearts of the school playground for a few weeks in 1974. Strange pizzicato strings framed the hiccoughed vocal, placing the singer somewhere between Ferry's vibrato and Bowie's slightly music hall London accent.

The album that followed, *The Psychomodo*, ended on the epic 'Tumbling Down', which almost matched the glorious portentousness of Harley's earlier orchestral pop. The album's single, 'Mr. Soft', bounced and lurched with a mad-eyed fervour straight out of Brechtian cabaret. The lyric was opaque, attacking aspects of its mysterious subject's personality. It also featured a baritone male chorus that oddly echoed 'Velvet Goldmine', an outtake from *Ziggy Stardust*.[353]

And then in 1974 came Sparks. The misfits' misfits. The one and only Sparks Brothers.

In 1969 Russell and Ron Mael had originally been called Halfnelson. It was Todd Rundgren, the singer/songwriter/producer[354] who helmed the Dolls' debut, who rechristened them. It was a play on the Marx Brothers, in tribute to Ron's vaguely Groucho-esque appearance and the humour in his songs.

When the two Californians arrived in the UK, they'd shortened the nom de plume to Sparks. They picked up some Brit rock musicians and soon created a unique niche in what was fast becoming a post-glam pop scene.

Their first and biggest hit, May 1974's brilliant 'This Town Ain't Big Enough For Both Of Us', established them as the oddest duo in pop history. For despite the band lineup of the time, Sparks would only ever really be Russell and Ron.

Ron's 'depressed bank manager' demeanour[355] was set off by a moustache which earned comparison with Charlie Chaplin or, more ominously, Hitler. (The Groucho aspect was oft overlooked.) When he stared sternly at the camera on *Top of the Pops*, it could be genuinely unsettling. This was the epitome of what a pop star *was not*.

---

352 Most definitely not Iggy & the Stooges' aural apocalypse.

353 'Velvet Goldmine' didn't see vinyl until 1975, on the B-side of a rerelease of 'Space Oddity'. But Steve Harley was acquainted with Bowie, having played acoustic versions of his own early songs at the latter's Beckenham 'Arts Lab' above a pub. Neither held much affection for the other. ('Oh him…' Bowie said dismissively, when Cockney Rebel were mentioned at a joint 1993 *NME* interview with glam fan Brett Anderson of Suede.) Harley was, however, friends with the equally egocentric Bolan, whose funeral he attended.

354 *A Wizard, A True Star*, as Rundgren modestly described himself on one of his albums.

355 Ron's own description, when promoting Edgar Wright's documentary film *The Sparks Brothers* (2021).

His pretty-boy brother, Russell, looked like a young Jim Morrison, but with a trademark falsetto that turned his brother's witty vignettes into pop anthems. 'This Town Ain't Big Enough…'[356] comprised oddly literate lines. So it continued, through a run of quirky hits – 'Get In The Swing' sounded like something Dietrich might have rallied the allied troops with – and a later career encompassing electro-disco and a concept album about *Seventh Seal* director, Bergman. Sparks have remained independent in a sense which most so-called 'indie' bands could never hope to touch.

In many ways, groups like Sparks and Roxy Music were timeless and indefinable - they were neither glam nor ham. They were so beyond the narrative that they were writing their own timeline helping bridge that gap between the end of glam's shapeshifting adventures and punk. They were not alone - there was plenty of other interesting wildlife rustling deeper in the undergrowth as a whole host of nearly bands were appearing on the horizon - like the wrong place at the wrong time, Doctors of Madness, Liverpool Roxy Music styled party band, Deaf School, the way ahead of their time goth precursors Gloria Mundi and the groundbreaking punky electric pop of Ultravox! - the latter being the closest to capturing a new starker zeitgeist with their human in the machine of Kraftwerk's robotic adventures in a live band format.

Meanwhile, Bowie had decamped to Europe with Iggy in June 1976, seeking new geographical, sonic and drug-free vistas that saw Iggy's debut solo album recorded in France. After completing *The Idiot*, Bowie and Pop travelled to Hansa studios in West Berlin to mix the album, and the pair of them lived in the walled city. The new sessions would result in Bowie's Jan 1977 groundbreaking Tony Visconti produced *Low* album, followed by the March 1977 release of the Bowie produced Iggy Pop album, *The Idiot*.

The two albums arrived just before punk and totally reshaped the landscape with their stark new horizons and monochromatic sound and would have a profound effect on goth with their innate darkness and future vision and their combination of experimental new tech like the first use of the Eventide H910 Harmonizer.[357]

Both album's melancholy, subdued mechanical cold detachment, their nudge towards the dance floor and their sonic bleakness and the profound influence of so-called krautrock and Eno's new sonic adventures, especially *Another Green World*, resulted in him being brought along for the trip after a chance meeting with Bowie after his May 1976 London show were a glimpse into the future.

Because *The Idiot* was recorded before *Low*, it has been referred to as the unofficial beginning of Bowie's Berlin period as its music features a sound reminiscent of that which Bowie would explore in his own Berlin Trilogy of albums. In a productive rush, they also recorded Bowie's *Heroes* and Iggy's *Lust For Life* months later.

---

356 A caffeine-nervous classic that Siouxsie and the Banshees chose to open their 1987 covers album, *Through The Looking Glass*.

357 When Bowie asked what it did, Visconti replied, "It fucks with the fabric of time."

All four albums were a pointer to the post-punk future, and their futuristic sounds are still astonishing to this day. For the teenagers fresh out of glam, the albums were shocking future templates and arriving just before the full tsunami of punk were a preview to the future that they too would take part in once they had been jolted into action by punk itself, but there was still some interesting diversions to navigate.

Chapter 10

Proto Post-Punk

The future is always arriving. The future is always embedded in the past. The post-glam malaise had some bright sparks (ha!) plus a whole host of groups who may never have broken into the mainstream. Music is littered with misfits, visionaries and ignored prophets. Glam wasn't the only story in town in the 1970s that would feed into post-punk and goth. As the decade attempted to make sense of the 1960s, there were many tangled strands that musically and culturally were part of the goth DNA.

In Notting Hill, the '60s trip never really ended. In the then-faded grandeur of the big townhouses, a hippy microcosm hung on with bands dealing a chemically driven revolution rock like Hawkwind, The Pink Fairies, Here and Now and The Deviants. Their rhetoric matched their music and their dealers were kept busy as they took the free festival spirit to its extreme.

The alpha band were Hawkwind who to this day exist in a parallel universe to the rest of society, tearing along with their tripped-out space rock and brooding, extra-terrestrial sound. Their strange and hypnotic music would be a key influence on groups as diverse as Killing Joke, Joy Division and The Sisters of Mercy as well as a new underground that clung on in the decades after the sixties. In their genius, Hawkwind somehow managed to straddle the lysergic excess of the hippie guerrillas with a driving, stripped-down rush of sound that was also very much a proto-punk template.

The group hit a genuine creative peak with their 1973 *Space Ritual* live album. It was a double album that defined space rock with a surging and dramatic series of songs and bizarre recitations on the universe. The bass played by the charismatic Lemmy drove the relentless tracks that swirled with primitive keyboards and surged with the dynamic of their two-drummer drum empire. This sound was very much their own and, when played at gigs, was accompanied by a futuristic swirling light show and famously their topless dancer called Stacia.

The already iconic Lemmy, had stumbled into singing their unlikely huge 1972 chart hit; the classic 'Silver Machine'. This was primarily because none of the rest of the band could sing in the correct key. Subsequently, Lemmy became the group's ipso facto frontman, which complete with his rough and ready biker image and charismatic presence would immediately become part of the alternative lexicon. Lemmy's presence seemed to touch every scene until he was unceremoniously booted out of the band for 'taking the wrong drugs'. The bass monster swiftly went on to form the much loved Motörhead, whose wall of sound, raw power and crafted songwriting was also highly influential in the post-punk wars.

Hawkwind's unique soup of psychedelia, drone rock and sonic hypnosis was a deep space swirl to lose oneself in. They provided a portal into a fascinating and unique early 1970s madness; a lysergic period of hope and technological aspirations.

They also offered a glimpse into the lunacy of a band that existed in both a chaos and a curated beauty. Hawkwind captured a time when rock music was full of drone, drugs and pure, creative weirdness. They were part of a new generation of bands who broke from the constraints of established songwriting structures and moved into the true progressive with a mesmerising dark energy.

In the unlikely West Yorkshire town of Wakefield, Bebop Deluxe were delivering a unique hybrid of glam and prog, yet shaved of all the excesses, with lyrical themes looking introspectively at the human condition. Much like Hawkwind, they also combined their sound with a hefty dose of sci-fi. The band, formed by singer, guitarist and principal songwriter Bill Nelson in 1972, may have had moderate chart success in their prime but would be a key influence on so many aspiring young guitar players who would be key players in the post-punk period.

Already a scene veteran who had played the same Hamburg clubs as the pre-fame Beatles, Glaswegian Alex Harvey somehow managed to weld hard rock with a prog twist. With his theatrical and narrative-based rock, his flirtation with Berlin 1930s cabaret of Brecht, and Weill's *Threepenny Opera,* and the visual madness of *A Clockwork Orange* glam, his sound was a distinctive and influential bricolage of ideas. The Sensational Alex Harvey Band showcased their musicianship and mastery of a hooligan prog but also had jaunty off-kilter pop such as their take on 'Delilah', and the iconic psychodrama of 'Framed'. Harvey's music would prove to be a considerable door-opener for many musicians, including the youthful Nick Cave who was a huge fan of this theatrical intensity.

Along with Gloria Mundi, Ultravox! may not have recorded till the early punk era, but they existed before it, inhabiting a brief new world of pre-punk progressive electronic tinged dramatic new music. By the mid-1980s, they had morphed into a huge, mainstream pop band, but their roots were laid elsewhere. Formed by Dennis Leigh (who would change his name to John Foxx) at the Royal College of Art, the band was initially named Tiger Lilly, releasing only one single, a cover of Fats Domino's 'Ain't Misbehaving'.

Shortly afterwards they became Ultravox! in 1976 after their initial plan to call themselves 'The Damned' had been thwarted by the newly formed punk band of the same name. Ultravox!'s music was a well-executed, timeless art rock with a futuristic and punkoid sheen. Signed to Island in 1976, their self-titled debut album was released in February 1977 and produced by Steve Lillywhite[358] and Brian Eno. However, despite sounding like it was very much of the moment and the band certainly looking the part, they were swamped by the incoming punk movement that was dominating the music press.

The band reacted with the punkier *Ha! Ha! Ha!* that is undoubtedly a great work, featuring their most punk electronic anthemic songs, like 'RockWrok', which managed to slip the word 'fuck' onto Radio One. Yet the single, much like the album, didn't manage to chart. The album also contained the classic 'Hiroshima

---

358 This was the first album that the legendary producer worked on.

Mon Amour' that was one of the first songs to grapple with the incoming musical technology and utilise the drum machine: a Roland Rhythm 77 on a song that later fused some of the caustic outrage of punk into their sound while still retaining their artfulness. It also eschewed the barre chord rush of punk, replacing it with their electric violin and keyboard-dominated soundscapes. Locked out of punk and two years too early, Ultravox! were one of the plethora of outsider bands that had a lasting influence on gothic and darker musics.

The post-glam hinterland saw bands exploring the theatrical and artful channels of performance like Doctors of Madness who may have been in the wrong place at the wrong time but were also one of the few hopes on the bleak glam horizon for a youth seeking a post-Bowie messiah, as Journalist Cindy Stern explains:

> Doctors of Madness were an important band and future faces like Dave Vanian and Gaye Advert were big fans. They were part of a lineage from glam to punk with the likes of Cockney Rebel, adding a more Burroughs-type vibe to the scene. A big crossover point for me was the Doctors gig at Middlesbrough in May 1976 with Sex Pistols supporting. Doctors of Madness were just breaking through but the scene that they had helped to pioneer was about to engulf them. They were just in the wrong place at the wrong time. I remember their singer Kid Strange, full of pathos, saying at the end of their gig, 'our time is up. How do we follow that? I am still not well but music helps!'
> The charismatic Kid Strange is one of those cult figures trapped in a limbo by his own idiosyncratic talent. 'I was trying to write folk protest songs but then I'm thinking about The Velvet Underground, and that very abrasive sound. I then got into a more avant-garde wall of noise with feedback thing that was just sheer two fingers up to up to the world kind of thing. In our heads, we knew what we were like and we were quite flamboyant. I had blue hair and the band had a look which were sort of street clothes but there was face paint, lots of flesh and odd-looking guitars. We weren't dressing for the stage but we looked different and we'd already taken on these names - I was Kid Strange and there was Urban Blitz, Stoner, Peter DiLemma.' [359]

The UK in the mid-1970s was full of these lost gems; ghost bands who had used the space created by glam to find their own direction. They ironically inspired punk but would be pushed aside and would fade into obscurity as a result, but that steady drip of ideas would re-emerge in the post-punk confusion. By 1975/76 there was an enormous wave of bands about to break, but all were rudely pushed aside by punk after Sex Pistols' defining appearance on the December 1976 Bill Grundy-hosted Today Show.

Even the prog scene was leaving its DNA in fertile young minds. Formed in the late 1960s in Manchester, Van Der Graaf Generator had gathered together with an experimental sound that was frequently lumped in with prog. However, they were very much on their own trajectory. Frontman Peter Hammill's jarring vocals were of huge influence on John Lydon and Public Image Limited and like French outfit Magma, whose polyrhythmic brilliance underpinned songs were written in their

---

359 Kid Strange to John Robb.

own bizarre fictional language, they seemed to exist in their suspended animation whilst informing those adventurous souls that dared to go there.

Not every band that forged their own path were left out of the mainstream. A vibrant underground scene in Germany of reparative experimental music that was often erroneously monikered 'krautrock' somehow found a crossover band when Kraftwerk had a worldwide hit with their 'Autobahn' song in 1975. Truly the sound of the future eschewing trad rock guitar and drums. Kraftwerk were true game changers turning existing norms upside down whose influence echoes through the generations.

Formed in the late sixties they had honed their sound down to a hypnotic pulse of melancholic melodies that created a very new European sound. The Dusseldorf-based band utilised new technology with the use of incoming affordable portable synthesisers like mini Moogs or the Korg MS-20 to push the pop culture boundaries beyond American guitars. Their minimalistic half man half/machine music would be a key influence in post-punk and goth, and their deadpan dark humour along with their fascination with esoteric subjects like the German motorway system on 1974's breakthrough *Autobahn* scored them a surprise worldwide hit.

The pulses of the radio entwined in their 1976 *Radioactivity* were a new extension in pop's lexicon and sonic texture whilst their sixth album two years later, *Trans Europe Express,* was inspired by inter continual train travel. A young Stephen Morris of the future Joy Division was captivated by their 'human meeting the machine' music and image whilst his future singer Ian Curtis was also entranced by the group. A whole host of future players in the many strands of goth and post-punk were taking their cues from the robots - like Depeche Mode, Virgin Prunes, early The Human League and many others in post-punk whether it was the group's minimalism or actual electronic textures

The cold wave term that would soon be used as an alternative phrase to describe some areas of goth was actually first used in the forward-thinking Sounds music paper on the 26th November 1977 issue in conjunction with Kraftwerk. The band, who had just released *Trans Europe Express*, were the front cover stars that week and snapped in a classic stark photo of core members Ralf Hütter and Florian Schneider that was captioned as 'New musick: The cold wave'. The phrase stuck and the following week music writer, Vivien Goldman, used the phrase again in the same weekly in an article about Siouxsie and the Banshees which also saw the Banshees describe their music as "cold, machine-like and passionate at the same time," perfectly summing up this modern dance.

The German post-war history was unique of course, saddled with war debt and not a considerable amount of guilt a broken nation had been split into two. Dealing with the future instead of the past the post-war German youth were forging their own music and culture which would have a profound effect on the future post-punk scene.

The 1970s German underground music ranged from proto-electronic to repetitive riffing bands with the famous motorik beat pioneered by Neu!, becoming a staple of alternative rock bands over the decades. Many of the groups took the possibility of repetition, as pioneered by The Velvet Underground, to its hypnotic logical extreme, sometimes with songs lasting up to twenty minutes, deconstructing one riff in an endless rush. There was also a prodigious use of synthesisers and new technology. Can honed down their rhythms into complex and hypnotic structures, courtesy of their late and great drummer Jaki Liebezeit. They specialised in long, atmospheric rhythmic pieces that the jamming band would then edit using their own studio as an instrument and with the incorporation of new technology that would be so integral to the post-punk mindset. After David Bowie (of course!) publicly name-checked many of these groups, a whole new musical world was opened up to his acolytes and fans.

Even Gotham city itself was casting a long shadow. New York in the mid-1970s was a city in crisis. Stumbling towards bankruptcy and famous for a high murder rate, it felt like a city having a nervous breakdown. Its very image, like the brooding walled city of Berlin, was a key influence on post-punk mindsets. Performance poet and musician Annie Anxiety recalls the city at its darkest:

> New York was bankrupt when I was a teenager and was on the verge of collapse while the federal government and the other 49 states were happy to let it do so. The place was dirty and dangerous but at the time I was, like most teenagers, too self-absorbed to see outside my immediate circumstance to what was actually happening around me. Rents were cheap which is always good for creativity – jobs were scarce, and trouble was plentiful. Don't know that spurred creativity – it's just how it was.

It was in this New York that a clutch of new noiseniks appeared in town. One of the most important was Patti Smith whose androgynous image and street image was a perfect backdrop to her poetry and music. Depending on where you sat, Smith was one of the harbingers of punk rock or the last gasp of 1960s counterculture. Smith provided inspiration, not only to many women who felt isolated by the rock'n'roll lads club, but to many men who also fell in love with her intelligence, steely music and intensity. Smith's classic 1975 album *Horses* was of enormous importance to alternative music scenes across the world, securing her status as a poetic and visual template for so many.

The CBGB club on the lower Manhattan Bowery was the hub for this new action and scene that would have a profound impact on punk and post-punk. The small cramped stage played host to bands such as Television, the wired Richard Hell, and Talking Heads. It also launched the classic gnarled pop of Ramones - a band whose influence remains enormous - visually with their oft-reproduced leather-clad appearance and musically with their minimalist yet melodic chainsaw rush. Musically, their high-volume, high-octane live gigs swept by in a rush of thrilling guitars, driving bass and a voice of heartbreak. They were fronted by the unlikely figure of Joey Ramone; a tall New Yorker with his face hidden by lank hair, gripping onto his microphone as though his life depended on it. The band have been the eternal garage band prototype since then.

Perhaps the most groundbreaking New York band of all were Suicide, whose influence over so much future musical culture was huge. The band took their name, not from provocation alone, but from the title of frontman Alan Vega's favourite Ghost Rider comic book titled *Satan Suicide*. Vega was also the first person to use the word 'punk' to describe the kind of music he was making. The duo were formed in 1968 by keyboard manipulator Marty Rev who dumped the guitar, bass and drums cliché of rock'n'roll for a primitive drum machine and a battered Farfisa organ, which, combined with effects units, made a ghostly and terrifying pulsating twitching psychosis.

Through this, they created lo-fi beats, rhythms and soundscapes that added a sense of turmoil and tension to their sound, whilst piercing the primal heart of rock'n'roll through circuitry. Alan Vega crooned and twitched his Elvis-from-hell vocals with his voice full of the terror of modern life. He would switch from a deceptively sweet croon to terror dread screams, creating an effect that was at once both hypnotising and terrifying and helming a stripped-down take on The Stooges' sonic nihilism without the guitars.

Suicide were the unheard soundtrack to America on the verge of collapse and a cultural shift. Their 1977 self-titled debut album was so unlike any music at the time that it confused almost everyone. Tracks like the electro shuffle of 'Ghostrider' and the terrifying 'Frankie Teardrop' were compelling listens but jarring in the music scene that surrounded them. Suicide were arguably 'too much' for most, yet the few that embraced them found that the band changed their perception of music completely and few musicians in the contemporary goth scene remained untouched by this strange and compelling release.

Suicide created futuristic and dangerous music, decades ahead of its time. Their sound still sounds like the future and still sits outside of established genres. Their stripped-down electronic pulse is all over post-punk, from Soft Cell's two-piece bedsit psycho kitchen sink dramas, to The Sisters of Mercy's rhythmic dread to Sigue Sigue Sputnik's repetition, Joy Division's spectral atmosphere to Big Black's relentless machine-like grooves. Their influence helped curate the gothic end of post-punk and the genre was the first to first embrace them. In one earlier failed experiment, the band had toured the UK with The Clash in the punk wars. On paper, this was a brilliant piece of booking however, Suicide were a musical step too far for the audience and the band were bottled off every night. At these gigs, there was a genuine air of danger showing how provocative and unsettling the band's music really was.

Another band who were operating beyond the established confines of genre were San Francisco's Chrome, who formed in 1975 and featured heavy elements of feedback and distortion. Their experiments in mixing synthesised noise with rock instrumentation marked them as part of the post-punk movement and as an unwitting precedent to the industrial scene. From the same city, Tuxedomoon mixed the distorted rush of punk guitars with a wheezing keyboard creating underground classic tracks that were harbingers for the eventual industrial scene, as well as being a counterpoint to the surrounding punk scene. Typical of many early innovators, Tuxedomoon have become a breathless footnote in musical history.

Cleveland's Pere Ubu had emerged in the early seventies and despite cult status was further proof of outsider cities creating idiosyncratic and strange scenes. They were a band so out of time that it is remarkable they ever existed. Music writer, Jon Savage saw the band, who had barely played any gig outside of Cleveland or New York, pitched into the heart of the UK new music scene, becoming an electrifying influence on a small but vital cabal of future music leaders:

> I saw Pere Ubu's first date in the UK when they came over in 1977 (supporting The Pop Group on April 28th at Manchester, Rafters). It was a couple of years since they had first released their records. I remember seeing members of Joy Division in the audience. Maybe they didn't get the idea of the high bass sound that night but Pere Ubu were very influential because they were dealing with post-industrial space, and there were all these link-ups between post-industrial American cities and Manchester which then was very much a post-industrial city then which links it up with all those rust belt cities like Detroit and Cleveland.

It's difficult to comprehend how astonishing Pere Ubu were when they appeared in 1975. The band, in many ways, were proto-post-punk; operating so far ahead of the game and in such splendid isolation. They were deliberately provocative and intellectual, having immersed themselves in pop culture and grown bored of the template becoming early dissenters to rock's fast-binding tapestry. With ominous bass guitar driven songs, they were creating a new, darker sound that would be a prominent influence on post-punk when the movement eventually arrived five years later.

Songs such as 'Final Solution' and 'Thirty Seconds Over Tokyo' are brooding classics – the former is quite terrifying in its lumbering build and the latter a manic, twisting affair that captures the innate dark terror and fear of nuclear war. Frontman David Thomas was a new kind of singer - a besuited behemoth with an acidic, lyrical wit and a powerful presence. While punk eventually managed to create an audience for Pere Ubu, it also managed to get in the way of their intelligent musical discourse.

These isolated pockets of scattered musicians left their ideas littered around the globe in the pre-punk mid-1970s for a new generation to use as templates. Prophets may never get a share of the spoils but their influence can be so profound.

Without each of the above bands, post-punk and goth would have sounded and *felt* so very different and it was going to be the big bang of punk that would create a new universe for them all to coexist in.

Chapter 11

THE PUNK WARS

The big bang of punk seemed to compress all culture before and then explode it outwards with a dark matter of ideas that would soon coalesce as what became known as goth.

Never had a youth culture felt as intense as the short sharp shock of punk. Its brief electric chock had now jolted and spiralled into countless tribes, each clearly defined and hostile to its rivals. The punk generation were now forging their own creative paths in a droog reaction to the Pistols' energy like the dystopian vision of Anthony Burgess's *A Clockwork Orange* come alive.

Punk was a creative playground and goth would be just one of the strands that came out of it taking its sex, style and subversion and twisting it with the sex and death dance to create new hybrid that would end up dwarfing punk in popularity. Whatever obsessions you brought into the Big Bang were fused with its energy and hurling out into the culture void.

Punk's psychodrama was empowering to so many. David Lett, the gravedigger from Hemel Hempstead, was now living out his vampire Iggy fantasies as Dave Vanian from The Damned, Susan Ballion utilised punk to combine a whiff of Thirties' Berlin *Cabaret* with the alien otherness of Bowie and Bolan to iconic effect creating Siouxsie Sioux. Punk gave these exotic creatures – and many more – the creative space to do what the hell they liked.

After punk hit, a new wave of impressionable and excitable music lovers were swiftly morphing into new and darker shapes, all in the shadow of the post-punk hinterland. Ian Astbury was hitchhiking around the UK following Crass, looking for a tribe to make sense of his life. Nick Cave and his school friends in Melbourne formed a school punk band called Concrete Vulture, finding a temporary home for their intellectual teenage rage. Bauhaus had coalesced in the art school in Northampton, whilst The Cure were inspired to create a new linear, angular sound that would increasingly add its own shadows. Joy Division would fumble around in the decay of post-industrial Manchester before inventing a whole new soundscape.

All new scenes need space for ideas to breed and percolate. In the 21st century, it's the internet. Back in the 20th century, it was either clubs or gigs and, in London in the mid-1970s, it was one shop in particular that gave a few stray youths the licence to dream.

Since 1971 Malcolm McLaren and Vivienne Westwood had run a boutique under various names at 430 King's Road in Chelsea. It was where creative sparks flew as wild ideas coalesced that would lead to punk and percolate into parts of goth.

In the great tradition of counterculture haute couture, clothes shops were at the core of British pop culture and its dandyish love of dressing up. The King's Road had been the epicentre of this pop culture style since the swinging '60s. Granny Takes

A Trip at 488 King's Road was the first psychedelic boutique in London. Later, The Chelsea Drugstore was cemented into pop culture by The Rolling Stones after a namecheck in their song, 'You Can't Always Get What You Want'. These and many other shops saw the area becoming the sartorial nerve centre, with its boutiques a magnet for musicians, models and hip teenagers.

By the mid-1970s, a cultural shift was afoot on the King's Road. Acme Attractions, a pioneering new wave stall, was founded by John Krivine and Steph Rainer in the basement of the Antiquarius Antiques Market and Beaufort Market saw a stall selling eccentric items called X Ray Spex was run by a pre-fame Poly Styrene.

430 King's Road was named Sex in 1974 and was the original game changer for a new (blank) generation. By realigning shock value clothes with music, it helped spark punk and post-punk culturally and aesthetically. Originally opened in 1971 by Malcolm McLaren and Patrick Casey as Let it Rock in the back of the Paradise Garage boutique, it was a stall that initially dealt in 1950s bric-a-brac collected by McLaren, who was fascinated with the decade. They then took over the whole shop and started selling Teddy Boy clothes created by Malcolm's then partner, Vivienne Westwood.

The pair were key players in the 1972 rock n roll revival before renaming the shop Too Fast to Live Too Young to Die and selling more rocker oriented gear, before finally becoming Sex in 1974. The new shop was now a clean break from the past with deliberate shock tactics that railed against social and sexual taboos. The self-designed clothes were built to confront with a mixture of rubber wear, outrageous outfits and ripped t-shirts that were covered in deliberately offensive slogans. Their famously scandalous self-screened t-shirts included images of the semi-naked cowboys,[360] provocative symbols such as swastikas, situationist quotes and images of Karl Marx all mixed together. It wasn't always comfortable, and it wasn't meant to be. Veering from rocker to rubber and from fetish to kitsch, it was deliberately and artfully provocative. The t-shirts were often shocking but always powerfully evocative; each item stunningly original and a minor work of art.

The iconic face of the shop was Jordan, who worked behind the counter. She had arrived in 1974 dancing down the King's Rd, vision in her see-through top, a ballet tutu and a '50s beehive that would soon morph into the iconic spikes. Arriving at the shop in her wild, idiosyncratic way she was instantly given a job. An instant icon with her Mondrian inspired face paint and her body as a blank canvas for her wardrobe exotica, she was a self-created walking work of art. Jordan was the first-ever punk rock anti role model and a major influence in the post-punk dress up.

Arguably, with her fearless attitude and artful dress codes, she was not just a punk icon but also the unintentional instigator of the eventual goth catwalk. The imperious Jordan was on a fast forward of clothes that were a mixture of rubber wear from the shop and her own pieces, creating a striking visual of a deconstructed ballerina from

---

360 From a 1969 illustration by the US artist Jim French.

hell. Her provocative look would make her one of the faces of the new punk scene alongside Sex Pistols, with whom she appeared with on their first TV appearance. [361]

A young (pre-Adam Ant) Stuart Goddard was similarly entranced by her presence and her dominatrix image and would leave her mysterious love letters dotted around the shop in 1976. A few months later, he asked her to manage the new band he was putting together: Adam and the Ants, whose future guitar player, Marco Pirroni, was another youthful teenage visitor to the shop:

> When I first went to the Sex shop in the autumn of 1974, Jordan had only just started working there. Vivienne and Malcolm hated working in the shop, so they got Jordan to be its face. I used to go in all the time and I got chatting with her. She said she used to like me because I bought the best things even though I must have been the youngest person in there. I started bunking off school and there came a point when I was in there every fucking day hanging out. They never offered me a job though. That would have been my dream.[362]

Jordan embraced the spirit of punk:

> Competition, not repetition always makes for exciting and challenging times. The main feeling that runs throughout for me is that punk was a great enabler. It wasn't meant to be easy. You had to know why you were buying the clothes. Often, I would tell people they couldn't have stuff because it wasn't right for them. Punk galvanised into action a stagnant youth that had had no focus and inspiration in their lives. It was an equaliser both sexually and aesthetically. Everyone was on an equal footing and no one was excluded either because they weren't pretty enough or the right shape. It also created a situation where male and female competed to look the best and could use the same weapons like makeup and clothes to outdo each other.[363]

Once released, Jordan saw this explosive energy scatter in all directions:

> Post-punk was really quite violent. These were the times when certain groups of people, like the National Front and skinheads, felt they could hijack the notoriety that punk had created and use it for their own devices, much like a parasite lives off a host. Although there are links to previous genres, perhaps with The Damned and Alice Cooper, I think that goth was more of a creation in itself rather than copying anything. I was, to be truthful, very unattracted to the New Romantics and found most of it to be far too contrived and pantomime-like. Power is in simplicity for me and the fussier it is, the weaker it is.

Like the future Uber-goths, Jordan saw herself as her own creation, a self-created work of art:

> I have been asked many times what my influences have been and to be honest, most of it came out of my head. I did see a small article in a fashion magazine when I was about 17 featuring Cleopatra-type makeup by a man called Serge

---

361 On Tony Wilson's groundbreaking TV arts show, 'So It Goes' which was filmed in Manchester in September 1976.

362 Marco to John Robb.

363 Jordan to John Robb.

Lutens[364] and I took the idea and exaggerated it many times. I also very much liked messing things up, like taking original '50s clothes and cutting or slashing them or wearing them differently - like see-through petticoats with nothing on underneath. I would deliberately ladder stockings and cut holes in my clothes. I used to wear ballet wear in the shop when I first worked there, and I cut too big a hole across a top and used a safety pin to attach it together again. My geometric face makeup was inspired by a combination of the works of an artist called Mondrian[365] and also from images from a book called *The People of Kau* by Leni Riefenstahl.[366] It took me quite a while to perfect that one as an art form for a face because it has to work naturally with your contours. I also really liked the Anne Bonney's[367] female pirate look and the pre-goth red contact lenses that I wore for quite a while that I had to get specially made for me. [368]

The Sex shop, with its mix of rocker styles served through an art school confrontation, had toyed with proto-goth darker styles before punk.

The first time I went to the shop, it was still called Too Fast to Live Too Young to Die. It had a big skull and crossbones outside. Inside it was all black. The imagery they chose was pretty out there, pretty scary. There was nothing else like it going on.

It was a Tuesday afternoon and Vivienne was in there and I asked her for some brothel creepers. I was thinking, fucking hell she looks incredible. She had white hair and she was wearing big leather pegs, and purple winkle-picker boots. It's one of those things where you walk away, and you don't understand but it keeps you awake at night thinking, what is this look?

I knew I had to go back again. I ended up going back in every week and sometimes bought things they were selling, like the slashed tee shirts or t-shirts with two bits of cloth sewn together, leather trousers, drapes, leather tee shirts, and jeans.

They had a pair of blue winkle-pinker boots which I really liked but they were not my size, so I bought some black ones. That was the crossing point, brothel creepers were now accepted because Mud had worn them on Top of the Pops but the winklepickers were really revolting, and they made people go eeugh! So I had to get them.[369]

Marco saw the shop mutate from McLaren's preoccupation with the 1950s to the confrontational fetish ethos that sowed the seeds of punk:

I don't think anyone had done a rock n roll shop before. There had never been a shop that sold drape jackets. In the '50s and '60s if you wanted a drape you had to go to John Dunn and Co and have it made. Also, with Malcolm and

---

364 Lutens is a French photographer, filmmaker, hair stylist, art-director and fashion designer. His 1973 series of photographs – inspired by the artists Claude Monet, Georges-Pierre Seurat, Pablo Picasso and Amedeo Modigliani – was shown at the Guggenheim Museum in New York.

365 Piet Mondrian 1872 -1944 was a Dutch artist who is one of the pioneers of 20th-century abstract art and his painting built around shapes have become iconic.

366 *Die Nuba von Kau* was a 1976 international bestseller for Leni Riefenstahl and is a follow-up to her earlier successful 1973 book *Die Nuba*. The photos in the book were stunning shots of African tribes, sporting powerful looks and geometric face makeup from the photographer who spent her younger years making films for Adolf Hitler.

367 One of the few female pirates Anne Bonney born in 1697 was of Irish descent and ploughed the high seas is search of booty until she died in 1721.

368 Jordan to John Robb.

369 Marco to John Robb.

Vivienne, there was a political thing going on. It was the first time I'd seen t-shirts with random slogans on them, You couldn't understand it though, because there was no statement saying what they were about and no manifesto. This made it even more interesting because you couldn't tie it down and that's what kept you thinking.

A lot of Teds used to go to the shop, but that tailed off after Malcolm had gone to see *Scorpio Rising*[370] at the ICA and he mixed that with Gene Vincent and the whole black leather thing which was not far from the next step which was the fetish stuff.

People now ask why did they do this stuff? Why did they do the black leather t-shirt? Why the chicken bones? Well, it probably doesn't come from anywhere. It's a random rush of ideas and someone else says that looks great. I don't think there was a bigger plan like they were doing these clothes to accentuate the revolution. Rock'n'roll clothes have always been revolutionary, to wear them is a revolutionary act and they played that up. [371]

The shop jukebox also played an important role in the cultural crash course.

The jukebox in the shop had things on that I'd never heard. I would put these records on and I didn't know who they were. There was no information, no cover and, of course, no internet or no book to look them up – and when you took the record out, there was nothing on it but you were intrigued by its sound and mystery. [372]

In late 1975 things shifted a gear when some other young scallywags who would hang around the shop had somehow got Malcolm to manage their band.

A moribund music scene was about to get a rude awakening.

At this point, Bowie was doing *Young Americans* which I thought was all right and Roxy Music were doing *Country Life* and *Stranded* – the whole dinner jacket thing - which I thought was great, although I preferred the more glam period. I was more into clothes then and I thought music was dead because there was nothing happening.

Then Sex Pistols appeared.

A few days later I went to Denmark Street. I was looking at guitars and I bumped into Vivienne, which was a complete mind fuck because there were two scenes – the King's Road scene and the music scene and they did not crossover in any way fucking whatsoever. So I thought, 'what's Vivienne doing in Tin Pan Alley[373]? And it turned out that she and Malcolm were managing the band. Now I was really intrigued. [374]

McLaren was now pitching the new young band built around Steve Jones and Paul Cook. These two young hooligans would drop by the shop, on the nick, and were looking for a manager. After adding Glen Matlock from the shop on bass, the

---

370 Kenneth Anger's 1963 biker film that managed to incorporate the occult, homosexuality, Nazis and even Christian themes into its mix that would have a profound influence on punk and, by extension, goth.

371 Marco to John Robb.

372 Marco to John Robb.

373 Tin Pan Alley was the nickname for Denmark Street. The name was borrowed from a similar area in New York City and was traditionally the home of music publishing offices and for years, the heartbeat of showbiz.

374 Marco to John Robb.

masterstroke was the addition of a freakish young waif John Lydon, who had been spotted on the King's Road by Malcolm's friend and rival, Bernard Rhodes.[375]

Lydon's audition involved miming to Alice Cooper songs on a jukebox in the pub. He was so unsuited to the role of conventional frontman that McLaren, with the prompting of Jordan, knew he was perfect. It was a masterstroke, the rag doll singer with his acidic tongue, spiked hair, sawn-off old man's clobber and penetrating, staring eyes would steer the band away from the established crowd-pleasing modus operandi and into a newly realised blend of truculence, hostility and anarchism. His stark, confrontational appearance brought a whole new approach to performance that would ignite everything.

> These black and white handouts had started appearing for an April 4 1976 gig at the El Paradiso in Soho. Jordan said, 'You have to come', so I went to see them. I hadn't bought a record for a year and I couldn't imagine what the fuck they would be like. It was in a strip club which was as perfectly vile as you could imagine, which I thought was really great, and I got in for nothing.
>
> I thought I must be going into some kind of theatre, but I went into a tiny room. There were about ten people there, some I'd seen before like Jordan, Malcolm, Sid, Vivienne and some of the band, and some people I'd never seen. Sid I knew a bit. He was a tall, geeky kind of bloke who was into Roxy and Bowie. He was very similar to me and all the other people of that age group that went to the shop. I was two years younger than the rest of them at that time and two years was a huge gap. First time I saw him was in *Honey* magazine where they used to do this thing where they would photograph fans at gigs and they had a picture of Sid wearing a gold lame drape at the Roxy Music gig at Wembley in October 1975.
>
> I remember seeing Vivienne at the same gig downstairs sitting in the stalls when Roxy were doing 'In Every Dream Home A Heartache', a really quiet song. She walked out shouting 'You're disgusting' over and over at the band. She was ushered out by the bouncers and I thought, 'Fucking hell! there's that woman from the shop!'
>
> Vivienne has always had this attitude of, 'it's my way or no way at all' with what's valid or what wasn't. Sex Pistols were the same and that April gig was the wake up call. They not only sounded and looked different but their attitude was really different. [376]

The band's ad hoc early gigs in London saw their fuck you attitude and non-virtuoso playing ability confusing many. Fired by a mixture of McLaren's pop-culture-steeped vision and the young singer's own wild ideas, a whole new template was being created. It wasn't long before a small scene and new youth culture coalesced.

> It was never packed. Fifty people turning up would have been unbelievable and it was always the same people – 15 people from around the shop and some other regular faces and the rest? I don't know where they came from. Maybe they were just coming to gawp at Lydon's mates.
>
> I also saw them play the Babalu Disco on Finchley Road on May 11 1976. It was the furthest out of town I had ever been and a real adventure up north. There

---

375 The future manager of The Clash.

376 Marco to John Robb.

was hardly anyone there either. Punk was not a scene. I was only just aware of The Clash forming. I didn't know about The Damned. They were both different circles of people. [377]

Throughout 1976, punk rumbled along, growing at its own rate until it was suddenly catapulted into the mainstream when Sex Pistols famously swore on the Bill Grundy show. The famous moment freeze-framed punk into cliché. That fateful evening Marco was on his way to another punk inner circle face's house:

> It was a Wednesday night and I was on my way to Soo Catwoman's place in Ealing. I didn't know the Pistols were going to be on telly. When I got there, she was saying they had been on and there had been lots of swearing. Sid was at the house as well. He didn't seem very happy about it. I think he started saying 'This is going to be everywhere tomorrow'. He had seen it and sussed out the impact. He was right. The day after Bill Grundy it went fucking crazy.[378]

That was the day punk went tabloid and presented as an idiotic belch, many of its ideas were beyond the grubby understanding of the tabloids. The very moment punk broke, it died.

> Suddenly punk's gone mainstream. I was a bit confused. I was happy that everyone knew what I'd been going on about for ages but what happens now? Before that, the whole scene had been completely underground and ignored. All of a sudden, bang! It then went crazy and all these bands appeared, but many of them missed that bit of intrigue, that bit of mystery and that bit of thought that went into the early bands. There was something underlying those early bands. There was some sort of vague aesthetic.[379]

Punk itself was now in a rush to get away from itself. Quickly, the scene was fracturing into micro scenes. As soon as punk arrived it was already post-punk...

377 Marco to John Robb.

378 Marco to John Robb.

379 Marco to John Robb.

Chapter 12

'WHAT WAS ONCE UNHEALTHILY FRESH IS NOW A CLEAN OLD HAT'

Post-Punk to a very Public Image

On 7 January 1977, Howard Devoto quit Buzzcocks. His parting shot was the perfect pithy statement:

> I don't like most of this new wave music. I don't like music. I don't like movements. I am not confident of Buzzcocks' intention to get to the dry land of new waveness, to a place from which these things could be said. What was once unhealthily fresh is now a clean old hat.[380]

Devoto was the first to leave the punk movement before most had even joined and he re-emerged a few months later in his new band - the art house post-punk Magazine. Punk was in such a hurry that it was already post-punk before it had even started. If Bill Grundy had turned punk into a 2D version of itself, then the darker hues of sex, style and subversion and that frisson of artful darkness were now being taken into new diablo directions by a host of new young performers. It oozed from Siouxsie and the Banshees, it was entwined in the style of Dave Vanian, it was at the heart and soul of the sex music danger of Adam Ant and it was part of the corrosive cordite of Public Image Limited. Mavericks were moving on and understating that punk was far more potent in its conception than in its delivery, and were creating their own idiosyncratic visions.

After punk's rush, Baudelaire's dark flowers were now truly beginning to bloom.

Post-punk was a fascinating period of reconstruction with no form and no rigid ideas. Into this primal space, a darker strand of music was leaving the 20th century. It didn't have a name yet. No one really called it post-punk or goth. It was mostly called 'alternative' music. The first new use of the adjective 'gothic' would occur 11 years after The Doors had been called it in descriptions of the atmosphere surrounding darker post-punk bands like Magazine, Siouxsie and the Banshees and Joy Division.

In a July 1978 review of Siouxsie and the Banshees, rock critic Nick Kent, furiously typed: 'Parallels and comparisons can now be drawn with gothic rock architects like The Doors and, certainly, early The Velvet Underground'. A few months later, in March 1979, he returned to the term, like a crow picking at a piece of verbal carrion, with his review of Magazine's new album *Secondhand Daylight* where he noted a "dank neo-gothic sound".

On 15 September 1978, Tony Wilson got in on the act when he described the new signing to his Factory label, Joy Division, as "gothic". The term now had traction,

---

380 From a press statement made by Howard Devoto at the time.

and five weeks later, a live review of Joy Division at the F Club in Leeds by music writer, Des Moines, in the leading music paper, Sounds, described them as 'gothic dance music' - tagging a fast-arriving future.

The mood was changing. There had been new tenebrous sounds on some of the big releases that spring of 1978. The Stranglers' third album, *Black and White* with its dark atmospherics and bass-driven starkness created a groundbreaking bleak post-punk atmosphere. A massively influential work that rarely gets the credit it deserves, it had a profound effect on many musicians like Joy Division bass player Peter Hook, who took a photo of The Stranglers' bass set up at their May 30 1978 gig at Stafford Bingley Hall. Taking his snapshot along to the local Manchester music shop, he bought a Hiwatt amp and Fender Precision bass like The Stranglers bassist JJ Burnel and began to perfect his own distinctive bass style.

While bands like Wire and Joy Division rightly get credit for taking punk into new areas, it seems strange that The Stranglers – who were far more popular and, in real terms, more influential – get left out of the narrative. *Black and White* was first, and as darkly bold and brave, and as influential, as any, and was embraced by a generation of musicians.

Post-punk was moving fast and splintering in different directions, as reflected by John Peel's must listen to BBC Radio One show. Up and down the UK, young bands were making their own sense of the sonic revolution as the culture, music and style were all personalised.

No one will ever agree at the exact point when post-punk and, by extension, goth and alternative, started. It could well have been when the Pistols fell apart and John Lydon had moved on to Public Image Limited. It could have been before that with Wire's iconic debut album and the thrilling way in which they twisted guitar textures into slabs of sonic concrete. It could have been Mark Perry's ATV trying to push punk forward into new angular shapes or with Siouxsie and the Banshees' November 1978 debut album. It could have been the punk generation reacting to the eternal gloom of living in the UK surrounded by the crumbling post-industrial and the imminent nuclear war.

The apocalypse party had started!

Perhaps post-punk's roots are older still. On 4 July 1976, John Lydon sat backstage at Sheffield's Black Lion venue and chatted to The Clash's young then-guitar player Keith Levene before a Sex Pistols headline show where The Clash were playing their debut gig as support. Both expressed dissatisfaction with the rock'n'roll nature of their respective bands and agreed to hook up in future and work together on something else.

Post-Pistols, Lydon phoned Keith Levene and, along with Jah Wobble, put together the groundbreaking Public Image Limited at his Gunter Grove flat in Chelsea. Whether it was already in his inner psyche or it was the pressure of the Pistols' collapse informing the situation, Lydon's flat was a dark space. The new band were not so much gothic, as a melange of left-field ideas, dub bass and hints of '70s German underground, but there was something quite shadowy about their vibe.

There was genuine dark stuff going on here and the flat somehow embodied it with its inverted crosses on the wall and the cruel, snark wit in the air, and some genuinely dangerous characters in the room. Poly Styrene was a neighbour who visited Lydon several times and remembers this darkness vividly:

> At the time, John lived around the corner from me on Gunter Grove and everybody adopted him as their friend. The venom in the country was directed his way and I had this empathy for him because of the racism I had experienced when I was younger. I went around a few times, but he didn't need much sympathy. Half of John hated being someone that everybody hated but half of him liked it. When you went around to his house, it was a bit on the dark side. It was part of John's image at the time. He was an anarchic character, a strange person. I don't think that he was bad himself but he always had an entourage. He was never on his own and it was the people he surrounded himself with like Jah Wobble – who I found a bit weird at the time. He was a bit of an odd bod and so was Sid Vicious who was always there. Sid came at me with a great big knife once. He was fooling around but it was scary.
>
> John had the anti-hero image that he played up to. Sid was just being dangerous and was a bit of a moron. He was the court jester but not a very good one. He would do bad things to make everyone laugh but in a very negative way. [381]

Like a post-punk version of Turner in Nic Roeg's genuinely unsettling movie *Performance*, Lydon had withdrawn into himself to ponder his next move. He'd become an almost claustrophobic rock star recluse. Sat in his flat plotting, he wanted a band that was to be something beyond rock'n'roll, a band that was stepping forward into the future and embraced his love of the esoteric.

There had been hints of this already in July 1977 when he had played his favourite songs on the Tommy Vance Show on Capital Radio. His playlist was a mix of prog, folk and dub and was far removed from the expected punk greatest hits. Filter this eclecticism and intelligence through the dark spectral vibes of paranoia that haunted Gunter Grove and the hangover from punk and the unique talents of Keith Levene and Jah Wobble, and you have all the ingredients that would make up Public Image Limited.

The late Keith Levene was a guitar virtuoso who had roadied for Yes and learned his chops from the prog titans. He took these lessons and created something utterly unique from them which was noticed by Wobble. 'Just watch his hands. He hardly touches the strings and makes these extraordinary sounds like he is playing electricity.'[382] Born John Wardle, and soon rechristened Jah Wobble by Sid Vicious, the self-taught bassist already had his own signature sound which favoured a heavy dub bass tone and which got him his nickname.

Sid himself had been earmarked as the original bassist, but he still had not got around to learning to play, so Wobble got the role with his fast-developing, bottom-heavy bass style which, along with Levene's chiming, metallic-glass guitar lines,

381 Poly Styrene to John Robb.

382 Jah Wobble to John Robb.

was key to making the new band's astonishing sound which was such a significant influence on many goth and alternative musicians.

The first warning shot of the genius to come was the band's debut October 1978 top ten 'Public Image' single. A seven-inch three-minute salvo and searing manifesto. The song rode along on the rumbling bass line, visceral guitar and Lydon's astonishing vocal. Public Image Limited were discovering a whole new sonic space whilst the iconic singer declared his clean break from the punk rock straitjacket.

Public Image's debut album, *First Issue,* released in December 1978, was a further dislocation of the music and the senses. Not particularly well received, then, by the press and punk scene alike, it stands the test of time. Lydon's poetic snark was perfect for a band that had quickly coalesced into something stunningly unique; a soundtrack to the psychic dancehall inside Lydon's head.

The album perfectly mirrored the punk come down – the grimness of the grey reality of real life that inevitably came to slap young dreamers in the face. The record set the template for future musical adventures and its shadow hangs over post-punk and goth.

Given the space to explore, Lydon revelled in the opportunities that Virgin Records provided. The label saw beyond the foul-mouthed punk persona and hoped for a potential future Bowie-type figure and a shapeshifting pied piper, leading his generation on a merry dance. His deep love of music, coupled with his eclectic and awkward nature and, conversely, his very anti-musicality, was key to the atmosphere of the band. Inspired by the open-ended cyclical jams of Can and the adventures of Captain Beefheart but with an added dark sarcasm, PiL would now discover new territory that sounded utterly alien to anything produced before.

Their follow-up album, a year later, was the stunning *Metal Box.* It was a game-changing dark disco that saw their music stripped away and stretched over three vinyl 12-inch singles cased inside a metal box. The deep dub grooves were very much at the forefront and their sound was taut and tense with the chiming guitars as far away from rock as possible. It arguably remains one of the greatest records ever made and a template for all adventurous musicians. By the time they had reconvened for their April 1981 third album, *Flowers of Romance*, Wobble was elsewhere. However, Keith Levene, with engineer Nick Launey, created a minimalistic drum-heavy album that was full of ghosts and spectral crashing and banging with a tribal thunder. After this creation, PiL resorted to a more mainstream sound, but their contribution had already been sealed.

In their wake, many bands swam upstream to make a virtue of punk's awkwardness. Howard Devoto's Magazine were creating their own literate gothic and their January 1978 debut single, 'Shot by Both Sides' with new hotshot young guitar player, John McGeoch, announcing his arrival as one of the key players of his generation, is one of the greatest debut singles of all time. With the music written by Pete Shelley, the song is a thrilling anthemic precursor for the darkly atmospheric sound of their debut *Real Life* album. Magazine was a different affair from the punk rank and file, pulling songs into new musical terrains, textures and atmospheres. Their sound simultaneously hinted at even prog, as well as post-punk, and cemented the band's cult status. Devoto's obtuse lyrics, dramatic subject matter, acidic, sarcastic vocal style, and oddly svelte sexuality, made him an unlikely post-punk icon. Their milestone second album, March 1979's *Secondhand* Daylight was a landmark release in the post-punk terrain and full of poetry and possibilities. Manchester was full of these dark shadows and upcoming bands who would embrace them.

In Newcastle, Pauline Murray from Penetration was typical of the many young musicians emerging out of punk and trying to create their own path. Her band may have had only a fleeting brush with success but with her distinctive monochromatic angular style and the band's stark music they were accidental post-punk, even goth, pioneers. Pauline's look – sharply cropped hair, heavy eye makeup and a stark image made her a mini punk icon and the band made a music to match:

> I am interested in things that can't be seen, problems that have no answers, and escaping from the things that hold us back. We were looking into the darkness to bring things to light!
> We were musical novices when the band first started and had no idea about writing songs. It was instinctive and primal. We were always pushing forward, trying to improve on previous efforts and it was a journey of musical self-discovery with no map other than our own creativity.
> Lyrically, I looked at subjects from many different angles and married the words, meaning and melody with the music. This can bring a depth and mystery and allows the listener to interpret their own meaning both intellectually and emotionally.[383]

Style-wise, attitude-wise, and music-wise, wherever you looked there were now bands accelerating away from punk's Year Zero. At the heart of punk was a band who were reinventing their influences into a darker serrated whole. From the singer's style to the band's distinctive music, Siouxsie and the Banshees were way ahead of the pack with a stark power and glacial sound that would be profoundly influential.

---

383 Pauline Murray to John Robb.

Chapter 13

SPELLBOUND

Siouxsie and the Banshees

Confronting the dark recesses of the mind in a swooping, swooning, captivating melodrama, Siouxsie and Severin, and their many Banshees, sang songs of desire and terror, light and shade, fragile beauty and the beat, and broken dreams and nightmares. Every groundbreaking filmic twist came with an alchemy of the soul and, always, with their singer's imperious grandeur and shapeshifting photogenic charisma.

Siouxsie is the intoxicating icon whose influence hangs heavy over all things gothic. Yet, despite her image, her music and her enduring presence casting a long shadow over the scene, 'goth' is a term that she and fellow Banshee, Steve Severin, both hate.

Understandably.

No musician wants to get boxed in by a scene that didn't even exist when they created their world. Forming in punk, and combining their fascinations with the possibilities of lysergic sound, arthouse film, alienation, claustrophobia and disturbed childhoods, with a love of esoteric music and the power of dark pop, the Banshees created a unique new music that was more Gothic than goth and that's an important distinction. This groundbreaking and confrontational sound was consistently threaded throughout their oeuvre.

Their debut 1978 album *The Scream,* created an escape from punk and was the template for a whole raft of bands from Joy Division, and U2, to The Cure. Supernatural black magic pop was layered with the sensuality of a sonic seduction and a dark shapeshifting soul that would go on to spark chart hits, like 'Happy House' and 'Spellbound' which were goth club staples for decades. It was a thrilling sound of esoteric influences that combined to create exquisite, off-kilter music which was unsettling, melodically lush and always adventurous.

Then there was Siouxsie: The Icon.

With her ever-changing style and photogenic charisma, the so-called ice queen inspired thousands of acolytes, both male and female, who dressed like her as they clattered through the '80s clubs.

Birthed from punk but with a more artistic and textural approach to their sound and style, the band quickly possessed a far broader lyrical vision and musical palette than their contemporaries whilst illuminating the sensuality of life or the dark shadows that lurked around it. Pushing way beyond punk's initial crude critique of existence, the band's vision quickly intensified and darkened, taking their music into new realms. This uncharted territory would prove to be an eventual big influence on goth and beyond. They had found a unique combination that hit an international raw nerve, seeing them hailed as musical and stylistic game changers, as the legions of Siouxsie lookalikes would later testify.

Before the Banshees coalesced in September 1976, Siouxsie [384] and band bass player, Steve Severin [385] were regular faces on the fledgling punk scene that was quickly growing throughout the long, hot summer of 1976. The pre-band Siouxsie was armed with a style and attitude entirely of her own creation and was already a micro-icon in a scene with no name. Her music and appearance would drip-feed into the future, all driven by her perfectly honed eye for outrage and orchid glamour.

Siouxsie was a central player in the Bromley Contingent; a bunch of hip, teenage pop culture obsessives escaping the South London suburbs in late 1975, just before becoming the first followers of Sex Pistols. Her exotic style saw a mix of dark cabaret glam, retro exotica chic and S&M daring. To these striking choices, she would go on to add an outrageous mixture of fierce stilettos, fishnet, Clockwork Orange makeup, cropped and dyed hair, rubber stockings, peek-a-boo plastic bras and a deliberately confrontational swastika armband.[386] It was this explosion of S&M, partial nudity and sexual provocation that Siouxsie turned into a work of art. Like an updated and extreme version of Hollywood silent movie-era vamps, such as, Theda Bara, [387] she would often be seen at early Sex Pistols events with her breasts exposed and her face painted in heavy, decorative makeup.

Siouxsie understood the cold seduction of glamour without the perceived necessity of sex and proved herself to be far more imperious than the ad hoc graffiti wardrobes of her punk contemporaries. Her striking persona acted as a powerful rallying call to women; highlighting the importance of female bodily autonomy that was already a key part of early punk. Throwing rock music's carefree sexuality back in its face, Siouxsie demonstrated how punk was a place where clothes were political statements and dressing up was a manifesto. She was no mere flicker of titillation, but a young woman very much in control of her own body and image. With her face painted 'with the obsessive skill of the truly possessed', she was the high profile leaderene of punk style, 'the female Sex Pistol' as some called her, and the instigator of a new kind of beauty which goth culture writer, Natasha Scharf noticed:

> I loved the energy and attitude of punk but there was something a bit different, a bit darker about Siouxsie; both musically and image-wise. If you listen to the early Banshees material, it had a very playful, almost nursery rhyme-like quality with very creative lyrics which really grabbed me. That playful quality extended to their image with Siouxsie looking like she'd fallen from the pages of a dark fairy tale with her strong makeup and theatrical clothing.[388]

384 Born Susan Ballion, 27 May 1957.

385 Born Steven John Bailey, 25 September 1955.

386 As influenced by the controversial 1974 Italian erotic psychological drama film, *The Night Porter*, starring Dirk Bogarde and Charlotte Rampling.

387 Early Hollywood sex symbol born in 1921 who died in 1955. Her striking image and her femme fatale roles earned her the nickname "The Vamp", later fuelling the rising popularity of "vamp" roles based in exoticism and sexual domination.

388 Natasha Scharf to John Robb.

Siouxsie and the Banshees were not so much goth as Gothic. Whilst goth has become a shorthand for the darker strands of post-punk, 'Gothic' has far better connotations for Steve Severin. He found himself personally more attuned to older art forms and architecture and the writing of Edgar Allan Poe and Baudelaire. Added to this (well) tailored definition was the music of The Velvet Underground and the rest of the (un) holy trinity like The Doors and The Stooges. With their similar sense of ambiguity and artificiality, Bowie and Bolan were also part of the DNA of the early Banshees.

Born in Guy's Hospital, Southwark, Susan was the daughter of a Belgian Walloon bacteriologist who had milked venom from snakes. He had met her mother, Betty, a secretary, whilst in the colonial era of the then-named Belgian Congo where her two older sisters – a decade older than Siouxsie – were both born. The family had then moved to the UK just before their youngest daughter was born. The grey skies of Chiselhurst on the edge of London were not welcoming for a child who felt continually uneasy about her home life, dogged by the sense of alienation that followed the entire family:

> I think that just because of the kind of family we were, there was definitely a sense of not feeling a part of the community, or of being neighbourly. I was very aware of us being different. My father had a drink problem, which also sensitised that feeling.
> Where we lived was very residential, and our house seemed different. To begin with, it wasn't red brick - it was white stucco with a flat roof. Everyone else had gardens with patios and neatly cut lawns, and we had these massive copper beech trees at the front, and a huge privet hedge. You couldn't look into our house. All the others were almost inviting you to look in - life in all its normality was being paraded. This probably wasn't the case behind closed doors, but that was the perception.[389]

For her young parents, the Post-Empire continental shifts in geography, climate and status had a profound effect. Grappling with the inclement cold climate and gloom of the perpetually post-war UK, Susan's young father turned to drink and cut an isolated figure within the home. The family's off-kilter background similarly added to the gathering sense of dread and dislocation in an unfriendly new country.

When Susan was nine, she was the victim of a sexual assault in the local sweet shop. The incident, in that still-closed world of the 1960s, was ignored by her parents. This shattering moment in her life gave her a disdain and distrust of the adult world; she now turned inwards and created her own imaginary space.

Susan would soon become Siouxsie.

In 1972, her father died as a result of his drinking. Even a remote parent's death is painful to process and Susan slipped into ill health, losing weight and ending up in the hospital with a bout of ulcerative colitis. Already a music fan, it was in the hospital that she had her pop culture 'road to Damascus' moment when she saw David Bowie performing 'Starman' on television. As for many other mesmerised UK youths, Bowie, the saviour, had arrived to bring glam rock's gospel through *Top of*

---

389 Siouxsie to leading pop culture journalist Michael Bracewell.

the Pops; the cathode ray conveyer belt of pop dreams. Post-hospital, there was no turning back:

> Music was always the one thing that made everything seem OK. It was a cause of happiness within the family, and laughter, and fun. My first love affair with a record was with John Leyton's 'Johnny Remember Me'. I was three or four when it came out, in 1961, and I used to have to get somebody to put it on the record player for me. It had these amazing, ghostly backing vocals, and a great melody, and was about a dead girlfriend, basically.
>
> As I got older, I loved a lot of Tamla Motown and a lot of R&B. Then there was the usual Beatles and Stones and I really got into *The White Album*. Pop music for me was definitely escapist but never studious.
>
> I was never attracted to being a very proficient singer or player. I suppose I was interested in creating a vision; in the same way that I was very drawn to tension within cinema and Hitchcock was my other early obsession - *Psycho*, and its score. So, there was that sense of trying to create an atmosphere: how sound resonates and makes an effect. That has always been very important for me.[390]

With her two older sisters feeding her pop culture, Susan was undergoing a journey. Leaving school in 1975, she would hang out at gay discos; safe houses where women could go to dance without enduring the leery fumbling of bumbling male youth. She soon followed her elder sister, who danced in clubs, to central London.

> The suburbs inspired intense hatred but the suburbs were also a yardstick for measuring how much we didn't fit in. I think the lure of London was always there. I remember my sister taking me to Biba on Kensington High Street; I bought a coat and used to gravitate towards going to London on my own. [391]

The dread suburbs, though, had one very crucial link to the beating heart of pop culture. They were where David Bowie had not only grown up but had also attended the same school as Steve Severin:

> The fact that Bowie came from Bromley was more weird than inspiring really. When he was in the charts with 'Space Oddity' in 1969, I was only in the third year but there was a lot of gossiping about his life at the school, like when he had driven a mini onto the school bandstand one lunchtime. I wasn't even that big a fan of 'Space Oddity' and after the hit, he seemed to disappear for a couple of years.
>
> I wasn't really aware of *The Man Who Sold the World* or *Hunky Dory* albums. He just wasn't on our radar until 'Starman' in 1972. A lot of people talk about their defining moment of seeing Bowie on *Top of the Pops* doing 'Starman' but my defining moment was Roxy Music doing 'Virginia Plain' in August 1972 because I could see and hear the progression from the kind of music I was into before. They were slightly prog but there was something more going on and that really appealed to me. You have to credit Bowie, though, he was always name-dropping people in interviews. That's how I got into reading William Burroughs *Naked Lunch* when I was 16. You were like a hawk. Any little snippet you leapt on it because there was so little of it.

---

390 Siouxsie to Michael Bracewell.

391 Siouxsie to Michael Bracewell.

We had a gang of us at school who were avid music devourers from 1969 onwards. One of our posse had an older brother who was stationed in Hamburg in the military. He became a junkie and came back to England in the late summer of 1970 and he brought with him the first Can album *Monster Movie*[392] and The Velvet Underground's *White Light White Heat*.[393] We listened to them one Sunday afternoon around a friend's house and it was like, 'What the fuck is this? It's brilliant!'

There was no way of finding out anything about them in those times - just little snippets in the music press about the Velvets but absolutely nothing about Can. David Bowie had nurtured Lou Reed's career and that became easier to find out about. Can came over in '71 and played somewhere in Uxbridge or Imperial College and it was just amazing. They came on and they started playing and didn't stop till then the end of the set. They were jamming what was going to be *Tago Mago*[394] and it was a revelation.[395]

Inevitably it had been The Beatles who had opened the pop culture door:

I had been a fan of music since I was about seven when I first heard The Beatles 'She Loves You' which my parents went to buy for me but bought 'Twist and Shout' instead. That was even better because it was really riotous, and I was hooked. I used to watch *Ready Steady Go*. I had to know who was in the band and the whole family trees of the bands. I was investigating and quickly was getting more underground than everyone else.

The Beatles and The Stones were talking about things in a broader way and they knew their place in culture but were simultaneously reacting against it. It would be like a pilgrimage to go to someone's house to listen to The Beatles' *White Album* because none of us could afford it because it was a double album. We sat down and listened to all four sides and then started again.

We were then swapping albums from The Mothers of Invention to Soft Machine. I never really liked any kind of hard rock. I was more into Zappa and Captain Beefheart and then as we got into our early teens we started going to the Windsor Free Festivals, the free concerts in Hyde Park where I saw Pink Floyd and King Crimson in 1969 and the Weeley Festival headlined by TRex and the Faces in 1971.[396] Our life was following music and bands and then we discovered drugs and that really was it.[397]

It was this promise of a more exotic world away from the suburbs that thrilled.

My sort of thing with the suburbs is different from everyone else's. Siouxsie grew up in Chislehurst, so she was more of a Kentish girl. Whereas, when I was ten, my parents moved to Bromley from London. It was so quiet and green, which

---

392 The classic 1969 debut from the band who combined psychedelic, free jazz and polyrhythmic world music into an astonishing hypnotic and influential whole.

393 The American band's 1968 second album saw a rawer more experimental twist on their sound.

394 The band's 1971 third album.

395 Steve Severin to John Robb.

396 Weeley Festival was held in Clacton On Sea, Essex on 27-29 August 1971. Rumour has it that this was where the 'wally' chant started.

397 Steve Severin to John Robb.

for me was just awful. I couldn't wait to get back to the city. Music was not just a musical escape for me but eventually a physical escape from the suburbs as well.[398]

Berlin[399], who would eventually become the youngest member of the Bromley Contingent, was immersed in the same cultural scene as Severin.

We all had a passionate, perhaps naive interest in culture, films, music and fashion. Warhol, Pasolini, Burroughs... I liked the movie *Cabaret*, especially Bob Fosse's directorial aesthetic mixed in with Isherwood's eye for detail which made it a brilliant recording of that era in Germany, so evocative and there seemed to be some correlation between that and London in the 1970s.[400]

However, for Severin, Roxy Music remained the ultimate era-defining band.

They looked fantastic and they sounded great. They plundered from the past and took it into the future, which was extraordinary at the time. They weren't afraid of doing a ten-minute song on their album. No one else was doing anything like that. There were so many influences and references that it was really intriguing. I went to see Bowie at Earls Court in May 1973. It was one of the last Ziggy shows. Of course, he would use *Clockwork Orange* as his opening music! It had just come out that summer. Amazing movie. Again, it was just like Bowie to be taking all the interesting stuff and cherry-picking the best bits and making something new from the patchwork.

There was now a split in our gang between the boys that didn't understand the Bowie/Roxy side of things and the rock side with their greatcoats and Afghans getting into Magma. We were cutting and dying our hair and going to see Roxy Music and just trying to find our own distinctive style. There were a lot of jumble sales and vintage clothes were popular at the time.

Even when punk started, we still felt we were on a different path. The Banshees would have happened without punk rock. While most of the protagonists of punk looked to American garage bands - Flamin' Groovies, MC5, The Stooges, the Dolls - or to the New York scene of Patti Smith, Television, Heartbreakers and Ramones as a benchmark, we, perversely, saw ourselves as taking on the baton of glamorous art rock like Bowie and Roxy Music - while incorporating a love for Can, Kraftwerk and Neu!.[401]

By now, Steve Severin was immersed in culture:

We read *Animal Farm* at school and *1984*. That was a big influence. When 'Jean Genie'[402] came out, Bowie said in one interview that the title was a mixture between Iggy Pop and Jean Genet[403] and I thought, 'who is Jean Genet? I have to find him.' There were films like *Rollerball*, *The Exorcist*, Hammer films with their quixotic soundtracks, Hitchcock was on TV with Bernard Herrmann[404]

---

398 Steve Severin to John Robb.

399 AKA Bertie Marshall.

400 Berlin to John Robb.

401 Severin to John Robb.

402 David Bowie's stunning November 1972 single. It was where Simple Minds got their name and rode roughshod on the same riff as The Sweet's 'Blockbuster' that came out the same week.

403 French novelist and vagabond playwright whose own life of vagrancy, prison, prostitution – before a flowering success as a writer – celebrates a beauty in evil.

404 American film composer who wrote many classic scores inlacing Taxi Driver, Psycho and the Twilight Zone.

soundtracks and there were underground readings with Burroughs that led me on to Ballard, Camus and Kafka.

All that music, cinema and books went into a melting pot that was finding your identity and what makes you different from everyone else. At that age, you are struggling to find yourself and your own unique personality, and you are deciphering it.[405]

It was this aesthetic quest that saw the shy but determined Severin find fellow travellers from his locale and companions who would soon become an integral part of the punk mythology. The infamous Bromley Contingent.

Named by music journalist Caroline Coon after she wrote about the coterie of exotic fans at the Sex Pistols gig in Paris on 3 September 1976, they were a loose confederacy of Siouxsie, Debbie Juvenile, Soo Catwoman, Simon Barker, Sharon, Tracey, Billy Idol, Steve Severin, Berlin, Tracie O'Keefe, Sharon Hayman and other long-lost names like Angel and Ruth. It was never a club or a gang, but rather a loose collection of like-minded people primed to provoke, with a music taste to match. They were the proto-goth shock troops defiantly dressed despite the ongoing grey of mid-'70s UK.

This suburban collective had a cultural arms race of its own with a keen swapping of records, clothes and ideas. It had all coalesced at the 18 November 1975 Roxy Music gig at Wembley Empire Pool. The gig was a catalytic moment, with so many of punk's future faces parading the aisles. Sid Vicious was in attendance in his gold lamé drape jacket, and this was the night Severin met Siouxsie.

The pair would become close, united in an artful disdain for most of the surrounding 1970s culture. Driven by art, adventure and punk's key impulse to escape from the suburbs, they would turn their backs on the suburban relapse and head for the neon thrills of central London. They began reinventing themselves, immersed in the thrill-seeking and the esoteric; anything beyond the suffocating boredom and hypocrisy of suburbia and, fittingly, it was the Roxy Music gig that would spark everything.

> That was the day I had decided to never work for anyone else again. So I quit my job and went to the concert. My friend Simon[406] knew Siouxsie vaguely and introduced us and the rest is history. That night she looked extraordinary. She had hired a mermaid outfit dress with a long tail, and she had short hair, cut like a crown of thorns, flipped upwards and all the tips were dyed red. A few people had dressed up, but no one looked like Siouxsie and very quickly after that she became part of the gang and a couple of months later, we saw Sex Pistols.[407]

Siouxsie remembers the gig vividly:

> I hired a costume from Berman's & Nathan's [408] - a cross between a mermaid and a chorus girl with purple sequins and a fish-tail train. I didn't get changed in the toilets at Charing Cross station, I travelled up to town in that outfit. I got odd

---

405 Steve Severin to John Robb.

406 Simon Barker – one of the Bromley Contingent.

407 Severin to John Robb.

408 Berman's amalgamated with Nathan's in the mid-1970s and became the world's largest Film, TV and Theatrical Costumiers.

looks, but if they saw you looking back, they'd turn away. I think that people sense that kind of single-mindedness and don't dare to approach you. But all that changed once punk was picked up on by the media. Then the public reaction was abusive.[409]

Pop culture was now accelerating. Eight weeks after the Roxy Music gig, Sex Pistols played an infamous show.

It's amazing how fast everything was moving in 1976. A few weeks after the Roxy Music gig I saw Sex Pistols for the first time at the Marquee on February 12 supporting Eddie and the Hot Rods. This was the gig where the Pistols broke the PA and got into the press for doing it. By that December, they had 'Anarchy' out and had done the Bill Grundy show and were front page news.[410]

That night at the Marquee, Steve Severin saw a new future and was instantly intrigued by the Pistols' musical iconoclasm:

This was the next step as far as I was concerned. Roxy were about to split up after the *Siren* tour, Bowie was in America and Bolan was not doing good stuff at the time. There was a void and here come the Pistols just in time.

Rotten was so obviously a star with charisma to spare. He was fantastic on the stage - all attitude. I'd never seen that before. Everyone else had something showbiz about them, something traditional but Lydon was a total one-off.[411]

Throughout 1976, Siouxsie and Severin and their colourful gang were at the core of the incoming punk scene. The Bromley Contingent were like a homespun British take on Andy Warhol's Superstars and would turn up at Sex Pistols gigs provocatively dressed. Their flamboyant style combined perfectly with the Pistol's music and attitude, creating a sense of the esoteric.

Bertie Marshall's infamous 'Berlin's Bondage Party' in May 1976 saw them literally come together in a wild shindig at his parents' house where the Styrofoam ceiling tiles were forever scarred by Siouxsie's whip in an evening of suburban decadence as they partied with Sex Pistols.

After a summer spent as attention grabbing audience members, it was time to move to the stage. The 100 Club Punk Special festival was announced for 20/21 September 1976. The festival was an attempt to create the impression of a burgeoning punk scene and bands were needed to make up the numbers. Now it was time for Siouxsie and Severin to cross the divide.

We had been looking for a way in but I don't think anybody thought we can do this. Siouxsie had been to a few auditions, answering ads in Melody Maker. Billy (Idol) could play the guitar and there was talk of him teaching me the bass. Siouxsie had been to Billy's house once and had done a version of the Velvets' 'What Goes On'.

---

409 Siouxsie to Michael Bracewell.

410 On 9 December 1975, Simon Barker saw the then unknown Sex Pistols as they played their second gig at the Ravensbourne College of Art in Bromley, supporting Newcastle-based glam-prog band Fogg. When Severin arrived later, the glowing Barker told him how brilliant the band were and added, 'The singer blew his nose on stage!'. With comparisons to Iggy and The Stooges and New York Dolls, Barker sent Severin up to the Marquee gig, telling him, 'at last we had a band we could believe in'.

411 Severin to John Robb.

The real plan came together when we found out about the 100 Club festival. We knew Malcolm and the Pistols and here was an opportunity. Siouxsie claims she went up to Malcolm and demanded that we play. The way I remember it was that Billy went up to Malcolm and said we got a band and could we fill a slot. Of course, we didn't have a proper band and then Billy backed out on the Saturday night when we were at Louise's[412] two days before the gig.

Nils[413] knew that we were attempting to form a band and he introduced Marco Pirroni to us. We had seen Marco around a lot and he could play the guitar so he was in. Then Sid said 'I will play the drums'. We said, 'Can you play the drums?' and he said, 'Does it matter?!'

On Sunday we were in The Clash's rehearsal studio in Camden for a ten-minute rehearsal. We bashed away, and Sid said, 'That's good enough, let's go to the pub'. On the Monday we were at the 100 Club playing the gig. It was insane.[414]

Marco vividly recalls how quickly the gig was thrown together:

I went to see Queen at Hyde Park on 18th Sept 1976 and I met Billy Idol who said he had written some songs for this new band with Siouxsie and Steve who I knew slightly. He was saying he couldn't do the gig now and 'You can play the guitar - can you do it?'. He didn't want to let his mates down and it was one of those get-out-of-it situations.

The next day I bumped into Siouxsie and Steve and they said, 'You can play the guitar,' and I said 'All right' and that was the extent of it.

We had one small rehearsal. The idea was to do a set full of cover versions of songs that they didn't like... Beatles songs, Captain Scarlet, Goldfinger, but they were songs I liked!

I said, 'We will never learn these songs tonight, it's impossible and Sid said, 'Fuck all that, let's make a big row!'

Naming the band after the Vincent Price film, *Cry of The Banshee*[415], they played a twenty-minute jam with Sid thumping away at the drums whilst Siouxsie intoned parts of the 'Lord's Prayer' and some of the songs from the rehearsal. The ad hoc band jammed with Steve Severin playing on a bass borrowed from Subway Sect and Marco adding a musicality on guitar. With a perfect punk rock disdain, they demolished rock classics like 'Smoke on The Water', The Beatles' dark and strange 'Helter Skelter' and a snatch of 'Twist and Shout'. Siouxsie fronted with the imperious glare of a stage natural, hiding those jangling nerves.

The gig was unimaginably important though. It was a defining moment of punk rock DIY with a denser, darker feel - a new direction in the aural confrontation. In the audience was the dancing scarecrow of John Lydon, embracing their simplistic beats and daredevil deconstruction of rock. For Marco it was job done:

---

412 Club Louise, 61 Poland Street, Soho, London.

413 The late Nils Stevenson was the brother of photographer Ray, and Sex Pistols' initial ad hoc manager and eventual Banshees manager.

414 Louise's in Soho was one of the gay clubs frequented by the early punk scene. Siouxsie Sioux had discovered it while visiting around Soho with her pretend girlfriend Myra. It became a key haunt for the burgeoning scene in 1976; a pattern replicated across the UK where gay clubs had a more accepting door policy, giving the freaks somewhere to go.

415 1970 British horror film directed by Gordon Hessler and starring Vincent Price as an evil witch hunter

Coming from a Velvet Underground background, I thought it would be a cool and easy thing to do - like the Velvets' 'Sister Ray' without even the riff. Sid had played the drums before and was pretty good actually. There was no structure to it. We just made it up as we went along, and I was quite good at that.

The Banshees thing was a one-off for me. I didn't want to be in the band. They didn't like me, and they didn't like Sid either! It was understood that they would do their own thing. It was their name and their band. [416]

The intended one-off performance was anything but. After the show, Steve Severin became embroiled in a clutch of important conversations:

As soon as we came off stage, two things happened. First, Kenny Morris[417] ran up to us. He knew Sid already from playing in Sid's band, The Flowers of Romance. He said he wanted to play the drums for us instead. We said we don't have any plans to do anything.

Then, the *Evening Standard* did a quick interview and we said we have split up because we were performance art. Then Nils came up and said, 'I want to manage you'. Basically, he bullied us into repeating what we had done.

The 100 Club was now the springboard. We thought, 'Wow we can get away with that!' What would it be like if we could play our instruments and write songs?! It was a blessing that we couldn't play!

Nils found us sometime in the Pistols' rehearsal room on Denmark Street while they were touring in Holland in early January 1977. Then, because of his connection with Malcolm, he became fast friends with all the Heartbreakers who were now in town. Leee Childers[418] gave Nils a table in his office at Track records and gave us money to pay for rehearsals – it was all very fortuitous.[419]

The already iconic-looking Kenny Morris, with his black clothes and perfectly destroyed black hair looked like a proto art goth before such a thing even existed.

Sid, who was one of my best friends, was drumming which he'd never done before and he was never going to do again. He told me, 'This is not what I'm about'. He knew he was destined to be a front person. His drumming reminded me very much of one of my favourite drummers, Maureen Tucker of The Velvet Underground.

After that, I played for a bit more in Sid's band and then I got a grade one at the Camberwell College of Art which entitled me to a year off so I joined the Banshees in January 1977.

That summer, I was also the assistant set designer with John Maybury[420] on the Derek Jarman film *Jubilee*. At the end of 1977 I told the head of the college I have a really big decision to make. The Banshees were asking me to sign this contract

416 Marco to John Robb.

417 Kenny Morris was the drummer for the first two Banshees albums and had rehearsed with Sid Vicious in his aborted Flowers of Romance band from 1976. He had played on songs such as the Sid originals 'Belsen Was A Gas' and 'Kamikaze'.

418 Childers was one of the Warhol crowd. He was also a photographer who had documented the Warhol scene and had managed Warhol's stage production, *Pork*. He was assistant to the artist at The Factory between 1982-84, and took photographs of visiting celebrities, counter-cultural figures and musicians, particularly of punk rock and new wave music stars, such as Debbie Harry, Wayne County and Sex Pistols.

419 Severin to John Robb.

420 John Maybury is an English filmmaker and artist who designed artwork for the Banshees and found fame making videos for the pet Shop Boys and Sinead O'Connor and many others.

with Polydor or do I go back to college and he said you should go ahead and sign the contract, which was the advice I wanted to hear.[421]

A few weeks after the 100 Club, Siouxsie and Severin hit the front pages of the tabloids after appearing with Sex Pistols on the now infamous Bill Grundy fronted Today show on 1 December 1976. It turned the striking-looking Siouxsie, with her cropped bleached hair and *Clockwork Orange* droog makeup into an overnight icon. Tugging at her braces, pouting icily at the camera and instigating the four-letter cultural standoff, she helped draw cultural battle lines across the UK.

With Peter Fenton now on guitar and Kenny Morris on drums, the Banshees played their first gig in February 1977 and were fast becoming an interesting proposition. They had the rudiments of an original sound with songs like 'Love in A Void' and 'Carcass'. However, after twelve gigs, Peter Fenton was sacked onstage for being 'too rock'n'roll'. He was replaced by John McKay, who brought his ground breaking guitar sound that changed the band's musical focus edging closer to what Steve Severin was looking for.

> What you do is eliminate what you hate. We didn't want guitar solos. We didn't want drum rolls. The first time Kenny had rehearsed with us, Siouxsie took away his hi-hats and cymbals and left him the snare and floor tom. It was about what you don't wanna do and what you are left with, which is hopefully unique.[422]

The young guitar player, as Kenny Morris suspected, added a perfect musical and visual symmetry to the band.

> It was me that introduced John to the group and all of a sudden we had it. We had the best group in that punk era possible. No one could match it. And I knew that.[423]

This was never a ram-a-lama punk rush – potential band members were played the soundtracks to *The Omen* and *Psycho* to give them an idea of what the band were aiming for. There was space between the instruments and Kenny Morris's sparse and tribal drums created a style that would become a staple for alternative and goth bands for years. John McKay's haunting chiming shard guitar and Severin's dive-bombing bass lines played in upstrokes created a stark musical backdrop. Meanwhile, Siouxsie's powerful Nico-esque voice hung above their sound with a spectral power. The Banshees were edgy and experimental but somehow managed to make their output highly listenable, deliciously dark and undeniably hypnotic.

> John McKay was a bit younger than us but he had the same sort of musical taste and he was smarter than the other guitarist. Siouxsie told him to make the guitar sound like the music in *Psycho*. He could translate ideas and very quickly he had his own sound and we became the band that made the first album. We then had a

---

421 Kenny Morris to John Robb.

422 Severin to John Robb.

423 Kenny Morris to John Robb.

year to write all the songs and play them on the road before we recorded which is important as songs are never right until done in front of an audience.[424]

With their sparse and deliciously cold music, the group was driven by their own, clearly defined aesthetic.

> Punk was more diverse initially and then it became a bit copycat Ramones without the humour. We always saw that it could be anything it wanted to be like The Pistols, Throbbing Gristle, Buzzcocks, and Wire had done.
>
> We were more post-punk really. Pere Ubu and Talking Heads had arrived quite early and then Devo released 'Jocko Homo' in 1976. All these bands were not what you would call typical punk bands, but they all had an aesthetic. I guess we were already on our own little path. It was sort of parallel with punk in that we already knew what we wanted to do.[425]

Often using minor chords and diminished scales alongside a dark subject matter, Siouxsie and the Banshees were compelling and enigmatic.

> For Siouxsie and me, it was rooted in our shared sense of black humour and a love of Edgar Allan Poe books and Vincent Price movies. Siouxsie would also get these anthology books like the *Pan Book of Horror*. Apart from the classics, there were not really any horror books until Steven King really.
>
> *Carrie* came out in 1976, so there was a sort of opening up in the cinema to horror with a darker side. Censorship was getting looser and people were able to show things in a much more interesting graphic way.
>
> Initially, you were thinking that we are moving into a more liberal time with an explosion of culture and music and suddenly reality hits – most of the rest of the country were not with you. We found this out touring outside of London. Play High Wycombe and you are in middle England and you'd think 'Oh fuck, that's who voted for Thatcher!'. The capital, had a completely different vibe to the rest of the country but everywhere we went there were always some people looking for something different.
>
> It was a pretty bleak time in Britain politically. We had just had the blackouts, the three-day week and we were just about to go down the abyss with fucking Thatcher.[426]

These pockets of provincial pioneers would soon be moving punk into post-punk.

> The bigger cities outside of London like Manchester, Liverpool, Glasgow, Edinburgh and Sheffield were where things were happening throughout 1978. You got interesting local post-punk scenes with the Bunnymen, The Human League, The Teardrop Explodes and all those bands coming up. They would define the town they came from.
>
> The Human League from Sheffield, played with us a lot. We were the first people to take them around the country. Cabaret Voltaire played with us a few times. Then you would see more factions with Rough Trade releasing Scritti Politti, The Raincoats, the Au Pairs and all those people.
>
> The band I liked the most at that time was Wire. I felt something in common with them. The difference was that we had a glamorous frontwoman fronting a

---

424 Severin to John Robb.

425 Severin to John Robb.

426 Severin to John Robb.

bunch of blokes which made us stand out but also held us back in many ways because of people's patronising attitude to us.[427]

The music industry seemed scared of the band with the fearsome frontwoman and its own ideas of sound and vision.

> They were a bit scared of us because we had our own views on everything. We didn't get a deal until June '78. They could understand Patti Smith as she was in a rock'n'roll band and a rock poet, but they didn't get Siouxsie. It was different. She looked like she couldn't be messed with on stage. You could see them thinking 'How do we market this?'[428]

Until their signing, the Banshees were an iconoclastic cult with a big live following. Fuelled by a couple of John Peel sessions and an outsider status they were enshrined as the untainted, unsigned version of the punk gospel.

> Looking back on those days, nothing can really capture quite how 'out on a limb' the primary people were. How brave it was, I suppose - without it seeming brave at the time; more a kind of recklessness.
> But the term 'punk' was so lazy and easy and inaccurate. The Pistols were different because they had Rotten – without him, who knows? And The Clash went at it in a way that was far more traditional – a kind of Keith Richards thing. I wasn't trying to be masculine and getting down with the boys, so the main difference between us and the rest was that it wasn't a solely male perspective. I think a certain amount of anger has been a fuel of mine, if you want – but also some sort of sadness, and plain mischief, of course.[429]

Once signed to Polydor, the band promptly scored a top ten hit with their 1978 debut single, 'Hong Kong Garden'. It was a perfect slice of curveball coldwave pop. Driven by its chiming neo-oriental McKay guitar motif, the hit, set in suburbia, was inspired by an incident involving racist skinheads at Siouxsie's local Chinese takeaway:

> I'll never forget it. There was a Chinese restaurant in Chislehurst called the 'Hong Kong Garden'. Me and my friend were upset when the skinheads would turn up and it would get really ugly. These gits would just go in en masse and just terrorise the Chinese people who were working there and we'd say, 'Leave them alone'. The song was a kind of tribute to the owners. I would definitely say that our early material, for at least the first two albums, was inspired by suburbia.[430]

The debut album, *The Scream*, was released in November 1978 and was a tenser and darker musical affair than the single. Its sense of dislocation and claustrophobia captured the cultural zeitgeist that made it a stark and original work that was a big jump ahead of punk. With songs that utilised space and dynamics in a thrilling and dramatic new way, the album was a precursor to post-punk and is as close as you can get to a template for the sound of goth. The songs were shivers of pristine darkness

---

427 Severin to John Robb.
428 Severin to John Robb.
429 Siouxsie to Michael Bracewell.
430 Siouxsie to Michael Bracewell.

and the production by new, young producer Steve Lillywhite was futuristic creating that powerful drum sound with reverbs and gates that would become so signature to the best bands in the 80s:

> If you just have a traditional rock band, what are the things that you hear? You hear the voice, and you hear some melody, maybe the guitars and unless you're Joy Division, or the Banshees before that, then not each instrument.
>
> I absolutely fell in love with Siouxsie and the Banshees and doing that album. In those days, we were like scared children putting on this big display of bravado and I was just the same but what you got in Siouxsie and the Banshees was a singer who was just, remarkable.
>
> Also, in terms of the guitar playing, people think The Edge and other guitar players created that sound, but of course, John Mackay came before all those people. He was the innovator. Listen to the beginning of 'Jigsaw Feeling' and it's like the beginning of U2's 'I Will Follow'. It's almost identical. Most bands at the time definitely used *The Scream* as a template.
>
> Kenny Morris is also such a unique drummer and it gave me the opportunity to experiment and create new drum sounds with this ambience thing. You can hear elements of the famous gated compressed drum sound that would be the go to eighties sound. Hugh Padgham was my engineer and he took the sound as well and then it was everywhere like on the Peter Gabriel album and he's claimed it, Hugh's claimed it, and I've claimed it![431]

The Scream is a truly arresting work with songs like the clipped tension of 'Overground' or 'Metal Postcard' with its rolling toms and brilliant monotony and a song that was created as a musical equivalent of anti-Nazi German artist, John Heartfield's[432] photo montages whilst also deconstructing masculine ideologies and societies' love of charismatic 'leaders' with striking, mechanical music.

> Lyrically the album is quite bleak. You've got to remember, we were very young then. We deliberately didn't make it too commercial. It was meant to be abrasive. We were into the idea of that Berlin decadence scene. That was the sort of culture we were interested in.[433]

The Banshees' own distinctive sartorial style matched the music and was also key to their wider influence and a big chunk of goth and alternative styles that would be born with the band's look and music.

> It wasn't spoken about. It just kind of evolved. We all started to wear black and Siouxsie would contrast. If you look at us on TV at the time on the *Old Grey Whistle Test*, all the boys are in black with Siouxsie is in a powder blue drape coat and a white scarf. We always went for that stark contrast. It was not a uniform but a unity to the way we looked which was very important and that came from following Roxy Music.
>
> The presentation was important to us. We went to the BBC in Manchester to film the *Old Grey Whistle Test* and we wanted white and blue lights and told them no

---

431 Steve Lillywhite to John Robb.

432 With his famous anti-Nazi and anti-Fascist photomontages, the Berlin-born John Heartfield was a 20th-century German visual artist who pioneered the use of art as a political weapon.

433 Severin to John Robb.

red, orange and green lights and we got them to change all the gels. Then we got our soundman to do the sound.

Because of that, of course, we would get a reputation for being the ice queen when, basically, we just knew what we wanted. We were assertive enough to say, 'No we don't want it like that. We want it this way' and that put a lot of industry people off – 'here's a band with ideas, stay clear of them!'[434]

Released in September 1979, the follow-up album *Join Hands*, was a tense, dense and even more claustrophobic affair that took the First World War as its inspirational starting point. It also explored the use of placebos in medicine in the track 'Placebo Effect'. 'Icon' looked at the destruction of paintings featuring religious images whilst 'Premature Burial' was 'ostensibly inspired' by Edgar Allan Poe's short story of the same name.

The album saw the band stretching their sound further into darker and even more enigmatic corners. The Banshees were moving way beyond punk and into tumbling lead lines, two note chords, MXR modulated guitars and minor keys. It was a record that was difficult to make and leaves bad memories for Severin.

It's patchy. It sounds like a band falling apart to me. Not that there are no great songs on there. If we had three more months, it would have been a different record - it's the second album syndrome I'm afraid. Occasionally Polydor would send an A and R to attend the sessions and we would say, 'That's all you are going to hear, you go on back to the office now'.[435]

The dense musical soundscapes of the album matched the mood of the band. The Banshees were beginning to drift into two distinct camps with the inner core of Siouxsie and Severin on one side and the rest on the other. Somehow, though, the album still managed to peak at number thirteen in the album chart,

It was a harbinger to the inevitable September 1979 split, a decisive and painful wrench that happened when John McKay and Kenny Morris walked out of a signing session at The Other Record Shop in Aberdeen before one of the first gigs on the album tour and took the train back to London.

That night, Siouxsie and Severin took to the stage with members of the support band The Cure. Together, they did an impromptu and vicious version of the 'Lord's Prayer' before denouncing the departed pair in an acidic and angry attack on 'the spineless prima donnas'.

The split left behind a series of question marks and 'what ifs?' with Kenny Morris going back to art school, film making and some low-level drum work, before resurfacing in 2014 as an artist in Ireland. Meanwhile, McKay eventually formed Zor Gabor with his long-standing girlfriend, Linda Clarke and released a brilliant if lost in the mists of time single on In Tape Records that retained that distinctive clipped guitar sound, and has since disappeared from view.

---

434 Severin to John Robb.

435 Severin to John Robb.

We didn't want to leave the band but there was no democracy. Me and John just didn't really get a say. I think when we left they thought that it was premeditated, which is just impossible. It wasn't the case. Initially, we wanted to see the tour through and maybe after the tour, we would leave. They were angry at the time but I have made up with Siouxsie since then. When I left the group I had offers to play from my old friend Adam Ant. But I actually couldn't bring myself to do it full time after being in such a great band. I just kind of needed to be out of the music industry for a while.

Later I did some drumming for Helen Terry then I went back to college and got a degree. I made some of my own records but I was not suited to the music business because I sometimes consider myself as a kind of a radical believer in the freedom of speech and expression. I am somewhere in the middle of being a Dionysian artist and an Apollonian type.[436]

The remaining Banshees were determined to finish the tour and cancelled a handful of dates whilst they returned to London to recruit a new lineup. They quickly added virtuoso drummer, Budgie, who had just recorded with The Slits for their debut album.

For the first session, the Banshees were still trying to patch up the lineup to finish the tour. I was sat in a rehearsal room with Marco who was stepping in on guitar to help out. I'd never met Siouxsie before. I had seen her live at Fulham Greyhound. I knew a bit of her sound but not the songs, so it was an initiation of fire. I was very much in at the deep end but they decided very quickly and said if you want to stick around you can be the drummer.

I was never sure why the others had left. It was so bizarre. Only Siouxsie would know. Having met John and Kenny afterwards on different occasions, I know they feel a sense of loss. They might have felt it was the right decision at the time but even shortly afterwards they realised it wasn't, but their pride would not let them back after hurting the original members.

It was unfortunate because it was a very strong band but when we joined it blossomed into something else.

At first, it was very odd. Whilst I was learning the songs we were also trying to find the guitarist to finish the tour. Everyone came down, name guitarists, people who had studied the first album backwards, Steve Jones came in, then lots of guitar players who didn't sound right until Robert Smith came back. [437]

With Robert Smith now on guitar, playing in the Banshees, and The Cure on the rest of the tour, it was saved. The experience would influence the young guitar player, moving The Cure towards their own darker direction.

Someone said 'Robert knows these songs', so we figured that he could do two separate sets on the rest of the tour as The Cure in support, and then with us. Nowadays, a band would pull the whole tour, but we only lost a week and then we continued. [438]

Post-tour, they recruited the brilliant young guitarist, John McGeoch from Magazine.

---

436 Kenny Morris to John Robb.

437 Budgie to John Robb.

438 Severin to John Robb.

I saw John McGeoch play on TV on *So It Goes* with Magazine and they were doing 'The Light Pours Out of Me' and I thought, that's the guy, he's fantastic. We cherry-picked the best of the generation to join the band. We had thought about another two potential contenders – Bruce Gilbert from Wire, also Geordie from Killing Joke – a band we saw right at the beginning of their career at the Moonlight in 1980 – they were fantastic, so loud and full on, but we realised that Geordie was not going to leave the band.

We had to kind of romance John McGeoch into leaving Magazine. For a while there, he was pretty loyal to Howard (Devoto) and then came to us. He was from Greenock, so nobody bullied him, not even Siouxsie![439]

When a band implodes, it can be a blessing in disguise - giving musicians a chance to break out from internal expectations and tension. With the virtuoso McGeoch now on board, and Budgie with his dynamic drumming, the band recorded their third album, *Kaleidoscope*, released in 1980.

Now free of their initial expectations, the Banshees were exploring new musical territories with the use of other instruments like synthesisers, sitars and drum machines as they stretched out their template. Like Joy Division's *Closer*, released the same year, this was an album that moved towards new horizons with a lightness in touch and an ear for captivating melody. There are touches of psychedelia and an understanding of a perfect shimmering and mysterious pop like on singles 'Happy House' and 'Christine' but there are still darker moments like on the spooked 'Tenant'.

We wrote everything in the studio which was a new approach for us. We would find the funny synthesiser in the corner that had been left behind by Godley and Creme and use it and come up with something different.

The new band developed pretty organically out of that. Budgie was on board fairly quickly. We knew what we were striving towards and when John joined it all fell into place. [440]

The Banshees' music was changing. They were moving away from the stark, confined sound that had defined them and they were now experimenting with a brooding and dark modern psychedelia. Their new guitar player was bringing inventive arpeggios, string harmonics and a disregard for conventional scales to the songs and adding effects like a flanger to create these unique soundscapes. It left Siouxsie in awe:

John McGeoch was my favourite guitarist of them all. He was into sound in an almost abstract way. I loved the fact that I could say, 'I want this to sound like a horse falling off a cliff', and he would know exactly what I meant. He was easily, without a shadow of a doubt, the most creative guitarist the Banshees ever had. [441]

Severin himself was enjoying the new colourful palette:

---

439 Severin to John Robb.

440 Severin to John Robb.

441 Siouxsie to Michael Bracewell.

I'd always liked the kind of softer – not wigged – psychedelia, the softer English pastoral Kevin Ayers and Syd Barrett stuff. That's what I was thinking of when writing things like 'Christine' – just the little bit of psychedelia in there both lyrically and musically affects stuff like that.

The only people it didn't work for was the Stones when they did *Satanic Majesties*. People forget that Tamla went psychedelic as well. That was a really interesting point in time. Everybody was extending tracks – 'Psychedelic Shack' by The Temptations is a great example of this. Hawkwind and the space rock side of things was a different way of taking this influence on board.

All this is what we had in mind with *Kaleidoscope* – to stretch out a bit and use a few effects. [442]

The two hit singles from *Kaleidoscope*, 'Happy House' and 'Christine', proved that the band had not lost their acidic pop touch, hitting the top twenty with dark, tripped-out pop masterpieces. This lysergic twist was provided thanks to an interest in LSD.

I like fun and I like 'up'. I loved LSD, yes. But you can't get the good stuff like you used to. You used to get very pure LSD, and I'm sure even that stuff wasn't half as good as it was in the '60s. Blue Window Pane is great. I've had Purple Haze, too. I've always had an amazing time. You can't hide with LSD. It's a truth drug. [443]

The new lineup were really gelling.

The original demos for 'Christine' and other songs were very different in approach but the vision for what they wanted to do with the Banshees was still intact. Had the original band done them it could have been very different.
I brought in a whole bunch of things I'd been listening to.
Unlike John and Kenny, I'd been in a lot of bands. I had a lot of other ideas from outside the Banshees, whereas that was their first band with one way of playing. [444]

Kaleidoscope, released in 1980, added light and colour without losing the band's distinct edge. The split had been creatively fortuitous.

We didn't have the 'Sturm und Drang' of the other two guys in there. We were now not doing tracks live in the studio. We were building them up bit by bit. It was much lighter in approach – not light-hearted just not too intense. We had had enough of that and it caused the band to fucking explode. It was different essentially in that it was just me and Siouxsie in the studio and our relationship was not like that brooding thing. It was more humorous and that was reflected on *Kaleidoscope* and we built the second band out of that. [445]

When *Kaleidoscope* was released, the music scene had changed. Punk had given way to the post-punk that the Banshees had pioneered. It was a time of glorious confusion of creativity and fantastically uncharted waters. Slowly, the micro scenes that emerged from post-punk would coalesce into new scenes and vistas. One of these

---

442 Severin to John Robb.

443 Siouxsie to Michael Bracewall.

444 Budgie to John Robb.

445 Steve Severin to John Robb.

was going to end up as goth; the dreaded g-word that the Banshees had both inspired and loathed. Despite this, Siouxsie would remain the fledgling scene's most iconic presence whilst treating it with a lofty disdain. It was an uncomfortable relationship for the unwitting icon:

> It was frightening. Even shop dummies were starting to look like me. Everywhere I went, there'd be bloody windows full of Siouxsies! Someone asked me how it felt to be the queen of goth. I said, 'That's rather like being known as the Prince Regent of Fools'. I hate all that. That wasn't what we were about at all. Gothic in its purest sense is a very powerful, twisted genre, but the way it was being used by journalists – 'goff' with a double 'f' – always seemed to me to be about tacky harum-scarum horror, and I find that anything but scary. There is a fun, flippant side to me, of course, but then I would much rather be known as the 'Ice Queen'.[446]

Despite this disparity and the band's refusal to be trapped, Siouxsie remained the number one style icon for the new scene.

> It was very weird. The Siouxsie lookalikes - we would call them 'Suzettes' and the gigs were chock-a-block full of them. Go to any alternative nightclub in any city around the UK and there would be half a dozen Siouxsie clones in there. Siouxsie was very uncomfortable with it but it was just another evolution.
> People forget there was a little phase where it was called positive punk. Southern Death Cult, Sex Gang Children and all those bands then sprung up – the dreaded g-word had not come into it yet. I'm not sure when that happened – probably with Bauhaus and then retrospectively with Joy Division who were called a gothic band which was weird.
> I don't mind anything being called 'Gothic' as that might refer back to the obvious influence of Edgar Allan Poe or Gothic architecture or Gothic painting – anything from the turn of the century. But when it comes shortened to 'goth', then I think of The Sisters of Mercy, Fields of the Nephilim through to Marilyn Manson and it's kind of a pantomime version.
> There are so many things in goth you cannot do, you have to fit a certain template and that was something we were fighting against in the late '70s. People could never understand why we didn't want to be associated with it – people would call Siouxsie the 'queen of goth' and she would say, 'No I fucking ain't!'
> But then I think of The Birthday Party who were pretty good – they got tarred with the g-word as well and they were something else entirely. [447]

For the Banshees, taking musical risks and stretching the template was at the core of their creativity. The peak of their foray into this dramatic musical brilliance was their 1981 fourth album *Juju*, with its defining hits 'Spellbound' and 'Arabian Knights'. *Juju* saw their guitar player brimming with ideas and his groundbreaking playing dominates, especially on tracks like 'Monitor' and 'Into The Light'. The Banshees had found a way of turning their innate darkness into pristine and perfect dark pop. Siouxsie went through a myriad of startling image changes and performed with

446 As told to Michael Bracewell.
447 Severin to John Robb.

a melancholic, misanthropic and introspective detachment that pulled the listener deeper into their music.

In 1981, Siouxsie and Budgie also debuted The Creatures, which saw Siouxsie's stark voice set against the drummer's stunning percussion for four intermittent albums: 1983's *Feast*, 1989's *Boomerang*, 1999's *Anima Animus* and 2003's *Hái!* that explored the possibilities of Budgie's incredible polyrhythmic brilliance with a more playful Siouxsie, whose distinctive voice collided perfectly with the battering percussive backdrops.

> The Creatures started at the same time as *Juju*, as an offshoot. The first couple of tracks were left over from a John Peel session and we played it live as part of the Banshees and it didn't become separate until we decided to do it. We went into the studio and Siouxsie had lyric ideas and I had some beats and we knocked it together in a weekend. And then we got on *Top of the Pops* and Siouxsie was where she should be – singing a mad song on the telly! [448]

The Banshees continued their explorations with 1982's *A Kiss in the Dreamhouse*, which added strings and extra instrumentation to their now rich and exotic palette. McGeoch's still-remarkable guitar work helped to create a sensuous playful listening experience. The textured sounds and swirling effects helped to create an altered reality.

With their psychedelic twist and breathtaking scope of musical ideas, the Banshees were very much in their prime. Sadly, it proved to be their last album with John McGeoch, who suffered a nervous breakdown due to the stresses of touring and drinking. After collapsing on stage during a performance at a gig in Madrid, he left the band in 1982, taking his unique textured guitar with him.

With Robert Smith back on board, the band released their biggest hit yet – a shimmering cover of The Beatles' 'Dear Prudence' that saw the original finger-picked guitar line transposed to a gothic arpeggio by Smith. There was also a further exploration of the psychedelics, with which Smith and Severin had dabbled at the time, with The Glove's 1983 *Blue Sunshine* album. 1984's *Hyaena* saw The Cure frontman's playful approach come to the fore before the stress of being in two groups and The Glove project saw him leave in 1984.

The band continued for another decade with albums like *Superstition*, then their covers album, *Through The Looking Glass* which signposted key influences like Iggy, Doors, Sparks, Kraftwerk, John Cale, and Bryan Ferry. They kept working on the fringes until their 1995 swansong and 11th album, *The Rapture,* which saw them continue to flirt and entwine with a bewildering array of musics. It was an ambitious late-period command of styles from orchestration to Indian instruments that had already hit pay dirt with 1988's astonishingly eclectic *Peepshow*, which is arguably the highlight from this later period.

By this point, Siouxsie had discarded her trademark big, spiky, black hair – which launched a million imitators around the world – and startled with a short bob,

---

448 Budgie to John Robb.

reminiscent of both Liza Minnelli and Louise Brooks. The accompanying promotional album tour saw the band's stage show at its most elaborate and ambitious. It was an extravagant, almost Vaudevillian set up with curtains, drop screens and a staircase-cum-catwalk along which Siouxsie strutted and danced. Many of the band members were similarly dressed in their ornate finery. Finally getting embraced in the USA, they stopped in 1996 before reconvening in 2003 when they released *Seven Year Itch (Live at Shepherd's Bush Empire)*.

Siouxsie's last release, so far, was her 2007 solo album, *Mantaray*, which was a critical success and a great album of industrial pop, with her voice as powerful as ever. She toured wearing her stunning Pam Hogg[449] designed catsuits and then, despite popping up at fashion shows and for her 2014 Meltdown live set, Siouxsie was noticeably absent for a decade.

Whilst many contemporaries such as The Cure and Nick Cave play stadiums, and Bauhaus have managed to reform for huge shows, Siouxsie maintained an imperious absence until, out of the blue, she announced a return...the reaction was online meltdown.

The Queen is back. She had been away for too long.

---

449 Even more outré than the late Vivienne Westwood, Pam Hogg has designed clothes for nearly all of goth royalty.

Chapter 14

FEEL THE PAIN

The Damned

It's October 2022 and we are in a sold out Manchester Apollo. The Damned's classic lineup reformation gig has finally gone ahead after being delayed by the great plague.

Not only are the band, with an average age of just below 70, at the top of their game, they are at the top of everybody's game. No band has the right to emerge like this, from the past, like supercharged cadavers with such a zest, explosive power and a sheer, wild musicality.

This is no mere lap of honour - and to be honest, that would have been enough - this is a righteous stomp, an explosive finale, that throws down the gauntlet to every other band on the planet. Somehow, and it's crazy to even think it, The Damned have returned, after decades, as one of the best rock'n'roll groups on the planet and possibly, typically of them, will snatch defeat from the jaws of victory and disappear into the night again like spectral ghosts drenched in the cordite whiff of adrenaline.

The set is culled from the first two Brian James helmed 1977 albums when they combined the glorious rush of prime time punk rock with a darker shiver that would be a key building block of goth.

Fronted then, and now, by vampiric, Byronic, baritone crooner, Dave Vanian, The Damned may have been one of the three founding bands of punk but were also true gothic pioneers who would eventually have their biggest chart successes in that era.

*****

Formed in 1976, by visionary guitar player Brian James, The Damned dealt a delicious and anarchic sound. Forged in chaos, throughout their extensive career, they have come to represent many things to many people. One of the original punk bands alongside Sex Pistols and The Clash, they delivered a very different, frantic and melodic rush of sound. Boasting elements of music hall, and a vaudeville Gothic melodrama with their high-octane brilliance, it all burned in the white heat of rock'n'roll genius. Throughout each era of the band, every member simultaneously pursued their own unique creative vision, often all at the same time, and a recipe for glorious disaster.

The Damned may never have been as big as those fellow punk instigators but the three bands were the core of the UK punk scene. They were created with a fierce sense of competition, inner tension and with a stylistic friction that proved to be so key to the scene's ethos. A lot of this musical unrest was attributed to the rivalry between the three key punk rock managers; Sex Pistols' Malcolm McLaren, The Clash's Bernie Rhodes and The Damned's Andrew Czezowski.

The Damned had moved quickly by virtue of being signed to the small indie label, Stiff Records. Being signed to a fast-moving indie had its advantages; they had managed to release that precious first punk single, but despite this, they would ultimately be hampered by lacking big label clout, unlike the two other core bands and were doomed for cult status.

The Damned were a band in a hurry. Their first rehearsal was on 6 July 1976, and just four weeks later they played their first gig, supporting Sex Pistols at the 100 Club. They were the first British punk band to release a single, on 22 October 1976, with the still-thrilling 'New Rose', which beat Sex Pistols' 'Anarchy in the UK' debut by four weeks. They were the first punk band to release an album, on 18 February 1977, and were the first to release a second album, that November. They were also the first punk band to tour the USA and were ultimately the first punk band to split up in early 1978.

The twin assault of their first two singles, 'New Rose' and 'Neat Neat Neat' have become punk rock classics. Both songs' infernal energy is as propulsive and compulsive now as it was when they were recorded in London's tiny Pathway[450] studios in 1976, months after the band had formed.

Dave Vanian's ghoulish stage presence and love of dark theatricality filtered through punk rock somewhat patented the soon to come dark style; certainly, in post-punk terms. He may have been 'camping it up', but Vanian had a genuine presence and a swashbuckling darkness about him. With his vampire-esque black suits, dark kohl-rimmed eyes, white face and jet black hair firmly greased back, Vanian was vamp-vaudeville.

In the band's early days, he would often wear a too-small leather jacket with a large, upturned collar that sat against his neck like outstretched bat wings. Vanian was always impeccably dressed and displayed an unusual fastidiousness in the middle of the punk rock wars that could be traced back to his love of the sartorial vampiric elegance of the bloodsuckers in his favourite films.

Never confined to one style of music, The Damned were built from an unlikely core of individuals whose tastes ranged from garage rock to prog, punk rock, psychedelia and epic film soundtrack. The band went on to capture this unlikely mix in an intermittent series of albums, played out over a tumultuous career.

Their 1977 debut album *Damned, Damned, Damned* was full of high velocity and high-octane rock'n'roll. However, these early efforts were not just tuneless thrashes. Brian James, the man once dubbed the 'inventor of punk rock' by The Clash's Mick Jones[451] was a great songwriter and guitar player. James provided witty vignettes and perfectly structured pieces that were played with a demented glee and a precocious musicality by the classic lineup. The album, though, even had a couple of proto-goth

450 Tiny Islington 8 track studio set up by the co-writers of the Arthur Brown hit,'Fire' and where the likes of Madness, Dire Straits and many others somehow recorded in its smaller than a front room space .

451 The pair met when Brian James spent a few weeks playing with Mick Jones› pre Clash outfit, the unfortunately-named London SS, who never played a gig but tried to get a band together, also with Tony James on bass. Brian talked about short, sharp songs and his hair was cropped, influenced by Lou Reed.

tracks on it. Driven by Brian James' sultry guitar arpeggios and the young singer's 'Phantom of the Opera' croon, 'Feel the Pain' and 'Fan Club' underlined an unlikely introspection and dank goth psychedelia.

The original lineup were a powder keg of raw power. Bassist Captain Sensible's wild stage antics – often seeing him dressed in a nurse's outfit or a tutu – were bizarre and gripping, often distracting from his brilliant playing. Meanwhile, Brian James cast a too-cool, skinny and ghoulish silhouette whilst looking somewhat like a sinister Keith Richards gunslinger. Drummer Rat Scabies was an explosive version of Keith Moon, full of audacious drum rolls and free jazz rushes, shackled into a high-octane punk rush that underpinned Dave Vanian's very non-punk, neo-Jim Morrison baritone croon.

Dave Vanian was born David Lett on 12 October 1956 in Newcastle but grew up in Hemel Hempstead [452] where his parents moved when he was a baby. The London overspill town was 24 miles northwest of the big city and rebuilt as a new town after WWII. The goth pioneer, he spent decades ensconced in his gothic world with his frontman duties being only a small part of his 24/7 nocturnal lifestyle. Before gaining notoriety, Vanian already lived in an interzone of flickering old movies, garage psych-rock and macabre bric-a-brac before even joining The Damned. A youthful New York Dolls and Roxy Music fan, he dressed in black with died black hair from the age of 14 before it was even a noir thing.

> I liked Victorian architecture and mourning rituals. Film noir was a big influence and rock'n'roll. I loved Gene Vincent, I liked Elvis but I always thought Roy Orbison had the best voice. Weirdly, they were all pallid with black hair. I was also into the imagery in those silent German movies, where the men are all over made-up and have blacked-out eyes.[453]

The perfect embodiment of pop culture, Vanian is proof that, in this world, you can become your alter ego. Within a few years, a large chunk of the goth subculture was taking its cues from him. He had changed his name from Lett to Vanian after a 1975/76 stint as a gravedigger, or 'a spiritual journey through the daisies', as he liked to term it, with his new name being a play on 'Transylvanian'. Despite his small frame, he was a very keen worker and it was a job that was perfect for him until The Damned began to take off in 1976.

Arriving fully formed in the band, he was one of the first male singers to wear black lipstick and black eye shadow, taking cues from the 1974 Andy Warhol's *Blood for Dracula, the* Italian-French horror film written and directed by Warhol acolyte Paul Morrissey. The film was one of the cult movies released under the pop artist's creative umbrella that celebrated the so-called trash aesthetic[454] that was of great influence on punk and post-punk. It starred 30-year-old German actor Udo Kier, who delivered

---

452 He was a year younger than Magenta Devine, who also came from the same unlikely place.

453 Dave Vanian to GQ magazine.

454 Warhol made over sixty of these films throughout the 1960s, along with his many famous screen tests that handled the issues of masculinity, eroticism, sexuality, boredom, beauty, excess, trauma and the progression of movement over time. These films are some of the most interesting and experimental works from the period.

a distinctive portrayal of Dracula that saw him play a slick and ghoulish character, sharply dressed with black, kohl eyeliner and lipstick, and struck a nerve with Dave Vanian who was in thrall to underground film and book culture:

> My favourite vampire movies are films like *Lemora: A Child's Tale*, for its lyrical strangeness, Andy Warhol's *Dracula*, Bela Lugosi's *Dracula* and Frank Langella's *Dracula* from the Balderston play. I liked it for its sincerity in depicting the Yorkshire people. And the strength of Mina Harker's character as played by Kate Nelligan, Gary Oldman's portrayal was superb in Coppola's *Dracula*.
>
> I was reared on predominantly Gothic fiction, black and white expressionist films from the twenties and thirties and my love for art and all things esoteric. These things worked their way insidiously into my subconscious until, to me, the graveyard pallor, the black lips, black hair and smoky kohl eyes, seemed perfectly natural. The reality was, that I was as far from the Gothic towers of Romantic fiction as I was to the moon, but I saw no reason why you couldn't aspire to a life less ordinary. There was, to me, nothing feminine about wearing makeup. I never thought of myself as wearing girl's makeup. It was 'male grooming' and you make the best of your features either way. Going on stage for me was almost like dressing down from my day to day life.[455]

By the late 1970s, Vanian was living this lifestyle around the clock. When the NME went to visit his Islington flat, they reported a full extension of his persona and one of the first proto-gothic spaces:

> It's a veritable shrine to Count Dracula and all of the vampire persuasion. The pitch-dark is split only by a candelabra and a dim red bulb. The walls are hung with collages of Dracula, '20s plastic face masks, a spiked ball and chain mace and bouquets of fake roses. Life-size painted china mannequins peer from the corners in black lace veils; severed china hands and skulls grace the mantlepiece. There's a church harmonium and a black telephone off the hook. From behind a curtain drifts the dulcet strains of horror movie soundtracks. Vanian (23) sits in a huge velvet armchair – white face, spiked collar, slicked back hair - sipping a Bloody Mary from a crystal goblet and winding up a clockwork mouse to entertain his black cat, Demon.[456]

For Vanian, this all appeared completely natural.

> It is with some irony that I am considered an icon since before joining The Damned my tastes in music, literature, art and any sort of sartorial style have since been noted for pioneering, and would have been the same in whatever profession I had chosen to pursue. So, it was perhaps in some ways accidental that I find myself in this position…why vampires? Elegance, suavity, intelligence, what's not to like? [457]

Musically, the singer was enjoying a different soundtrack from his contemporaries with several singers and crooners making a big impact and influence on his own distinctive style.

---

455 Dave Vanian to Alex Barker.

456 From the NME.

457 Dave Vanian to Alex Barker from Fashion Alternative website.

I tend to listen to mainly soundtrack music and albums without singers on. Music is the thing for me more than singers. Yet I have always liked the singers from the '60s such as Scott Walker. He has most definitely been an influence, not just for his singing but also for what he has done. Not his commercial hits as such, but the albums that he made of Jacques Brel material, those cutting edge songs that he recorded. Obviously, there would have to be a bit of Jim Morrison in there because he is another baritone. I loved some of Paul and Barry Ryan's stuff and that is why I eventually recorded their hit 'Eloise'. And even people like Tom Jones, those big-sounding singers who you don't get so much these days. As a singer, those are the type of things that I would probably cite.

Funnily enough, I didn't go to many concerts when I was young. I kind of wandered into music almost by accident. Eventually, I went along to see bands like New York Dolls but sadly I never did get to see David Bowie. I saw Doctors of Madness who were pre-punk and then ironically some years later, we got to do a tour with them. They were just at the wrong time really. That whole kind of Bowie era was ending, and they were just a little bit late in their timing. I loved that early era of Roxy Music with Eno. Some of the tracks on the first and second Roxy albums to me are quite punk rock in their attitude. It's different and it really goes for it. I think that without those types of bands, things would have been different. Also, in there are Iggy & the Stooges and Beethoven and Wagner but the thing I listen to the most is Nico. [458]

Dave Vanian first appeared on the music scene radar in early 1976. His inquisitive nature had led him to discover the Sex shop on King's Road one Saturday afternoon early that year, resulting in Malcolm McLaren introducing him to Rat Scabies a few weeks later, which further resulted in Vanian being introduced to a confusing scene of young hopefuls.

Asked to turn up for a vague 'audition/rehearsal' by Scabies, Vanian walked into a room of young people with no band name other than the jokey Masters of The Backside. This was a loose collection of new faces put together by Malcolm McLaren in his attempt to create a scene around his other young charges, Sex Pistols.

The audition seemed to be built around Chrissie Hynde. The young American was playing the guitar and looking for a vehicle for the songs she had been writing whilst working behind the counter in Malcolm and Vivienne's shop. Somehow, the much-changing and short-lived ad hoc band ended up with two singers, Vanian all in black and the long-lost Dave Zero all in white; much to the bemusement of Vanian:

> Malcolm was overseeing it. There was another singer who I only know as Dave, it might have been Dave Zero. He had perfectly white hair, so we looked like a couple of dominoes! We did a whole pile of '60s garage-y numbers with Chrissie Hynde on guitar, but it never went any further. [459]

Rat Scabies paints a vivid picture of the ebb and flow of pre-punk bands:

> I used to hang out quite a lot with Chrissie Hynde and go shoplifting with her. She was looking for a band. She had done some stuff with Johnny Moped [460]. She

---

458 Dave Vanian to UK Music Reviews website.

459 Dave Vanian to Alex Barker.

460 Semi-legendary, gonzoid garage punk band from Croydon and friends of Captain Sensible

had been working with music writer Nick Kent on this thing but they had fallen out. Malcolm then made this band up and had decided that Chrissie was going to dress up as a boy and she would sing and play the guitar even though she had just started playing, but all we did was just play covers like the Pistols did.

At that time, me and Brian James had also spent a week rehearsing with Mick Jones and Tony James as London SS but that didn't work out as they didn't think I looked right! Brian said to Mick that if they didn't want to work with me then he was off to do something with me instead and that's what we did.

Initially, it was slow progress trying to get a lineup together. There were not very many people around at the time. Captain Sensible was a mate from Croydon Fairfield Halls where we were both toilet cleaners and was still doing the Johnny Moped thing and wearing velvet jackets with his hair like Marc Bolan and being very muso! I was on the way to a Masters Of The Backside rehearsal, so I grabbed him. When he came down Malcolm didn't have an immediate thing with him but he did have a bass guitar and an amp, so he was in. Malcolm's first comment on seeing the Captain was 'Oh my God what an unsightly creature!' [laughs.] He was like, 'But never mind, put him in the band'. It was all a bit un-together.

Now we needed a singer. Dave had been going to Malcolm's shop and had come down to the Masters Of The Backside rehearsals before The Damned where we also had another bloke who was a singer called Dave White whose stage name was going to be Dave Zero. It was hilarious. He was totally the opposite to Vanian, and the idea was to have two different kinds of singers - one completely macho and dark and the other doing the opposite. Dave Zero was a hairdresser from Bromley and totally effeminate. He was absolutely brilliant- one of the most wonderful, witty people I ever met, and I've never seen him since.[461]

The bizarre lineup was fumbling in the dark; trying to make sense of a loose collection of eccentrics. New boy Captain Sensible was feeling his way into band life on the bass; not his first choice of instrument but he was captivated by the situation:

At the audition, I remember particularly playing 'I Can't Control Myself' – The Troggs song. It was really funny with the two singers with Dave already having his whole look. They both started and stopped singing at the same time. It would have been incredible onstage. Can you imagine! Me, Chrissie and Rat were staring at each other while they were doing it. It was unbelievable- especially when you consider Little Jimmy Osmond and that sort of bollocks was what was going on at the time.

The two-singer lineup lasted about two weeks, I think. Then The Damned started which was down to Brian. He was looking for his preferred kind of lineup. I think he picked a good one, mind you. I would say that wouldn't I [laughs]. We all added our own thing, not only musically because that was down to him, but personality-wise – in terms of everyone being extreme in their almost cartoon character kind of way.[462]

Brian James had been waiting with his master plan to create a raw, classic rock'n'roll band:

I had this idea of a perfect band and I knew what it should sound like. Rat had a mild flirtation with this thing that Malcolm was trying to put together and that's

---

461 Rat Scabies to John Robb.

462 Captain Sensible to John Robb.

how he met Dave Vanian, which was cool. It had a few names like Mike Hunt's Honourable Discharge – Chrissie liked that joke. Rat lasted one or two rehearsals and he thought 'fuck this'. That band was a strange fucking thing. They dallied with that for a week or two and then me and Rat got onto the serious stuff of recruiting people for our band, and Rat brought down the Captain so that was the bass player sorted out.[463]

The ad hoc Masters of The Backside was never going to last; there were too many agendas and directions. However, early punk was full of these loose arrangements. A bemused Captain Sensible explains:

I didn't know who I was auditioning for because everything was in a flux all the time and everyone was playing with each other. One minute Tony James was in a band with Brian, then Chrissie Hynde was in a band with me and Rat, and Brian wasn't there. It was all mixed up. We were just trying each other out to see who got on with who. It was a very interesting period and we were all drinking together. It was a funny little community, down the Nashville Rooms, Portobello Road. To be quite honest, in 1975/76 music was so bad and in the hands of the 20-minute-long drum solo wankers and whispering Bob Harris types that you thought whatever you were doing was so exciting, but you never thought it would ever get anywhere. You never thought that the music press would write about you. Record companies would never touch with you with a barge pole. I just liked doing it. It was so exhilarating and such fun. [464]

Gradually, out of the flux, Dave Vanian saw things begin to coalesce:

Basically, Rat wanted me to meet Brian and Brian's words were to Rat, I believe, 'He looks like a singer, we'll try him out!' So, I auditioned for The Damned and the other guy who was asked to audition never actually turned up. I was the only one, so whether they actually liked me...!? [465]

'The other guy' was future punk royalty.

In April 1976, me and Brian were in the Nashville [466] and John Beverley AKA Sid, walked in with a gold lame jacket, looking like the total star. We said, 'He looks good' . Brian had seen him before on the number 31 bus and knew his face. Then a quarter of an hour later, Dave walks in, and Brian said, 'There's another one' I said I know him already, so we asked him along for an audition as well, and that's how it all came together. We auditioned Dave at the church hall on Lisson Grove, just round the corner from the dole office where everyone seemed to be signing on. The 'other guy' was Sid Vicious, who was meant to come down for an audition, as well, but never turned up.[467]

This new band masterminded by Brian was a different proposition from the ad hoc bands.

Brian had all these songs he'd been working on. He wanted to fulfil this dream of getting an album together. He was looking for the right people to work with, with

---

463 Brian James to John Robb.

464 Captain Sensible to John Robb.

465 Dave Vanian to Vive Le Rock Magazine.

466 Long gone venue in Kensington, London ‹The Nashville Rooms› was a key pub rock and punk space.

467 Rat Scabies to John Robb.

the same attitude. Up to that time, he'd never found anyone, but in Rat, he found the perfect drummer. I guess, in me, he found the perfect singer who'd give vent to his songs. Immediately when I heard him play the guitar, I wanted to work with him. He was an amazing guitarist. There's only so many guitarists who don't sound like anyone else and instantly when they play you know who they are. I'd always been a big fan of Johnny Thunders and he reminded me of him in a way. He had the same kind of attitude. I liked that, and I liked what he did.

Of all the band members, I imagine I had the least experience. Rat had been in several bands. Brian was a little bit older than the rest of us and he'd been in bands previously, whilst Captain had been in bands with Johnny Moped. So, I literally just lied my way into the business. I lied that I'd been in a couple of local bands out of town. I knew I could hold a tune though 'cause I could sing along to a record, at least I thought so! [468]

The new movement that had been predicted by Brian James was finally beginning to happen. There was now a hunger for short, sharp songs.

There was a feeling that something was going to happen, Brian always said you could see it was coming. I think people wanted bands playing very loud and have energy and that was what we wanted to do. I always presumed I couldn't have been the only one who wanted this and when you saw the Pistols and Jonesey – there was other people with the same attitude and you were not the only one who was angry about what was going on, who couldn't get a job and not have any money. [469]

The new band already had a name provided by Brian: The Damned. It was a perfect summation of both their (eventual) wilful madness and the artful, darker undertow that always stopped them from collapsing into comedic excess. He had taken the band's name from a 1969 Italian-German, Luchino Visconti film of the same name. [470] It was a dark movie of moral decadence, sexual neurosis, aesthetic death wishes and political opportunism, all of which greatly appealed to Brian.

I had the name and I had wanted to use it for a long time. I liked it because of the decadent thing. There was also a couple of British black and white films called *Village of The Damned* and *Children of The Damned*, which I also liked – films about mothers who become pregnant with strange, threatening children based on the 1957 John Wyndham book, *The Midwich Cuckoos*. [471]

According to Captain Sensible, the band's set fell together quickly:

Brian had some songs from his previous band, Bastard, and he had some new ones. We rehearsed a set and played our first gig four weeks later, in July, with the Pistols. The set lasted 45 minutes but once we were on stage with the old adrenaline pumping, it was about 20 minutes [laughs]. Early on, if the promoter

---

468 Dave Vanian to Vive Le Rock Magazine.

469 Rat Scabies to John Robb.

470 Originally titled in Italian, *La Caduta Degli Dei, 'The Fall of the Gods'* starring Dirk Bogarde.

471 Brian James to John Robb

booked you for an hour, we'd have to play the set again because it was all so frantic – people never noticed if we played the same songs twice anyway![472]

At last, the music revolution that Brian James had been willing to happen was erupting:

It seemed to me that music had lost touch with the street. There was no dirt or nitty gritty. The only bands at the time I thought were worth bothering with were those like The Pink Fairies. They had a really good spirit. The real stuff was in the States as far as I was concerned, the New York Dolls, The Velvet Underground, MC5 and The Stooges. They were my heroes and the beginning of what became known as 'punk'.

Someone took me to see the Pistols play early on in February 1976 at a party. They played a Stooges song and I just thought 'wow'! At that time, I was still in a band called Bastard and we just couldn't get a gig anywhere. We even moved to Belgium, where people were more relaxed and more into that sort of music. I just remember that when I first saw The Pistols, I thought they were the perfect band for what would become The Damned to make our debut with.

Punk exploded after the Bill Grundy *Today* show, when it hit mainstream consciousness, but was quickly tabloid cliché.

We all found ourselves caught up in this monster that became punk. In my opinion, punk became one-dimensional, which is a pity because as much as it was liberating, it also shackled us. That was a shame because I feel that it wasn't about anything other than the music originally. The attitude came with that because we were so excited and so driven by it.

The movement got ruined in so many ways. Initially, it was so optimistic and seemed like it was really going somewhere then, all of a sudden it was like 'this is what it is and we're going to give it this name and you should only listen to that and blah blah blah'. I often wonder if the Grundy show had never happened, how different history could have been. Which is ironic really when you consider that swearing on TV is almost de rigueur today. [473]

It was in this new cultural warzone of early 1977 that The Damned released their debut album. It is often regarded as one of the great rock'n'roll records and is easily up there with The Stooges and the MC5 as a rush of great primal guitar music, but there were moments of vaudeville gothic in amongst the wild energy. Even sceptical fellow punk musicians, such as, Marco Pirroni were impressed:

I did have my initial doubts about The Damned but 'New Rose' was great and the next single, 'Neat Neat Neat', was fantastic. I generally didn't like their vibe, but I always thought that Dave Vanian looked really cool with that Andy Warhol

---

472 Captain Sensible to Dave Jennings from Louder Than War.

473 Dave Vanian to Alex Barker.

Dracula look. The Damned were not playing by numbers. It was not just 1,2,3,4. It was very well-written songs like the MC5 and The Stooges had.[474]

The album's insane energy was captured by Nick Lowe's shrapnel production. Yet, it also hinted at a musical progression with a few moments of gothic melodrama that helped make the album outstanding and visionary in the musical landscape. Tracks like 'Fan Club' and 'Feel The Pain' were proto-goth in their melodrama and really allowed the singer to stretch his ghoul baritone. Vanian sang the slower Brian James songs with a dark relish and, added to his vampire style and moves, was patenting goth a couple of years before it appeared.

> I think it's an amazing album. I can look at it totally from the outside as I didn't write any of those songs. I was just fortunate enough to be the singer.
> Brian wrote some amazing stuff, totally different from other bands that were around at the time. I'm really proud of being the singer on that album and if I hadn't been the singer, I would definitely have gone to see that band. I don't sit around and play it but recently I saw some footage of us from 1977 playing in Brighton. I was worried about how we'd look but I was glad I watched it. The film quality was really good, and I thought, that band looks really exciting, I'd go and watch that band now.[475]

Captain Sensible was surprised by the album:

> To be quite honest, I was shocked that anyone liked it! Not that I didn't like what we were doing. I just didn't think anyone else would. The reaction we had been getting at out of town places like the Nag's Head in High Wycombe was not necessarily any indication of where we were going. What pissed me off though was that my picture was not on the back cover because I was facing away from the camera and I was covered in cake on the front! I thought 'If this is the only album I ever make- I might as well get my picture on it!' I went straight to Paddington St station and got some passport photos taken. I cut them out and gave them to the bloke who was doing the artwork and said, 'Stick that on', I can't show my auntie Sadie the album and say, 'I'm on this' all she would say, 'Oh Ray, you can hardly see your face on the pictures!' [476]

The Damned spent 1976/77 on the road. Whether supporting T. Rex or headlining their own tours, they existed in an endless blur. The music industry fully expected them, like all their contemporaries, to collapse from fatigue or simply run out of songs and, because of this short-term thinking, six months later, they were back in the studio recording their second album, all before the bubble burst.

The *Music for Pleasure* album has been maligned for decades. The band hate it and it has gone down in history as one of the great examples of the 'second album

---

474 Marco Pirroni to John Robb.

475 Dave Vanian to Alex Barker.

476 Captain Sensible to John Robb.

syndrome'. Yet it's far better than that. Encased in a great Barney Bubbles[477] sleeve that disguised the band members as a Kandinsky painting, it was produced by Pink Floyd drummer Nick Mason.[478]

The album is a lost classic. Some of the songs, like 'Problem Child' (a punky take on the spook chug of Syd Barrett's 'Astronomy Domine'[479]) and 'Don't Cry Wolf' are great, whilst 'Alone' is spectral studio brilliance. Following this was 'You Know' with the freeform jazz sax of Lol Coxhill, which sounded stunning. The album's brilliance was finally vindicated when it was played at the 2022 reformation gigs. At the time, the album was mistakingly slated by critics and fans alike, and the band limped on. Rat Scabies quit to be replaced by future Culture Club drummer Jon Moss, before Brian called a halt to the band while sat in the pub in February 1978.

> It's never fun when a band splits up. Especially if you are a former toilet cleaner and that occupation now seems like the only option you have left.
> This was the terrible situation I found myself in shortly after we'd delivered the album to Stiff Records. The recording sessions had given me very little joy as we were barely talking to each other by that point. Our leader Brian James had written an amazing bunch of anarchic tunes for *Damned Damned Damned,* but, compared to that, his new material was decidedly lacklustre and that, added to the fact that he wasn't keen on playing anyone else's songs, was pretty much the cause of all the conflict.
> We DID all agree on one thing though – that rather than rehash the first album time after time, The Damned should go on a sort of musical adventure, changing and developing with each new record. That was the reasoning for Pink Floyd's psychedelic ex frontman Syd Barrett being appointed producer but somehow we ended up with Nick Mason. I still think we could've made an interesting spaced-out punk-psych record together – if Syd had had his head together enough to attend the sessions. [480]

The Damned were seemingly no more. They played one last show at the Astoria on 8 April 1978. Even Rat Scabies got up to play along with new drummer Jon Moss.[481] The gear was, of course, trashed at the end of the set in a symbolic full-stop.

Without their founder and creative driving force, it looked like there would be no comeback. Brian himself was already moving forwards. Sensing the psychedelic revival to add to his profound love of garage rock, he formed Tanz der Youth with ex-members of Hawkwind and Warsaw Pakt. With a typical Brian sense of vision, he

---

477 The late Barney Bubbles was a groundbreaking graphic artist who had designed record sleeves for Hawkwind and many others.

478 The band apparently wanted Syd Barrett, yet he was a burn out at the time, living in a hotel room surrounded by flickering TVs.

479 From Pink Floyd's 1967 *Piper at the Gates of Dawn* debut album.

480 Captain Sensible to Grauzone website.

481 The future drummer of Culture Club.

described the band as: 'transmagical; the sound of the 1980s'. They released a great debut single, 'I'm Sorry I'm Sorry' which was sadly overlooked, and fizzled out.

A couple of years later, he was back with a new band, the rock'n'roll überlords with a certain gothic twist; Lords of The New Church - a punk supergroup formed with Stiv Bators (The Dead Boys), Dave Tregunna (Sham 69) and Nick Turner (The Barracudas). The band had Brian's fingerprints all over it. They were conceptual rock n roll; they had a look - dark gothic and bedraggled – and played a unique droog, yet grandiose and melodic, rock'n'roll.

Initially, Brian's former colleagues were in disarray. Scabies formed The White Cats whilst Sensible put together King, and they seemed on the fast track to the rock'n'roll gutter; just another bunch of musicians who got close to success before the inevitable burnout. None of this was a surprise for Sensible:

> 'What kind of new band would I put together now?' was the question I was asking myself and the answer was right there in front of me. Why not attempt the psych/punk experiment? That is exactly what I did with the short-lived King, who, although we had only done a handful of paid gigs were starting to sound as though we had something. This was at the point when the phone rang. It was my ex-colleague Rat Scabies, who'd been offered some money for a London show if we could get some kind of Damned lineup back together. Being totally broke I didn't need much persuading, I can tell you.
>
> As ex-guitarist of the Johnny Moped band, I fancied a go at six strings again. So, we called up our old mate Lemmy to play bass and knocked together a setlist of Damned and Motörhead favourites during a short boozy rehearsal. The reaction of the audience on the night of the performance, that September 1978, was splendid, so we arranged another show…and then another…and well, you know the rest. [482]

Signing to Chiswick Records, the reformed Damned of Vanian, Sensible and Scabies, with Algy Ward joining them on bass, recorded and released their third album, *Machine Gun Etiquette*. The album was full of anthems that combined the rush of punk with Vanian's gothic croon. Songs like 'Love Song', the joyous 'Smash It Up' and the dripping with candelabra goth keyboard chime of 'I Just Can't Be Happy Today' maintained their varied musical approach. The album caught the imagination of the punk movement that was now re-emerging as the more rudimentary second wave and was the band's first chart record.

Their righteous 1979 *Old Grey Whistle Test* appearance remains an iconic moment in punk rock. The band performed in all their chaotic glory. Vanian flitted around like a debonair vampire whilst Scabies was a blur of drum trills and the Captain seemed rather inebriated while shouting 'we're a punk band' down the mic. New bassist, Algy Ward, played along, utterly bemused by the chaos unfolding around him.

---

482 Captain Sensible to John Robb.

Further exploiting this dark side and Vanian's pioneering sense of the dark, the band's next album, released in November 1980, was the gothic-drenched *The Black Album*. This was the first time that Vanian's vampire Victoriana began to dominate, and his influence can be heard all over the album as they moved away from their punkier rushes. Their new dark-tinged, jaunty vaudeville was perfectly captured on 'Waiting for the Blackout'. Similarly, the lush melodic 'History of The World Part One' provided a glorious vehicle for Vanian's rich voice. The real statement of the album was the ambitious seventeen-minute-long song, 'Curtain Call', that sprawled across one whole side. This was a track that exorcised Vanian's theatrical demons as well as the Captain's love of prog rock. For Vanian, this was a defining release:

> By the time we got to *The Black Album*, we had all realised our songwriting strengths and where we were going. It all came together so well. We were pushing boundaries and it was a very exciting time.
>
> Recording 'Curtain Call' was a move that could have buried us. We were a band that was known for doing songs that were fast, full of energy and under three minutes long. Then suddenly you've got this seventeen-minute track, laden with atmospherics. We saw it as being truthful to who we were and hopefully, our audience would see that and, of course, they did. We weren't writing music for other people and their approval. We were just writing good music for the sake of good music. With 1982's *Strawberries*, we were bringing in all the music that had influenced us in the first place. We're all heavily influenced by the first garage bands of the '60s like The Seeds, The Shadows of Knight, The Doors, Strawberry Alarm Clock and hundreds of others. Then there's obviously MC5 and The Stooges, while Captain is heavily influenced by prog bands and Terry Riley and all kinds of odd stuff. He also loved Bolan and glam and all those influences just seemed to bubble up and it became *Strawberries*.[483]

Sensible himself was now a bona fide solo pop star with a faintly ridiculous number one with his cover of Rodgers and Hammerstein's 'Happy Talk' from the *South Pacific* musical. It was a long way away from Vanian's more gothic vision for the band and, added to the Captain's solo commitments, saw the guitarist quit.

Post-Sensible, The Damned became a self-fulfilling prophecy. They would finally have the biggest hit of their career at the height of goth in 1986 with their cover of Barry Ryan's 1969 single, 'Eloise', which swiftly lodged at number three in the charts. The band, then built around the core of Rat Scabies and Dave Vanian, amped up gothic. Vanian was now in full on Byron mode that saw him draped in gothic finery; dressed in frills and leather and with an added white streak in his hair. According to Rat Scabies, this was the era of 'selling Vanian by the pound'. The singer saw different:

---

483 Dave Vanian to Dave Jennings, Louder Than War.

I was always a big Scott Walker fan. That was why I did 'Eloise', because of all those grandiose melodramatic '60s songs, I loved all those. I thought it was a shame no one was doing those anymore. My main influences have always been film music. It's something I have more of than anything else, and it tends to filter in. I tend to think of moods in music which is different than writing a three-minute pop song. Things like John Barry, Morricone, John Carpenter. It's endless. [484]

The 1985 album, *Phantasmagoria*, came resplendent with its gothic album cover photo of Susie Bick [485]in Kensal Green Cemetery. The Damned were now a central pillar to the emergent goth culture that their singer had unwittingly pioneered and stylised a decade before. Driven by 'Eloise', the album reached number eleven and was the band's highest-charting album to date.

Brian James, whose vision and songs had created the band, watched on in admiration as they were achieving the biggest successes of their career:

> I think they've done great. Some of what I hear by them appeals to me and some doesn't, but I've always admired them for doing what they wanted to do. Full marks to them for that.
>
> They kept the true spirit of punk and I think that's why so many people love them. The key thing with The Damned is that they kept changing, they never conformed and that's what punk was always meant to be really. They also picked up fans through their different periods which I feel makes them important too. They had the original punk fans. Then they were one of the most important gothic bands. Then there was their sort of psychedelic period and their comebacks.

After 1986's weaker *Anything* album, the Captain re-joined the band as they maintained a cult status. Losing Rat Scabies for the second time, they employed a new drummer – Pinch – who somehow managed to organise this most chaotic of bands into a machine. They then released *Not of This Earth* (1995), *Grave Disorder* (2001), *So, Who's Paranoid?* (2008) and gradually inched their way back up. More recently, The Damned have hit a purple patch, easily selling out London's Royal Albert Hall in 2016; a venue that was made for them with all its historical theatrical gothic grandeur. The band even scored a 2018 top ten Tony Visconti produced album, *Evil Spirits,* and have become unlikely national treasures. Indeed, they have been ambitious enough to end 2019 with the Vanian-driven theatrical gig 'An Evening of a Thousand Vampires' at the London Palladium; perhaps the most gothic gig of them all and a culmination of his unique and influential vision.

> It was just sheer accident, not by design, that we all ended up in the same group. I think that's what set us apart. Basically, other bands were all like-minded individuals and consequently looked the same as The Clash, and The Jam… but

484 Dave Vanian to Vive Le Rock Magazine.

485 Future wife of Nick Cave and the owner of the leading gothic high-end fashion line The Vampire's Wife.

we were all extremely different from each other in every way. Where we came together was our love of music. In fact, it's still the same now; Captain and I like each other but we really don't have that much in common. But when it comes to music, it's a magical thing. It's a weird thing, and I think it's the very differences that make The Damned work. That's why the music was pulled in all different directions too. It was quite a democratic process. There's very rarely any arguing. It's like what sounds good rather than who wrote what.[486]

The Damned were forged by punk, yet inspired and pioneered much of goth. Throughout their zigzagging, high octane, vaudeville career, their Vampiric frontman has continued to rise above it all, and from the coffin, with the loveable madness of his black clad, gothic cool, which made him one of the true pioneers of the form.

---

486 Dave Vanian to Vive Le Rock magazine.

Chapter 15

RIDICULE IS NOTHING TO BE SCARED OF

Adam Ant

In the forbidden zone just after punk, there were all kinds of heavy manners of wild and wonderful performers acting out their personal psychodrama and dark art on stage and creating new music from fringe ideas. None were more captivating and darkly intense as Adam Ant.

At his first show at the London ICA in May 1977, Adam was a striking individual who hid his handsome face behind a leather mask and performed 'Beat My Guest' to a shocked audience. From that point onwards he upped the ante.

With his kabuki face paint, intense performances and the freak zone of ant music for sex people, he presented unique and confrontational ideas with strange songs laced with sex and a twisted sense of humour. Adam and the Ants were a spectacle and the ultimate in underground music. His image and music was to have a profound influence on the goth alternative that was beginning to coalesce at his gigs and the eventual king of the wild frontier was going to have a big impact on the scene.

Emerging from the Big Bang of punk, The Ants [487] S&M aesthetic was primed for delivery. With an intense theatricality, their early period is arguably the template for what subcultural treats were to come. Similarly, Adam's pop stardom in the early 1980s, complete with a technicolour tribal pop, would become the gateway drug for a generation of young music fans who would go on to embrace the emerging goth culture; the same culture that had taken so many of its cues from the early Ants.

His early performances were quite unlike anything else at the time. There are striking images of Adam as a fetishistic work of art, dressed in full leather, kilts, Seditionaries clothes, black lipstick, *Clockwork Orange* eye makeup and that kabuki face paint. Topping it all were his defiantly non-punk Romani curls. His challenging appearance combined with provocative performances to create a powerful impact.

In the wake of Sex Pistols' breakthrough and after Siouxsie and the Banshees finally got signed, the early incarnation of Adam and the Ants inhabited the true punk underground. They were the only band left who seemed to understand Malcolm McLaren's 'Leaving the 20th century' rhetoric, with Adam a willing disciple of the visionary manager's ethos and ideas, as well as being a furtive regular at his King's Road shop.[488]

Already an astonishing performer with a manic and dangerous edge, Adam seemed to embrace the sex and danger at the heart of punk, further developing its provocative

---

487 The initial lineup of Adam (vocals and occasional guitar), Andy Warren (bass), Dave Barbe (drums), Mark Ryan (guitar) and Jordan (vocals) was known as The Ants until October 1977 when they became Adam and the Ants.

488 'Leaving the 20th Century' was the Situationist slogan and a book about the vibrant anti-art, anti-capitalist energy of the original International Situationist texts. The philosophy was integral to McLaren and his vision of punk.

nature and creating a goth prototype. Pushing buttons, he sang of Italian futurists and masochism, and sex as art, on songs such as 'Physical (You're So)' , 'Beat My Guest','Whip in My Valise','Ligotage' and 'Bathroom Function'.

The inner core of Ant fans that began to appear at the shows were a heavy duty and well-dressed crew of travelling rogues who followed the band up and down the country. The Soldier Ants were a clandestine gung-ho gang of real characters who were created a S.E.X. spectacle, sporting early post-punk Mohicans, kung-fu slippers, makeup, heavy duty belts, Ants or Seditionaries t-shirts, all of which were exquisitely documented in *Vague* fanzine. Typical of those fans was Stuart Green: 'I was one of these people who followed Adam all over the north of England. Ee by gum, have I got some stories to tell of fighting skinheads whilst wearing mascara . . .'[489]

The band oozed a delicious, erotic elixir of darkness, making them clear precursors to the sex and death cult of goth. Their confrontational imagery and music would inspire Killing Joke, Southern Death Cult, Sex Gang Children and many others who would pick up on the powerful impact of the early Ants gigs and the tribal rhythms of their next period.

Fittingly, it was right at the initial spark of punk on Nov 6 1975, whilst still called Stuart Goddard, that Adam Ant became the first person whose life was changed by the incoming revolution. That night Stuart was playing bass in a band called Bazooka Joe which had formed earlier that year. An art school band, they were dealing a rock'n'roll revival on the fringes of the London pub rock circuit. They featured founder Danny Kleinman[490] and future members of punk band the Vibrators; Pat Collier and John Ellis, the latter of whom was a school friend of Adam's. Another band member was Dan Barson, whose brother, Mike gained fame as the keyboard player for Madness.

Bazooka Joe were surfing on the fringes of the brief rock'n'roll revival that had arrived alongside glam after the Bo Diddley, Jerry Lee Lewis, Little Richard, Bill Haley and His Comets, The Glitter Band and the MC5 Wembley Arena show on 5 August 1972. Malcolm McLaren was also at the concert, selling clothes from a stall and representing his then 1950s clothes shop, Let It Rock. McLaren and the small coterie of new rock'n'roll fans loved the sex and wildness of the form and the dandified flamboyance of the Teds themselves. For him, it defied the worthiness of 1970s prog which he saw as sexless and dull.

The 1950s revival also fed into the glam gene pool and the likes of Roxy Music, whose '50s on steroids camp saw Bryan Ferry with his own take on the quiff and a certain glitz twist on their louche styling. The brothel creeper shoe[491] had also re-entered the nation's pop culture. Bazooka Joe were part of this artful and playful take on the 1950s.

---

489 Stuart Green to John Robb.

490 Kleinman went on to design all the title sequences in Bond films.

491 Brothel creepers, or 'creepers', are the famous British shoes with a thick crepe soul. They were initially created for desert warfare during World War II to prevent troops from burning their feet in the sand. They became fashionable in the post-war period before being adopted by the Teds and then punks.

The band were kind of like a Sha Na Na-esque rock'n'roll thing.[492] We did songs that were all about B movie/science fiction films. It was very intelligent, but it was during that fucking awful pub rock period, where there was no one any good apart from Dr Feelgood. We had a small following including these 15-year-old kids who would become Madness.

At the time I was at Hornsey art school. Sid Vicious was there as well. I've got a book of Sid's stuff somewhere. He was good, actually. So many rock bands come out of art schools. They were the only place to get subsidised to create. To survive I also did loads of jobs like a groundsman, demolition – fucking anything to pay for the band. Out of that I bought my Precision bass. The art schools were a cultural jolt and a big part of our history. Ray Davies had been to my college. Paul Simonon, who is a great painter, went to art college, Pete Townshend, John Lennon, Stuart Sutcliffe, Glen Matlock as well because you would get subsidised to create art and also make music because you had time to start a band up.[493]

That November evening, the support band was a new band called Sex Pistols making their debut gig. The young group bristled with attitude as they made the short walk from their rehearsal room on London's nearby Denmark Street to St Martin's Art College on Charing Cross Road.

The tiny, fifty-capacity top-floor room in the college saw a few students milling around. That evening they would accidentally witness the moment that would change the sound of the 1970s. The startling-looking young support group had already done a quick soundcheck that made a big impression on Adam:

I'll never forget it. They came in as a gang. They looked like they couldn't give a fuck about anybody. Jonesy was tiny and looked like a young Pete Townshend. Glen Matlock had paint-spattered trousers and a woman's pink leather top on. I watched them soundcheck and then play. Malcolm was at the front, orchestrating them, telling them where to stand.

There weren't many other people there, about a dozen including Vivienne Westwood, Michael Collins and Jordan who all worked at Sex and Andy Czekowski.[494] They did 'Substitute' and 'Whatcha Gonna Do About It?' with the lyrics changed to: 'I want you to know that I hate you, baby'. Then John lost interest. He'd eat sweets, pull them out and suck them and just spit them out. He just looked at the audience, glazed. It was mesmerising. [495]

Malcolm McLaren was already thinking outside the box. The tried and tested pub circuit with its mundane beer culture was not for him. His early manifesto would fit the future goth scene as well:

It was not necessarily a plan to play art colleges first and avoid the pubs. I just hated beer. And that's all you got in those stinking pubs in Anglo-Saxon land. Art school preached a noble pursuit of failure. It was part of the legacy laid down

---

492 Sha Na Na were an American rock'n'roll revival band whose short appearance at Woodstock festival in 1969 sparked a revival of the interest in the1950s in the USA.

493 Adam Ant to John Robb.

494 Future manager of The Damned, he also opened the Roxy punk club in 1976.

495 Adam Ant to Jon Savage.

by William Morris: art for art's sake, which we attempted to create and indeed succeeded at one level. We made ugliness beautiful.[496]

Inevitably Sex Pistols quarrelled with the headliners. There was tension; a generation gap separating the 20-year-olds from the 18-year-olds. For Adam, though, the gig was a life-changing moment. An astute observer of pop culture, he felt the electricity of the young band. That night, he would become the first person from outside the Pistols' inner circle to be converted to the manifesto of punk rock. He would soon quit Bazooka Joe and re-emerge six months later in a new band briefly called the B-sides, which was then renamed The Ants, fronted by the reinvented Adam Ant.

*****

Born in Marylebone on 3 November 1954, Goddard was an only child of Romani descent.[497] His father, Leslie Goddard, had served in the Royal Air Force and worked as a chauffeur, while his mother, Betty Kathleen Smith, was an embroiderer for the designer Norman Hartnell.[498] Adam remains proud of his background:

> I have my foot in the gutter and my head in the stars. I never liked this dole queue martyrdom of punk. Downtown Abbey? I say, 'Fuck you!' My grandmother was in service as well, and I say, 'Fuck you', to the middle classes who didn't give a fuck about these people.'[499]

Adam grew up in the De Walden buildings - a communal block surrounded by the wealthier St John's Wood, until his parents divorced when he was seven. His mother then brought him up while now working as a domestic cleaner for people such as Paul McCartney, who lived nearby.

At primary school, he was a difficult child with serious anger issues who once threw a brick through the headteacher's window. His saving grace was being placed under the supervision of a quite brilliant teacher, Joanna Saloman. She was impressed by a charcoal drawing he had done and encouraged him to develop his abilities in art. Adam would always credit her as the first person to recognise his artistic skill. It was her son, Nick Saloman, who also went to the same school and was the future underground psych musician, Bevis Frond who taught Adam how to play guitar.

> He was two years older than me and a hippie but didn't take drugs. I was into soul and reggae and he introduced me to Hendrix, Argent, Queen and music like that. He was very instrumental in that he taught me a lot about all that kind of music and how to play.[500]

After school, Adam attended the Hornsey College of Art, where he initially studied graphic design. Taking several specialised courses on Futurism, Feminism and the

---

496 Malcom McLaren to John Robb.

497 Adam was one of many proud Romani, tracing his roots back to the wandering tribes who left Rajasthan in India centuries ago.

498 Clothes designer for the Royal Family.

499 Adam Ant to John Robb.

500 Adam Ant to John Robb.

History of Art, it was the erotic arts given by Peter Webb that had a big effect on him in his second year.[501] It was a direction that would infuse his future evocative music. The college's inspirational tutors were not confined to Peter Webb, but also Allen Jones[502] the artist, whose own work was highly erotic. Jones made artwork and sculptures of women dressed in high heels with rubber outfits and whips in their hands. His course concentrated on sexual imagery in artwork which would leave a lasting impression on Adam and his striking graphics for badges, record sleeves and posters for the band a few years later. The courses opened up a whole new world with a new set of images and ideas. He devoured book after book and looked at hundreds of slides, utterly fascinated by the subject:

> I was studying pornography in art with the leaders in the form. In 1974, Peter Webb had gone to private collections around the world to see the works by the great masters that are never normally seen because they are judged to be too erotic. He wrote a book about it called *The Erotic Arts* that I thought was marvellous and was a big influence on me. Hans Belmer[503] and also many female artists affected me as well.[504]

In 1975, Adam married fellow art school student Carol Mills, moving in with her parents in Muswell Hill. It was a suffocating situation that, when coupled with the seismic effect of that November's Pistols' gig and his instinctive lurch towards the incoming punk movement, would manifest itself in a nervous breakdown. Adam was diagnosed with anorexia nervosa and attempted suicide.

In escaping his home, his band and his marriage, he kept himself alive.

After discovering Sex on the King's Road, Adam became fascinated with their increasingly esoteric, erotic and confrontational designs. He was also secretly in love with Jordan. With her dominatrix image and pop culture smarts, the face of the shop was his ideal woman. Adam sent her a series of anonymous love letters that eventually saw him publicly outed, as the late Jordan recalled:

> I was sent all these letters and I still have them. There were about fifty of them and they were anonymous. One day we were in the shop and there was someone in there looking a bit nervous and Michael Collins, who managed the shop, said 'I bet that's who has been writing them'. We asked him to write his name and immediately recognised his handwriting. He confessed and told me about his band. I went to see them play their second-ever gig on the King's Road at the Man In The Moon pub. The gig was a disaster and all the audience left, but I thought it was brilliant. Adam looked stunning. He had a bondage mask on and was dressed in leather and rubber. He was magnetic and I became his manager.[505]

---

501 Peter Webb has written an academic study of the Erotic Arts and has frequently been called to give evidence at trials on pornography.

502 Allen Jones RA is a British pop artist best known for his paintings, sculptures, and lithography. He was awarded the Prix des Jeunes Artistes at the 1963 Paris Biennale. He is a Senior Academician at the Royal Academy of Arts.

503 German artist from the 1930s known for his life-size statues of pubescent female dolls.

504 Adam Ant to John Robb.

505 Jordan to John Robb.

With their new manager in place, the band developed their sound and image with an intense sexuality and a visual nod to sadomasochism and the more outré items from the Sex shop. In 1977, Adam was on a creative rollercoaster. There are endless bootlegs of demos of quirky songs, written during a creative hyperdrive. Most of these songs have never been released. They are endlessly fascinating, imbued with an artful invention, intelligence and a quirky structure that saw them stray far away from the rest of the post-Pistols pack. Adam's music, presence and image were a realised version of the artful erotic in which he was so fascinated. This heavy duty intensity was, by turn, embraced by the young punks who were looking for a new underground godhead to plug the gap left by the fast-imploding Sex Pistols.

With Jordan sometimes performing with Adam on stage, singing/screaming the vocals on 'Lou',[506] the pair of them would provide a terrifyingly, yet brilliant, stage spectacle and style, creating a presence and genuine connection into the heart of punk.

In 1977, the Derek Jarman[507] film *Jubilee* captured the early Ants on camera. *Jubilee* was the acclaimed director's own personal interpretation of punk. Jordan took on the starring role and Adam performed a physical, twitching version of 'Plastic Surgery', dislocating his knee in the process. The film's freakishness was a snapshot of the decadence and madness of the mid-1970s that would partially feed into the primordial goth soup. *Jubilee* is an awkward yet captivating timepiece. The anarchic movie had an awkward gestation period that saw the Banshees bail when Siouxsie saw the bad press coming and they only appear on a flickering TV screen in the final cut. Despite this, it has its own energy, as a defiant Adam explains:

> I got so much stick for being in that film. I got slated by the music press, who considered us as some sort of jerk-off band, part of Derek Jarman's imagination. Malcolm McLaren said to me at the time, 'I'm not sure about Derek Jarman, he's a bit arty but he's the only person with the guts and the energy to make the fucking film'. Derek didn't make any money but he was a very artistic person. For me, *Jubilee* gets better with age. It's now a classic.[508]

Another rising star in the film was Toyah[509] with a shaved head and wearing rubber waders playing the part of a character called 'Mad':

> It's a wonderful film made by an incredibly sensitive man. It was his take on the early punk scene that had happened in Andrew Logan's warehouse party which was full of very colourful characters next door to him on Butlers Wharf in London.[510] I think Derek was a very human person and was not scared of

---

506 A song about the disappointment of a recent Lou Reed concert in London.

507 The late film director whose films such as *Sebastiane* and *Caravaggio* explored avant-garde and historical homosexuality. He was an ardent campaigner for gay rights and an outspoken and fearless figure, both artistically and politically.

508 Adam Ant to John Robb.

509 The future singer, Toyah Wilcox.

510 Sex Pistols had played a famous party at the flat of sculptor and performance artist Andrew Logan, on Valentine's Day 1976.

facing anything. If he was alive today, the work he would be doing would be phenomenal with that explosive energy and that ability to project.[511]

Bizarre, good-looking and arriving without anyone's permission, Adam was, of course, hated by some of the music press. Some of the early reviews were breathtaking in their vitriol, creating a siege mentality that only added to the defiant micro scene that was building around him and capable of selling out big venues in London, with ease. With a lineup beginning to solidify, the Ants were sounding like a serious proposition. The addition of a new young drummer, Dave Barbarossa, was key:

> I had played a gig as a support band to Adam and the Ants when they started. A few days later, there was a knock at my front door. Adam and Jordan were stood there. Everyone was open-mouthed. They must have been the two freakiest-looking people in the country at the time. They looked amazing. They absolutely blew my fucking mind. I had never seen anything like it in my life! Can you imagine? I'm fresh from school and I open the front door and Adam and Jordan are there all in black leather saying, 'You're playing the drums for me'. They were like Martians asking me to play with them and I could hardly say no![512]

With the addition of charismatic 17-year-old guitar player, Matthew Ashman, joining the band they now had the perfect lineup locking in with the quirky intensity of Andy Warren on bass. The early demos were quickly ditched and were replaced by new material. Finally signed by Decca, the band's 1978 debut single, 'Young Parisians', was a surprising release. While many expected angular noise, what they got was a jazzy, music hall, dark cabaret lilt. This was a curious, yet brilliant, pop oddity with a quirky melody and tongue-in-cheek lyrics.

> 'Young Parisians' was about being on a train and there was a French bird that I liked and met, and she liked Patti Smith, who was popular at the time. I had also seen this film about getting nipples pierced, and about Andy Warhol, and I was sitting on the train fantasising, and it all came from there.[513]

Adam and the Ants were already very much on their own (war)path. They were pushing away from punk cliché and into their own Ant world.

> To me, punk rock was never about Dr. Martens and drab clothes or uniforms. It was about high fashion and the working-class looking sharp and different. A new attitude. That was also the case with the music. Everybody was trying something different.[514]

The band looked great: DIY-bizarre. They matched their music by looking sharp and angular. This was a style that, like all great bands, perfectly matched their music.

> It doesn't cost you anything to dress up, get a shirt – do it up: the boots I made myself – the makeup was very inexpensive. The hair would be a thousand quid if you went into some chi-chi barbers with a picture of someone's hair and said, 'Can you do this?'. But the thing is, you could get it done for fuck all if you had

---

511 Toyah to John Robb.

512 Dave Barbarossa to John Robb.

513 Adam to John Robb.

514 Dave Barbarossa to John Robb.

developed it yourself, because it was part of your style, part of your sartorial thing. I would think about the great slogans on the Anarchy shirts from the Sex shop. Malcolm put these phrases on the shirts, and we would say, 'What's that French shit!?'. They were the champion nickers, but they used it brilliantly and they used it right.

As a punk, I didn't adhere to the Seditionaries' way of doing things. Malcolm was an influence but I never wore things like the bondage straps in the normal way. The clothes were not disposable either. They were permanent. Everything I have ever done, from the clothes to the graphics I have kept it all.

Now signed to Robin Scott from M's new label, Do It Records, the band released their second single 'Xerox' in 1979 with it flip-side - the S&M and Allen Jones-influenced track, 'Whip in My Valise'. The track's anthemic, sexy darkness was a harbinger of sex goth and cemented their status as the last great cult band in first wave punk.

Our second single, 'Xerox'[515] was about the idea that you take from the best and then make it yours. It was about David Bowie, in a nice way. I felt that it was a dedication to him and how he had made a career out of it.[516]

Adam's sex and S&M fetish artwork for the band flyers, posters, badges and cult collectable pin badges was like a secret code into another world. A world that only sex-warrior aficionados could understand making it like a punk rock Polari.[517] Dave Barbarossa was impressed by Adam's attention to detail and creative and also his live intensity.

Adam was prolific. Brilliant. It was like playing for a God. He had such confidence and bottle to do what he did. He would look at me and say, 'You're a soldier, I'm relying on you, don't fuck up'. You would go through a brick wall for him, which you did at the gigs, with all the bottles and the gob. 'Keep playing, keep playing', he would say. And we would because he was a leader.

Gigs were like a derby football match. Although I was there to do a job and concentrate, I felt like everybody else, nervous and excited. Maybe the skinheads were coming to cause trouble that night? Who was going to get carted off in an ambulance? Would we get through it without the show being stopped?

We had some really extreme fans and Adam was completely wild when he performed. It was quite something to see. He could be menacing, intense, unforgiving, merciless – an absolutely fascistic, dictator frontman. It was his alter ego. By day he used to wear that green mac and National Health specs and be all meek and mild. At the gig, he would start putting his makeup on and do press-ups and punch the wall and then bang! He would go onstage and go berserk.[518]

The artful defiance and insect intensity was spelled out on their own manifesto.

---

515 'Xerox', was released in 1979 was a more punkish affair than the debut.

516 Adam Ant to John Robb.

517 From the Italian word *parlare*, Polari is a cant slang prominent in the then gay subculture and also used by actors, circus and fairground showmen, sex workers and criminals. It possibly dates back as far as the 16th century and has a curious connection with Punch and Judy, who traditionally used Polari to converse.

518 Dave Barbarossa to John Robb.

We are 4 in number; we call our music Antmusic; we perform and work for a future age, we are optimists and in being so we reject the 'blank generation' ideal; we acknowledge the fanzine as the only legitimate form of journalism, and consider the 'established' press to be little more than talentless clones, guilty of extreme cerebral laziness; we believe that a writer has the right to draw upon any source material, however offensive or distasteful it might seem, in pursuance of his work; we are in tune with nothing; we have no interest in politics; we identify with no movement or sect other than our own; there are no boxes for us or our music, we are interested in Sexmusic, entertainment, action and excitement, and anything young and new; we abhor the hippy concept and all the things that surround the rock n roll scene; we admire the true individual; and above all the destruction of the social and sexual taboo; finito muchachos. [519]

The idiosyncratic band cemented their dangerous cult status with their astounding, yet critically damned, October 1979 debut album, *Dirk Wears White Sox*. An innovative and darkly unsettling work, *Dirk* is a gallery of grotesques and art school rock at its very best, full of strange brew atmospheres and jarring music that would be a key influence on goth. The bass-driven songs combined disco and punk funk rhythms with experimental lyrics and strange short stories. The songs were laced with dark humour and a taboo-challenging artfulness, all sung in the most English of voices.

It was recorded in an old school studio in Primrose Hill. We just went straight in and did it. I had to produce it myself because no one else wanted to at the time. I didn't know what I was doing, but I had the sound in my head.

It just about sits in the post-punk era. The songs are very simple like Joy Division and that kind of stuff. Songs like 'Family of Noise' and 'Animals and Men' were basic but, fuck me, the vocals were difficult. They made us stand apart. We recorded the backing tracks live and I put the vocals on after. I was listening to the Beach Boys, the Byrds and The Beatles at the time – I fucking love them.

If you listen to the voices on *Dirk*, there are complex three-part harmonies. I've never done harmonies that complicated since then.[520] Songs like 'Cartrouble Part 1' seemed a real challenge to people, but I always liked its long intro. I had all these demos like an artist doing a sketch. Once the demo is done, it's just a question of finishing the idea off. Once the paint is down, it's done. Metaphorically, you have to know what colours are right and build it up. It's where you take it that counts. When you have finally recorded the song, it's done, finished.

Making that record was a labour of love. I thought it was going to be a number one and I was thoroughly disappointed when it didn't make it.[521]

Lyrically the album was fascinating. It contained the hilariously spiteful 'Catholic Day' about the assassination of Kennedy, the curious 'The Day I Met God', the almost autobiographical 'Family Of Noise'. It name-checked the Futurist Manifesto and the Italian movement's leading lights on 'Animals and Men', where Adam celebrated 'Marinetti! Boccioni! Carra! Balla! Palazzeschi!'

---

519 From Adam and the Ants Manifesto, 1978.

520 Adam Ant to John Robb.

521 Adam Ant to John Robb .

There was a lot of art school influence in there. At college, I had studied Futurism. I was learning this amazing stuff. I was working with Palazzeschi before he died.[522] I was very influenced by these guys but not everyone understood what I was doing.[523]

Musically, the debut album was sophisticated. Adam understood that the band were working to their core strengths:

Dave came from the soul boy period and maintained his own style. If you listen to 'Cleopatra', he made that track with his drumming. He was so tight. If you watch him drum, he has a straight back, straight as a rod, which is the sign of a good drummer. Andy Warren would play bass with a metal plectrum. He could be intense. He used to belt me in front of the audience when we were pushing each other around on stage. One day he went smash! right on my jawbone which was a great performance.[524]

Integral to the energy of *Dirk Wears White Sox* was the wild and carefree young guitar player, Matthew Ashman.

When I recently listened back to the album, I released how much I loved him. When we were touring at the time, it was very intense. We were in the trenches together. He was like my little brother, a little Norman Wisdom. He looked great. We liked to dress good but with Matthew, if they had designed the perfect good-looking punk rocker in a leather jacket and jeans, they would come up with him. 'Why do I have to turn up for rehearsals!?' he would say. 'Because you are a professional!' we would reply.

He would have these party tricks that he could never get right, like he would get a fag out and say, 'I'm gonna chuck this in the air and catch it right in my mouth. If you don't believe me, watch . . .' and he would always miss and then do it again and again, and after about forty goes give up.

He was this pretty little Sid Vicious; gorgeous, beautiful, but his attitude was pure punk fucking rocker, and he's now dead and that's not fucking right. They were all great guys – the previous guitarist, Johnny Bivouac, and bass player Andy Warren. We would take the piss out of each other all the time, but if the National Front turned up and we had a ruck, we stuck together. I remember a Rock Against Racism gig when 200 British Movement turned up and 'cos we were going nowhere, we couldn't be beaten.[525]

The album was perhaps too artful and sexual for the more monochromatic post-punk climate and the resulting reviews were mixed.

The *NME* didn't even take the trouble to review the album on its own. It was shared with Throbbing Gristle and the headline said 'the burks that lurk in the corner of your psyche,' – that fucking hammered me. The *NME* was powerful then, but the album did 20,000 in the first week and was the first independent album chart number one.

---

522 Italian Futurist poet who died in 1974 and was famous for his grotesque and fantastical poems.

523 Adam Ant to John Robb.

524 Adam Ant to John Robb.

525 Adam Ant to John Robb.

The press didn't like the S&M stuff. They didn't like my humour. They didn't like my graphics. That music journalist Nick Kent was the worst, he wrote, 'If Adam can get away with S&M crap then he can get away with anything'. But these writers, because they were so far up Joy Division's arse, had never heard of Allen Jones or Andy Warhol or the pop art movement. They couldn't understand what I was doing. It was not even in their zone. 'Cartrouble' was about my dad, who was a chauffeur. He got a new car to drive people around in and got up really early to go to work. He was always dressed in his cap, and he took a life of shit. People treated like him like a subhuman. The music journalists would never understand that world.[526]

The song the music press misunderstood the most was 'Deutscher Girls', missing the camp humour of the lyrics and making lazy assumptions.

The press claimed it was a Nazi song but the inspiration came from the Mel Brooks film *The Producers*.[527] What you write about doesn't make you that person. It was also a song about Hitler's niece who refused his advances. She killed herself and it set him off on his path. My question was about the death of this girl and if it hadn't happened, could it have saved the world?
I was interested in taboo subjects but if you do a song like that then everyone claims you are a Nazi – oh come on! have you never seen the film, *The Producers*! I'm not having the Nazi claims. My old man saw Belsen. Dave Barbarossa was from Mauritius, and as someone with Romani roots, I find that sort of thing offensive.
Vivienne Westwood talked to me about the Nazi thing when I got a lot of misdirected stick for it. She had the shirts with swastikas on them in the shop. This interviewer had asked her about it, and she killed the guy stone dead when she said, 'we are not afraid of Nazis in this shop…'[528]

In a sense, the press misconceptions only hardened the band's reputation. The punks saw the Ants as the last great outsider band, and they continued to grow in cult status with the lack of a major deal adding to their mystery and exclusivity. However, it made life more difficult for the ever-ambitious Adam.

It's all very well being the anti-hero on the outside, but, because of the press, I couldn't get signed to Sony for three fucking years. You really need the press when you start. Everyone else was getting signed – even the Banshees. We were the last band to get a record deal.[529]

Put down by the press, ignored by the record labels and trapped in fierce cultdom, Adam was at a crossroads. Being the number one bizarro act in the country meant intense celebratory gigs but the flipside was violence. In the suffocating conformity of the late 1970s, the UK had been shaken up by punk and aggro was commonplace. At gigs, the band's pioneering image and music often clashed with the strait-laced locals and by the autumn of 79 the band was falling apart. Adam and Dave Barbe

526 Adam Ant to John Robb.

527 Mel Brooks' 1968 black comedy satire was his directorial debut and about a theatre owner and accountant who, as part of a scam, decide to stage the worst musical centring on Adolf Hitler and the Nazis to make a flop and claim back the insurance.

528 Adam Ant to John Robb.

529 Adam Ant to John Robb.

demo'd up some never released funk tracks and, apart from a one-off show at the Electric Ballroom on New Year's Eve, it looked like the end. Believing he could do so much more, the singer knew he had to make changes.

On the 27 October 1979, Malcolm McLaren and Adam Ant had both attended the same wedding in London. The wily ex-Pistols manager asked what he was up to. Adam talked about the *Dirk* album and how it had failed to break out of cult status. Malcolm was intrigued. He recognised that Adam just needed someone to light the touch paper. Six weeks later, he would become Adam's manager.

It was going to be a short-lived yet explosive ride.

Adam handed Malcolm a thousand quid in cash raised from the New Year's gig at London's Electric Ballroom to manage him for a month. In return, he received a cassette containing seventeen eclectic tracks and was told that it would help him understand the construction of songs and to use them to find his own style. The tape was a multi-coloured collection of musical brilliance from the likes of Elvis, the Village People and Buddy Holly.[530] It opened up the imagination and vista of pop potential that fired up Adam's mind and would eventually, after a long and tortured year, lead to the creation of a new Antmusic. Malcolm understood Adam's current complexity was too much for the mainstream and talked of Pirates and Native American warriors. He planted seeds of ideas that Adam would make his own.

> Malcolm was great. Him and Vivienne were always full of these sayings, 'Johnny Rotten is a poet. You won't learn anything from David Bowie, boy'. He then listened to *Dirk* all the way through. He would stop and say, 'What's that song about, boy?' and I would have to tell him, and he would say, 'Right, next one!'. 'The Day I Met God' – and the lyric bout the size of God's knob was a bit too much for him. Malcolm then looked at the record sleeve and said, 'What's this cover?' and I said, 'It's a woman walking . . .' He said, 'No, no, no! You got good looks and muscles. Put that on the cover'. He said, 'What do you want to be? A cult? That's all right, but if you want to go to the top you are going the wrong way about it – put your face on the cover and in colour.
>
> No one in the business had taken any notice of me until then but Malcolm was really interested in what I was doing. He talked to me about songwriting and the tricks like scanning the syllables in the songs. He said, 'when Elvis sings, 'Since my baby left me…', listen… it's six then seven syllables – listen to these singers and the way they sing'. He then pointed out the song structure – verse-chorus-solo chorus-verse. He said, 'listen to 'Blue Moon' by Elvis and sing it. All this would eventually feed into 'Dog Eat Dog' and the new songs. It simplified what we did and made it into songs.[531]

The rest of the Ants were initially bemused by the sudden appearance of the legendary architect of punk in their lives:

---

530 The full track listing was as follows: 'Wipe Out' – The Surfaris, 'No Problem' – Chet Baker, 'He's The Fatman' – The Hawks, 'Mystery Train' – Elvis Presley, 'Blue Moon' – Elvis Presley, 'YMCA' – Village People, 'Hot Dog' – Taps Miller, 'Cast Iron Arm' – Peanuts Wilson, 'Tear It Up' - Johnny Burnette, 'Hello, I'm Back Again' – Gary Glitter, 'Where Were You' – Lloyd Price, 'Broadway Jungle' – The Flames, 'Got To Pick A Pocket' – Ron Moody, 'I'm Not Tired' – Cliff Bennett, 'Rave On' – Buddy Holly, and crucially, Burundi Black and also Belly Dance Music from Farid El Atrache.

531 Adam Ant to John Robb.

I don't know exactly why Adam brought Malcolm McLaren in. To produce a video, I'd heard. We were rehearsing and we were going, 'Fucking hell! Malcolm McLaren is coming to see us – the godfather of punk'. And he came in, in an immaculate pin-striped suit and we thought, 'Fuck me, here's this geezer who gave us our lives. This is the geezer, the man!'. We played the set for him and he spoke to Adam. We were not involved. Then he came down to another rehearsal room, the one next to Swanky Modes in Camden Town, and came out with this revelatory thing which was, 'Why don't you let the band do the music, Adam, and you do the lyrics?'.[532]

Barbarossa was stunned at the prospect of the band being asked to write songs. They already had a songwriter with a vision and had never written their own material before.

Writing our own songs? This was a revolution. We were happy to play Adam's songs. We had done the album. We were a great band and Adam wrote great songs and suddenly, this other great bloke has come in and turned it upside down. Adam was as staggered by this as we were. I remember the silence in the room as we all took it in and Malcolm, looking from one person to another with that satanic grin he had.

Adam must have thought, 'That's Malcolm McLaren saying it, so he must be right'.

Then Malcolm very carefully siphoned us three off from Adam and gave us all this ethnic music to absorb and be influenced by. At the same time, he gave Adam books on pirates for lyrical content. Malcolm was very serious about what he was doing.[533]

The Machiavellian manager soon started to peel the band away from their leader. Scheming and creating - he had a cunning plan. And it now didn't involve Adam. The next rehearsal saw the band quit one by one in front of the singer who was left heartbroken by the mutiny.

We had tried writing with Adam for a couple of weeks and then Malcolm started to suggest to us that we should be in our own band and he would find another singer. Our heads were turned. Up till then, Adam had been the man, but here was Malcolm McLaren saying this. Malcolm put a lot of pressure on us to stand on our own two feet. I couldn't believe what was happening. I'd been given a chance to lead my own band by the geezer who invented Sex Pistols. So, we left Adam, which was heartbreaking. We went on to do Bow Wow Wow, which was great. But Adam trumped us because he is a great songwriter.[534]

The Ants without Adam were reconstructed by Malcolm as Bow Wow Wow. The new band were fronted by the 14-year-old Annabella Lwin who had been discovered singing in a laundrette. Part glorious technicolour tribal pop, part celebration of the power of pirated music and part dubious machination of the young singer, Bow Wow Wow were a culmination of Malcolm's new ideas that he had also been feeding

---

532 Dave Barbarossa to John Robb.

533 Dave Barbarossa to John Robb.

534 Dave Barbarossa to John Robb.

to Adam as well as being a front for Malcolm and Vivienne's new clothing collection – the pirate look.[535]

Meanwhile, Adam was left licking his wounds. Without his band of willing droogs, but with a perfect manifesto handed to him by punk's Fagin, he had two stark choices. One was to pack it in; the other was to move fast.

> At the time of the mutiny, when they left, it was annoying, but it ended up being good for me, and good for them as well. It gave them a chance to play in their own band. Matthew was a great guitar player. He needed to be heard and he also had that Mohican. It was the best Mohican there ever was and it needed to be seen.[536]

The night his band left him and distraught, he rang up Jordan who rushed to the singer's flat. She made it clear that there was only one man to turn to suggesting Adam recruit the young guitar player who had hung around the Sex shop and was part of punk's inner circle but was still waiting for his proper break. Adam leafed through Jordan's address book and set out across London with her, looking for a man called Marco and pushed a letter through his door.

After he had played the guitar for the Banshees at the iconic 100 Club gig in 1976, Marco had been in the almost-made-it lineup of punk band, The Models. They had a minor hit in 1977 with 'Freeze' before Marco, one of the few on the scene who had actually learned to play, moved on to the post-punk underground band, Rema Rema whose brilliantly obtuse art punk he had now lost interest in.

Marco had grander visions than being in the underground. A fan of Roxy Music, he was looking for a style revolution, an art school pop that was also mainstream. Something like the proper pop stars he had grown up with. The intriguing experiments of Rema Rema did not fit this vision.[537]

> After Rema Rema I thought, 'I don't want to do this anymore. I'm not arty or dark'. A week later Adam contacted me. I had seen the original Ants loads of times. Jordan was managing them then and I thought if Jordan is managing them, they must be really good, but it wasn't, so I forgot about them for some time.
> I'd been out all-night trying to get off with some girl who I never got off with. When I got home there was a note pushed through my door where I lived in Harrow with my mum and dad, saying, 'Call me on this number – Adam'. I knew him a bit but not that well. I was thinking, 'How did he know my address?' I phoned him up, and he said, 'What are you doing?' And I said, 'Nothing, why?!' He then said, 'Are you working with The Banshees?' and I said no, so he replied, 'That's good, because I'd like to talk to you about something'.
> He was cagey about it. He said there's a situation that's happened and we got to meet, and I'll tell you all about it. So I met him the next day, but it wasn't that clear.

---

535 Malcolm and Vivienne's rebel aesthetics and themes would fly past. From Teds to rockers to punks, they delved into historical highwaymen, pirates and buccaneers for inspiration. The pirate look was their first catwalk show and Vivienne followed this up with ethnic and primitive looks that she'd seen in the pages of National Geographic magazine.

536 Adam Ant to John Robb.

537 Rema Rema are well worth checking out. Their 'Feedback Song' is a great slice of dramatic feedback (from Marco) drenched piece of dark post-punk. They would become Wolfgang Press who also left a catalogue of great music.

I thought, 'I don't really want to join the Ants – that would be a real step backwards – but then again, maybe if I did join the Ants, I could change it, not go back into punk - make it something different. Maybe Adam doesn't want to go back to punk and maybe go forward?

Adam said, 'We had Malcolm giving us advice and I got thrown out of the band!' And I said, 'What!' This meeting was two days after he had been thrown out, and he was laughing about it. He said he walked into a rehearsal one morning and the band looked awkward. Mathew was the first to say, 'I don't want to be in the band anymore. . .' and Adam said ok and Lee said, 'I'm with Matthew,' and Adam was, like 'Oh fuck', a bit shell-shocked, then he said the immortal words: 'It looks like you and me Dave'. And Dave was like, 'Er, no!'

He said I'm thinking of not using the name and not doing any of those songs anymore. I said keep the name! It's your name and do some of the songs that are good. Then he started banging on about all these ideas that Malcolm had and gave me this cassette of stuff that Malcolm had made for him that they were supposed to steal all the best bits from.

I thought, fuck it we'll do it instead. Initially, Adam was a bit, 'I dunno about taking Malcolm's ideas'. And I said, 'Fuck it, if they are good, we'll have them . . . if you paid Malcolm a grand then the ideas are yours now!' We looked at Malcolm's notes and cassette of songs to listen to. We took the Burundi drums and the war chants, and we filled the rest of it in ourselves. We did it completely differently from Bow Wow Wow, although I liked them. We moved pretty fast as there was this whole kind of big thing with Adam trying not to be bitter and to not cause a rivalry. I didn't have any songs written that we could really change, so we started from scratch with two guitars. The very first one we came up started with a song title that Adam had called 'Kings of the Wild Frontier.'[538]

The pair quickly built a band and hit the road. The race with Bow Wow Wow was on.

We jettisoned *Dirk*, apart from two tracks, because I didn't really like the album. The Ants were now adding glam to punk rock and it was really working. We had this manager called Falcon Stuart;[539] who got us a deal with Sony pretty quick. I don't know what they thought they were signing. It was a really odd time. It was this transitional period when there was no more punk and the guys at the record companies were trying to find things that were punk but were also not punk. I think they thought they were signing a Killing Joke, who were quite big at the time. [540]

Meanwhile, Bow Wow Wow had got off to a head start and were first out of the blocks by a couple of weeks with July 1980's debut mini album [541] 'Your Cassette Pet'. The lead track, 'C30 C60 C90 Go!' was Malcolm's attempt at provoking the music industry that was, at the time, in meltdown over home taping. [542] The Burundi-driven drums and frantic melodies were filled with a crackling energy that may not have stormed the charts as expected but made the band widely discussed.

---

538 Marco Pirroni to John Robb.

539 Former manager of X Ray Spex.

540 Marco Pirroni to John Robb.

541 Regarded as a single by the UK charts due to its sole availability on cassette.

542 It was a cheeky song with lyrics from the manager about the joys of home taping - then the current bugbear of the music biz.

Bow Wow Wow were Malcolm McLaren at his most manipulative. The band, of course, looked striking; beautifully dressed in Vivienne's tricorn hats and her first post-punk collection of glam pirate threads and ethnic patterns. The music perfectly married Malcolm's concepts to Vivienne's clothes and Dave Barbarossa's drums and Lee Gorman's elastic bass playing. Mathew Ashman, who had the swagger and rock star arrogance, delivered fluid guitar lines that danced around Annabella's yelping, youthful vocals. Their musicality inspired many. One such admirer was John Frusciante, the future guitar player with Red Hot Chili Peppers, who bought a white Gretsch Falcon guitar in tribute to the one played by Ashman. Johnny Marr was also watching.

> One of the major charismatic guitar players of that time was Matthew Ashman. Every girl I knew was fucking in love with him in Bow Wow Wow. A lot of people when they went out to certain clubs at the weekend in Manchester looked like they were in Bow Wow Wow. His playing and style were key.[543]

Coming up quickly, though, were the new Adam and the Ants - would the audience dare go with their new bold technicolour pop vision?

> What we wanted to do was make pop records and sell singles, but Sony wanted a big cult band. They were a bit baffled and I said, 'No, look – remember the 70s, remember T. Rex? We don't think they were ironic or funny. We think they were great. Remember they sold lots of records and made loads of money? That's what we want to do. We've starved already.' In the middle of the meeting, label boss Maurice Oberstein came in and sat on the table and said, 'These are these guys who are doing the African drumming thing? 'Kings of the Wild Frontier'? great song – let them do what they want', and then walked out! And that was it!
> We wanted to make music like 'Virginia Plain' – which, when you heard it, you thought, 'What the fuck is this?!' We wanted to sound like we were from another planet and yet be totally accessible.[544]

As they swiftly worked up their ambitious new sound, they toyed with a new look. When it came to the pop apocalypse, Adam, consulting his notes from Malcolm, went down a decidedly more colourful route, both musically and stylistically. With his iconic white stripe on his face representing a warrior going to war, his hussar jacket from Bermans and Nathans costumers that was a nod to the 1968 *Charge of the Light Brigade* film starring David Hemmings and an added swashbuckling pirate style, his appearance matched the album's gleeful, musical brilliance.[545]

The band's new logo was the warrior Ant/Native American brave hybrid that was designed by former Bazooka Joe colleague Danny Kleinman and caught the new Ants. The debut July 1980 'King of the Wild Frontier' single grazed the bottom end of the chart but the band's breakthrough moment was their glorious performance

---

543 Johnny Marr to John Robb

544 Marco Pirroni to John Robb.

545 The famous Hussar jacket had previously been used by the actor David Hemmings for the 1968 film, *The Charge of the Light Brigade*. The iconic Apache war line – the white line painted across Adam's face – was a declaration of war on the music industry.

of 'Dog Eat Dog' on *Top of the Pops* on 16 October 1980 which sent the single to number four in the charts and the Ants Invasion had started.

The medium of television was ideal for their new style and Adam's warrior cheekbones with the attendant thundering swagger of the Burundi[546] drums. Decades later, the power of their beat is still breathtaking and, shares that same tsunami of sound and that daredevil, can-do rush of all great pop and the enveloping sound of the track is as powerful as Sex Pistols' *Never Mind the Bollocks*. Released in November 1980, the *Kings of the Wild Frontier* album was an unexpected explosion of pop art, punk vision and 3D cinemascope pop/noise. It was a collision of music from glam to movie soundtrack and from punk to pop art. The album saw Adam go from the cult monochrome of *Dirk*'s dark, dank yet enthralling world to a glorious vista of sound. There was feedback, war chants, twanging guitars, tribal rhythms and yet a perfect polished yet weird pop. Lyrically, Adam remained outside of pop expectations, writing songs about warriors, survival, sex and empowerment and a Native American culture that was the ultimate symbol of resistance to the American machine with an empathy and artful eye for the beauty of that culture.

Adam was in a curious position. One moment he was the S&M star of his personal micro cult, the next, he was the biggest UK pop star since Marc Bolan. It was a transition perfectly detailed by former Ant acolyte Tom Vague in his Vague fanzine, capturing that moment when the band that is your life morphs into something else and the dwindling army of soldier ants leave the building without their dose of frisson from their former warrior icon.

The vast panorama of the wild west and piratical adventures proved to be the ultimate escape from the claustrophobia of the UK. Here was a band that was brash, wild and colourful and sexy. It would have a considerable impact on goth, where warrior style was to become a key influence.

The band's immense power forged a whole new pop template and by Christmas, the UK was engulfed in Antmania. The 'Antmusic' single entered the charts the same week as John Lennon and the '60s dream was assassinated by Mark Chapman. Lennon was on sale again and dominated the charts, but Adam easily held his own. A huge hit in early 1981, 'Antmusic' was a song of empowerment and affirmation; the sound of someone standing up against the cultural tide. It was a display of what pop does best. The 'Kings of the Wild Frontier' single flew back up the charts to join 'Antmusic' and the album was number one for twelve weeks.

1981 was Adam's year.

Meanwhile, Malcolm was hoping for a media storm akin to that instigated by Sex Pistols for Bow Wow Wow. He was still toying with ideas that were like grenades. Initially, it worked and there was a brief flurry of controversy but the band were not crossing over. Their first full-length album, October 1981's *See Jungle! See Jungle! Go Join Your Gang Yeah! City All Over! Go Ape Crazy!* created a storm when the now 15-year-old Annabella was photographed naked on the cover, in a recreation of the

---

546 Copped from Burundi Stephenson Black's 'Burundi Black'.

1863 Manet painting, *Dejeuner Sur L'Herbe* (Lunch on the Grass). McLaren was always looking for trouble and had muddied the waters.

Bow Wow Wow album charted at number 26 while *Kings of the Wild Frontier* has already gone down in history; a white stripe painted across the face of pop culture. The sheer avalanche of great ideas and delivery made Adam and the Ants one of the most innovative, weird and wonderful bands to ever top the charts. It was also a portal into another culture, through which many future goths wandered.

By 1982, Bow Wow Wow had broken free from their manager's grip and went on to have bigger hits like their cover of 'I Want Candy' which was produced by Joan Jett collaborator, Kenny Laguna. The song, stripped-down of the tribal flux that initially made their music so interesting, was a great piece of bubblegum rock n roll with Ashman's slashing guitar sounding great.

Eventually, constant touring tore them apart. The flop of their final album 1983's, *When the Going Gets Tough, the Tough Get Going*, produced by glam legend Mike Chapman, was the end. They fell apart later that year with the boys in the band putting together Chiefs of Relief with the Sex Pistol's Paul Cook, and Annabella going solo.

Adam had won the great pirate pop battle. Malcolm was unflinching, though, and he continued to see him as his own proud creation: 'I was the one who turned Adam into a male Cinderella. I laid it out to him to think of yourself as a pirate, think of stories about Geronimo,' he cackled.

After the battle was won there would still be big hits to come for Adam, the follow-up November 1981 *Prince Charming* album played on the idea of Adam as some kind of dashing futuristic pop star – a latter-day Ziggy Stardust with an added sci-fi dandy swagger. The title track of the album, alongside 'Stand and Deliver' remain his biggest hits and Antmania continued for another year.

Disbanding the Ants and retaining Marco, Adam went solo for 1983's *Friend or Foe* which mixed some of the tribal rush with a slicker sound. Later albums like *Strip* (1983) and *Vive Le Rock* (1985) produced by Tony Visconti, and his Live Aid appearance that year which was all too brief saw Adam in the pop firmament without the dominance of that wild breakthrough. Later albums like *Manners and Physique* (1990) and the solo *Wonderful* (1995) saw diminishing chart returns before everything eventually unravelled with Adam's well-documented struggles with depression and mental illness.

'It was like having a fist smashed in your face,' he claimed about his illness, and yet in the last decade, Adam has pulled himself through and released a 2013 comeback album, *Adam Ant Is the Blueblack Hussar in Marrying the Gunner's Daughter*. He also tours consistently with a powerful celebration of his back catalogue and the huge hits that were both pop and underground art combined. With sell-out world tours played to devoted fans; Adam is the great survivor.

In a remarkable career, he was the bridge between the end of glam, the beginning of punk and the brave new world of post-punk and the gateway to the goth scene that he was a key influence on. In many ways, Adam was the last glam rock star, the visionary who understood that there was a place in pop culture for sex, art and wild ideas.

And when he sang 'ridicule is nothing to be scared of', it was perhaps the greatest pop culture truth of them all.

Chapter 16

NEW DAWN FADES: MANCHESTER & JOY DIVISION

'Joy Division are dancing music with Gothic overtones'

- Martin Hannett, 1979 [547]

The lingering echoes of the explosive Manchester post-punk scene are long gone. The sounds are consigned to box sets and dusty memories, leaving behind nothing but ghosts and shadows. The Manchester of Joy Division is now a place of urban myth. The post-industrial city centre of abandoned warehouses and smoke-blackened terraces have been converted into flats or demolished to make way for the 21st-century city 'that is never finished.'

The modern Manchester is no longer the first world's first post-industrial city but the world's first post-punk city. It is a metropolis culturally and architecturally inspired by a musical legacy; a legacy that was driven by the futuristic music and thrust of Joy Division whose very Gothic sound cast a long shadow over the city itself as well as the post-punk and goth alternative.

The Manchester post-punk revolution had its own agenda that was inspired by the vision of a clutch of maverick musicians, designers, photographers and writers. Watching above them all, propelling the scene, was local TV presenter and culture enthusiast, Anthony H. Wilson with his Factory Records label.

From Peterloo to the modern world's first vegetarian society, from splitting the atom to being the first modern industrial city, Manchester was always a city in a rush. It was also a city of ideas that fermented genuine revolution from the suffragette movement to Karl Marx's research for *Das Kapital* in the city centre Chetham's Library.[548] Manchester has always birthed ideas, poets and writers such as Thomas De Quincey, whose 1822 *Confessions of an English Opium Eater* painted a florid account of the pleasures and perils of opium addiction whilst another more dystopian vision was presented 140 years later by Mancunian Anthony Burgess with 1962's *A Clockwork Orange.*

The post-punk period somehow combined all these different elements and was another evolutionary chapter in the city's creative mindset. The revolution was now in music and its vibration is still felt to this day musically, culturally and even in the city's modern skyline.

Of course, Joy Division were never a goth band but they were certainly gothic and their pulsating bass-driven melancholia and poetic depictions of the dark side of being human were a profound influence on that scene. The Manchester based band,

---

547 The first use of the word 'gothic' in describing a post-punk band.

548 The oldest public library in the UK.

formed in 1976, were the gateway to post-punk and turned the music scene on its head when their debut *Unknown Pleasures* album that came out on 15 June 1979.

There would be few bands in the future goth scene that did not take something from the Joy Division sound - whether it was those melancholic melodic bass lines, that baritone vocal style or the death disco motorik rhythms of the drums or the grappling with modern technology in Martin Hannett's futuristic production. To this day Joy Division still sound like that future and in the goth world they retain a key influence on its sound and vision and its emotional heart and soul.

Manchester itself had a head start on post-punk.

In the summer of 1976, Buzzcocks staged the two infamous and totemic Sex Pistols shows at the Lesser Free Trade Hall where many of the future bands were inspired on the night and the post-punk Manchester music scene coalesced. The following September, Anthony Wilson gave the Pistols their first-ever TV appearance on his cutting edge TV arts show *So It Goes*. These two events were enough to trigger a new and highly different version of the new wave to erupt in the city. As the dust from punk itself settled in the next few years, bands such as Buzzcocks, The Fall, The Smiths and Joy Division created something new from the musical debris. However, it was Joy Division that made the initial move into a new and distinct post-punk sound with a dark energy.

> Joy Division had a soundscape which completely validated what the band was putting out. It was the ultimate act of that alienation. Even before Ian died, it set up an alternative environment when you listened to it. It was a shadowy night time. That was before you even heard a word or the sound of Martin Hannett's production or Hooky's bass, Steven's drumming or Bernard's very metropolitan approach to the guitar - making it sound like metal or like the concrete you were growing up around.[549]

The powerful, dark and stunningly original sound of Joy Division was explored through songs of alienation, hurt, and the sense of being lost in the sprawl of the city and this audible fragility would make a defining impact.

The real revolution of punk had been to turn fans into musicians. Empowered by ideas, Joy Division were typical of their generation, fumbling for direction and liberated by punk's clarion call. Peter Hook and Bernard Sumner were two school friends excited by the possibilities of punk after the Sex Pistols gig in June 1976.

> For a lot of people, punk demystified music and brought it down to our level. The energy of it was so genuine. Punk was like being a child in Toys R Us! Bands were forming and playing a gig the next day with no songs. They were buying instruments and making a racket. The day after Sex Pistols gig, I went to a shop called Mazels in Piccadilly, Manchester - which is long gone now - and said to the guy 'I want a bass guitar', and he said, 'which one?' I said 'well, which one's a bass?!' He picked me out a Gibson SG copy and it was absolutely terrible; it would have been more tuneful for me to have banged some strings into a plank of wood! I played the bass because Barney had the guitar, so we needed a bass. Being

---

549 Johnny Marr to John Robb.

a punk band, we didn't have two guitarists, which was funny because we had only seen one punk band, but you wanted to look like the Sex Pistols.[550]

Before that, Hook had been trying to find a soundtrack in the mid-'70s.

> Before punk, I was listening to heavy metal, not Black Sabbath but Deep Purple, Led Zeppelin – pretty much the same as Barney. Then I got into John Cale weirdly before I knew about The Velvet Underground. A kid at work loved his stuff and he lent me the solo albums. I then soon got to realise that there were all these different kinds of music going on and that got me into Cockney Rebel and Roxy Music – whose first album is my favourite record – which led me to Bowie and I then got into weird types of music that took you away from heavy metal which by now seemed a bit obvious.[551]

The empowerment of punk now meant that, you too, could take to the stage.

> There were no parameters, none of us could play but that didn't matter. When we started, all we wanted to do was play the punk music we heard at gigs. It was all 'rararara' and all sixteenths because you were young and had loads of energy. We weren't bothered about being musical at first. It was more important to just do it and write songs quickly to improve. At first, it was me writing the lyrics because Barney never really wrote lyrics until later and we hadn't found Ian yet.[552]

This sheer gung-ho amateurism was key to the inception of post-punk. Instead of the time-honoured learning of rock classics, a whole generation of musicians were self-taught and, with a wilful self-determination, were adding their own instinct to a ragbag of ideas. These were ideas grabbed from 'teach yourself' books or from mates who knew a chord or two. Even to this day, Peter Hook admits to knowing no cover versions and having to turn down an audition for The Rolling Stones after Bill Wyman left because he only knows one style of playing; his own:

> Barney could play the guitar a tiny bit. He had a book, so I got one about teach[ing] yourself bass and it told you to put stickers on your guitar which was great. When they wore off with sweat, I painted it with Tipp-Ex instead, so I knew where the notes were. Added to that was the enthusiasm of playing; that soon got you around any problems.[553]

The fledgling group fully coalesced in 1977 when they amalgamated with another ad hoc out of town band led by a charismatic local music fan. They had previously seen him at Sex Pistols Free Trade Hall gig, wearing a jacket with 'Hate' painted on the back.

> We used to see him at all the gigs. There were only a few people who used to go to everything, and he was one of them. I can't remember the first conversation, but I actually got to know him quite well before he joined the band. We would be stood together a lot. Me and Barney had our band and we needed a drummer

---

550 Peter Hook to John Robb.

551 Peter Hook to John Robb.

552 Peter Hook to John Robb.

553 Peter Hook to John Robb.

and singer and we knew he had a group and he needed a bassist and guitar player, so we made it work.[554]

Born in 1956 in Macclesfield – a small silk manufacturing market town 20 miles away from Manchester, Ian Curtis was the intense and intelligent grammar schoolboy who fell in with the self-deprecating, self-styled Salford oiks. The same town would also eventually provide them with a drummer when fellow Macclesfield local and krautrock fan Stephen Morris would bring his off-kilter and precise style to the lineup.

Ian Curtis had a bit more musical nous about him than his new friends. He had a large record collection and scoured local shops for pop culture ephemera. An avid music lover and a big fan of David Bowie, he was also ensconced in krautrock[555] and had been savvy enough to the musical underground that he was photographed in the t-shirt of cult space rock band Nektar[556] in 1975. Like so many other musicians mentioned before, Ian Curtis was also a disciple of the dark triumvirate of Iggy Pop, The Doors and The Velvet Underground.

Armed with a fierce knowledge of the possibilities of music, he was actively seeking out new sounds and performances. He attended gigs from the likes of David Bowie on the classic Ziggy Stardust Tour of 1972 and travelled alone as far as the Mont De Marsan festival[557] in the south of France in 1976 when it was headlined by Eddie and the Hot Rods.

What Ian Curtis brought to the band was a new artful edge, a deeper record collection and a sense of direction. What he can't possibly have known, was that the creative fire he unknowingly lit beneath the Salford lad was going to truly rage.

The band initially called themselves Warsaw in a tribute to the David Bowie track 'Warszawa' from his 1977 *Low* album. After making their debut at Manchester's long-lost Electric Circus on 29 May 1977, they played on the fringes of the local punk scene at venues such as the Squat or Rafters. Peter Hook smiles. 'The bands we were trying initially to sound like were the punk bands that we played with like Eater, Slaughter and the Dogs, The Worst or Buzzcocks.[558]

Close friends like Mark Reeder[559] knew Ian Curtis from working in record shops in town where he would seem him almost every day.

> I knew Ian from when he worked briefly in Rare Records on John Dalton Street. He was also a regular in our little Virgin Records shop where I worked in town. He'd always come in his lunch hour to listen to new records, as did future Joy Division manager Rob Gretton and also Tony Wilson. I had no idea Ian could

---

554 Peter Hook to John Robb.

555 The less than right on term for the German underground scene of bands like Kraftwerk, Can, Neu, Cluster and Harmonia and many others who were bending rock into bold new shapes. The German term for the scene was Kosmische Musik.

556 English prog band based in Hamburg who were parallel to the German underground.

557 The first punk rock festival in Europe held in August 1976 with headliners Eddie and the Hot Rods, Pink Fairies, and the just formed The Damned. Supposedly, Sex Pistols were invited but refused.

558 Peter Hook to John Robb.

559 Reeder found fame in 2015 with his *B-Movie: Lust & Sound in West-Berlin* film about his life on the cutting edge music scene in his adopted city.

sing. I was actually very surprised to see him up on stage fronting Warsaw. He didn't seem like the type. He always appeared to me to be quite reserved.

I was really impressed, and they immediately became one of my favourite Manchester bands, together with Buzzcocks. As usual, when I went to the Electric Circus[560], I was pretty messed up; mostly on a mix of speed, Carlsberg Special and vodka and lime, so I don't recall everything exactly. But I remember Warsaw's music as being quite fast and hard but not really punk in the 1-2-3-4 fashion, but still rough and aggressive, Manchester style. We had a lot to moan about and it all came to play in the music. I remember they were quite individual sounding. Ian had sound problems and he didn't have a very loud singing voice that could sustain through bad equipment. That was something that would always plague the band.

I was really impressed seeing him on stage and more so with him being able to surprise me like that. I thought 'he kept that quiet!' I know Ian was fascinated with history and I thought many of their songs had underlying 'historical' themes, which also interested me although I couldn't hear what he was singing about most of the time.[561]

After playing the local circuit and being mostly ignored, the band took a few months off to rehearse at TJMs rehearsal rooms based at the long-demolished 35 Little Peter Street, around the corner from where the Haçienda would eventually emerge. This was then a forgotten corner of Manchester in which the heart, soul and birthplace of the band and new city sound was being nurtured.

The promotional video for 'Love Will Tear Us Apart' was eventually filmed in TJMs. It provides a glimpse into the recent past of redbrick spaces with wooden floorboards, dirty windows and damp walls. Young bands like Joy Division were perhaps unconsciously soundtracking the surrounding dereliction and, ironically, would eventually spark its regeneration. Their music and cultural cache were to empower the city in so many ways. However, at the time of recording, post-industrial Manchester was filled with boarded-up industrial units, old warehouses and the broken remnants of a decayed industrial powerhouse. Surrounding the rehearsal room were old gas works and long-lost pubs like the Gaythorn – with its outside toilets.

This was the crumbling heartland of the broken-hearted Victorian remnants of a bygone Manchester. It was here, in this old warehouse, that the young band revised their set and wrote new songs in a burst of creative energy in a transformation that would eventually change the shape of music. With a new set, they eventually made their live debut at Pips under the new name, Joy Division, on 25 Jan 1978.

The band's new name would raise eyebrows with its reference to the Nazi death camps,[562] a reflection of the dark interests of many at the time, with Nazi paraphernalia, literature and books fascinating post-punk youth. The long shadow of

---

560 Key Manchester venue that closed in 1977.

561 Mark Reeder to John Robb.

562 The band's name is taken from the 1955 novella *The House of Dolls*, written by Ka-tzetnik 135633. Thought to be a young Jewish girl who was captured in Poland when she was fourteen years old, she was forced into sexual slavery in a Nazi labour camp as part of one of several 'Joy Divisions'.

the Second World War still hung over Europe and many people were darkly obsessed with this lingering hum of evil without embracing the ideology. This residual fear was threaded through the lyrics of Joy Division, joining thew sense of alienation, pain, disgust, confusion, and loneliness, all in Curtis' perfect prose.

> Everyone thinks it was Ian who came up with the name, but Barney had been reading books about Nazis. Ian was reading *The House of Dolls* which wrote about the areas in concentration camps in which women were forced into sex slavery, and that's where Barney got the name Joy Division. Barney also came up with an idea about using Rudolf Hess for the subject matter of our earlier song, 'Warsaw'. He was interested in Hess escaping the Nazi regime and crashing his plane into Scotland. We were heavily into reading about that stuff at the time.[563]
>
> In those months at TJMs Joy Division wrote the backbone to what would be their classic debut album, *Unknown Pleasures*. Rehearsing twice a week, they honed their sound down.
>
> In that period, the first couple of songs we wrote weren't punky ones. There was one called 'The Kill' which has never been recorded by Joy Division although later on, we used the title for another song which was ok but not as good. The next one we wrote was 'No Love Lost' and then 'Leaders of Men'. Ian would sit there listening to us play with his bag of lyrics. One day he looked up and said to me that it sounds better when I played high up the neck on the bass, so he could hear what I was playing – and that's how I got my sound. As a musician, it was great to hear Ian use a lot of the bass line melody for his vocals. Ian would say 'that sounds good, that works. Barney, can you put some guitar on that? Steve play tribal drums...' and fucking hell there is the track! It was amazing.[564]

Ian Curtis' role appears to have doubled as an ad hoc conductor, nodding at the bits of music he liked or suggesting changes before placing his lyrics into the melee. He would also lend the band albums that they hadn't heard before, like The Doors and other underground artists. Creatively, Curtis not only suggested the high bass lines, but nudged the band towards a unique atmosphere and sense of space within the music, worlds away from the claustrophobic thrash of punk. The group were now surprising themselves with their own creations. They finally had their own sound with the bass moving into a melodic lead role.

> JJ Burnel from The Stranglers was a huge influence. I went out and bought the same amps as him after seeing The Stranglers playing the whole of their *Black and White* album live at Stafford Bingley Hall in May 1978. I also started playing the bass by my knees because I had seen Paul Simonon from The Clash do that and, because I'm obsessive about whatever I do, I have to do it to the max.
>
> We were now playing together all the time. The experience made us really improve. The more you write, the better you get, and because you are so prolific when you are young, you just to do it well. It was not a matter of learning to do it, it just came to you and you started playing different things. It's easy when you start. The

---

563 Peter Hook to John Robb.

564 Peter Hook to John Robb.

more we played, the more sophisticated we became and to be honest, we became very sophisticated songwriters and players very quickly after only six months.[565]

The young band were learning about each other, and their different backgrounds were fast becoming strengths. It was purely instinctive and yet somehow, this powerful, sensitive music was coalescing to reflect the emotional tides hidden just below their gruff, northern surfaces.

What happened was Barney and I were very working-class and not very arty. Ian was working-class but leaning towards middle class and he was arty. Steve, who had now joined on drums, was really eccentric, but you didn't care. As long as you could write songs you didn't analyse them. I was in good company because Barney was really good, Steve would do something really good and Ian would put brilliant lyrics on it. Everyone was pushing everyone else. The reason Joy Division sounded so fantastic was that each member brought something unique into the songs. [566]

The key to this new sound was the space between the instruments whilst everyone was playing lead lines - a staple of post-punk, as Peter Hook explains:

Bernard heard space and liked it, but Ian didn't always like the space and wanted the guitars to fill it in! I was just playing the bass and keeping my head down. I was happy just to be in a band but after 'The Kill' was written, we were inspired to move in that direction. We knew where to go because that was the sound.[567]

The previously ignored band were now starting to get noticed, which initially surprised Mark Reeder.

One day, Rob Gretton came into Virgin, and said, 'I saw the best band in the world last night playing their first gig when I was DJing at Pips. I want to be their manager'. I asked him what the band were called, and he said Joy Division. I'd never heard of them. That Saturday, Tony Wilson came into the shop, as he always did a few minutes before closing time and he said, 'I saw the best band in the world the other night, you would love them'. I asked him who it was, and he said, 'Joy Division'.

I was now suddenly really curious about who this band were. They had no records out but had obviously made an impression on two people who I thought had pretty good taste in music.

Then I went to see them. I couldn't believe my eyes. It was Warsaw, but under a different name! I asked Ian why they had changed their name and he said because they didn't want to be confused with that really crap band from London called Warsaw Pakt, who had recorded and rush-released a really rubbishy record within 24 hours, a few months before.

Compared to other Manchester punk bands of the era, they sounded really different. Even more so than Buzzcocks and Magazine, who in themselves were each quite individual. It was so unique and original and creatively produced. Their performances were special too in retrospect because the band didn't really jump about like other punk bands and they dressed differently too. They were

565 Peter Hook to John Robb.

566 Peter Hook to John Robb.

567 Peter Hook to John Robb.

dressed down. Bernard just stood on the spot chopping at his guitar, and Hooky would stand there, legs akimbo and Ian would do his manic dance. It was very entertaining to watch.[568]

Without any decision or discussion, Joy Division were now forging in a new direction. Their futuristic sound was rattling around the damp warehouse rehearsal room in the cold winter of 1978.

> We never talked about music. We would write a song and say to Ian 'can you put some lyrics to that?' It was only when Ian started influencing us musically that we gained another dimension. He was into Iggy Pop and Lou Reed. I had never heard of Lou Reed even though I was a John Cale fan! I didn't even know 'Walk on The Wild Side'. Ian would bring us these records like *Raw Power* and *Metallic KO* and *Lou Reed Live*. We didn't get into The Doors until everyone said we sounded like them a year later, so Ian brought a Doors record for me and Barney to listen to and we said 'fuck! we do sound like The Doors!' and then we started playing 'Riders on The Storm' in soundchecks and no one noticed the difference! Ian was very nice. He was never really very pushy with the band. He would lend you things, but he wouldn't give you the record and say this is what the bass line should sound like. He would give you the record and say listen to this it's fantastic and you would be 'ok' because you liked him and trusted him, and you would go and listen to it. He may have been manipulative, but I like to think not! He was always the one who was leading. He had the best record collection. Steve, on the other hand, was into Frank Zappa, Captain Beefheart – shit like that, which was difficult for a punk, and not the music for me or Barney. We tried it, but we didn't like it. We were stuck with what we liked.[569]

A pop culture autodidact, Ian Curtis would spend hours reading in the back room of his new house in Barton Street, Macclesfield, where he had moved in with his new wife Debbie. The house was just around the corner from his workplace at the nearby Macclesfield Unemployment Office and close to his local pub, the Prince Albert. At home he would read Dostoevsky, Nietzsche, Gogol, Kafka, Jean-Paul Sartre, Hermann Hesse and *Crash* by J.G. Ballard, the latter about car crash sexual fetishism. Another favourite was Ballard's 1975 work, *High-Rise*. There was also William Burroughs, whose books, *Naked Lunch* and *The Wild Boys*, which were two of Curtis' favourite works.

Burroughs 'nuclear style' prose and apocalyptic, non-linear style of writing dropped the reader into the middle of a world of unease. This world with no formal start and finish would be a profound influence on the young singer. He was also lapping up *New Worlds* – the sci-fi magazine containing columns and stories written by Ballard and other leading lights of science fiction.[570]

Like Siouxsie Sioux, Curtis was fascinated by the anti-Nazi photomontages of John Heartfield. All these dark culture bombs helped to push his imagination. Hoovering up the esoteric literature, he located these books and magazines in the counterculture

---

568 Mark Reeder to John Robb.

569 Peter Hook to John Robb.

570 The magazine had been edited by Michael Moorcock in the 1960s.

hubs in town: House on the Borderland; Orbit on Shudehill; Bookchain in Peter Street; Paperchase; the left-wing Grassroots bookstore; or the bookshop in Stockport where future music journalist Paul Morley worked.

This stark and powerful culture was having a profound effect on Curtis' young mind. It was all clearly evident in the notebooks of lyrics and ideas that he would always carry with him. Through his voice and lyrics, he would eventually capture the intangible unease that lurked just below the surface of society; ultimately capturing the personal and the universal and vice versa.

Music journalist Jon Savage had just moved to Manchester and was writing about post-punk for the long-lost *Sounds* music paper, which was so often at the cutting edge of the post-punk period and explains the evocative power of Ian Curtis.

> Ian Curtis did not seek conventional narratives but strived instead to create a situation in which the emotion came from the response of the narrator. As the lines shifted from the universal to the personal, the 'I' was often trapped, as in a Greek tragedy, by forces outside his control.[571]

This dark and deeply personal subject matter didn't always permeate through to the rest of the band, though.

> We were light-hearted about life. We would mess about as boys do but when we were writing it was very serious. The music was serious because in your mind you wanted to be successful. If I listen to our earlier punk stuff and then listen to the later stuff, it's like fucking hell, what a difference. When our producer Martin Hannett heard the material for *Unknown Pleasures*, he must have gone 'how come this lot came up with this!?'
> If someone brought that to me now, I would go mental because it was so good. Ironically, we didn't tape hardly anything when we rehearsed. The only way we would keep a song was if you could remember how it went in the next rehearsal. That does freak me out now because we lost a lot of things. The even sadder thing was that, when we did eventually get a cassette recorder, later on, we would have just one cassette and then tape over things when it was full. There is no early Joy Division left because we had no money to buy cassettes.
> We were very prolific and wrote quickly and we were dumping stuff. We would be writing a song a week and then it would be – 'get rid of that one it's shit'. It was as simple as that. It was a very quick turnover.[572]

The new music was now taking a darker twist due to the singer's cultural preoccupations. This change permeated through the band to such a degree that the musicians were inhabiting their own playing styles.

> It was the subconscious influences that were around you. We were growing up in Salford and Manchester and they were not very joyous places. We were working-class, skint and angry. The whole place was dark – literally – with the three-day week and the crumbling infrastructure. It was heavy, and you were frustrated. You were intense and serious about everything, ridiculously so.

---

571 Jon Savage to John Robb.

572 Peter Hook to John Robb.

The music scene was very middle class, very arty and controlled by hippies like Martin Hannett or Tony. They only wanted people who were like them and we were like 'hiya, fuck that!' and they were like, 'we don't want them, we want people like Buzzcocks, people like Howard Devoto' – nice hippie people. Ian would go and kick at the doors to get the band noticed. When he was like that, he was an animal. He was really passionate and really believed in what he was doing. He was right, though. We were better than most of the other groups.

Ian was the most selfless person I've ever met. He was our biggest fan and he lived and breathed the group. He is the only lead vocalist I have ever met who would say 'do you want to write the lyrics?' And I would say 'mine are a bit crap and yours are fantastic', but he fucking meant it. He would say 'write the lyrics and I'll sing them'. He was a generous spirit, and I have never met anyone like that as a singer. You would look at his lyrics and they were brilliant. He never, to my knowledge, did a shit lyric. I wrote most of the lyrics for 'At A Later Date' and 'Novelty' and compared to Ian's they are crappy lyrics – luckily for me, the music is great.[573]

Recorded in 1978 at Pennine Sound Studio in Oldham, their debut *An Ideal for Living* EP was released on their own Enigma label as a seven-inch record. Its stripped-down sound captured a band edging away from their punk roots. The EP's artwork – a black and white drawing by Bernard of a blond Hitler Youth member beating a drum reflected their darker interests that brought some local criticism. The following year saw the twelve inch-only release printed with the less controversial scaffolding cover.

'The Nazi stuff? The Pistols were doing it, Siouxsie was doing it, everyone was doing it. It was all about the fashion and had nothing to do with being a Nazi. You thought it looked cool. It was stupid of course.[574]

Mark Reeder clearly remembers the single being hand-delivered to the Virgin Records shop:

When they finally released *An Ideal for Living*, Ian proudly came into the shop with Bernard and gave me a box of EPs to sell. I thought it was a great record, even if the sound was pretty flat. It also had a very thought-provoking cover. A few months later when I moved to Germany, Ian sent me a demo cassette tape of what was going to be their first album that had been recorded for RCA Records. I remember Rob Gretton had a real battle trying to get that tape back off the label when they left to sign to Factory. It had some of the songs that eventually ended up on *Unknown Pleasures*, but one of my favourite songs on the tape, 'They Walked in Line' was sadly missing from the finished album because Rob thought it would give off the wrong impression.[575]

The EP created a small stir, picking up a bit of radio play from John Peel and a couple of awkward interviews in the local press where the surly musicians collided with earnest young journalists. RCA had not been a good experience so they signed to a

---

573 Peter Hook to John Robb.

574 Peter Hook to John Robb.

575 Mark Reeder to John Robb.

new label with a keen aesthetic that had been set up by their manager Rob Gretton with Tony Wilson, and Alan Erasmus called Factory Records that saw this unique collection of individuals combining with the band to create a dark, uncontrollable magic with a strong Manchester and northern ethic.

The cast was set.

With Factory Records, Tony, now calling himself Anthony Wilson was using his fame as a local TV presenter and his own maverick vision to create a powerful pro-Mancunian set up. He had turned down a move to the media heartland of London and decided that the capital would have to come to him. His vision and, more importantly, his drive were key to the success. With his dynamic enthusiasm and media connections, Wilson created a space for Factory to exist. The label vision was reflected by local graphic designer, Peter Saville and his stark artwork for the sleeves that saw him create an art that underlined the stark power of the music.

Proving that all great bands are just part of a larger team Joy Division also had manager Rob Gretton's no-bullshit, unconventional approach and maverick producer Martin Hannett's groundbreaking ideas of sound and unconventional recording methods that still sound futuristic to this day. The local post-punk media also contained two future stars who held the same mindset. *NME* stringer, Paul Morley, whose writing propelled the band forward and photographer Kevin Cummins, whose iconic photos of the band on the Epping Street bridge (in Manchester's Hulme) in January 1979 freeze-framed their image and music forever.

> The session was for an *NME* feature on new Manchester bands written by Paul Morley. In many ways, we were blagging it, and making it seem like there was more of a scene than there was to get the double-page spread. When I asked the band what they wanted for the shot, Hooky and Barney suggested standing at the bus stop in Hulme but that was never my intention.
>
> I wanted the shots to match the band and their music. I'd decided that I would never photograph Ian smiling. The famous photo of him smoking the cigarette at the same session has the rest of the band in the background taking the piss and trying to put him off but he knew what he wanted in the shot and so did I. I told him to think about something else and ignore the rest of them. The photo on the bridge is perfect. It's become iconic because it sums up their music.
>
> Hulme, at the time, looked like a broken East European city; the bonus of the snow really added to the shot. We wanted them to look like very serious young men and they went on to make music to match the images. It was visually intimidating. It was media manipulation. Black and white suited them. Hooky says when you think of Joy Division, it's as a black and white band.[576]

Jon Savage had moved to Manchester after Anthony Wilson got him a job at Granada, and he replaced Paul Morley, who had moved to London as the Manchester scene writer. Jon was now the main music writer in the city and was covering the scene for Sounds.

---

576 Kevin Cummins to John Robb.

The hip end of London was going into a Scritti Politti/Prag Vec moment which was dreary beyond belief. I didn't like it. It had no glamour, no excitement and no sex. It was just kind of post-structural theories about music – dull as ditch water I'm afraid. It was time to go. I made the move when Tony Wilson got me a job at Granada TV, knowing that I would be writing about Joy Division for *Sounds*, so it worked out for everybody. At the same time, Paul Morley moved down to London. He had been writing about Joy Division and now I was the person writing about them.

I had already been up to Manchester to see Pere Ubu's first date in the UK in May 1978. In the audience I remember seeing members of Joy Division. So later when I finally heard Joy Division, I thought Pere Ubu were parallel with the high bass sound and because they were dealing with post-industrial space from their home city of Cleveland. There were all these link-ups between post-industrial American cities and the Manchester of the time with its own post-industrial atmosphere.

The next thing I'm living in Manchester and I got a letter containing a cassette saying: 'My name is Rob Gretton, I'm the manager of Joy Division and I'm sending you a copy of their new album. You may have heard their first EP *An Ideal for Living* – it's crap'. I really liked the way he wrote the letter. I thought it was really funny.

It was Joy Division's time. They had just finished recording *Unknown Pleasures* – which don't forget was not that big an album when it first came out. Nobody in London was that interested in what was going on in Manchester. Despite Paul Morley and myself, there was still a huge media divide between the north and south. Pete Shelley said it very well when he said that the bands in the north were like the animals in New Zealand and got on with developing because they were left alone there!

Joy Division were just a local group then, but I thought they were terrific because they helped me to make sense of Manchester. I had a white label of *Unknown Pleasures* which I played constantly and that really fixed in my head what Manchester was like. It was very much like the Charles Salem movie;[577] very grey, lots of space and yet claustrophobic. Also, one of the first things Wilson, who smoked pot for Britain, said to me was that Manchester was about getting stoned. He said London was all about speed before it went to coke. This changed the music in the cities. Tony said we smoke loads of dope up here and we like the first Public Image album and our own music.

At that time Manchester was in the James Anderton[578] police era where, if you were out in a car, you would get pulled. It was horrible, particularly if you smoked dope which made you completely fucking para when you went out at night.

I definitely thought that Joy Division were psychedelic. The auto-suggestion by them was totally trippy. They had that slow drowning wet Sunday in Manchester vibe, which was un-fucking-believable. Joy Division were so good. Something that people forget about them is how uplifting they were because they really rocked. They made you want to move around. They could swing and be heavy as hell.[579]

---

577 The 20 year old director captured this particular era of Manchester with his 1979 *The Factory Flick* film. It was based on Liz Naylor's article in Manchester City's *City Fun* fanzine and features music from *Unknown Pleasures*.

578 James Anderton was 'Gods Cop'; a Bible-driven chief of police with his own 'moral' agenda.

579 Jon Savage to John Robb.

Another sensitive former northern soul using extreme music to understand himself was the late Genesis P-Orridge of Throbbing Gristle.

> When I first saw Joy Division, it was in Hemel Hempstead [580]. In my memory, it was the classic image of Ian wrapped around the mic and looking into space. I remember very vividly, as I was watching, he seemed to become almost semi-transparent and all the people and everything around began to fade away. I got this very strong sense of disconnection seeing him. It was not connected with reality and not fully of this earth.
>
> The only time I had felt that before was in 1965 when I met The Rolling Stones as a teenager at a TV studio. I sat with them for a while in a cafeteria and the same thing happened with Brian Jones. He seemed to be present and yet everything around him was not present. It was as if I was seeing someone in a slightly different dimension, like a hologram.
>
> Ian Curtis gave me the same feeling. He was only present by an effort of will. There was a strong sense of disconnection from everyday existence and especially a strong, unusual, special feeling at that moment on the stage. [581]

Recorded in Stockport's Strawberry Studios with Martin Hannett, Unknown Pleasures changed the sonic landscape. Some of the band may have been thinking they were going to record a raw rock record, but they were in for a shock as Martin Hannett simply saw them as a blank canvas for his own unique vision. There was a lot of space in Joy Division's sound and they were a gift to a producer because they didn't have a clue. They didn't argue. I think I'd had the new AMS delay for about two weeks. It was called 'Digital'. It was heaven-sent for this and I shaped their sound.[582]

It was this space in their sound that would intrigue Hannett who would explore it fully with his digital delays and production style. His experimental mindset – perhaps forged by his chemistry degree and enquiring, scientific mind – was to be of great influence on the young band's music.

Initially credited as Martin Zero, few producers have such a signature sound. The Mancunian maverick had a couple of credits to his name like local punk band Slaughter and the Dogs and the iconic Buzzcocks' *Spiral Scratch* EP debut which saw few hallmarks of his future futuristic style.

His work on Joy Division was going to make him a legend.

Part of the Manchester music scene's inner circle, Martin Hannett had been doing live sound at gigs around town and was an original partner/director at Factory Records. Working with Joy Division gave him the opportunity to craft this astonishing new soundscape. Hannett was keen to experiment with drum sounds, studio effects and recording techniques, creating a stripped-down, yet cavernous-sounding record with shapeshifting reverbs and delays that would be come key for so many goth bands.

---

580 5 November 1979 – Joy Division were supporting Buzzcocks.

581 Genesis P-Orridge to John Robb.

582 Martin Hannett to Jon Savage .

His love of the motorik rhythms employed by the German underground of Neu! was integral to his new, stark methodologies. 'The insistent cyclical rhythms created in real-time, on real kits, buzz and vibrate all kinds of interesting sounds and with flanged and phased guitars, pulsing bass and muted synthesisers create a soundscape,' he pondered and to achieve this, he experimented with Joy Division, bringing in synthesisers and his beloved digital delays. Hannett commented that 'when digital effects came in at the end of the 1970s, there was a quantum leap in ambience control. You had as many flavours as you could invent.'

Remarkably *Unknown Pleasures* still sounds like the future and retains the shock of the new after four decades. So much of this was down to the producer turning the songs inside out, taking them beyond rock music as he treated them with an array of these filters, echoes and AMS digital delays. Most noticeably, it was his collection of BBD echo devices all of which he had amassed over time, and called his 'bluetop echo and delay boxes', that were put to good use.

Hannett collected delay units, the most important being the Advanced Music Systems (AMS) DMX 15-80. At the time, it was a state-of-the-art piece of studio equipment, being the world's first microprocessor-controlled 15-bit digital delay. Many of the effects had never been heard before and some were invented by Hannett himself, who would pester gear manufacturers with ideas and designs for gear that became staples in future studios. In addition to this, he also made use of analogue tape-echo units such as the Melos EM-110 Echo Chamber, which he used for cruder echo sounds somewhat akin to those used in dub reggae, of which he was something of an aficionado.

Bernard already held an interest in synths and had built his Transcendent 2000 himself from a kit he had sent for in the post. Hannett now added more synths like the ARP Omnis, several Jen SX1000s and an International 4600 synthesiser modular synth to add further textures to the band's sound.

Unknown Pleasures and the follow-up, *Closer*, were Hannett's production masterpieces. The ethereal sound kept the band's dark, driving atmosphere and the bass guitar's central position in the mix. The dislocated dark disco drums were anchored to the washes of strange background sounds, creating a futuristic soundscape.

Hannett created the cold, harder, yet emotional textures that would be such an influence for the post-punk and goth scenes. Some of his working techniques were way beyond convention, from his use of delays or to getting Stephen Morris to take his drum kit apart and record each drum separately.

> At that time, he wanted complete separation. He wanted the bass drum on its own with nothing, no spill, so he could treat it one way and treat the snare drum another way. He wanted it as clean and as treatable as he could get it, which meant you couldn't really play the drum kit because you would get spill. And you could forget playing the cymbals. You had to basically take the drum kit to pieces and play each bit separately. At the time I thought he was just doing it to drive me mad – which he did, quite successfully.

The end result was great, but I don't think he knew what the end result was going to be, he just had this idea and forced it through. Occasionally he'd let me not do that just to save time, but if we were in all-night, he'd mess about taking the pedal to pieces because it squeaked but I liked the squeak!

Initially, Peter Hook and Bernard did not like the Hannett sound, preferring something rawer and heavier.

Me and Barney thought that Martin Hannett had absolutely fucking ruined the album. I'm so glad we didn't get our own way though! Martin was a producer. He was an adult. We were kids. I was an idiot [laughs]. We didn't know our arse from our elbow. It was like finding a diamond and using it to pick your teeth. Martin heard us, and he heard something fantastic. The same as Rob. The same as Tony. We were completely oblivious to it.

When we made the album, we didn't know what to do. Much as I had hoped for the live sound, Martin made the songs sound delicate. He made it so you could listen to them again and again. Martin added stuff because he recognised that the songs that we were writing were very mature and beyond our years. Maybe Martin finished off what we had started and made the record unique and timeless.[583]

Giving himself carte blanche to override the band's wishes, Hannett took Joy Division on a quantum leap with Ian Curtis as a willing participant. Ian would sit in with the producer while they created the astonishing soundscapes.

Martin adored Ian and they got on really well together. Ian was so nice to everybody. It was me and Barney annoying Martin with Ian saying, 'That sounds great Martin'. Ian was with him all the way and understood what he was trying to do.

It's interesting to contrast *Unknown Pleasures* with the Warsaw bootleg. It's quite weird because it's the same lineup but a different producer – the demos were done by Richard Searling and the contrast between that and *Unknown Pleasures* was huge. Somehow, when we got to Factory and Martin Hannett, we had gained an edge in our playing as well. I don't know where that edge came from. I can't tell you. I mean we didn't get meaner or poorer.[584]

In many ways, the naivety of Joy Division was part of their glory. The band were feeling their way into this new sound - a sound that they had personally instigated - and that Hannett had fully realised. Their youthful approach to their intense and serious music was part of what made them so magical as Peter Hook understands years later.

The interesting thing about us was that we didn't really know how to do it properly. When we did a song like 'Isolation', Barney would play keyboards and there would be no guitar for that part – the same with 'Love Will Tear Us Apart' – we didn't think of dubbing the guitar on after or bringing another member in. The way we had our sound made us more vulnerable. Other bands would have had more musicians fighting for space, but the way we had it would heighten your frailty and that was a good thing.

---

583 Peter Hook to John Robb.

584 Peter Hook to John Robb.

When it worked, and you got it right, it was fucking gold. We didn't know what made it work. When I went back to playing the songs years later and got in a rehearsal room and tried to figure out how the tracks worked, I was thinking, fuck that's very clever. It was created in a subconscious way and that was the beauty of Joy Division. Barney was magnificent, and Steve was magnificent and so was Ian. I was pretty good.[585]

Unknown Pleasures became the cult release of the year and was soon set as the benchmark against which every alternative band was measuring itself. It was not just the sound or the stunning artwork[586] but it was also the emotional content of the album, and its stark, beautiful music that was a sharp turn from punk without losing its cutting edge, energy or power.

It is still an astonishing record, made by a band who had no idea how good they were, with a singer who didn't live long enough to see how important they would become. Its bass-driven soundscapes utilised space, emotion and melancholia in ways that other generations of bands are still trying to unravel.

Unknown Pleasures became a template for a whole new kind of rock music that would affect all future alternative music scenes, making Joy Division underground icons across the UK. Young fans like Ian Astbury, the future singer with The Cult, felt its impact, keenly explaining: 'Year Zero for me was Joy Division; more so than the Pistols'.

Meanwhile, the band were already working on their second album in early 1980, with a clutch of songs – 'Atrocity Exhibition', 'Passover', 'Colony', 'A Means to An End' and '24 Hours' – already written and being played live. '24 Hours', 'Colony' and 'Sound Of Music' along with a very early version of Love Will Tear Us Apart, were also recorded for a John Peel session in November 1979. There was a noticeable style change with the creeping use of synthesisers on newer and more atmospheric songs like 'Isolation', 'Heart and Soul', 'The Eternal' and 'Decades'.

On Jan 21st 1980 Joy Division played in Berlin for the only time. 58 people turned up for the show in the city that held a deep fascination for the band and especially Ian Curtis. It was the city where Bowie and Iggy had famously lived in 1976, recording the classic series of albums. Joy Division's dark fascination with the war and the capital's strange vibes remained inescapable and those Berlin albums would be a core influence on Curtis. The band were brought over by Mark Reeder who had moved on from working at Manchester Virgin record store to Berlin and was now Factory's young representative in the city and Europe.

Ian was fascinated by Berlin – but the show we put on at the Kant Kino was disastrous. Here they were coming to Berlin and nobody would entertain them. The gig was atrocious, the sound was awful and Ian was shouting for the monitors to be turned up – he couldn't hear anything, the crowd couldn't hear anything

---

585 Peter Hook to John Robb.

586 The image of successive pulses from the first pulsar discovered, PSR B1919+21—often referred to in the context of this album by its older name, CP 1919. The image was found in the 1977 *Cambridge Encyclopaedia of Astronomy* by Bernard Sumner and the colours were reversed by Peter Saville, turning it into the iconic image that perfectly captures the album's contents.

and someone shouted, 'Can you turn the vocals up?', in German at them because everyone thought Bernard was German because he called himself 'Bernard Albrecht' on the first record. [587]

In March 1980, the band started recording their second album, *Closer* with Martin Hannett at the Britannia Row studios in London. It saw a move further into sound sculpture, being less dense than the debut. The album possessed beautifully constructed, elegiac layers of sound and subtle textures created by the mix. Ultimately, this approach resulted in unique atmospheres that took some time for the band to appreciate.

> At first, I was like, head in hands, 'Oh fucking hell, it's happening again'. It's *Unknown Pleasures* number two. Martin had melted the guitar with his Marshall Time Waster as we nicknamed it.[588] It made it sound like somebody strangling a cat, and to my mind then, absolutely killing the song. I was so annoyed with him and went in and gave him a piece of my mind, but he just turned around and told me to fuck off.
>
> In the end, I realised that things like having the bass lower in the mix was Martin's way of giving it a subliminal melody and making you listen to it and hear something else in the track. When you listen to the record, you initially concentrate on the vocals and then you wonder what's that beautiful thing in the background and it was the bass playing the melodies.
>
> I was also using the six string bass for the first time. Sound-wise, Ian knew much more of what he wanted than Bernard and I. Although, in a letter I've seen he says he didn't like *Closer* which surprised me as he got on so well with Martin. This time, though, when we were in the studio, we watched Martin, and we thought we could do this if we learn.[589]

On release, *Closer* was treated as a monumental work with its spectral sound turning rock music into a thing of haunting beauty. Its stunning sound was a veritable reinvention of the wheel and so future-perfect that, to this day, it still sounds five years ahead.

The backdrop to all of this, though, was the decline of Ian Curtis's health. He had started having epileptic seizures around 1978 and these would worsen throughout 1979 and 1980 respectively. Exacerbated by the demands of touring and his poor medication, his ability to handle his condition worsened. Many people have remarked that his on-stage dancing, where he would hypnotically flail around in mesmerising, shamanic shapes, resembled seizures. As his condition worsened, there were times when he collapsed on stage and had to be carried off. His private life was also falling apart. His 1975 marriage to Debbie was floundering at the same time as he had struck up a deep friendship with a Belgian journalist, the late Annik Honoré.

Life was coming to a head for the young singer. On one hand, all that he had strived for, creatively and artistically, was working out perfectly. He was widely recognised

---

587 Mark Reeder to John Robb.

588 The Marshall Time Modulator is a classic analogue delay and modulation unit from the mid-1970s. Designed by the late Stephen St. Croix (aka Stephen Marshall), it became popular for its ability to produce deep flanging and crazy modulations.

589 Peter Hook to John Robb.

as the leading light of the post-punk generation, a genuinely talented and poetic soul with an iconic voice and stage presence. However, his health problems, and the problems of his personal life were, figuratively, tearing him apart. It was in this flux that the band recorded their defining song, 'Love Will Tear Us Apart'.

> We wrote 'Love Will Tear Us Apart' fast. We would practise for an hour and a half on the Wednesday night and three hours on a Sunday. On the Wednesday, me and Steve had the riff and the drums and we played them over and over again and Barney had the keyboards. Then Ian went to the corner to do the lyric and when we came back on the Sunday he had done the lyrics and there was the song! It only took an hour and a half to write and I still get money from it 35 years later and it's still revered. It's amazing how you can do something for a couple of hours that lasts a lifetime. Most Joy Division songs were written fast – 'Shadowplay' was written in a couple of hours as well.[590]

With the album ready for release that summer and an American tour booked by the late Ruth Polsky, who was the main driver for getting British post-punk bands into the USA, it felt like a band on the brink of breaking out of cult status. Ian Curtis, though, was falling apart. Following a failed suicide attempt, he had to take time out at Anthony Wilson's home in the Derbyshire Hills. The rest of the band were oblivious to the seriousness of the singer's problems.

> We were young lads and when you were from the north in those days, you didn't talk about that kind of stuff. Lads didn't talk to each other about emotions in the '70s. Of course, when I read the lyrics, later on, I realised that there was a real tormented soul there, but at the time, despite everything, we just didn't see it. He wasn't there on the floor, curled up in a ball, with his head in his hands. He was actually, most of the time, acting quite normal. We didn't know much about the illness. We would have stopped the band if he had wanted to, so he could recover, but Ian was the one who was the most driven. The idea of stopping the band and everything he had worked for would have been a non-starter for him.[591]

On May 2 1980, Ian Curtis played his last concert with Joy Division at High Hall in Birmingham University. Sixteen days later, in the early hours of 18 May 1980, after viewing Werner Herzog's 1977 film *Stroszek* [592]and listening to Iggy Pop's album *The Idiot*, the singer hanged himself with the washing line in the kitchen of his house at 77 Barton Street, Macclesfield.

He was only 23.

Two weeks later, the 'Love Will Tear Us Apart' single was released. The song, with its iconic, lilting, bass-driven melody, is the sad epitaph to the singer and the band.

Ironically it became their first hit record.

'The suicide was a permanent solution to a temporary problem', says Hook, 'We would never know what he wanted. We never asked him. We never talked about it to my knowledge'.

---

590 Peter Hook to John Robb.

591 Peter Hook to John Robb.

592 Herzog's brilliant oddball film about an ex-prisoner, a little old man and a prostitute, who leave Germany to begin a new life in a house trailer in Wisconsin.

Ian Curtis's tragic death left an endless series of 'what ifs?' and broken hearts. It turned him into a tragic icon while the rest of the band continued under a shadow as New Order, whilst Joy Division finally became a mainstream success.

Decades later, the influence of Joy Division is everywhere, the band has become a worldwide staple. Their melancholic and beautiful music combined a romantic, poetic vision with a dark energy and has made them the touchstone band for generations of young musicians.

If there was any form of closure for the remainder of the local scene, it could have been the sad day of Anthony Wilson's funeral in 2007. The Factory boss had died of cancer at 58 and the Hidden Gem church in the centre of Manchester was packed for a poignant funeral which he had designed from his death bed; Anthony Wilson even giving his coffin the last Factory number – FAC 501.

The church was packed with people from all walks of life; from gangsters to church leaders and from musicians to family to media folk. As the coffin passed for one last time, Joy Division's 'Atmosphere' wafted over the church PA.

There was not a dry eye in the house.

Perhaps a little more was also grieved that day; not only the death of the powerhouse that was Anthony H. Wilson but for a lost youth, the passing of an era and the genius of the song that was filling the room.

A room filled with melancholy, sadness and lost love.

Chapter 17

'THE WRECKERS OF WESTERN CIVILISATION...'

Industrial Music

From underground mail art to stadiums, from jarring noise to neofolk, the journey of industrial music has been a wholly unlikely one. In a psychic parallel with goth and often entwined with it, the industrial scene has explored its own darkness. Deconstructing the musical norms, industrial could vary from found sound, metal percussion, and musical concrete to freak electronics, sound collage, and stygian drones whilst often dancing to its own dark disco. Over the decades it has morphed, endlessly restless, into neofolk, stadium industrial, industrial metal, dark matter techno or remained resolutely underground.

Playing with the dark contrast between new technology, found sound and post-industrial themes and a fascination with the darker sex and death corners of the human psyche, it could be confrontational poetic melancholia or expose uncomfortable areas of the human condition. Meanwhile goth - while dark, would tend to explore its themes with more traditional instruments and its lyrics, often poetic, would deal with internal battles of depression, existentialism, sex, death and romantic vistas and relationships on a less detached more human level.

What started as an esoteric, almost performance art, with incidental jarring music has become a dark matter blockbuster, with its influence on huge bands like Nine Inch Nails and Rammstein seeing it inhabit a whole new meaning while many of its key players remain creatively active exploring their own obsessions deep in their own rabbit holes.

*****

On 18 October 1976, an arts collective called COUM Transmissions caused tabloid uproar after they staged a challenging art event called 'Prostitution' at the ICA venue in the heart of London and the British establishment.[593]

Attending 'Prostitution' was the controversial late Tory MP, Nicholas Fairbairn[594], who took the usual professional umbrage at what he saw: 'The wreckers of Western civilisation...' he sneered. It was a remark which became the Daily Mirror headline the following day, and going on to say, 'It's a sickening outrage! Sadistic! Obscene! Evil! The Arts Council must be scrapped after this!' His remarks became headlines in the Daily Mirror the next day.

---

593 The ICA was founded to establish a space where artists, writers and scientists could debate ideas outside the traditional confines of the Royal Academy.

594 Scottish MP dogged by sex scandals and known for his flamboyant dress sense.

The press reaction forced Ted Little, the chair of the ICA at the time to defend the exhibition and the controversy it caused, explaining that the venue had a duty to provide a platform for the contemporary avant-garde.

Built around an unconventional couple, Cosey Fanni Tutti and Genesis P-Orridge, COUM Transmissions confronted, subverted and challenged social conventions and the hypocrisy of 'decency'. That night, their event consisted of assemblages of rusty knives, syringes, bloodied hair, used sanitary towels, press clippings, explicit photos of Cosey Fanni Tutti cut from porn magazines and graphic photo documentation of previous performances in Milan and Paris. The event was the last performance by COUM and also the first performance of their new music project, Throbbing Gristle[595]. Bizarrely, also on the bill, that evening was the early punk band Chelsea (billed as LSD) with Billy Idol on bass:

> The Arts Council put on a thing where Genesis P-Orridge had a grant to do an arts show. He had these pictures of Auschwitz, James Hanratty and all these people hanging in jails. Our manager at the time, John Krivine[596], also managed Genesis (P-Orridge and I used to meet him a lot at the time in his called shop Boy, and he asked us to play the gig. [597]

At the start of the Throbbing Gristle performance, Genesis took to the mic and delivered a speech full of doom and destruction. As he began his dark diatribe about the decay of humanity, Peter Christopherson took his place behind his tape machine, Chris Carter got behind his keyboards and Cosey Fanni Tutti settled herself onto a wooden chair to handle a guitar. The following set consisted of weird sub-psychedelic taped sounds and random keyboard noises, all played while Genesis P-Orridge intoned his lyrics and gripped his bass guitar.

Musically, this was a pungent and powerful stew spiked with taped material selected by Christopherson – some of which was genuinely unsettling, some sexual and some a musical concrete[598]; all of which was put into the sonic blender for maximum effect. Meanwhile, Genesis howled or sang dark and provocative lyrics softly over the top, his voice treated with effects. It was a shocking leap into the future and an early incarnation of the seductive and yet frightening electric pulses and noise surrounded by the cut-up confrontation of the dark debris of the present that Throbbing Gristle would go on to hone down.

It also made the growing furore around the then-incoming Sex Pistols seem rather tame.

Sex Pistols and Throbbing Gristle make an interesting juxtaposition. At the time, they were both unpinned grenades, about to bounce around British culture. Both

---

595 Northern slang for an erect penis - darkly funny and unsettling at the same time - perfect for the project.

596 Krivine had met Genesis at Hull University in 1968 and located the building that became their first art space. He moved to London and opened the influential Acme Attractions Clothes shop on King's Road that later became Boy. He also managed the early Generation X and his old college friend's early projects.

597 Billy Idol to John Robb.

598 Or a Musique concrete - the french term for Musique concrète a type of music composition that uses raw material for sound which is then treated with processors and tape montage.

were a result of the decade's stuffy reaction to the high-water mark of the post-counterculture freedoms fought for in the 1960s. By pushing further, both bands had the ability to shock the establishment to its core.

In the end, it was Sex Pistols who broke into the mainstream. Nonetheless, Throbbing Gristle managed to have a long and enduring influence, creating a genuinely groundbreaking sound with challenging ideas in a startling and unsettling project that was far away from the more conventional guitar rush of punk rock.

Throbbing Gristle drew on a much wider variety of influences than many of their contemporaries. In their mix were '60s psychedelia and happenings, the electronic pulse of Kraftwerk, the prog-pop of Roxy Music, the textures of John Cage and the repetition of The Velvet Underground alongside hippy acid test jam bands and freak happenings and Antonin Artaud's Theatre of Cruelty. Also influential was Lou Reed's groundbreaking *Metal Machine Music*; a record that had been released as a deliberate 'fuck off' to his record label and an album that was a noise record of guitar drones that, of course, found a small percentage of fans who loved it for its hypnotic quality. There was also a nod to the polyrhythmic groove of Afrobeat king, Fela Kuti, and an embrace of free jazz, musical concrete, Dadaism, experimentalists and hippy-era trance bands.

Left-field literature also had a place within Throbbing Gristle's world, with William Burroughs' contemplative darkness, Friedrich Nietzsche's nihilistic theory and as ever, 'the wickedest man in the world', Aleister Crowley, all having influence in the band's output. This cultural potpourri helped to create a new and unsettling inspiration for a musical performance utilising technology, science and future noise. In curating their ever-changing sound, Throbbing Gristle reflected the filth of the establishment back at itself in a whirlwind of ideas and a crash course in extremist art.

They had arrived at the cusp of punk but were the final revenge of the hippies. The disappointment at the failure of the counterculture revolution helped to create a darker black hole art. However, this art swiftly accelerated away from hippy culture and into a twisted zone of contemporary mischief-making.

That late night at the ICA in 1976 sparked something and in the next couple of years, Throbbing Gristle became the ultimate cult band inspiring fellow noiseniks or earnest young men in military gear to spray symbols on their shared houses as they became consumed by TG's metal guru.

Musically a whole clutch of talented outsiders became immersed in the new electronics, noise, and confrontational content and creating their own interpretation of an edgy culture of impenetrable and challenging sound collages and blip electronics on what would become a journey into what would become labelled industrial music (after Throbbing Gristle's Industrial Records label.)

From its early sonic confrontations, industrial would later develop through countless hybrids, never flinching from embracing the darkness of its own provocative roots and yet always maintaining an appreciation of the stunning beauty in that darkness.

In 2020, what constitutes industrial music is so varied that the term is almost redundant. It could refer to the pioneering work of Throbbing Gristle or the esoteric micro scene built around idiosyncratic individuals with a unique world vision like David Tibet,[599] Steven Stapleton[600] or the late John Balance.[601] The now defunct American label, Wax Trax! Records further sculpted the vision of the genre by releasing the industrial metal of bands such as Ministry and Revolting Cocks. Then there were was the rock-based, industrial dance of the million-selling, stadium-filling bands who primarily concerned themselves with industrial's aesthetics while crossing it with heavily treated trad rock guitars such as Depeche Mode, Nine Inch Nails, Rammstein, Marilyn Manson and even Prodigy. Contemporary industrial also incorporates the diverse raft of decades of deconstructed bands like Einstürzende Neubauten, Swans, Fad Gadget, Front 242, Ministry, Laibach and The Young Gods, all of them utilising the sound and vision to create new sonic space.

The twilight world of Throbbing Gristle's art guerrilla underground sparked a proto-scene that blossomed in the post-punk era when the DIY climate and desire for a new post-rock soundtrack was particularly strong. This growing atmosphere created a platform for many of these new creatives. Operating outside the system, many of the early industrial artists formed their own semi-anarchic network of independent record labels and DIY fanzines. They exchanged audio cassettes, ideas and 'mail art'; the latter referring to their art-dangerous, artistic missives that were sent via the unknowing postal system.

With its roots in the 1970s this furtive underground had seen several other obscure pioneers explore performance art, primitive electronics, distortion, radio frequencies, pulsating electronics, tape noise and even Nazi shock horror imagery to create genuinely unsettling music and art culture. Aside from Throbbing Gristle, there was the late American percussionist and performance artist Z'EV and key influential figure of sound/noise Boyd Rice alongside volatile performer Monte Cazazza (who, even for the underground, was regarded as a maverick's maverick) with his potentially dangerous anti-social aesthetic (and sound collages to match), all of whom were following similar creative paths.

Throbbing Gristle got to know Monte Cazazza after Genesis P-Orridge and Cosey Fanni Tutti read about him in a 1974 issue of *Vile* Magazine. He was the Valentine's Day cover boy, holding a dripping bloody heart that looked as though it was torn from his own chest. They began writing to each other and their mutual fascination for the dark side inspired a meeting in California.

Cazazza is key to the original aesthetic of the industrial form, not least for coining the slogan 'Industrial Music for Industrial People' in the mid-1970s, which Throbbing Gristle would later appropriate for their Industrial Records label slogan, shortly before it was abbreviated to the term 'industrial music'. It became a catch-

---

599 Born David Michael Bunting, 5 March 1960. Tibet was the founder of Current 93, former member of Psychic TV and cohort in the death-folk of Death in June and many others.

600 Recording under the name Nurse With Wound, Steven Stapleton explored all kind of textures from drone, dark ambient, industrial and noise and beyond.

601 The late John Balance was the co-founder of Coil as well as playing and collaborating with Death in June, Psychic TV, Current 93, Chris & Cosey and many others.

all term for the label and then a whole scene of similar creatives, fascinated by the artistic possibilities presented by violence, sick imagery and the darker side of life.

A mysterious shapeshifting figure, Cazazza pioneered experimental noise collages in the mid-1970s and broke all established musical rules when creating his new musical narrative. His work mixed a fascination with porn, necrophilia, the phallus, blood, death and Nazism, all adding layers of genuinely unsettling weirdness to his work and making him one of the true catalysts of the form.

It was uncomfortable art and deliberately so.

Yet it was Throbbing Gristle who would make the biggest impact across the music scene as The Smiths guitarist Johnny Marr pointed out, 'the godfathers and the most revered band was always Throbbing Gristle. I saw them play a lot; there was something distinctly different about them.'

It all coalesced in Hull, of all places. COUM Transmissions were founded in 1969 at the University by Salford-born Neil Andrew Megson. The smart and darkly inquisitive student had become interested in the 'beyond' culture of Frank Zappa, the Velvets and the occult in his 1960's school days at Solihull school - a grand looking overachieving place with an endless list of alumni. Megson's defining moment came when he dropped out of Hull University in the summer of 1969 and drifted down to London. It was here that he spent a few months living in the Transmedia Explorations commune in Islington.

The extreme fringes of the counterculture of the late '60s were full of such fascinating and failed experiments in living. These experimental lifestyles affected many British alternative movers and shakers that would find their voice in the cultural wreckage of the pre-punk and punk eras. So much of the '70s, and then punk's eventual anarchic mindset and intellectually abrasive art, found its roots in these revolutionary if grubby, environments.

Transmedia Explorations was an offshoot of Exploding Galaxy who counted Derek Jarman as one of its fringe members. The 1967 collective, who had performed happenings at the Alexandra Palace, were living in the Balls Pond Road house of artists like Paul Keeler and David Medalla – whose bubble machines had been of the groundbreaking late 1960s UFO club experience[602].

Far from the frivolous hippie utopia he was looking for, Transmedia was serious business. Commune members lived under a strict regime that was designed to shock them out of their routines and conventional behaviour. It was during this rigorous deconditioning that Megson began to formulate his own ideas to recreate back in Hull. Deliberately disconcerting, Transmedia members were forbidden from sleeping in the same place on consecutive nights, food was cooked at irregular times of day and all clothing was kept in a communal chest with members wearing something different each day.

---

602 The UFO club was the key psychedelic club in London where the early Pink Floyd had played and showcased the tripped-out effects that were like an early version of the provocative multimedia art that Throbbing Gristle would ramp up a decade later.

He fell out with the commune when he discovered that the leaders, as ever, received preferential treatment. He also disliked the lack of music and left for a short stay at his parent's new home in Shrewsbury. Whilst back in Shropshire he conceived the idea of COUM where he planned to implement many of the Transmedia art/life concepts he had experienced in London. A key concept involved thinking of himself as a 'transmedia' persona; a transitory human form, a creative energy source having the potential to express and exist through, and in, any medium.

Returning to Hull in the autumn of 1969, Megson and college buddy, John Krivine started the Ho-Ho Funhouse art space by the Hull docks. The charismatic, now bearded figure and his followers staged a couple of COUM events to bemused Hull locals. These happenings were based on Tom Wolfe's 1968 New Journalism book, *The Electric Kool-Aid Acid Test* which detailed time spent with Ken Kesey's Merry Pranksters as they drove across the 1964 America in their famous painted bus, tripping on LSD and performing their acid tests.[603]

Having earlier befriended Megson at an acid test party, local flower child Christine Newby would move into the Funhouse art space where she was promptly renamed Cosey Fanni Tutti.[604] Meanwhile, Megson now became Genesis P-Orridge, in a reference to his favourite food.

The ad hoc group soon moved to their new base on the historic Prince Street in Hull city centre where they created a new commune in one of the old houses. It was not quite the hoped-for hippie utopia with attendant poverty, grime and old-school male/female attitudes pervading in the damp old building but the collective's fervent imaginations saw them stage several performances in the early 1970s. Unflinchingly challenging sexual content, they were inspired by their fellow counter-culture mavericks like Fluxus[605] and the Viennese Actionists[606] they had met on their travels.

COUM's deliberately provocative art happenings mixed sex, violence, maggots, dildos, syringes of blood, nudity and all manner of provocative actions like masturbation – sometimes with an added chicken. The collective believed in chance, intuition and improvisation as techniques for creating 'pure' art. They used deliberate shock tactics to awaken and shake the senses. Soon enough, there was a sonic twist to their performance as Cosey remembers:

> Music was part of my life before COUM. As a teenager, I was closely involved with the local underground music and art scene in Hull. My father built radios and created strange sounds during the process, and, coupled with my uncle, who

---

603 Documented in Wolfe's book were Kesey's adventures, observing the USA through the prism of acid. Kesey had just found fame as the author of *One Flew Over the Cuckoo's Nest* and was a pioneer of LSD experimentation. The bus, driven by Neal Cassady, was a riot of new ideas, mad pranks and Day-Glo painted proto-hippies inventing a new America.

604 Partly after the title of Amadeus Mozart's 1790 opera, *Così Fan Tutte*. All this period is brilliantly documented in her autobiography 'Art Sex Music'.

605 An international, interdisciplinary community of artists, composers, designers and poets during the 1960s and 1970s who engaged in experimental art performances which emphasised the artistic process over the finished product.

606 The Actionists believed in art as a direct confrontation. Happenings often saw participants masturbating or covering themselves in faeces, inciting a strong reaction and resulting in arrest.

lived with us, played his guitar and harmonica. So, I was kind of primed for sound from an early age. [607]

There was no central focus or aim for the group and ambiguity was key; COUM could be anything at any time. Whether they were supporting Hawkwind at Bradford St Georges Hall in 1971, self-publishing flyers, posters and magazines or creating art pieces, COUM were a force of creativity. They began to stage deconstructions of music, such as 'Marcel Duchamp's Next Work', in which volunteers bashed bicycle wheels 'conducted' by P-Orridge or Paul Woodrow,[608] accompanied by slides and written instructions. Where Duchamp rendered mass-produced objects useless by transforming them into art, COUM transformed the same art object into a totalitarian object; a musical instrument.

After 1973, their left-field confrontational art and their habit of shoplifting in order to survive inevitably attracted the attention of the local constabulary and the heat was on. It was time to move to London.

Genesis and Cosey found rooms in an art commune called SPACE in Hackney's Martello Street which they called the Death Factory. It was here that P-Orridge would meet highly influential American writer William S. Burroughs. He, in turn, introduced the young man to left-field performance artist and writer Brion Gysin[609] whose use of the cut-up technique[610] was a great influence on P-Orridge.

In 1974, the collective started to shift their focus more towards sound and music after meeting Peter Christopherson; a man who they nicknamed 'Sleazy' because of his fascination with their project's confrontational sex media. Cosey began to work as a stripper and as a pornographic model, consciously participating in the process of commercial image production. She explored pornography as an art form - viewing art as encompassing sex, porn, music and media. The collective would use such examples as ammunition in their commentary on society.

Sleazy, working for sleeve designers Hipgnosis,[611] had begun by designing graphics for the wayward art pair whose performance art shows across Europe were becoming increasingly provocative. In their explorations of sex and violence, they had begun to masturbate on stage, sometimes putting lighted candles in Cosey's vagina.

After meeting Chris Carter, they became Throbbing Gristle on 3 September 1975, the date deliberately chosen by Genesis P-Orridge for being the 36th anniversary of the United Kingdom joining the Second World War.

> When we shifted from COUM Transmissions to Throbbing Gristle, we were also stating that we wanted to go into popular culture. Get away from the art gallery context, and show that the same technique that had been made to operate in that

---

607 To The Quietus.

608 The co-founder of the Canadian artists' collective, W.O.R.K.S. (We Ourselves Roughly Know Something).

609 Fringe Beat and British-Canadian painter, writer, sound poet, performance artist and inventor of experimental devices.

610 Whereby the text is cut up and rearranged to create a new text. The concept can be traced to – at least – the Dadaists of the 1920s, but was popularised in the late 1950s and early 1960s by writer Burroughs.

611 Art design group who designed sleeves for many large bands of the 1970s, including Pink Floyd, T. Rex, ELO, 10CC and many others.

system could work. We wanted to test it out in the real world, or nearer to the real world, at a more street level – with young kids who had no education in art perception and either empathised or didn't; either liked the noise or didn't. A little mini-Dada movement, eh?

It was a process of reduction. We decided we didn't want a drummer, because that would immediately anchor us in rock history. In the beginning, we hit my bass strings with a leather glove to provide a rhythm. Chris Carter started building drum machines and weird gadgets. Sleazy Christopherson experimented with tape machines and cut-ups because he was into Burroughs. Cosey wanted to play lead guitar, which at the time was unheard of for a woman. We got one from Woolworths, but she said it was too heavy. So, we took an electric saw and cut off the excess wood and that's how she ended up with that shape of guitar.[612]

After the ICA event, Throbbing Gristle would become a counterculture guerrilla raid on good taste. They created a music and art piece so full of ideas and strange new sonic textures that they have taken decades to unpick. Their November 1977 debut album *The Second Annual Report* was released on their Industrial Records label. A mixture of live and studio tracks, the album is astonishing in its otherworldly assault, making for compulsive and uncomfortable listening.

Follow-up 1978 single, 'United'/ 'Zyklon B Zombie', was a fantastically bizarre release that jolted the listener into another sonic dimension. The flip-side was the deliberately provocative reference to the Zyklon B poison gas used at Auschwitz extermination camp; the war's dark shadow was still lingering on the fringes of music culture. Creepy and provocative and yet oddly playable, the single was a standout release in a year of standout music.

With a heavy underground reputation, the band, now dressed in army fatigues, were a byword for extremes in music, creating something as sublime as it was grotesque or morbid. They were showing how art could indeed be both a mirror and a hammer. [613]

The 1978 album, *D.O..A: The Third and Final Report of Throbbing Gristle*, is considered by followers to be the band's most perfect statement. Recorded under duress, the album was played out with the backdrop of the personal tension in Cosey's relationship with Genesis that had imploded and she was now with Chris Carter. From the desolate, touching and very personal 'Weeping' to 'Hamburger Lady' – a song about a hospitalised burns victim – it was a deeply unsettling journey. The dark subject matter would become a key inspiration for much of the twisted muse of future industrial. Musically, the collection of esoteric tape loop grooves, found sound, background conversation and half-snatched atmospheres is, yet again, compelling in its off-kilter brilliance.

I first became aware of Throbbing Gristle in the late 1970s. I was pretty much used to hearing abstract avant-garde music from 1972 and the Faust Tapes but Throbbing Gristle sounded quite unlike anything that I had ever heard before.

---

612 Genesis P. Orridge to The Guardian.

613 It was German playwright Bertolt Brecht who came up with the phrase 'Art is not a mirror held up to reality, but a hammer with which to shape it.'

They were really dark and demanding. Their releases were hard to acquire and the mythology surrounding their performances only enhanced the desire to possess their records and see them live. I was lucky enough to obtain a coveted copy of Live at The Death Factory bootleg, of which only 50 copies were pressed. Mine is number 20. This was the recording of their gig at Manchester's Factory Club on the 18 May 1979, which Ian Curtis told me he had been to see. He would commit suicide exactly one year later.

In November 1980, Throbbing Gristle came to Berlin to perform at the SO36 club and the gig was a thrilling masterpiece recorded for the promoter, Burkhardt Seiler from Zensor Records, by Dimitri Hegemann. This recording eventually became the album *Funeral in Berlin*.

I took the band around West Berlin to have their now infamous photos taken at Checkpoint Charlie and the brutalist buildings of the former Oberkommando der Wehrmachts Headquarters at the Reichpietschufer.[614]

20 Jazz Funk Greats, released in 1979, was a subversive, neo-mutant, dirty disco release that was still primed to shock with its sinuous, electro grooves that were verging on the commercial. The deceptive album cover saw the group dressed down and standing on Beachy Head in East Sussex, a notorious suicide spot, capturing the mood of the album perfectly – all coy innocence disguising a darker and provocative undertow, as Genesis P-Orridge points out:

> I've been involved in a total war with culture since the day I started. I am at war with the status quo of society and I am at war with those in control and power. I'm at war with hypocrisy and lies, I'm at war with the mass media. Then I'm at war with every bastard who tries to hurt someone else for their own sake. And I'm at war with privilege and I'm at war with all the things that one should be at war with basically. As my mentor used to say: 'I feel your pain, I feel your shame but you're not to blame.[615]

Fractious and intense, the first phase of Throbbing Gristle could never last and, in 1981, after four years of remarkable and imaginative dark exploration, the first phase of Throbbing Gristle it was over. As Cosey explained, 'TG broke up because me and Gen broke up'.

Genesis P-Orridge and Peter Christopherson went on to form Psychic TV with the unheralded musical genius of Alex Fergusson from the punk band ATV. Their psychedelic trip would see them entwined with the then-current goth scene. Their best known song, the haunting and melodic psych guitar of 'Godstar' – about the late Rolling Stones icon Brian Jones – became an unlikely hit, reaching number 29 in the charts, transforming Genesis into a very unlikely fringe-pop DarkStar.[616] Eventually, their long and sprawling career would see them release 100 albums and pioneer acid house in a whirlwind of ideas and concepts.

Meanwhile, Cosey Fanni Tutti and Chris Carter continued to record together under the names of Chris and Cosey, Carter Tutti and Creative Technology Institute

---

614 Mark Reeder to John Robb.

615 Genesis P-Orridge to The Guardian.

616 Genesis P-Orridge died in 2020.

and Carter Tutti Void, continuing to refine their music into an hypnotic electronic perfection to this day. Cosey's 2017 unflinching autobiography *Art Sex Music* provided a vivid account of her whole trip.

After leaving Psychic TV in 1983, Christopherson put together Coil with his partner and fellow Psychic TV member, the late John Balance. Their music was laden with a powerful atmosphere as they pursued their vision of creating a 'ritual music for the accumulation of male sexual energy'. Armed with brilliantly produced albums that were full of brooding drama, they would eventually mutate towards a heavier, drone-like sound, twisted with a powerful melodic touch and a heavy dance floor heartbeat.

Their debut EP release, *How to Destroy Angels*, is a mesmerising piece of percussion and electronic proto-drone, played on subtly fluctuating gongs. This piece of music would prove to be hugely influential on the modern drone scene and to bands such as Sunn O))). The debut 1984 Scatology album is a landmark in the genre; a groundbreaking work that crossed industrial with a certain whiff of post-punk and a musicality that saw its bold and dark soundscapes fully realised. Their version of 'Tainted Love', with Marc Almond on vocals, utilised a slower groove for a deceptively uneasy primal listen.

Later albums like 1986's *Horse Rotorvator* saw the band take an even darker and slower approach that only served to underline their unique atmospherics while 1991's *Love's Secret Domain* was drenched in post-acid house hedonism and was a near-dance record. When John Balance died on 3 November 2004, after falling from a two-story balcony at his home, it opened the door for Throbbing Gristle to reform in the same year to great acclaim. They would perform intermittently until Christopherson himself died in 2010.

✵✵✵✵✵

Maverick music always works best in isolation. There is something fascinating about the idea that the post-industrial cities were breeding grounds for this esoteric activity. In the internet age, it's nearly impossible to understand this sense of cultural isolation, yet there was a time when these strange micro-collectives operate with no idea that anyone else was out there.

Sheffield in 1974 was far from pop culture's focal point, but that didn't stop Cabaret Voltaire from pushing the boundaries of music and taste, creating a homemade electronic noise. They took their conceptual cues from William Burroughs, J. G. Ballard, and Tristan Tzara,[617] creating their own proto-industrial sound. Along with Throbbing Gristle, they are considered key pioneers of industrial music. Initially composed of Stephen Mallinder, Richard H. Kirk, and Chris Watson, the group was

---

617 The Romanian and French avant-garde poet, essayist and performance artist who died in 1963.

named after the early 20th century nightclub in Zürich that served as a centre for the early Dada movement.[618]

Initially inspired by the art school prog-pop of Roxy Music, the stripped-down art aesthetic of The Velvet Underground and the futuristic, electronic pulses of Kraftwerk, Cabaret Voltaire began in 1973 by trying to make music with reel to reel recorders, playing with recorded sound and a music concrete. There was, quite literally, no one else out there doing it. The band would spend hours in Chris Watson's attic, recording ideas. They created all manner of lyrical skreegh and cut-up rhythms with found sound and layers of collage. Often, these would be placed over rhythmic patterns, and treated with their trademark effects. This sonic bricolage would eventually be integrated and appreciated by many generations of musicians, each finding new areas of influence in their sound. It took years, though, before anyone caught up with them.

In 1975, the group played their first gig. The set finished with Stephen Mallinder being admitted to hospital after an audience altercation. Their esoteric music was played on two synthesisers, guitar, and occasionally, clarinet as well as a rhythm generator, and the EMS[619] - which was used for treating the voice and organ,– which proved too much for some. Cabaret Voltaire were breaking auditory barriers with several of the tapes pre-recorded with different sound sources; from jet engines to random noise collage, all heavily treated with sound effects. The [band]'s process of using tape loops to build up these collages expanded into processing and distorting other instruments and vocal lines, recording them onto hundreds of cassettes in an archive of imagination.

Finally finding an audience in post-punk, Cabaret Voltaire were sharing bills and the 1978 *A Factory Sample* EP with Joy Division. That release tied together the new northern post-punk underground of Sheffield and Manchester into one fascinating whole. They then signed to Rough Trade in 1978 capturing the antagonistic underground spirit of the time on their debut EP with tracks like 'Do the Mussolini (Headkick)' that set their agenda.

Their breakthrough single, 1979's glowering, dark, distorted and uneasy 'Nag Nag Nag', somehow managed to turn Cabaret Voltaire's experiments into a distorted dance floor hit that was big in the proto-goth clubs at the time. The band's darker sound was driven by an atmosphere of paranoia, an interest in conspiracy theories, political control and the use of drugs – both to free and inhibit the individual. This helped to create an air of mystique around the band as they explored this mixture in their first three albums that set the stall, not only for them, but for industrial music as a whole. 1979's *Mix Up*, 1980's *Voice of America* and 1981's *Red Mecca* albums became template releases for all acolytes of industrial musics.

---

618 Dadaism was an art movement that emerged during the ravages of WWI and was a reaction to the bloody mess of Europe's war. Rejecting ideas of logic, reason, and aestheticism that were dominant in a modern capitalist society, Dadaist artists were fascinated by nonsense, irrationality, and staged anti-bourgeois protest in their works.

619 Named after the new portable version of Peter Zinovieff's remarkable electronic music studio and synthesiser the EMS that would modulate and treat sound into baffling and brilliant new shapes.

Cabaret Voltaire had made their own nod towards a neo-pop direction with the introduction of top producer Flood on their 1983 *Crackdown* album. The release was their intellectual left-field tussle with an almost pop sound, adding their slant to a more commercial and less dense sound. Depeche Mode would also take their fringe to the mainstream after Martin Gore saw Neubauten perform, it inspired their music and the way he dressed too. Gone were the neatly creased trousers and in came the black leather and S&M bondage gear. Another British band who were heavily inspired by Neubauten were The Test Department.[620]

As the original wave of industrial bands added a musicality to their sound, there was an opportunity for darker and even stranger beasts to emerge from the undergrowth. An ad hoc loose collection of musicians built up around David Tibet, Steven Stapleton and John Balance making artful and challenging music beyond ego, all supportive of each other's projects and explorations.

Few people on this loose scene had not worked with the idiosyncratic and fascinating David Tibet. Picking up his nickname from Genesis P-Orridge, he remains the only full time member of Current 93. The project, which started in the early '80s, was named after one of the many tenets of Aleister Crowley's Law of Thelema.[621] Initial recordings with twisted tape loops and disorientating distorted vocals to the fore formed a disorientating collage. Tibet then went on to pioneer a darker, pagan-folk soundscape in a series of captivating releases. In a complex and fascinating career, he has played on and produced on a huge list of cutting edge releases with a roll call of creative powerhouses including Steven Stapleton of Nurse With Wound (who also plays with Current 93), Death in June, Steve Ignorant of Crass, Boyd Rice, Little Annie, Björk, Nick Cave, Shirley Collins, Rose McDowall of Strawberry Switchblade and even Tiny Tim.

Tibet, like many in his immediate circle of musical accomplices, was on a trip of unflinching intellectual ideas, spirituality, politics and philosophy, set to an ever changing soundtrack that could be sparse, noisy, ugly or beautiful; but never boring. Since 1986, he has pursued an 'apocalyptic folk' direction, mixing traditional elements with experimentation. Guided by his spiritual leanings and his esoteric tastes in music and literature, 2006's *Black Ships That Ate the Sky* is a neofolk masterpiece. It started, like most of his projects, with a phrase and an idea. The album explored Tibet's own growing spirituality and interest in Christian mysticism with songs that have a glowering folk darkness and smouldering beauty.

Current 93's vast number of albums cover a huge array of themes that touch on so many ideas. There is a deep interest in Christianity, Buddhism and other folk and religious mysticism, as well as folk traditions, witchcraft and art and Aleister

---

620 Mark Reeder to John Robb.

621 The central philosophy of Thelema is summed up in two phrases: 'Do what thou wilt shall be the whole of the Law' and 'Love is the law, love under will'. The two primary terms in these statements are 'Will' and 'Love', respectively. In the Greek language, they are Thelema (Will) and Agape (Love). Using the Greek technique of isopsephy, which applies a numerical value to each letter, the letters of each of these words sum to 93.

Crowley, whose dark and arcane theories of magick and self-will have been key in industrial music.

Fellow musical travellers, Nurse With Wound, have also pushed boundaries. They have always been fascinated with the outer limits of sound and music as a form. Formed by Steven Stapleton in 1978, they experimented with noise sculpture and sound collage through forty albums across an astonishing array of styles and influences. Music writer Richard Foster caught one of the band's rare live outings at Incubate Festival in Tilburg Holland 2012:

> The Incubate show was magical and disconcerting. One immediate impression was that they seemed quite happy to crack on without any fuss at all. Nothing suggested Stapleton and co had been away for over twenty years. And despite the trippy backdrops it felt more like a private rehearsal than a big show. The trio seemed to have a total confidence in being able to suck the crowd into their otherworldly, sometimes gnomic stew of electronics, wyrd samples and obtuse instrumentation.

Stapleton has created many sonic vistas and worked with many collaborators, including James Thirlwell of Foetus, William Bennett of Whitehouse, Rose McDowall, Annie Anxiety, John Balance and most regularly David Tibet of Current 93; all the while creating a music that is impossible to define. His creativity utilises a whole gamut of influences ranging from The Beach Boys to pagan folk and from Latin to soundscape. All releases are brilliantly laced with a dark Dadaist humour and an enticing surrealism.

This next wave of industrial musicians were moving deeper into a darker sound and the outcome wasn't always pleasant. Whitehouse were formed by William Bennet, the former guitarist from Essential Logic – the post-punk band formed by Lora Logic, the original saxophone player of X-Ray Spex.

While studying at Glasgow University in 1977, Bennet had become fascinated with the works of Karl Fogg. This obsession was instigated after a meeting with the future boss of indie label, Postcard Records, Alan Horne, who was translating the banned author for his fanzine, *Swankers*. Bennett claimed that he was going to play 'the most brutal and extreme music of all time'. It was an aim he undoubtedly achieved, creating a bleak, haunting and distinctly uncomfortable music. This output was partly influenced by the often-overlooked music of Yoko Ono, cranked with an intensity and a dark and ferocious noise. Whitehouse dealt with the taboo and the discomforting with a genuine, unsettling darkness. There were references to sadistic sex, rape, misogyny, serial murder, eating disorders, child abuse, neo-Nazi fetishism and other forms of violence and abjection. It was uncomfortable listening and a journey into the darkest corners of the human psyche. The self-styled power electronics outfit didn't flinch from controversy as Bennet continued to work with a series of collaborators. These ranged from the omnipresent Steve Stapleton who lent his talents to many industrial bands, to Steve Albini who engineered several of their 1990s releases. Many questioned his moral motivation, but Bennett had his own explanation.

It's simply what I'm interested in. It's what I like reading about, watching and participating in, to some extent. I wouldn't do things that I wasn't interested in. It's just personal interest, obsessions, if you like. Nothing is sacred, as far as I'm concerned. I wouldn't not do anything. There's no taboo that I wouldn't be quite happy to break if I thought it would make for some good music.

Death in June took this confrontation even further. Built around Douglas P, whose roots lie in the left-wing late-1970s punk band, Crisis, the band have flirted with controversy. Accusations of neo-Nazi leanings are frequently thrown at them due to their use of Nazi-related imagery. These images are deliberately provocative and emerging from a fascination with dark aesthetics; in the blurred world of industrial, it's often hard to define meaning and intention in the creativity. Understandably, the debate still rages.

Death in June have endured various lineups that have shapeshifted through many styles of music and performance, all before helping to pioneer the move from industrial to neofolk/pagan on their 1983 album, *The Guilty Have No Pride*. With its acoustic guitars and references to European history, it jarred with heavy percussion and electronic pulses. It is an oddly off-kilter, yet successful amalgamation of disparate musical ideas. After this release, Death in June would go on to experiment with electronic dance music and help pioneer the martial industrial form[622] throughout a long and varied musical sojourn.

The fervent industrial underground was full of fascinating activity, built around labels like Third Mind Records; a UK indie label born from post-punk fanzine culture that decided to release some of the music they were writing about. Label head honcho Gary Levermore even had his own band, Bushido, whose haunting music has a timeless floating quality to it. Levermore can also be credited for signing Canadian industrial band Front Line Assembly and British singer-songwriter Bill Pritchard.

Back in Sheffield, there were further green shoots of creativity appearing in Cabaret Voltaire's shadow. Klive Humberstone from In The Nursery was one of many people drawn to the city's raw and futuristic music scene; a scene built around a dystopian and sci-fi vision, cultivated in the post-war, concrete city centre. 'I came to Sheffield in 1979', Humberstone remembers, 'and more than half the audience were in bands themselves. The music scene there made you want to produce music and there were plenty of territorial rivalries, but it was invigorating at the same time'.

The Human League were just one of these bands. Initially, a quirky, sci-fi, underground band armed with reel-to-reels and a weird sense of post-glam humour, their early music was unintentionally left field. They found art in the trash aesthetic and were taking comics and old glam rock singles as seriously as the heaviest cultural theories. Their 1978 debut single, 'Being Boiled', was released on the inventive Fast

---

622 Martial industrial is a syncretic offshoot of industrial music characterised by noise, dark ambient atmospheres, neofolk melodies, dark wave tunes and neoclassical orchestrations as well as the incorporation of audio from military marches, historical speeches and political, apolitical or metapolitical lyrics.

Product label[623] and is a fantastic record. The song is a mash of future keyboard noise and sparse and darkly futuristic sci-fi overload. The baritone vocals came from new singer Phil Oakey[624] who had 'alternative' pop star written all over him. From his asymmetric fringe to his makeup, his enhanced glamour predicted the flamboyant future pop by a couple of years.

When the band spilt into two, the songwriters recruited Glenn Gregory on vocals and turned themselves into Heaven 17, a smart pop band with a penchant for cutting-edge technology. Meanwhile, Phil Oakey kept The Human League name and enlisted two teenage girls discovered in a Sheffield nightclub, Susan Ann Sulley and Joanne Catherall (aged 17 and 18 respectively) helping turn the band into one of the biggest pop groups of the early 1980s. Under the watchful eye of Martin Rushent who was arguably the best producer in punk, having worked with The Stranglers, Generation X and Buzzcocks, together, they created a unique, distinct and best-selling pop sound.

Meanwhile, another former The Human league singer, Adi Newton, was soon to have his own project off the ground; Clock DVA. It was a band that reflected the steel city's fascination with *Clockwork Orange* and its dystopian vision of the future. Added to this was an outsider spirit fostered by the disappointed generation came of age among the decay and dereliction of the late 1970s. Formed in 1978 by Newton and Steven 'Judd' Turner, Clock DVA married the sparseness of industrial music with black dance music and were one of the precursors to the future goth soundtrack of EBM. [625] Clock DVA were a fascinating proposition that combined the Sheffield scene's love of tape loops, rumbling bass, distorted noise, dark drones and robotic detached vocals that all helped to create a futuristic sci-fi sound.

Meanwhile, In The Nursery had set out on a unique musical journey that started with intense noise, then martial military beats before creating a beautiful, almost symphonic soundscape.

> Sheffield was now full of bands looking for a new way. We certainly didn't consider ourselves as part of an industrial scene in much the same way that Cabaret Voltaire and Test Dept didn't. There was a certain affinity with bands like Dead Can Dance,[626] who were using early samplers in a similar way to us and projects like This Mortal Coil for their use of classical instrumentation. Joy Division and post-punk artists such as In Camera, Rema Rema and A Certain Ratio were elements that we brought with us when we had re-located to Sheffield, but the creative scene within the city (not to forget the stunning surrounding countryside) was a defining influence.

---

623 One of the great post-punk labels, Fast Product, were based in Edinburgh and released the likes of The Mekons, Scars and The Human League whilst maintaining an artful critique of the music scene. They ended up managing The Human League.

624 He replaced the artful Adi Newton whose own band Clock DVA's musical adventures are a key influence on EBM and industrial.

625 Electro body music.

626 From Australia, Dead Can Dance explored archaic instrumentation and diverse musical genres in an ongoing, elegant musical adventure.

We were feeding off the sonic atmosphere still lingering from the likes of Cabaret Voltaire, Clock DVA and The Human League whilst developing our craft with like-minded compatriots including Hula, Chakk and They Must Be Russians.

In The Nursery's journey into industrial music was almost forced upon them as Nigel Humberstone recalls:

In retrospect, I think the appeal of so-called 'industrial music' was born out of necessity. We couldn't afford fancy drum kits or percussion but were impassioned by the desire to make interesting sounds, so opted for a more DIY approach. Striking a rusty metal bed frame with a spanner and putting the microphone through an old tape delay was both exciting and functional. That 'sound' approach extended to the studio where we'd record the sound of a lift door slamming and use it as a percussive effect.

Nigel and his twin brother Klive quickly moved on to military/martial style beats before becoming immersed in classical, as they remember:

I started going to see classical concerts at Sheffield City Hall in the mid-1980s, anything by the Halle Orchestra. I especially liked the programmes that included music by Stravinsky, Bartok, Mahler and Wagner. I spent most of the evening watching the percussionists – the timpanis and snare. I felt the timpanis in particular, were used too sparingly. That's when the idea hatched to use this type of percussion as a driving force throughout an entire song. We sourced a couple of Premier timpanis and that's when tracks like 'Compulsion' began. We were incorporating very early and basic sampling techniques that were powered along with strident marching snare and driving tympani.

In Coventry in 1977, a young Martin Bowes was about to set off on a long musical journey as Attrition. He would go on to create his own musical niche and cottage industry. If punk had sparked his creative surge, it was the new technology that arrived just afterwards that helped define the sound he was making, as he explains:

The punk 'anyone can do this' attitude I took literally. I was, and still am really, a total non-musician, in a traditional sense anyway. Punk and then post-punk led me into the industrial scene but it was Cabaret Voltaire who were a big influence on my starting to play.
There is a dark undertow to their music where it shares the themes of sex and death with goth that fascinated me. I loved the early "goth of Siouxsie, Bauhaus, Sisters and Sex Gang Children. I combined all this with punk lyrics dealing with animal rights or racism, but I also write from my dreams, and sex, death, religion and philosophy.

Like all styles, industrial would subdivide into new ideas and genres; subgenera that were often a million ways away from the source. It travelled through a myriad of musical styles and created many post-industrial micro scenes such as dark ambient, with its quixotic drones and necromantic soundscapes. Some groups had taken their cues from Throbbing Gristle, painting an otherworldly canvas that was further explored in the introspective and cavernous spaces of the new technology via groups like Lustmord and Nocturnal Emissions. That extreme tech was termed power electronics by Whitehouse to describe their atonal noise rush. However, the term became its own scene with several shadowy outfits creating their version of the anti-melodic, electronically generated noise-scapes in a music that was dense and captivating. Even more noise-dense was Japanoise, a loose catch-all for post-industrial outfits from Japan who created varying types of caustic electro-cacophony; bands such as Merzbow and other under the radar outfits.

Meanwhile in the opposite direction was the neofolk pioneered by the likes of David Tibet and Whitehouse themselves that saw a whole plethora of artists delving back into the folk history and music of Europe for influence. They crisscrossed their music with pagan or folk references and held a deep interest in Europe's pre-Christian ideas, the same kind of quest for an idyllic pre-industrial, pre-Christian Europe that had been the heart and soul of the 19th century's Romantic ideals.

The dance floor had always been a prime conduit for goth industrial culture and in the mid-1980s it was the turn of EBM to dominate club floors with its minimal structure and clean production. Electro-Industrial music delivered a grittier, more complex and layered sound with distorted vocals and cranked beats. This pounding dance floor of new genres found its own space with bands like Skinny Puppy, Front Line Assembly and Nitzer Ebb, who combined stripped-down, machine-driven dance throbs with stark imagery and a dance floor ethic. Utilising the influence of the German band D.A.F.[627] and other industrial forefathers like Cabaret Voltaire, these artists created a pulsating, electronic whole. Inevitably, this would further subdivide into scenes like dark electro with its horror soundscapes and grunted, distorted vocals. Later, aggrotech would develop with its emphasis on aggressive beats, prominent lead synth lines and lyrics of a dark nature.

Formed in Vancouver in 1982, Skinny Puppy were perhaps the first band to pioneer the industrial rock crossover. The band were, in turn, a big influence on Trent Reznor of Nine Inch Nails and Marilyn Manson, showcasing their powerful music in increasingly elaborate and macabre live show. Initially a dark synth band, they moved deeper into pioneering electro-industrial with distorted vocals and samples from horror films and radio broadcasts mixed between loops and conventional rock sounds. Formed by Ogre and Cevin Keybut, it was the addition of the classically trained Dwayne Goettel that helped them leap forward. However, Goettel's tragic death from a heroin overdose in 1995 saw the band end with their final album, *The Process*, before reforming ten years later. Their defining album *Remission* twisted industrial music with gothic overtones that seeped into the band's look, stage theatrics, and atmospherics.

EBM itself was a phrase coined by Ralf Hütter from Kraftwerk in an attempt to describe the brave new world that they almost solely created. This became a dance floor oriented, electronic music that was pioneered by the classic 'Verschwende Deine Jugend' and 'Der Mussolini' by D.A.F. alongside Die Krupps tracks like 'Wahre Arbeit, Wahrer Lohn' and 'El Macho y la Nena' by Liaisons Dangereuses.

---

627 Deutsch Amerikanische Freundschaft or D.A.F. were an influential German electropunk/Neue Deutsche Welle band from Düsseldorf, formed in 1978.

Similarly, 'Body to Body' and 'U-Men' by the ubiquitous Front 242 and the work of the aforementioned Throbbing Gristle, Cabaret Voltaire, and newer bands like Portion Control were all of great importance.

Front 242 were pioneers. In borrowing Ralf Hütter's, 'Electronic Body Music' phrase to describe their *No Comment* EP, they had unwittingly named this emerging genre. Formed in 1981 in Leuven in Belgium, they pioneered the style and were a profound influence on a new scene and strand of electronic music whilst embracing the emerging new technology to create their music and graphics. The new EBM genre was later typified by a new wave of outfits such as Vomito Negro, Borghesia, The Neon Judgement, ª;GRUMH, A Split-Second and The Invincible Spirit.

Belgium was at the epicentre of this frantic scene, with its most successful wave of bands playing what was termed new beat; essentially a slowed-down EBM. The new style was invented by accident in the Ancienne Belgique club in Brussels, when DJ Dikke Ronny played the 45 rpm EBM record 'Flesh' by A Split-Second at 33 rpm, with the pitch control set to +8. The crowd still danced and new beat was born. It was further tempered by influences from bands as diverse as The Neon Judgement, as well as new wave and dark wave acts such as Fad Gadget, Gary Numan and Anne Clark.

The key labels in the form were spread worldwide, with Antler Subway, Play It Again Sam, the German Zoth Ommog, the North American Wax Trax! and the Swedish Energy Rekords furthering EBM's distribution. However, it was the Brussels-based Antler Subway that released so many of the scene staples; a defining track was 'Move Your Ass and Feel the Beat' by Erotic Dissidents. was a defining track. They also released works by the likes of other key groups like Taste Of Sugar and Nasty Thoughts.

The UK-based Nitzer Ebb were a conundrum. They were certainly not a new beat band as they were far too aggressive for the form. Nevertheless, they brought a UK-centric feel to the party whilst sticking with the genre's rapid sequenced sounds and hard percussion. Perhaps they might be better included in the EBM bracket with the likes of Front 242, Revolting Cocks, Blue Eyed Christ, Cat Rapes Dog, Kode IV and Insekt – many of which were released via KK Records, a label that also released the mighty Numb, Front Line Assembly and Controlled Bleeding. Also British, Cubanate, who formed in 1992, were an industrial band from London whose fusion of distorted rock guitars, techno percussion and breakbeats made them sternly powerful dance floor governors and intense purveyors of a new beat. Their first gig was with the esoteric techno duo Sheep on Drugs, whose own twisted and colourful sojourn as electronic misfits merits praise. Cubanate found a perfect home on Wax Trax! and, for a decade, were perfect stentorian purveyors of the harsh possibilities of the technical utilisation of robotic digital pulses.

Canadian band Front Line Assembly combined rhythm-driven music with the powerful and harsh guitars of American hardcore, creating an intense new dynamic to an already frenzied scene. Subsequently, the scene would further develop in the late 1980s through the Wax Trax! record label. The industrial imprint grew out of a record shop of the same name and spawned a whole raft of bands like Ministry, My Life with the Thrill Kill Cult, Revolting Cocks, Front 242, KMFDM, Pigface and many more, reading like a roll call of the new scene of the time. From its humble beginnings to relocation in Chicago, it became a label in 1978 and quickly became the definitive label that helped forging the EBM scene in the USA. Discontinued in 2001, Wax Trax! Records has since reopened in 2014 under the guidance of Julia Nash, daughter of original co-founder Jim Nash.

Notable releases on the label include Ministry's key 1987 album, *The Land of Rape and Honey*. The release utilised jackhammer beats and a dark distortion to create a heavy and intense direct sound helping to define the new label's aesthetic. Fronted by Al Jorgensen, the band had moved from their earlier electropop direction (heavily influenced by UK bands like New Order and Depeche Mode) into a far darker and dicier chemical proposition. Jourgensen also acted as a producer and brought the same level of wilful intensity he brought to his own band to all the projects he mixed in the Chicago studio.[628]

Follow-up albums like 1989's *The Mind Is a Terrible Thing to Taste* and *Psalm 69* epitomised Ministry's duel success at making dark, heavy artillery music that somehow charted top thirty in the USA. They also became central in the goth-industrial crossover and laid down the path for industrial's unlikely journey into the stadiums. The other key big crossover album on Wax Trax! came from Revolting Cocks' 1986 album *Big Sexy Land*; with is an alchemy of Wax Trax! industrial, sampling, hard rock, EBM and strong synthesised beats which captured the attention of devotees from multiple scenes.

Naming themselves after an early EP from New York's Swans, The Young Gods emerged from Fribourg in Switzerland. Their lineup of drums, keyboard/sampler and Franz Treichler's Jim Morrison-style baritone vocals saw the band create a powerful, stark soundscape. They also released an astonishing clutch of records in the late '80s that were produced by Swans member Roli Mosiman. The razor-sharp production only added to their dark, powerful intensity; and the reduction of metal by sampling the guitars and placing them at unlikely juxtapositions. The band's powerful drums played off against the sampled guitars and the battery of treated sounds in a genre-busting combination that was best captured on 1992's *TV Sky* album.

Before industrial figurehead Graeme Revell became a Hollywood score composer with credits including *Daredevil*, *Sin City* and *Pineapple Express*, he fronted Australian industrial outfit SPK who made a noisy splash with their metal percussion-driven deconstruct of ideas.[629] What had once been considered experimental and 'fringe' had by now seeped into the mainstream. As Revell notes, 'aggressive noise elements can become part of popular culture'.

---

628 Interestingly, next door to the studio, the formative acid house scene was starting.

629 Ideas from the likes of Jean Dubuffet, Marcel Duchamp, Jean Baudrillard, Michel Foucault, Walter Benjamin, Marshall McLuhan, Friedrich Nietzsche, and Gilles Deleuze.

I remember also when SPK came to play in Berlin. They were staying at the flat in Kreuzberg where Anton Corbijn also designed the cover artwork for *Dr Mabuse* by Propaganda.
Graeme's first question was, do I know of a butcher's nearby?
I thought they wanted to buy something to cook, but they came back with a huge blue waste sack, full of stinking innards, which they told me they intended to throw at the audience during their gig in SO36.[630]

With added rock riffs, industrial managed to penetrate the mainstream with stadium industrial bands like Nine Inch Nails, Marilyn Manson, VNV Nation, White Zombie and Rob Zombie. Industrial metal artists such as KMFDM, Fear Factory and Gravity Kills would all similarly reach enormous audiences.

Nine Inch Nails frontman Trent Reznor was the key instigator in this later crossover – taking industrial, ramming it into the American top ten and releasing the highly influential four million-selling *The Downward Spiral* in 1994; an album that redefined intensity. Nine Inch Nails simultaneously retained the darkness of the underground and the self-loathing of grunge, adding it to the machine-like grind of the music's claustrophobic rhythms. Reznor then crossed this with the big guitars of rock without losing any of the distorted, crushing weight of the original form.

We shouldn't forget the impact that bands like Einstürzende Neubauten, The Cure, Soft Cell, Anne Clark, Joy Division had in Germany, where the GDR authorities. I started the ball rolling with the two illegal gigs of Die Toten Hosen and the TV shows that I had been involved in like The Tube and, through these shows, a new crop of younger bands were allowed to emerge like experimental/ proto industrial bands like AG Geige emerged and were tolerated to a degree, although they were initially denied the coveted "Einstufung" (or permission to perform). Towards the end of the '80s, Young GDR bands like Die Vision, Feeling B or Die Art emerged. One of the members of Feeling B (Flake) eventually joined Till Lindemann and Richard Kruspe in the early '90s to form Rammstein.[631]

Industrial hip-hop was a very wide catch-all term for musicians who were working on the 'darker side of music' and crossing it with the newly emerging scene of hip-hop beats. New York's Public Enemy, whilst not industrial hip hop, had certainly created an industrial wall of sound with their overlaid loops and astonishing dark sonics. In the UK, Adrian Sherwood was producing heavy and dark dub soundscapes like those of Tackhead, creating slabs of sound that may have helped push Justin Broadrick and his grindcore Godflesh project into new sonic vistas. Godflesh, themselves, would become another influence on adventurous metal bands; cross-pollinating and cross-polluting the culture.

Some of industrial's micro-genres were bizarre, self-fulfilling prophecies like witch house. The micro-genre of bands like Black Ceiling or Salem added occult themes to dark electronics incorporating a bricolage of bizarre dub hip-hop crossovers and weird samples to create a very creepy dark atmosphere.

630 Mark Reeder to John Robb.

631 Mark Reeder to John Robb.

Far from the underground and now just another shade of the mainstream, the industrial gothic hue was everywhere. TV adverts or Hollywood blockbuster films like *Terminator* are also couched in industrial's trappings. Arnie played a future cyborg, a post-industrial robot who looked like a pumped-up member of some industrial goth band. It was a long way away from the 'wreckers of civilisation' but the film's dystopian vision of the future, whilst shockingly close to a late twenty-first-century reality, also matched the dark visions of early industrial pioneers.

For the mainstream, industrial culture is an attractive wardrobe and mood change. A clatter of metallic percussion or some distorted noise, a darkening of the lights or studded belts – it's the mainstream's take on a complex and provocative culture with all of the visuals and none of the content.

Beyond that fringe though, the scene's architects continue to plough their idiosyncratic grooves.

Chapter 18

'I MUST FIGHT THIS SICKNESS... FIND A CURE'

The Cure

Like a riddle, wrapped in a mystery, inside an enigma; The Cure are a rare jack of all trades that are somehow masters of them all. From their initial late '70s forays into bedsit post-punk to their early '80s darker trips followed by their descent into the art of darkness of 1982's *Pornography,* then that shock swerve to a Day-Glo lysergic pop and the charts and back again they have always remained convincing in a way that leaves Robert Smith and his merry men as a 21st-century stadium band still retaining their smudged makeup gothic imagery and music.

From recording some of the darkest music ever committed to vinyl to enjoying those commercial hits, Robert Smith has been guiding The Cure through decades of diverse musical imagination. Like Smith's childhood idols, The Beatles, The Cure have always been adept at so many styles of music. Being trapped in one genre was an anathema to The Cure frontman and his ability to make sense of such diversity is at the core of his creativity. The band's sound and image has seen them become one of the key gateway bands to goth culture whilst denying any affiliations to the form and meanhile making some of the most important albums of the form.

Being Robert Smith is like being perpetually locked in a bedroom of insecure neurosis, emotional poetry and a playful imagination. Slipping in and out of dreams and nightmares and existing in a cocoon of escapism and a life unfettered by the day to day, Smith is a modern-day Peter Pan in suspended animation; a Robert In Wonderland repeatedly falling down the rabbit hole. Meanwhile, his music accompanies his alternating nightmares and Day-Glo adventures, creating a soundtrack that swings between existential gloom, hallucinogenic pop and perfect articulations of the mysteries of love and life.

In 2022, The Cure played a stunning arena tour as unlikely national treasures. Two hours of triumphant, glacial and eclectic brilliance. 39 years earlier, they were in the middle of their *Pornography* tour, playing some of the darkest music ever that saw the band at their most bleak and impenetrable. The monochromatic stage lighting of white and shadow framed the band as they dealt a stark and emotional music from their fourth, darkest and densest album. *Pornography* was not just an airing of new, stunning music, but a pinnacle for The Cure's explorations into the visceral heavy. This was a music that was so punishing that the band couldn't sustain its intensity and would fall apart shortly after its release.

The ever-changing group had already lived three musical lives since their 1978 debut single, 'Killing an Arab'. Initially, they produced an angular, stripped-down, post-punk art-pop on their debut *Three Imaginary Boys* album - a breathless, teenage rush that placed them in the smart set of new wave art-pop bands like Buzzcocks, Wire and XTC.

The Cure had followed this with the twilight zone, bedsit bohemia of the following *Seventeen Seconds* (1980) and *Faith* (1981) albums. Both were dealing bass-driven songs that incited a hypnotic, melancholic, textural bliss. *Pornography* was the 1982 culmination of this initial journey; a dark and heavy LSD-fried work of apocalypse and breakdown. It would quickly become the hardcore fans' favourite album and a key goth, industrial and even black metal influencer. The band now had the image to match. Post his stint in the Banshees, Smith along with bass player Simon Gallup upped the style ante was a mix n match of exploding black hair, dark clothes, studded belts and smudged makeup making the pair of them style icons for an emerging new scene.

Few bands dare to tackle truly dark and depressive imagery and even fewer emerge from the other side with some level of sanity. Or survive at all. From Syd Barrett to Joy Division to the *Holy Bible* Manic Street Preachers to Nirvana, various degrees of disintegration have been explored musically, all with varying emotional results.

Pornography is rightly considered a masterpiece in the alternative music canon. The album is a work of dark, early 1980s psychedelia; a lysergic journey of pounding drums, searing guitars and grinding bass that is mind-altering in its ambition. The album is filled with sensual shapeshifting and throbbing melancholia, was not a goth construct. However, much like Joy Division – their closest musical relative at the time – it has become one of the foundations of the whole scene. While the band were certainly looking the part, Robert Smith never felt comfortable with the goth tag.

> We didn't invent goth. That's a myth. We were a raincoat band[632] in those days. That was the term that was around at the time. Now I suppose it's all been lumped together as goth and we've actually achieved this status of legendary goth gods.
>
> Around the time of *Pornography*, we had a sound and a vision, and that's been turned into this notion of goth. But it wasn't around at the time we were doing it. I don't think we invented it. It was bands such as The Sisters of Mercy who came after us. They were goth. And Danse Society, who supported us on a British tour we did in '80 or '81. Those bands were responsible for goth. They cited us as an influence, but they just took it a step further. We had just done *Seventeen Seconds* and *Faith*, and if you look at the photos from that time, they certainly don't scream 'goth' at you. I wore the same black and grey raincoats for two years running. That's all I wore. That's not really goth. I suppose Simon looked the part during the *Pornography* period. He wore black leather and studs, red neckerchiefs and very black eyeliner, and his hair got really big. [633]

Goth or not, *Pornography* itself was a stunning experience of melodramatic melancholia. It had been two years since Ian Curtis's suicide and The Cure were now the poster band for the new dark. Built around stark beats that switched from

---

632 'Raincoat bands' was a catch-all term for the darker indie bands that were emerging in post-punk. Mainly groups from the north would wear raincoats, reflecting the inclement weather. Echo & The Bunnymen always seemed to be encased in them and Ian Curtis often sported a long mac. Smith himself also had a grey mac that he wore for a couple of years while in the band.

633 Robert Smith to Guitar World.

relentless drum machine patterns to pounding, almost tribal rhythms, the album was driven by the now cranked up bass, close to the stark four string soundscapes of The Stranglers' *Black and White* period. Smith's intense, economic guitar work delivered the vivid arpeggios and the drumbeats were thuddingly and effectively simple recorded with the full-room ambience adding to their avalanche of sound. Robert Smith's harrowing vocals pulled the listener deeper into the band's despairing vision. He saw the album as a creative funeral pyre – a deliberate helter skelter dive into making the heaviest, most intense album possible; the last stand with everything piled up high before the band imploded.

The album starts with the powerful landslide sound of 'One Hundred Years' which opens with the line, 'It doesn't matter if we all die', wailed in hopeless desperation. A thrillingly powerful piece of music, drenched in despair and emotion, it is in turns both haunting and beautiful. The song is also gloriously heavy, with the clattering drum machine and an incessant, wailing guitar line hooked around hanging grinding bass notes. An anti-war piece, it is full of angst and exasperation at the pointlessness of it all. Musically grinding, the powerful, seething song climaxes over a pungent drum loop. It is a perfect exercise in jagged noise but with a yearning, melodic yet molten vocal. It's a thrilling introduction to the album and a whole new sound for The Cure. It set the tone for the rest the album with the tribal thunder of 'Hanging Garden' and the album's title track becoming standards of the newly emerging goth scene.

The band had delivered a fantastic work; a vivid and hallucinogenic nightmare and a piece of modern psychedelia, filled with frayed nerves. Even the album's front cover is an intense experience. The band are presented in a semi-smudged photo, looking like dark haired ectoplasm in a blur of red and black, creating a spectral gothic presence which was apt for a band that were literally, do or die.

> I had two choices at the time, which were either completely giving in and committing suicide or making a record of it and getting it out of me. I really thought that was it for the group. I had every intention of signing off. I wanted to make the ultimate 'fuck off' record, and then sign off the band. I was in a really depressed frame of mind between 1981 and 1982. The band had been touring for about 200 days a year and it all got a bit too much because there was never any time to do anything else.[634]

The recording sessions were fraught with a powerful intensity that mirrored the madness of the time. To save money, they slept in the office of their record label and Smith noted 'there was a lot of drugs involved' as they gobbled LSD and drank relentlessly. The effect of these indulgences was amplified by working through the night, with the group leaving at midday looking 'fairly deranged'. Somehow, they managed to make an album that was not a mess, but powerfully focused and darkly attractive. It was held together by their frontman's still intact instinct for pop, no

---

634 Robert Smith to Never Enough.

matter where his steely, determined and seductive vocals took him. Their dense opaque new sound had reached another level.

According to drummer Lol Tolhurst, 'we wanted to make the ultimate, intense album. I can't remember exactly why, but we did'. 'Intense' was the key word for defining their best work so far. The prevailing end of the world mood of the times was amplified by the escalation of the Cold War and the tension of the early Thatcher years. That surrounding intensity was the ultimate measure of the album's worth and, if it meant burning bridges, losing friends or yourself, it mattered little. Art was everything.

> At the time, I lost every friend I had; everyone, without exception because I was incredibly obnoxious, appalling, and self-centred. I had channelled all the self-destructive elements of my personality into doing something. [635]

Born near Blackpool in 1959, Smith had moved to the London satellite of Crawley when he was three years old, still retaining a fondness for the venerable seaside town:

> I have such strong memories of Blackpool that I don't know if I would want to go back: the promenade, the beach, and the smell, it's a magical memory, that evocative time of innocence and wonder. My earliest memories are of sitting on the beach. I know that if I went back, it would be horrible. I know what Blackpool's like – it's nothing like I imagined it was as a child. I think I would like to go there when I'm older because then I shall probably have similar impressions because I'd be more decrepit, and my eyesight would be so poor. Even now, things are becoming impressionistic![636]

Like Syd Barrett, Smith reflects on the strangeness of the English suburbs, where every dream home is a nightmare. Also, like Syd, with wild hair and smudged eyeliner and a penchant for dark and obtuse pop Robert Smith is a very English construct. Unlike Syd, though, Smith has shuffled into his early sixties with his sanity intact, still framed by his trademark exploding hair and smudged lipstick and still looking iconic – and that's one hell of a trick to pull off.

It was his late older brother Richard, ten years his senior and a renegade hippie, who had introduced the more fragrant sounds of the 1960s to his youthful sibling. Robert, already hooked onto The Beatles by his older sister, was now embracing Jimi Hendrix, playing 'Purple Haze' over and over, lost in its ethereal, electrical magic. He even went with his brother to the second Isle of White Festival in 1970 where he missed Hendrix perform, having been banished to their shared tent whilst his sibling made the most of the free love at the festival.

In the 1970s, Smith found his own culture bomb when he was fired by the 1972 'Bowie playing 'Starman' on *Top of the Pops*' moment. This was followed by immersing himself in a whole host of glam rock like T. Rex, Slade and The Sweet as well as the guitar brilliance of Rory Gallagher who performed the first live gig Smith attended on his own in 1973. His real love, however, was Thin Lizzy, who he saw

---

635 Robert Smith.
636 Robert Smith to The Guardian.

ten times in that period. There were other notable influences from the surreal wit of Spike Milligan, the flickering brilliance of singer-songwriter Nick Drake, the prog art-pop of Roxy Music and, later on, the Sensational Alex Harvey Band and their harlequin-wardrobed guitarist, Zal Cleminson.

Precociously intelligent, the young Smith had already met future Cure drummer Laurence 'Lol' Tolhurst on a school bus in 1964. While at the free-thinking Notre Dame Middle School in Crawley, the pair would form a band a decade later called Obelisk, with Smith on piano, future Cure bassist Michael Dempsey on guitar and Tolhurst on percussion. They never played a gig and in January 1976, whilst at their next school, St Wilfrid's Comprehensive, they morphed into Malice. They added local guitar hero Porl (now Pearl) Thompson to the lineup, playing covers and learning the chops.

With the oncoming furore of punk engulfing their comfortable world - thanks to the efforts of John Peel and the music press – they dropped all the covers in January 1977 and renamed themselves Easy Cure, after a Lol Tolhurst-penned song.

The young Smith had his perceptions changed after seeing Buzzcocks and then The Stranglers at the local Red Deer in Croydon. The latter, on 20 January 1977, was of enormous influence.

> Elvis Costello was an influence. So were The Stranglers. They both had really good songs, and I suppose that's what appealed to me. I mean, I really liked Sex Pistols. They were brilliant to hear at parties. And The Clash were awesome live. I cut my hair after they released 'White Riot'. But The Stranglers were my favourite punk band, even though you knew they were old and just pretending a lot of the time. But then, so were a lot of other people. They just did it better. Elvis Costello was a cut above as well. The way he used words and the way the songs were put together was so incredibly simple. Yet when I was trying to do that, I found it really difficult. It gave me something to aspire to. [637]

Lol Tolhurst was also turned by punk:

> Before punk, there was no real model for what we were doing, because the mid->70s was mostly prog rock and disco. In January 1977, we were rehearsing in Robert's parents' annexe three times a week. I remember reading *Melody Maker* and seeing an advert for The Stranglers playing at the Red Deer in Croydon, so we got in the band van and went to see them. I remember Robert and myself dancing wildly at the front, fuelled by much lager. It changed everything, because we could now sense a way forward. After that, we saw The Stranglers fairly regularly. I remember the first Clash album. It was something completely different for us. The energy of punk completely resonated, and that idea that something had to change. Of course, we put it through a slightly different lens because we were more isolated than somebody who was living in the capital. We took longer to register how things changed. [638]

The Cure were fired by punk without actually being punk. Inspired by the energy and the low entry level of the form, they were part of the endless generational

---

637 Robert Smith to Guitar World.

638 Lol Tolhurst to Record Collector.

disagreement of what punk actually was. They were sauntering away on their own distinct path, thrilled by its energy and ideas eventually creating their vision; much like fellow suburban maverick, Kate Bush, who also dealt in dreams and sensuality in a parallel creative world.

Original singer, Peter O'Toole, quit in 1977. After several fruitless auditions, Smith stepped up to the mic and his then Pete Shelley-style vocals dominated their first set of demos for Hansa Records.[639] The recordings came about after they answered an advert for new bands, placed by the label that had found success with Boney M and Child. These demos from the new four-piece of Dempsey, Smith, Thompson, and Tolhurst sound surprisingly adept, with the group's tight and melodic punk rushes hinting at Buzzcocks melodic, buzz saw-guitar love bites hysteria. Fortunately, they slipped out of the impending contract after the label refused to release 'Killing an Arab' as the debut single, insisting that the band concentrated on covers.

With the newly simplified name of The Cure, they became a three-piece after Porl Thompson left to attend art college.[640] The minimal trio's new stripped-down sound was captured on the Spring 1978 demos of 'Boys Don't Cry', '10.15', 'Fire in Cairo' and 'It's Not You'; all recorded at Chestnut Studios in Sussex.[641] The demo cassette was sent to several labels, with none replying aside from Polydor Records' scout Chris Parry. He had signed Siouxsie and the Banshees and The Jam in the punk wars and was on the lookout for something fresh for his own new label, Fiction Records.

Hooked by the mood and atmosphere of the demo, Parry got in touch with the band and, after seeing a gig in Redhill, promptly signed them in September 1978 hustling them a couple of supports with Wire, which helped to neatly place them in the newly emerging world of highly intelligent post-punk pop/noise. Their then dressed down look – tricky for record label marketing - matched the new post-punk no thrills music and disdain for the superficial fripperies of showbusiness.

Whilst Fiction were finalising their distribution, The Cure released their debut single, 'Killing an Arab' on Small Wonder Records in December 1978. The indie label, owned by Pete Stennett, and operated from his record shop of the same name in Walthamstow, was a starting point for so many great left-field bands of the time such as Bauhaus, Crass and The Cravats.

'Killing an Arab' received great reviews, with an early *NME* article perfectly capturing the young band as 'a breath of fresh suburban air on the capital's smog-ridden pub-and-club circuit'. The song, however, was not without controversy. Despite its well-documented intent, the title has become problematic over the years. Musically, though, it was clever and artful pop with a twisted and intelligent take on the 1942 Albert Camus novel, *L'Etranger* (*The Outsider*). The lyrics condensed the book's themes of morality, spirituality, the moral codes of society and the

---

639 Recorded in October 1977.

640 He would re-join the band a few years later on guitar in 2005.

641 The session paid for by Ric Gallup, owner of a local record shop where the band hung out and brother of future bassist, Simon Gallup.

worthlessness of life itself into two-and-a-half minutes. The book was structured around a random murder, an act which played with Camus' ideas of existentialism and the absurd. 'Killing an Arab' was Smith's personal take on such ideas and of the meaninglessness of ultimate choices. In the murderous act, the race of the victim is, as Smith explained, 'immaterial'.

That sense of futility, morality and being the outsider would remain strong themes in so much of The Cure's songwriting. The subtlety and deep themes of the lyrics were beyond mainstream understanding. Years later, the song had been taken so far out of context that the band even changed the title to 'Kissing an Arab' on one tour, proving that artful and clever writing is all but destroyed once it leaks out into the wider world. In 1987, The Cure's *Standing on a Beach/Staring At The Sea* singles compilation ran into a wall of controversy in the USA, resulting in it being stickered with the following statement from Smith: 'The song 'Killing an Arab' has absolutely no racist tones whatsoever. It is a song which decries the existence of all prejudice and consequent violence. The Cure condemn its use in furthering anti-Arab feelings'.

This sense of futility in the Camus book is something Smith has personally returned to several times in his lyrics and interviews. That sense of emptiness played a large part in the post-punk generation's mindset. Smith, himself, has often artfully refuted the suffocating norms of society; religion, the establishment, the monarchy, capitalism and the world at large.

Their debut *Three Imaginary Boys*, released in May 1979, is a time capsule album of the tense, scratchy, staccato, angular art-pop of the band at this time. A collection of sharp and angular songs with intelligent and obtuse lyrics, this was high-IQ post-punk pop music that had seen the band positioned as a quirky, John Peel favourite.

Produced by Parry and engineer Mike Hedges, the songs' sound levels were not where one would expect; guitar solos were deliberately loud, the bass or drums in unexpected places and with the claustrophobic vocals combined together to deliver an intense and unusual music. It was a sound that Smith hated, believing that it lacked depth and substance. Driven by Michael Dempsey's bass and Smith's spidery guitar lines, songs such as 'Accuracy' shine with a stark emptiness and spooked atmosphere. 'Grinding Halt', written by Lol Tolhurst, had a great, circular bass line. 'Another Day' was a perfect post-punk song about boredom, 'Object' tackled sexism whilst 'Subway Song' was a detached song about murder in a subway. Similarly, the disdain of 'So What' created a deep sense of detachment. The band's jerky minimalism and close intensity was underlined with a breathless take on Jimi Hendrix's 'Foxy Lady' that added a late seventies urgency to the classic.

Not only did Robert Smith feel dissatisfied with the music, but he didn't like the artwork either. Chris Parry had felt that the band were so imageless that he decided to make this a feature of the group. The obtuse artwork saw the band (presumably) represented as a fridge, a vacuum cleaner and a standard lamp. Lol Tolhurst would often joke that he was the vacuum, Robert the lamp and Michael the fridge. Years later, Smith still felt uncomfortable with the release:

It's my least favourite Cure album. Obviously, they are my songs, and I was singing, but I had no control over any other aspect of it: the production, the choices of the songs, the running order, the artwork. It was all kind of done by Chris Parry without my blessing. And even at that young age, I was very pissed off. I had dreamed of making an album, and suddenly we were making it and my input was being disregarded. I decided from that day on, we would always retain total control. [642]

Michael Dempsey was also unsure about the album as he explains.

Like many novice producers, Chris had a particular affection for the instrument he'd played himself which were the drums, so a lot of the recording process seemed to be spent on drum sounds. We did Peel sessions which perhaps captured better the spirit of the times. Yet when I listen to *Three Imaginary Boys* now, it seems strangely right, at least in the context of what was to come. To its credit, it does have a lot of space and it feels well-engineered and balanced. It represents The Cure before Robert was fully able to assert his vision, at a time when we had no control at all. This is evident even in the record sleeve featuring the infamous fridge, vacuum cleaner and standard lamp. Polydor used their in-house designer Bill Smith to assemble something. Every part of the design was beyond our control, apart from a few credits we were permitted on the sleeve. [643]

Despite these disappointments, the album reached a respectable 44 in the UK charts and the band sold out a residency at the Marquee club with Joy Division supporting. Their acclaimed second single, 'Boys Don't Cry', was released in June. It was a smart and stripped-down piece of perfect guitar-led post-punk pop with heartbreak lyrics, neatly contrasted over an upbeat melody.

That autumn, the imperious Siouxsie and the Banshees, who were always seeking interesting support bands, took The Cure on their *Join Hands* tour, alongside a young Scottish band called Scars. It was a great break for both young bands and would be a game-changing opportunity for The Cure. Smith had already met Banshees bassist, Steve Severin, at a Throbbing Gristle gig at the YMCA in London on 3 August 1979, when Severin proposed the support opportunity. Severin had enjoyed the 'Killing an Arab' single, which had been given to him by Chris Parry, and Smith already liked the Banshees.

The tour would have a profound effect on The Cure and being pulled into the Banshees web would affect both bands in very different ways. For Smith, it was the start of a journey into a darker, more intense music and style and also provided an inspiration as to how to be in a band that made music on its own terms. The Banshees striking style also subconsciously inspired him to begin the slow morph into his iconic look of the tousled hair bomb; all smudged lipstick and eyeliner, crafting one of the most coolest on the alternative scene.

The Cure played the Banshees first date in Belfast on 5 September and all seemed to be going well, yet the fractious headliners were about to blow up. The tour quickly fell apart after three dates, culminating on the 7 September 1979 at the

---

642 Robert Smith to Rolling Stone magazine.

643 Michael Dempsey to Record Collector magazine.

Capitol Theatre in Aberdeen. Banshees guitarist John McKay and drummer, Kenny Morris, walked out on the tour. The Banshees were in crisis. It was the release day of their second album, *Join Hands*, and, instead of a triumphant tour, cementing the reputation of one of the most innovative bands of the post-punk era, it hit the headlines for opposite reasons. The tour was now in tatters. The gig somehow still went ahead with The Cure extending their set, before Siouxsie came on stage and tore into the two renegade members before The Cure then returned to the stage and played a handful of songs, including three new ones from the upcoming *Seventeen Seconds* album. The atmosphere remained tense and strange and Siouxsie and Severin soon re-joined them on stage for a version of the Banshees' 'Lord's Prayer' jam.

Any lesser band would have fallen apart at this point, but the Banshees were never a lesser band and rushed back to London to audition for a new drummer who turned out to be Budgie and the search for a new guitarist led to phone calls made to Marco Pirroni and to Steve Jones from Sex Pistols. In their enforced downtime, The Cure recorded their next single 'Jumping Someone Else's Train', a pithy look at youth culture which was the last of their jaunty power pop offerings and the last recording with Michael Dempsey on bass.

Siouxsie came down to the recording sessions to sing backing vocals for the B-side, 'I'm Cold', and to inform Robert that he was now in the Banshees. Smith had his work cut out as the tour reconvened with the reconstituted band at Leicester De Montford Hall on Sept 18th. He was now performing in both The Cure and the Banshees, playing the 'electric sitar': an Ovation Breadwinner guitar.

Working with the juju queen and her charismatic courtiers had its effect on Smith both artistically and stylistically. It also compounded the frontman's stress with two sets a night proving exhausting. After a fight in a Newcastle hotel, he locked himself in his room and, in his unhappiness, wrote the rest of the upcoming *Seventeen Seconds* album lyrics.

> On stage that first night with the Banshees, I was blown away by how powerful I felt playing that kind of music. It was so different to what we were doing with The Cure. Before that, I'd wanted us to be like Buzzcocks or Elvis Costello - the punk Beatles. Being a Banshee really changed my attitude to what I was doing.[644]

The tour changed everything and at its end Robert Smith played the rest of his new, darker, more introspective songs to the band. Bassist Michael Dempsey wasn't keen and left to join Fiction Records' label mates, The Associates.

Seeking a new bassist, Smith recruited a friend of the band, Simon Gallup, who had made a cult name for himself in local punk band Lockjaw, the first band to release a punk single in the Crawley area. Unlike Dempsey, Gallup liked the sketches of the new Cure songs; songs that were perfectly built for his trademark driving bass lines. This combined with his then JJ Burnel-influenced[645] stage persona helped to create a new dynamic for the group. Gallup would fit seamlessly into the band. He

---

644 Paytress, Mark. *Siouxsie & the Banshees: The Authorised Biography* (2003).

645 Bassist from The Stranglers.

was the perfect foil on the stage, thanks to his energetic presence and skinny rocker look that contrasted perfectly with the band leader, creating the iconic, visual core. The new lineup change also saw Matthieu Hartley brought in from Gallup's then current band, The Magspies, with an array of the synths with which Robert held a keen interest.

The keyboard textures and drones were central to the new Cure sound. There was space in the new sparse and minimalist songs, creating a creeping, spectral, ghostly sadness. This was a subtle music that was concerned with building moods instead of short sharp shocks. The Cure were now creating a patient melancholy that somehow struck a nerve to become bedsit classic. The bass played a key part in driving the melodies of the new songs and the detached ghostly vocals were intoned over the top, alongside chiming guitar lines. This was a whole new style of music that utilised a Nick Drake introspection, crossed with the stripped-down steeliness of David Bowie's *Low* and Joy Division's dark adventures.

> It was a very exciting time. We had a new band and new songs and we were more certain of the direction we wanted to go in. Robert had an old organ at home with a very simple drum machine in it and a cassette recorder. He would use that to demo all kinds of stuff both with and without the band. It was very simple and minimal, and it worked great as a sketchpad for ideas.
>
> Robert would perhaps present an idea he had been working on at home, so we would then expand on it. 'A Forest' was done like this in rehearsals and we worked out all the parts. Robert would sing what he had ready at the time in a live show and maybe improvise a bit. When we recorded with producer Mike Hedges, the final lyrics were put in place. The words were nearly always the last thing.[646]

'A Forest' was the key track of the album. Built around a cyclical, driving bass riff and haunting vocal, it feels as though the whole record is building around its spectral atmospheric. Its chiming guitar and synth drone creates an unsettling, ethereal sound. It's a wonderful song to get lost in and was a big hit in the alternative clubs for years to come. It was also the band's first top forty single.

The *Seventeen Seconds* album, released on 2 April 1980, was startling with its minimalistic music; creating perfect, brooding atmospheres. The subtle nuances and emotional delicacy of the new songs were hypnotic; each instrument held its own clearly defined space in the sound. The band also took advantage of the new technology of guitar pedals and synths to create nuanced textures.

The band consider *Seventeen Seconds* to be the first true Cure record and its proto-goth, gloom-core template fitted neatly into the new dark. This exploration of a new, shadowy music was a reaction to their debut album.

> A lot of the debut album was very superficial. I didn't even like it at the time. There were criticisms made that it was very lightweight, and I thought they were justified. Even when we'd made it, I wanted to do something that I thought had more substance to it.[647]

646 Lol Tolhurst to Record Collector.

647 To Adam Sweeting of Spin Magazine, July 1987.

This new subtle, minimal music was full of perfect contrasts. However, you could still dance to its icy slabs of futuristic, post-punk disco. The songs' subtle shifts and sense of space were produced by a band that was starting to edge out towards the darker limits.

The Cure delved deeper into their new sound with their third album, *Faith*, released in April 1981. It continued on these darker themes and textures, but with an increasingly introspective and gloomier sound. This was predominantly built around the hypnotic repetition of the bass, merging with the darker hues of a more thoughtful release. An exercise in soul searching, the album touched upon Smith's confusion with the ideas of faith, life and death, tackling heavy themes with a heavier music.

Driven by the leadoff single – the almost punky chug of 'Primary'– the album hit number fourteen in the charts, cementing the band's reputation. The smudgy cover shot of Bolton Abbey, taken by former and future member Porl Thompson, matched the textural music. It is an immersive work, as was Robert Smith's intention.

> I've always tried to make records that are one piece, that explain a certain kind of atmosphere to the fullest. If you're gonna fully explore something, you need more than one song to do it. That's why I always liked Nick Drake's albums or Pink Floyd records like *Ummagumma*. I like a lot of music that is built around repetitions - Benedictine chants particularly and Indian mantras. These musics are built around slow changes, they allow you to draw things out.

Faith was born of post-punk's urgency to create a new kind of rock music. The Cure were one of many bands who were turning rock inside out. The album was filled with a haunting beauty and a dark sensuality at which the band were now so adept. Another patient album of mood and emotion, it possessed subtle shades and textures that paved the way for a music of emotion and real depth, without ever breaking down.

Unlike the eight days spent recording *Seventeen Seconds*, *Faith* had a longer gestation as Smith and producer Mike Hedges found its creation difficult. They went from studio to studio, trying to capture the funereal feel of the original, homemade demos. They were desperately searching for the right atmosphere, which was so key for an album draped in death, the abandonment of faith and the Catholic upbringing of Smith and Lol Tolhurst.

After the album, Mathieu Hartley departed, and the band reverted back to a trio who honed down their live performance to a perfection of intensity. The constant touring and heavy subject matter were so emotionally draining that they would sometimes leave Smith in tears at the end of gigs. The Cure were now entering a darker and more serious space. The late 1981 single, 'Charlotte Sometimes' had a heavier, more haunted feel, and can be seen as the bridge between *Faith* period Cure and a hint of something darker and more lysergic on the horizon. The song was based on a children's novel of the same name by English writer Penelope Farmer. Published in 1969, it was the story of a girl who imagines she is someone else. This was exactly the kind of mental shapeshifting that would appeal to a psychedelic mindset.

When the band entered the studio for their fourth album, they were determined to create a massive and terrifyingly dark spectacle that would engulf the listener with its sound. Smith instructed new producer Phil Thornalley to make *Pornography* 'virtually unbearable'. Together, they cooked up a twisted and thrilling work of ferocity and strange shapes, matching the energy within the band at the time. They cranked up this sensation by dropping LSD to help explore the starkest of terrains in an altered state. Years later, the album still resonates with fellow musicians like Mogwai's Stuart Braithwaite.

> It's hard to pick a Cure album because they're one of my favourite bands. They are one of the few bands that has made brilliant albums in very different styles. *Pornography* is a pretty unique record in that is just so insanely bleak, so hopeless but also really self-contained and perfect. It's not got a shit song on it, it's absolutely brilliant in that respect. It's just a suffocating, druggy, bleak amazing record. [648]

Recording *Pornography*, Smith was on a Dionysian trip into a desolate emotional place. Such a journey had turned Jim Morrison into a bloated poet before he died in a bath in 1971 after a chaotic night out in the French capital. Ian Curtis's own trip into his psyche was a similar one way ticket while creating some of the greatest music of all time. The attendant soundtrack and art accompanying these apocalyptic journeys is hypnotic and fascinating, yet lives can be destroyed on these dark shamanic campaigns. *Pornography* is the sound of a band on the edge of a nervous breakdown. Songs are like fragments of dreams or shards of nightmares and are powerful, wrenching musical and lyrical affairs.

Playing live in 1982, they pushed the album even deeper into the dark. Smith barely strayed from his microphone – a terrifying shape caught in the stage lights. He appeared as an explosion of black hair, an apocalyptic rag doll delving deep into emotional ebbs and flows. All was captured by his charismatic voice, face frozen in concentration. Simon Gallup was dealing his proto-goth rocker look, swinging and driving the grinding bass. Meanwhile, Lol Tolhurst pounded out the mechanic beats. The atmosphere in the venues was dank and explosive; a stunning reproduction of the album.

On 27 May, towards the end of the European leg of the tour which had been an intense affair, with the band and crew all on tenterhooks, Robert and Simon had a fight in a Strasbourg nightclub and the band fell apart. It was patched up a few days later for the last show in Brussels, but then the bass player was gone. The inner sanctum of the band had been breached and Robert and Simon did not speak for eighteen months.

Smith could well have been heading for pop casualty territory, another burnout. Saving his sanity, he pulled back from the brink and swerved away from the demons that had been tormenting him and his art. After a one month detox, he revisited a leftover instrumental demo from the album, then called 'Temptation'. Smith then

---

648 Stuart Braithwaite to The Quietus.

recorded a slightly trippier pop version, which would then morph into the electropop of 'Let's Go to Bed'.

The new, lighter Cure had been Smith's escape from the clutches of creative darkness and tapped into his natural skill of writing perfect, twisted pop songs. For the hardcore fan, it was a surprise. After *Pornography*, there had been a hope for more introspective yet heavy pieces, but the emotional and mental strain on the band had been too much. It was The Cure's astute manager, Chris Parry, who had subtly persuaded Smith into a change of direction and a different musical style. The challenge presented by Parry had been to write a pop song. It was a challenge duly accepted. The attempt to curveball the intensity and dark glamour of their Gothic phase worked, and it was time for The Cure and their leader to explore other sides of their creativity.

> When I took 'Let's Go To Bed' to Fiction and played it to them, it was like silence. They looked at me, like, 'This is it. He's really lost it'. They said, 'You can't be serious. Your fans are gonna hate it.' I understood that, but I wanted to get rid of all that. I didn't want that side of life anymore; I wanted to do something that was kind of cheerful. I thought, 'This isn't going to work. No one's ever gonna buy into this. It's so ludicrous that I'm gonna go from goth idol to pop star in three easy lessons.[649]

'Let's Go to Bed' saw Tolhurst switch from drums to keyboards and marked the period where The Cure became a post-Gallup pop duo. The single spurred Smith onto writing the far more accomplished pop hits like 'The Walk' and the now-iconic, jazzy, breezy pop of 'The Lovecats' which hit the UK top ten in 1983.

The Cure had now finally escaped from themselves.

Robert Smith was now a surprise pop star pin-up and his smudged lipstick and iconic presence became pop mainstream. Like a 1980s Marc Bolan with the same wonderful, nonsensical lyrics and makeup-clad persona, he was soon cosmic dancing on *Top of the Pops*, as though he were centre stage in some madcap, lunatic-pop freak show.

The first album of this new Cure was 1984's *The Top*, which was virtually a solo album from Smith. The singer was accompanied, only in part, by the faithful Lol Tolhurst on keyboards and Andy Anderson on drums whilst blasts of sax were provided by the ever-returning Porl Thompson. From the dark, twisted, neo-metal of tracks like 'Shake Dog Shake' to the deceptively childlike pop hit of 'The Caterpillar', the album managed to combine the new pop of The Cure with a dripping psychedelia; which showed that all the previous years' acid adventures had not gone to waste.

There were also further adventures in the Banshees. Smith returned to playing on a tour after John McGeoch had left. He then played on their 1984 *Hyaena* album and on the band's biggest hit, a cover of The Beatles', 'Dear Prudence'.

The Cure toured the world to consolidate the success of *The Top*, but it was not until the return of Simon Gallup for the next album, 1985's *Head on The Door*, that

---

649 Robert Smith to Rolling Stone magazine.

the band became a whole again. The album saw the band's musical mood swings swerve backwards and forwards as they managed to combine the pessimism and optimism inherent in their muse, creating a sense of danceable gloom. It was their breakthrough release in the USA and set the stage for their particularly eclectic and sprawling *Kiss Me Kiss Me Kiss Me* double album released in 1987. The Cure were on the way to becoming huge. They were adored in France where their poetic angst struck a chord with its cultural heritage of Baudelaire and the melancholic leanings of the French Romantic poets.

The double album would become their first top 40 in the USA, driven by the perfect modern, sombre, pop rush of the crystalline 'Just Like Heaven', their most successful single to date and made them the goth pin ups for a new generation of mall kids. The USA was embracing the post-MTV generation of new British pop. The Cure appeared as the sulky yet playful distant cousins of that invasion, armed with the director Tim Pope's perfectly weird and captivating videos.

In the USA, the band were seen as pioneers of the goth look to a new generation of American youth. It's a measure of their mainstream impact that Smith would arguably become the template for (known fan), Tim Burton's hit film, *Edward Scissorhands*. To be embraced in a country where Halloween was larger than Christmas was rather useful. Smith, of course, never saw himself as goth, nor as a style pioneer:

> I started wearing lipstick because it made me feel confident and more attractive. I'm completely featureless without it. But on stage, I always used to lean my mouth on the mic and shut my eyes, so I wouldn't have to see the people. And at the end, I'd come off with lipstick smeared all over my face, so I thought I might as well go on with it like that and make it look intentional.[650]

Breaking big, the band developed the knack of dealing a sensitivity into huge arenas. In their unlikely mainstream success, they were creating the soundtrack and style for a huge army of thoughtful teenagers.

However, it was 1989's million-selling *Disintegration* which brought the band into the true big league. Smith had the confidence to return to his twisted inner psyche and created an album that embraced the deep gloom of their Gothic heyday and yet some of their most shimmering perfect pop moments. It reflected the singer's personal despondency of the time but added a sense of space and a sheen of pop sensibility to the darker moods. *Disintegration* saw a return to their bleaker, more anxious sound, with its driving beautiful bass lines and textural keyboard washes. The beauty of Smith's off-kilter guitar work similarly returned, making *Disintegration*, for many fans, their ultimate album.

Many tracks were timeless, such as signpost singles 'Lovesong', which reached number two in the US singles charts, and 'Pictures of You', 'Lullaby' and 'Fascination Street' also impacting. All were exploring several styles but were simultaneously sounding like The Cure. Robert Smith's wonderfully distinctive English voice still cut through the middle of the creative madness.

---

650 Robert Smith to Q Magazine.

At the time of *Disintegration*, I was worried about getting older. I was getting closer to thirty and it worried me. I know that it's just a number in your head but there have to be points in your life when you reassess where you are going, but I'm used to the idea of getting older now. I don't mind at all. In fact, I can't even remember how old I am now!

I still feel though, ultimately, everything is really futile; everything I do is really meaningless. One day we will all be dead, and this will all mean nothing. Maybe all this is worse than having a real job, getting tired and collapsing at home in front of the TV, really knackered and with no energy to think about things.[651]

The album saw the awkward firing of Lol Tolhurst during its mixing stage. His drinking and perceived lack of commitment to the band had been hanging in the air for months. It was a painful decision for all parties.

Lol was a pissed-up wreck in the end. He didn't notice what was going on. There was a time when this girl came backstage to meet him and even had a painting of him on her back and he didn't even notice she was there. It's really sad with Lol, he did used to live for that side of it all the time and it was destroying him.[652]

The following album, *Wish*, in 1992 was a huge international hit and their biggest seller to date, rising to number two in the American charts. It was the band's commercial peak and was driven by big hits like 'High' and the perfect pop creation of 'Friday I'm in Love. Late-period Cure has seen the albums become less and less frequent with 1996's *Wild Mood Swings* being far less well received by long-term watchers. The general slowing down in the pace of the band saw them slip slightly away from their commercial peak. 2000's *Bloodflowers* was seen as a sombre return to form by critics; the third part of the dark trilogy of *Pornography* and *Disintegration*. Meanwhile, 2004's self-titled album was produced by American nu-metal producer, Ross Robinson added a stark and heavy undertow to the sound.

The group's most recent album, 2008's *4.13 Dream*, brought them closer to modern soundscape bands like Mogwai and Godspeed You! Black Emperor reflected in the atmosphere and the protracted nature of songs and textures; something of which The Cure themselves were pioneers. Despite their success, Robert Smith has retained an enigmatic distance from the circus. As he explains, the unique internal dynamics of the band are freeing, rather than restrictive:

I don't feel trapped by my image. We're not stuck here being in The Cure full time. If you imagine The Cure is like that building over there, then we can get out of any time we like. The Cure is definitely more of a band than just a couple of individuals. I'm not meant to be the focal point. The band is democratic, but they know I'm the boss and have the last say on everything, but it's not like the Bunnymen these days with Ian McCulloch – who has a great voice and is a great songwriter, but the young guys are so in awe of him. I wouldn't want that in The

---

651 Robert Smith to John Robb.

652 Robert Smith to John Robb.

Cure – the others knock me off my perch. I need the band as I'm a self-conscious person and I couldn't do videos unless the rest of them were behind me being equally silly. I was working on a solo album but then I thought what's the point? I get a real buzz working with these people.

For Smith, being in The Cure means never having to grow up:

To tell you the truth, we never really thought about it. Some people are cool when they get older. Neil Young is cool but it's not like I'm Mick Jagger. There's no showing off to do. All I have to do is shuffle across the stage.

The thing is, I don't feel that image is me. I've shaved my head three times and I didn't feel any different inside. It's just something on the outside of me. It's odd that people think that image is me.[653]

Currently playing breathtaking long sets, the band has a new album chalked in for some time in the future. It's a tantalising wait for the release that is mooted to be their heaviest yet. The Cure remain omnipresent yet are a defiantly non-mainstream presence. Their melancholic vistas fill arenas with their almost childlike Wonder In Alice-land psychodrama and glorious freak show shenanigans. They remain a monolithic touring machine in a celebration of their exhaustive and stunning back catalogue.

Smith, at sixty plus, looks great in his definite hedge backwards iconic styling. His voice and music have become timeless and have remained, at turns, desperately dark, playful, romantic, ferocious, tripped-out or simply pop bliss.

The Cure create a high-decibel, immersive world and their music has crossed post-punk, dream pop, synth-punk, psychedelic rock and remain one of the key influences on post-punk and goth. However, the band keeps moving, maintaining their remarkable journey into the forest.

---

653 Robert Smith to John Robb.

Chapter 19

THE NAUGHTY NORTH AND THE SEXY SOUTH

If that first clutch of bands who were moving out of punk were exploring their dark entries without being 'goth' it was different in the new club scene that were spreading a new gothic gospel that was still called 'alternative music'. As the bands began to percolate out of punk, two seminal clubs appeared miles apart underlining quite separate convergent evolutions of the soon-to-be goth scene.

While The Batcave in London is arguably more famous, the first and equally influential club was Le Phonographique (or 'the Phono') in Leeds. Like all northern cities at the time, Leeds was gripped with the post-industrial decline accelerated by the new Margaret Thatcher led Tory government. The city was full of broken warehouses and soot-stained buildings that added to the malaise plus the terrifying spectre of the Yorkshire Ripper or the NF right-wing skinheads who were always loitering adding a level of fear plus the weather that made it 'a coat colder' as they said in Yorkshire.

> Things were dark and gloomy but the youth still needed to dance.
> Goth was a response to the immediate landscape of derelict mills, windswept moors, *Wuthering Heights* meets post-industrialism and socio-historical factors like the Cold War and mass unemployment of Thatcherism. It was also about reacting against the prevailing mainstream style of the day – bright, shiny, happy, dress-for-success Thatcherite yuppie materialism – by preferring to look like a gloomy consumptive poet with one foot in the grave. It was very much a reaction to life in the 1980s, retooling the beat and psychedelic subcultures of previous generations for harsher, more brutal times. It's endured as a scene and an aesthetic in which misfits and outsiders can belong and celebrate their weirdness.[654]

Starting life in the late '70s as The WigWam, Le Phonographique was tucked away in the Merrion Shopping Centre. The 1979 name change and move towards an alternative club night saw it pick up on the city's emerging post-punk culture. Watching and learning was future The Sisters of Mercy frontman Andrew Eldritch, who would occasionally work the decks with partner and club DJ Claire Shearsby with also Marc Almond, Anni Hogan[655] and other DJs. Mixing jagged post-punk with glam and the grittier end of rock n roll the dance floor they forged would help Leeds become the initial Gotham city.

Famously, the Phono had a unique dance floor, with a central mirrored pillar that helped create the so-called 'two-steps-forwards-two-steps backward' dance. People

---

654 Ben Graham to John Robb.

655 Singer and keyboard player Anni Hogan studied piano before attending Leeds University in 1979 to study politics where she met Marc Almond and David Ball. After moving to London she sang with Marc and worked with Paul Weller.

would preen themselves in the mirror as the lack of space brought them face to face with their own reflection - a perfect addition to any club!

Online music writer Michael Johnson, who founded the *Nemesis To Go* website, appreciates the Phono's legacy:

> The Phono has a greater claim to being the key club of the early goth scene. If The Batcave had not existed, goth would still have happened – maybe without the camp, glammy elements, but it would have happened. Without the Phono, I'm not so sure. Certainly, it played a much bigger part in the creation of a distinctly goth style of music, while The Batcave probably helped the look to evolve, not least because it got itself on television.
>
> In *Streetstyle*, Ted Polhemus presents goth as the exclusive creation of the London club scene – specifically, the people who opened The Batcave club in 1981. He sums up the birth of goth in just eight words: 'A small clique decided to paint it black.' With all due respect to Ted, it was a bit more complicated than that. Goth was equally about punks in black leather jackets going to gigs in pubs as it was about club kids glamming it up in Soho.
>
> Leeds Phono was open before The Batcave and carried on for years after The Batcave shut. It played host to many of the key bands of the early goth scene. The Sisters of Mercy even wrote a song about it – 'Floorshow'.
>
> Most of the early bands came from the north: there was a big cluster around Yorkshire, a few more in the north-of-London commuter belt (UK Decay in Luton, Bauhaus in Northampton) and very little in London – Sex Gang Children were unusual in being a London goth band. Even Specimen, the house band at The Batcave, originally came from Bristol, which made them the real outliers of goth.[656]

All British youth culture is born out of space - whether it's a clothes shop like Sex on King's Road or, in this case, The Phono in Leeds, which also had a support network of other key venues in the city. Leeds was buzzing at the time. The Warehouse[657] had regular live bands and the Faversham pub was at the heart of the LS4 and LS6 postcodes where most of the scene hung out. It could also have been the clothes shops dealing in dark fabrics like X (on Call Lane), Bad (on New Station Street), and Other Clothes (in the Empire arcade) or it could have been the huge flea market that was manna from heaven for DIY clothes makers. Maybe Leeds's post-punk was twisted by the progressive university attracting a clutch of visionary students who created bands like Gang Of Four and The Mekons as well as Andrew Eldritch.

For once Leeds was where it was at and the cultural head start saw the city move quickly.

The scene had been forged by the tireless local promoter called John Keenan, who had founded the F Club as a punk rock gig night in a common room at Leeds Polytechnic in 1977 before it became its own venture in town[658] The groundbreaking venue had been the city's Erics or Roxy - a space to thrash out the future. It was

---

656 Michael Johnson to John Robb.

657 Leeds version of the Haçienda or the Danceteria.

658 F Club had moved to the basement of Brannigan's nightclub down the bottom end of town near The Dark Arches, a complex of vaults under Leeds railway station.

where all the cutting edge punk and post-punk bands played giving the watching new audience of students and the wild youth from the endless surrounding towns a culture head start. Soon it was hosting its own post-punk festival that platformed many of the prime movers in the soon-to-come goth and post-punk breakout.

Futurama Festival began in 1979 as a post-punk showcase at The Queens Hall in Leeds. Festivals were few and far between at that time and punk nor its bastard children had been acclimatised to big venues or expansive stages.

Originally billed as 'The World's First Science Fiction Music Festival', John Keenan's Futurama was looking towards the future[659] with a mix of bands and sci-fi films. The Queens Hall, being an old taxi and bus shed, was cold with diesel-stained concrete floors that smelt oily creating an unsuitable if genuine post-industrial edge to the proceedings. It suited key performances from PiL who played unheard material that would soon become their debut album. Also at the peak of their powers were new band Joy Division who sounded like they belonged five years in the future and the rest of the lineup was full of other future players like Cabaret Voltaire and Orchestral Manoeuvres In The Dark.

Goth wasn't a thing yet but in subsequent years, due to the bands coming our of the north, the follow-up festivals found themselves increasingly at the darker end of that post-punk spectrum. Shadowy music proliferated at Futurama and by the time it worked its way south in 198 to Stafford Bingley Hall, the line-up now included Bauhaus, Theatre of Hate, Virgin Prunes, the early Simple Minds and Bow Wow Wow, boasting the type of bands that resonated with early goth audiences.

Futurama 3 in 1981 felt like a real gathering of the clans drawn to a freezing cold ice rink at Queensferry near Chester. The audience had a distinct look that was growing out of punk into a mixture of post-punk, raincoat and goth styles and the Sunday bill was a smorgasbord of this new scene headlined by The Damned with Dead or Alive, Southern Death Cult, Gene Loves Jezebel, Nico, Sex Gang Children, Stockholm Monsters, The Danse Society, The March Violets, Membranes and more. As The Fall had sung recently 'The north will rise again' and its take on post-punk was creating a darker sound that was about to be labelled goth.

Back in the sexy South, London had another and very different tale to tell.

An archetype gothic city. An organic being, a pulsating metropolis with a tangle of streets with dense shadows and mysteries ingrained in its very filth and neon, the city contrasted a futuristic skyline, cobbled retreats, brooding Victoriana and a foggy pea soup mythology.

In its then-fading Victoriana with shadows of Sherlock Holmes, Dickensian dandies and romanticised street urchins, London was a festering contradiction. The city had nurtured the swinging '60s, punk rock's electric shock and some of the adventures of post-punk. It held the heartbeat of street fashion and was the hub of pop culture,

---

659 This futuristic twist went so far as to include hippie space rock band Hawkwind on the first bill – who were always associated with science fiction writers like Michael Moorcock.

updating its trends at a whim. Decades of redevelopment may have smoothed many of the rough edges, but the dank atmosphere of the capital remained.

London was a culture magnet. Typically, many of the important figures in the burgeoning post-punk scene, like Siouxsie Sioux or Robert Smith, were commuting in from outlying towns and far-flung suburbs. Each arrived with their own dreams, desires and expectations of the big city. Others were exotic migratory fauna from the other side of the world, like The Birthday Party, who had arrived from Australia, breathing fire and brimstone through great mangled riffs and wild poetry into the then-moribund scene of 1982. The markets like Camden were a draw for weekend visitors buying the new styles, and endless Europeans were drawn to the capital to buy Dr. Martens and grab a gig.

London was an easier place to live at the time. The dole and cheaper housing created a space for art to thrive and there were ad hoc jobs and a 'twilight hours' existence. Nick Clift, who had played in post-punk combo Ski Patrol, was now working at Rough Trade distribution and was holed up in an old Victorian house in Shepherds Bush that was a typical microcosm of the new noise. The base had a figurative revolving door that saw the likes of Nick Cave, his then partner Anita Lane, Jim Thirlwell (AKA Foetus), and Ian Lowery of Folk Devils[660] and many others all sharing a communal atmosphere and amenities.

> Guests at the house during Winter – Spring 1983 included: Blixa Bargeld who was a fantastic character cutting a striking figure with his gaunt cheeks, safety pins and wellington boots and ragged leather waistcoat/trousers ensemble; Marc Almond who was just down from Leeds and was a loose cannon, but good fun; Stevo - who financed most of these people with his Some Bizzare label; Michael Gira of Swans; Rowland, Mick and Tracey of The Birthday Party; Lydia Lunch; music scribe Barney Hoskyns; and Beate Bartel and the ladies of the German band Malaria. The huge over-run back garden was where Cave did a few interviews for the *NME,* whilst Jim Foetus's bedroom was awesome, decorated top to bottom with Lenin- era iconography, flags, banners, constructivist artworks, weird figurines and gruesome serial killer arcana.
>
> Nick Cave was only supposed to be there for a week but stayed for several months, much to the growing resentment of the rent-paying members of the house. He was in a bad way in those days, with no money to speak of, constantly mooching groceries and scrounging smokes, practically everyone in the house smoked Marlboro reds. His favourite and apparently only pair of shoes were falling apart and held together with duct tape. His extracurricular lifestyle would definitely explain his mood swings, irritability, and generally sullen behaviour towards me

---

660 Ski Patrol had been formed from the ashes of two Sunderland college bands (The Wall and The Debutantes) and best known for the quite brilliant 'Agent Orange' – a loping, menacing song built around a hypnotic bass line and punk-funk drums. Moving to London in 1979 and, along with fellow Ladbroke Grove agit-dub-rockers Red Beat, the band joined the Malicious Damage roster – the same label that launched Killing Joke. After Ski Patrol, frontman Ian Lowery put together Folk Devils in the Autumn of 1983 after a chance encounter with guitarist Kris Jozajtis at the popular Brixton venue The Fridge. Folk Devils' dark melancholy was imbued into their looping, explosive punk blues. Their moody, captivating songs ran with an adrenalised energy that caught the attention of John Peel and Ray Gange – the star of The Clash film, *Rude Boy* – who managed them and self-released their first single 'Hank Turns Blue'. Lowery's disaffected, paranoid, often elegiac gutter poetry perfectly complimented their bass-driven swamp rock and claustrophobic howl. Inevitably this kinetic, abrasive energy would burn out and the band fell apart. Lowery died in 2001, something of an unsung legend of the era.

and others in the house, and he appeared to resent having to ask for the things he needed, mostly cigarettes and amphetamines, which I could afford because I was working full time at Rough Trade. He also resisted the basic principles of communal living, like washing up your breakfast dishes. 'I don't do chores' was his only explanation.

That said, even then he was, you know, 'Nick Cave', tortured artist, charismatic, tall, thin, massive shock of backcombed raven-black hair, a druggy Aussie lilt in his voice and at times he could be extremely droll, charming and entertaining. Plus, I think The Birthday Party were on the brink of imploding, so uncertain times all round. But for all his faults, when his band played live, to this day I don't think I've experienced anything quite so magnificently primal, libidinous, anguished and visceral, and hardly any of it in standard rock n roll 4/4 time. Antipodean swamp rock blues, I guess you could call it.[661]

It was in these (un)safe houses that the new culture was being created with music soundtracking experimental lifestyles. These were a few brief years when all possibilities were on the table and the future was coalescing in the chaos. On the other side of London, John Lydon's Gunter Grove flat had already had a similar revolving door of striking guests tested to the max by Lydon's unique dread intellect whilst Killing Joke were forged in the then-faded stucco housing of Notting Hill and Brixton even had streets of bohemia.

London drew people in. It was a place to escape small town suffocation or even escape from yourself. Typical of this was a young Bristol mover and shaker called Ollie Wisdom [662], who moved into town and in July 1982 opened a club with Jon Klein at Gossips on 69 Dean St in Soho. It was one of the few alternative venues in early '80s London where the New Romantics, who were more aspirational than underground and taking the glitz and glam from Bowie and not his more dystopian traits, hadn't gained a toehold and it offered a very different space from mainstream discos.

Christened 'The Batcave', it originally ran for five months every Wednesday and was created as a dark droog version of the Bowie nights. It was not initially a goth club, but a club built around Wisdom's fishnet vision. The Batcave originally specialised in a mish-mash of cutting edge music, from new wave to glam rock – played by DJ Hamish MacDonald – and live sets from upcoming gothic bands that would help the culture grow into a new aesthetic.

Both The Batcave and the Phono were pioneering in their use of multimedia. Films or videos from bands were projected onto screens, providing a pulsating visual backdrop, an aspect that was particularly important to The Batcave.

While Ollie was the face and organiser, Jon Klein was the art director, befitting a club with a strong sense of aesthetics. The London venue sent out a statement of intent – 'No Funk, No Disco', was its early manifesto to give it a cultural

---

661 Nick Clift to John Robb.

662 The seminally influential Ollie Wisdom died on August 23, 2021, aged sixty-three.

distance from rival London clubs and soon the term 'Batcavers' was spawned for its clientele, DJs or performers.

The Batcave was a breeding ground for darker, artier bands. Ollie and Jon's band Specimen utilised the space they had created, while it also hosted Sex Gang Children whose singer, Andi Sex Gang, was one of the early scene faces. Specimen themselves had originally formed in Bristol in 1980 and played the local scene before making the big move up to London in 1982 where they created the club in their own image. Their style, especially that of their iconic keyboard player, Johnny Slut, has resonated through the decades. With a blur of teased deathhawk hair, fishnets and makeup, they took the proto-goth look to a new extreme which was much covered in the mainstream media like on Channel 4 TV's 'The Tube', the mainstream press and even London's local TV news. This all helped to spread the new style across the country, giving Specimen.who only released a clutch of singles dealing in their 'Death Bowie' music as Ian Astbury described them, a big cultural impact. The club may not have been the first but its high profile was a game changer and a template for future clubs. It also saw a more dressed up, more decadent take on goth thrive in the capital and create a different aesthetic.

Post-Specimen, Jon Klein would play the guitar with Siouxsie and the Banshees from 1988 to 1995 whilst Ollie Wisdom joined many other travellers and post-goths in the seasonal exodus to the Goa beaches in India, where he went on to become a key face on the Psytrance scene.[663] Here, the booming electronic music was like a DayGlo extension of the keyboard-driven, electronic club culture of the early goth scene filtered through the acid house love of repetitive beats with an added psychedelic feel, and was a natural extension of his fascination with club and dance music. Joining them at the time in the southwest Indian heat was Youth from Killing Joke and several other seasonal émigrés from the UK and its decidedly gothic, overcoat climate.

The Batcave itself had quickly bred its own scene of integral bands. Alien Sex Fiend was one of these. Their singer Nik Fiend (AKA Nicholas Wade) helped to run the club as a space for creative darkness.

> I wasn't the barman as people sometimes say. I ran the place. The band already started making music and we had come up with our name and artwork and so on before The Batcave. The club, though, was the perfect place to lay the golden egg. It fitted with the way we were thinking at that time. It was almost like the club had been invented specially for us. At that time in 1982 we were into The Cramps, Bauhaus, Killing Joke and The Birthday Party, and watching B movies on TV or at The Scala cinema in King's Cross. I didn't want to compete with those things – I wanted to do OUR version of them. The Batcave was a hybrid of all of those things plus glam rock.[664]

Alien Sex Fiend had emerged out of the swampland of post-punk culture with a defined sound that has proved to be influential. Along with Mrs Fiend (AKA

---

663 Psychedelic dance music originating from the Goa beach parties' drones and trippy sounds, built over high tempo beats.
664 Nik Fiend to The Quietus.

Christine Wade), Nik Fiend created dance floor fillers of electronic industrial grind with heavy samples, loops, dub flourishes and manic vocals. You can hear the echoes of their best known song, 'Ignore the Machine' – a goth club dance floor filler – in many other bands. Their music and white-face, unsettling performances must have had a marked influence on Marilyn Manson and many other shock rockers in the new millennium. However, it was their mix of dance floor aesthetic, wonky weirdness, B Movie aesthetic, dark psychedelia, a theatrical nous and a pulsating electronic savviness that continued to mark them out as an important scene band.

Their initial 1983 cassette-only release, *The Lewd, the Mad, the Ugly and Old Nick*, recorded with Youth, set the stall. Their debut album, *Who's Been Sleeping in My Brain*, showcased their deliciously kooky tone and set the band travelling on their own, very distinct musical path fusing the electro-shiver of Suicide with the theatrical shock rock of Alice Cooper. With much of their output defined by singles, their story is best told on compilations like *Drive my Rocket*.

The Batcave saw the darkly dressed clientele of the new cult rub shoulders with the many musicians that would soon form the musical pillars of their scene. These visitors to the club would include Robert Smith and Siouxsie Sioux as well as Steve Severin, Bauhaus, Foetus, Marc Almond and Nick Cave. Andi Sex Gang was a frequent attendee:

> I had no involvement in running The Batcave, but, like many of the other musicians, I frequented the place because we were invited, and they played great music. Everyone used to go there, especially before it got hugely popular. No matter what level a band was on, in the club everyone was equal. The scene was already emerging and The Batcave came along at just the right time offering a gathering place and a platform launching pad for Specimen and a few other bands. They did a damn fine job marketing that club but make no mistake…the scene was already in place before The Batcave.[665]

One of the key architects of what would become goth, Sex Gang Children had already been filling the capital city with their powerful cross of art, cabaret and tribal post-punk noise. Their frenetic songs were driven by a melodic and heavy post-punk bass whilst their frontman dealt a flat-topped and flamboyant combination of Bowie and Brecht. Their dark cabaret elegance was streaked with a punk rock intensity and an undoubted bacchanalian rumble. The band had the early goth staples of the pounding tom-toms and powerful tribal rhythms.[666] The audience at these early shows was almost as intense and Sex Gang Children were one of few London bands of the era who could match the new crop of emerging northern bands such as The Sisters of Mercy and Southern Death Cult.

---

665 Andi Sex Gang to John Robb.

666 'Tribal' influences included early Siouxsie and the Banshees drummer Kenny Morris. Listen to their 1978 debut album, *The Scream*, particularly to the poundingly repetitive tom-toms on tracks like 'Metal Postcard (Mittageisen)'. Then the new Adam and the Ants 'Kings of The Wild Frontier' warrior rhythms.

The band had a more authentic history than most. They were part of the capital's post-punk scene, exploring firebrand creativity in the squat and bedsit land that sprung up in places like Brixton. The latter had become a punk squat magnet with a whole cast of characters drawn to the area by its sulphurous air of creative danger and gothic Victoriana. Famously, it would be Andi Sex Gang's Brixton home that was christened 'gothic' and by extension, Andi picked up the affectionate nickname 'Gothic goblin' from Ian Astbury, helping to give the whole genre its unwanted moniker.

> My flat in Brixton wasn't a squat. I had stopped squatting by that time, but it was large, Victorian and cheap. Popular cultural history has it that Camden was the hotbed of post-punk and goth culture, which is absolute rubbish...it was a bunch of shops that sold gothy clothes manufactured in sweatshop factories and sold to tourists. The real action happened in Brixton. A lot of bands and artists lived there, including Tony and Pat (Death in June), Luke and Lester (Crisis/Theatre of Hate), Abbo (UK Decay), Ian and Billy (Death Cult), Under Two Flags, Hugo (Gang of Four) and Sarah Jane (Communards).
>
> They all moved into my street.
>
> It was.... alive!
>
> That whole neighbourhood was full of creative people, stage designers, independent filmmakers, and actors.
>
> That whole period was brimming with revolutionary fervour and you were afraid to leave London even for a few days, just in case you missed out on some big change, some musical coup d'état. It seemed that everybody wanted to throw out the old rules and push the boundaries, set new standards, and raise new flags...this was a cultural war and Brixton at that time was at the centre of it all.
>
> The best clubs were all in and around Soho. Gossips, which hosted Billy's, The Batcave and Alice in Wonderland were the most well-known and loved. Wow, just talking about it reminds me of how attitudes have changed. We have fallen asleep and blindly accepted the bondage of commodity. But, never lose hope, never give up the fight.[667]

It was in this creative flux that Sex Gang Children were born. Their name was derived from the gang in William S. Burroughs' novella, *The Wild Boys: A Book Of The Dead*.[668] and had come c/o a suggestion by Malcolm McLaren for a name for a band fronted by Andi's friend on the London club scene, Boy George. He soon dropped the name after [669] Jon Moss, the band drummer, went to L.A. on holiday and took some demo tapes with him. 'I remember getting a postcard from Jon from L.A. saying, everyone liked the music but 'I don't think America is ready for the Sex Gang Children name,' remarked George.

---

667 Andi Sex Gang to John Robb.

668 'Sex Gang Children', as a conflation of the juvenile gang's activities, was the brainchild of Sex Pistols/Bow Wow Wow manager Malcolm McLaren. It was originally floated by Boy George as the name for his band, before he fixed on the far less transgressive Culture Club.

669 Boy George was putting together his own band after a stint dancing with Bow Wow Wow under the name of Lieutenant Lush.

Initially Andi Sex Gang had tried to persuade Boy George to keep the monicker. However, George's desire for mainstream success would not sit comfortably with the controversial handle, so Andi took it instead.

> The band was originally called Panic Button, but it was just me really and a carousel of wandering minstrels. I was looking for a name change. The songs were developing – as was I – and with the right lineup at that time, we needed a new name to reflect the music, something bold, unique and strong.
>
> When I first heard the name Sex Gang Children from a mate of mine at the time, he was running off a list of names he was thinking to use. I told him to use the name. It was perfect, but he insisted he was going to stick with the name Culture Club and suggested that I should use the name for my band. Thank you, George.[670]

The newly christened Sex Gang Children started their furtive journey on the scene with their music full of scurrying, twitching rhythms and great ideas. They may have lacked The Cure's pop nous, Adam Ant's pop star pin-up appeal and The Cult's ability to tap deep into the inner rock sanctum, but that was never the point. For Andi, this was a deeper statement with its roots in art/glam. A genre he had admired long before the days of punk.

> My life before music can be categorised into three stages – artist, criminal gypsy, political miscreant. The result of my nature reacting to the circumstances that surrounded me at any given time...cause and effect. As a child, I grew up with quite a variable exposure of music that influenced me in one way or another, ranging from Edith Piaf to Johnny Cash. My own discoveries came with Bolan, Bowie and Roxy Music and from there on the floodgates just opened up. However, even though I had always felt a natural affinity towards music, as a child it was painting that was my first form of expression. When I was four years old and still in infant school, the head teacher submitted some of my works to the Arts Council and the local newspaper, which resulted in getting some of them exhibited in their annual art exhibition at Slough Town Hall. As the exhibition primarily featured adult artists only, it was good exposure for me at that age.[671]

Typically, of many of the important figures on the scene, it was a reaction to a strong religious upbringing that would spark something deeper and darker.

> I was actually incredibly religious as a child, but more as a self-dedication to the idea of the human as a higher self, and I lived my life dedicated to that end. So, the stage was set for disappointment, conflict, and downfall with all the established institutions around me, especially the Catholic Church. All the perfect ingredients for a music artist. After a few years in my early teens involved with an older gang, I eventually made the move to London. It was either that or end up in prison like most of my older mates. Apart from the odd foray with a guitar, I still hadn't got involved seriously with music. I had always loved the bass, it was my favourite instrument when I was a child, I saw something in it that I felt hadn't really fulfilled its true potential. It wasn't until the late 1970s with the likes of Joy Division and the Banshees that I saw that instrument's potential realised.[672]

---

670 Andi Sex Gang to John Robb.

671 Andi Sex Gang to John Robb.

672 Andi Sex Gang to John Robb.

It was this idea of the bass guitar finally fulfilling its key role that is one of the integral components of the post-punk sound. So many groups pushed the instrument up in the mix and its sound was grittier and tougher than ever before. The bass was the spine to so much of the music of the period. With his head full of all these innumerable influences and ideas, it had been punk that had sparked the singer into action.

> Sex Pistols album had a big impact on me. I was still living in Slough. Like most other kids there, I believed the tabloid hype and didn't take punk too seriously. Then one afternoon, one of my older mates sat me down and said, 'You've got to listen to this carefully', and track by track he took me through the whole album, pointing out every defined vocal pronunciation, guitar sweep, lyrical juxtaposition and how it all made such perfect sense. I left that room with a new sense of enlightenment. I had also realised The Pistols were serious, they were not just 'grown men playing in a band to be famous' with nothing more to offer other than their shock tactics. They were REAL. They had DIGNITY. They had set a new standard and had made an album that redefined music within popular culture.[673]

Sex Gang Children's dramatic catalogue of bass-driven, tribal-pounding, scuttling, twitching songs was a thrilling circus of ideas. They possessed an intensity that was interspersed with moments of pure sparse beauty. This can be most clearly seen in tracks such as their cover of Marianne Faithfull's 'The Ballad of Lucy Jordan'. The band were moving their music into a deeper, darker and more theatrical tradition, much like fellow artists Virgin Prunes who were adding their own pagan rites and chants to the mix. Both bands were delivering a forbidden poetic decadence that added burlesque and vaudeville stylings into the canon. This dark take on burlesque is a key strand for a culture born out of nocturnal clubs. Its powerful sexuality, S&M flavourings and feminine control appealed to the post-punk crowd who were keen to break down established barriers.

This resurgence of interest in the theatrical and provocative made Andi Sex Gang all the more keen to assemble a band. However, with the post-punk gene pool of young hopefuls on his doorstep, he didn't follow conventional routes of recruitment:

> I advertised and auditioned people. I also just stopped people in the street if they had a certain look and feel about them. I had a kind of a press gang thing going on, but I didn't care. I was on a mission. I stopped when I felt I had the right team on board for what was needed. It was never about technical ability so much; I was looking for heart and feel in my musicians.

Sex Gang Children were a distinctive force from the off. Their first release was the 1982 cassette-only live album, *Naked*, which captured their set, honed by their regular appearances at the Hammersmith Clarendon Hotel. By early 1982, they were regulars at the faded thirties art deco venue[674]. *Naked*, created the buzz and the first vinyl, the four track *Beasts* EP, was released in the summer of 1982. It hovered

---

673 Andi Sex Gang to John Robb.

674 Its large upstairs ballroom would also eventually play host to the Klub Foot nights; the main club in the psychobilly scene.

around the indie charts for a year despite an initial artwork hurdle, as the band had not obtained permission for the Diane Arbus[675] photograph on the picture sleeve.

Sex Gang Children were very much in the ascendancy. Their next single, 'Into the Abyss', was released that autumn, preceding their spring 1983 album, *Song And Legend*. The album's popularity was aided by the epic 'Sebastiane' which was a classic of the period. The single played with the imagery of Derek Jarman's celebrated 1976 art film of the same name with its dialogue entirely in Latin, its cinematic portrayal of the martyrdom of St Sebastian, semi-crucified and riddled with arrows,[676] was overtly homoerotic. This iconic scene adorned the single's artwork, while the song itself is a haunting lament with Andi Sex Gang's mannered vocals draped around Ginnie Hawes' atmospherically doleful violin.

The song's lyric is obscurely allusive and it fitted the tenor of 1983 debut album *Song And Legend*, drenched in atmospheric echo by producer Tony James[677] and songs themselves that were full of poetic takes on what would become goth rock motifs: sexual and religious imagery; the tomb; totalitarianism; even Ivan the Terrible.

Just at the point of breakthrough, however, things began disintegrating. Drummer Rob Stroud was first to depart, simply not turning up to a show then resurfacing in Aemotii Crii. Sex Gang Children then added former Theatre of Hate drummer Nigel Preston to the lineup and, in September 1983, a one-off deal with the independent Clay label brought a new single, 'Mauritia Mayer'.

The band were still in the middle of recording the album when Nigel Preston also quit to join The Cult. They soldiered on to release a new single, 'Draconian Dream', before collapsing, leaving Andi Sex Gang to continue solo with his own unique vision.

*****

Looking for a new direction in the complex flux of music, a new young writer from the fanzine world called Richard North joined the *NME*. With him, he brought his vision of a new scene which he called 'Positive Punk' in his February 1983 'Punk Warriors' call to arms feature.

It was an attempt to realign punk with its original ideas of sex, style and subversion, away from – what North believed to be – the more negative aspects in which the genre was now wallowing. Living in the London squats, Richard North was one of the many writers,[678] who were documenting the emerging new scenes that were

---

675 Arbus was an American photographer whose suicide in 1971 had ended a controversial career dealing in strange, powerful and disturbing images of outsiders in the USA. She offered a sideways glimpse into another aspect of Americana – a perfect reference point for the artful outsider band.

676 According to Holy Roman Catholic Church accounts of the lives of the saints, Sebastian survived his multiple arrow wounds to be later bludgeoned to death – a 'double martyrdom'. Jarman's film enhances and exaggerates the homosexual/masochistic element inherent in Church-sponsored depictions, such as that by the painter El Greco.

677 The bass player and driving force behind punk band Generation X who eventually ended up playing bass in The Sisters of Mercy.

678 Along with Tom Vague from Vague fanzine, and Tony D from Ripped and Torn, and Mick Mercer from Panache.

trying to come to terms with what punk was and could be. In this squat punk world, bands as diverse as Adam and the Ants were embraced for their sex music freakishness and yet somehow co-existed in people's tastes with the anarchist band, Crass.

Crass, themselves, were an art manifesto. They sprung from the loins of punk but dealt in the avant-garde with their stunning albums, painting a perfect utopian ideal. Crass also released several other bands on their label, Crass Records, such as The Mob, whose 'No Doves Fly' was a haunting, atmospheric anti-war anthem that would nestle in many proto-goth record collections. Zounds was another such band, whose single, 'Demystification', was an underground classic. The label also released Rudimentary Peni, whose dark and twisted blasts of sound were driven by an off-kilter bass, concrete guitars and screamed vocals that were unlike any other band ever heard.

The London squat scene was also typified by bands like Rubella Ballet, who bucked the trend for young men dressed in black with a colourful, exuberant appearance. They offered an unsuspecting lightness in the dark and made records to match. Later on, The Cravats brought their Dadaist punk to the scene before morphing into The Very Things, whose heavy bass-driven, humorous releases like 'The Bushes Scream While My Daddy Prunes' were fringe goth club favourites.

It was this melange of new noise that zine writers were documenting on a quest for a true spirit of punk, as Richard North recalls.

> The 79-83 bit between punk and goth was really interesting. I liked the make up, breakdown, safe when dangerous, follow the heart and unconscious mind, heaven and hell and kiss and tell bands like Bauhaus, Wasted Youth, Flesh for Lulu, UK Decay, and Psychedelic Furs. Groups that promoted sensual style and re-action. Primal magic. Occult chemistry. And (no logic to the) soul. I also liked Crass and some of the anarcho bands who talked (and walked the talk) about beating or subverting the reality of the 9-5 work/play/sleep conveyor belt (rather than just escaping it for a few hours). [679]

This mish-mash of reactions to the loose energy of the times saw the glam dislocation of Bauhaus nestling in the same record collections as the dark London troubadours Psychedelic Furs or Wasted Youth who were a fantastic anomaly with dark troubadour romantic hues blending with a proto-goth and an urgent post-punk whilst wearing the hearts on their leather sleeves. Johnny Marr, ever the pop culture fanatic was watching keenly:

> I saw Wasted Youth a few times supporting The Only Ones. They looked like me and my mates and straddled the rock'n'roll and proto-goth scenes that also inhabited the London '80s scene. Pre-Southern Death Cult Velvet freaks. They became Flesh for Lulu who actually supported The Smiths once.[680]

Respect was also given to older bands like The Only Ones who were musical misfits whose melodic rushes dripping in a glorious decadence had been birthed from the

679 Richard North to John Robb.

680 Johnny Marr to John Robb.

late 1960s underground but had thrived during the punk and post-punk period. Despite living a hedonistic, chemical lifestyle, their frontman Peter Perret balanced a fascination with sex and death with an eloquent, beat-up beat poetry. Like French artists romanticising the grave, they produced beautiful, poetic, deathly songs, topped with Perrett's velvet voice. The classic track 'Another Girl Another Planet' is a fine example of this romantic, gothic duality.

In London, this mish-mash of squats and pop-up venues were a long-lasting conduit to the new interpretations of punk as Richard North explains.

> My favourite places were The Batcave and the anarchist centres at Wapping and Harrow Road; venues that were removed and apart from the standard gig circuit and all that entailed. I come from a club background, as a kid, I used to go to my local place, the California Ballroom, Dunstable, which was to funk what the Wigan Casino was to Northern Soul – coach loads from Slough and wherever up every week. So, I also liked the Wag Club, Heaven, et al.
>
> During punk, for a while, I lived and hung out with some of the people who would later become known as the Kill Your Pet Puppy Collective – Tony D,[681] etc. It was a very social and creative time. The place I shared with Tony and others, Westbere Road in West Hampstead, was something of a hub. All kinds of cool and crazy people would pitch up on, seemingly, a daily basis. Bands, writers, TV crews, vagrants. The interaction fuelled the creativity and vice versa, of course. For us, the early '80s were another punk Spring. Punk at that time became a way of life for an increasingly large and motivated group of people. Moreover, folk were, to paraphrase Malcolm McLaren, creating an environment in which they could truthfully run wild. We were making scenes that took people away from the confines of school and work. Instead of just listening to records in isolation and going to the odd gig, people were having life adventures.[682]

Growing out of these strands was a scene of bands reacting to what they believed to be the negative interpretation of punk by the rougher edged Oi scene. North's defining *NME* 'Positive Punk' feature became the manifesto for this proactive take on punk energy and was built around the bands, Brigandage and Blood and Roses. Rather than lighting the touch paper for the revolution, it cracked open the door through which future goth bands could sneak, while the two featured bands were marooned.

Brigandage seemed to have all the right credentials. Fronted by the charismatic Michelle, who was a known face on the punk rock scene. She had been photographed at the front of the queue for the September 1976 100 Club Punk Festival in her leopard skin top, inking her into the pages of punk history. The band created a wall of sound with songs that captured their love of magic and anarchism. One can easily feel the hallmarks in their music of what would later be termed goth; the euphoric meeting the melancholic.

---

681 Tony Drayton had moved to London from Glasgow in the punk days and his Kill Your Pet Puppy fanzine was a key publication on the new underground.

682 Richard North to John Robb.

I wrote the Positive Punk article for the *NME* in January/February 1983. At that time, there were three distinct groupings in the punk scene. The Oi-sters and Herberts, who were basic and gumby-ish punk music, fashion and behaviour. The anarchos, who were like a mass of black, in terms of clothes and demeanour. And then you had a loose, nameless collection of punks and former punks who were colourful, and full of, it seemed, vim, dash and go-ahead spirit. These folks tended to go to see roughly the same bands and attended the same sort of clubs. I wrote about many of the bands and places, ranging from The Batcave and the Specimen, to The Mob who were sort of anarcho-plus.

It was obvious that something was going on, and the *NME* asked me to write a piece about it. Originally, I didn't use the name 'Positive Punk', or any umbrella term. But the paper needed an easy hook to snag readers. Positivity, I suggested when asked, was a common denominator, so hey presto… a little alliteration goes a long way. Of course, Positive Punk was a disaster. As soon as something is named, people have a target to attack. Also, factions within the scene quickly appeared.

The style magazine *The Face*, for instance, did a Positive Punk piece, but Sex Gang Children refused to become involved – because they couldn't control it. Their noses had been put out of joint. The big wigs in the scene, your Sex Gangs and Southern Death Cults, had suddenly been usurped, or so they thought, by upstarts like Brigandage and Blood and Roses.[683]

Weeks after the Positive Punk article in the *NME*, Brigandage lost their bass player which saw Richard join the band in a potential case of poacher-turns-bass player! However, 'Positive Punk' could never last.

Overnight, the atmosphere changed from togetherness to suspicion, jealousy and loathing. This would probably have happened in any case, unfortunately the Positive Punk article greatly accelerated the process. As far as I am concerned, Positive Punk described the 'Passage of a few People (wearing makeup and top hats) through a Rather Brief Moment in Time'. I think it was accurate. In hindsight, the music wasn't great, which was probably the real downfall. And then it turned into goth, with even worse music.[684]

Positive Punk was a false alarm, but all over the UK, bands were springing up inspired by the energy and opportunity of punk. Everywhere you looked, there were feral and dark bands casting their mini shadows in cheap rent Victoriana. There was space in the capital city for reinventing yourself and the opportunity to truly live the piratical dream. All of which helped to sculpt the template of an English Southern goth.

Despite the north/south divide in the cultural wars, a band that had appeared in 1979 and came from neither area and from a small market town in the East Midlands had already defined goth despite their own protestations.

683 Richard North to John Robb.

684 Richard North to John Robb.

Chapter 20

ALL WE EVER WANTED WAS EVERYTHING

Bauhaus

One night in 1979, John Peel played a record.

It was like nothing else anyone had heard before.

For 9 minutes and 36 seconds, this mysterious and entrancing sound filled the airwaves and made time stand still. It was a song that married the adventure of post-punk with the space of dark dub. It understood glam but added a shivering spectral shimmer. Its skeletal structure was built around a haunting descending bass line, bizarre guitar skreegh and neo bossa nova beat. It was filled with a linear and thrilling tension. The baritone vocals were sung with a high-cheekboned lucidity about the thirties film star who had perfectly portrayed Dracula – Bela Lugosi.[685]

'Bela Lugosi's Dead', the debut single from Bauhaus, was released that August and, for many and arguably is the first goth single. Of course, the band deny the tag. So they should; no one likes to be saddled with a scene. But somehow, with its new sense of theatrics and its powerful textures, it sounded like it was breaking away into a new musical territory. The ghostly, mesmerising song was a daring and powerful debut statement and, arguably, one of the most groundbreaking musical manifestos of the post-punk period.

Even more remarkable the fact that the band had written it in their first rehearsal.

Bauhaus 1919 (as they were then known) had only been in existence for a few weeks and had just played their first gig on New Year's Eve. On 26 January 1979, the band took a short trip to Beck Studios in Wellingborough, Northampton to record a demo that would eventually become the infamous single.

'Bela Lugosi's Dead' was one of five tracks recorded live during the session; an early snapshot of the band that would soon captivate so many worldwide.[686] The speed at which the band coalesced is astonishing.

> We were all broke, but we chipped in for this little sixteen-track studio with all this homemade gear within weeks of starting the band. We recorded 'Bela' with other tracks – 'Some Faces' and a song called 'Harry'.[687] We recorded and mixed five tracks in four hours.

---

685 Fittingly born in what is now Romania, Béla Ferenc Dezső Blaskó, known professionally as Bela Lugosi, was a Hungarian actor famous for his portrayal of Count Dracula in the 1931 horror classic Dracula, Ygor in Son of Frankenstein and many other horror films from 1931 through to 1956.

686 Influence is an awkward barometer of a group's worth, but Bauhaus' distinct artistic direction touched a diverse cross-section of musicians throughout the generations. Musicians such as Savages, Nirvana (Kurt Cobain was quoted as saying he had played his Bauhaus records so much that they 'were all scratched up'), Mogwai, Marilyn Manson, AFI , Nitzer Ebb, Skinny Puppy, My Chemical Romance, Ministry, Chris Cornell, Tool, Nine Inch Nails and Massive Attack (who play a great cover of 'Bela Lugosi's Dead') all describe Bauhaus as an influence.

687 Including two additional tracks: 'Bite My Hip' later reworked as 'Lagartija Nick' and a first recording of 'Boys' (although this version was not to grace the single's B-side). To celebrate the session's ruby anniversary, the 'Bela' session was released in its entirety in November 2018 by Stones Throw Records.

When you walked into that studio, it was quite an experience. It was like walking into somebody's living room with tacky 1970s wallpaper and an old carpet on the floor. It was run by a real character who was then in his fifties called Derek Tompkins who we would work with for years. Derek was a chain smoker; 60 cigarettes a day and we'd all be smoking in there as well so we literally couldn't see each other over the other side of the room. He'd just open the back door and spray some of this lemon spray in the room and we'd all start again. He'd get a throbbing headache from all the smoke and always had a big tub of aspirin; to counteract the effects of the chain-smoking.

They were fun times – especially when we recorded 'Bela'. That was recorded in the first or second take, all done live. Pete had a stinking cold, but the vocals sound great. That was it, we were on our way.[688]

Hooked by the pure escapism and empowerment provided by unhinged glam rock and the wonky end of pop culture, exotic local art school dropout Daniel Ash had asked old primary school friend, Peter Murphy to make some music with him. Initially, this was because he looked the part, rather than for his vocal abilities. Abilities that no one, not even Murphy himself, knew he had. Until their first rehearsal. Then they knew..

They really knew.

They then recruited a youthful Kevin Haskins to drum for them days later. The band fell into place quickly when his big brother joined on bass.

David came to see us rehearse really early because his brother Kevin was our drummer and said he had to be in the band. So, we got rid of the bass player that we had, and David was in. A few days later I called David up and I said 'I've got this riff. It's a really haunting riff, and I'm not using normal chords'. And he said, 'That's really weird you say that. I've got this lyric about Bela Lugosi, the actor who plays the vampire'. I said 'Really? That's interesting.

In the next rehearsal, David gave the lyric sheet to Pete. Kevin started playing that bossa nova beat right off the back. I started playing the riff and Dave came in with the bass line – and Pete sang pretty much as you hear on the record and boom! It was written immediately.

It was just magic right from the get-go – we didn't have to work it out. It was very strange; we had it within about half an hour. The dub feel came from David and Kevin who were always playing tapes of dub which introduced me to the whole reggae thing.[689]

Dub and reggae first became entwined with punk after Don Letts had played it at the first-ever punk club – the Roxy – DJing there in early 1977. Cult reggae giants like Big Youth were punk favourites and the melodica playing of Augustus Pablo would also have an influence on many groups at the time such as New Order, Bauhaus and Gang of Four. Originating in Jamaica, the music redefined the bottom end and the bass guitar and was full of new effects and reverbs. It also utilised 'drop outs' to create the kind of 'space' embraced by these new young bands and Daniel Ash.

---

688 Daniel Ash to John Robb.

689 Daniel Ash to John Robb.

I never thought of 'Bela' being dub but I guess there is something there. I nicked the riff but I'm not going to tell you what it is from as that will spoil it. It's based on a very, very, very well-known pop song that's really slowed down with some tricks with the tuning as well.

I remember coming back and playing the song to my Mum. Normally I would play things like *Never Mind the Bollocks* to her and she would say, 'Very nice Daniel, very nice. You're not one of those Sex Rockets, are you?' So, she obviously wasn't listening – because if she was listening…she would've hated it. But my Dad loved 'Bela'… 'I like that one, it's something you can tap your foot to - and you can hear the lyrics!'

Ash senior was right. There was something within the sombre and funereal drone; a twist of the darkly humorous atmosphere of sex, dread and death that listeners instantly grasped. It was little surprise that 'Bela' became one of the template tracks for decades of dark adventure, making Bauhaus, arguably, the alpha band in the so-called goth scene. Mont Sherar was a DJ in Florida who picked up on the game-changing song:

Bauhaus broke away completely from punk into their own ideas of abstract fantasies and imagery. Sonically, all four members are totally unique. They dared to make a new sound and it remains timeless music. The track 'Bela Lugosi's Dead' is, without question, on my list as one of the greatest dance tracks of all time. There is just something beautifully perverse about dancing to something as dark and macabre as this song. It pretty much sums up the entire genre perfectly. Although their entire catalogue is brilliant, to say the least, this one track is all you need to know what 'goth' sounds and 'feels' like and if you stare at the album cover, you know what it looks like too.[690]

The song itself, with all its brooding imagery, also came with a big dose of British irony.

It was a very tongue-in-cheek song, which sounded extremely serious, very heavyweight and quite dark. But the essence of the song, if you peel back the first layer, is very tongue-in-cheek – I sing 'Bela Lugosi's dead, undead' – it's hilarious. The mistake we made is that we performed it with naive seriousness! That's what pushed the audience into it as a much more serious thing. The intense intention going into the performance actually overshadowed the humour of it. Because of that interpretation, the Gothic tag was always there, and of course, we eventually found ourselves playing to our reputation. That's really why Bauhaus didn't have a longevity, because we were just clicking with energy. But when it came down to thinking about what we were doing, we realised that we were pandering to the audience, to what we thought the audience would like. [691]

Few groups arrive as fully formed as Bauhaus and few manage to make an impact as powerful as this, especially so early in their careers. Even fewer manage to do so coming from a small market town like Northampton. A shoe-making town of

690 Mont Sherar to John Robb.

691 Peter Murphy to Alternative Press.

200,000 people,[692] lying in the flat fields between London and Birmingham, literally middle England, where not a lot goes on,

> Northampton was not key to what we did. It could have been anywhere. There were other factors – at that time, unemployment was through the roof, the crap weather, the drudgery. Music was always a way out. That's why you get so many great bands in England - the weather is shit. If you're in Southern California, everybody's out and about doing stuff. In England, you either go to the pub or you started a band. You can hear it in the music. If you listen to Bauhaus stuff it's not exactly tiptoe around the fucking tulips; not exactly tying a ribbon around the old oak trees. We were pissed off![693]

Sleepwalking and suffocating, Merrie England had somehow survived the 1960s when the margins of what was culturally acceptable had shifted. Ash remembers The Beatles and The Stones unbuttoning a starchy top button in stuffy post-war UK, hair creeping down towards their collars,

> Originally, of course, it was The Beatles. I'm giving away my age now. Beatlemania. I stuck my face against the TV screen when they were on with the volume on full. 'What is that screaming sound, I love it! Why is everyone screaming?' I was really young, like eight years old. It must have looked very funny to my parents when they walked into the room.
> The first music, though, that really affected particularly Peter Murphy and myself – and we had been friends since we were ten years old – was glam rock. As soon as T. Rex came on to the scene, and then the whole Bowie/ 'Starman' thing on *Top of the Pops*, I was sold. Then it was Roxy Music, the first couple of Lou Reed albums and Iggy Pop. I was hooked – *Raw Power* is still one of my favourite records - after hearing all that, then we knew.[694]

With Bowie at the helm of its teenage rampage, Glam was the fantasy future of sci-fi pop, promising escape from the grey drudgery of the 1970s and Murphy and Ash were just two more skinny freaks open to the dangerous possibilities it threw in the face of glum seventies England,

> Pete and I first met at St Mary's Catholic School, a secondary modern. We were best friends from the get-go; we loved the same music. We were on a strict diet of David Bowie, T. Rex, Lou Reed, and Iggy.
> The school was really rough. We were getting beaten up all the time. The teachers and the other kids were shit. Me and Pete were the little arty-farty kids sat at the end of the class who weren't into the sports cliché thing. We'd be doing painting and all the other kids would be playing football. So, we had a connection right from the start.
> We weren't faking it. We were pissed off. All that shit we'd gone through at school, the hypocrisy of the Catholic faith - all of that stuff is mixed into the music. Those kids who were going to church on Sunday were the ones kicking the shit out of

---

692 Northampton is also the area where the iconic Dr. Martens factory was based – a boot that soled so many feet in the post-punk era.

693 Daniel Ash to John Robb.

694 Daniel Ash to John Robb.

each other on Monday morning. All of that stuff came out in our music five years later in our songs like 'Stigmata Martyr'.[695]

At school, we couldn't dress glam; we all had to wear school uniforms. One Monday morning, though, when we were sixteen, Peter turned up with a perfect bright orange Ziggy Stardust haircut and he was getting beaten up in the playground and all this crap.

I'd always arrived late at school 'cos I couldn't fucking get up in the morning. When I got there Peter was trying to flatten his hair down and was getting so much grief. I saw him, and I went, fuck, that looks fucking brilliant. That is the best fucking haircut. You look exactly like Bowie. And he said, 'thank you so much, everybody else is giving me shit. The girls are taking the piss out of me and the guys are beating me up'. He was still trying to flatten his hair and I said: 'Fuck that! Stick it back up again. It looks fantastic'.

We always had that connection. We both loved dressing up and wearing makeup and all that stuff.[696]

Northampton's proximity to London meant that pop culture was tantalisingly touchable but a relatively lonely obsession.

In town, there were twelve to fifteen people that looked different. Everyone else looked like blockheads. There were a handful of Bowie boys or you were jocks or chavs as people now say. These fifteen people, male and female, 17-20 years old, looked like they were in Roxy Music or were David Bowie. They completely stood out. They looked absolutely amazing. Perfect haircuts, perfect clothes, doing the '50s rockabilly thing, wearing the crepes, but they were not Teddy Boys; they'd taken it somewhere else, it was mixed in with what would become the punk thing. Everywhere they went they'd get beaten up, and they'd have to have their own parties, so they wouldn't get their heads kicked in. I think that was happening all over the UK, with little pockets of interesting people. And then the punk thing happened and – boom. These people were the beginning of all that.[697]

Ash had been playing the guitar from an early age, or at least that was his intention. It all began with him picking up a six string in 1972, as ever, inspired by Bowie:

I was fifteen years old in 1972. It was just when Bowie was coming out with the Ziggy thing. My dad took me to Shaftesbury Avenue and bought me a Fender Telecaster copy because I kept going on about a guitar. It was £25. When I got it home, nothing happened. I couldn't be bothered to play it. I'm really lazy and I just used to look at it. I would be falling asleep with it and I'd wake up in the morning holding the neck of the guitar. It looked amazing. It was a starburst colour. I remember cutting out plastic stars and sticking them on it.[698]

Daniel Ash's love of art led to his attending Nene College of Arts in Northampton, where the rest of the future band, apart from Peter Murphy, was hanging out. Art

695 There is much to be said for the influence of the religious backgrounds of many of the prime practitioners in the goth scene. The contradiction between religious guilt and a perceived moral hypocrisy between the church and one's reality was prime for artistic interpretation. Many of these frustrations were played out against foreboding religious imagery that simultaneously attracted and repelled.

696 Daniel Ash to John Robb.

697 Daniel Ash to John Robb.

698 Daniel Ash to John Robb.

schools were a key part of British pop culture where creativity filled young minds with new ideas and possibilities.

> Pete didn't have the luxury of going to art school. Because of his financial situation with his parents he had to get a job straight away at a printing factory. What art school did was to completely decode you from the nine to five mentality. To be honest, I didn't need decoding; I was already there mentally. I was never going to get a nine to five. I just felt completely at home in art school. You could be yourself. Mind you, musically, the majority of students were listening to crappy music; that horrible progressive rock stuff.
>
> I remember David J being there. We were one year apart, and we crossed each other in the hallway. We were the only two wearing drainpipe trousers because the punk thing had just happened; all the others were wearing the flappy, hippy flares. So we'd always say hello. There was a connection right there.
>
> All the other guys at art school were trying to play like Jimi Hendrix. I was too lazy to attempt that. I also thought, 'what's the point in sounding like Hendrix, he's already done it?'
>
> And then the whole punk thing happened, and I thought, yes, I can do this, I can do the three-chord thing, and that's when it all started. It was the punk thing that spurred me on. Seeing Steve Jones up there on the telly and thinking what an amazing sound he gets with that Les Paul. Incredible. And that's when we started playing together.[699]

Before Bauhaus, Ash and the Haskins brothers had been playing in numerous local bands. Like many young musicians, they earned their chops by playing covers, with the occasional David J original thrown in Typically, by spring 1975, their youthful ad hoc band had typically fallen apart, only for a new outfit, Grab A Shadow, to emerge. While this project was initially influenced by Steely Dan, the fast-changing year of 1976 was having a profound effect on both the group's music and their trousers. The new energy of Dr Feelgood's late Wilko Johnson with his machine gun style of guitar playing increased the young Northampton band's intensity.

In the autumn of 1976, David J found himself intrigued by a Xerox flyer he had found for a new band called Sex Pistols. The band were playing Oxford Street's 100 Club and he and brother Kevin in tow, promptly made the 90-minute trip to the capital. Like so many like-minded pioneers of the future post-punk generation, he was inspired by the energy; the spectacle and the artful brilliance of Sex Pistols, rushing back home to recreate them on his own terms. The Haskins brothers now reconvened as the punkier The Submerged Tenth playing a mixture of covers and a couple of originals with Janis Zakis newly christened the punky-sounding Vince Venom by David J.

Their fertile young minds were fired by punk; a genre and mindset impinging on their mid-1970s glam rock music world. The Sex Pistols being the ultimate alpha band were an electric shock of inspiration for David. Unfortunately, Daniel Ash didn't get to see the Pistols. The gig he was planning on attending, at the Northampton cricket club on 9 October 1976, was cancelled.

---

699 Daniel Ash to John Robb.

There was a huge buzz in our world about them coming. I was so excited, but they didn't show up. So when I saw the Pistols on *Top of the Pops*, in July 1977 doing 'Pretty Vacant' I was so fucking happy. They were really breaking the mould. Later on, when Bauhaus had started, we were all living in the same house in Northampton. If I'd had a heavy night and woke up with a stinking hangover, I would put on *Never Mind the Bollocks* and it would get rid of it. Everyone else thought I was a total loony when I put it on as loud as possible, but it was total adrenaline.

Punk put things on another level. It was so exciting. I loved The Damned as well - they were underrated, 'New Rose' was the perfect single. Also, The Only Ones, that single, 'Another Girl, Another Planet'- fuck, it's brilliant. And also Television, Richard Hell and Neon Boys. I loved that stuff, the Ramones and the rest were brilliant. So that whole thing when it hit really affected me.[700]

The Submerged Tenth entered 1977 in search of a second guitar player. Daniel Ash would re-enter the fold, just before the band collapsed and regrouped as The Craze in early 1978.

The Craze was a reaction to everything that had gone before with the exception of T. Rex. All the punks loved T. Rex. Marc Bolan had no problem telling the world that he thought he looked fucking great. The prog rock guys were hiding behind this bushy fucking hair and a pair of flared Levi's and looked like shit. Whereas Bolan wanted to look great and so did the punks in their own way; they wanted to look sharp. It was a big part of it.[701]

The Craze were already moving away from the punk template and adding elements of jazz, reggae and dub to their stripped-down sound - elements that would emerge in Bauhaus later on albeit with a darker twist. However, yet again, the young band fell apart, leaving Daniel Ash on his own. Now bitten by the performance bug, during the summer of 1978, he began looking for like-minded souls and decided to get in touch with his old school friend:

I knew it had to be Peter. I had no idea of what he would sound like. I just thought he looked great. I thought 'he's just got to be in a band'. The band that I had been in with Kevin and Dave had just split up; the three of us went in three different directions. We didn't even phone each other up to say the band was over. So, I was sort of pissed off. I had nothing to do. I was working at a petrol station. I was going to phone Peter on a whim, after not seeing him for a few years, but then I remembered where he lived. So, I just got in my Ford Cortina Mark II, which cost me £50 from my maths teacher at the school and drove ten miles down the road to Wellingborough[702]. I knocked on his door and he had just come home from work when he answered. And I said: 'Hey, do you want to be in a band?' He said, 'fuck yeah'.

So that was it, I got this little rehearsal room, just Pete and myself, and I had this 15-watt amp. I had this echo unit and he started singing words out of *The Sun* newspaper, and I'd be playing this reggae riff, which ended up being a song called

---

700 Daniel Ash to John Robb.

701 Daniel Ash to John Robb.

702 The town near Northampton where Pete Murphy grew up and where Dr. Martens were made.

'Harry' because it's about Debbie Harry. He started moving around straight away, and it was only a matter of time before it clicked and I thought: 'this is it; this is the one'. [703]

Now with Kevin Haskins on drums, it only took a couple of weeks before brother David came to a rehearsal and had a word with Ash.

Dave took me aside afterwards and he said: 'the band's fucking brilliant… the singer is a diamond, but you've got the wrong bass player…' I thought – 'you're not fucking joking' because this bass player was useless for us. Dave was in for the next rehearsal and the rest is history. The chemistry was there and that's something that's out of your hands. Because it's like The Beatles – how did those four guys meet up? The Stones? How did they meet up? They were meant to meet up. The same with us – we were meant to meet up.[704]

From a suggestion by David J, the band initially titled itself Bauhaus 1919. The name was taken from the German art school which operated in Weimar from 1919 to 1933 under the leadership of Walter Gropius, combining crafts and fine artsand creating its own powerful aesthetic. It produced modernistic, all-encompassing visuals that proved a powerful influence on 20th-century culture. The 1919 suffix would soon be dropped.

The newly-named band played their first gig at the Cromwell pub in Wellingborough on New Year's Eve 1978. The local punk scene was thriving, all built around local clothes shop Acme and punk nights at the Paddock Pub in the village of Harpole (occasionally frequented by John Peel.) The Paddock held gigs by the likes of second wave punk favourites Discharge and The Exploited and was run by future Bauhaus manager Graham Bentley.

Bauhaus then spent the early months of 1979 tightening up their sound and aesthetic in the local pubs of Northampton. In July, they headed to London for their debut capital city show at the Music Machine in Camden. This was closely followed by a gig at the famed punk venue, The Nashville in Kensington. They played a small support slot, beneath punk poet Patrik Fitzgerald [705], The Teardrop Explodes and The Wall. The next London gig was in September with Gloria Mundi,[706] a proto-goth band whose intense, darkly theatrical performance that night was arguably quite an influence on them.

Graham Bentley[707] had already, at Daniel Ash's invitation, filmed the band at an early gig at The Romany pub in Northampton. After recording 'Bela Lugosi's Dead' Bentley filmed the band again; this time at their rehearsal room, miming

---

703 Daniel Ash to John Robb.

704 Daniel Ash to John Robb.

705 One of a handful of punk poets Patrik Fitzgerald never got the mainstream acclaim of a John Cooper Clarke but his Safety Pin Stuck In My Heart to this day remains a classic tune.

706 Gloria Mundi are one of the great lost bands of the scene. They are certainly a proto-goth band and a bridge from punk to the later scene, especially in terms of visual imagery and songs of isolation, sexuality, and aggression. Scene documenters like Mick Mercer claim that they were the first goth band but had arrived too early. They eventually morphed into the electro cabaret band Eddie and Sunshine before disappearing.

707 Bentley had met Daniel Ash through his work as an accountant. Daniel's father, Arthur, was one of his clients.

to their five track demo. The idea of using video as a means to showcase oneself and obtain a record deal was a radical one. As forward-thinking as his employment of this technology was, Bentley was getting ahead of himself as few labels had the equipment to play the videos!

The band fell together quickly, forging their own sound,

> I treated the guitar like a piece of wood with six strings on it and developed it from there.
>
> Obviously, I learned three or four chords, but I couldn't be bothered to learn one scale. I still don't know the scales. I would make up chords, particularly on my 12-string acoustic guitar. If somebody asked me what they were, I'd have no clue, but I'd just find them, and they would sound good. The idea of learning to read music or learning scales is boring to me. You've got to learn how to play a barre chord though, otherwise you're really in trouble. Things like our song 'Dark Entries', I mean that's just one note on the E-string just going down four frets, that's all it is, but it works, it works really well.
>
> So, it's funny, all these guys at art school were learning to play whatever that guy in Yes was doing. There was also all that shredding nonsense – then there's me hitting one or two strings, and it works. All that other stuff is just ego-wanking; boring. All it's saying is 'Look how fast I can go…' It was boys' stuff and I was much more interested in impressing girls, not boys. Girls have no interest in that sort of stuff and nor did I.[708]

The rudimentary yet imaginative approach was also applied to the drumming.

> There were some great drummers in post-punk. Like Stephen Morris from Joy Division and Kenny Morris from Siouxsie and the Banshees. I liked how Stephen played sixteenth notes on the hi-hat and how he used this wonderful electronic drum called the Synare drum which I ran out and bought immediately! With Kenny Morris, I loved how he would use the tom-tom drums rather than hi-hats and cymbals and create that tribal sound.[709]

Like most of the emerging post-punk generation, Bauhaus were turning their lack of equipment and rudimentary skills into to their creative advantage.

> We were all anxious to get the band going. As soon as we'd got three chords, we were off.
>
> Sound-wise, it was a combination of having no money and a limited amount of gear. We were making the best out of the fact that we couldn't play very well. That was the story of post-punk. New Order/Joy Division also had a very simplistic way of playing but it worked. You made do with your limited ability and it progressed from there.
>
> That's why we all loved Iggy and The Stooges who were so ahead of their time. Or the MC5's 'Kick out of The Jams' – that stuff's fucking brilliant. It's not complicated, it's to the point. It was the opposite of that pompous crap that was happening in the early 70s. Not the glam stuff 'cos that was brilliant, but the prog rock stuff that was way over complicated. The bottom line is if it's not sexy,

---

708 Daniel Ash to John Robb.

709 Kevin Haskins.

then I'm not interested. I used to love funk as well. I still do to this day. I think it's brilliant. Perfect. It's sexy. The girls love it. It's fucking hot. It's the opposite of the prog rock guys who were always in the kitchens with big fucking beards even when they were 18 years old and wearing big, baggy jumpers, talking about politics and drinking real ale. You know, that crowd. So, we were reacting to all of that.[710]

At such an early stage, it's unusual for a band to have so well-defined a sense of its diverse sound and style,

People would ask 'how did you get the idea of all wearing black?' We didn't ever talk about it. It just happened. It was organic. I would wear black because I was always tinkering around with motorcycles, plus it looked good. I think it's the same with the rest of the bands that came out of post-punk. It was like, we're not going to look like fucking hippies and look like we were queuing for a bus. We wanted to look sharp like The Clash – who looked great – and the Pistols; they all had something going. Ramones as well, in their own way, had this image. It was the opposite to the whole boring, hippy, prog rock shit.

You can see it in the early photos, Kevin's trying to look like one of The Clash and me and Pete are trying to look like Bowie; or at least glam rock.

There was a heavy Bowie/Iggy influence with the vocals, I don't deny that. David was an anchor; he liked a real cross-section of music. The thing I liked about David was that he was ahead of his time at art school. He loved Dr. Feelgood first when all the scumbag hippies were listening to Yes and Genesis. He got punk first. I loved punk as well as soon as I heard it. We all knew what we liked. Most importantly, we didn't want to sound like anyone else.[711]

Clearly defined, the young band were brimming with confidence. Daniel Ash, now armed with the 'Bela Lugosi's Dead' demo, was ready to go to London early in 1979 and meet the music biz; who, as ever, were behind the beat on these strange new sounds.

Initially, I just booked meetings with four or five big major record companies like EMI, RCA, Decca and somebody else. I went with the acetate of 'Bela', under my arm, and got on the train down to London. I actually got interviews with these big A&Rs and they all said the same thing, 'This is great. It's the sort of thing I listen to when I'm at home but it's not going to sell'. I knew they were going to say that, but I was always in a fantasy world and I thought they might just get what we were doing.

So, we ended up with an indie label, Small Wonder records, which was run out of a tiny little record store run in Walthamstow in the east end of London by Pete Stennett. I took it into the shop and Pete, who was smoking a joint, looked up

710 Daniel Ash to John Robb.

711 Daniel Ash to John Robb.

halfway through the track and said 'This is fucking great. You've got a deal. There's no money for promotion, but I'll give you a 50/50 split and take it from there'.[712]

Small Wonder were one of the seminal post-punk labels. Initially a record shop best known to the post-punk generation for its weekly ad in the back of the *NME*, it had blossomed into one of the key labels of the period. They had made a name for themselves with an idiosyncratic roster including Crass, The Cure, The Cravats, Punishment of Luxury and Fatal Microbes; providing a perfect launch pad for the weird and wonderful.

Finally released late that summer, 'Bela Lugosi's Dead' was one of the alternative songs of the year. It was released at a point in time when goth didn't yet exist. Music and bands like this were still considered 'alternative' and very much an exercise in post-punk art rock. With the help of heavy rotation from John Peel the band's music and style would soon prove key in creating a whole new strand of alternative culture. After the impact of the debut, Bauhaus signed with 4AD records, finding a good home for their artful endeavours.

The label, initially called Axis Records, was funded by the bigger Beggars Banquet imprint and was operated by Ivo Watts-Russell and Peter Kent. Initially, 4AD was a testing ground for esoteric ideas and the only band to make the eventual graduation from 4AD to its bigger umbrella label were Bauhaus. After that, 4AD carved its own niche running parallel to Beggars Banquet, releasing work from the likes of The Birthday Party, Cocteau Twins and Modern English. The label's distinctive, modernistic and beautiful artwork, provided by the late Vaughn Oliver, packaged a whole clutch of dark art and intense music, integral in the foundations of the future goth and '80s art rock scenes.

'Bela' was one of the big songs of that year, a permanent fixture at the top of the indie charts and the band were promoted to Beggars Banquet where they started to explore both their commercial and artistic sides, combining them to pay big dividends and break out of cult status.

Now with big label backing, the band went out on their first major UK tour supporting current new wave favourites Magazine as they promoted their third album, *The Correct Use of Soap*. The two groups would seem like post-punk polar opposites decades later but, at the time, it was a perfect example of the cross-cultural pollination that was the reality of the period before tribal lines were forged.

In the meantime, two more singles underlined the band's diverse musical palette; the deceptively simplistic dark punk rush of 1980s 'Dark Entries' followed by that summer's spooked and sparse single, 'Terror Couple Kill Colonel'.[713]

This restless creativity helped to define the band. Throughout their short career, they never settled on one specific style. Bauhaus were always style-shifting with an art school ease, and always making each move their own. Their impatient imagination was underlined on debut album *In the Flat Field*, released by 4AD in October 1980.

---

712 Daniel Ash to John Robb.

713 A song whose title was taken directly from a newspaper headline detailing the case of a murder that had taken place in West Germany.

Recorded in Southern studios, the claustrophobic tiny recording environment captured the band perfectly. The recording facility was built into a shed at the back of the Wood Green home of producer John Loder with the drums set up in his front room and the amps in the hall. Loder's production style was a particular influence on a host of artists from Crass to Steve Albini. The place had form; Crass, On-U Sound System, Fugazi, The Jesus and Mary Chain and Shellac would all record astounding records there over the years- cutting edge music recorded in a shed! In that suburban house, Bauhaus recorded and self-produced an eclectic and iconic debut album. There was adventure in the bleeping syn drum and atmospheric soundscape of 'Spy in The Cab', the grinding leviathan that was 'Double Dare' with its gnarled bass line and the haunting, anthemic rush of 'In the Flat Field' was astounding. There was the spindly and oppressive 'A God in An Alcove', the neo-glam stomp of 'Dive' and the loopy swing of 'Small Talk Stinks'. Completing the creation was the kooky grind of 'St Vitus Dance' and the lolloping bass-driven 'Stigmata Martyr'; the latter being a Black-Sabbath-esque song dripping with religious symbolism and frayed nerves. The album displayed the eclecticism that was core to the band's aesthetic.

> It was very deliberate. Why would you want to sound like someone else? If we were working on something I would go 'hang on, that sounds like so-and-so' and knock it on the head; take it another direction. I remember when I discovered the e-bow[714] – that was a godsend – it took the guitar away from being a normal sound and I used it a lot.
>
> It was very early on in 1980, I went to the local music store and I saw this little chrome thing on the top shelf. It captivated me when they explained it. As soon as they did, I grabbed it and said, 'how come these things aren't selling like hotcakes?' And they said, 'because it's so small people think it can't be worth £100'.
>
> The whole band loved technology. I remember Kevin got one of those little drums where you can affect the sound. After that, the syndrum and the e-bow became very much a part of the Bauhaus sound. There was also this other thing called the Sustainer which has the same principle as the e-bow. With that, you can hit all six strings and they'll resonate for as long as you want. They're amazing with guitars. You can do an individual note and it will howl on three different octaves of feedback or you can do a whole chord and it will go on forever with controlled feedback, perfect. All this stuff at your fingertips really suits me.[715]

The album was groundbreaking and became a template for so many musicians from the emerging goth and alternative scenes and still echoes through the decades. The UK music press, though, was somehow less than keen on Bauhaus with some commentators being particularly vicious, reporting that the band were pretentious.

---

714 The e-bow, or 'electronic bow', was a defining tool for the guitar player. A small handheld device, it was invented by Greg Heet in 1969. It was the original monophonic, handheld, electromagnetic string driver, creating vibrations and drones on the guitar strings that made a distinctive and eerily compelling sound.

715 Daniel Ash to John Robb.

However, in reality, all great music is pretentious. Pretending is the key; it signals the imagination running riot, instead of being timid and scared.

Misunderstanding their muse, the *NME* pigeonholed the band as 'Gothick-Romantick pseudo-decadence'. Writer Andy Gill described the album as 'nine meaningless moans and flails, bereft of even the most cursory contour of interest, a record which deserves all the damning adjectives usually levelled at grim-faced 'modernists''. Dave McCullough of *Sounds* was also negative, 'No songs. Just tracks (ugh). Too priggish and conceited. Sluggish indulgence instead of hoped for goth-ness. Coldly catatonic'.

While the mainstream media were not fully on board the underground embraced the album, enjoying its inventive soundscapes and sending it to number one in the alternative charts . It was sexy and breathlessly inventive with each track becoming its own entity as each musician played in unconventional and inventive ways. The band was hardly wallowing in misery- Bauhaus were about sex and dance. The core to their sound was black music like dub, soul and funk, influences they acknowledged on the dance floor groove of March 1981 single 'Kick in the Eye', contrasted by follow-up, the dramatically stark ballad 'The Passion of Lovers'. Both singles were further proof of the band's dexterity and a perfect prelude to their second album released that autumn.

An ambitious work, *Mask* saw the band stretching their sound with new flavours and textures, showing their ambition and focus in one of the great British art rock albums. *Mask* is, perhaps, Bauhaus at their peak; there is a stunning diversity to their music. Their imagination was running riot, yet the work had a narrative structure with the tracks fitting together perfectly. All four points of the band compass firmly fit together in that perfect post-punk way; everyone has a lead role, and working to serve the song.

Firmly established as a big cult band, Bauhaus always understood the power of pop. They may have been steeped in art school adventure, but this was a band birthed in the warm glow of early 1970s *Top of the Pops* episodes and the power of the seven-inch single. It was inevitable that, they would they pay homage to this glorious pop culture period with their 1982 top twenty cover of the totemic 'Ziggy Stardust'. This scored them a brilliantly dark, camp *Top of the Pops* appearance, sending the accompanying third album, 1982's *The Sky's Gone Out*, to number four in the charts.

Now mainstream, the band performed 'Bela Lugosi's Dead' during the opening credits of the hit movie *The Hunger*.[716] This, coupled with Pete Murphy's endless appearances on TV ads for Maxell cassette tapes,[717] saw Bauhaus on the brink of a breakthrough. Inevitably, though, the closer they edged to their yearned for success, the more the band fractured. The cracks in their perfect makeup were underlined on their fourth album, 1983's *Burning From The Inside*, recorded at the famed Rockfield

---

716 The 1983 erotic horror vampire film directed by Tony Scott, starring Catherine Deneuve, David Bowie, and Susan Sarandon.

717 Maxell created quite a stir with this series of TV adverts that saw Murphy stylishly sat in an armchair with his hair and frame literally blown away with power of cassettes.

studios in Wales under somewhat strained circumstances. Murphy missed much of the initial recording due to a bout of viral pneumonia yet, contrary to the reports of the day, he did eventually contribute vocals to all the album's tracks aside from 'Slice of Life'.

Following the album's promotional world tour, tensions in the band were reaching breaking point. These issues came to their denouement when the band chose to end their tour with two shows at London's Hammersmith Palais. The gig of 5 July 1983 would be their last.

For Peter Murphy, it was a bittersweet split. The band had reached their peak and pulled the plug.

> The performance was quite intense and overwrought. We were at the height of our career and there was a decision to split, so I wasn't expecting the gig to be triumphant. I felt like I was jumping off the edge of a cliff into the sea. There was an audible gasp when the audience saw us come out; we knew how fervent they were. But between the band, there was a lot of juvenile but dark, repressed, negative energy – sort of: 'We are the crème de la crème and we can do what we like, we can split up or we can record a fart as a track on an album'. I had to get out of that. But it was the end of something I had worked very hard to achieve, so it was very bitter. It was never going to be violent – it was gentlemanly, all stiff upper lip and respectful. One of the band members, though, chose to close the show with the words 'RIP', and that was not cool: it was as though we were some death-oriented, Munster-rock band, and it cemented the perception of us as this graveyard rock thing, later to be identified as goth. I always thought of Bauhaus as the Velvets gone holy, or The Sweet with better haircuts. [718]

A week after the Hammersmith gig, *Burning From the Inside* was released and reached number thirteen in the charts, proving a frustrating coda to a powerful career. Ironically, the album was the band at their most ambitious and diverse. From the mystique of one of their best singles, 'She's in Parties', to the incendiary riffs of 'Antonin Artaud' and the bizarre twenty-one second instrumental 'Wasp', the band were still moving forward. Tracks such as the waltzing 'King Volcano', the sorrowful 'Who Killed Mr. Moonlight' (a lament for the fast-fading band perhaps?), the baroque 'Slice of Life', 'Honeymoon Croon', 'Kingdoms Coming' and the dramatic arpeggios of the protracted title track cemented the album's importance in contemporary music. If there was one thing that typified Bauhaus at the very end of their time it was that they had no definitive sound, marrying their disparate styles to hang together as one band.

Post-Bauhaus, Peter Murphy cemented his musical cult status, initially joining forces with Japan bassist, Mick Karn. Together, they recorded an album as Dalis Car before Murphy set out upon a long solo career. Somehow, he never became the mainstream star that his matinee idol presence and velvet voice demanded and he retained his respected cult status whilst moving to Istanbul and converting to Islam.

---

718 Peter Murphy to The Guardian.

Meanwhile, Daniel Ash, together with then current flatmate Glenn Campling, turned his part-time project, the artfully brilliant Tones on Tail into a fully-fledged recording and touring unit,the duo replacing their Doctor Rhythm drum machine with Kevin Haskins. The band recorded one highly recommended album of macabre, twisted minimal pop to underground applause before breaking up following an American tour in 1984.

During this time, David J had released two solo albums and collaborated with other musicians. He also meshed his creativity with fellow Northampton resident, the iconic comic book artist Alan Moore, in the short-lived band The Sinister Ducks.

It was in this fractured environment that a Bauhaus reformation was mooted. A rehearsal was planned but Peter Murphy failed to show up. The ensuing jam sounded so good that the three core members decided to carry on as their own separate entity. Subsequently, in 1985, Love and Rockets were born debuting with a powerful version of The Temptations' 1970 classic, 'Ball of Confusion' that became a club smash in the USA. The band achieved further success with 1989's 'So Alive' which hit number three in the American singles chart. Buoyed by this freak mainstream success Love and Rockets went on to record seven albums of twisted freak-pop that diverted the dark humour of Bauhaus into a glowing world of glam-psych. They became incredibly popular in the USA, far bigger than Bauhaus had ever been. However, they never lived up to the totemic, cultural force of Bauhaus, who were now regarded as the alpha band in the now-worldwide goth scene.

The band's influence was so enormous that if some common ground could be found between the members then they could surely cash in on their own legacy. Finally, in 1998, they reunited for the 'Resurrection Tour' which was passionately received and saw them returning to top form like undead sonic vampires. They reunited again in 2005 for a stunning set at the Coachella Festival that opened with a cadaverous Murphy being lowered upside down to the stage, singing 'Bela Lugosi's Dead' in a brilliant piece of theatre. The celebratory gig, in front of their biggest ever audience, was the perfect springboard to a new world tour leading to the surprise release of a new album, 2008's *Go Away White*. Written and recorded in a tense studio session, the album was surprisingly good in parts, considering the band's long break. There were plenty of flashes of the old magic but, before release, the band had imploded yet again.

Bauhaus was dead. The bats had left the belfry. Or had they?

In 2019, Peter Murphy and David J toured a Bauhaus set while Daniel and Kevin (without Glenn but with Kevin's daughter Diva playing bass) toured their *Tones on Tail* album as Poptone. It seemed as though the band were as fractured as ever. By the end of the summer, Peter Murphy suffered a heart attack on stage during a New York residency show. Perhaps this event put things into sharp focus for the disparate band as they suddenly reformed to book a world tour that saw them play their biggest ever UK show at the Alexandra Palace , the band delivering a perfectly shimmering set of their mad, bad and dangerous to know classics.

Somehow they still looked the part and those songs birthed in the flat fields of Northamptonshire echoed around the famous old 10,000 capacity North London Hall. Inevitably the projected world tour fell apart as the wheels came off again and the band went back into a volatile limbo leaving their mystery and reputation intact. Their unique chemical composition that was both so creative and yet so destructive was perfectly summed up by David J:

> You have a test tube, and you pour in one chemical, and you pour in another chemical, and something happens. It starts to bubble. Pour in another chemical, and it starts to bubble a bit more. You pour in a fourth chemical, and it bubbles really violently and then explodes. That's my answer.[719]

---

719 David J to SuicideGirls website.

Chapter 21

LORD OF CHAOS

A Dark and Beautiful Playground: Killing Joke

With a fierce intelligence and a thirst for esoteric knowledge, Killing Joke is like no other group. Formed in the post-punk fallout, they quickly found their own musical route, combining the space of heavy dub with a concrete guitar, tribal funk, neo-classical melodies and Panzer tank riffs. They combined the riotous intensity of punk with a heavy groove undertow and wild-eyed apocalyptic vocals, splicing the two with a chainsaw guitar.

This unique band are a multifaceted and magical combination of four very different personalities, each bringing their personal voodoo into a brooding whole. Birthed from punk and alchemised in the multi-cultural hothouse of Notting Hill in the late 1970s, they soaked up the intensity of punk and added the surrounding space of dub and funk to their alchemical mix. They would then set out on one of the most unusual musical journeys.

Killing Joke are fronted by one of rock's great shamanic figures; the wild-eyed Jaz Coleman who, for years, was considered by onlookers to be an unhinged if charismatic voice, ready and expectant for Armageddon. These days, as bassist Youth likes to point out, the singer was 'right all along' and his paranoid visions from the band's early days now sound like 21st century news headlines as his dark visions become a bleak reality.

Killing Joke were forged in the swirling possibilities presented by punk. Once formed, each member of the band would bring something unique to their infernal chemistry.

> Our intensity is intrinsic to the sound and who we are and what we are into. We're like four points of a compass. We pull in four different directions and that makes it whole. We each have our influences and sometimes they crossed over. Youth was listening to disco; Geordie was listening to Pete Townshend and Zal Cleminson and I was listening to Gene Vincent and Jaz had studied classical music but loved punk. What we agreed on was heavy dub reggae and music having to have a groove.[720]

That disparate intensity resulted in the production of a series of dark and apocalyptic records that captured a very different side of the punk fallout.

> Their sound is unlike anyone else there has ever been or will be. They are truly unclassifiable. Certainly not goth but definitely dark. Call them what you will, their influence is felt by almost all bands in the realm of alternative music - even if there are those who don't realise it. Without them, there wouldn't be a lot of what goth and later on industrial came to be. They fused funk, dub and disco

---

720 Paul Ferguson to John Robb.

grooves with the fury and power of heavy metal. All this with an apocalyptic script that gave their fans an almost supernatural strength to make it through the dregs of life. As a DJ, you could never go wrong with Killing Joke. They appealed to everyone. Everyone who had a backbone that is. [721]

Their influence has been enormous, with an unlikely roll call of musicians and genres inspired by their sound and vision, from Nirvana to post-punk, industrial, dance, goth and modern American metal, each taking their cues from the curious band who were dance floor staples in the goth clubs. Killing Joke always understood the art of dance and shackled their infernal visions onto heavy duty grooves.

The band have gone through several permutations over the years but when the classic lineup of Jaz Coleman, Geordie, Youth and Big Paul reconvened in 2008 (after working together intermittently), that strange and powerful voodoo once again filled the room. Individually, they have a power but together they have something sulphurous; a dark magic and pungently dense sound that few bands can match. When the classic band are together, their performance is more of a ritual than a standard music concert.

> Killing Joke is a dark and beautiful playground. It's an amoral place. There are no boundaries. It has a complete honesty. We can see each other as we really are. Nothing is really planned.[722]

Killing Joke is not an average band with an average agenda. The classic lineup's extracurricular activities of conducting orchestras, producing multimillion selling bands, making pagan jewellery, recording with Arabic musicians and even writing national anthems, somehow feed into their muse and are as unlikely as they are diverse.

Frontman Jaz Coleman is a fiercely intelligent and rather dangerous intellectual. Garrulous and friendly, he can switch to wild-eyed and confrontational in an instant. Coleman understandably has a fearsome reputation and his stage performances are like nothing else. Born in Cheltenham in 1960, Jeremy Coleman is from a high-achieving family with an English father and an Anglo-Indian mother of half-Bengali descent. His older brother, Piers, is now a leading British-American theoretical physicist[723]. Jaz believes this drive for creativity, knowledge and rebellion was in his genes.

> My great, great, great grandfather was Mangal Pandey who led the insurrection against the British in 1857[724]. He is revered in Mother India as one of the great nationalists. Then there's B. N. Pandey, who wrote *The Breakup of British India* and was very close to Gandhi. My grandfather was in the 1962 war with China. He executed two of his own men for not going forward. He also believed in a global revolution.[725]

---

721 DJ Mont Sherar to John Robb.

722 Jaz Coleman to John Robb.

723 British-born theoretical physicist working in the field of theoretical condense matter physics.

724 :)

725 Jaz Coleman to John Robb.

Whilst brother Piers followed an academic path into mathematics and science, his parents wanted Jaz to succeed in music. This saw him study piano and violin under Eric Coleridge, head of music for Cheltenham College. By the age of seventeen, Jaz was a member of several cathedral choirs in England.

> My grandmother saw me moving to music in the cradle, and decided I had an oral, visual intelligence, as opposed to an academic one. Rock came to me on a certain day in my life. Before that, there was just classical music. Rock had been in the background. Back in Cheltenham in my youth, I used to see Brian Jones of The Rolling Stones on a fairly regular basis. He was fairly close to my uncle Bob. They'd been to school together and they moved to London together in the early '60s. When he came back, Brian Jones stayed at my parents' house on several occasions. My parents made a point of playing The Rolling Stones records to me, but I wasn't interested in rock music. I went off on an orchestral course to study the violin. I met this viola player who said to me 'Don't you listen to anything else other than classical music?' and I said 'no'. And she said, 'Have you ever heard any experimental rock music?' and I said 'No, no, not at all'. And so, she invited me back to her room and she'd got all these tapes ready. By tapes, I mean reel-to-reel tapes. Not cassette tapes. Then she said to me 'Have you ever smoked marijuana?' and I said 'NO!!!' I was absolutely horrified and shocked as an innocent. So, I ended up listening to this music, getting high and losing my virginity all in one go.[726]

In conversation, Coleman stares you in the eye, testing out your resolve. He laughs the death rattle cackle of a man who has always predicted this wild and unfettered end of times. Fascinated by the corporate machinations destroying the planet, he remains on a lifelong quest for his truth. Coleman is obsessed with the power of nature and the responsibility of the human race. In conversation, his speech is peppered with references to history, religion, philosophy and ancient and modern theories of the beyond. He currently lives on a small island in the Hauraki Gulf, near Auckland in New Zealand. It's a remote spot where they have banned mobile phones, citing 'the signals affect the bees'. Not only fronting the behemoth of Killing Joke, he conducts orchestras and has been chosen as Composer in Residence for the European Union, writing music for special occasions. He also records Arabic music in Cairo and is involved in endless musical, intellectual and philosophical projects that are far removed from the banality of the normal band process.

For Coleman, Killing Joke is the ultimate space and only a derangement of the senses, he says, can create this kind of ritualistic intensity:

> It's a completely different thing from the classical entity. When I'm conducting, my mind is on fire. I have to anticipate everything and conducting orchestras is a more cerebral process. It's mathematical. With Killing Joke, you're trying to get into a state of frenzy. They are different mediums – they are both music but that's where it ends. The styles are reflected in the two aspects of me – one part of me is an individual, a hermit, and the other part is a communist who likes to share

---

726 Jaz Coleman to Mudkiss website.

music with people – Killing Joke is the collective and classical is one person's vision.[727]

Killing Joke were formed in 1978 in London's Notting Hill. At that time, it was still a bohemian area of West London, a place where all kinds of interesting and artful madness occurred in its then-ramshackle, large Victorian houses.[728] In the 1960s, the cheap flats had been home to a vibrant colony of artists, musicians, bohemians, drug dealers and misfits. The area was like New York's Greenwich Village or San Francisco's Haight Asbury - a proto-hipster area of drugs, left-field art and music; a veritable melting pot of ideas.

The whole area is riddled with pop culture history. It was where Eric Clapton formed Cream and where Jimi Hendrix died of a barbiturate overdose. Van Morrison sang about Notting Hill in the song 'Slim Slow Slider' from his *Astral Weeks* album and writers such as Michael Moorcock, J. G. Ballard and Colin McInnes all drew inspiration from, and wrote about, the area. Meanwhile, Nic Roeg and Donald Cammell immortalised it in their 1968 cult film, *Performance*, starring Mick Jagger - a classic capture of the area and the wreckage of counterculture. In the late 1960s, space rock kings Hawkwind had drifted together in the decaying Victoriana while flying the flag for an idealistic hippy festival free spirit. In the mid-1970s, The Clash had also formed around Notting Hill, surrounded by the huge reggae sound systems that rumbled through the night air. This ongoing cultural mix was intoxicating.

> Notting Hill was our tribal area. It was an area of dissenters and thinkers, and now it's just full of bankers and wankers. It was the first cosmopolitan experiment in this country. Its sacred land. It's where a lot of punk started. It was where the punky reggae party started when Don Letts brought punk together with Bob Marley and the whole spring in punk's rhythm section changed. We used to rehearse there, and The Clash would be upstairs rehearsing, but we didn't used to speak to each other at that stage, but later I became great friends with Joe Strummer. We used to live in squats then. It was the only way you could afford to do your music.[729]

All these Notting Hill culture clashes would later be identifiable within Killing Joke's sound. Music of differing cultures and genres hung in the sticky night air, affecting the soul and psyche of Coleman who had moved there from the regency charms of Cheltenham.

It was also into this melting pot of cultures and ideas that, in 1978, 'Big' Paul Ferguson became the drummer in the Mat Stagger Band. The drummer had arrived in London from Wycombe where he had settled after moving around the world with his parents whose work had taken them many places, including a stint at the Pentagon. Hoping to attend art college, Ferguson made the move to London but

727 Jaz Coleman to John Robb.

728 Notting Hill had a long association with artists since 1870. In the post-war period, its large decaying houses were subdivided into cheap flats and rented by the newly-arriving Caribbean families. This often led to exploitation by landlords such as the notorious Rachman. The area saw a tension that culminated in the 1958 race riots instigated by Teddy Boys. A whole hippy scene had coalesced around Hawkwind in the '70s and its vibrations were still apparent in the post-punk period.

729 Jaz Coleman to The Quietus.

ended up joining a band. Music had been of paramount importance to him since the late 1960s

> The first single that I ever bought was the ska classic 'Monkey Spanner' by Dave and Ansell Collins. There was a big skinhead scene at the time and a lot of horrible fights. The first albums I possessed were *Are You Experienced* by Jimi Hendrix and the *In the Court of The Crimson King* by King Crimson which made a huge impression on me. Then it was Roxy Music's *For Your Pleasure* after seeing them on the *Old Grey Whistle Test* – that was jaw-dropping. I'd never seen anything like that, also Alex Harvey was big for me, as was older music like Gene Vincent.[730]

Wycombe was a part of the busy live music circuit, with the venue The Nags Head hosting many gigs in the drummer's formative years. However, while Ferguson saw Dr Feelgood, he missed the famous Sex Pistols 1976 gig.

> I started playing the drums when I joined the Royal Grammar school combined cadet force where I elected for playing the snare with the military band. The school had a very strong tradition of military service and was completely covered in tombs of old boys who fell in the Great War. It was strict, but times were changing. The pupils now had longer hair even if the teachers hated it. The staff were in their caps and gowns and the youth were all scruffy and into T. Rex, The Sweet or Gary Glitter. There was a real animosity going on. The year above mine locked all the masters in the common room and broke into the school armoury and marched around the school with guns until someone got hurt and the police came. Despite this, I managed to sleep my way through school. I wanted to be a drummer and I wanted to be an artist and I spent my time drawing drum kits on my notebooks. I always had a fascination with drumming and fire.[731]

By 1976, Ferguson was already in his own band called Beowulf, which included Roy and Martin Jones, brothers of 1980s pop star Howard Jones. He then moved on to Pink Parts, who covered songs like The Velvet Underground's 'Waiting for The Man'. They also wrote their own songs with many of the lyrics written by Ferguson, who would later do the same for Killing Joke. Pink Parts were fringe players on the freshly emerging punk scene, playing local gigs and even getting as far as supporting Adam and the Ants at the 100 Club.

> When punk came along, I got rid of my Afghan coat [732]and out came the white t-shirt with 'Rat Scabies' daubed on it! My friends for the most part thought I was crazy, so I would take the bus up to London on my own as much as I could and join in the mayhem at the Marquee or wherever.
> I was trying to get into St Martins art college to study painting and I moved to Dulwich in London with my girlfriend and looked for a job on a building site whilst looking for auditions for bands. The first band that came up was the Mat Stagger Band and I went to the audition instead of an interview at St Martins and we hit it off. He was into this Nigerian afro rock reggae, but I could only do it

---

730 Paul Ferguson to John Robb.

731 Paul Ferguson to John Robb.

732 The traditional overcoat of the Afghan people, the sheepskin coats were first imported to the UK in 1966 by Craig Sams and were sold in hippie boutiques like Granny Takes A Trip. When The Beatles wore them for Magical Mystery Tour they became a fashion and a signifier for hippie culture.

the way I could do it. Maybe he saw me as a blank canvas, and he sat down and showed me how to play that style for a gig at the Nashville that was in a couple of weeks. [733]

The Mat Stagger Band was also looking for a keyboard player. In a stroke of luck, Paul had just met the intense young Jaz Coleman who was new in town. Despite winning several classical music prizes, punk had turned Coleman's head in 1977 and he had left school with no academic qualifications and promptly moved to London. Three days later Coleman met Paul Ferguson and he played keyboards on one session for the Mat Stagger Band before the pair decided to create something of their own. They just needed to find the right brethren to join them.

> When me and Jaz met there was some sort of strange attraction. It didn't work out with Mat Stagger but we carried on playing. We hit it off. There was a strange fascination. I think I've read him saying it was a mutual disgust! But whatever, we ended up spending a lot of time together. Musically, we were poles apart. His record collection and mine were pretty much the antitheses. It was obvious that we wanted to play together though and so I sort of finagled him into the Mat Stagger band, but it didn't go that well because he didn't have much of a feel for reggae. We were sat in the pub with Brian Taylor, who would become the Killing Joke manager, and we just felt it wasn't right, so we called Mat Stagger and blew out the next gig and told him we were leaving. In retrospect, it was a pretty shitty thing to do but we felt we were on a mission and nothing could get in the way of it.
> I'm going to call it the grand illusion and it still exists between us all. I'm not saying that we verbalise it that much anymore, but we had a distinct sort of programme about what it should be. Whatever we were talking about, once you get into a room, your musical limitations dictate what you are going to do. [734]

In the old time-honoured style, the duo placed an advert in the *Melody Maker* 'musicians wanted' back pages. Instead of being confronted with a tidal wave of hopefuls, they received a couple of replies from guitarist Kevin 'Geordie' Walker and bassist Martin 'Youth' Glover.

> We knew they were out there, our brothers, our soul mates. We needed to find people who had right-sided brain capacity. They had to have a natural aptitude for the mystery tradition and be revolutionary musicians and have an innovative style. This is a tall order that we were talking about, and the only way we could find these essential criteria for these two people, was magic. [735]

Perhaps more than the music, it was that mutual interest in the power of this magic that bonded these unlikely individuals and their future colleagues

> Magic was our common ground. It was important because Jaz and I needed to attract the people who were going to carry this through with us. We tried and held auditions and got a few professional musicians or wannabes. We were looking for

---

733 Paul Ferguson to John Robb.

734 Paul Ferguson to John Robb.

735 Jaz Coleman to Mudkiss website.

the people who also had the spark, the certain undefinable thing that would make this band something special and we liked to think we did that through ritual.

When I was at art school, I was hanging out with somebody that was heavily into the OTO.[736] I'm sure he was far too young to be a member of it, but I made a short 8mm movie with him in the Octagon in High Wycombe. I was dressed in a white sheet with a crown of thorns, banging a drum leading a sort of funeral procession down through the shopping centre on a Friday afternoon market day. I then got into it more deeply. I started to look at books about ritual, sigils and geomancy. Being raised a Catholic meant that the rituals fascinated me, but it was actually that performance that really sort of brought it home. It spurred me on into looking into the Hermetic Order of the Golden Dawn[737] and stuff like that. When Jaz and I met and started talking, that's where we found our common ground. He and I started studying magic together and started performing some lesser rituals.[738]

With Killing Joke there was a bigger and more quixotic power. The rituals of religion and magic interrelated with a music performance to build something that was not only beyond but also powerful.

When we came together it was about the music putting us in a place where we could channel something greater than ourselves, something greater than just rock'n'roll. A large extent of that is now unspoken. We have each had our separate and distinct experiences. Before we get on stage we come together as an entity and focus on bringing down the fire. Sometimes we are just a band playing on stage. Sometimes we are not, and we create something else.

Geordie is totally unique. He is an evolving one-man orchestra. The guitar often starts the song. Sometimes it has started from a drum beat and sometimes it's

---

736 Ordo Templi Orientis (O.T.O.) is an international fraternal and religious organisation founded at the beginning of the 20th century.

737 A secret society devoted to the study and practice of the occult, metaphysics, and paranormal activities during the late 19th and early 20th centuries.

738 Paul Ferguson to John Robb.

THE ART OF DARKNESS

come from a bass lick but for the most part, there are these chords and it's a case of, let's see what we can do with them.[739]

With magic added into the equation, it was always going to be a very different process finding the rest of the band members. One of the new arrivals was Martin 'Youth' Glover – a former soul boy who was now deeply immersed in dub and punk. Born in 1961, Youth had been touring on the national UK punk circuit in one of the smaller bands. He was also at the fringes of John Lydon's Gunter Grove scene; listening to heavy dub whilst hanging out with the arch snark.

At seventeen, Youth had already dived headfirst into the punk scene after surfing the possibilities of mid-1970s music culture.

> In 1977 I had just left school. I had just returned from a summer job in the South of France on a British run campsite. I was what was known as a 'Soul boy', going to discos in London like Countdown and the Global village. The look was very proto-punk. It was Bowie pegs or tight jeans, winkle pickers or jelly sandals. Later it got more eccentric with army uniforms, black bin liners and safety pins. Although it was not well documented, soul boys in London were the precursor to punk. I heard a lot of people talk about the Roxy punk club, but I never went.[740]

Mid-1970s soul was a huge influence on UK pop culture. Post-glam, it had provided a fruitful escape route for both Marc Bolan and David Bowie. Musically and stylistically, soul was one of the drivers for UK youth and in the playground culture of secondary schools where it dictated fashions and saw the hipper kids practise their dance moves whilst smoking fags in the dinner breaks.

This background of black music was important, not simply for Killing Joke, but most of the best music emerging out of punk and into post-punk. It was not just soul, but disco and dub bass lines that were giving the young listener a proper grounding and teaching them about groove and space. For the time being in 1977, however, it was punk that had been captivating.

> Punk rock was exploding in London and I was missing my chance and I couldn't wait to get stuck in. I had caught a bit of the fever before I left, and it tasted fresh. Prior to this, I thought there was no point in doing music as a career choice as I thought it had all been done, how were you going to top the Stones or Led Zeppelin or The Beatles, Bob Marley, Heatwave? It was futile trying, although I was writing songs by then I thought it was all over and my best bet was my other love, 'Art', so maybe art school was my future.' [741]

Youth never made it to Wimbledon Art College, even though he had been accepted. Hooking up with old schoolmate Alex Paterson, [742] they were swept up by the oncoming punk scene.

> Punk taught us the future had only just begun. Alex and I started going to lots of gigs. We would take speed, blues, and drink pints of snakebite and we would walk

---

739 Paul Ferguson to John Robb.

740 Youth to John Robb.

741 Youth to John Robb.

742 Later of The Orb.

all over London to gigs getting free entry at the Camden Music Machine and see a few bands every night at the Marquee or the Nashville, and even Croydon Greyhound. Croydon was tricky as I had an unusual look at the time – my top half was pure Elvis slicked back hair with sideburns but my bottom half was bondage trousers and a bib.

It was at this time I auditioned for a band. I answered an ad in *Sounds* looking for a bass player. I hadn't actually ever played the bass guitar in my life, but I could play the guitar a bit. Luck was on my side as there were about eight guys queuing up outside this room and they were all a lot older than me – mid-twenties at least; they seemed ancient to me – and none of them were punks.

I got my chance and feebly explained how my bass had been stolen at a party the week before, fortunately, the guitarist, 'Riff', had a spare Rickenbacker copy. I kept my eyes on his hands and followed his strumming. For some unbeknown reason they immediately said, 'you're in the band' and then 'we start rehearsing Monday for our tour supporting The Adverts...do you want to move into our flat in Tulse Hill?' without blinking I said 'Yes! I'll move in tomorrow!' [743]

Things were moving quickly for the teenage bass player.

Ten days later, The Rage were on 32 date UK tour supporting The Adverts and The Saints. Wow, and I was still a virgin. The Adverts single, 'Gary Gilmore's Eyes', was on the ascendancy and the shows were packed and I very soon developed a huge crush on their bass player, Gaye Advert. Although she was friendly, and I would get the odd shy smile she was firmly attached to TV Smith. The Adverts were much older, they were in their twenties and they were going through a classic 'coping not very well with fame and success' story. They were a great band and TV Smith had a lot to say and he really meant it. Gaye was icy-cool-beautiful and indifferent on stage, and her bass playing was great. The Saints were an amazing band. They still had long hair and looked like junkies in old raincoats, not unlike Ramones but with more chords.[744]

The Rage were having the time of their lives playing with these six-month-old veteran punk bands. Time moved fast in punk and a few months felt like an eternity.

The Rage had a strict no drugs/no pot policy – 'hippy stuff' they sneered when we came across it. I was too young to really question it, but it didn't bother me, I was having the time of my life on half a shandy in a club! The band was formed by John Towe, whose claim to fame was that he was the original drummer in Generation X. He had known The Adverts from the Roxy and was a determined, ambitious, driven man and a nice guy. Later he replaced Laurie Driver in The Adverts who he had taught how to play. Unfortunately, our guitarist wasn't a nice guy and very soon upped sticks to form the first punk super group called the White Cats with Rat Scabies from The Damned. Meanwhile, on tour, I lost my virginity to a girl from the DHSS, in Jayne Casey's[745] squat in Liverpool. Eventually, I got spotted by punk svengali, Jock McDonald at a gig at the Acklam hall and he invited me to join John Lydon's younger brothers' band, the 4 Be 2's

---

743 Youth to John Robb.

744 Youth to John Robb

745 Jayne Casey is a Liverpool scene legend whose band Big In Japan were freakish looking and sounding and pushed the envelope in the city. These days she is a prime mover in the big positive changes that are being made to the city with areas like the Baltic Quarter.

and that got me on my first record, 'One of the Lads', produced by John Lydon and released on Island which grazed the top forty. This was all before I joined Killing Joke, and that was the end of my innocence.[746]

Killing Joke also had a guitar player. Born in 1958, Kevin 'Geordie' Walker had moved with his family from Newcastle to Milton Keynes in Buckinghamshire, 45 miles northwest of London. He had lost his hometown accent by the time he moved to London itself to study architecture but nonetheless, it resulted in his nickname. After seeing the ad placed by Jaz Coleman, he joined Killing Joke in 1979. It was the first band that he had played in. He was also fascinated by the esoteric. Geordie fitted.

> Killing Joke – it involves mysticism. It involves changing the world. It involves changing our lives and it pulled us all together. This was even before we found Geordie who has really been the music of Killing Joke ever since, and Youth – look how he shapes the sound. When we all met, we all agreed on what we didn't like, so maybe it was the negatives that formed us.
> Since then, Youth has become a druid and is very well-versed in all sorts of rites and rituals and Geordie takes astrology and numerology very seriously. I'm the one that really doesn't involve myself in it very much anymore. I feel like in many respects, we weren't in control of what was going on around us and we were drawing a lot of bad stuff out as well as the good, so I felt like I didn't want to be around that energy anymore. [747]

Spirituality was always part of Jaz Coleman. It was just a case of finding what to embrace.

> When you take into consideration that I'm from an atheist family, I chose out of my own free will to become a part of a church choir and a cathedral choir because loved sacred music and ritual in all its forms. I also ended up with a massive passion for the occult in my earliest years. By the time I was nine I had a lot of occult masterpieces that I was studying. By the time I was twelve, I was pretty well-versed in astrology. I wanted to know if there is any truth in magic. I wanted to see it. I wanted to see supernatural things happening and so in my early teens, I decided to study magical traditions in all their forms all over the world. And that's what I have done. I have written so much about it. You could get my studies into three books the size of *Lord of the Rings*.[748]

Now rehearsing, the early Killing Joke already had their own agenda. According to Coleman, their manifesto at the time was to 'define the exquisite beauty of the atomic age in terms of style, sound and form'. Even the band's name came loaded with meaning.

> The killing joke is like when people watch something like *Monty Python* on the television and laugh, when really they're laughing at themselves. It's like a soldier in the First World War. He's in the trench, he knows his life is gone and that within the next ten minutes he's gonna be dead ...and then suddenly he realises

---

746 Youth to John Robb.

747 Paul Ferguson to John Robb.

748 Much of his work is detailed in his dense but enthralling autobiography/manifesto, *Letters from Cythera*.

that some cunt back in Westminster's got him sussed – 'What am I doing this for? I don't want to kill anyone, I'm just being controlled.'[749]

The new band spent a few months in preparation and then played their debut gig on 4 August 1979 at Cheltenham Witcombe Lodge, supporting The Ruts and The Selecter. From the get-go, they were dancing on fire. In the primordial creative soup of post-punk, the possibilities were endless. Taking cues from this musical cross-contamination, Killing Joke were already fusing a contrasting bag of styles. These included dub, punk, left field, krautrock, funk and disco. However, the tribal undertow and intense charisma of Adam Ant were of equal influence.

> I remember Adam Ant's 'Car Trouble' and 'Never Trust A Man with Egg on His Face' made a huge impression on us. The early Ants had that sort of bondage thing going on. Adam Ant dressed in a raincoat with PVC trousers and wore makeup. The audience was completely spikes, chains, and mohawks and was very intimidating and he had a sort of control over the audience which was, of course, very impressive to us.[750]

John Lydon's Public Image was of even greater importance.

> In a funny way, the two Johns – John Peel and John Lydon – were responsible for Killing Joke bursting onto the world stage in such a short period of time. John Lydon's death disco, in the original lineup of Public Image with Jah Wobble, was already on a similar track to us. Their first two albums were so important. We got a tape to him because he was friends with Youth and he became passionate about Killing Joke and talked about it in the press a lot.[751]

PiL's adventures into dark dub made them fellow travellers.

> PiL's 1979 *Metal Box* is a masterpiece. It's a monumental work. I thought they just got that whole art punk thing perfect. They fulfilled the promise of punk. They were a big influence. And there was Dennis Morris's[752] packaging of it in a metal film box with three 12-inches.
> I was also into Lee 'Scratch' Perry at that time. The atmosphere, the ambience and the mashing up of everything on albums like *Super Ape* was unbelievable. Subsequently learning that he was doing that on a little eight-track mixer with the barest minimum of equipment was mind-bending. It certainly illustrates what any great dub album does: which is taking backing tracks from other records and productions and reinventing them, alchemising them. It's just blinding. The other great dub producer is King Tubby. What he does with the dubs and the way he reinvents is just revolutionary, but he was more bass and drums focused. With Tubby, the crispness of the hi-hats and the drums really set him apart. He still remains one of the great innovators of the genre. Augustus Pablo - the great melodica player and great master of melodies and when they worked together it was special. I remember listening to the *King Tubby Meets Rockers Uptown* album when it came out in 1977. It was in West London where Killing Joke was squatting. You'd go into a very small, dark living room at the bottom of a

---

749 Jaz Coleman to John Robb.

750 Paul Ferguson to John Robb.

751 Jaz Coleman to The Quietus website.

752 One of the key photographers on the punk scene.

Victorian house in the basement. There was very minimal lighting – just shadows. You'd be rammed up next to loads of other people with a tiny little bar at the back and smoke from ganja weed. It was an amazing place to hear that sound – the bass would just penetrate your bones.[753]

Now with the perfect lineup, Killing Joke formed their own Malicious Damage label in Notting Hill with their late manager Brian Taylor in September 1979. The label released their debut *Turn to Red* EP, which was steeped in a PiL flavoured post-punk dub. The release came in a stark sleeve featuring the Centre Point building on Tottenham Court Road and was designed by graphic artist Mike Coles who has continued to work with the band for decades, designing their highly distinctive sleeves to give the band a complete individual brand warp.

We got friends to stand in front of the BBC and push the first EP into Peel's hand as he walked in. Peel thought the record was a set up, like a famous band like The Stranglers masquerading under a different name, which is why he dropped by the first Peel session recording to see who we were. With his support, it was only ten weeks from us getting together to the first gig selling out. It all happened fast. By the time we were really kicking into our career, punk was gone completely, and we were the only voice really for rebellion.[754]

That sense of rebellion was caught on the band's eponymous 1980 debut album that captured a heavier, darker sound that caught the claustrophobia of the new decade and the nuclear war paranoia of the time. Its bleak soundscapes were equal to Joy Division's intensity,[755] but with the addition of a heavy duty rhythm, which helped to create songs like 'Wardance' – an apocalyptic dance floor classic that swiftly became a goth club staple.

Killing Joke's unique calling card was this combination of dance floor aesthetics and the dark intensity of the punk apocalypse. Lyrically esoteric and intense, they created a shamanic dance rock classic with bone-crunching and incessant riffs.

The following year's *What's THIS For...!* saw the band create a wall of sound that was almost impenetrable. Its sleeve art was equally disconcerting, being a burnt-neon photograph of a side street in Norwich, featuring the back of a lone figure in shorts, peered at by several questioning heads, emerging from the archways of buildings.

The raw music was skilfully balanced by the band with engineer and drum recording expert Nick Launey whose trademark huge drum sound really added something to the sonic tsunami. The production also allowed light into the huge rhythms and caustic riffs and was a perfect capture. Crucially, the album also managed to retain those dislocated dance rhythms that were so key to the band's style. A prime example of this was the totemic and anthemic single culled from the album, 'Follow the Leaders'. It was an avalanche of powerful drumming, Giorgio Moroder pulses and a huge chorus. Its equally strong flip-side, 'Tension', hit a perfect heavy duty funk groove, cranked with the band's own dark power.

---

753 Youth to the Skinny.

754 Jaz Coleman to John Robb.

755 The two bands shared three iconic gigs together in 1980.

Killing Joke were now a yardstick for the intense and primal. Their live performances were enthralling. Calling the gigs, 'gatherings', Coleman was the heavily made-up conductor of the mayhem. They created an astonishing spectacle and were much embraced by the goth scene for their intelligence as much as their dance-friendly, dark music.

1982's *Revelations* was recorded by legendary German producer Conny Plank and was the pinnacle of this early period. The album was a relentless, grinding and powerful release that made a strange and coruscated pop music from their heavy groove and rhythmic nous. The intensity of the band and its surrounding aura was now, inevitably, beginning to take its toll.

Fearing an impending apocalypse, Jaz Coleman fled to Iceland to become a classical composer and work with some of the burgeoning local bands. His sudden departure meant that the remainder of the band had to perform the new single 'Empire Song' on Top of the Pops with a roadie in a beekeeping suit standing in for the absent singer. Soon afterwards, Jaz was followed to Reykjavik by Paul and Geordie.

Meanwhile, Youth had been sectioned after he was found walking down the street naked after a strong acid trip. With his world and his band falling apart, he quit to form the more dance oriented-project Brilliant with Jimmy Cauty. Their twin bass-driven dub-funk dance-rock saw them signed by Bill Drummond, who would later go on to work with Cauty in KLF. Brilliant were produced, bizarrely, by Stock, Aitken and Waterman, but the album was not a huge success. After Brilliant ended, Youth became a dance producer and re-emerged as one of the most successful pop producers of modern times with a list of credits including Crowded House, Kate Bush, The Verve and many others.

With Jaz returning from his Iceland doomsday sabbatical and with Youth out of the picture, the band recruited a new bass player – Paul Raven. Growing up in Wolverhampton where his father, Jon, was a well-respected folk singer and author, Raven had cut his teeth in the local power-pop band The Neon Hearts and played with glam rockers Dogs D'Amour before finding his home in Killing Joke. The new revitalised lineup recorded their fourth album, 1984's *Fire Dances*, before hitting a commercial streak with 1985's swirling, melodic, moody and majestic *Night Time*. The latter included their top twenty hit singles – the brooding and melodic 'Love Like Blood' and the classic 'Eighties', whose guitar line was famously 'borrowed' by Nirvana for their hit song 'Come As You Are'.

Somehow finding a commercial space for their brooding apocalyptic muse, Killing Joke had retained the darkness and pagan mystery that was so appealing to the primal end of the goth scene. It was a quality hard to sustain and the band were starting to lose direction with 1986's over produced *Brighter Than a Thousand Suns*. It was an album of awkward gestation, seeing its synth-heavy sound lose focus and its follow up, *Outside the Gate*, saw the band reduced to a core of Jaz and Geordie after Paul quit and Raven asked for his name to be removed from the credits. The album fared little better and saw them dropped by Virgin Records, leaving the band to self-release their 1990 album, *Extremities, Dirt & Various Repressed Emotions*, a return to their heavier sound before they imploded in 1991.

In the meantime, Youth's highly successful career continued to blossom. However, the dark magus magnet of Killing Joke was still tugging at his heartstrings. When he met Geordie during the compiling of 1992's Killing Joke anthology, *Laugh? I Nearly Bought One!*, he suggested re-joining the band and was welcomed back into the fold. He played on and released their next two albums 1994's *Pandemonium* and *Democracy* on his own Butterfly Records label. The reinvigorated band added some elements from the trance world with which Youth was now familiar and combined this with other, more varied styles still embedded in the Killing Joke atmosphere but with even more intensity. Back in the top 20, *Pandemonium* saw the masters return to lord their sound over the new industrial metal scene which had used them as their one of their templates. It was one of their best-selling albums to date and Killing Joke were reanimated by this surprise mainstream embrace of their dark and off-kilter music.

Indeed, the prophets were now being honoured.

Democracy, was a more introspective and optimistic release, introducing acoustic guitar into the mix. The album made less of an impact and the band then took its longest hiatus to date, with Jaz Coleman becoming more embedded in the classical scene and Youth continuing his run of production success before returning for 2003's *Killing Joke* album, which famously featured Dave Grohl on drums; a sort of payback for Nirvana's 'borrowing' the 'Eighties' riff. The album, which was focused, intense and heavy, saw the partial return of Raven on bass, sharing 4-string duties with Youth and Geordie. The hard-hitting album was full of the dark and pessimistic visions of Jaz Coleman. The western world had entered a dangerous period, which the singer saw as a validation for his own beliefs and the prophecies in which he immersed himself. 2006's *Hosannas from the Basements of Hell* was an even denser, heavier work and would be their last release with Raven, who died in Geneva the following year while working on the *Weird Machine* album with French industrial band, Treponam Pal. The tragic death of the bass player would have a profound impact on the disparate wanderings of Killing Joke and it was at his funeral that big decisions were made.

> Everything came together when we all met at Raven's funeral. It was funny the unifying effect it had on all of us. It made us realise our mortality and how important Killing Joke is to all of us.[756]

Sparked into action, the original lineup buried their differences. Back in the rehearsal room, there was something about the original four musicians; each possessing that dark magus that made them so enticing. Of course, Raven had been integral in the band and was there for some of their biggest successes, however, the various lineup

---

756 Jaz Coleman to Terrorizer Magazine.

changes and different drummers used since the now-returned Paul Ferguson, who had left in 1986, underlined the dark voodoo of the classic four.

This new phase in the bands' history was marked by the dark trilogy of 2010's *Absolute Dissent*, 2012's *MMXII* and 2015's *Pylon*. These were albums that saw the band add another level of accursed intensity to their infernal muse. Instead of sounding dated, they sounded at the forefront of a new era of rock music which had in turn been influenced by the band's older, heavier sound.

This dark trilogy of albums was full of apocalyptic songs and wild-eyed visions that married the band's heavy, neo-industrial wall of sound with gurgling dance rhythms and tribal patterns.

The focal point of their changing sound remained in Jaz Coleman's intensity. His dark visions in the age of flux may have been draped with a lining of hope but were tempered with a mighty dread. These recent albums reflect this dark vision, yet the ever-erudite Coleman sees the great change in a more positive light.

> All the remote viewers I know, myself included, cannot penetrate beyond. These times are about getting our collective dreams in order, restoring the biosphere, the idea of wellbeing as opposed to economic growth, the idea of partnership and co-creation with fellow human beings, moving away from national boundaries and more towards what Schiller and Beethoven were saying in some of their work. If we can concentrate on what it can be, the dream of clean streams, of reforestation, of permaculture, of disengaging all the banks – identifying all the majority shareholders of the top hundred corporations and dismantling them. If we start dreaming of a fairer system and defining what an elite should be which is an intellectual powerhouse and not international bankers.[757]

Jaz laughs that wild laugh and stares as he explains.

> The way I perceive a Killing Joke concert – it's a spiritual experience for myself to get into that state of grace. Music is the theme of mantra. I'm not into organised religion at all but I always liked what Fela Kuti did in Nigeria which was playing music like it was a temple. Maybe we will evolve into a time where we will be performing for idealistic and spiritual reasons alone and not for monetary reasons. I can't see the point of contemplating extreme life extinction. It's good for nothing. It's nihilism in the absolute even considering it. It's in many different calendars though – the great unveiling, the sky and the earth coming together. We are heading towards the Eschaton and no one really knows what's going to happen.[758]

With that, Jaz lets out one last manic laugh, at the killing joke...

757 Jaz Coleman to John Robb.

758 Jaz Coleman statement.

Chapter 22

RELEASE THE BATS!

Nick Cave

There he is, the Black Crow King, immaculately besuited, with his jet black hair swept back into the darkest of dark waves on stage singing songs that combine poetry, heartbreak and wild imagery to thousands of spellbound fans in arenas and stadiums across the globe. His band are an extraordinary collection of similarly besuited elder statesmen droogs and the pictures they paint with words and music both captivating and complex and yet wildly popular. Somehow their leader has gone from confrontational wild-haired shaman to elder statesman of all that is atramentous and artful, in a career curve from talented cult troubadour desperado (fronting the Australian noiseniks The Birthday Party) to 21st-century stadium-filling icon.

Without losing any of his brooding poetic power and songwriting nous, Cave has easily adopted the role of the wise elder icon. Currently fronting an astonishing live show that matches the theatrical brilliance and cinematic narrative of his songs, his performances are part showbiz spectacle, part emotional power and part intimate confessional. In more recent years, a sense of dignified grief and loss has also been present in his live performances and songs, due to the tragic death of his son, Arthur Cave in 2015.

Thanks to Cave's sensitivity, raw power and a command of dark energy, he has become one of the major artists of the present times. A full on obfuscous baroque brand whose instantly recognisable sound and spectral shadow permeates anything to which he turns his quill. From writing books, music, and screenplays to being a style icon with his own online shop, Cave is the ultimate 21st-century creation, combining a deep tradition with a modern portfolio. Perhaps more Southern (hemisphere) gothic[759] than goth - a term that he naturally despises - Cave remains one of the key icons in this shadow world.

It's been a long journey from the wild and fierce early The Birthday Party gigs that set a new benchmark in the possibilities of rock. Fronted by a much younger and wilder Nick Cave, The Birthday Party arrived in the UK from Australia in 1981 on a one way ticket to self-destruction. They were armed with their own dark vision of a musical future; a sound where Shakespearean drama collided with Byronesque poetry and a gunslinger style. The young band delivered an artful violence and melancholic beauty, creating a highly original and addictive sound.

In the late 1970s, a darker and more intense strand of post-punk was formulating in towns across the UK. Worldwide, similarly, isolated pockets of like-minded

---

759 American Gothic is a 19th century literary genre filled with grotesque characters, dark humour and an angst ridden sense of alienation.

thinkers were following suit; micro scenes of kindred souls who had been touched by the darker corners of glam and proto-punk. All were now being empowered into action by the ferocious drive of punk rock.

In the world of late 1970s Melbourne, Australia, a clutch of highly intelligent and well-educated hoodlums were poised to veer off the rails and create one of the scariest rock'n'roll bands of all time. Through their kinetic distillation of sex, death and danger and their breathless, agitated urgency, the band would enjoy bumpy success after changing their name from The Boys Next Door to The Birthday Party.

Within a couple of years, and about to break into the big league, they imploded. Their final two twelve inch releases of 'The Bad Seed' and 'Mutiny'[760] are arguably the two most enthralling, dense and propulsive rock records ever released. Complete with skittering rhythms, slowed-down heavy grooves and Cave's stunning poetic skreegh, the songs make for compulsive listening. The frontman's charisma and devil-may-care attitude elevated Cave to the status of a scraggy-haired pied piper, leading the bedsit desperadoes and poetic souls of the early 1980s underground scene on a nihilistic march to bedlam.

Live, The Birthday Party were a full on confrontation. Cave would mentally attack the audience with his fearsome lyrics and delivery, then physically assault them with his pointed boots. The band would zigzag behind him with their unique and powerful melange of garage punk fury, howling noise and free jazz skronk. Their wild and deeply intelligent music was built around bassist, the late Tracy Pew, whose too-tight leather trousers, large cowboy hat and angular moustache, made him appear like a psychotic member of the Village People. Swaggering with a combination of killer and camp, his gnarly, heavy, swing bass cranked the band's fetid blues into a demonic danger zone. To his side, stood the charismatic agitated figure of Rowland S. Howard poised with a trademark cigarette in his mouth. The shrapnel twang of his guitar slashed across the bass gnarl, creating a whole new lexicon of noise. Meanwhile, multi-instrumentalist Mick Harvey would stare sternly at the surrounding chaos whilst holding the centre either on guitar or later with shattered drum motifs.

This wild landscape provided a perfect canvas for Nick Cave's explosive poetry. He was a flickering, twitching, rag doll with wild hair and dead men's suits. His stage antics created a dangerous energy and a narcotic stained havoc which he accompanied with lyrics of dark romance and wilderness narratives, delivering them like a man condemned.

No group had taken rock'n'roll so far and so deep. With each tenebrous twitch, the band were waltzing into crazier and wilder territory. They seemed to arrive fully formed in the UK, ready to assault audiences and senses in equal measure. It was like they had suddenly appeared from hell as they burned with an energy that could never last, yet, while it remained, provided a certain illicit thrill consumed with an outsider spirit.

---

760 Both EPs released in 1983.

I've always had this incredible feeling that I don't belong here in the UK and that I actually shouldn't be here. That I'm an imposter here. I almost feel that if they ever found out what I really felt about England they would string me from the nearest tree and burn me.[761]

With that sense of dislocation and creative anarchy and a music that was teetering on the edge of collapse, the band made a profound impact on everyone that saw them. Johnny Marr caught their legendary shows at the Haçienda in 1982/83.

You couldn't ignore The Birthday Party when they arrived. As a guitar player, I had to take notice of Rowland S. Howard and a lot of what Nick was doing forced you to change your perceptions. They were different. They were Australian. They were impenetrable. They were noise. They were sexy. They were confrontational. They were mysterious. They were druggy and they were kind of slightly intangible and they were a riot, like at those two gigs.[762]

After that initial explosive foray into the UK, they relocated to Berlin in 1982 and their last two EPs hinting at what could have been a defining third album, at the same time sounding like a band that were never going to get there. In the German capital, they had inevitably fallen in with Blixa Bargeld, his band, Einstürzende Neubauten, and their surrounding German art crowd. Still divided by the wall, the city's claustrophobic madness and 24-hour lifestyle managed to infect even The Birthday Party's wild aesthetic, driving them to new highs; chemically, musically and visually.

At least, until the wheels came off.

Inner band tension, their intense lifestyle and Cave's yearning for a different sound would pull the band apart. The Birthday Party would finally split in 1983.

Music writer Julian Marszalek believes that the powerful core of Nick Cave's creativity and imaginative performance is a force that lies at the heart of his wild intelligence and that his academic background that proves a good education doesn't always mean a safe career:

I suspect that a lot of it comes from his early upbringing. He was raised in an academic household. His mother was a librarian. His father taught English and Maths and introduced him to classic literature at an early age. I should imagine that his own academic background – he was a day boarder at Caulfield Grammar School, where he was also in the school choir – also plays a part. He also went to art school. I don't think that you can study art and literature to that degree and not try to apply that to your own work. He's always positioned himself as an artist and I think that's been evident right from the early days.

I remember seeing The Birthday Party for the first time. It was at the Clarendon Ballroom in May 1982 in London just after they had arrived from Australia. My overriding memory is of the intensity of the performance. This wasn't entertainment in a song-and-dance fashion. This was something verging on performance art.

---

761 Nick Cave being darkly amusing to John Robb in 1989.

762 Johnny Marr to John Robb.

Where does that intensity come from? I think that ultimately, he's being honest with both himself and his audience. Anything less is a fraud and he knows it. I've never seen him do a shit gig. Ever. Some of his albums are below par – I'm thinking of *No More Shall We Part* and *Nocturama* – but the gigs to support them were always amazing.

He lives those songs.

Here's an example: I saw him at Reading Festival in 1990 and his delivery of John Lee Hooker's 'I'm Gonna Kill That Woman' was so intense that he took the whole audience with him. I've never seen anything like it – he and the band took the song right down and a hush fell on the crowd. It was a total seduction of tens of thousands of people and when the band crashed in it was like having your head slammed against a wall. See also his 2013 Glastonbury performance of 'Stagger Lee'. It was just like in The Birthday Party days, he wouldn't have been able to deliver a song like 'Dead Joe' by looking at his shoes.

Marszalek also feels that Cave's intensity of delivery is also matched by an ingrained work ethic:

I interviewed him in 2008 and I asked him about his work ethic and motivation. He replied that he feels 'compelled to work', that he'd get up in the morning, go to the office, keep office hours and pretty much drag the art out of himself. I think that's quite telling. He's not someone who sits on his arse waiting for inspiration to hit. He's very methodical in his approach and I think it's one that he shares with many authors.

I remember reading an old interview with Ian Fleming who said that he wrote two thousand words a day when writing his Bond novels and I think that Cave sets himself targets like that. It's interesting that he views his output as 'work'. It's a real protestant work ethic and maybe that's something else he got from Caulfield which is, after all, an Anglican school.

Also, at the risk of entering the realm of cod-psychology, I think that the death of his father at a relatively early age had an effect. He was told of his father's death by his mum as she was bailing him from a burglary charge. He himself said that his father 'died at a point in my life when I was most confused' and that 'the loss of my father created in my life a vacuum, a space in which my words began to float and collect and find their purpose'. [763]

Cave concurs that his father dying in 1978 had a profound effect on him:

The things I love. The things I hate, the things that really affect me. I felt those things forming right down to the type of music and literature I liked. I don't feel they've progressed particularly since that time and that was pretty much the time my father died, and I think that's not coincidental. [764]

Nick Cave was born in 1957 in Warracknabeal, Australia — a boondock town of some 2,000 souls, known for its statistically improbable abundance of highly freckled redheads. Midway between the dusty small towns of Wycheproof and Dimboola, it lies 330 km northwest of Melbourne. Later, the family moved to Wangaratta, a small

---

763 Julian Marszalek to John Robb.
764 Nick Cave to The Guardian.

cathedral[765] town 100 km closer to Melbourne and best known for, fittingly, being near the site of outlaw Ned Kelly's last stand.

Like Jim Morrison in the 1960s, Cave was a deeply intelligent and literate misfit with a phenomenal drive. His music tastes were initially moulded by his older brother Tim and his prog rock leanings. That was until the young Cave discovered glam rock with T. Rex, Alice Cooper, and the Alex Harvey Band all gaining his support before, digging a little beneath the surface he discovered the (at that time hard to find, certainly in Australia) cult music of Lou Reed, New York Dolls, Kraftwerk, Roxy Music and The Doors.

> I find that out of all the art forms music is the most reliable in the sense that I could put on, for instance, Van Morrison's *Astral Weeks* now after a few years and all the feelings and associations are still welded together with that record. That's what I hope my own records can do. Same as when I play a Stooges record – there's a distinct feeling to it that makes me want to be like I used to be when I listened to those records. That's kind of incredible and it doesn't really happen with anything else. [766]

Cave was an extrovert bad apple at school and, while his natural charisma and artistic flair had seen him ponder becoming an artist, it was rock'n'roll that would prove to be the inevitable magnet for the young man. Joining with a loose cabal of like-minded souls, he put together a band called Concrete Vulture in 1974, taking on the role of lead vocalist with fellow school choir member, Mick Harvey on guitar. They were then joined by other students including Phill Calvert on drums. Concrete Vulture would play covers of David Bowie, Lou Reed, Roxy Music, Alice Cooper and the Sensational Alex Harvey Band - the Scottish band who were incredibly important to the young Australians who loved them for their combination of glam, hard rock prog, theatrical dark cabaret and narrative, literary stylings.

When school ended in 1975 and with Cave now at art school, the reprobates decided to keep playing and added friend and schoolmate Tracy Pew on bass. Already mining the distinctive musical seam of the new rock generation gap, they were finding more thrilling sounds beyond the mainstream radar at Chris Walsh's, Pew's best friend, house. Here, furtive listening sessions would introduce them to the delights of The Stooges, Pere Ubu and other pre-punk cult figures.

It wouldn't be long before they caught wind of the oncoming punk explosion. There was the eponymous Ramones' 1976 debut album, followed by Patti Smith's *Horses*, The Damned's 'New Rose' single and then Sex Pistols and The Clash, all meeting the eager young ears of the collective. In 1977, they would also be discovering homegrown bands like Radio Birdman and The Saints[767].

Remarkably, these Australian bands, like punk rock marsupials, had defied their relative cultural isolation with a convergent punk rock evolution in the pre-internet

---

765 Cave sang in the cathedral choir.

766 Nick Cave to John Robb.

767 Their classic singles included 'I'm Stranded' and Know Your Product' two of the greatest songs of the punk rock genre.

era and were spearheading a local micro scene of homegrown punk rock. From Brisbane, The Saints had a sneering, snarling attitude behind their propulsive and melodic brilliance which undoubtedly had a profound influence on the young Cave. To substantiate the band's importance, there is a great photo of a very young Cave, mesmerised, at the front of The Saints show at the Beverley Crest Hotel in Melbourne in April 1977. Their galvanising rush of sound is something he remembers to this day:

> The Saints were kind of godlike to me and my colleagues. They were just always so much better than everybody else. It was extraordinary to go and see a band that was so anarchic and violent.

Now calling their band The Boys Next Door, the young group's set was now peppered with punk and proto-punk covers like Ramones' 'Blitzkrieg Bop', Patti Smith's 'Gloria', and Alice Cooper's 'I'm Eighteen'. By late 1977, they had finally started writing their own typically teenage punk songs to add to the set, like 'Sex Crimes' and 'Masturbation Generation'. They performed at booze-stained halls on the local circuit, which toughened them up quickly and saw them signed to new imprint Suicide Records, a subsidy of big Australian indie Mushroom Records, who released their debut single - a manic version of Nancy Sinatra and Lee Hazelwood's classic 'These Boots Are Made For Walking'.

While the rest of the scene was catching up with Ramones' fuzzy imprint in 1978, The Boys Next Door were already moving on, covering more complex songs like Iggy's 'China Girl' and Lou Reed's 'Caroline Says'. They were moving away from the punk clichés toward the dark, proto-Gothic Berlin period Bowie/Iggy albums and then into the early twitchings of post-punk.

Melbourne now had a busy scene of wired local bands who were pushing The Boys Next Door to their peak. Playing locally were the long-lost bands like Primitive Calculators with their artful spontaneity and the melodramatic drama of Crime & the City Solution. The latter's charismatic frontman, Simon Bonney, would cast a powerful shadow on the young band.

Another young band who had made a big impression on the early Melbourne scene were Young Charlatans. They were also quickly moving away from punk's pulsebeat. Yet after only 13 gigs, they had split; their charismatic young guitar player Rowland S. Howard had already reviewed The Boys Next Door favourably in a local zine and joined them in the summer of 1978. In doing so, he instigated a crucial gear change, bringing his mercurial talent to the group. Howard's skills and talent would also push Cave into a creative arms race whilst Howard's unique guitar style helped move the band from their punk trajectory and into new territories. With his loose playing, use of feedback and wide-ranging tastes, he began incorporating free jazz and raw blue soundscapes into their post-punk rushes.

Rowland Howard also added his own songs to add to the band's repertoire. At the precocious age of sixteen, he had written the spooky and dark 'Shivers'. The song was a popular live track for Young Charlatans and was quickly added to The Boys Next

Door's set. It would, in turn, become one of their best known songs. Cave gave the song a powerful and emotive performance, harnessing the artful theatrics of one of his teenage idols, Bryan Ferry, whose influence he often acknowledges: 'I was a huge fan of Bryan Ferry as a kid; he had a massive influence over me in the way I looked and sounded - the whole thing.'

The Boys Next Door's performances now matched their music. With a fast-developing taste for religious imagery, literary references and a fledgling interest in narcotics, they were invoking a sense of tension and surrealism into their music. Their new songs were firmly replacing the youthful, punk rock capers of songs like 'Masturbation Generation'. The following year, they recorded and released their one album, *Door, Door* on the Australian label, Mushroom Records. Cave personally hates the record. Its songs aren't fully formed or especially dark and some of the recordings are almost pop punk in nature with a melodic take on punk that sometimes sounded more like The Undertones than any of the darker spaces they would eventually explore. Cave also does a rather convincing Joey Ramone-style warble at times and the album is almost acne youthful.

> We were like clean-cut youngsters. We didn't know what we were then. There are a few photographs of us powdered and preened. We were like a lightweight punk band picked up by a record label and put in the studio by some guy who didn't understand us with a fat cigar in his mouth. In some ways, I'm glad that this happened because the whole process was so repellent to us that it changed us considerably.[768]

There are several moments when The Boys Next Door hinted at more and audibly moved away from punk rock's garage template. The near-ballad of 'After A Fashion' hints at future directions and the funereal, fairground, keyboard-driven verses and wild choruses of 'Dive Position' are striking, as are the dark and strange vistas of 'I Mistake Myself'. The album also included that take on Rowland S. Howard's 'Shivers'. Released as a single, it didn't get airplay due to its references to suicide. A brooding and tragic ballad, Rowland S. Howard had written a song with such maturity and deep intelligence that it surpassed the usual reach of a 16-year-old. It was also a wonderful opportunity for Cave to explore the dark corners of his voice.

Post-album and frustrated by industry hurdles, the band elected to pack their bags and head to London. The lure of the British capital now far outweighed their status in the 200-strong local scene centred around Melbourne's St Kitts Hotel. London was the epicentre of post-punk musical creativity and seemed to be a place that would embrace ambitious young bands like The Boys Next Door; a band that was struggling to break free from the straitjacket of the then more culturally conservative Australia.

They played their final pre-move gigs at the Crystal Ballroom, Melbourne in late 1980. Then they grabbed their plane tickets and guitars and, on 25 February 1981, headed halfway around the world. Before they left, they had renamed themselves The

---

768 Nick Cave to John Robb.

Birthday Party; prompted by Cave perhaps intentionally misremembering a non-existent birthday party scene in the Dostoyevsky novel *Crime and Punishment*. In a 2008 interview, Rowland S. Howard gave his own recollection:

> The name The Birthday Party came up in a conversation between Nick and myself. There's this apocryphal story about it coming from a Dostoyevsky novel. It may have had various connotations, but what he and I spoke about was a sense of celebration and making things into more of an occasion and ritual.[769]

The band's expectations of a vibrant and welcoming British scene were not fulfilled. Living as a struggling band in the poverty and grey skies of London and still playing their Boys Next Door songs, they turned their disdain onto the current scene that left them feeling empty. Cave often talks about a 1981 Echo & The Bunnymen gig in London that they attended and somehow found insipid. Their fierce disappointment with the UK scene would drive the growing intensity that was infecting their music. As Mick Harvey explained to Julian Marszalek, the UK's bleak early 1980s environment clearly impinged on their art:

> The Birthday Party's music was more a reaction to what we saw in the music scene when we arrived in the UK and what was happening artistically in what we perceived as some kind of scene and a common area that we might have had with other musicians. To us, the new wave and punk and stuff was about artistic freedom and getting to the heart of the matter and doing all the other stuff that came with it. When we got to the UK in 1980, punk was long gone, and it had gone in different directions as either a fashion accessory or being commercialised. Obviously, there were still certain things that were holding up and we were trying to hold on to our artistic values. There weren't that many bands holding a hard line artistically and that was something that we were really disappointed about and this was an artistic response.[770]

A few weeks after the Bunnymen gig, they saw The Cramps. The primal ooze, wild abandon and musical collision of sex, death and rock'n'roll lit something deep in the young Australians' souls. Cave keenly embraced The Cramps' twisted Americana as an adjunct to his own nascent Southern Gothic persona.

Despite everything, the dark intensity and narcotic eroticism of The Birthday Party was beginning to take hold at a cult level in the UK. Combining the band's coarse reactions to the harsh realities of the UK's grey climate and disappointing soundtrack with their visceral and gripping re-embracing of The Stooges, whose songs they would cover with added ferocity, they pushed their new songs, sound, and style far beyond their recent recordings.

Now signed to 4AD records, The Birthday Party were part of an intriguing roster of artful, darker, post-punk bands of which they were initially, the most obtuse. 4AD itself would become an important cornerstone in the darker arts of the underground scene, having already released Bauhaus and had making a name for itself with artful groups and a powerful aesthetic.

---

769 Rowland S. Howard to Mojo magazine.

770 Mick Harvey to Julian Marszalek, The Quietus.

The Australian band were swiftly growing into their role as agent provocateurs. Cave's style was now as explosive as his stage demons and the band's cranked music and Oxfam-suited, rocker-from-hell look were making them an iconic presence on the micro scene. Now creating havoc in small clubs, the band were also growing into their own roles with Rowland S. Howard's increasingly wired guitar playing matching his glaring stage presence and a wild kinetic madness that was all held together by Mick Harvey.

> I don't know what Mick's actually doing back there but I believe that he's organising what goes on a bit. He has a bad temper, a very bad temper. He's like a kind of conductor, really – I guess he's keeping everyone on their toes. He's scaling out what key every song is in to certain other people.[771]

In April 1981, The Birthday Party released their debut album proper, *Prayers on Fire*,[772] which captured their frustrations with their new home and their penniless bohemian madness in a zig zag wandering record of seething imagination. 'The album was a kind of reaction to the major disappointments we felt when we went to England,' Cave sneered, adding, 'We began to see a vision and I don't think we were positively influenced and we certainly didn't want to be like the English new wave pop groups of the time.'

Stylistically, the album goes from songs full of manic leering glee to a frenetic, boiling frustration. Receiving a whole raft of creative inputs from the band itself, Nick's girlfriend Anita Lane, and Rowland's girlfriend Genevieve McGuckin who both added a holistic, female depth to the wild alpha male explosive, the album was a communal splurge. The band had embraced its creative and cultural extended family of friends with their music, books, and ideas all added into the melting pot. Heroin and alcohol were also becoming an increasing part of the equation for some of them, only adding to the wildness of the album.

The defining leadoff single, 'Nick the Stripper' was written solely by Cave and was a song that oozed a grotesque humour and dripped a carny storytelling. It was accompanied by a disturbing video of a ritualistic dance, with Cave stripped semi-naked as a sacrificial victim, dancing around a burning fire, and surrounded by a *Lord of the Flies* style savagery. Another key track was 'King Ink' with its sense of space, drama and deep literary intelligence and a lumbering dark tempo, hinting at the oncoming musical dramas.

Their spitting, swirling, intellectual disgust was channelled into the wild and untamed songs that dripped in imagination and deadly desire. These themes were being embraced by the emerging alternative and goth scenes who loved the band's wild imagery, style and hair. By the time of the release of their next single, July 1981's iconic pounding 'Release the Bats', the band were already huge on goth club dance floors with their anthemic slice of wildness. Produced by Nick Launey, who

---

771 Nick Cave to John Robb in 1989.

772 1980 had seen the release of The Birthday Party album initially credited to The Boys Next Door and then to The Birthday Party that captures the state of flux between the two bands and the vastly different new sound that was emerging.

had made a name for himself with big drum sounds on PiL's *Flowers of Romance* album, the track sounds enormous as it staggers around with a jazz blues riff and is a veiled nod to The Batcave club in London that Cave had personally frequented.

'I will say that recording a song called 'Release the Bats' with people who looked like vampires was pretty fucking exciting,' laughs Launey years later. The track broke the band out of cult status. The swaggering stripped-down blues and dark humour caught the feel of the moment and it became an anthem for the darker scene which it both celebrated and sneered at.

Cave was now moving quickly, his literary aspirations lacing his songs with dark narratives, undoubtedly fired by his narcotic intake. Somehow, he retained his work ethic in the middle of the chemical madness and was moving apart from Rowland S. Howard creatively. Cave was losing interest in singing the guitar player's songs and darkly surreal lyrics. The creative schism would eventually break up the band, but the initial tension only added fuel to their musical pyre.

London could not contain such a feral outfit, and it was no surprise that in the August of 1982 they relocated to Berlin – then a city wrapped in Cold War unease and hedonistic intent. It was a move inspired by a meeting in June 1981 with Einstürzende Neubauten's Blixa Bargeld, who was then at his most wired and skeletal. Cave had initially seen Bargeld and Neubauten on a television performance whilst on tour in Amsterdam:

> He was the most beautiful man in the world. He stood there in a black leotard and black rubber pants, with black rubber boots. Around his neck hung a thoroughly fucked guitar. His skin cleared to his bones, his skull was an utter disaster, scabbed and hacked.

On meeting, it emerged that Bargeld had never heard of The Birthday Party. Cave, however, was inspired by the German singer's freeform approach to creating music; a music that operated beyond the structures and strictures of rock'n'roll. It was music created from found objects and clattering metal that sounded as though it was at war with the world, and a sound that was kicking against the empty rhetoric of punk rock with a blowtorch of new intensity.

In Berlin, their friendship saw another creative surge.

The next Birthday Party album, *Junkyard*, was an explosive and thrilling affair. Recorded on a return trip to Melbourne in 1982, it was a big jump forward as the band stretched their fabric with glorious wild abandon. Inspired by American Southern Gothic imagery and dealing with such extreme subjects as an evangelist's murdered daughter, it was a release full of the scuzzed-up blues, dark ballads and vivid poetry which had seen Nick Cave establish himself as the ultimate king crow frontman.

One of the defining albums of the year with its explosive cordite riffing, deep dark emotions and heavy duty grooves, the album caught the band in full flow with an explosive collection of songs that was a rare moment of auditory danger. Far more than just aimless noise though, it was angular, powerful and terrifying. If their new buddies, Einstürzende Neubauten, were operating outside of rock, deconstructing the chaos, The Birthday Party's trick was to use the comparatively conventional guitar, bass and drums format and artfully wreak the same creative havoc.

The band were now in full throttle. The bass was really dark and hip-swingingly heavy, whether it was played by Tracy Pew or by Manchester's Barry Adamson – a man who had made his name with Magazine and was a perfect choice of bass deputy whilst Pew was in jail for three months on a drink driving charge. Roland S. Howard's guitar was firing off in all directions, cutting and slashing, its ferocity exacerbated by his onstage presence, which saw his wiry frame skitter backwards and forwards, cigarette clamped firmly between his lips. Meanwhile, Mick Harvey's role as the straight man surrounded by chaos was key to the band's delivery. Whilst his bandmates were falling off the precipice, he was keeping his act together while moving from guitar to the drum stool owing to Phill Calvert's departure from the melee to join The Psychedelic Furs.

Recorded by band collaborator Tony Cohen in late 1981, *Junkyard* was mixed by the man of the moment, Richard Mazda and also involved Nick Launey who knew how to get that big drum sound. Mazda had previously delivered a great sound for The Fall on the 'Lie Dream of a Casino Soul' single and was in high demand. The sound was enormous and loud, yet had plenty of space in which these urgent masterpieces could breathe.

Junkyard was a creative coup d'état.

The diverse songs lurched from the hellish skidding of 'Dead Joe' to the deadly shakes of 'Blast Off' via the lethal, visceral thrill of 'Hamlet (Pow Pow Pow)'. There were the swaggering thrills of the monstrous 'Big Jesus Trash Can' that combined Rowland S. Howard's toxic guitar lick and Nick Cave's now-perfect raucous death-rattle scream to startling effect. Meanwhile, the dark and smouldering gothic balladry of 'She's Hit' jostled for space with the swing-time howl of '6 Inch Gold Blade'.

Junkyard set a new benchmark for music that dared. It was gothic carnage and a perfect soundtrack for the nihilistic romance of the times. It was also an astonishing leap forward from a band whose earlier work was already pushing the barriers of musical expectations. The band's chaotic music matched their lifestyle and their intellectual yearnings were driven further by the nihilistic yet creative lifestyle they were living in Berlin where they had been embraced by an artistic community in hyperdrive. In keeping with the music contained within *Junkyard*'s grooves, the sleeve art was painted by custom car designer Ed 'Big Daddy' Roth, whose cartoon cover was lewd, loud and a deceptive swerve from the music inside.

With his wild-eyed imagery and astonishing rush of words, Nick Cave had very few lyrical peers. Only The Fall's Mark E. Smith and a handful of others could run him and his jagged, literate imagery close. Immersed in dark literature, Cave was constructing a uniquely dark and dangerous poetic worldview.

Deeply ensconced in his Southern Gothic world, Cave's wordplay was already extraordinary. A gifted wordsmith, his dark-stained lyrics were thrilling and dripping in a black humour as each line fired off a cinematic series of ideas. Cave was beginning to emerge as a modern-day equivalent of the French Romantic danger poets, such as

Baudelaire, Rimbaud and Lautréamont. He was dealing with the same darkly putrid imagery yet finding the beauty in the filth of life mashing abandon and melancholy or heaven and hell together into a stinking, rotten heap. He was cleansing his soul by confronting the filth.

Nick Cave was certainly living the life; a laureate of artistic dislocation, celebrating the spontaneous and living in the full beam of the moment. A great writer will always tackle the big questions – life and death, God and the Devil, the dark and the light. Baudelaire once said, 'I can barely conceive of a type of beauty in which there is no melancholy.'

He would have loved The Birthday Party.

Working at this pace and intensity, there was only ever going to be one conclusion. The vortex that the band had created was threatening to swallow them up whole, and the group was starting to fracture. Their nihilistic swirl had fired their music to new heights, but their metaphorical and physical assault of audiences and art was now being embraced by the crowds they hoped to repulse. The awaiting audiences began to adore the band's wildness, leaving them trapped by an unlikely expectation for the thrill of confrontation.

Cave held his audience in total disdain – in one interview, he shook his head at what he saw as 'the most cretinous audience'. Trapped by expectations and internal band tension, the band was at breaking point. If moving to Berlin had given them a new impetus with which to create their last two EPs, it was to be short-lived. Their last hurrah consisted of two 4 track, twelve-inch singles, recorded in the same Hansa studios where Bowie and Iggy had made their legendary records.

Creative and personal tensions were sky-high with Cave and Howard moving away from each other, and this explosive and menacingly powerful music ultimately proved to be the perfect epitaph. The ever-creative Cave was now pushing the band away from the carny of chaos and into an embrace of dark spaces in sound. He was seeking tensions, textures and dynamics within their explosive noise; places to leave space for his rush of lyrical images. The implied threat of unease in these late-period songs was a direction he would fully explore when the band split, following their last ever show in Australia that June.

Within weeks, Nick Cave was looking for people to be in his new band with the initial intention of putting out a solo EP on Mute Records, entitled *Man or Myth*. Cave had new influences at play and new directions to travel in. Like many at the time, he was reacting against the Year Zero of punk, searching deeper into musical history for darker and more thrilling musical fixes. Cave found this inspiration in corners previously ignored by the punk generation; such as his new favourites, the Walker Brothers, Hank Williams, Van Morrison and a pile of old blues records.

With his trusty lieutenant Mick Harvey, Cave put together a uniquely talented new lineup for his initial post The Birthday Party band. On hand were Mick Harvey, Jim Thirlwell, Barry Adamson and Blixa Bargeld with producer Flood at the controls.

If there had been hints at a sparser, slower sound on the last The Birthday Party records, then the new music truly explored that same taut and brooding space.

Gone were the charismatic guitar slashes of Rowland S. Howard, gone was the confrontational car crash sound and gone were the skittering rhythms, all to be replaced by a darker and sparser set of Nick Cave songs that still held the same tension as The Birthday Party but were now stretched tight like a tripwire. The new outfit began to coalesce with Barry Adamson remaining to play his bass. Joining him were Blixa with his unique guitar tones, now a key part of the sound with the Neubauten frontman simultaneously playing in both bands. Blixa confessed to hating the guitar, preferring to play 'anti guitar' with its odd tunings. Nonetheless, he proved to be a highly effective counterpoint to Cave's songs.

> Blixa's very much in a world of his own. He plays whatever is necessary. He understands the beauty of economy and restraint. Blixa also has a bad temper, if he wants to stop playing and take his jacket off halfway through a song and then continue to play then he does. It would be very much a compliment for you to say that you see him as a kindred spirit to me. Einsturzende Neubauten's new album is great. I love him as a guitar player and I love him as a person. He continues to intrigue me, that guy, he's a very wise person." [773]

Their debut release, *From Her to Eternity*, was released in June 1984 and is an album full of brooding, darkly cinematic pieces. From the hollering blues of the title track – which remains a staple of the Cave set decades later – to the nightmarish cover of Leonard Cohen's 'Avalanche' and the haunting death knell blues of 'A Box for Black Paul', this was an album that set the stall with its unique and apocalyptic visions. The 1985 follow-up *The First Born Is Dead* saw Cave explore his Southern Gothic obsessions embracing Elvis, the Bible and the dark blues of America's inner psyche , forged in the imagination of the sticky heat and rolling thunderstorms of the deep south, filled with lyrical images and matching musical metaphors.

It takes nerve to release an album of cover versions, the artist placing himself on a level with Bowie and Bryan Ferry (via *Pin Ups* and *These Foolish Things* respectively). However, Nick Cave's 1986 *Kicking Against the Pricks*, its title a reference to the Acts of the Apostles,[774] was a confident move. When in possession of your own sound, you are granted the privilege of reshaping the works of others. The album held surprising choices like 'The Carnival is Over' from fellow countrymen, The New Seekers[775] –a long-time favourite of Cave's from his childhood. There was also a nod to his beloved Alex Harvey with a cover of 'The Hammer Song', giving the band a chance to stretch out and give a nod to a formative hero.

With his life spiralling out of control in a mania of drugs and alcohol, Cave somehow managed to retain his work ethic for 1986's *Your Funeral... My Trial*, which he has often claimed to be his favourite of the earlier solo period releases. Similarly, 1988's *Tender Prey* was somehow pulled together under the same difficult circumstances yet opened with the song that has come to define much of his solo

---

773 Nick Cave to John Robb.

774 Acts 9: 4-6, KJV King James Bible.

775 The beautiful, dark melody is borrowed from a traditional dark Russian folk song called Stenka Razin.

career – the terrifying 'The Mercy Seat', a song of a man about to be executed by electric chair that dripped biblical imagery.

Many of the band members were living wild and chaotic lives. The exacerbating effect of drugs added into this volatile mix yet created a Molotov cocktail of possibilities, as music writer Julian Marszalek explains:

> Drugs have probably played a part too – mainly heroin, speed and alcohol. I remember both Mick Harvey and Kid Congo Powers telling me about the speed during the recording of the Bad Seeds *Tender Prey* album. The East German secret police were flooding West Berlin with industrial strength speed that would keep you up for 2-3 days. Harvey said he tried it once but stopped after the horrific comedown but that Cave and Blixa were well into it. Kid Congo recalls that the night the Berlin Wall came down near Hansa Studios where they were recording. He says the streets were flooded with thousands of celebrating Germans, so he went back to the studio to tell Cave to take a look. Cave reportedly declined as he was deep into recording while also speeding his nut off. That's quite telling.[776]

1990 saw Cave move to Brazil to live a new life with journalist Viviane Carneiro, subsequent *The Good Son* album saw him pull himself back from the dark intensity of the lifestyle documented on previous releases and return to classic songwriting through the single 'The Ship Song' and the lush melodies of his dramatic and touching duet with Blixa, 'The Weeping Song'.

1992's *Henry's Dream* and 1994's top ten album *Let Love In* saw him perfect his songwriting craft before he released the startling and brilliant and conceptual work, *Murder Ballads* in 1996 and reaching number 3 in the charts. The album established Cave as a major dark star and featured a mixture of traditional and new songs that were hooked around the ideas of crimes of passion and songs about love and murder. It was Cave's most extreme evocation of the theory of love and also gave him his first proper hit single, 'Where the Wild Roses Grow', thanks to his duet with Kylie Minogue that he first talked about years before.[777]

> I'd like to write songs from a woman's point of view, I like the idea of being given an exercise, It would depend on who I was writing for, if it were Lydia Lunch it would be quite different from Kylie Minogue….I must say I would like to write a song for Kylie one day,' [778]

In 1997, Cave took a creative swerve with the stripped-down and minimalistic *The Boatman's Call* – his tenth studio album. The album saw a series of powerful, emotionally charged songs sung plaintively over sparse piano parts as the singer attempts to seek solace in spirituality. It would be four years before the now-clean Cave returned with 2001's *No More Shall We Part*, a mature album that saw the band's playing talents really flower in a lush and enthralling work. A couple of years later Blixa Bargeld finally ended his tenure with the Bad Seeds, mysteriously departing

---

776 Julian Marszalek to John Robb.

777 The famous video suggests Cave murdering the pop singer with a rock in a brilliantly dark and erotic film clip that drips with implied sex and the Romanticism of death.

778 Nick Cave to John Robb in 1989.

without a word after recording 2003's *Nocturama*. A year after losing their talisman guitarist, the reshaped band released twin albums *Abattoir Blues / The Lyre of Orpheus* with the darker, heavier twisted blues of the songs of *Abattoir Blues* and the gentler songs of *Lyre of Orpheus* exploring both sides of the singer's muse.

Perhaps as a means of getting the heavier music out of his system, Cave then started a side project, Mini Seeds. The new band quickly developed into Grinderman, so named after a Memphis Slim song, and was a return to the darker and more feral side of the now iconic singer. They released two albums, either as a nod to his wild youth or as an explosive expression of musical midlife crisis, depending on your viewpoint.

In the middle of Cave's side project, they found time to release the fourteenth Bad Seeds album, 2008's *Dig, Lazarus, Dig!!!* It was a concise distillation of everything that was great about the band. It also marked the swan song for Mick Harvey; the faithful lieutenant and last link to The Birthday Party who left the band in 2009.

Post-Harvey, the band saw another shift with Nick Cave now working even more closely with another old home town friend, Warren Ellis, who had joined the Bad Seeds in 1993. Also from Melbourne, Ellis was playing in the acclaimed Dirty Three whose live sets of enthralling instrumentals alternated with shaggy dog stories from the equally shaggy Ellis who was now the key collaborator in the Bad Seeds. The marked shift in the sound and a new level of success saw Nick Cave move into the mainstream.

This move into unbridled success was sparked by 2013's nuanced and textured, *Push the Sky Away*. The album's subtle shapeshifting songs were full of subtle drama and magnetic melodies that managed to be both sophisticated and atmospheric. Perhaps Cave's finest release, the album features an evocative set of songs with an emotional twist and great storytelling, such as with 'Higgs Boson Blues' which saw him extend beyond his normal lyrical concerns or the iconic 'Jubilee Street' – a grand and powerful song that builds to an epic climax. The period was captured perfectly in Iain Forsyth and Jane Pollard's *20,000 Days on Earth*, a semi-fictionalised documentary film of a 24-hour period in the life of Cave. The film leans away from all the established clichés of music biographies and covers the times prior to, and during, the recording of *Push the Sky Away*.

> For Cave, the creativity was still as intense if framed differently.
> It's very different now than when I was in The Birthday Party, but I still come off the stage completely drained. It's kinda incredible that sometimes before you go onstage you feel nothing at all, and as you blunder up the stairs it's incredible how excited you can become.
> Writing is an intuitive thing; certain lyrics are just kind of right and I feel like I'm being given gifts – like the way that they come to me never seems to relate to how I feel at the time. Sometimes I can wake up in the morning and feel really strong and inspired and sometimes I feel really dead without anything at all. As I said, the song is given to me as a gift in the way that it's suddenly there."[779]

779 Nick Cave to John Robb.

2016's *Skeleton Tree*, was already recorded and then later reworked, following the tragic death of Cave's fifteen-year-old son Arthur, who died in an accident on his hometown Brighton cliff tops. The previously recorded songs already covered themes of death, loss and personal grief and were amended to incorporate Cave's mourning processes and the acknowledgement of his terrible loss.

Now an arena act, Cave has managed to maintain the sense of intimacy within his newer songs, even when performing them in big venues, whilst his older, more explosive songs, transfer riotously into huge arenas, making his live show a spectacular affair. The band perfectly convey all the dynamics of their vast back catalogue and Cave's charismatic presence fills the arenas; his preacher-man persona is now a mainstream icon. It has been a long and strange journey from small town Australia and is one that has not yet ended. 2019's *Ghosteen* was his third number UK one album in a row and proved that Cave's relentless creativity was in no danger of depleting as he took another creative swerve with an album of subtle shapeshifting and minimalistic atmospheres. Yet again, he found an emotional honesty and a powerful divinity in his work, dealing with harrowing grief and life, and death.

For decades, Nick Cave and the Bad Seeds have continued to release a remarkable series of albums, all in diverse styles and with astonishing lyrical content. The sheer volume of words and songwriting is staggering. Through his powerful imagery and emotional content, marking Cave out as one of the finest lyricists of his generation. His iconic status has been achieved without ever compromising his unique and unholy vision; a vision that makes him one of the central pillars of modern gothic.

Chapter 23

'I AM NOT AVANT-GARDE; I AM A DESERTER'

Blixa Bargeld, Einstürzende Neubauten and the Reinvention of Berlin

Destroying the 'do-re-mi' of established songwriting, Einstürzende Neubauten do not fit into the conventional musical narrative. Like the Berlin of their '70s youth, the band, whose name means 'collapsing new buildings', were once stateless. Detached. Reconstructed.

Their name reflected the post-war West Berlin of quick builds and a city full of building material. Using these found objects to create their sound, they celebrated their artistic 'no man's land' with their own distinctive style. Their early music crafted jarring rhythms and an addictive cacophony from sheets of metal, drills and a minimalist guitar as they deconstructed rock music into a primal, urban symphony, whilst their later releases explored silence and a sensual, subtle beauty. Charismatic band leader Blixa Bargeld's image was as confrontational as his music and his lyrical German language poetry that he would deliver with a garbled intensity, a subtle phrasing, a clipped, crooned delivery or with his trademark inverse screams.

Initially dressed in tailored S&M rubber with the occasional codpiece and the wildest mane of backcombed hair, he was the central iconic, skeletal, provocative figure of the early clattering claustrophobic sound before moving towards dark suits and the sombre, elegiac, yet sharp, style of the nuanced and textured later years. It made him an exotic yet unintentional goth icon - an unwanted status that was further underlined after playing the guitar with Nick Cave and the Bad Seeds for twenty years.

Formed from post-punk in the Cold War Berlin of the late 1970s, Einstürzende Neubauten perfectly captured the contradictory tension of the city. The capital was in a permanent political limbo whilst surrounded by the communist East and encased by the Berlin Wall, creating a unique landlocked island that was full of wild art and all-night parties defying the political inertia. Caught between the East and the West, the wall was the physical manifestation of the tense post-war standoff that must have seeped into the band's unique muse. The totemic and imperious Bargeld remains an acidic and darkly humoured character that was central to this attractive and dangerous Berlin.

> How much this city is an influence is hard for me to explain. I've always lived here. Berlin is point zero on a scale and everywhere else was different. Would the music be any different if I came from London or Melbourne? I don't know. It's certainly an urban music. The changes of the city have affected certain

things I talk and sing about but it doesn't necessarily affect the music. But as a child of the post-Second World War era, and the resulting division of Germany and Berlin, I'm, of course, hugely influenced by my upbringing.

When I started Neubauten, I hadn't left Berlin for two years. There was this law at the time that was pretty unique in that it said that if you didn't have a proper address, you had to report to the police so they could find you. I had lost my passport, and the police were looking for me. Without a passport you didn't exist anymore. It was quite a chaotic life. But in a positive way.

The first time I left the city was to play a concert in Hamburg, and I was shocked by how different that city was. The whole punk revolution had been and gone by then, but Hamburg was a violent city with the squatters fighting the police. There was a chaotic, violent atmosphere on the scene there which did not exist in Berlin, despite some big confrontations in Kreuzberg.[780][781]

Neubauten were the realisation of this geopolitical void. Their initial soundscape of clattering metal, driving bass, cassettes of noise and Bargeld's clanking, rusty guitar and his distinctive, howling vocals was stunningly original aided by their own added unfettered imagination. They would then move further into a neo-classical beauty playing with silence and texture, with an added mischievous Dadaist deconstruction for good measure.

The duality of Neubauten's sound was deliciously shocking. The music was brutal, beautiful and startlingly original, with the guttural power of the German language delivered at a time when the Anglo-American musical axis dominated. You could feel the audible power and emotion that embraced the intensity of living on a fault line. Few could match the band's deconstruction of rock, leaving them hailed as forefathers of many scenes with which they have little in common.

Neubauten have enjoyed a stunning journey in the tradition of fellow German composers such as Stockhausen, who, at his peak in the 1950s, had also moved way beyond the barriers of musical convention. There are arguably no bad records in their arsenal – just a thrilling musical trip with a group who have seemingly endless ideas of outrageous brilliance that unintentionally soundtrack Berlin's own journey from political scrapyard to leading 21st century city.

There was a noise around my generation that aroused fear, a noise which could cut through the sky. Neubauten shows in the early '80s took a lot of work. Driving in a little van to a city, then going to the scrap yard, finding the instruments and setting them up on the stage, playing the concert, leaving the instruments in the backyard, and driving to the next city. You can only do this for a certain amount of time. It was very intense but necessary.[782]

The band were following a decades-long tradition of German progressive writers and musicians. These were innovators like fellow Berlin Dadaist artist Kurt

---

780 An inner-city area of West Berlin, Kreuzberg was predominantly working-class and included a large proportion of Turkish immigrants. By the 1970s, it had become the squared and radical part of the city.

781 Blixa Bargeld to John Robb.

782 Blixa Bargeld to John Robb.

Schwitters[783], whose Merz collages in the 1920s were created from scraps and objects collected from the streets of his hometown of Hanover. Although the fragments were scavenged, Schwitters carefully arranged and affixed them to a painted board with glue and nails, transforming them into works of found art. Einsturzende Neubauten would create their aural sculptures in the same way - sonic art instead of visual art. While Chuck Berry influenced much of rock n roll, Neubauten were the self-styled deserters operating in a space where the likes of French literary theorist, philosopher and linguist, Roland Barthes[784] or the ideas of Romanian philosopher Emil Cioran[785] and the works of composer John Cage[786] were of creative importance. Finally, there was also the influence of the eclectic thinking of German philosopher, Walter Benjamin[787] and his theory of the destructive personality. The latter perhaps a model for Bargeld's own artistic goals and practices.

The ghost of Antonin Artaud also hangs heavily in the band's sound. The early 20th-century French playwright of Greek blood established his undiminishable place in theatre history with the publication of his 1938 manifesto *The Theatre and Its Double,* which opened with a call for:

> 'The communion between actor and audience in a magic exorcism; gestures, sounds, unusual scenery, and lighting combine to form a language, superior to words, that can be used to subvert thought and logic and to shock the spectator into seeing the baseness of his world'.

This theory of art-shock was integral to Neubauten waking up their audience. When sieving these kinds of ideas through the detonation of punk, the result is an artful nitroglycerine. Adding the early 1970s experimentation of krautrock and a European non-Anglo-American method of music making into the mix, the resulting sound was urgent and very 'of the moment'. This music accidentally caught the gloom of the Cold War but with an explosive originality reacting against the seemingly impending apocalypse that it sometimes sounded like.

Neubauten were breaking new ground, moving away from the so-called krautrock or, more fittingly, the Deutschrock scene of the early 1970s. Like the wonderful Faust working in their isolated commune in Wumme creating a new musical language all of their own utilising song fragments and pulsing electronic

---

783 Born in Hanover in 1887 and died in Kendal in1948. Schwitters was a multi artist who made an impact on dadaism, constructivism, surrealism, poetry, sound, painting, sculpture, graphic design, typography, and what came to be known as installation art.

784 French philosopher (1915 -1980) Barthes was a literary theorist, essayist, philosopher, critic, and semiotician.

785 Born in 1911 and died 1995, Emil Mihai Cioran was a Romanian philosopher, aphorist and essayist who dealt in pervasive philosophical pessimism, style, and aphorisms. His works frequently engaged with issues of suffering, decay, and nihilism.

786 John Cage (1912 - 1995) A pioneer of indeterminacy in music, electroacoustic music, and non-standard use of musical instruments, Cage was one of the leading figures of the post-war avant-garde.

787 Walter Benjamin (1892-1940) was a German Jewish philosopher, cultural critic and essayist. An eclectic thinker, combining elements of German idealism, Romanticism and Western Marxism.

drones to mesmerising effect, they in turn, were a continuation of the musical concrete[788] pioneered by early electronic musician, Pierre Schaeffer[789].

Kraftwerk had remoulded music into a new German narrative, or 'shaking off their American head', as their Ralf Hütter had said at the time.

Neubauten would shake that head clean off its shoulders.

This was a band operating on its own terms. They were never 'industrial', but industrious. They were never 'noise', even in that early period. They were also never 'ugly', as there was beauty and subtlety to their art. They were creating soundscapes and space and were tearing apart their cultural landscape in the process. The band rejected the trad rock pulsebeat that had dominated post-war pop culture and created a visceral new tradition.

Blixa Bargeld was born Christian Emmerich in West Berlin on 12 January 1959 and grew up in Friedenau, in the Schöneberg district of the split city's American sector. He attended the Paul-Natorp-Gymnasium Oberschule, where his wilful and highly intelligent mindset saw him become both president of the student body and expelled for firebombing the school.

> One of the reasons I got kicked out of school was because I had started a fire. My expulsion had already been decided upon anyway, so I didn't have anything to lose. But I was still the student body president and tried to enforce my pseudo-democratic rights by decorating a 'Schülermitverwaltungsversammlung ', a kind of student council assembly, with a firebombing – in which no one was hurt – because I was no longer allowed to take part in the assembly.[790]

The inquisitive, long-haired, teenage Bargeld was conducting musical explorations into the more experimental end of mid-'70s rock.

> I grew up with Can, Kraftwerk, Neu!, Cluster, German electronic music and avant-garde. My first record was Pink Floyd. The second was Can. I had a guitar pickup from when I was thirteen, and I was making experiments with tape recorders, opening them up and fiddling around with the insides, taking the pickup and putting it on kitchen equipment and then recording it on a tape. I would never have guessed when I was thirteen that I would have become a professional musician. It seemed so far away as to become a reality in my personal life.[791]

Leaving school, it would not be long before he found the artful playground of post-punk Berlin, giving him plenty of space for his adventures. It was an intimate scene of bars, venues and shops between Kreuzberg, Schöneberg, and Charlottenburg, where a small and fascinating community would coalesce. It was in this new community that Christian Emmerich became Blixa Bargeld. He took 'Blixa' from the name of a German brand of blue felt-tip pen, and 'Bargeld' from the German

---

788 Music concrete is a type of music that utilises recorded sounds as raw material. It is a sound that is detached from source – an acousmatic sound – a sound without an apparent originating cause.

789 The French composer, engineer and musicologist had invented the aforementioned music concrete in post-Nazi Germany.

790 As Bargeld recalled in Neubauten's oral history, *No Beauty Without Danger.*

791 Blixa Bargeld to John Robb.

for 'cash', with a nod to German Dada artist Johannes Theodor Bargeld[792]. Like punk in the UK, this was a time of reinvention. New names, new styles, new ways to live in a city caught in the spotlight of history.

This was the Berlin that Mark Reeder reflected in his 2015 film, *B-Movie: Lust and Sound in West Berlin 1979 – 1989*, which perfectly captured a city in a creative flux. Reeder had moved from Manchester to Berlin in 1978 at the age of twenty. He had a keen outsider eye for the city, and many of the characters are in his film. Berlin was the apogee of cool for a young, pop culture obsessed Mancunian.

> All I knew about Berlin was what I had seen in Cold War movies like *Funeral in Berlin* or *The Spy Who Came in From the Cold*. The four allied powers still occupied the city, and it was full of draft dodgers, transvestites, hippies and weirdos. There were constant student riots, the spectre of Baader-Meinhof[793] and protests of all kinds. It was seen as where a military confrontation would obviously take place, ultimately leading to a nuclear holocaust. More importantly, was that I knew that Iggy and Bowie had put Berlin on the map and recorded magnificent and atmospheric works there. Before their arrival, Berlin was mainly known for being a political city. I thought there must be something about it to make Bowie make such moody music like that. At that time, I wasn't aware that he had also become infected by Cluster, Can, and Tangerine Dream. By the time I went to Berlin, I was hoping to find these rare and obscure electronic and krautrock records that you couldn't buy in the UK. Things like Popol Vuh, or Guru Guru.
>
> Of course, we Britons in the '70s had some romantic TV idea of what Berlin must be like, but that was the Weimar Republic *Cabaret*-ized Berlin of Christopher Isherwood, and Berlin actually looked nothing like that when I got there.
>
> Bowie had changed all that sonically. He made Berlin sound interesting. His instrumental side of *Low*, which he recorded in Berlin, was otherworldly. I loved it and played it to death. 'Warszawa' is, for me, still my ultimate Berlin soundtrack. I discovered it sounded just how Berlin looked at that time. Bullet-riddled, confined and desperate.
>
> The *Heroes* album cemented the sound of Berlin even further, and I think it was the pinnacle of Bowie's career. I thought it was a masterpiece. Iggy's records were somehow different, even though they were recorded here. They were a little more conventional and easily accessible. In their own way, they became a soundtrack for the city too, especially 'The Passenger', which you would hear almost everywhere.
>
> But Berlin only became musically alluring after the success of the *Heroes* album. Of course, there were internationally established artists already living here, such as Tangerine Dream or Klaus Schulze, but they were musicians from a different era.[794]

The cultural oasis of the shops and esoteric bar culture fascinated Mark Reeder who turned up in town in 1978:

792

793 The Red Army Faction or the Baader-Meinhof was a West German left militant organisation founded in 1970. They came out of student protest and were opposed to what they saw as the Nazis retaining power in post-war West Germany.

794 Mark Reeder to John Robb.

My first impression of what to expect from Berlin was the next morning after my arrival. I stumbled upon a small pub at the end of the street. I walked in and saw a couple of workers sitting around drinking coffee and schnapps. There was someone at the bar. Nervously, I asked, 'Do you speak English?' The person turned around and stood up, and it was a six-foot transvestite with full horrorshow makeup. I realised at that moment; this is normality in Berlin. I was in a totally free city, where you could be whoever, and do whatever, you liked. I immediately felt at home.

The clubs and bars were a diverse and weird mixture of old, dingy, student and hippy haunts, and up and coming new wave bars with bright neon lights. Places like SO36 or Excess were just concert venues, but what happened outside and in the surrounding bars made the area exciting. The Tschungel was exceptional and exclusive; on the outside it looked like a fashionable up-market private club, but in fact, it was the watering hole for the real Berlin arty scene. Posers and fashionistas were equally as welcome as filmmakers and decrepit punks in rubber wellies. It was the Berghain[795] of its day; almost impossible to get into if you didn't know the people at the door, and yet very welcoming for those creatives who contributed something to the scene in some way. It was here that the new wave avant-garde was radically different. They broke all the traditional rules of rock n roll. Malaria![796] or Neubauten were refreshingly original.[797]

In June 1979, Gudrun Gut, Bettina Köster and Claudia Skoda[798] opened a clothes and design shop at Goltzstraße 37 in Schöneberg. The name of the shop was Eisengrau or 'iron grey' in English. The name was taken from the colour of the paint in tins left by the former tenant, which were broken open and used to paint the shop.

We sold dyed shoes and T-Shirts from New York by Karin Luner, second-hand clothes and Berlin designers like Claudia Skoda and Susanne Wiebe, whose clothes we had on commission. Wolfgang Müller[799] also sold his fanzines in the shop. Out of sheer boredom, I put up a knitting machine and designed my own knitwear. It was lots of grey and colours that didn't match. Weird patterns, simple hems, fringes and those popular multicoloured knit pants for men. Later, when Bettina quit, I continued the store with Blixa Bargeld, and we also sold the Eisengrau Allstars Tapes, which were live and rehearsal recordings of mainly early Einstürzende Neubauten but other bands as well, like Die Tödliche Doris.[800]

---

795 The key techno club of the modern city.

796 Malaria! were the Berlin-based, experimental electronic band formed in 1981, from the ashes of Mania D. Mark Reeder would become their manager.

797 Mark Reeder to John Robb.

798 Key players in post-punk Berlin Gudrun Gut formed Mania D then Malaria, with Bettina Koster whilst Claudia Skoda is a fashion designer and Beate Bartel founding member of Einstürzende Neubauten and of Mania D

799 The founder of the multi-media performance art group Die Tödliche Doris.

800 Gudrun Gut to Electronic Beats website.

Another important shop was Zensor Records, which was founded by Burkhardt Seiler[801] It brought in all the underground records which had been heard on the John Peel show via BBC World Service into the city:

> Back then, he was still selling records from a vendor's tray. Among many others, I bought the first Throbbing Gristle album there. And he had all those incredible seven inches! I also got the first Daniel Miller single[802] and the B-52's' 'Rock Lobster' from him. Today a single only serves as a promotion for the album. Back then, it was a means of communication that managed to connect the most faraway places.[803]

Beate Bartel was at the heart and soul of this new scene with the shop and was keen to put a band together. In post-punk Berlin, you could be asked to join a band because you looked the part, as Bartel remembers. 'Eva Gößling[804] and I found Gudrun so interesting to look at that one night at the SO36; we asked her if she would like to join our new band, Mania D.'

The Eisengrau shop cellar was soon turned into an ad hoc rehearsal space. This was where Blixa's former schoolmate N.U. Unruh[805] started jamming with him, sometimes with the then-youthful 14-year-old, future, band kingpin, Alexander Hacke, looking on. This was the epicentre of a thriving local underground.

> The legacy of the '80s in Berlin was created by all those little-known bands who fell into obscurity as the decade progressed. All those who had been involved in actually creating the so-called Berliner Krankheit (Berlin illness) such as MDK, Seen Links, Schlosser Rechts, Leben und Arbeiten, Notorische Reflexe, or Die Todliche Doris were each equally as important in forming the sound and image of the Berliner scene as much as Neubauten and Malaria! were. Because of them, years later, it became fashionable to do a Berlin album (if you could afford it) at Hansa Studios. Bands like Depeche Mode and Killing Joke made Berlin albums, as did U2 in the final hours before the Wall fell.[806]

The New York No Wave scene was also making a significant impact after Brian Eno had curated the 1978 *No New York* compilation album. This exotic new underground of bands was having a profound effect on the Berlin micro scene.

> I first heard Brian Eno's No Wave compilation on John Peel, which significantly impacted Berlin. Musically, with Mania D, everything boiled down to the three of us, Bettina, Beate, and me. For a while, there also was Isabel, our front woman. She was a skinhead and looked great. She was in a relationship with Tabea Blumenschein, who later did much work with Die Tödliche Doris. We rehearsed in the basement of Blixa Bargeld's storefront apartment in

---

801 He is the founder of the Zensor record shop and of the Zensor record label.

802 'Warm Leatherette'/ 'T.V.O.D' – The Normal, April 1978.

803 Gudrun Gut to Electronic Beats website.

804 Eva Gößling was the sax player and singer from key 1979 Berlin all-girl band Mania D.

805 Born Andrew Chudy, he had freshly returned from Amsterdam where he had studied for several years to become a piano tuner.

806 Mark Reeder to John Robb.

Langenscheidtstraße. Blixa wanted to start a band, as well, and asked us if we were interested in joining. We said, 'Sure we do!'[807]

The new, ad hoc grouping made their debut gig at the Moon club in Berlin on 1 April 1980. Symbolically, the gig occurred twenty days before the roof of the Kongresshalle – a symbol of American liberty in Berlin – had fallen through, underlining the potent power of the symbolism in collapsing new buildings. Blixa was already one of the hallowed, hollow faces on the flickering late-night post-punk scene. His wiry and intense presence, bug-eyed vocals, inward screams and scratched, chopping guitar would soon become synonymous with the city's post-punk sound.

That night, fifty people watched as Neubauten performed improvised music to Super-8 films. Andrew Unruh was already experimenting with found percussion, and his soon-to-be sold drum kit. Meanwhile, short term founder members, Beate Bartel on bass, and Gudrun Gut, prefaced their own future electronic efforts by introducing a Korg MS-20 synthesiser into the sound. The two women already had their own Mania D. project and would play a handful of gigs with Blixa before they left to concentrate on their own band.

After Gudrun and Bettina had left the early Neubauten lineup, the new band were reduced to a core of Blixa and Andrew Unruh, who sold his drum kit and started making percussion with bits of metal liberated from a local skip and experimenting with found sound; like a modern-day Henry Cowell.[808]

The fledgling band began to find their own distinctive direction of total performance, art and kinetic sound, including a quite brilliant June 1980 appearance under the Berlin Autobahn, which they filmed. This performance in the concrete wasteland was a powerful statement beating the inside of a pillar of the Stadtautobahn bridge, turning the very fabric of the city into a musical instrument, and playing the veins of a concrete organism.

The gig was released as the 38-minute *Stahlmusik* cassette, packaged in a metal sleeve. The inner artwork of the release also saw the first appearance of the band's distinctive logo – the Toltec Petroglyph. The ancient design has seen variations on its form from Stonehenge to Native American lore, and was spotted by Bargeld in a book whilst looking for a striking mythological symbol.

Their first recordings, issued on various cassettes and limited to twenty copies, reflected their deconstruct of sound that, initially with guitar and drums, was constructed with a No Wave post-punk, minimalism that already sounded distinctive. The band quickly found a tension and discipline, utilising it on early

---

807 Gudrun Gut to electronicbeats.net.

808 In the early part of the 20th century, Henry Cowell's percussive and convention-defying piano pieces dripped atmosphere and a new kind of tension. Another precursor to Neubauten's sound was American composer, Harry Partch. Partch's belief was that everything you learned about music is wrong. His random tunings and clanking percussion were delivered through home-made instruments, strange timings, outsider music and deep interest in so-called primitive cultures.

pieces like their debut vinyl single, 'Für den Untergang', with its menacing, pounding, scratching guitar.

> The main shift was the vocals and the use of our own language. No one had really bothered before, but that's because of the broken tradition. The previous bands usually avoided the issue altogether. You have many instrumental bands in that so-called krautrock scene – Can had initially had an American as a singer – or they didn't sing at all. It took even Kraftwerk a long time to open their mouths and sing in German on 'Autobahn'. The starting point for Neubauten was more that we didn't have anything. I didn't really have the choice to say, 'I am doing this, I am doing that, or maybe I should play (an) organ.' I didn't have any of these things. I couldn't afford any of those things. It was more about the logical consequence of *what* can we obtain that was lying around in the Berlin streets at the time. It certainly didn't start out as an artistic concept to say, 'let's do something different.'[809]

The band's developing textures and unique percussive units were crafted by the addition of FM Einheit[810] , whose physical stage presence was an essential part of the band's performance. The core unit was now starting to collect members. Mark Chung from The Abwarts initially joined on bass alongside the teenage whizz kid from the Kreuzberg streets, Alexander Hacke[811]. Hacke was a youthful musical powerhouse who had initially learned to play the drums along to The Stranglers' *Black and White* album before becoming a multi-instrumentalist. Initially, Hacke did the band's live sound, adding random noise on cassettes to their performance before moving onto the guitar. In the mid-1990s, he switched to bass and, according to Blixa Bargeld, became 'a musical director of the band.'

Bargeld's anti-guitar style was integral to the early band's identity. His chopping rhythm was filled with disdain for guitar clichés. He would play the guitar as he would another piece of found sound, hacking the noise and vibrations of the instrument into new textures. For Neubauten, the sound of a deconstructed electric guitar was just another fascinating sonic texture, along with eventually: fire, wood, wire, sand, oil drums, old drills, rattling chains, phone interference, a shopping trolley, bags of leaves, the swilling of wine and plastic pipes.

Blixa Bargeld was also seeking out new ways to use voice and language. This vocal dexterity conveyed new meanings to the sound and beyond the restrictions of speech itself. It was a fascination with words that initially saw him construct and deconstruct the German tongue. Like Artaud, who had been inspired by the Balinese theatre, Neubauten were concerned with breaking language down, attempting to find a more profound emotional depth beyond the trappings of

---

809 Blixa Bargeld to John Robb.

810 FM Einheit had joined Neubauten along with Chung from Abwarts. The short-lived band had left two key German post-punk albums, 1980's *Amok/Coma* and 1982's *Der Western Ist Einsam*. These were albums of stark, percussive and smart punkish renunciations of the western dream and the divided Germany. They were very much part of the post-punk wave of German bands loosely lumped together as Neue Deutsche Welle.

811 At the time, Hacke had a local notoriety as the then-boyfriend of Christiane F, a woman who found fame as the subject of a book and film, documenting her life as a drug addict on the Berlin streets.

established verbiage. Bargeld's recorded vocals were undoubtedly not the treated rock voices of contemporary music; such voices are of limited range and have a dislocation from the very flesh into which they were born. His own vocals, enunciating and chewing on the very syllables of sound, developed into far more lyrical, poetic and textural shapes.

In the early 1980s, Einstürzende Neubauten became the house band for the new Berlin dark art scene. As Bargeld noted, 'In Berlin, there was a successful art scene at that time. Everything was entwined and intermingled. Everyone was getting along. It wasn't separable, yet the chaotic energy was useful.'[812]

This new Berlin came together at the1981 Geniale Dilletanten festival, held in Berlin's Tempodrom venue, which had opened in 1980 next to the Berlin Wall. The event was a signifying moment for the feverish underground scene. It was typified by the use of brute noise, German language, provocative Super 8 films, cheap photocopied fanzines, independently produced samples, and designs that challenged 'good taste' plus a new wild language for figurative painting and sculpture created by artists opposed to the prevailing zeitgeist in Germany.

That night, playing with Einstürzende Neubauten was Die Tödliche Doris, who continued to push their minimal electronics and Dadaist guerrilla cabaret, filled with explosive and brilliant ideas, lasting from 1980 to 1987. Their stripped-back, skeletal recordings, such as 'Tanz Im Quadrat', still sound futuristic to this day.

Also on the bill were Der Plan, who had formed in an art gallery and performed in surreal costumes, singing ironic, sarcastic lyrics. Meanwhile, Freiwillige Selbstkontrolle (F.S.K) were busy rejecting the idea of authenticity, and Palais Schaumburg were dealing their synth-driven atmospheres with the bizarre trumpet accompaniment and atonally recited vocals. Playing one of their early shows were West German duo Deutsch Amerikanische Freundschaft or D.A.F., who sang over tough, dirty disco drums, coupled with synth pulses in a stage show caught between ecstasy, frenzy and tumult. There was now a scene of sorts, and Mark Reeder was part of it:

> My band, Die Unbekannten, also performed at the now-mythical festival. Our music was miserable and quite dark and gloomy. We were doing songs about Cold War life in the walled-in city. I suppose that's why some consider us in Germany to be the godfathers of goth. We were absorbed into this new German scene probably because we were equally dilettantish and different. At this time, I first met Blixa. It was perhaps through Gudrun Gut, somewhere in our little scene at venues like Kant Kino, Tschungel or SO36? The Berlin new wave avant-garde scene was still in its early days at this point. Only a handful of bands were around, Mania D or Einstürzende Neubauten. Although I had had virtually no success at all in trying to promote Joy Divisions records to the German media, I firmly believed that my Throbbing Gristle loving friends in Berlin would love the dark sound of Joy Division too, once they got to see them perform live and so earlier that January, I managed to talk Rob Gretton into

812 Blixa Bargeld to John Robb.

bringing Joy Division over to Berlin, and they performed to around 58 people in the Kant Kino.[813]

The catch-all term 'Neue Deutsche Welle' (New German Wave) was first used in a record shop advertisement by Burkhardt Seiler in the German magazine *Sounds* in August 1979. The phrase was picked up by journalist Alfred Hilsberg whose article about the movement titled 'Neue Deutsche Welle — Aus Grauer Städte Mauern'('New German Wave - From Grey Cities' Walls') was published in the same magazine in October 1979. The new scene encompassed a whole host of bands – from the aforementioned groups, Grauzone, Neon, Die Krupps, Weltklang, Scratis, ZaZa, Pyrolator and many others.

Meanwhile, following their own trajectory, Einstürzende Neubauten were releasing game-changing music. They released the 1980 double 7" vinyl *Kalte Sterne* and then the album *Kollaps* in 1982, which had a clattering, claustrophobic rush that mirrored the artful intensity of Berlin at that time, and perfectly signposted the furthest sonic frontiers of the post-punk period.

Some of these recordings were later compiled on the brilliant *Strategies Against Architecture 80-'83* collection where the frenetic claustrophobia snapshots the times perfectly.

It was almost inevitable that Blixa Bargeld and Nick Cave's paths would soon cross. A June 1982 Neubauten concert at the Meervaart concert hall, as part of the Amsterdam-Berlin festival, was famously filmed live for the arty VPRO channel on Dutch TV. Watching in a Hague hotel room, Cave was instantly captivated by their music and performance and decided to get in touch. The very idea that a concert such as this could be broadcast on live TV is quite something. Mark Reeder was there doing the live sound:

> I was there mixing live sound with Malaria! And Neubauten. Also performing were the Neonbabies, White Russia and transvestite blues singer, Hot Java. Neubauten arrived only with Blixa's guitar and Mark Chung's bass. They got a van, went to a local building site, and acquired some 'instruments.'
> Alexander Hacke also 'borrowed' three Amsterdam city bollards - large metal posts which stop cars from falling into the gracht (canal) - and placed them centre stage, directly at the front, so everyone watching the telly could see them. Unknown to the band, in the audience was also the mayor. After the show, bemused, he said, 'You have to take those bollards back from where you got them, otherwise there will be big trouble' (and they did!).' [814]

Watching the TV, Cave was intrigued by what he saw. He made contact and became fascinated by Neubauten and the like-minded Berlin scene and would soon move The Birthday Party to the city. In 1983, within months of Cave's arrival, Blixa was playing the guitar in the dying embers of The Birthday Party. He became part of the ever-shifting final lineup of the band and performed on their last recordings.

---

813 Mark Reeder to John Robb.

814 Mark Reeder to John Robb.

When Nick Cave reconvened as the Bad Seeds, Blixa became a vital member of the band, winding his guitar into new shapes whilst still leading Einstürzende Neubauten and enjoying the freedom of musical expression that Cave afforded him.

> If Nick had asked me to join his band on clarinet, I still would have said 'yes'. But the thing is, I have always looked at the outside techniques of what is considered 'normal' use of an instrument. What is the word in English... when the rabbit runs back and forth...? Zigzag! This is how I play, using this zigzag strategy to make music that nobody would expect whatsoever. Although the music was very different in The Birthday Party and then the Bad Seeds, I could still play the guitar without actually playing it in any conventional way.
>
> The general understanding of song structure I got from working with the Australians. I learned about songwriting from their working process. They come from a completely different musical background. Mick Harvey and Nick Cave were in a school band where you learn to play other people's songs, and, in that process, you learn how songs are constructed – how songs work and don't work. That's certainly not my tradition. My tradition was improvisation – like Can or electronic music – and that's a different knowledge. Working with the Bad Seeds, I learned more about the songwriting side. When I started Neubauten, it was always a hundred per cent spontaneous and improvised.[815]

In the Bad Seeds, Bargeld was still treating guitar with his customary disdain, creating a sense of unease and of disturbance with his playing. During recording sessions, he often placed his guitar on the floor, playing it with bows or electric razors. As he explains, such an approach could only be delivered by someone who hated the guitar or, at least, hated what most musicians play on the instrument. 'I thought it was a good decision to play the guitar because I claimed my hatred for playing the guitar in several interviews. It's probably good to play an instrument out of hatred of what other people do with it.'[816]

In 1983, with Einstürzende Neubauten now signed to Some Bizzare Records, they released their more structured second album, *Zeichnungen des Patienten O.T.* which saw the dominating metallic textures collaged with found sound and recordings of Hamburg fish market. A haunting Armenian folk song was meshed into the beautiful and powerful 'Armenia', which was, perhaps, the first hint of a more ambient and haunting melodic future sound. The bass guitar now drove songs, as the band started to create a spine for the textural explorations.

Their live performance were now sheer spectacles and genuinely dangerous. With sparks flying and shards of metal at centre stage, there was a streak of malevolence and a wilful art delivered as both a mirror and a hammer.

At a 1984 London ICA show, they hit music media headlines. As a part of 'A Concerto for Voice and Machinery', they clashed with the venue over the decision to market the show under their name alone as, originally, Blixa Bargeld was only

---

815 Blixa Bargeld to John Robb and to tone-deaf.com .
816 Blixa Bargeld to John Robb.

supposed to appear three-quarters of the way through to intone live favourite, 'Sehnsucht', over and over into the mic. When he did, drills and percussion were used to batter the stage and venue, freeze-framing the band in the music press' eyes as an art riot that would go on to define them in the media for years.

Over the decades, Einstürzende Neubauten have made a surprising impact, despite their music being created beyond cliché. Initially, the releases had been dense and percussive, but 1985's *Halber Mensch* saw a sparser, more industrial dance-tinged work. The stripped-down sound saw them combine their noisier instincts with the strict discipline of spartan electronic, neo-industrial dance. Bargeld was also singing more melodic parts with poetic phrases, moving away from his screams and strangulated earlier delivery. The album marked a shift in their thinking as they pulled away from the pain and pleasure of cacophony towards explorations of space and even silence.

1987's stark and blues tinged *Fünf auf der nach oben offenen Richterskala,* and 1989's *Haus der Lüge* continued this journey. However, it was the aptly named *Tabula Rasa*[817] that saw the significant sonic shift to a more seductive textural sound that kept the same tension but finely coiled and with a delicious restraint. Bargeld signposted the change by moving from his rubber scarecrow look to a wardrobe of black suits. They would then deliver an album of lush, beautiful songs to match this sartorial shift and a new sonic manifesto.

Newly emboldened, the band would return with 1996's *Ende Neu*, exploring many hypnotising subtle textures. The lead track, 'The Garden', concerns itself with German national identity and is a damp and coldly beautiful piece of haunting, sparse music with a hypnotic vocal.

The new fascination with silence was underlined by 2000's *Silence Is Sexy* – a 70-minute masterpiece. The title track is stripped to as near silence as the band can get and uses the emptiness as an instrument. In the sparse introduction, where the silence is deafening, you can hear the striking of a match for a post-coital cigarette. This subtlety underlined the standout tracks with Bargeld fascinated by the sound of silence.

817 Latin for 'clean slate'.

Silence Is Sexy – the song – is, in fact, a total contradiction, because silence becomes audible as tension. John Cage tried to direct the listener's concentration to all the sounds that are there when you think it is silent. It's a kind of Zen idea, a philosophical statement…I wanted to make silence itself as audible as tension.[818]

On 2004's *Perpetuum Mobile,* the band explored air utilising the wheezing and sighing sound from car tires to air compressors. This was combined with the band's new-found love of plastic tubes, electric fans and weird and wonderful wind instruments to explore the subtle shifts in tone of the moving molecules of the hiss and rush of atmosphere.

In 2007, Blixa Bargeld had suddenly left the Bad Seeds after a twenty-year stint, leaving him more time to concentrate on his main project. The resulting album was *Alles Wieder Offen.* A well-crafted yet experimental work that was very listenable, with the subtlety and intelligence of older musicians not resigned to reliving their past sounds. There are even moments of pop-lightness on the album, like the neo-dance floor hit 'Let's Do It A Dada'. It is undoubtedly an album crafted by veteran musicians at the top of their game. The subtle textural shifts continued to fascinate Blixa Bargeld:

Someone said it's like the songs have become inverted. I like that. It's the same motivation and attitude as before. The song structures are deconstructed from within. They remain intact but are fragile and fractured.[819]

Neubauten still defy gravity. 2014's *Lament* was a masterpiece of ideas and conceptual brilliance. The album was a sprawling affair that looked at the madness of the First World War. Working with archive sound recording, they added a varied collection of musical and theatrical ideas. The album was beautifully researched – a key element in the Neubauten creative process –with the resulting work appearing like an aural documentary painting a picture of the pointlessness of war. The band were explicit in making profound points about the history and futility of war itself, all without the necessity of slogans.

In 2020, Blixa Bargeld is an unlikely national treasure in Germany, enjoying TV appearances where he cooks meals with exclusively black-coloured ingredients. Alexander Hacke is constantly on the road with his partner Danielle de Picciotto making captivating violin and drone led art-scapes.

Neubauten, most of whom are now in their sixties, released 2020's *Alles In Allem,* which saw the band sounding almost conventional and a long way away from the apocalyptic industrial of their formative years. Still fronted by Bargeld, now resplendent in his sparkling mascara and long hair, the band, like Berlin itself, sit a long way from their post-war post-punk roots and yet are comfortable in their textured new sound with added strings and Blixa singing beautifully. The

---

818 Blixa Bargeld to John Robb.

819 Blixa Bargeld to John Robb.

conventional is now experimental, as someone once sang, and they lose none of their power and sensuality and ability to surprise and to engage.

Decades in, and even with an added melodic touch, the band are still the deserters.

Chapter 24

VOODOO IDOLS

The Ballad of Lux and Ivy
(Exploring America's Underbelly with the Cramps and the Gun Club)

The singer, who goes under the bizarre handle of Lux Interior, is doing his gonzoid Iggy whilst dealing a ghoulish baritone with a Vegas croon, then switching to madcap slapback hiccough whilst he staggers across the stage in his high heels and PVC leggings. He's drenched in red wine and stardust in a display of near naked, near the knuckle public madness whilst singing like a liquorice Elvis. Meanwhile, whilst her husband disappears off the stage and into the aching vortex of psychobilly psychodrama, the six string from hell is dealt by a gum-chewing, stoic, cool as fuck, gold tiara-wearing, gunslinger ice queen peering out from under her nest of red medusa curls. Her name is perfect, Poison Ivy - the tough, beautiful and brilliant guitarist who runs the band with a gimlet stare and who has influenced a whole swathe of young musicians.

Lux and Ivy defined rock'n'roll, and their trip into the heart of the darkness of the form, whilst entwined each other and to The Cramps for nearly forty years defines the greatest love story of them all.

Like the taste of fresh strychnine, The Cramps were switchblade dangerous and filled with a stylistic, stripped-down yet lysergic take on backwoods redneck rockabilly. They were unique - a psychedelic band playing primitive rock'n'roll. At the core of the band were Lux Interior[820] and Poison Ivy[821]. The glamorous, scowling couple met as tripped-out hippies in 1972 and set out on a deeply personal and creative journey, scouring the grubby underside of American culture for inspiration and somehow being embraced by the goth scene for their style and their sex beat sound.

Rather than following the LSD clichés, they immersed themselves in raucous and intoxicating primal rock'n'roll. They also found creativity in kitsch, art in rubbish and beauty in the discarded. Their fanatic fascination virtually invented a high-decibel music culture that embraced a trash aesthetic. The Cramps may have ostensibly dealt a stripped-down lascivious rockabilly, but their interpretation was sieved through a certain chemical consciousness.

The Cramps' distinctive and fantastically filthy guitar was an inspiration to every band with any poison in its soul. As Jim Reid, the singer of The Jesus and Mary Chain says, 'I remember listening to The Cramps before we started the band and

---

820 Born Erick Lee Purkhiser in Akron Ohio on 21 October 1946 died 2009.

821 Poison Ivy Rorschach born Kristy Marlana Wallace in 1953.

their sound was something that me and my brother were fascinated by. The feedback and Poison Ivy's guitar was a big influence.'[822]

At their heart, they were the missing link between psyche, psychedelic and psychobilly.

The Cramps were never goth, yet goth would have been aesthetically and musically different without the band and their style, sound and voodoo vibe.

This is the story of the band whose songs about raw sex were a celebration of the power of the Devil's music. The irony is that at The Cramps' core is one of the greatest of all rock'n'roll love stories with a couple who were together for thirty seven years.

This is the ballad of Lux and Ivy.

*****

In astrology, there are certain combinations of people that should not work. They would not fit in with the social order, and they would cause trouble. They may start a revolution, or they'll cause trouble, or they'll set things on fire. I think we're definitely the kind of pair that they would have tried to keep apart. Together we cause a lot of upheaval. From our point of view, though, it's creation. We're creating things.

I don't know what you'd call what we are. We're not married. We're deeply in love and feel like we've been together for more than this lifetime, but we're not aware of any particular ritual that would consecrate it in a way that makes sense to us. We sure don't need to make it any kind of institutionalised situation. Nature upholds our bond.

There's not anything that we deny each other. I'll always hear somebody say, 'Oh, I'd like to buy that, but my wife would kill me', or vice versa, and I'm, like, 'God, what is that?' We don't feel that either one of us has any right to say anything about the other's needs. We just have to trust that person and what that person is entitled to. Fortunately, we happen to like a lot of the same things, but even if we didn't, that shouldn't matter. We're both real free-thinkers. We're nice to each other. There's all those reasons why we're together, but I think it's also karmic. We're karmically entwined.

He's easy to love. He's someone I can get crazy with; I knew that about him right away. I thought: 'Oh boy, what's gonna happen now? Something exciting!' It's still happening.[823]

Astrology got this one right. The inseparable pair were explosive together. Such a cordite creative core could only result in the construction of something as feral and genuinely dangerous as The Cramps.

We're different in a lot of ways. I tend to fly off the handle and go crazy and start screaming, and she tends to be a bit wiser, calmer and more patient than I am – before she starts going wild, too. I think she's a lot classier than I am, but I think I've gained a lot of class from her. It's hard to figure out how we're different

822 Jim Reid to John Robb.

823 Poison Ivy to The Independent.

because we're together all the time, and we always do everything together. In a way, it's kind of one thing, me and her, but she's also very much an individual and very strong. She grows like a tree. She's faceted like a diamond. There are a million sides to Ivy, and I just love all of them.[824]

The then Erick Purkhiser was born in 1946 in Akron, Ohio[825], the bleak northern lakeside city which has, over the years, provided a surprisingly large amount of interesting music; Chrissie Hynde, Devo, Black Keys, Rachel Sweet and also Pere Ubu, who were from just down the road in Cleveland.

He was of the rock'n'roll generation who were swept up by the electric madness of the form. His younger brother, Michael Purkhiser, was nine years his junior and remembers the young man who used to watch, listen and absorb the American TV and radio personality Ernie Anderson[826] who had a profound effect on him. Anderson, in turn, had based his act upon the larger-than-life antics of Cleveland radio personality Pete Myers.

Better known as Mad Daddy, Myers reached the peak of his popularity at WHK[827], hosting record hops and live after-midnight shows dressed in a Dracula costume. A mixture of cheap kitsch and rock'n'roll wildness that impacted the future Cramp.

Such ghoul madness struck an artistic nerve, and fired-up he left Akron for California in the late '60s to pursue art at a very of the time freak college. His younger brother, who played in various hometown groups, remembers receiving a letter from him.

> Basically, he said, 'I want to do what you're doing. I want to play in a band and make music like you do.' I thought that was pretty cool because I always knew him as an artist and as a music lover but not as a musician or performer.[828]

Still pursuing art, Erick arrived in California at the tail end of the hippie era in 1972 drifting around the liberal Sacramento State College, enrolling on niche courses, baffled by the strange college he was now attending.

> Saying it was a college is stretching it a bit. You'd get credit for just going there and everything. It was just a bunch of weirdos. It was crazy. Half the teachers were fucking the students and getting paid for it. It was really a great time, those days and a really creative environment.[829]

The then Kirsty Wallace was also at Sacramento State College.

> It was a very strange art department in Sacramento at that time. The whole student population was made up of hippies, and they were into witchcraft and metaphysics and everything else. I was doing a class called Art and Shamanism.

---

824 Lux Interior to The Independent.

825 Akron is home to the most presidents and the most serial killers in US history. It is also the rubber city where America's tyres are made.

826 The American TV and radio personality portrayed 'Ghoulardi', the host of a late-night horror show in Cleveland in the early 1960s.

827 Cleveland radio station - the 15th oldest station still broadcasting in the United States.

828 Michael Purkhiser.

829 Lux Interior to the *Independent*.

The textbook for that class was called *The Sacred Mushroom and the Cross*[830], and the subject of that book is how the real topic of the Bible is the Amanita muscaria[831] mushroom and that Christ is a metaphor for this magic mushroom. The kind of instructors we'd have would say: 'I haven't seen you in class for a while; what grade d'you want?' And we'd say, 'Well, I guess an A', and they'd say, 'Okay.'

So those were crazy times. It was just a very loose, very unique situation, and we met in that environment. We met in a very free way, and we fell in love very quickly.[832]

The couple first met when one afternoon when Lux picked up the then-19-year-old Kristy Wallace when she was hitchhiking near the college. The pair sparked immediately. For Erick, it was love and lust at first sight

Decades later I said to my friend who was with me that day, do you remember when we picked up that really pretty girl hitchhiker and your dog Wheezer jumped all over her? Well, I've been jumping all over her for the past 35 years, and we have a band called The Cramps! That first time I saw her, she was walking down the street, hitchhiking, and she was wearing a halter top and short shorts with a big hole in the ass with red panties showing through. We both just went, 'Who-o-o-oh!' We pulled over, and I think I had a hard-on about three seconds after I saw her![833]

Even in the bohemian atmosphere of the college, Erick and Kirsty had stood out and she was already aware of the charismatic long-haired figure loping around the college. Their paths were inevitably going to cross with a powerful kinetic spark that occurred that warm afternoon.

I'd just started college, and one day I was hitchhiking back from the campus to my apartment when Lux and a friend of his gave me a ride. I'd seen him around the campus, and I thought he was extremely exotic. He would have these pants, and each leg of the pants was a different colour. That kind of thing fascinated me. Because it was the beginning of the new term, we had catalogues to look at to see which classes we were going to take, so we were sat there comparing to see if we'd be in any classes together.

I was then sitting in the Art and Shamanism class when I saw Lux walking in. It was a very large class, too, because everybody knew the teacher got high. I was sending out psychic brainwaves of, like: 'Sit by me! Sit by me! Sit by me!' And he did. He came straight in and sat next to me. We were making small talk, and I said, 'It's my birthday', and he pulled a drawing out of his portfolio and gave it to me as a birthday gift right then. It was a female figure, but it was very abstract expressionist. It had a lot of physical energy that I can't describe in words. I don't know if it was past lives or what, but I felt like I'd known him all my life. It wasn't like we'd just met. We were just together constantly, and we were pretty much out

---

830 The book relates the development of language to the development of myths, religions, and cultic practices in world cultures. The book argues, through etymology, that the roots of Christianity and many other religions, lay in fertility cults and that cult practices, such as ingesting visionary plants to perceive the mind of God, persisted into the early Christian Era.

831 Better known as the Fly Agaric - the classic red mushroom with white spots on it,

832 Poison Ivy to The Independent.

833 Lux Interior to LA Weekly.

of our minds constantly, to be honest. We didn't come to the surface for quite a long time. [834]

From the moment they met, the pair were inseparable. Their psychic energy, high intelligence and willingness to experiment was now amplified by their mutual encouragement.

I asked her: 'What is shamanism?' and she explained it to me. I thought, boy, that sounds pretty interesting. I think I'll take that course. And then, when I showed up for that class, she was there as well!

I remember the first day of that class; the teacher had us all sit around in a circle on the floor and hold hands. It was some kind of weird exercise, some mumbo-jumbo crazy cult thing where there was supposed to be energy which would fly around clockwise, and then he made it go counter-clockwise. It was great, it really worked, but just holding hands with her, I felt about a thousand times the energy that I was getting from him.

She's incredibly beautiful, that was the first thing I noticed. And then when I talked to her, she was incredibly smart, too. We just had a bond. A week and a half, maybe two weeks later we started living together. We just couldn't hardly stand to be away from each other. People would even tell us: 'That's not right, it's not healthy, you guys shouldn't be spending all your time together.' And they tell us that to this day.[835]

A further deep interest in the arcane corners of rock'n'roll bonded their deep partnership.

When we first met, all we wanted to do was go to rock'n'roll shows. And at that time, going to rock'n'roll shows in Southern California was great 'cos everybody got dressed up like crazy. It almost didn't matter who the band was because the audience was more interesting. I'd wanted to be in a band, and she played the guitar, and we got this idea within days of meeting each other: that we should have a band.

This was a while before the group actually happened. All my life, I'd been to see rock'n'roll bands, but I'd never quite been in one myself until I met Ivy. I remember her saying, 'Well, we should do that', and I'd say, 'Well, yeah, I guess we could do that', and she'd go, 'Of course, we could do it!' I think we just talked each other into it. If I hadn't met Ivy, I might still be just going to rock'n'roll shows.

She's really courageous, and she's really smart. At first, when we started out, we just wanted to have fun. We didn't want to have anything to do with the business part of all this band stuff, but when we had the band in the future, every time we've tried to have somebody manage us, it's been some kind of a bad experience, so she took over managing the band, and she really does it great. That's why The Cramps were around for a long time, because she cares about it and she's capable of unbelievable acts.[836]

At that time, Erick was not yet the fully formed psychobilly godhead. Both he and Kirsty were archetypal late-period hippies, arriving at the tail end of the movement.

---

834 Poison Ivy to The Independent.

835 Lux Interior to The Independent.

836 Lux Interior to The Independent.

Five years after the summer of love, California still had lots of opportunities for free love and psychedelic adventures. These were still mind-expanding times with a plethora of ideas and boundaries pushed by psychedelic drugs. The hippie lifestyle was something that Erick – with his long wavy hair and scraggy beard – was fully embracing, 'I was the hell of a hippie. Every weekend you could go to the park, drink jugs of wine and dance around and play one-string guitar for hours out of your mind on drugs.'[837]

Now with his new partner in crime, he had someone with whom to share his counterculture lifestyle and music.

> I guess we took a lot of acid together. That's probably considered a hippie thing, and we listened to a lot of T. Rex and New York Dolls. We also dug early Alice Cooper. Anybody who was just sexy and wild and played rock'n'roll, we dug it.[838]

Their quest for new horizons and sensations saw them get turned on to older music styles, such as rockabilly.[839] Instead of the contemporary rock music or the usual soundtrack for acid-fried hippies, they went deeper into the past and into the heart of musical culture.

> When we were living in Sacramento, we met this Mexican guy who collected black vocal group records and he turned us onto that. That's what started us collecting records from junk stores and getting doo-wop records. Then we just sort of discovered rockabilly.
> Because there were no reissues out then, like there are now, the only way you could get the music was to find the originals and learn about it that way. So we just learned about that music, and we fell in love with it.[840]

In 1973, the course at Sacramento ended, and they were forced to jump state for a mysterious, still-unspecified reason, 'There was a, uh, legal issue in California,' Kirsty recalls darkly, 'But I don't want to elaborate on that. We just had to get out of town.'[841]

Moving back to Akron to work out what to do with their lives. The pair worked in odd jobs in the rubber city and plotted their next move. They watched films and the more prominent bands who were coming through town at the Akron Civic Theatre. They bought junk from garage sales and flea markets and scoured their neighbourhood for rare albums and battered 45s. They also started to piece together a band of their own from this bric-a-brac of ideas and influences.

> Akron was very inexpensive to live in. So, we had this gigantic three-storey house for the two of us. We used the attic for rehearsals and getting some kind of ideas for a band. We must have talked about the band before in Sacramento, though, because I actually bought Lux the fuzz pedal we still use, which is a Univox

---

837 Lux Interior to Creem magazine in 1980.

838 Poison Ivy to Graham Russell.

839 The earliest form of rock'n'roll, rockabilly, dates back to the 1930s. It started as a deviation from country and was a fusion rock'n'roll and hillbilly.

840 Lux Interior to The Independent.

841 Poison Ivy to Gary Mulholland.

Superfuzz[842], from a pawn shop. His brother sent him a Student Prince guitar, and I taught him 'Baby Strange' by T. Rex.

In Akron, we were both working in a circuit-board factory. Really boring with a really fascist boss. We weren't cut out for that kind of work; we're too delicate and sensitive! Although, one of the early interviews we did a couple of years later with Nick Kent for the *NME* he thought we said surfing-board factory.

I kinda hate to say that's not true.

Through record collecting, we were getting more and more passionate. Being exposed to music that most people weren't. There wasn't much going on in the 70s that really thrilled us. The New York Dolls had broken up, T. Rex wasn't what it was before. I think being together — not just as a couple, but as partners in crime — you can get each other wound up in a way that a lone person can't. We convinced each other that it was viable to have our own band and that everybody would think it was cool. It was kind of a delusion except that we succeeded with it.[843]

Akron saw them refine their vision in its rubbery isolation. After seeing the New York-based band, Television, at a gig in Cleveland in July 1975, the duo's ears pricked up, making them realise that something was going on in the Big Apple. The Television gig[844] was not only a prime example of the oncoming New York musical shift, the pioneering local band support band, Rocket from the Tombs[845] pointed to be an advanced local scene as well.

Rocket from the Tombs had formed in the post-industrial wasteland of Cleveland alongside another fascinating proto-post-punk band, the electric eels,[846]proof that cutting edge music could be incubated in small town America by unknown, idiosyncratic oddities a few years ahead of the pack. The electric eels' drummer Nick Knox would eventually join Lux and Ivy in New York City, drumming with The Cramps for decades. Cleveland with its fervent micro scene were only 39 miles away from Akron, but it may as well have been 39 thousand miles for the couple who were so lost in their own world.

One thing people assume, is that we knew those people. We didn't. We weren't aware of them playing, except that we saw Rocket from the Tombs supporting Television in a hotel in Cleveland. We didn't meet any of them until we moved to New York. We knew nothing in Ohio except our stupid jobs and mainstream gigs. We didn't know there was an underground. So we had to get out of there.[847]

New York may have been nine hours away by car, but its lure was getting stronger.

---

842 One of the classic fuzz pedals it is an octave fuzz using two germanium diodes to produce the square wave clipping and used by the likes of J. Mascis, Josh Homme and Kurt Cobain and many others.

843 Poison Ivy to Gary Mulholland.

844 The 24 July 1975 gig was at the Piccadilly Inn, Cleveland. The support band, Rocket from the Tombs, had formed four weeks before and later splintered into Pere Ubu and The Dead Boys. It was also Television's first gig outside New York City, a year after they had formed.

845 Rocket From The Tombs soon morphed into Pere Ubu and became a prime influence on darker post-punk UK music.

846 The electric eels only played five gigs after being inspired to form a band after a 1972 Captain Beefheart gig. However, their ultra-confrontational stance and rudimentary punk noise attempts at free jazz have left them permafrozen with a cult reputation as one of the great lost bands.

847 Poison Ivy to Gary Mulholland.

After that Television gig, we did the nine-hour drive from Akron twice to New York in 1975 and saw the Ramones and Television play. So we knew it was all there. We would get a few days off work, take speed, drive there, see the bands, and drive back. There'd be nothing left of us when we got back to Ohio. But those two trips convinced us we had to move. We had enough money for a hotel in New York for two days, and couldn't find a place to live. So we slept the third night in the car at a truck stop in New Jersey and said, 'If we don't find somewhere tomorrow, we'll have to forget it and go back to Ohio.' That day we found our apartment. So we moved in and proceeded to starve. But that was okay. We had to be there.[848]

The impossibly glamorous pair with their singular vision quickly became lurking shadows of the flourishing micro New York City proto-punk scene. They began hanging out in the city's bombsite local culture hubs among the ruins of the pre-yuppie takeover of lower Manhattan. Lux soon found himself a part-time job in the rare records store, Musical Maze, on 23rd Street and 3rd Avenue. Famously, the building's water heater was downstairs and was painted to look like King Tut's sarcophagus and the store was a focal point, selling records to local students who also grabbed their new *NME*s freshly imported from the UK while looking for the latest releases.

It was whilst working at the store that Lux met the magnetic, Bryan Gregory[849] who also worked there. The pair hit it off. Even though Bryan had never played and had no obvious musical ability, Lux asked him to join the band. Like Lux, he was an artist and a music freak, which was enough. Through a misunderstanding, Gregory bought himself a guitar instead of a bass and, more through embarrassment than anything else, didn't point out his mistake. And so, the twin guitar no-bass musical attack of The Cramps was born by default.

The Detroit-born Bryan Gregory was an artful construction and within a year of joining the band, he would be a veritable cadaver pin-up and eventual cult goth icon. His two-tone hair formed a follicle curtain that would dramatically half hide and half expose his hollowed face that looked like it was carved from granite. Dressed in a rubber fetish-billy wardrobe and draped in bone jewellery and swinging his trademark polka dot flying V with a cig stuck in his gob, he was the band's rudimental Brian Jones - the style overload Godstar and his hero from The Rolling Stones and where he took his first name from.

A proto-goth ghoul, whose guitar hero look has never been bettered; the guitarist was a profound sartorial influence on anyone who fancied pushing the style envelope at the time. Like his idol, Bryan Gregory added the final flavour to The Cramps' feral yet perfect compositions. His fuzzed-up blocs of guitar filth were dealt whilst he was flicking cigarettes from his mouth into the crowd. Sometimes he even played with his hands over the top of the guitar and made no attempts to play conventional chords. He acted as the perfect foil to the rockin' bones power couple at centre stage.

---

848 Poison Ivy to Gary Mulholland.

849 Born Gregory Beckerleg, 20 February, 1951 – January 10, 2001.

I met Bryan on our mutual birthday on February 20, 1976. We were almost the same size and could fit into each other's pants and shoes. We understood each other because we weren't the boy/girl next door, and we'd both already been through a lot and knew how to hustle tooth and nail to survive. We could be our scary selves without horrifying each other. My fondest memory is of tripping on acid together in Central Park that summer. We were never quite able to sustain that high.

Bryan's creative forte was more visual than sonic — when we met him, he had just moved to New York to pursue a graphic-arts career. He loved art, jewellery making, decorating — I think it was the visual aspects of The Cramps that appealed to him most. Lux and I had come to New York in 1975 with a mess of songs and crude home demos, and a plan to take over the world, but I think it was mostly our exotic looks and Flying V guitar that lured Bryan to join us. When we gave the guitar to him, he immediately decorated it with polka dot price stickers and painted our name in fancy script on the case, and you know what? It looked hot![850]

A bundle of contradictions, Bryan lived life on full gas, as Ivy recalls.

Bryan was more enigmatic and incongruous than imagination would allow. Once, in a packed coffee shop, he pulled a switchblade on a booth full of square businessmen who were snickering about him, but on another occasion, he whined that he couldn't leave his apartment because the neighbourhood teen toughs followed him down the street teasingly singing 'Sweet Child in the City'. A sense of adventure led him to let Lux dangle him upside down by his ankles from a 17th-floor high-rise window 'just to see what it's like', yet he despised touring because of his fear and hatred of 'foreigners'. He thought rockabilly was 'goofy' but said we made it work 'cuz you're so weird'. We had a brief, intense relationship, and I don't think any of us knew what hit us. At one time, we all wanted to be in a band that people were afraid of offstage. He was a true DMF — Detroit Motherfucker.[851]

The new band's first jam took place in the Musical Maze record store cellar, by the sarcophagus, in April 1976 with Bryan's sister Pam Ballam on drums.

When we first went into the basement to jam, we didn't know how we'd sound. So, we just did it. We didn't have enough going on to discuss it! With Bryan, we just connected, though. It was a chemistry thing. There was never a plan.[852]

Pam lasted a few months before she left and was replaced by Miriam Linna[853], another Ohio renegade from the Cleveland music scene and Rocket from the Tombs inner circle. She remembered already being asked to join the band whilst she was still hanging out in Kent State back in Akron when Lux had sidled up to her in a record store and asked her to join. She had initially spotted the exotic singer a few weeks before at a local April 1975 show in Akron by The Kinks due to his stand out turquoise shoes. Lux introduced her to Ivy and asked her to play the drums for the

---

850 Poison Ivy.

851 Poison Ivy.

852 Poison Ivy to Gary Mulholland.

853 Still active Miriam Linna Linna owns one of the world›s largest private collections of vintage paperbacks, including complete runs of Avon, Beacon, Signet, and others. She has written her autobiography.

band he was forming, which was about to move to New York. She told him that she had never played the drums, but this, somehow, made him more enthusiastic.

Finally a few months later she was on board and played The Cramps' debut gig on 1 Nov 1976, at New York's legendary CBGB venue. Opening for fellow Ohio band, The Dead Boys, the show saw them enter the fervent New York band scene, where they would quickly gain a following,

> It was easier than you'd imagine; that's why we feel so grateful and so fortunate with the scene that was there at the time. Monday night was audition night at CBGB, but not everybody could get on. We did straight away because we'd just made friends with The Dead Boys, who were really hot at the time. They headlined this audition night, and we played our first show to a packed club. Many people saw us, as chaotic as we were, including the key punk and new wave booker, Peter Crowley who booked Max's Kansas City.[854] He loved us and immediately booked us. Hilly Kristal, the boss of CBGB, thought we sucked, which we probably did. But Peter loved us, and we started playing Max's regularly, supporting bands like Suicide.[855]

Now called Poison Ivy, she acknowledged how the New York scene quickly embraced The Cramps:

> We got a following just from those gigs. We put these flyers up all over town, and that's where the 'psychobilly' tag came from that. We thought it up and put it on the posters just to get people interested in us. It clicked straight away. The biggest break was when Ramones saw us and dug us, and then they let us open for 'em. Their audience loved us. New York was just a magnetic Mecca for people in 1976/77, and there was just this swell of energy. We were hanging out at CBGB and Max's every night of the week, and so was everybody else. It was a swirl of creativity.[856]

Paying the bills working as a dominatrix at the now-demolished Victoria Hotel in mid-New York because it 'paid better than being a waitress', Poison Ivy was adding sex and money to the band's coffers as they played around New York City with a virtual residency at Max's Kansas City. Their first big break came when Richard Robinson, producer of the Flamin' Groovies classic 'Teenage Head'[857], demo-ed the band in April 1977. The recordings caught the already-in-place Ivy driving guitar twangs playing against Bryan's chords that were more standard and less noisy than later on. Lux's vocals took on a higher yelping pitch as he was still trying to find that voice, whilst Miriam honed her lack of drumming skill to a Mo Tucker perfection, inventing The Cramps pounding heartbeat.

A few months later, in August, Miriam Linna left the band and was replaced

---

854 Open from 1965 to 1981, a nightclub and restaurant at 213 Park Avenue South in New York City, which became a gathering spot for musicians, poets, and artists.

855 Poison Ivy to Gary Mulholland.

856 Poison Ivy to Gary Mulholland.

857 From San Francisco, Flamin› Groovies are the great lost band in rock'n'roll - armed with a series of classic singles they were playing Merseybeat for decades after it had faded and had honed it down to a perfection.

by Nick Knox,[858] whose straight-backed tight drumming held the band together, creating the classic lineup that would see him remain on the drum stool until 1991.

Finally, with a settled lineup, The Cramps' twisted psychodrama created a distinctive sound that chimed perfectly with the punk and post-punk scene. They also looked fantastically cool. Lux had the Iggy moves down and would emerge as one of the world's great wild singer/showmen. Ivy had perfected her sneer from behind her mass of red curls, and her exotic wardrobe had its own linear, sharp style. Nick Knox's impassive deadpan cool thousand-yard stare from behind his sunglasses after dark was equally iconic. Meanwhile, Bryan Gregory's chiselled features appeared scary and unreal as he worked on his glam corpse look.

They also made a music to match.

Their filthy, primal rock'n'roll saw them embraced by the punk scene, and now signed, they released a couple of early singles on the Vengeance label, the first of which was 1978's 'Human Fly', flipped with a cover of Roy Orbison's 'Domino'. This was followed by a cover of The Trashmen's 'Surfin Bird' and a B-side cover of Jack Scott's 'The Way I Walk' - all missives of timeless danger. Once signed to IRS, these singles were included in their July 1979 *Gravest Hits* 12" EP with an added fifth track of their cover version of Ricky Nelson's 'Lonesome Town'.

Their first full album, *Songs the Lord Taught Us*, was produced by former Box Tops singer Alex Chilton who reproduced the band's genius monochromatic vision perfectly. It is a rare record that creates a world of its own with a personal, timeless vision. Recorded in Memphis, it paid homage to rock'n'roll's spiritual home.

> Early on, we had almost collected every Sun label single. When I first met Ivy, we drove all the way across the country to visit Memphis. We went to the Sun warehouse. We were really in awe of that building and of Sam Phillips.[859] We had to stay overnight in the studio because we got locked in when we met him. It was like a dream or something. Could this be happening? We were told he never comes to the studio, but he showed up with a chainsaw to cut down the vines that had grown up over his name plaque. It was a magical experience. We didn't talk to him too much. But we told him that we had every Sun single, and he says, 'Well, you know something?' And we said, 'What?' And he just says, 'You're lucky.' He had these huge glasses on that magnified his eyes until he looked like a monster from outer space. He was a real character.[860]

In the tiny Sun Studios, they recorded a mixture of their own compositions like 'Zombie Dance' and 'I Was a Teenage Werewolf' and covering (and totally unzipping!) tracks like Johnny Burnette's 'Tear It Up', Link Wray's 'Sunglasses After Dark' and Little Willie John's 'Fever'. The album was a dramatic slice of primal rock'n'roll that somehow caught the confusion of post-punk and a history of experimentation. It had switchblade riffs, filthy feedback, pounding drums and those distinctive hollered

---

858 From Cleveland, Nick Knox formerly of the electric eels was born Nicholas George Stephanoff on 26 March, 1953 and died 15 June, 2018.

859 The Sun Records boss and record producer who discovered Elvis Presley.

860 Lux Interior to Gary Mulholland.

vocals. Digging deep into the primal swamp that had birthed rock'n'roll, The Cramps somehow souped it up with a post-punk feel and their own psychedelic vision. The songs were drenched with Bryan's feedback and distortion, adding to Ivy's twanging perfection, their brutally simple thudding drumming and Lux's perfect thrillbilly vocals.

Released alongside the single 'Garbageman' in March 1980, their impact was swift. The alternative clubs loved the heartbeat thud of their primal ooze. They also loved the band's style, with its sex and death stylings, which would become a key influence on the early goth scene wardrobe. The album felt dark. They looked and sounded dangerous. Their dark vibes and cordite sense of danger made them look and feel part of the broad church of goth, and their pounding rhythms and sensual sex beat were instant goth club favourites. There was an attractive darkness around the classic filthy twang of Link Wray's heroic guitar lines that Ivy had always loved: 'He was initially my biggest influence, and he still is. He sounds like the guitar at the end of the world. So austere. And yet so much drama. He makes the most out of the least.'

The Cramps' own music was at once terrifying and enthralling. Later on, they delivered a more camp, kitsch sound, but their early releases captured an enticing, sexual noise that was genuinely dark and off-kilter. Arriving entirely out of context in 1980, they sounded like a document from a nether world. The album cover photo saw the band at their corpse-like best – a perfect statement of this most purist of groups with their faces freeze-framed by sex and poverty. Like all great bands, you wanted to be in this all-night gang, this nocturnal crew.

At a tangent to goth and inspired by The Cramps, a psychobilly scene now sprung up consisting of bands like The Meteors, King Kurt, and Demented Are Go! who were far more linear in their approach. The new psychobilly scene was forged in adrenaline and quiff riffs. The Cramps, however, dealt in mystery and a sense of the exotic. They also drew upon their own psychedelic depths and other more subtle nuances that were picked upon by a diverse selection of other, very different new music makers. The Jesus and Mary Chain adored them, and one can hear The Cramps style fuzz and feedback all over their sound. Pete Burns of Dead Or Alive was obsessed with Bryan Gregory and his bone style, whilst the London Batcave club scene also made them a virtual house band in terms of spooked ideas. When The Birthday Party saw The Cramps just after they themselves had arrived in London, it changed everything. For a small coterie of freaks, their impact was immediate and decisive, especially in the UK, where music author Nina Antonia first saw them.

> The Cramps invoked a backwater Mid-West creepiness and were the first people I met who talked about Ed Gein,[861] who was the inspiration behind *The Texas Chainsaw Massacre* film. Bryan Gregory was incredibly spooky and played on it. Ivy went for a medusa look; no one could pull an evil eye like that gal! Lux turned

---

861 American serial killer of the 1950s who fashioned furniture and artefacts from his victim's remains. This fascination with American serial killers was a cult interest at the time. Somehow, UK serial killers and murderers were never deemed as 'cool'.

on the Anthony Perkin's *Psycho* routine of good-boy-gone-bad, and Nick Knox was like a surly shadow, very stylish. They used to put candles on their amplifiers until Lux's hair went up in flames one night. I rode the hell-bound train with them for a couple of years. They were the first people that I saw wearing bone jewellery. At that point, everyone was Bram Stoker's children. Lux was painting voodoo symbols on his chest, and Siouxsie was singing about Voodoo Dolls. You could see their influence all over the scene.

The exotic quixotic band toured Europe on the album, and their impact was profound. From the bone jewellery to the graveyard chic, they were a key sartorial influence on the emerging goth scene. Their stripped-down fuzz tones were replicated across the continent and the band seemed to be in the driving seat of their hot rod, but things were not what they seemed.

It was absolutely the worst time. We'd just toured Europe, and they made up this stuff about Bryan leaving our band to join a voodoo cult! Crap that we wanted nothing to do with because it wasn't true. That was terrible. It ended up breaking up that lineup because Bryan couldn't take it anymore.[862]

In May 1980, Bryan quit and drove away with a van full of band equipment before re-emerging in Beast, the band he put together with future The Gun Club, The Sisters of Mercy and The Damned member, Patricia Morrison,[863]. Beast didn't have much impact, and afterwards, his releases were intermittent, in projects such as his Legal Weapon, Dials and Shiver. The maverick guitarist sadly died from multiple organ failure in a Florida hospital in 1991. Years later, Lux speaks fondly of his long-lost comrade in arms:

They're all really great memories. Bryan could just do so many weird things. He was just such a weirdo at first. Later on, he became... more of a rock star, unfortunately. But at first, he'd go out onstage, fold himself up in the yoga lotus position, and run around on his knees. Then he'd spin around on one knee and jump into the audience, which was so dangerous. He would really frighten people. That lineup was a real four-pronged attack.[864]

Ivy has more pragmatic memories of the guitar player.

On a soul level, the affair was over by 1979, after we had started touring and recording regularly. Without a passion for and understanding of, the fundamental forces influencing The Cramps, a combination of too much hard work, chemical haze and backstage leeches who drove Bryan to the next bright, shiny object in his path and a pursuit of so-called social relevance. I'll never forget the high-flyin' Bryan that few people had the privilege to know, before he stopped being a rocker and became a 'rock star' . . . the way he walked, the way he talked, the way he rocked.[865]

---

862 Lux Interior to Gary Mulholland.

863 Born in 1962, goth icon Patricia Morrison was part of the LA punk scene in her mid-teens. She co-founded LA scene band The Bags in 1976, before moving on to Legal Weapon and then, in 1982, The Gun Club. She subsequently joined The Sisters of Mercy and then The Damned whose singer, Dave Vanian, she is currently married to.

864 Lux Interior to Gary Mulholland.

865 Poison Ivy statement.

The band overcome the loss of Bryan with the addition of another charismatic guitar player, Kid 'Congo' Powers.[866] The young guitarist was poached from LA band, The Gun Club, where he played bass. The Gun Club were starting to forge a reputation with a fanbase similar to The Cramps. They had their own obsession with Americana which they, too, had twisted into a post-punk template in their case built around the visionary talent and haunting vocals of singer Jeffrey Lee Pearce. His voice was a swooping, swooning spectral presence that floated over his band's charcoal blues. It was a voice of quivering emotion and deceptively angelic beauty that somehow caught the urgency of punk rock and crossed it with the primal rush of the blues.

Whereas The Cramps were serving up obscure old rockabilly and junkyard kitsch with a don't eat stuff off the sidewalk twist, The Gun Club were digging into the feral blues and spectral melodies of the great American hinterland. This mix of post-punk urgency and the deep soul of the fading American dream was vital to the band's sound. The Gun Club produced a solid clutch of albums before frontman Jeffrey Lee Pierce died in 1996 at the age of 28.

Born in 1958 in El Monte, a working-class industrial suburb East of Los Angeles, to a Mexican/American mother, Jeffrey Lee Pierce moved to Granada Hills in the San Fernando Valley, where he attended the Granada Hills High School, participating in the drama program, acting in plays and writing several of his own brief experimental pieces. In the mid-1970s, rock'n'roll would impinge on the young Pierce. Sparks and Roxy Music enticed him into the fringes of glam, yet he also had a love of Genesis and a curveball passion for reggae after attending a Bob Marley concert. His reggae passion even saw him travel to Jamaica to explore the music deeply. The trip left him ambivalent about the music's relevance to American culture. This would give him the idea of exploring his own musical roots. His infatuation with reggae had overlapped with the emergence of punk rock. Pierce became a fixture on the Hollywood scene as a writer for the Slash fanzine and initially, to a lesser extent, as a musician. His growing interest in American blues was counterpointed by a deep dive into the minimalism of the No Wave movement in New York City.

The initial rush of energy of punk had worn out for Pierce as the music became more formulaic. Like the more inquisitive punks in the UK, he was ignoring the Year Zero[867] part of the manifesto and, like The Cramps, looked further into the cultural underbelly of his own nation. The two bands were working in very similar ways.

Pierce discovered the Delta Blues and planned to fuse its haunting raw power with the rush of punk rock. He melded the two primal forms into a revolutionary new sound putting together The Creeping Ritual before changing the name to The Gun Club, with the new name being given to him by his roommate, former Black Flag vocalist Keith Morris.

---

866 Born 27 March, 1959 as Brian Tristan, he has played with The Gun Club, The Cramps and Nick Cave and the Bad Seeds and is currently touring with his own band The Pink Monkey Birds.

867 Named after Pol Pot's wiping out of all old culture in his dictatorship of Cambodia.

Jeffrey Lee Pierce's stage persona was the perfect talisman for this synthesis. He was a charismatic figure under a mop of dishevelled bleached hair whose intensity effortlessly held the room. Joining him in the new band was a youthful Kid 'Congo' Powers, Don Snowden, (at the time a music critic for the *Los Angeles Times*) and Brad Dunning, now a prominent designer and writer. It was the first of many lineups for the band over the next decade and a half.

Pierce utilised his connections with Blondie, whose American fan club he ran, to help the band get a head start and a record deal. Ward Dotson joined in place of Kid Congo, who had then just joined The Cramps. The band's debut, *Fire of Love*, sounded otherworldly, and it dripped with a beauty, atmosphere, and the dark mysticism that lay at the heart of the American soul. It was a cult favourite with the goth scene in the UK echoing through the decades and influencing bands like The White Stripes and the late Mark Lanegan, who idolised Pierce and became close friends with him. A critical success, it set the band up on a cult level that they underlined with the following year's *Miami* album, released on Blondie guitarist Chris Stein's new Animal records label.

With their third album, *Las Vegas*, The Gun Club added a polish to their sound in a nod to the mainstream alternative without losing their own innate raw beauty. The crossover was intangible, and the band fell apart in 1985 with the singer forming the Jeffrey Lee Pierce Quintet and the rest of the band coalescing as Fur Bible.

There would be reformations, new lineups and acclaimed albums as Pierce's phantom creativity jolted through the decade before he died in 1996. His journey had left behind a musical legacy and a series of albums that captured his mercurial genius.

It was from this mercurial background that Kid Congo emerged, ready-made for his new slot in The Cramps. Already imbued in this arcane world of long-lost culture, he knew exactly where to place his guitar in relation to Ivy's. The self-produced second album, *Psychedelic Jungle,* was a deep dive into their swampy ooze with an added lysergic fug over their deep 1950s roots. This psychedelic twist joined the dots between primal rock'n'roll, '60s acid trips and the fringes of the post-punk future with the same sort of off-kilter vibe that PiL had caught on Metal Box but utilising arcane old rock instead of old dub and krautrock as its template. It retained the fifties gonzoid backwood beats but somehow melded them with a tripped-out psychedelia infusing the tracks with a post-punk futuristic rush.

Somehow The Cramps sounded like both the future and the past.

At the same time, on an album where half the songs were obscure covers, it was the ultimate expression of their avowed record collecting picking out the jewels from the cutout bins and making them into their own diamonds.

Ivy's guitar sound is perfect – she remains one of the great guitar players, her guitar tone was hugely influential and came complete with a perfect understanding of the hip grind of the six string, as Lux's lascivious hollering brilliantly frames the album's tripped-out weirdness.

The band would never feel quite as dangerous again. Their next album, the 1983 live release, *Smell Of Female,* recorded at New York's Peppermint Gardens, saw them perfectly indulge their B movie direction. Dressed in gold lamé and oozing raw sex, but with less of the danger of their inception, this was The Cramps that appeared on UK television and toured big venues. They were now a huge cult band and would remain so for the rest of their career, with various lineups, but always with their aesthetic perfectly executed.

If they had lost their early period's danger and genuine freakishness, they remained incendiary outsiders. They were a band that existed outside the music business, apart from, all contemporary fashions. After a bust-up with their label, IRS records, their releases were mainly compilations and live albums, and it wasn't until 1986 that they released a new studio album, 1986's *A Date with Elvis,* and then 1990's *Stay Sick.*

Their fallout with the vampiric music industry saw the band exist as primarily a live outfit with brilliant live shows highlighting Lux in rubber and high heels, as he executed the perfect Iggy-gone-feral stage act where he would hump amps, climb on PAs, and roll on floors, all the while delivering perfectly spooked slapback vocals. To his side, Poison Ivy retained her stoic ice queen cool, playing tough guitar lines whilst surrounded by the various new members who came and went. For years, they were one of the great live acts and a festival highlight until their last live show at the Marquee Theatre in Tempe, Arizona, in November 2006.

Even the undead have to retire. It was the end of The Cramps, but their vision remains unimpaired. Endlessly copied but never equalled, they were one of those rare bands with a perfect idea and never strayed from it.

The Cramps' legacy looms large over rock'n'roll – perhaps because they were the perfect summation of the sex, style and subversion at the core of the form. They may never have been mainstream, but their DNA is spattered everywhere where rock'n'roll really matters.

Lux and Ivy semi-retired to their new home in LA, which became a shrine to their film and music obsessions until Lux died unexpectedly aged 62 in 2009. Following his death, Ivy perfectly described her beloved partner of four decades at the memorial service:

> Lux seemed like a creature from another world, with one foot already out of this dimension. As much as we might wonder, 'Where are you now?' we can also wonder, 'Where on Earth did you come from?' Now that's a mystery!

Chapter 25

FIRST, LAST AND ALWAYS

How Post-Punk Leeds Created Goth and The Sisters Of Mercy

My terror of being on stage is other people's entertainment. It's the function of that terror to make myself uncomfortable and, with that, pull bits of myself out. I have to be in a slightly altered state of mind to get up there and bring out a forbidden side of me. Normally unsociable I stalk the stage with this monstrous shadow that is much bigger than I am, and that's why I suppress my normal self.[868]

Of course The Sisters of Mercy were not a goth band.

It's a term their enigmatic frontman despises with acidic derision.[869]

But then who was!

What was it about Leeds[870] , though, that saw the city as one of the prime movers in forging what would become the so-called goth culture? Whilst other cities on the M62 corridor, had their own journey out of punk, like Liverpool which dealt its post-punk melancholia with the Gothic (north) west coast splendour of Echo & The Bunnymen, and a clutch of sartorial renegades like Pete Burns and Jayne Casey, and Manchester had the game-changing Joy Division creating great melancholic musical narratives, there was something different going down in Leeds.

West Yorkshire post-punk was Gang Of Four stripping the trad from rock whilst the other side of the city's midnight was doing the opposite but with a dose of irony and dark playfulness. This new hybrid scene was embracing the then discredited 'trad rock' and merging it with a post-punk narrative and the stripped-down throbbing genius of Suicide whilst embracing new tech. Driven by local club DJ Claire Shearsby - the John Peel of Leeds - with her defiant ear for rockier sounds turning the floorshow onto a different narrative, Leeds had its own trip.

This was a city where The Stooges, Suicide, glam and rock were celebrated instead of being sniffed at by UK post-punk where the very notion of 'rock' had been considered dead. The 'race against rockism', was sparked by the *NME* and used to beat away any rock tendencies.

Leeds, however, ignored the media memo.

The city was the heart of a new 'dark alternative' culture, with its take on post-punk being strikingly different from other places across the UK.

At the core of this new scene lay a shadowy, charismatic Colonel Kurtz figure who had turned himself from a Clark Kent style student studying Chinese at the local Uni

---

868 Andrew Eldtrich to John Robb.

869 Far too smart and far too knowing to be pinned down by a 'scene', Eldritch laughs at the tag or takes it down with a pithy sneer. He went as far as dressing in white suits and white baseball gear to destroy his unwanted prince of goth darkness tag.

870 Termed 'Gothic city' by the Yorkshire Post in one of the early uses of the term.

by day into an ubermensch rock star by night and was named after the adjective for weird and sinister or ghostly: Eldritch.

Rock was so sniffed at by the post-punk snobs that it was there for the taking. Ziggy was still playing guitar for the glam droogs from the north and Bowie had left a complex set of cultural messages in his wake. The Spiders From Mars were actually from Hull and that northern twist had given Bowie a fire that, melded with his future sci-fi visions and artful androgyny, had created something unique.

The Sisters would be a direct descendant of this.

By the early eighties, nothing was left to be inspired by, that had not been ransacked, apart from rock. For the Leeds inner circle, rock's gonzo grind was a portal into an artier take on the dystopian noise. It's no coincidence that Eldritch's nickname was Spiggy - a tongue-in-cheek Ziggy reference to the new kid in town who liked loud guitars but was smart enough to weld them to a drum machine and create something futuristic from the old model.

Ziggy would have been proud.

Sparked by nights at the Phonographique club, Leeds was about to fuse guitar noise with a post-punk sensibility. This would, in turn, birth many bands who dressed distinctively in black, with winklepickers, long hair and leather, filtered with a knowing cool. Alongside these developments, nearly everyone began integrating drum machines into their Trad Rock - a digital futurism fusing the unlikely combination of rock with a dislocated disco that was spearheaded by The Sisters of Mercy.

If there was ever a band that embodied all the mystique and contradictions of this outpost of post-punk, then it was the Sisters. Shrouded in dry ice, the band were built around a drum machine called Doktor Avalanche and their enigmatic frontman, Andrew Eldritch.

Inspired by glam rock, forged by punk and spat out by post-punk, Eldritch comes from an uncompromising time when bands rewrote the copybook and genres were at their most malleable. The Sisters of Mercy were a post-punk band spliced with rock music and it was groundbreaking when they aligned these rock flavours to a drum machine's cold, digital pulse and a combination as radical as any of their contemporaries' hipster choices of influence. Just ask Steve Albini[871], who used them as a template for his mighty Big Black, or a whole generation of Leeds, and then worldwide bands, who embraced this rock with a different sensibility, saving the form from a slow death. As the original Sister, Gary Marx[872], explains, this was putting the rock back into punk rock.

> The decision to openly say we were 'rock' was intentional. It was a direct response to what we saw as the prevailing trend among many of our contemporaries for stating the opposite. By virtue of being incapable of making a standard rock

871 Another high IQ visionary moving to a big city university with an acidic disdain creating a band built around a drum machine and industrial dark guitars, Albini was a big fan of The Sisters .

872 Then known as Mark Pearman.

sound, we arrived at this uneasy hybrid. I couldn't play a guitar solo even if I wanted to. So what you were left with was an amalgamation of the electronica of Kraftwerk, The Human League, Suicide, and the simplicity and power of The Velvets, The Stooges, The Cramps and Hawkwind. Everything we loved but had no idea of how they fitted together, if indeed they did.[873]

In one stroke, The Sisters of Mercy managed to bridge the gap between Lemmy's grinding snarl, Suicide's spectral horror, and new dance floor technology's cold precision. Defined by Eldritch's captivating neo-baritone, their songs were driven by deceptively simple, heavy bass lines, shimmering or driving guitars, and the binary clatter of a drum machine. They delivered a unique mystique with dark humour and a northern mystery that was as compelling as Joy Division at their peak on the other side of Peaks[874].

There was a starkness in their sound, which, coupled with great songwriting and Eldritch's voice created a unique pulsating vision thing. Aided by a minimalist, clever wordplay the songs are littered with literate references, lyrical hyperlinks and clues like a Dylan with a razor blade. There is an innate understanding of the brilliance of paring the muse down to dumb in a celebration of the lizard ridiculousness of rock but with a sucker punch of deep intelligence that hooks the listener into the chief Sisters' world. The lyrics have a Philip K. Dick sci-fi sheen, an apocalypse now of TS Eliot and a hidden sly humour in their literate switchblade and minimalist slash and burn. They were full of nuance and meaning yet also a texture and sensuality. Like the stark and haunting music, the words were pared to the bone but still deeply nuanced and layered with meaning. These were songs of heartbreak, politics, drugs and of love and fury. Their surrounding artwork was equally striking, comprising of stark and powerful graphics designed by the singer that looked somehow both sci-fi and classic.

> There was always something architectural about the Sisters. A fascination with ruined temples and other buildings permeated their imagery like on the 'Reptile House' E.P. which featured a richly textured and carved temple from Angkhor Thom, Cambodia to their video for the single 'Dominion', shot around the spectacular classically-inspired rock-cut tombs of Petra. The band located its music in ambivalent landscapes, among ruins, in places of decay, sparking the idea of reaching beyond the known and habitable to make connections through time. This spoke to me, and the music and the remains of medieval buildings where I lived, such as Bayham Abbey and Winchelsea Grey Friars Church, seemed to exist in their own exotic universe and carried a similar sense of possibility. [875]

*****

---

873 Gary Marx to John Robb.

874 Named after the 7th-century Anglian tribe, the *Peacsaetna* (‹Peak Dwellers›). The Peak District is the soggy highlands that separate Lancashire and Yorkshire.

875 Alex Woodcock (Doctor of Medieval Sculpture).

Andrew Eldritch was born Andrew William Harvey Taylor on 15 May 1959 in Ely, Cambridgeshire.

> I tended to be an introverted kid. I used to read a lot of books. I never had a normal job, either. I never did warehouse or office work. I have never had to fit into a team, although, as a band, we obliviate ourselves into the whole and become this small sniper platoon.[876]

Like his predecessors to the lizard throne, Eldritch's reinvention left few clues to his past, and he is often reluctant to discuss these matters in interviews. Reading between the lines, it appears his father was in the air force, creating the classic dislocation of the 'forces child'. This fractured instability often leaves rock n roll as the only home for the over-educated and rootless.

> When I grew up, my father was stationed all over the world. He was posted to so many places, and I went to so many different schools. It makes you very adaptable and very mobile. I'm happy with that life making coffee in plastic cups in dressing rooms and airports. I've got china in the cupboard, but I never use it. [877]

In 1978, he arrived at St John's College, Oxford, to study German Literature. One year into his course, the 19-year-old Deep Purple and Ramones fan with shoulder-length red hair moved to Leeds, where he studied Mandarin Chinese.

It was his first time in the north.

However, he dropped out after realising that part of the course entailed studying in Beijing for a year. Instead, he discovered the F Club, punk gigs and signing on the dole where dark dreams had space to fester in the late 1970s bedsit culture. It was in this hinterland between student grant and the dole queue that Eldritch was already sketching out a band as a concept.

> Before I moved to Leeds, the only time I had a band conversation was at Oxford University in the room of my best friend. The Psychedelic Furs' first album had just come out, pulling the rug from under our feet. That's what we would have sounded like if they had not already done it.
>
> I had the idea of The Sisters before I had the band. I had the t-shirt before we made a record. I didn't project it very far forward. We only planned it up to the point where we were played on the radio, and that was the job done. Then we wrote a couple of good songs, and things started to find their own direction.[878]

Stuart Green was part of the Leeds alternative scene and remembered the new face in town.

> Andrew Eldritch was a southerner who came to Leeds to study at the Uni and immediately copped off with the siren of the Leeds punk scene and Debbie Harry lookalike, Claire Shearsby, who was and remains the town's punk DJ. So there was immediately some envy directed towards him. He was, and remains, a difficult guy to know – and I'm speaking as someone who has known him from his first days in Leeds. He was super smart - he was studying Chinese, for fucks sake! And

---

876 Andrew Eldtrich to John Robb.

877 Andrew Eldtrich to John Robb.

878 Andrew Eldtrich to John Robb.

quite a cocky guy. I used to think he was plain arrogant, but the wisdom of age makes me realise that he is quite shy and also a little sociopathic.[879]

It is this dichotomy that makes Eldritch a fascinating figure. On one level, a charismatic, brooding, minimalist modern Romantic poet; on the other, a well-read, introverted aesthete using his lack of conventional musicality as a creative tool.

> I think primitively, and I have no musical training. It's the same with Peter Hook; he can't play any other songs at all, and he has the best bass riffs other than mine. Leeds is where I decided to be instinctive. It's about what my fingers play rather than my brain. My brain might want to be Mozart, but it could never be. My first guitar had two strings on it, and I remember whole days and whole nights on the floor of very sparsely furnished council house, hammering out riffs on two-string guitars and writing songs.[880]

Post-punk was about the imagination and ideas above ability with no boundaries which gave Eldritch the best platform for his imagination.

> Like most people of my generation, I was not so much changed, but enabled, by David Bowie doing 'Starman' on *Top of the Pops*, which was unbelievable. I was not enabled to be the president or a politician. There was nothing else I could do. I am committed to a life sentence of rock-ary. All I have done since punk was be in a band. Music changed me - like every other person I knew. We reacted to the world because it weighed heavily on us. Maybe this was because of the Cold War, and we didn't expect to live for long. Also, we didn't expect normal employment because half of us had no skills, and the other half didn't know how to apply our skills.[881]

Late '70s Leeds had a unique culture flux. Local music heads were entwining with the vibrant student culture of Leeds University, where lectures from former situationist and head of art, TJ Clark, helped form a powerfully creative atmosphere of genuine political discourse and a destruction of artistic boundaries that affected many bands of the era. Everyone wanted more from their culture.

> I was interested in that notion of post-punk that the music writer Simon Reynolds spoke of in his book, *Rip it Up and Start Again: Post-punk 1978-1984* where he defined the form as 'less a genre of music than a space of possibility.'
> This makes sense to me.
> As crazy as I was for punk rock, the fact was that after taking away the attitude, the speed, and the aggression, it was nothing new. Thus, it threw out a challenge to us kids. Talking Heads, Blondie, Gang of Four, PiL etc., all took their inspiration from disco and reggae and for a time, for some people, 'rock' became a dirty word. But what if it still turned you on? Our answer was what became known as goth. Unconsciously, I guess, the post-industrial landscape of Leeds, like Manchester, was also an influence as well as Bowie, Iggy, punk and glam. We had all gone for our first nights out at Bowie/Roxy clubs. With the punk scene in Leeds being so small, we regularly boarded coaches to Pips in Manchester.

879 Stuart Green to John Robb.

880 Andrew Eldtrich to John Robb.

881 Andrew Eldritch to John Robb.

There was a bit of a divide between the kids who had grown up in Leeds and the students who incubated in the scene. Gang of Four and The Mekons led the student scene. Great bands that they were, they took themselves incredibly seriously, while we were more interested in sex, speed and The Stooges and looking good. So, while the students hung around the Poly and Uni, we spent Monday nights at clubs like the Phonographique and Thursdays at The Warehouse, where an unselfconscious scene grew up around us. Aside from Joy Division - the Banshees and early Adam and the Ants were massive for us. We would roam all over the North of England, seeing both bands. Hell, some of us even went to Amsterdam to see the Banshees and The Cramps.

Influenced by all the above, the 'look' developed. There was no meeting where we all decided to grow our hair and get Cuban heels, (although I remember future Sisters bassist, Craig Adams, searching for about six months for a pair), leather trousers, waistcoats and cowboy hats, but it happened. Then a journalist, or Ian Astbury, gave us a name - 'goth'- and everyone groaned.[882]

This new scene coalesced around influential gigs signposting the road to the future.

Sex Pistols' 1976 'Anarchy' and The Clash's 1977 'White Riot' tours had played in Leeds, and they were big. Then there was the tiny basement Cellar Bar for us kids born in Leeds, and the Stars of Today club[883] in the Poly common room, promoted by students.

Total attendance? Fifty, at a pinch.

Then John Keenan started promoting at the Poly and brought all the coolest bands to town. I have great memories of early Slits, Jayne County, and the Banshees gigs. Suddenly there then seemed to be thousands of punks in Leeds. John Keenan was then kicked out of the Poly, so he started the F Club, which he kept going for five years or more, bringing everyone to the city. The F Club is where we all met and formed lifelong friendships. Interestingly at the time, there were not many punk bands proper in Leeds; the best was SOS which featured Jez Allan and Terry Lean, who went on to form, Girls at Our Best.[884]

The Siouxsie and the Banshees gig at the F club[885] on 6 December 1977 was a signpost for the new local sensibility but it was the visit of a young group from Manchester that would make the real difference. Stuart Green was one of a clutch of people who were there the night Joy Division came to town and electrified a tiny audience at the F Club at Roots in Chapeltown on 27 July 1978.

The gig was so early in their history that they were billed as ex-Warsaw. There can't have been more than thirty of us there. John Keenan used to let people in for free if they helped the bands with their gear. The first sign we were in for something special was our mates, Harty and Plumby, were raving about the soundcheck

---

882 Stuart Green to John Robb.

883 The club was where key scene driver Claire Shearsby started DJing punk records and also The Stooges album she got from Leeds library, kick-starting the scene's obsession with the band. Her eclectic playlist is arguably where the Leeds scene was sparked and inspired the dance floor and created the 'Leeds sound'. When she took a break, Eldritch would take over for a bit and 'all he ever played was Iggy Pop, David Bowie and Gary Glitter.'

884 Stuart Green to John Robb.

885 John Keenan's new night whose name stood for 'fuck the Poly'.

where Joy Division had played 'Riders on The Storm' - what you wouldn't give for a recording of that! [886]

The importance of this singular gig and their follow-up show on Oct 20 1978, in sparking something in Leeds, cannot be exaggerated.

Joy Division showed us a different way. You didn't need to change the chord for the chorus; drums and bass can be lead instruments. After the bands finished, we always gathered around the bottom of the stairs at the club entrance to discuss what we had seen. I will never forget the look on everyone's faces after each gig, eyes shining, falling over each other to try and work out what they had just seen. Andy Taylor/Eldritch was one of them, Danny from Salvation another, and two members of the new Leeds band, The Expelaires. The effect of those gigs was immediate. The Expelaires, who were the best players in town, were transformed.[887]

Eldritch himself is rather more ambivalent about the famous Joy Division gig, preferring, rightly, that The Sisters of Mercy are seen as firmly part of a new northern post-punk consensus of bands on their own terms.

I never saw Joy Division, and if I did, I don't remember it, but I loved the first album. I had their poster on the wall. We were not to the side of Joy Division; we came from the same space as them, with The Stooges, Hawkwind and Suicide as the background. We were from a similar part of the world, with similar pressures on us, and it was natural that we came up with something vaguely similar, emitting a moody vibe. There were whole swathes of the country that were making that kind of sound. In The Sisters, we called it 'the M62 sound' because of the motorway connecting us to The Teardrop Explodes, Comsat Angels and all the other bands we grew with. That part of the country is narrow, and we were on the same trains and buses; we were connected.[888]

John Keenan, a proactive presence, pushing the local scene with bands that were ahead of the curve, recalls the growing influence of Joy Division on the Leeds scene.

I liked their rough and moody approach but didn't think they would be a huge band until I saw them play at my Futurama Festival on 8 September 1979 in Leeds. The dark and echoing hall suited their music perfectly. It was then that I realised that they were a potential stadium band. The music press was then peppered with dark, atmospheric, black and white photographs of Ian Curtis and co mainly taken by Kevin Cummins[889]. It's such a shame that Ian departed before they could reach their potential.[890]

In this small scene of gigs and endless nights at the F Club, future bands revolved into each other's orbits and Gary Marx inevitably bumped into Andrew Eldritch.

My first conversation with Andrew Eldritch was at the F Club where we talked about politics. It was nothing philosophical or highfalutin – just survival stuff. I

886 Stuart Green to John Robb.

887 Stuart Green to John Robb.

888 Andrew Eldritch to John Robb.

889 The leading rock photographer of his generation, Kevin Cummins› shot of Joy Division on the bridge in Manchester framed the band forever.

890 John Keenan to John Robb.

sussed relatively early on that his views were more informed and nuanced than the average punter you'd bump into watching The Angelic Upstarts. Leeds city centre could be volatile back then, with the National Front being very active and visible, and he aligned himself with what would be seen as the arty left, personified by The Mekons and Gang of Four. That was my leaning as well, so a few flashpoints sort of threw us together.

I liked the fact that he stood his ground – mental strength rather than an action hero. He always had balls, and the more I got to know him, the other traits, like his sense of humour, started to show through.

Our backgrounds were poles apart. To me, he was posh, although I was left mainly to guess at the precise nature of his upbringing. I pieced it together from the few school photos he'd have around the place and the odd slip he'd make. In all the time I've known him, I have never heard him mention his father in any context; only once did he tell me anything about his mother. As far as I was aware, he had no contact with them as an adult.

All this points to a complicated, troubled person, but that wasn't really the 20-year-old I met; he had an easy manner about him and always liked to have a chat with the people in the corner shop.

He was not what I would ever term 'aloof'. He seemed at home in Leeds for whatever reason. I suppose the caricature became a Prince of Darkness figure. Still, whatever else was fermenting in his head, he was just the scrawny kid who had dropped out of university and always trounced me at Scrabble, and who I happened to be sharing my biscuits with.[891]

The scene was close knit. Dressing 'weird' in the late 1970s was a life-threatening affair that ran the gauntlet of the clenched fists of drunks that saw the alternative youth coalesce around a handful of pubs and clubs where the 'Tetley Bittermen'[892] didn't stray.

For years we kept clear of pubs and the town centre in general because you were taking your life in your hands if you were a punk. By 1980 we had started to frequent the Faversham pub, which, being near the Uni, was a student pub and safe; and you could walk to the Warehouse and the Phono from there.

By 1982 we ruled that pub.

Venue-wise it was The F Club in its various homes, and club-wise, it was The Phonographique on Monday nights where it was maybe 50p in and £1.50 a pint, probably less. And there was the Warehouse, of course. This was a much larger space and where Marc Almond famously worked in the cloakroom. Thursday nights might have started as a student night, but we took it over. Bands started to play. And you made sure you looked good down there.

It's important to remember that we didn't know we were creating a scene that people would still be talking about nearly forty years later. We were typically competitive kids who wanted to sound better, look cooler and do something no one else was doing. No one was holding 'goth nights'.

Amphetamine sulphate was essential; we all took too much speed. Also, John Keenan was the key with F club and his Futurama '79 festival. Ask anyone who is as old as me and was a punk in 1977 in Leeds. They will all say the same thing;

891 Gary Marx to John Robb.

892 A tongue-in-cheek nickname for beer-drinking local lads who would attack anyone dressing outside the 'norm'.

John Keenan built the playground, let us all play in it and encouraged us to the max.[893]

The omnipresent John Keenan was perfectly placed to see the whole of post-punk unfold in front of him, played out at his various gig nights.

Many people claim to have invented goth, but it was a movement that only came together in 1983. The germination of the Leeds Gothic scene started around 1980 with The Expelaires, who signed with Zoo Records[894]. They were like the house band of the F Club, and Joy Division heavily influenced them. Craig Adams, the rhythm guitarist-cum-keyboard player, then formed a Soft Cell-ist electropop duo called Exchange before becoming the bass player in The Sisters. The Expelaires guitarist, Dave Wolfenden, later joined Red Lorry Yellow Lorry and The Mission. I think the pivotal moment for Eldritch was when I put The Cramps on with Nightmares In Wax

One of the Sisters' early gigs was at Futurama 3 in 1981, where they played a 20-minute version of The Velvets' 'Sister Ray'. Also on the bill were Theatre of Hate, Bauhaus etc. so the roots of the goth scene were already in place. Several other local bands were part of that scene which I called 'Dark Wave' at the time, like The Danse Society from Barnsley and Music for Pleasure.

In the second half of 1983, around the same time as The Batcave was operating in London, I started a 'dark wave' club called The Dungeon Club at Tiffany's, which, after a few gigs, moved to The Bierkeller. The night featured dark and doomy bands (many of them interchanged with The Batcave in London) alongside rockabilly bands and reggae bands. In September 1983, I promoted my fifth Futurama Festival, which included many of these groups with the Bay City Rollers for a touch of light relief.

Howard Corry at the *Yorkshire Evening Post* asked me what the theme would be, and I jokingly replied, 'It's probably all a bit Gothic Horror.' The headline for the reviews was 'TWO DAYS IN GOTHIC CITY'. The term 'goth' became widely used after that, and Leeds became known as 'goth city'.

The Sisters became prominent in what later became the goth scene. Bands like Bauhaus, Killing Joke and Siouxsie and the Banshees were the early forerunners of that music and, I suppose, The Doors and The Velvet Underground from the previous generation. They had practically influenced everybody, including Joy Division and Echo & the Bunnymen.[895]

A thriving band scene, Futurama Festival, clubs and pubs; something was stirring in Leeds.

You had that New Romantic thing which none of us got into because we weren't really into the re-tooled disco. The Banshees, The Cramps and the Ants still influenced us. We had been brought up on Bowie and punk, and in those days, you defined who you were by how you looked. Eldritch looked like a Ramone and loved Patti Smith. He had a great collection of t-shirts and a great cassette collection which he filed in strict alphabetical order.

---

893 Stuart Green to John Robb.

894 Liverpool indie label run by Bill Drummond and David Balfe who released early cuts from The Teardrop Explodes, Echo & The Bunnymen as well as the semi-legendary 'Iggy Pop›s Jacket', by the Liverpool band Those Naughty Lumps.

895 John Keenan to John Robb.

Clothes were a big deal. The look happened gradually. I wanted a frock coat and ended up with a Nehru Jacket whilst Claire Shearsby made Andy (Eldritch) his. I remember Craig Adams searching for ages for a pair of winklepickers and walking into my room one day pissed off and saying in all seriousness: 'In the 60s, everyone wore them, so why can't I get a pair now?' [896]

Clothes, as ever in the UK, were hugely influential. In Leeds, this meant a mish-mash of lingering rock'n'roll elements with hair grown out from punk styles. The hard-to-find black drainpipe jeans were ever popular, as was the staple black leather jacket. Then there were wide-brim hats, paisley shirts (as a nod to psychedelics) and those elusive winkle pickers. It was rock but filtered through a post-punk youth who were too young for initial punk but keen to create their own aesthetic in their own city. In this flux of post-punk style and music, the Sisters coalesced to become the house band for this new Leeds. According to Leeds music writer Jane Hector Jones 'They distilled the violence and aggression of the times into something cold and hard and reptilian, but with a love and fervour for music that was absolutely born out of the club's arty anarchistic DIY.'

Yet, it was humble beginnings for the band.

It started with a group of people jamming in the basement of the Red Rhino record shop in York[897]. I was one of them. Andy (Eldritch) played the drums. I left. Gary Marx replaced me. Then the two of them went into a studio to record the first single.

The Sisters were terrible for ages. Then after a couple of years, with help from The Psychedelic Furs (another band we all loved), they turned into this amazing thing. In regard to the local sound, The Sisters articulated this best; our scene wasn't anti-rock, and we despised the term 'rockist'. Craig was unashamed in his love for Hendrix, Motörhead, and Led Zep – 'Kashmir' was a pivotal song. The Sisters wanted to create a considerable noise. And they did. They wanted to make a new kind of rock music. This is really what goth is about. It was taking cues from Bowie, punk, The Stooges, Iggy's Berlin albums, The Banshees, The Cramps, Magazine, The Furs etc. The desire was to reinvent rock music, and, in my opinion, goth music is the last great leap forward for British rock'n'roll; the last time it actually sounded new, and the Sisters' *Floodland* album would be the monument.[898]

The Sisters of Mercy filtered their music through a wide range of musical sounds and styles. The new electronic pop of the then underground The Human League and the proto-post-punk of Pere Ubu were within their dark, art rock adventures. As unlikely as it sounds, the two bands shared a key bill in Leeds.

It was just after I moved to Leeds, and I remember seeing the best gig I ever saw in my life, Pere Ubu supported by The Human League on the tiny stage of the F Club[899] where all the new bands played. I practically lived in there. That

896 Stuart Green to John Robb.

897 Key indie record shop set up in York by Tony K and his wave - ibs the main outlet for obscure and cutting edge vinyl and released a clutch of bands as well.

898 Stuart Green to John Robb.

899 Dec 7th 1978.

night is my favourite gig ever. I'm still haunted by the dual genius of it. The Human League had their screens up showing episodes of Thunderbirds and did their version of 'You've Lost That Loving Feeling', and it was hauntingly beautiful and achingly great. They reinvented music. Pere Ubu were also important to us in many ways. We didn't want to be Pere Ubu, but I loved how the trained jazz musicians in the band didn't play like jazz musicians. If I were a trained jazzo, it would be hard to play that simply.[900]

Fired up by the diet of cool gigs and kicking their ideas around, the new band now had a name that came from the soundtrack of Robert Altman's film *Mrs* (1971), which featured the Leonard Cohen song 'Sisters of Mercy' which became their handle, 'because calling ourselves 'The Captains of Industry' wouldn't have been as funny' guffaws Eldritch.

At the outset, Andrew was drumming, and both of us were having a go at playing guitar and singing. By default, Andrew proved to be the better singer, meaning I became the guitarist. Given that the models for bands with drummers who also did lead vocals represented a veritable punk hit list – 10cc, Genesis, The Eagles and The Carpenters – it was inevitable that we'd embrace the available technology of the drum machine. The extra benefits we could hardly have known at the time were that we could rehearse in Andrew's bedsit and, therefore, for free. Given his largely nocturnal lifestyle, he could stay up programming, playing and writing whatever the time was without fear of the neighbours kicking off—all very mundane but essential in keeping us going in that sprawling first year.

When we actually came to play live, that's where the drum machine revealed itself as such a master-stroke. If you play small venues or further down the bill, there's always the hassle of trying to get the sound half decent. Rather than all that messing about, setting up drums or negotiating with the bands above you to share gear, we just plugged in and pressed go. Given how chaotic everything that went over the top of the drum machine could be, it also meant the train always stayed on the tracks, and the emptiness of the stage counterpointed this relentless barrage.

I remember travelling to an early gig in York on the train to play a gig, and we only took the drum machine, our guitars, leads and a fuzz box each. We plugged straight into the PA's DI boxes, and it was job done. The sound and stripped-back look singled us out for good or bad.

We provided a model for a band with programming that wasn't just playing synth-pop. Other groups from the Leeds area soon followed suit. Andrew got really into the drum machines and writing the drum patterns, and he spent ages working out ways to chain more than one box together. Eventually, the technology improved, and we stepped up through the various models Roland brought out. I will never forget standing in Tiffany's in Leeds next to Andrew the first time we put the Roland 808[901] through a PA. We were sound-checking, and he had just programmed a drum track for our cover of '1969' complete with handclaps. It sounded immense, and the pair of us just looked at each other and burst out laughing.

900 Andrew Eldritch to John Robb.

901 Widely used the 808 was brought onto the market in 1980. It was the go to drum machine for early hip hop and its rhythmic upgrade meant percussive breaks and a powerful kick drum sound were part of its assault.

There were few sweeter moments.[902]

The Sisters had already recorded their debut single in 1980 at RicRac Studios, a small shed-like space in Wortley, a run-down industrial area south of Leeds. They sang a song each; Gary Marx on 'Watch' and Eldritch on the main track, 'The Damage Done', which was hooked around a looping guitar line taking the place of the bass because of the band's lack of equipment. This was threaded around a dirty rhythm guitar played through a cranked practice amp and some rudimentary drumming from Eldritch sounding[903] like a drum machine whilst singing in an early version of that iconic voice.

Even at this primitive stage, plenty of The Sisters of Mercy's hallmarks were in place, and Eldritch's distinctive vocal line nails the song with his haunting delivery. The single may be lo-fi and cheaply recorded, but it still has a powerful, intoxicating hint of the profound, dark mystery to come. Eldritch hates the single. Gary Marx, however, remains a little more ambivalent:

> 'The Damage Done' indeed! Listen, whatever Andrew says, it was the best record we'd ever made at the time. It was obviously overtaken by some distance as soon as we made a second one. Back then, there was a will to do, rather than a plan, as such. In that sense, it makes it more my personality driving things than Andrew's, which could be part of the reason he chooses to dismiss it. I had more energy than ideas, and Andrew just seemed happy to have found an outlet for his bedroom doodles. Listening to the single has never been the most rewarding way to pass seven minutes of your life, and it was mainly helpful in cementing our working relationship. It was almost like producing a child together and deciding to stick together to at least see it reach adulthood. The thing Andrew has cause to be most grateful for is that it gave us a reason to create the packaging and the logo[904] which obviously has long since come to represent 'Brand Eldritch'.[905]

Post single, the duo fleshed out their lineup with proper musician Craig Adams adding that distinctive heavy bass minimalism to the sparse electro primitivism of the ubiquitous Boss DR55 Dr Rhythm drum machine that gave the new band their USP.

> Craig was the only person on the Leeds punk scene with any musical training. He was his own man and had kept his hair longer than the regulation punk length. He liked Sandy Denny and loved The Stooges and Motörhead. For ages, he was known as 'Hippy Craig' but won't thank me for telling you that. He played keys in The Expelaires and then left them because he wanted to play bass like Lemmy. His bass sound defined the early Sisters, for me. He is the best bass player of his generation, and he never played two notes when one will do.[906]

---

902 Gary Marx to John Robb.

903 They borrowed the drum kit from Jon Langford of The Mekons/The Three Johns.

904 The back of the single sleeve has the iconic Sisters artwork plus font already in place and designed by Andrew Eldritch and the classic The Head & Star logo also designed by Eldritch from the "Dissection of the head, face and neck" from *Gray's Anatomy*, super-imposed on a pentacle perfect for t-shirts with its stark black and white like Ramones or Motörhead's classic logos.

905 Gary Marx to John Robb.

906 Stuart Green to John Robb.

The new trio finally played their first gig, a CND benefit, on February 16 1981. They were supporting Thompson Twins in their tribal funk pre-pop hits stage at Alcuin College in the University of York. They then made their Leeds debut at the Warehouse and a week later at the F Club of course, supporting Altered Images before spending the year honing down their sound at various local supports before the 1982 release of their second single, 'Body Electric'[907]. The single with its nod to Walt Whitmans 1855 poem, saw a big jump in quality with the distinctive drum machine dealing perfect dance floor crisscrossed with lead bass line/chiming guitar and chopping grinding guitar chassis that would come to define them with Eldritch's resonant knowing sonorous vocals of grandeur defining the song.[908]

But it was the third single, 'Alice', backed with the menacing and grindingly brilliant 'Floorshow' – a song about Le Phono club which broke through. Fleshing out the lineup with the addition of Ben Gunn[909] on the second guitar the song was an instant underground hit with the combination of deft writing, magnetic croon, and a lingering darkness that made The Sisters of Mercy the band of the moment. It put the spotlight on the band who were celebrating and deconstructing rock, who were as much Brecht as Alvin Stardust, and as much TS Eliot as The Glitter Band. They dared to embrace all culture and combine the gonzoid with the intellectual on the shivering exquisite 'Alice', which took ten minutes to write in Eldritch and Claire Shearsby's then flat, and transformed the band.

> Andrew often cites 'Alice' as the real gear change, and of course, it was in all sorts of ways but probably most specifically for him. I remember its birth being slightly different to previous songs. Typically, if Andrew was working on something, you'd hear him endlessly playing the guitar line and looking for whatever variations to piece together a loose song structure. In those early days, we had no home studio facilities beyond the most basic cassette recorder.
>
> Around that time, Andrew had befriended a couple of guys in the Psychedelic Furs after a 1981 gig in Huddersfield and had demoed 'Alice' with their guitarist John Ashton using his gear, which was super hi-tech as far as we were concerned. My memory is that he stayed with John in London and came back with this completely new song mainly formed – even the rough demo sounded fantastic. Unlike other earlier tunes where Andrew wanted help, or I instantly felt like there was something I could add here or there, this was a complete take. John was duly given the producer role for a trip to KG studios in Bridlington to record it correctly, and my memories of the sessions are that it was all a breeze. I think John may have come up to Yorkshire with a car full of kit and finished the home recording. He was a top bloke and vastly different from our prior experience working with an outside producer like on 'Body Electric' where the producer wasn't really our choice, and we'd clashed and wasted time pursuing his ideas and bowing to his supposedly superior knowledge. I think Craig came close to punching him more than once.

---

907 Released on Jon Langford's CNT label.

908 The band now had stage names Ben Matthews became Ben Gunn in a nod to Treasure Island, Mark Pearman mixed glam rock and socialism to be branded Gary Marx, Andy Taylor mixed sci-fi with high brow for Andrew Eldritch which is also from an Old English word used to describe the otherworldly, weird, ghostly, and the drummer got the best name of them all, Doktor Avalanche.

909 AKA Benjamin Matthews.

Because the demo for 'Alice' had been so good, the recording process was very relaxed. It's a track with real strength in its core ingredients and didn't need any overdubs. I spent more time on the other main track, 'Floorshow' which represents the peak of the Mark One Sisters as an entity for me, but there's no doubt it was that opening hi-hat pattern from 'Alice' that followed me around the nightclubs for the next few years.[910]

Ever restless, 1983's follow-up, *The Reptile House* EP, was a daring work which pulled back from the floorshow anthems, creating a sparse and brooding cinematic soundscape. The brooding bass and cimmerian space that surrounds the tracks created a unique and powerful atmosphere that Gary Marx saw as his singer's first truly personal project.

Andrew was someone who naturally wanted to assume that controlling role. It didn't bother me, and it was perhaps most evident within the confines of the studio environment. *The Reptile House* was his pet project, really. He still didn't have the studio know-how to get the more up-tempo stuff right which was very evident with the next release, 'Anaconda', but given the space and the dirge-like quality of most of that set of songs, he was in his element. He could whack up the reverbs and delays and indulge himself. As for songs, the collection is a bit flimsy but as a set of atmospheric soundscapes, it's great, and I love the production. Some of them were things we hadn't done or didn't go on to do, live, so there wasn't a significant input from us as a group on those sessions. In a more standard career, it would have been seen as an Eldritch solo release, I suppose, but he has always loved that idea of it being The Sisters, this renegade organisation. Ben[911] took it as a personal affront, being restricted to his one or two guitar parts across the five songs, forming part of that little power struggle. Sadly, there was only going to be one outcome to that particular fight.[912]

One of the hallmarks of the Sisters was their love of cover versions, where the band would take unlikely songs and unzip them, finding hidden undercurrents in their perceived pop banality.

Our songs are set in a wider world, I think. We definitely project onto a worldview that is invariably mine. Often the times don't matter. You just represent yourself with your worldview. Most songs are just 'boy meets girl, whilst with our songs, it's true there was also a lot of 'boy meets girl, but someone got stabbed'. Some people live in a much smaller world, and they can't see beyond someone getting pregnant and wanting a mortgage, but that has never been in my world.
We covered Hot Chocolate's 'Emma' to say to the press, who were accusing us of being a 'goth band' because of my baritone, that here is a song that you would dismiss as pop, yet it is as full of angst, suicide and darkness as anything we could do.
With The Sisters of Mercy, there was no plan. We would certainly have done it differently if it had been done properly. I would probably be like the person from The Darkness or Freddie Mercury, more confident and flamboyant, and would have written fewer words in the songs because it's hard to sing too many words.

910 Gary Marx to John Robb.

911 The latest addition to the lineup Ben Gunn was in the band from 1981 to 1983 and left after recording 'Temple Of Love'.

912 Gary Marx to John Robb.

To make it easier for myself, I should have written songs like Depeche Mode and go 'ah huh' every now and then.

The songs I am proudest of paint the most complete picture with the fewest words, an engaging picture with very few strokes of the palette knife. I'm probably frightened by prose, people who write rock n roll and punk rock are particularly utterly inept, yet it can still be great. I'm also very fond of instrumentals. I'm a massive fan of John Carpenter.[913] He paints a similarly engaging and complete worldview with very few strokes of his palette knife.[914]

Very much in the driving seat and with this vision, Eldritch was stretching in different directions, but the band's curious chemistry was already primed to boil over.

The band was a democracy and it helped that Craig was uncomplicated and undemanding in what he expected from his involvement. Providing he was left to make an unearthly racket, he was usually pretty happy. Andrew and I had already had time to feel our way into a way of working, an understanding that allowed him to occupy the driving seat for long stints without me feeling the need to grab the wheel. The problems primarily arose from having a fourth member – it didn't seem to matter who that extra person was; we always encountered problems. Who knows what would have happened if I'd learned to play the guitar to a level of competence where I didn't need someone to cover for me sooner?[915]

The first of those fourth members, Ben Gunn, left in the autumn of 1983, just as The Sisters of Mercy were establishing their sound with their just recorded 'Temple Of Love' single. The release saw them construct their biggest anthem yet with its glowering atmosphere and enormous chorus and a song that rereleased ten years later would become their biggest hit. Replacing Gunn was a Liverpool gun for hire.

What happened was that Dead or Alive, who I was playing with in Liverpool, had signed to CBS and were making an album, and I left. CBS was talking to Andrew about the Sisters, and Andrew mentioned that they needed a new guitarist, and they told him, 'You should try out this guy from Liverpool'. So, I went over to meet them, and we chopped up some lines, smoked cigarettes and talked crap about football and music, and they offered me the job of playing the guitar!

Andrew gave me a pre-release of the then upcoming 'Temple of Love' single, which was all right, but then I turned it over and played their version of the Stones classic, 'Gimme Shelter', and then I thought 'Oh yeah, I like this', that was what sold me on the idea of joining the Sisters. Being in Liverpool, all my contemporaries had chart hits, so I didn't pay much attention to the indie charts and all I knew of them was that I had a girlfriend who liked that kind of music, and I heard things in nightclubs which were not called goth clubs at the time.[916]

Now on board, Wayne Hussey brought his unique, melodic touch and 12-string sensibilities to the sound that could be first heard on the new 'Body And Soul' single that was the band's first hit proper. The new guitarist helped to precipitate a move

---

913 American filmmaker, screenwriter, and composer. Carpenter's films are characterised by minimalist lighting and photography, static cameras and his distinctive synthesised scores.

914 Andrew Eldritch to John Robb.

915 Gary Marx to John Robb.

916 Wayne Hussey to John Robb.

away from the stark post-punk landscapes and threaded baroque melodies and a more trad rock twist into the Sisters sound.

> I don't think there was any kind of consciousness about what we were doing and how we would sound – not on my part, anyway. I didn't come in there intending to change the sound. That was something that happened organically. I just played the way I played with my 12-string guitar, which changed the sound of the Sisters. As a band, it was a weird set up. Gary and Andrew lived in the same house, and they wouldn't talk to each other, so me and Craig ended up being the conduits between them.
>
> I had only been with them five weeks, and I was on the tour bus with Craig and Gary, and they said, 'We want to leave. We don't want to work with Andrew anymore. Do you want to come with us?' I said, 'Hang on a minute. I've only just joined, and I'd rather stick to this for the time being.'
>
> It's no secret that Andrew and I didn't get on. I was the antithesis of Andrew. I'm talking about thirty years ago, and he may have changed. Andrew is very educated. He thinks first before he does anything. I was an animal of instinct, and, at that point, I was very hedonistic and living the lifestyle. I loved being on tour. Initially, it worked between us, and that tension produced good stuff – listen to 'Marianne' or 'Black Planet' – it worked, but life's too short to have to live with the tension all the time. [917]

Despite all this and now signed to a major, the band somehow recorded with a difficult gestation, the 1985 debut album proper *First and Last and Always* that hints cryptically at Eldritch's long-term relationship breakup. The album is considered a classic of the form and was the release that finally changed everything,

> I suppose the album broke the band in both senses, but I would never blame that on anyone's perfectionism. Andrew had become the sole manager of the group after periods earlier in the band's life when either we'd shared the role or we had drafted people in to 'man the office'. This had a two-fold effect; firstly, it created mistrust between all of us over financial matters. More importantly, in terms of the actual music, it meant Andrew hadn't written any new songs. He had immersed himself in this managerial role, wading through legal papers and living out some weird parallel life where he talked to International Corporations all day. He maintained that we should book the studio and, once locked away inside, he would be able to rattle off material without a problem.
>
> So began the process; firstly in Stockport at Strawberry Studios[918] and later in Goring-on-Thames. The band worked on backing tracks with producer David M Allen[919] through the day while Andrew either slept or scribbled down ideas. An engineer was kept on call 24 hours a day in case Andrew wanted to work on something when the stars aligned. Within two or three weeks, the bulk of the music was recorded, but still little or no sign of lyrics from Andrew. While most of the Sisters' lyrics were Andrew's, I had contributed in the past, so I offered a few ideas to tracks that were already taking good shape – even going so far as to

---

917 Wayne Hussey to John Robb.

918 The studio opened by 10CC and was named after The Beatles' Strawberry Fields and where Joy Division recorded most of their work.

919 English producer working in Gothic, electronic and indie who worked with The Cure, The Sisters of Mercy, The Chameleons, Depeche Mode, The Mission, The Associates, The Human League and many others.

record rough guide vocals to try things out. Andrew didn't feel able to use the lyrics, which in itself wasn't a problem, but as time wore on and no alternative was offered, tensions arose. Again, it was partly because there were financial implications for all of us over who wrote material; publishing royalties were suddenly up for grabs. Whereas in the indie label phase of the band, all money made was put back in to make the next thing we did bigger and better.

When slowly, snippets of Andrew's half-formed ideas began to emerge, there was a feeling that lyrically and melodically, they were nothing like the standard we'd come to expect from him. We were faced with the prospect of saying 'yes' to his ideas, which we didn't necessarily think were doing the tracks justice or delaying the album's completion indefinitely.

On top of that, you were effectively saying, 'here's tens of thousands of pounds for you, as well for making a bollock of my song.' The longer it went on, the worse the situation became. The rest of the band and the producer became irritable and disinterested. As the supposed delivery date for the album drew ever nearer, Andrew's behaviour became increasingly worrying.

He was taking more significant quantities of speed to squeeze extra hours out of every day, but still, the results were limited. This particularly vicious circle continued until, one night at Genetic studios, I was told he wanted to perform a vocal and would I sit in the control room as I usually did whenever he sang for real. Throughout the band's life, whoever else was present, it was usually down to me to say how a vocal take was going. After he mumbled a few lines, he came into the control room, ricocheting off the walls as he entered, and at that point, I told him the sessions were over, we were pulling the recording, and the album would not be completed as promised.

He argued briefly but then said the decision was on my head and that I would have to tell the record company – it has a habit of making me sound overly noble and heroic when I recount this part of the tale. Still, in reality, it was a simple decision. He was my friend, and he was ill. I could see us completing an album on time and it being sub-standard, with Andrew suffering an even bigger breakdown as a result. What was the point? I wasn't a slave working for WEA. What was the fucking point?[920]

The band were now fracturing over various fault lines. Would they split? Who would work with who? Would the situation resolve? In this situation of creative tension, working methods can be unconventional.

We had a 4-track recorder portastudio, and I worked on songs that I would give to Andrew on tapes, and he would like some songs, not others. It was the same with Gary Marx and Craig – they would have a go, and Andrew would have his own thing.

Andrew would work through the night, and I would work through the day. We had two engineers and Dave M. Allen, also switching between night and day – the poor lad! I remember one day I had some spare time, and I had this new thing that became 'Marianne', and I did the whole thing – guitars and the bass. Andrew came in and said, 'what have you done today?' I played it and he said, 'I don't like this much. It sounds like the Banshees', and I thought, whatever, and I returned to the hotel. The next morning, I came in, and Andrew was not there,

---

920 Gary Marx to John Robb.

and we got the tapes up, and he had finished the vocal on both songs, and they sounded great.

I know Andrew is not fond of that period of the band. He doesn't play songs from that time; if he does, they are unrecognisable, which is fair enough; that's his artistic choice. But for me, there was beauty built out of that tension. But it's not a way of life I like living, to be honest. We didn't get on. I know I annoyed him, and the feeling was mutual![921]

Finally finished, the album was a hit and captured the curious alchemy of the band well. Somehow, *First and Last and Always* hung together, and the songs worked, despite their unconventional recording and construction. The opening track, 'Black Planet,' is a perfect chiming slice of melancholic baroque pop. 'Marianne' is a darkly beautiful creation, full of tension and melody; it remains a perfect piece of lugubrious pop, where each party plays to their strengths. Wayne Hussey's guitar chassis is coated with a captivating magic, and Eldritch's perfect, shimmering vocal delivers a poetic emotion drenched melody, whilst songs like 'Walk Away' further underline the sense of heartache and sadness. The foreboding doom-laden baritone of Eldritch creates the album's overarching atmosphere, and the chiming 12 string guitar, rococo melodies and swooping choruses make a captivating whole. Despite the incessant drama, the album went top twenty and enjoyed worldwide success. There was an audience waiting to embrace their new and quixotic music. The recording may have been a strange world of fleeting shifts and high tension, but life on the road was a different affair.

There are a million stories but being on tour was easier, even if it meant the band were together all the time, but you find your own space despite bust-ups and a lot of booze and drugs being involved. Out on the road, there were clashes, and at times I would drunkenly leave the band or find myself waking up in some strange bedroom and thinking, 'What happened last night!' and then remember that I had left the group and would have to say, 'Please take me back!'[922]

It was great though and we were really good live. The thing that held the band together was actually the drum machine. When Craig and I played, we played slightly ahead of the beat because of the speed we were taking, and it was quite an interesting style that really evolved.[923]

Despite worldwide acclaim and big album sales, Wayne Hussey knew that the band's innate tension was always going to catch up with them.

The situation between Andrew and Gary Marx became increasingly uncomfortable to the point where Andrew gave Craig and me an ultimatum, 'It's Gary Marx or me!'

Me and Craig were road dogs who lived for going on tour, and we were really looking forward to it, but then Andrew said to me, 'Ok, it's your job to tell Gary to leave because you were the last to join the band!' and I had to call and tell Gary

921 Wayne Hussey to John Robb.

922 Wayne Hussey to John Robb.

923 Wayne Hussey to John Robb.

he was out of the group. To this day, people blame me for kicking Gary out of the band, but I was just the messenger.[924]

Gary Marx's last gig was at the Top Rank, Brighton on April Fool's Day 1985 before filming The Old Grey Whistle Test a few days later and then he was gone. At the end of the tour Wayne had gone as well.

We had carried on touring, and we even did the Albert Hall[925]. We were then planning to do a second album. I had done a bunch of tunes on my portastudio in Hamburg, where I was staying for a month with Andrew, working on the new album. He didn't like any of my new tunes. Fair enough, but they were good songs like 'Wasteland', 'Sacrilege', 'Severina' and 'Witches Brew', which would go on to make up the bulk of the eventual debut album of The Mission. Andrew was giving me very skeletal songs – drum machine patterns and a very primitive bass line and saying, 'Can you work with that for me?' This was difficult because I couldn't feel enough movement in the bass. It was a frustrating time. Then we went back to Leeds, and I started rehearsing with Craig, and on the first day of rehearsal, I said, 'The Andrew stuff is fucking rubbish, and I'm leaving.' We continued for an hour or two, and we decided to find a new singer for our songs which ended up on the first Mission album.[926]

Gary Marx remains philosphical.

It's easy to paint Wayne as the villain of the piece, given that the band imploded so soon after his arrival, but as I've said, it was more to do with a
fourth member messing with that equilibrium. It mattered not whether it
was Ben or Wayne, really. Only the nature of the clashes changed; who
bore the brunt and how much was at stake.

What differed with Wayne's arrival was that he was a very capable musician, so Andrew finally had someone who could do things he couldn't. That undoubtedly excited Andrew, at least on one level, and clearly had implications for me as the band's most ardent non-muso.

While I agree that Wayne brought in all these extra textures and flourishes, I happened to love the black and white of the earlier sound. Gang of Four were among the best bands I ever saw, and their guitarist, the late Andy Gill was the main focus for me – there are traces of his influence on the earliest things I did with Andrew, but that was mostly born of necessity rather than design. I'd do those sorts of dissonant stabs or bash the guitar and it was more a compositional necessity than any adherence to a modernist agenda.

What also changed was that Wayne had come from a chart band background. He was used to having an allowance for stage clothing and being extremely image conscious. His arrival meant there was an element of competition for Andrew, for the first time, of who would be the most recognisable face of the band. This was something of no interest to two punk kids like Craig and myself. Wayne also loved the idea of playing the rock star, which meant the drinking and drugs escalated, especially on the road.

The added pressure Andrew was under, as this prominent cult figure by then, and the fact that Wayne, as he later proved, was perfectly capable of being successful

924 Wayne Hussey to John Robb.

925 The Wake gig at the Albert Hall was on June 18th 1985.

926 Wayne Hussey to John Robb.

without him, pulled the four of us every which way over that brief time, but we managed to hold it together. Would the three of us set up on our own and leave Andrew to be the solo artist he seemed destined to be? Would Andrew cut his ties with the punk past and enjoy this technicolour future with Hussey as his cowboy-hatted partner and the only musician actually worth hiring?[927]

Post Sisters and free of the tension, Gary Marx formed his own band, Ghost Dance:

I don't think it could be said that I had a plan after the Sisters beyond inviting Anne Marie Hurst from Skeletal Family[928] to sing the songs because I knew and liked her. It quickly made sense to my mind, at least, to help put some distance between the Sisters and me in one key aspect of what we did was with a woman singer.

The music was going to come out somewhere near the stuff I'd just done on *First and Last and Always* because that was how I played, and I didn't know any other way of playing. I wasn't really in a position to say, 'I'll go funk now' because I didn't have the musical chops. The initial lineup was a trio with a drum machine – that made sense to me. That fourth member thing was probably still at the forefront of my thinking.

I had been a 20-year-old idealist when the Sisters kicked off. By the time I formed Ghost Dance, all sorts of external factors were in play, and my motivation wasn't always so clear-cut. I was conscious of picking up a reputation within certain parts of the industry for being a trouble-causer. I foolishly went out of my way to try and be obliging for a while. I think if The Mission hadn't been a runaway success and the Sisters Mark II had bombed, things could have been different and the path I took with the band might have been less overtly commercial. In that first year or so, that wasn't so much a factor, and I was happy to be back in a band, writing songs, recording and releasing them without stressing too much. I was pleased for the group to grow up in public similar to when the Sisters had released 'The Damage Done. [929]

Post Sisters breakout, Yorkshire in the 1980s was the epicentre of a surge of bands. Leeds was full of future faces. Some, like Marc Almond, who had moved from Southport to be at college in the city, had been at the core of the scene Djing before forming Soft Cell. His aesthetic black clad image and the duo's Suicide style lineup were forged in Leeds and its particular obsessions. Their mix of electro, northern soul, and a nocturnal melancholy with a dark sexiness was a perfect parallel to goth while their dramatic songs were also locked into the floorshow.

Being in Leeds at that time was a big part of it, of course, and we also had this five year art school background studying performance art and films at college in Leeds. This is what Soft Cell grew out of and where I first met David Ball who had moved there from Blackpool. [930]

927 Gary Marx to John Robb.

928 Skeletal Family were from Keighley and formed from the ashes of local punk band The Elements. They took their name from the title of the song 'Chant of the Ever Circling Skeletal Family' from the 1974 David Bowie album *Diamond Dogs* and had released two studio albums *Burning Oil* (1984) and *Futile Combat* (1985).

929 Gary Marx to John Robb.

930 Marc Almond to John Robb.

Yet, it was also the faded grandeur of his seaside background that played into his narrative:

> I didn't realise till later on that working as a stagehand in Southport theatre and getting to meet all these northern pantomime impresarios and strange theatrical characters would be so influential. It was the real tail end of that variety world and it became a part of my psyche. The first Soft Cell album resonates with that culture. I also loved northern soul, which was a staple of that part of north.[931]

Another child of the revolution, Marc, was a glam kid in a new darker world. After hearing Marc Bolan on the John Peel show in 1970, he had even changed his name. The sequinned glitz and esoteric outer space imagery seemed oddly familiar to someone who had grown up in the showbiz-stained world of a seaside town, and even now, there are traces of that era reflected in his music.

> The '70s were my time with people like Jobriath[932] and that sense of musical theatre I loved. Look at all the amazing musical changes then: rock at the beginning, then progressive, then glam and Bowie and Bolan coming along and changing your world. Bowie told you about Lou Reed, Iggy Pop and Jean Genet. After that, it was punk and post-punk, then disco and then the electronic disco of Giorgio Moroder and then the post-punk disco thing. In Soft Cell, we had all those seventies references. I'm really a child of those times though I don't know how to categorise my music. People say 'cabaret pop', but I never know what to call it. New romantic, for me, was punk and glam rock reinvented with an electronic, futuristic slant.
> When 'Tainted Love' was a massive hit in 1983, I felt we had lost our way. It was great to have that enormous hit, but I thought it was essential for us to move on and, although Dave might not have agreed, to commit commercial suicide. We could have ended up being stuck with that gang of bands from the eighties, always being known as one of those. We had to move out of that. That's why I did the Mambas and worked with Nick Cave and Lydia Lunch[933]

The new Leeds was throbbing with skewed guitars and drum machines. Cassandra Complex were a stimulating local outfit that found a success in Europe with their own take on the new sound. Singer Rodney Orpheus paints a picture of prime time Leeds.

> Nowadays, people think of the term 'post-punk' as being something positive and exciting, but then it was more like a moan: 'Oh, punk's over, and we missed all the excitement.' But, at the time, if you walked around Headingley on a sunny afternoon, you'd literally hear music coming out of a basement rehearsal space on every single street. If you had asked anyone then what the 'Leeds sound' was, that was easy - it was fuzz guitars and a drum machine, and a shared love of The Velvet Underground, The Stooges, Hawkwind, and Suicide.
> I remember walking from my house on Ashville Avenue to our basement studio on Victoria Road one day. On the way, I bumped into Wayne Hussey (who lived on the same street), heard Red Lorry Yellow Lorry tuning up, and caught the end

---

931 Marc Almond to John Robb.

932 The great lost star of glam rock who had the image and the hype but not the required songs.

933 Marc Almond to John Robb.

of a Three Johns session (they lived next door to our studio). Then afterwards, I went down to the Faversham for a drink with Andrew Eldritch.

What a time to be alive! [934]

Deep in the heart of the Sisters inner circle were The March Violets. They met at Leeds University in 1981, where band leader Simon Denbigh shared a house with Craig Adams. Denbigh was considering putting together his own drum-machine-led band, but with the added twist of dual male and female vocals. He was already a key part of the Sisters' experience, mainly through being the 'nurse' to Doktor Avalanche, and his musical and technical abilities had been a key part of the band's development over the years.

With The March Violets, he quickly constructed his own combination of dark irony, hard rock and acidic punk. The band produced several influential records in the period fronted by the twin vocal attack of himself and Rosie Garland[935]. This charismatic combination saw their early singles released by Eldritch on his Merciful Release label. Singles such as 'Snake Dance' and 'Walk Into The Sun' were cult classics on the burgeoning scene and became firm John Peel favourites. Forged in glam and fired up by punk, Simon Denbigh was another aesthetic-driven child of the 1970s whose adventures in the Leeds post-punk scene bore strange fruit:

> Pre-punk, I danced to Mud, The Sweet, T. Rex and Bowie at the youth club disco. I liked Iggy, The Velvets and Hot Chocolate. Punk changed me, and that was it forever. I went to some very early punk gigs and bought some 7" singles: New Rose, Spiral Scratch and Anarchy, as well as stuff by The Vibrators and The Boys. John Peel made me the man I am. He was one of the most incredible things for British music ever. Look what's happened now that he's gone. The whole thing's collapsed.
>
> I'd always wanted to do something different with male and female vocals; at the time, there was only Meatloaf or Peters And Lee doing it! I didn't want a backing singer. I wanted a partner at the front. The drum machine came from rehearsing and realising it was convenient. The Dr Rhythm I used was the first programmable drum machine. It only had four sounds in it and no midi, and it ran on batteries. Earlier bands like Suicide were quite laid back with their drum machine sound-wise, whereas we were trying to do it more punk speed, so it had to be fast, 160 BPM.[936]

The Three Johns had a scuffed Dr. Martens in both Leeds camps[937] whilst creating their own distinct style birthed in the vibrant atmosphere of the pubs like the Fenton and the Faversham, where post-punk idealism and politics were part of the smoky air. Live, they were great fun. Their drum machine seemed as pissed as they were as they bumbled around like three bamboozled bees, fired by cheap booze and high ideals.

---

934 Rodney Morpheus to John Robb.

935 Now a novelist of some renown.

936 Simon Denbigh interview with Classic Rock.

937 Guitarist Jon Langford was in The Mekons whilst being friends with the early Sisters and lending them equipment.

Somehow their alcohol-stained surrealism made complete sense. There was a method to their madness—a purity to their idiot savant genius where art brawled with politics and whiplash chords. The Three Johns may not have had the aesthetic napalm of Gang Of Four, whose brilliant songs were frequently discussed and dissected with a white-hot political intellectualism. But with Jon Langford's skewed blues guitar and John Hyatt's Bolan-esque vocals, they produced a glam tinged, Beefheart-glued vision of artful madness that was equally compelling. Their musical output was driven by the now familiar drum machine that gave the nod to a Gothic backdrop combined with Gang Of Four's post-punk shrapnel. John Hyatt, the band's singer, was central to the Leeds post-punk ferment and ponders the city's idiosyncratic take on the new noise:

> We spoke our greatest truths as jokes, and our jokes, with a straight face, and it could get chaotic. I would be standing at the back screaming, "Oh God, oh God", whilst bassist, Brenny tanned Langford's backside with his bass whilst Langy shouted, "Spank me with your typewriter!"
> I am pleased to say The Three Johns never fitted in. This was problematic in terms of getting critical attention because we needed to fit into a categorisation. We didn't help, though, as we played the part of being Karl Marx speaking through the Marx Brothers.[938]

This northern family of noise had further participants. Formed in the early 1980s, Red Lorry Yellow Lorry were scene pioneers, crossing classic underground rock'n'roll with the adventure of Wire and the revolutionary rock of the MC5, The Stooges and brooding drones. Their tight, claustrophobic sound, with dark, foreboding vocals and guitars switched from fuzzy to glacial, and clicked in razor tight-time with the omnipresent Yorkshire drum machine. They created an electronic death disco clatter that stopped the band from tipping over into Trad Rock, remaining allied to the heavy, post-punk bass and the innate darker hues that made these bands so compulsive.

Red Lorry Yellow Lorry's propulsive, powerful rock was signed to Red Rhino and their debut single, 'Beating My Head', was picked up by John Peel and kick-started a run of singles that were indie chart top fives. This established the band as big underground favourites. Their debut album, *Talk About The Weather*, was their creative and commercial highpoint and the best document of the band's sound and cemented their large cult following.

West Yorkshire was full of these leather-jacketed droogs with their guitars and drum machines, drinking and speeding in the Faversham and sometimes becoming yet another band adding to the distinctive geographical sound. There was a whole new ecosystem of scene bands – like Salvation, who formed in 1983, bonding over a love of Lou Reed's Metal Machine Music, Cabaret Voltaire and drum machines. The singer was Danny Horigan, who roadied for The Sisters and sang under the name Danny Mass. They played their debut gig in 1985 and dealt a self-styled psychedelic

---

938 John Hyatt to John Robb.

goth sound, picking up on the non-paisley sonic patterns of Leeds' post-punk. Their first release was on the Sisters' Merciful Release label, delivering their definitive *Diamonds Are Forever* album in 1987. Decades later, Salvation are still with us, a visceral reminder of that early 1980s time zone. Yet more Faversham regulars, Rose Of Avalanche were, yet again, John Peel-approved dark noise that coalesced around two big indie chart singles 'LA Rain' and 'Goddess' and would peak with their second album, *First Avalanche,* released in 1986.

Growing up in Keighley, Skeletal Family were another of the Yorkshire dark diaspora. Initially sparked by glam rock, the band were further proof of the power and reach of 1970s David Bowie inspiring youth in far flung corners of the UK. Even the name of the band was a homage to Ziggy. Taken from the song, 'Chant Of The Ever Circling Skeletal Family' from Bowie's 1974 *Diamond Dogs* album.

Forming from the remnants of local punk bands they swiftly built up a following with songs like the haunting 'She Cries Alone', the punky rushes of 'Promised Land' and the brooding dark baroque pop of 'So Sure' all given a distinctive power with unexpected chord changes and Anne-Marie Hurst's powerful vocal.

Their debut, *Burning Oil*, album was released by the key York based indie label, Red Rhino who were based at the record shop of the same name. A snapshot of darker post-punk it was number one in the indie album charts in August 1984. Signing to Chrysalis the band then released Restless and Just a Minute before they began to unravel with Anne-MarieHurst joining up with the fresh out of the Sisters, Gary Marx in his new Ghost Dance project.

Band bassist Roger 'Trotwood' Nowell pinpoints how deeply embedded glam was in their psyche.

> Glam was were it all started. When I was around 11, my mates and me went camping in the woods at the top of the village. There was probably 6 of us and we took a radio which we had on all day. Alice Cooper's 'Schools Out' and David Bowie's 'Life on Mars' were getting their fair share of plays. I fell head long into music after that - the heavier side of things. I would wear a great coat and have an album under my arm, taking the piss out of the soul boys at school/youth club. Then punk arrived via Sounds, NME and Melody Maker. It was at the time when I was about to leave school and the country was pretty fucked up. Everyone was offering job advice for my future. What future?

Punk seemed to bring everyone together. For us The Cure, Banshees and the Clash had survived the first round of punk and were then being joined by new bands like Killing Joke, Joy Division, Bauhaus, The Bunnymen. Then there was Southern Death Cult, The Sisters of Mercy, March Violets, Sex Gang Children, Theatre of Hate and us of course! being added to the mix. This to me was the real second wave of Punk.

Like so many of their generation it was punk that gave the band the energy and the stage to create their own culture.

> We were the kids who went out and bought guitars after punk and formed bands. They were great times, no job, records in the indie chart and touring round Europe doing what we loved doing. We didn't have any money and we didn't really care.

I don't know why Yorkshire or Leeds was such a hot bed at the time. Liverpool, Manchester always had good bands, as did Glasgow. Until then Kiki Dee and Smokie were the best Bradford had to offer. Maybe it was down to people like Nick Toczek[939] in Bradford or Richard Rouska in Leeds who did his fanzine. So even if you didn't make Sounds and the music press people still could find out who you were.

Adding to this bubbling gene pool was the fracturing Sisters mothership. In November 1985, Wayne Hussey, still in Leeds, was now enjoying his freedom from The Sisters of Mercy and began searching for potential vocalists to front his new project. He considered Johnny Copson from The Expelaires, Simon Denbigh, Peter Murphy and Sal Solo before Craig Adams suggested Hussey himself should step up to the mic. 'Craig said, 'You're better looking than me, and you can sing.' I'd done backing vocals before and sung in the school band in Bristol, so it was not alien to me,' he remembers.

With a settled lineup, Hussey and Adams were initially mooted to be calling their new band The Sisterhood, despite both sides in the great schism agreeing not to use the Sisters' name. Eldritch kiboshed this with a hastily recorded release with James Ray on vocals as Eldritch could not contractually appear. 'Giving Ground' was released under the same name, on the same day, as Wayne Hussey and Craig Adam's debut show in London, forcing them to a last-minute name change. Settling on the name of The Mission, the phoenix rising from the ashes started to find its own ground.

> We already had an audience, which was quite intimidating and it took a lot of speed and drinking to have the nerve to play. We did the support tour with The Cult because Billy Duffy was my best friend at the time. We had no money, and they took us on their bus, which was very generous of them. I found my feet when we played Birmingham Powerhouse as The Mission. That night, how can I say? I lost myself entirely in the role of being a singer for the first time. That was the changing point for me and really when I started to grow into it.[940]

The Mission would become one of the biggest bands on the scene, releasing a run of successful albums that followed their 1986 *God's Own Medicine* debut. The album set the staple for their melodramatic, melodic anthems, with Mick Brown from Red Lorry Yellow Lorry replacing the drum machine. Produced by Tim Palmer, who Wayne Hussey knew from his Dead or Alive days, the album swiftly broke through with its mix of Gothic darkness and Trad Rock stylings and a keen ear for a pop hook.

The follow-up albums continued their penchant for a chiming epic crafted songwriting that bridged the gap between Echo & The Bunnymen and the gothier end of post-punk. 1988's *Children* and 1990's *Carved in Sand* both reached top ten status in the UK. This was all off the back of a run of hit singles which saw Hussey's knack for natural melody reach its triumphant peak. The band also developed a reputation

---

939 Key punk and post punk promoter in Leeds
940 Wayne Hussey to John Robb.

for a daredevil rock'n'roll approach to life which created a legacy of legendary tales of hedonism. Hussey's loveable and roguish charm made them approachable to a big audience whilst still retaining a certain whiff of the dark stuff.

> We lived it 24/7 for the first couple of years. It was pretty intense. All the people I knew took drugs for fun, not because they were oppressed or emotionally sick. When we did the third album, the band was divided into three camps: the drinking camp, the 'making spliffs' camp, and the fast drug camp. When you're not in the same mind space anymore, it becomes... not together. When Simon Hinkler left the group mid-tour, I was coughing blood. I was in a bad way, so I went to the Herefordshire countryside, lived in a barn, and stayed there for a year recuperating.[941]

Meanwhile, the post-split Eldritch was not wasting any time and was now working on *Floodland*, later seen by many as his masterpiece. Initially composed and recorded by the singer with virtually no assistance from anybody else, it was an ambitious and groundbreaking work and, for many, marks the zenith of the Sisterly orbit.

The true masterstroke was bringing in Jim Steinman to produce the album. The producer, who had made his name with Meatloaf, was noted for his grandiose production and huge sonic vistas. His appointment raised eyebrows as his style differed from the Sisters' dark minimalism, but he soon turned out to be the perfect choice to realise Eldritch's soundscape vision.

> Sometimes I made a Sisters record where no one else mentally and physically showed up. Sometimes the lineup puts in a lot of input, which I like. I like it when the lads and lasses in the band have been good enough to say that they can't work with this bit or that bit and get involved. Musicians are a funny breed, aren't they? They have an innate misunderstanding of the relationship between power and responsibility, so some learn the easy way, and some never learn. Some people are unilaterally irresponsible and are the only ones sad enough to do the same job. Most people in the real world don't do one job for that long. We have done pretty well working in the Sisters – some people have gone off to do better, and some people have left and think that they hate me, but in many ways, it's a mirror held up to themselves.[942]

Demo-ed in his new home in Hamburg on sequencers and computers, *Floodland* was a continuation of the technology, dark rock and baroque that had always been at the core of the Sisters' genius. Steinman's eventual tsunami-size production helped to create the masterpiece. With many of the songs unintentionally themed around water, personal grievances and the recent band split, Eldritch's intellectual prowess is plastered over the release that billows with ominous power and the shivering dramatic soundscapes of film soundtrack.

Take *Floodland*'s magnificent opening 'Dominion/Mother Russia' which oozes drama over a descending guitar line, or the second single, 'This Corrosion' which starts with a dramatic choir before hitting a vast club groove that builds the enormity

---

941 Wayne Hussey to John Robb.
942 Andrew Eldritch to John Robb.

and creates a big dance floor anthem and top ten chart hit. The song was a glowering statement about the band's new-found freedom and, perhaps, a withering putdown of former colleagues. For promotion, Eldritch, now dressed all in white, created a new-look Sisters with a quick phone call to former The Gun Club, and then Fur Bible bassist, Patricia Morrison, who added a whole new dynamic to the band.

Released in November 1987, *Floodland* was a big seller and set the Sisters up on a global level. It was a remarkable Lazarus-style comeback with an ambitious album full of shadows and powerful, huge, dramatic sounding songs that filled clubs worldwide.

The follow-up, 1990's *Vision Thing*, saw another lineup change, with former Generation X bass player Tony James replacing the outgoing Morrison. Co-written with unknown guitarist Andreas Bruhn, the band (initially consisting of Eldritch, Bruhn and Morrison) was about to enter the studio when Tony James was suddenly called up. Since then the band have become a touring machine with no releases.

> The stakes got higher, and by the time we did the third album, we were an international priority of Phonogram with enormous budgets for videos and albums, American and European management and the responsibilities that come with that. At that point, we kind of bought the ticket to ride. We then got to the point where we said, 'It's not for us.' We are not waiting for a record deal. I'm happy for this situation. On the upside, it certainly means I don't have to spend months in studios trying to pin down definitive versions of the songs. Recording can be disappointing; you can end up with something sung terribly because that's how it happened on the day you recorded. I'm glad that not having record company machinations involved in it enables us to shake it up and I hate being trapped by that, 'you invented a genre nonsense'.[943]

Eldritch still writes songs. The Sisters of Mercy still tour the world, selling out big venues, headlining festivals, and play these new songs - songs they never record. The lack of new releases only adds to the band's continuing enigmatic aura.

> I don't feel the driving need to release stuff. I'm introverted. I don't feel the pressure of outside forces to open the window and play it to the world. I will do it if it's convenient, but I always find something else to do.[944]
>
> Whilst the Leeds scene itself is now consigned to rumour and memory of a game-changing time when its clubs and bands drove a new musical narrative and art was goth central, the enigmatic Eldritch remains just out of focus, lingering in the shadows and one step ahead.
>
> Meanwhile, just up the road in Bradford, a very different scene was emerging in a very different city.

---

943 Andrew Eldritch to John Robb.

944 Andrew Eldritch to John Robb.

Chapter 26

VAGABONDS: BRADFORD

New Model Army and Joolz

The imposing Gothic splendour of Bradford's long-crumbling Victoriana is a lingering reminder of its 19th-century boom time. By the late 1970s, the city had suffered the all too familiar story of post-industrial meltdown. However, its brooding skylines, faded facades and multiracial makeup helped to forge a creative melting pot that was primed to nurture a distinctive post-punk period.

Never as creatively mainstream or as fashionable as its neighbour Leeds, the city's brief moment in the popular culture spotlight had been in the mid-1970s. Local lads Smokie had substantial successes with songs like 'Living Next Door to Alice', and Bradford native Kiki Dee was the first white singer to sign to Motown records.

In the 19th century, the booming Bradford was a city of immigrants, complete with its own German quarter. In the early 1980s, it would be a mix of musical immigrants and locals, such as New Model Army and Southern Death Cult, who would be central to the goth and post-punk cultures without either band being goth archetypes. In a city of former glories and ghostly empty warehouses, a loosely linked scene of bands would emerge and become key players in the new alternative culture.

As indomitable as the hills surrounding them, Bradford-based New Model Army have carved out a long career on their own creative terms. The band, built around the imposing Justin Sullivan, emerged on a powerful trajectory from post-punk. Initially, with a tough and concise Ruts-meets-Stranglers with a twist of Tamla Motown direction, they snuck onto the fringes of the new alternative scene as one of the most challenging bands to categorise.

Over the decades, their music has incorporated a very English folk, a sliver of northern soul, the clank and grind of post-punk and heartfelt honesty. All has been layered above rock-solid beats and pounding toms. Thriving outside the music business, they have commandeered a huge loyal fanbase – thoroughly defining the term 'cult band'. They may not have been goth by definition but were a staple part of the soundtrack of the clubs. New Model Army are not so much a band but rather the story of Sullivan and the high profile poet and writer Joolz Denby. Comrades in arms, they worked towards the same powerful vision. It was a common vision that would open a space for fellow restless souls to create music outside of society's established constraints.

New Model Army have become synonymous with Bradford, despite Sullivan originating from the south of England. Putting down roots in the city, the grey slate houses of Bradford's New Cross Street are typical of the city. Built to last, they defied weather, the economic crash and decades of industrial history, all ingrained upon their solid walls. In one of these houses, the Bradford post-punk scene coalesced. Rented by Justin Sullivan after leaving Bradford university, he shared the house with his then-partner Joolz as they plotted the band and her poetry. At the time, Joolz was the high priestess and motivator of their micro scene, and their relationship is at the core of Bradford's post-punk story.

In the cellar, bands, including Southern Death Cult, would rehearse. Comedian Little Brother appeared to lodge in the same house, as did the late legendary rock journalist Seething Wells, who was often crashed out on the settee. All manner of waifs and strays would drift through. It was a space that not only nurtured a music scene but a space that nurtured a new mindset; you could create in Bradford. There was no longer a perceived necessity to move ten miles east to Leeds or move to London to find fame and fortune. The house's out of town clientele was a microcosm the immigrant city built in the 19th century through the sweat and toil of outsiders, creating a Victorian megapolis with their bare hands. Aki Nawaz, then Southern Death Cult's drummer, continues to celebrate the cultural value of the house.

> It was a gathering place for creative misfits, castaways, the homeless, Satan's slaves, the lost and never found; it was such an interesting place that even the insects had names, the flowers spoke, and the sound of water was a language.
> If you could draw a picture, you would need to invent new colours. It was a 24/7 human supermarket with more drama than Bollywood, Hollywood and Lollywood. A blue plaque should be placed, but no death date![945]

New Model Army were formed in 1980. The band were built around their granite-faced frontman and were unrelenting harbingers of impassioned and powerful music, delivered with a palpable, visceral power. Their tightly constructed songs with rough-hewn melodies initially came armed with a running bass, raw guitar and tight, melodic songwriting full of wisdom and eternal melodic prowess. Over the decades, they have defied time and fashion and built a loyal and huge following across Europe with their heartfelt songs full of vim, vigour and passion. Their lyrical depth was equally as unwavering, writing songs concerned with life, spirituality and the enormous questions of existence.

They were swiftly adopted by the new northern alternative and the fringes of the so-called goth scene. They quickly built up a reputation as a fierce live band with a charismatic totemic frontman whose emotive interior created songs that oozed undeniable humanity.

Not short of an opinion and disinterested in showbiz frippery, the band emerged from the northern city in a blur of snarling songs, sharp haircuts and the soon-to-be infamous clogs.[946] They were a key band in the sleeping bag era of music obsession when fans shaved the sides of their heads and took to the road to follow bands from one end of the country to the other. Far more than a band, New Model Army were a

---

945 Aki Nawaz to John Robb.

946 Made by Walkley Clogs in Mytholmroyd, near Hebden Bridge in Yorkshire, the traditional clogs were initially worn by the band, then picked up by their following as a defining symbol of the band's rugged outsider-ness and Yorkshire cultural roots.

lifestyle. They were nonconforming preacher men, surrounded by the timid church mice of early 1980s pop.

Justin Sullivan was born into the Quaker community of Jordans in Buckinghamshire, a village that boasted a barn made from the timbers of the Mayflower.[947] He was also the grandson of Canadian novelist, engineer and explorer Alan Sullivan, an ancestor who shared Justin's relentless work ethic.

> I was raised in a Quaker household and still have a lot of respect for Quakerism, while I have also written several of the most un-Quakerly songs ever made, like 'Vengeance''The Hunt' and 'One of The Chosen', the idea that there is a spiritual aspect to life seems to me so obvious that I don't need to question it or join any particular clubs or creeds, or cults to express it.
>
> To me, God is Nature, and Nature is God, so I guess I'm a pagan of some sort, but in the end, even the nonsense 'Religions of the Book' – Christianity, Islam, Judaism – have a mystical wing that is interesting, not so much in the words of some prophet or other, but in the very principles of light and love. So, they're all really the same. It's all simple, easy, and obvious, and we're all aware of that at some level. It's the power-brokers of religion that like to make it complicated because they have their own different agenda.[948]

This unconventional historical background seeped into Sullivan's creativity, with lyrics and titles littered with 17th-century references even the band's name would come from Thomas Fairfax's English Revolution militia which formed in 1645 and fought in the English Civil War. Thomas Cromwell was one of their commanders, and their puritanical zeal saw them win the war, a fervour that is reflected in the impassioned intensity of the band. Justin Sullivan's own stage name, 'Slade the Leveller'[949] was taken from a socialist rebel in Cromwell's English Republic. With reference points such as these, it would be easy to misunderstand the band, presuming they were part of the clutch of post-punk bands that emerged in the early 1980s to carry on punk's perceived political agenda. For Sullivan, his songwriting was always far broader than this.

> It was always a music press misconception that we were some sort of Chumbawamba, Billy Bragg, The Redskins, Rage Against The Machine-type political band and that we existed only to put across a message. From the start, there were also songs about life, sex and personal relationships. People may notice the political statements, but it was the minority of our output.[950]

Justin Sullivan moved north to study peace studies at Bradford University in 1976. He dropped out after a year to drive Transit vans loaded with engine parts, fridges and videos to Pakistan. In 1980, he had met the charismatic local poet, biker, tattooist and force of nature, Joolz, and was immediately sparked into action by her vision and drive.

---

947 The same ship that carried the first English settlers to America.

948 Justin Sullivan to the Westworld website.

949 The Levellers were a political movement during the English Civil War (1642–1651) committed to popular sovereignty, extended suffrage, equality before the law and religious tolerance.

950 Justin Sullivan to John Robb.

The imposing figure of Joolz is key to the post-punk story of New Model Army and Bradford. Another emigre, she was born Julianne Mumford in Colchester in 1955. Her family moved around with work before finally settling in Harrogate when she was 11. In 1975, aged 19, she married a local biker, Ken Denby, and fell in with the local biker gang Satan's Slaves.[951] Frustrated with the biker gang's strict rules, she dyed her hair pink and left to become a bouncer. She worked as such at the punk shows at Bradford's Queens Hall before conquering the local poetry scene with her spoken word pieces. The chance meeting with Joolz kept Justin Sullivan in the city.

> There are two or three reasons why I stayed in Bradford. I had dropped out of university after a year. I then met Stuart[952] and then Joolz and started doing all this stuff. The other is Bradford itself. I find it an interesting city. Bradford's population went from 15,000 to 150,000 in ten years in the 19th century. It was a boom town. If you go back more than five generations, no one is actually from Bradford. It's a town that was built by immigrants from the rest of the UK and then from abroad. No one cares where you come from in Bradford. In some places, you have to be three generations before people are accepted, but that's not true in Bradford, and I like that.[953]

After meeting Joolz, Sullivan, who had played in several earlier ad hoc bands, was empowered to make his own music. It was handy that his youthful bassist, Stuart Morrow, was a bass prodigy.

> Stuart Morrow was an extraordinary talent. Basically, everything started for me when I bumped into him in 1977 in some youth club in Bradford. We started various bands like Misfit and Hustler St before forming New Model Army in 1980. I had met Joolz in a cheap nightclub in 1979, and we started talking about stuff, and within a short time, we were a couple. We are still very close soul mates, but we have not been a couple for a long time. We would bounce ideas off each other right from the start. I would never have started the band properly if I had not met her. I owe her a lot as she moulded this into something. Everyone who comes across her knows she is forceful and makes things happen. She is also a public person as well and a writer and an artist who is very visible.[954]

New Model Army were not only inspired by several strands of punk but also by a broad church of music, from The Who to Sullivan's deep love of Tamla Motown.

> I'm a northern soul fanatic. My first love is Motown. I'm not a massive fan of rock, and I know that's a heresy to say that when you're in a rock band. The arrangements and not the songwriting are all steeped in this. On the other hand, my favourite albums are The Who's *Quadrophenia* and Kate Bush's *Hounds of Love* which create self-contained worlds. You submerge yourself into that world. They are not background albums, and you have to listen to them. That's me. I don't do background music.[955]

---

951 Satan's Slaves is a 'one percenter motorcycle club' founded in Shipley, a suburb of Bradford in 1967.

952 Stuart Morrow – the original New Model Army bassist.

953 Justin Sullivan to John Robb.

954 Justin Sullivan to John Robb.

955 Justin Sullivan to John Robb.

Their first gig was in Bradford in October 1980 before the hard-gigging band honed down their sound on the newly emerging circuit of post-punk venues. Their gritty determination was married to the knack of writing pithy and powerful songs that utilised Sullivan's melodic touch and Morrow's busy bass lines, giving them a distinctive sound. With his powerful stage presence and brooding, intense appeal, Sullivan is often seen as the band's key member. However, he prefers to be a team player in a fluctuating lineup.

> I think I was lucky in who I met – Stuart in 1977, Joolz in 1979, and then three years later, I met Robert Heaton.[956] These were exceptional people. I thought it was normal to meet people like this. Artists of this calibre. Now I realise all three were exceptional, and I was lucky.
>
> I always think it's a band, but other people see it as just me because I'm the only continuing member. On one level, I don't believe in democracies in bands; on the other, I think they work by consensus, which is that the person who argues their point the most strongly persuades everyone else into doing it. Everybody thinks that's me, but I'm in the minority most of the time![957]

Signing to Abstract Records, who already had the Three Johns and was also home to 1919, Hagar the Womb, UK Subs, and The Outcasts, as well as the "Punk And Disorderly" album series, they released their 'Great Expectations' single in 1983 and were given airplay by Radio 1's John Peel and the release of their debut 1984 *Vengeance* album saw them break through.

There is always something gripping about powerful, uncompromising songs delivered with such a sense of conviction. The album's title track, with its impassioned chorus of 'I believe in justice, I believe in vengeance, I believe in getting the bastard…' was a fierce declaration of a personal justice that was in direct opposition to the punkier peace ideals of the time. The song was a club favourite, and the album was full of similar driving pieces of music, like the bass-driven 'Smalltown England' that captured the suffocating claustrophobia of the UK. 'Christian Militia' was the song from which their fervent fan base, who had started following the band from gig to gig, took their name.

In February 1984, the band performed on Channels 4's *The Tube*. The programme thrived on controversy but somehow flinched at the lyrics of 'Vengeance', and the band had to play 'Christian Militia' and 'Small Town England' instead. It was a great appearance; the seething and intense band looked fantastic and genuinely dangerous despite the sniffy introduction from presenter Muriel Gray referring to them as 'the ugliest band in rock'.. The leering singer was kitted out in a dandy red military jacket and leather kecks, delivering his pithy sermon with the bass player jiving next to him, delivering those distinctive bass lines. Meanwhile, new drummer and multi-instrumentalist Robert Heaton held it all together, making the band a perfect power trio.

---

956 The band's long serving drummer and co-writer who died in 2004.

957 Justin Sullivan to John Robb.

The audience, sporting an array of proto-gothic hairstyles, were wildly chicken dancing[958]. There was an air of confrontational violence and defiant exuberance about the proceedings as the defied the snarky music media. The *Tube* appearance sent their *Vengeance* mini album to number one in the indie charts, pushing the more media-friendly Smiths from the top spot.

This flurry of success saw the band signed to EMI, who released 1985's *No Rest For the Wicked* album and the band's debut top 30 single 'No Rest'. The single saw them perform on *Top of the Pops,* where the powers that be flinched at the band's t-shirts that sported the slogan: 'Only Stupid Bastards Use Heroin', making them cover the offending word in white tape, in the typically petty way of the early 1980s BBC.

Weeks into the No Rest album tour, Morrow quit the band and was replaced by 17-year-old Jason 'Moose' Harris. The perfect triangle was broken, leaving Sullivan to power through the decades with various lineups, never once losing his vision. The perfect outsiders, New Model Army, were a lifestyle, with their fans having their own look and style of clogs, sawn-off clothes, tattoos in a time when body art was more taboo and myriad variations of longer hair and grown-out punk spikes. At festivals where the band often headlined, it appeared as though a pagan army had arrived in the fields.

Their 1986 *Ghost of Cain* album was produced by the legendary Glyn Johns[959] and saw them stall at number 45 in the charts, but they still built their rabid live following. 1990's top 20 *Thunder and Consolation* album was the band's commercial high water with Reading Festival appearances that saw them become the stand out band at the event with their music pouring out of cars and minivans across the campsites. Their then mix of an added green and ghostly English folk to their impassioned poetic polemic helped pave the way for Levellers, who would take their version of this synthesis into the top five of the album charts.

The band's work ethic was impressive. 1989's *Thunder and Consolation* had its title taken from a 1663 book by a 'revolutionary' Quaker called Edward Burroughs, undoubtedly as a nod to Sullivan's roots and saw the top 30 singles 'Stupid Questions' and 'Vagabonds'. 1990's *Impurity* saw the band immersed deeper in their folk crossover, adding Ed Alleyne-Johnson on violin. This gave them a bigger and more diverse sound that saw them at their peak with songs that became anthems for a new offshoot audience of crusty, rave and new-age travellers. Many listeners in these new scenes had travelled through the punk and goth scenes hit the road and never returned home - the logical conclusion of grabbing sleeping bags and leaving home for months on end, following bands.

Part of the New Model Army fanbase joined the new traveller community. They hit the road in converted vans, benders and buses and having no set destination was

---

958 The de rigueur dance of the time - elbows out flapping like chicken wings - great for movement and great for causing a bit of argy bargy.

959 Glyn Johns had worked with The Who, The Rolling Stones and famously The Beatles *Get Back* sessions. His drum sound was totemic...a few mics placed near the kit instead of the usual battery of mics.

integral to the lifestyle. This way of living aligned with a new look of unlaced army boots, army fatigues, dreadlocked hair, dogs on ropes, caravans, and some unshakable hippie flavours that would define what would become a huge movement. It was initially soundtracked by bands such as New Model Army and Levellers but soon incorporated a mixture of post-rave dance music into the scene, like Ozric Tentacles, Eat Static and Senser.

New Model Army had been central to the sleeping bag culture, and many travellers had cut their teeth on the road with the band. However, the band's puritan work ethic and roughly hewn songs would initially seem to be at odds with the freewheeling new agers. New Model Army's wilfulness runs very deep. Justin Sullivan sees it as a welcome by-product of their era.

> It comes from punk rock, and almost every band that comes out of that era has got that streak of wilful perversity. As our recent *Between Dog and Wolf* album title hints, things are not entirely tame, and we are not entirely predictable, and it is important to retain that. It's something that Neil Young has done throughout his career. When they think they know what you are going to do, give them the opposite. That attitude is in Joolz, and it's in all of us.

New Model Army are still an important and popular slot at the many festivals that have sprung up in the wake of traveller culture, like Levellers' own Beautiful Days festival. Their own gigs capture this close relationship between the band and fans that has been there since the start; a fierce family of true believers on and off stage. The New Model Army following are as dogged and loyal as the band. One such dedicated fan, Jase, explains that despite being a member of the most intense crew, each band had its own mob:

> Most bands had a following with a nickname – The Sisters of Mercy had The Sisterhood, God Squad and the Sausage Squad, New Model Army fans were the Militia, Balaam and the Angel were the Sperm Bank, Fields of the Nephilim had the Bonanzas and later The Psycho Vikings, Ghost Dance had the Spook Squad, Salvation - the Jivers and Killing Joke were followed by the gatherers. The Mission had The Missionaries, later The Eskimos. Play Dead went one better by having two rival followings one of which was the Stay Dead crew who ensured that some gigs were like war zones!

New Model Army themselves remain indomitable and on their own trajectory. Whole musical movements have risen and fallen, and the band remains true to their muse. Still creating and pushing the boundaries of their sound, the band's most recent albums, *Between Dog and Wolf* (2013), *Between Wine and Blood* (2014) *Winter* (2016), *From Here* (2019) have arguably been their best works. It is this dogged creative attitude that makes them as special as ever.

The current New Model Army is a band peaking decades into its career. Their songs have the glowering storm clouds of the Bradford hills but yet remain drenched in feedback, passion, and the sound of those moors and mill towns. Their sense of urgency and anger is unfaltering and remains a sensation that only the genuinely awake can feel and their tireless creation of a space for fellow creatives saw many a band lurking in their cellar like in our next chapter...

Chapter 27

FLOWERS IN THE FOREST

Southern Death Cult

In 1981, a young punk rock drifter called Ian Astbury had emerged on the scene in a blur of Native American[960] clothing styled with fierce post-punk nous, a tomahawk mohawk and tribal makeup.

He was undoubtedly a striking presence.

With guitarist David 'Buzz' Burrows, bassist Barry Jepson and drummer Aki Nawaz[961], Southern Death Cult looked and sounded startling for a brief flicker of time. A force of nature, they swiftly made an impression on the scene. However, they imploded as suddenly as they had arrived, leaving behind memories of intense gigs, dramatic wardrobes and a set of mystical and powerful songs, demos and sessions. These musical remnants were thankfully collected on an eponymous album as evidence of the biggest band on the goth scene that flickered and fired and then crashed and burned.

The combination of Native American philosophy and a dark, euphoric post-punk was powered by tribal beats, spectral guitar and driving bass lines. This killer combination made them clear heirs and natural successors to the new underground throne, a role recently vacated by Adam Ant's mainstream success.

Southern Death Cult were full of wild-eyed belief, and the young band's gigs were intense and colourful celebrations. Their set at the Futurama 4 Festival at the Deeside Leisure Centre in Queensferry (12 September 1982) saw a band at the top of their game. Ian Astbury cut an imperious, domineering figure. His shamanic dancing and powerful voice defined the romantic idealism of the young new generation, who were yet to be labelled.

Six months later, the band would be no more.

Bradford was the birthplace of this fleeting band, which was sparked shortly after Ian Astbury pitched up in town. He was sofa surfing whilst hitchhiking around the country, keenly following the Crass/Poison Girls tour of 1981, looking for idealism in anarcho, seeking to make sense of his life in the warrior remnants of punk rock.

Born in 1962 in the suburban greenery of Heswall in the Wirral,[962] Ian Astbury is one of the last great rock n roll romantics. He is a firm believer in the magical and transcendental power of music, the mystical communion that remains untainted

---

960 The underlying fascination with Native American culture was entwined into punk. Malcolm and Vivienne played with its themes and Adam Ant fully embraced them. The warrior rebel culture certainly chimed with punk and the style looked great but the deeper philosophy of living in tune with the planet and the anti-imperialism ideas were considered strange at the time but have become very much part of the modern mainstream.

961 Born Haq Nawaz Qureshi.

962 20 miles from Liverpool, Heswall was the birthplace of John Peel and Andy McCluskey of Orchestral Manoeuvres In the Dark.

from the cynicism of modern times. 'You get a truth when watching your favourite band. It's just you and them. There's no filter.' [963] as he explains.

In 1973, when he was eleven, his parents moved to Hamilton in Ontario, Canada, which gave him a dislocated cultural cache. After moving back to the UK five years later, he was culturally trapped between the two opposing rock cultures of his youth; a mixture of the Canadian radio rock and the claustrophobic post-punk sounds of his new British home.

> I never had a cultural identity. My mother was Scottish, my father was from Birkenhead, and I was growing up in North America. So, I just made it up as I went along. The guiding stars were always music. There was Bowie for so long. Then Sex Pistols came along, but the early 80s were the Year Zero for me. Joy Division, Public Image and particularly Crass were all very personally important. People my age were the younger brothers of the punk scene and bands by about five or six years, and that's quite a huge gap in terms of the age difference. In 1977, the first wave punks were in their early twenties, and we were in our young teens. We were in the audience. Learning. We picked up instruments because of the Pistols and those bands. Our lineage and heritage goes back to those shows.[964]

Unlike many of his new British friends, Astbury's years of living in Canada had also imbued him with a love of very different music, with rock classics like Led Zeppelin and even Genesis nestling into his record collection. After his mother got cancer, the family had moved back to the UK to Glasgow to be near her family, where he excelled at football. His mother died on his 17th birthday, and he tried to find himself with a short 29-day stint in the army before leaving and becoming immersed in the ferocious local punk scene.

> My mother died on my birthday, and a few days later, I was in the British Army. It was like going to prison. It was a real wake up call in the world of men and what men do. I realised that I wasn't really part of mainstream culture. I felt outside of everything. When I came out of the army a month later, I was into punk rock full on, 24 hours a day. That was my lifestyle. I first saw The Clash in 1978 in Glasgow, and then I saw The Stranglers, The Damned and Ramones there. It was such a spectacle, especially being in Glasgow at the time. It was so exotic. It was mind-blowing. It was transcendental. It still stays with me. They are the most amazing performances I've ever seen or probably will ever see.[965]

It was also in Glasgow where Astbury fell in love with The Doors after hearing 'The End' from the iconic 1979 *Apocalypse Now* film soundtrack[966]. This was a moment

---

963 Ian Astbury to John Robb.

964 Ian Astbury to John Robb.

965 Ian Astbury to John Robb.

966 Never has a film been so perfectly timed. 1979's *Apocalypse Now* was a take on Joseph Conrad's 1899 book Heart Of Darkness updated to the Vietnam war and questioned the morality of war and western civilisation. Military fatigues and dog tags were everywhere from the Combat Rock Clash to the underground due to a fascination with the film which, whilst being an ostensibly anti-war exercise, was more of a psychedelic movie, a sprawling acid trip with a backdrop of war gone insane, aided of course, by the soundtrack, filled with pop culture references and remnants of The Doors' oeuvre. In one fell swoop, the film gave Jim Morrison's band a new lease of life and connected them with post-punk culture. It made the band central to the strand of post-punk that would become alternative and goth and broke The Doors into the big time outside the USA just over a decade since they had ended.

he describes as a 'religious experience'. A moment that, for him, complimented the influence of the surrounding punk rock culture.

> At the time, I was also into music that we weren't supposed to listen to as punks, like The Doors and Led Zeppelin. Those guys had also once been young and pissed off and driven once. For me, there were many similarities between the punk ethos and those bands before they became the super juggernauts. I wasn't listening to the common wisdom at the time – the 'I hate Pink Floyd' philosophy of punk rock. It's interesting now to see what kind of records stand up in people's collections. So many punk rockers that I grew up with now listen to Pink Floyd and the more tripped-out stuff and are also exploring a more tripped-out philosophy.[967]

After his father moved back to Canada, Ian and his brother moved to Liverpool to continue their post-punk adventures in the city they had partly grown up in. He fell in at the tail end of the vibrant local post-punk scene and spent time in the final moments of Eric's [968] observing its strong cast of characters; Pete Burns, Julian Cope, Pete Wylie, Jayne Casey, Ian McCulloch and various Ant fans. He was stunned by the vibrant and wild characters that made the city's scene so distinctive whilst coming to terms with the powerful impact of punk.

> We were kids when punk came. We were young. I hadn't developed. I was reaching for myself. I hadn't found myself, so it was really earnest. If there is a criticism for being young and earnest, then yeah! I'm guilty. I was exploring everything, and I wasn't afraid to put it into my music, the way I dressed and the way I looked.
> I was a year younger than most of my peers, so I didn't see the Pistols, and I didn't see The Clash until 1978 because I had been in Canada. Punk rock split my skull open and introduced me to a different way of being and a breaking away from the mainstream. All of a sudden, you were in this different field.
> There were amazing conversations I used to have. People used to think that punk rock was all about degenerates or just being anti-establishment, but there was a lot more going on. There was a lot of philosophical stuff. People were really exploring things.
> Growing up with Bowie, Iggy Pop, and punk rock - that's where my philosophical part came from. I don't want to cheapen it by giving it a tag, but maybe it was the quest, search, or whatever. I was always inquisitive – 'what's round the next corner?' I could never really just stay in one place physically or mentally. There were other influences coming in by now. Joy Division were incredibly important. Ian Curtis was such an icon for us, for me, anyway. If you listen to bands in the early '80s, a lot of the singers were going for that kind of baritone Jim Morrison/ Ian Curtis vocal style. For me, Echo & The Bunnymen definitely were. The energy of punk rock fused with that.
> Then there was Adam and the Ants. *Dirk Wears White Sox* has as much to do with goth as Siouxsie and the Banshees. I was more into the tribal end of goth because I was into Native American imagery. There was a whole sect of kids like me who were into World's End gear, they would become Southern Death Cult

---

967 Ian Astbury to John Robb.

968 The key punk club in Liverpool opened in Oct 1976 with bands booked by the legendary Roger Eagle. The Liverpool post-punk scene and its mythological cast of characters grew out of the venue that closed in March 1980.

fans because we were into our version of the tribal imagery. When I was living in Canada when I was really young, I grew up around indigenous native Canadians. They were the most rebellious kids at my school. I was absolutely taken with them. They had no respect for authority. They didn't have any concept of it.[969]

The late 1970s UK 1970s had been an enormous culture shock for Ian Astbury. All the optimism of North America was dashed by the cultural dislocation of the old country. The political and social ferment created a simmering tension that was felt in every city. If Canada was a big space with big dreams and ideas, the UK felt squashed in. The refuse was piled high on the streets, and the empire's dashed dreams were turning into dust. All of which was matched by the dark British cynicism reflected in punk.

> When I came back to England, there was this horrible Thatcherite cynicism and dystopia after she got into power in May 1979. I was coming out of a very optimistic culture in North America at a time when the music had been very rich with the Stones at their height and bands like Queen touring. They were considered to be dinosaurs in the UK, but they were still doing really good work for me. Punk rock grew out of a kind of psychic hole in the culture, and people just filled it with DIY colour and expression. It was very individualistic. That was until Oi![970] came along, and everybody was wearing leather jackets. Before that, everyone had completely different ways of dressing, thinking and being. Class wasn't important. Race wasn't important. Gender wasn't important. If you were a punk, you were a punk. That was it. It didn't matter where you came from. I didn't even ask people. If I had a bottle of cider, I'd share that, no problem. We used to be trading clothes, records and stuff, and that stays with you.[971]

Punk was the place that this much-travelled youth could finally call home. The vibrant Liverpool punk scene, with all its colour and flamboyance, was a great grounding for the young man. He was getting noticed and even chosen by Lin and Paul Sangster to be the singer in Liverpool band Send No Flowers, but the arrangement came to nothing. Doreen Allen - the key player in Liverpool's post-punk and goth club culture, recalls the awkward pre-rock star teenager.

> I certainly have memories of a young Ian Astbury from when I worked at Eric's. He looked about 12 when he came to the matinee shows with his mate. I was a bit of a 'mother hen' to them as they looked so much younger, and I would give them posters and badges for nothing! Ian was the quiet one and always seemed to hide behind his chatty mate. Out of all the people I knew from Eric's, I would have lost all bets on Ian turning out the way he did! I didn't actually realise years later that Ian, whom I had taken under my 'wing', was Mr Astbury, but I couldn't forget those eyes. In fact, when he was a kid, I thought he should have been in the film *Village of the Damned!*[972]

---

969 Ian Astbury to John Robb.

970 The brutal form of street punk that was inspired by the original punk wave.

971 Ian Astbury to John Robb.

972 Doreen Allen to John Robb.

After losing his bedsit in Liverpool and opting to hit the road in 1980, Ian Astbury became part of the raggle-taggle collective of idealistic young minds who would follow Crass and Poison Girls around the country on tour. He comfortably fitted into the world of the sleeping bag-carrying, hitchhiking, young punk buccaneers.

It is safe to say that there has never been a group like Crass. Appearing in the punk fallout, they had come together in Dial House on the edge of London, in Epping Forest, where the young Astbury would stay for some time. With deep roots back into the counterculture idealism of the 1960s, they were an extension of an Avant art community with band drummer Penny Rimbaud at its core.[973] Crass taught young listeners about pacifism, vegetarianism, feminism and other key values and ideas. They did this with groundbreaking music that varied from cleverly constructed yelping punk thrash to artful layers of sound.

Crass delivered a genuinely thrilling, angry punk rock of searingly political songs that sang of hope and anarchism with vital and urgent anger and poetic compassion. Each album came wrapped in brilliant artwork from the incomparable Gee Vaucher. The hand-painted pieces resembled political collages, and each release was a crash course in the counterculture. If Sex Pistols had sung about anarchy, Crass were offering explanations to young ears. The cult band were a powerful and perfect eye-opener to Ian Astbury, who loves them to this day:

> Crass! I saw those guys 36 times. I used to follow them around. They had a huge influence on me. I remember being at their Dial House HQ[974]. It was like an open house. Singer Steve Ignorant was sitting in the tepee outside. I think it may have been Eve Libertine from Crass who gave me the book Black Elk Speaks[975] and said, 'Read this,' I was about eighteen. I sat and read the book and it gave me a map of what I was picking up on at a certain frequency. At Crass house, all sorts of fascinating people were coming and going. As a nineteen-year-old kid with a mohawk, how can that not have an effect on you? It's only now that people understand Crass a bit more and what they were trying to do. Maybe you must go through a few life cycles to understand that it's not just shouting. That it's not just a superficial explosion of something that's exciting but with real depth. Being around Crass was mind-blowing. They were one of the few bands that asked those questions. They tried to give some kind of context to the energy of the music and the times.
>
> People always said that if you weren't there for those three months at the height of punk in 1977, then you weren't there at all. But I don't agree. To me, punk was just a 'get in the door' moment that lead to a real moment. We are all made of atoms, and if you split the atom, the energy is always there.[976]

973 Penny Rimbaud had been politicised by the police crackdown on the Windsor Free Festival that had damaged a close friend of his, Wally Hope. He had seen the hippie dream turn sour and it was thanks to future Crass vocalist Steve Ignorant that he was sparked into a new musical action. Through music, he would move away from the stencil campaign they had previously been waging on the London Underground with thought provoking slogans, turning their efforts into a band.

974 The ramshackle house on the edge of London near Epping Forest was bought for a small amount of money in 1964 by Penny Rimbaud which operated an open-door policy for idealists, free thinkers and artists to this day.

975 Black Elk Speaks, is the 1932 book by American poet and writer John G. Neihardt, which relates the story of an Oglala Lakota medicine man.

976 Ian Astbury to John Robb.

Operating outside the rock n roll framework, Crass would play fan-promoted gigs in small towns and overlooked cities of the UK. They would arrive at venues with a big picnic hamper and share food, endless cups of tea, and ideas with their young fans. They would talk about esoteric subject matter, opening up the imaginations of their followers.

The autumn tour of 1980 had pitched up in Bradford at the Sweatbox. Also on the bill were the equally interesting Poison Girls, whom the charismatic, Vi Subversa, fronted.[977] In town for the gig were the usual mixture of Crass acolytes, local punks and sleeping bag-carrying travellers, including the young Ian Astbury, fresh from a stint in Belfast and then known as Ian Lindsay.

> I was on the road following the tour around. I didn't have anywhere to stay, but I met these kids that night; they said, 'We've got a room in our house. If you ever need anywhere to live, come and stay here. We've always got a room.' The idea of moving to Bradford then... was like growing up in New York and ending up in Oklahoma! That's how I ended up staying at New Model Army house[978]

The gig's promoter was a young Bradford Pakistani punk called Aki Nawaz. Aki's cultural mix made Ian Astbury's transatlantic cultural confusion look like a doddle.

> The long journey of an immigrant can never be sure; its end is unpredictable. We arrived on these shores with the great promise of the former colonial masters that gold would be growing on trees, but our lives had been suffocated and oppressed to such a degree that every bit of our rich culture was seen as backward.
>
> For example, when we watched Legs & Co do their thing on *Top of the Pops*, my mother would shout: 'switch it off, bloody 'bashtaard' society, no shame!' That would have us running towards the black and white television set, attempting to switch it onto the 'white noise' channel to save our souls. Our culture simply did not permit this decadence where women were used as sexual objects. It was not because our parents were 'overzealous Victorians'. They just had some values which we did not understand at the time. However, we grew up in a liberal but disciplined household with secrets but also a traditional Muslim upbringing.
>
> Racism was rife inside the streets of the tiny back-to-back houses, but somehow we bit our tongues as they ran away shouting, 'Pakis go home.' Punk rock emerged, and never in their wildest dreams could my parents have envisaged that it would arrive on their doorstep, inside their home and inside the soul of their eldest son, who was supposed to be the role model for the rest of the children. Within a few months, I was pogoing to the Sex Pistols live at Knickers Club in Keighley[979] and then going back to school in the morning where we would register, leave through the back door, and congregate at a friend's house, listening to punk records.[980]

Learning drums as he went along, Aki quickly formed a teenage punk band called Violation. With his dedication, they were soon making something out of nothing.

---

977 Vi Subversa, born Frances Sokolov in 1935, was already over 40 when she made her stage debut. She died in 2016. A powerful presence with her feminist, anarchist and socialist leanings she was a fundamental driving force behind the band and also Crass who she befriended after moving in near them in 1979. Both groups presented a new way of thinking and Vi Subversa was widely accepted by the teenage punks who embraced her age, her powerful femininity and her brilliant music.

978 Ian Astbury to AV magazine.

979 The Dec 19th 1977 gig at the unlikely named club was one of the last original lineup Sex Pistols shows in the UK.

980 Aki to John Robb.

Future Southern Death Cult members Barry Jepson and David 'Buzz' Burrows were also in the band, playing bass and guitar, respectively. Violation's brief adventure began when Aki harassed the manager of Bradford St Georges Hall for the support slot for The Clash on 29 January 1980. Some start!

With things moving quickly, Violation were on the lookout for a proper singer. They noticed a new face on the scene after the Crass/Poison Girls gig, a piece of punk rock driftwood that had been washed up in the New Model Army house.

> I had made the move to Bradford. My flat in Liverpool off Lark Lane that I shared with Mark Jordan had gone, and I needed somewhere to stay. I found the house the kids mentioned at the gig and went back to Bradford. It was New Model Army's house. They gave me the room. The house was made up of musicians and artists, and poets. It was a really cool house. This band was rehearsing in the basement, and Joolz told me to sing for them. They liked me 'cause they liked the way I looked. That was the beginning of Southern Death Cult. I was 18 years old.[981]

The Bradford scene was small, and Violation had spotted Ian Astbury and noted he was upstairs at the New Cross Street, where they were rehearsing.

> One Sunday afternoon whilst rehearsing, Buzz said that he had seen the guy who was staying upstairs at a 'new romantic' club the night before and thought he was a great dancer and that he also looked great and if he could sing, it might just be worth checking him out. So, Ian was invited down into the basement to rehearse, and that's the beginning of the band and Southern Death Cult. We started to work immediately. The vibes were fantastic. Ian's personality was very warm and brotherly, and we all gelled. We dropped the name of Violation, and Ian thought of Southern Death Cult, taken from his interest in Native American culture.[982]
> We worked as a team. Barry and Buzz got on with the major writing. Ian got his lyrics together and started to contribute to musical writing. In all honesty, I did not have a clue about music or even drumming or its purpose but made up stuff that, for me, was a drum pattern creating some mood for the others to write upon. Buzz and Ian would begin to get t-shirt designs together as I managed to get the college printing workshop to print them after hours and illegally. In those days, everything was done on 'dole budgets!'
> The first gig we did was a TV recording for Yorkshire TV at the Bradford Royal Standard in July 1981. Unfortunately, it wasn't televised, and we never saw the results. We played our first official gig at the 1 in 12 Club[983] on Sunbridge Rd. I recall it was a very interesting response from the small audience. It was not the 'wow' factor but a genuine 'this is something really special.'[984]

The band were now also forging its own aesthetic beyond punk.

> The band's identity was growing, with Ian attaching himself to the Native American look. I also decided to paint some white stripes across my face for the first gig. The gig was great, and after the usual late curry and dropping everyone

---

981 Ian Astbury to AV website.

982 The term comes from the Southeastern Ceremonial Complex, a mound-building Native American culture.

983 Bradford 1 in 12 Club is a local institution – a venue run on co-operative lines that has survived for decades.

984 Aki Nawaz to John Robb.

off at home, I went home totally shattered. In normal circumstances, I would clean myself up before going in the house as Dad usually waited for me to get back and lecture me about how even the 'animals are asleep.' This time I thought I would get away with it as it was about four in the morning. I crept up the squeaky steps into the loft bedroom with a sigh of relief that my father had not woken up. I was wrong, as suddenly I heard my father's slow, beautiful, tranquil footsteps coming upstairs. I quickly removed the black DIY 'Destroy' t-shirt from my back, and the door opened. My father stood there with the 1950's antique-looking clock raised to head height in his right hand. He was angry I had come home late and even more furious when he saw the makeup on my face and left the room shouting.

"Bloody hell, what the hell, five generations of the family and I get the bloody PUFF, wearing bloody makeup Bloody puff!' His accent echoed in my head – I had never heard him say the word 'puff.' In all honesty, I never thought he knew about the gay community![985]

Fortunately, things were moving quickly for the band. They recorded a demo that scored them a May 1982 John Peel session from the ever-supportive DJ. Post-sessions, labels were interested, key support tours were offered, and sold out headline shows awaited. Aki was thrilled:

The band was just growing and growing. The gigs became like events. A movement was being created as we made bridges with other bands. We also kept the grassroots approach alive as played small off-the-wall venues like in the Lake District, which became like outings with maybe up to 100 or so followers turning up. The gig in the Lakes was fantastic until it exploded in violence with about 20 or so Nazi skinheads turning up. They got completely battered by the following, who were from all over the country. We had a few Asian and Afro Caribbean Punks in the contingent as well, and every time, without exception, we beat the skinheads back to their rat holes.[986]

The band then signed to Situation Two records – a mini label set up by Beggars Banquet. The timing was perfect. There was a genuine interest in a band with flamboyance and substance, something dressed up, tribal and a little esoteric. They picked up two quick support tours, central to the gathering of the new clans and the emergence of goth culture. One was with Theatre of Hate in the summer of 1982, and the other was a huge UK tour with Bauhaus the same year. These were tours that saw the torch being passed. This was a flame that burned bright in the eyes of young idealists who would travel up and down the country to see the bands, as culture writers like Tom Vague would document so beautifully in his Vague [987] fanzine.

The band and the fans had the same striking look; a mix of off-the-peg and DIY homemade clothes, a loose uniform of army boots, post-punk clothes, shaved mohawks, paisley shirts, crimped hair, Native American beads and junk shop finery. Southern Death Cult had caught the moment. The band sounded great. Their tribal

---

985 Aki Nawaz to John Robb.

986 Aki Nawaz to John Robb.

987 The key fanzine in the early days of the culture with long well written pieces from the heart and soul of the scene and well worth tracking down.

pounding and the widescreen sound was the next chapter in post-punk. Their style marked them out as the scene veered in their direction and the totemic, charismatic, idealistic Ian Astbury was the new ace face who truly believed in the surrounding culture. Ian Cheek of *Tongue-in-cheek* fanzine recalls just how special they were:

> I first saw Southern Death Cult in Keighley. I remember the uplifting, jubilant, tearful effect it had on me. Here was a band who had lived a little, despite their youth, who between them had suffered the isolation of the military, of racism, of spending a childhood being whisked from city to city, nation to nation, but who had come together in a celebration of life and a damnation of oppression. Southern Death Cult were never just another band.[988]

Upender Mehra was a keen fan from the Midlands. Like Aki, he was a young punk with a Pakistani background looking to make sense of the UK. Punk and post-punk music was the glue that held his and so many other young lives together and briefly. Southern Death Cult was the tribe with their multiracial following.

> I first saw Southern Death Cult supporting Theatre of Hate at Digbeth Civic Hall, Birmingham, in the summer of 1982. Visually and auditory they were like a juggernaut to the senses. They were so much more than just 'the band.' This was the first real tribe to which anyone, from anywhere, could immediately belong. It was a new northern sound and look that captured punk escapism, away from any pigeonhole or drab grey reality of Thatcher's inner city.[989]

In 1982, the band were at the top of its game. Ian Astbury was doing his shamanic shuffle dance across the stage and had a mesmerising presence and the group to back it up. Their debut December 1982 single 'Moya/Fatman' was one of those classic seven-inch singles of the time, full of the drama and excitement that dominated the post-punk discourse. A spaghetti western crescendo with aching vocals it hit number one in the indie charts. It seemed that the band were on the cusp.

> Our London Heaven show on 21 February 1983 was our biggest show yet. I recall a massive queue waiting for tickets, and when we got inside the venue, we heard it had completely sold out of 1,200 tickets.
>
> The vibes in the venue were massive, and I think it was the first time we actually did feel nervous as we took to readying ourselves in the usual manner. Ian would be preparing his Native American makeup, Barry and Buzz making sure their private parts bulged on the right side of their trousers and me? I was just exercising for that hardcore naive and unfocused tribal drumming. Pre-gig was always difficult for me because I knew I had to work hard with those drums. It was the only time I wanted to be left alone so I could prepare myself mentally and physically.
>
> As I came up for the 50th press-up, I heard a voice say, 'Is that what you do all the time?' I looked back; it was Bono from U2. They were on the verge of big things but not there yet. 'Just loosening up', I replied in a thick northern accent. I was too shy to say anything else and just smiled. I have always suspected that the band had influenced U2 in terms of presentation and passion, hence why they

---

were there. The gig went down great. It was like all the other gigs where we put everything into each one and were extremely self-critical of ourselves.[990]

Southern Death Cult were on the fast track to being huge. Yet five days later, Ian Astbury disbanded the group after a show in Manchester. All that promise evaporated as the band fell apart. Their impact was huge, but their time was short.

> Things were not too good inside the band. Ian had started getting a lot moodier, whilst Buzz always felt left out of the decision-making process, and Barry was very strong at getting his own way. Me? I just carried on working. If I was a problem, I did not know what I was doing wrong but continued to work hard as my Pakistani background taught me. I just wanted to prove something to my father and make him happy, and he, although completely against this career, had come around, as his friends had seen the band's success.
> Socially it had all seemed fine. Ian would come round to our house, and he liked my mother, who looked very much like a Native American woman. The band would all be given helpings of curry and learned Pakistani swear words. My mother called Ian 'Kotha Cir', which meant 'horse head' after the Mohican Ian had, which looked like a mane of a horse to her.[991]

Eighteen months after they formed, and with the band on the cusp of an enormous breakthrough, they suddenly fell apart. Aki was heartbroken:

> I was standing outside my family house on Cecil Ave crying when I heard that Ian had decided to leave the band. I went into overdrive and tried many ways to contact him and speak to him. I did not understand and wanted to know exactly what the problem was and how and if it could be resolved. I was truly shocked and hurt. Southern Death Cult meant everything to me on many levels. It was a love affair that I was dedicated to and absolutely obsessed with. The chemistry, outlook and ideas had not even been explored fully. We had not even reached half our potential, and Ian had decided to throw it all away.[992]

Perhaps a band such as Southern Death Cult could never last. The intensity of the group and their sudden successes subjected the young band to many new pressures and expectations. Their sole self-titled album was posthumously issued by Beggars Banquet in 1983 and compiled studio outtakes, the single and some demos and live recordings by the band as a snapshot of 'what ifs'.

Moving quickly, that April, Ian Astbury had already called up the services of Mancunian guitarist Billy Duffy, who had befriended the singer on the previous summer tour with Theatre of Hate. Coming from Wythenshawe - Europe's biggest housing estate to the south of Manchester, Billy Duffy had been a youthful fringe member of that city's post-punk music scene. He once spent an afternoon in 1978 writing songs with Morrissey in the legendary Manchester punk band Ed Banger and the Nosebleeds and played one gig with the semi-legendary outfit. A teenage Duffy also taught Johnny Marr how to play the guitar and remains firm friends with the fellow Wythenshawe guitar hero to this day. He had since moved to London to

990 Aki Nawaz to John Robb.

991 Aki Nawaz to John Robb.

992 Aki Nawaz to John Robb.

work in key King's Road clothes shop, Johnson's, and had joined peak-time Theatre of Hate before getting the sack on the aforementioned summer of '82 tour.

Now that Ian had moved to London to start working with Billy, the rest of SDC tried to pick themselves up. Aki, Barry and Buzz put together Getting the Fear, with former founder member of Danse Society, Bee (Paul Hampshire), on vocals. Bee's androgynous looks and charisma had seen him as one of the faces of the Blitz club scene and with Psychic TV. The new lineup looked good, and the early releases added a poppy sheen to Southern Death Cult's styling. The press was buzzing, and they had a brief moment in the sun, but it soon faded.

> We did not have that 'magic'. The new band went into some dark corners of the human psyche, which was great for a time, but never matched the excitement and confused spiritual honesty of Southern Death Cult. We were all part of that chemistry, but Ian, as frontman of Southern Death Cult, had brought it all together with his passion and alternative vision. A great frontman always inspires and attracts people who yearn for more out of life, and Ian became a symbol of that.[993]

Billy Duffy recalls that frontman quality as well from the moment he first saw the charismatic Ian Astbury when Southern
Death Cult supported Theatre of Hate in 1982.

> The band's name was great, and the first time I heard them was when he walked on stage. Me and Stan Stammers from Theatre of Hate were watching them play at Keele University. It was their first support on the 1982 Theatre of Hate tour. Ian looked amazing, like Daniel Day-Lewis in *Last of the Mohicans*. He had a loincloth on and moccasins with bells on them. People were dressing pretty flamboyantly at the time like Adam Ant who had gone from rubber into I'm-a-Jolly Roger a couple of years previously, so it wasn't that mental for people to be flamboyant. But even so, Ian was striking.
> Their opening song was 'The Crow', and I remember the whole intro. It started with a tribal drum beat from Aki, the d'ga-d'ga-d'ga of the drums and then the bass starts, and Buzz did that weird guitar line and then Ian does his little dance across the stage, his little Indian thing, and the bells are jangling. The first time I heard him open his mouth was – with 'We are Southern Death Cult. And this one's called The Crow.' And then he started singing. And me and Stan went, 'What the fuck is *that*?' because his voice was twice as loud as the band. He is actually physically a loud human being with a very powerful voice. And he just overpowered – it was just stunning.[994]

On the rest of the tour, a friendship grew between the pair – a friendship of two very different individuals that would form the core of one of the most enduring rock bands of the past few decades – The Cult.

> I was the only northerner in Theatre of Hate, so me and Ian just gravitated. I thought Southern Death Cult were gonna be as big as U2 or The Smiths, who

---

993 Aki Nawaz to John Robb.
994 Billy Duffy to John Robb.

were starting with Johnny. To me, they had all the makings of a band that was gonna do well. In Theatre of Hate, we had our limitations, but we were doing ok. After the tour, I was kicked out of the band and ended up unemployed in Brixton. I went back to selling clothes in Kensington Market and signing on. I had spent all my money on my Gretsch guitar, and I was living with Theatre of Hate's merchandise guy, Little Ian, in Brixton, in Clifton Mansions on Coldharbour Lane. There was a bit of a scene there, and I was playing around with my neighbour, Abbo, from UK Decay which ended up with him doing a band called Furyo.

Ian's brother Brian came down from Bradford to London and had mutual friends in Brixton and found me. I had an inkling summat was weird when Brian said, 'Ian wants to come down from Bradford and see you. Are you gonna be around?' I didn't think much of it, but Ian came down with a plastic bag full of clothes and an overcoat and stayed at the flat. That was when Ian dropped the bomb, saying, 'I'm leaving Southern Death Cult. I don't want to be in the band anymore. I don't think it's gonna last. The personalities aren't gelling as a band, and I want to do something that's going to last.'[995]

It was a bold move that Billy Duffy understands in hindsight.

I knew there was something slightly off because they had about five attempts to record 'Fat Man' and 'Moya', didn't they? And they could never find the right blend. I remember mixing the sound for them at the Rock Garden once at a gig[996] – so we were close. I lent them my Gretsch for the recording of 'Moya' – all the feedback – that's my guitar. And I remember going to the studio and just hanging out. We were all mates, but I detected a separation between the band and Ian, but that might just be Ian's personality. Something was weird. Apparently, Ian had seen me play some Jimi Hendrix stuff when Kirk Brandon wasn't about during a soundcheck on the Theatre of Hate Tour. I was just goofing off playing more rock stuff. And Ian, having grown up much of his life in Canada, had an ear for rock. He was very punk, but he had listened to American and Canadian FM radio, so he wasn't afraid of that music. When he saw me play Hendrix-y stuff on a Gretsch, with a rockabilly hairdo it clicked something in his mind, and he was like, 'I wanna work with that guy.'[997]

It was at that moment, at the soundcheck, that The Cult concept was born. The idea of fusing the esoteric side of the underground and the idealism of punk rock with classic rock – sounds obvious now but was almost a heresy at the time. Within weeks, in April 1983, the band came together with Jamie Stewart (bass) and Raymond Taylor Smith (later known as Ray Mondo) on drums, plucked from the Harrow post-punk band, Ritual. It was a bold move.

Ian just had faith in me and said we had better write some songs. And I'm like, 'Oh fuck!' because all that Theatre of Hate music which – I'm an immense fan of – was all written by Kirk and not me. I'd never really been a writer. I was in a room and it was a bit like The Rolling Stones manager Andrew Loog Oldham locking fucking Jagger and Richards together in 1964 and saying, 'You're not coming out

995 Billy Duffy to John Robb.

996 April 15th 1982.

997 Billy Duffy to John Robb.

until you've written a song!' I kinda shit myself and went, 'Oh Christ!' Ian's left Southern Death Cult – y'know, a very happening concern – to form a band with this idiot, and I hadn't written a song since I wrote with Morrissey when I was seventeen![998]

The new band was forged quickly and had to fight for its reputation. That July, they released their debut *Death Cult* EP. The release was a bridge between the tail end of their previous projects. With songs referencing Native American Ghost Dance religious movements as well as the writings and teachings of spiritual leader Wovoka[999], it is a snapshot of the spiritual yearning of the time. 'Brothers Grimm' was a song that Billy Duffy had left over from his sessions with Abbo.

Another track referenced *Apocalypse Now*, underlining the film's enormous impact at the time with the film's chic now infusing the scene with Billy Duffy wearing his green Vietnam War-era (5th Special Forces Group) beret flash alongside tiger stripe fatigues.

In September 1983, Ray Mondo was replaced by Nigel Preston, formerly from Duffy's old band, Theatre of Hate, for their next release, October 1983's 'Gods Zoo' which was their last as Death Cult. With their ambitions to break out of the underground, they decided to simplify the name further, becoming 'The Cult' in January 1984, just before appearing on Channel 4's *The Tube*.

The music matched the symbolic stripping-down of the name. Attempting to move away from the post-punk that had birthed them, they were one of the first bands to go back and re-examine rock music like AC/DC and Led Zeppelin. It was a risky strategy at the time.

> Rock was taboo in the UK in the '80s for the little clique who drank in three pubs in London and who ran the British music business. They seemed to think, 'Guitar solos are bad. All rock is bad.' It was a bit Orwellian. And we just reacted against that, and we evolved into more of a rock band. Organically if that's who you are, and if you want to express yourself as a writer in any authentic way, you can't fake it for too long. Trying to write in a manner that isn't truly yourself is just faking it.[1000]

For Billy Duffy, it wasn't until they wrote 1984's 'Spiritwalker' that they felt like they had the music to match their ideas and potential. The single still retained the mysticism of the early work, but there was growing rockism to their sound.

> It came together with that song. I remember many bands were doing better than us at the time: Sex Gang Children, Danse Society, and Killing Joke. Our peers were actually having hits. Everybody had been on *Top of the Pops,* and people were looking at us going, 'Hey – when are you gonna have your hit?' 'Spiritwalker' was our first indie number one, which was, at that time, a relevant milestone. And

998 Billy Duffy to John Robb.

999 Born in 1856, Wovoka (the name translates as wood cutter) was also known as Jack Wilson. He was a religious leader from the Paiute who founded a second episode of the Ghost Dance movement - a circular dance to reunite the living with the spirits of the dead.

1000 Billy Duffy to John Robb.

then we tried to come up with the next thing but blundered a couple of times with 'Go West' and 'Resurrection Joe'.[1001]

The initial success of 1984's 'Spiritwalker' pushed their debut *Dreamtime* album up the charts, and the band started to find their feet. The album still had some of the mystery of Southern Death Cult, as shown on tracks such as 'Horse Nation' with its lyrics taken from Ian's favourite book, *Bury My Heart at Wounded Knee*.[1002] Similarly, 'Spiritwalker' covered themes of shamanism, while the Hopi Ceremonial Butterfly Dance was referenced in 'Butterflies'. This may have been a rock record, but the content differed from the rest of the pack.

> Spiritwalker was paraphrasing a traditional Native American prayer song that I melded with Buffy Sainte-Marie's 'Starwalker', which is such a dignified song and sung with a voice of such power. Everyone around us was getting into hard drugs, and I went into books and film. I remember going to see American Indian Movement leader Russell Means speak on a lecture tour in the early '80s. I found him to be an enigmatic speaker but very inspiring. He was a holy man in real life. Later, I met him and had a sweat ceremony with him, which was very powerful. Spiritwalker' came out of a spiritual quest, although I wasn't even conscious of it. I wasn't objectifying myself or thinking about what my process was. I just found myself being drawn towards specific energies and performers. I pulled information from them, and it came out in my writing. My writing at that time was just so naïve. I didn't even finish school properly. I didn't have a command of the language. Sometimes my writing could be very simplistic. But I thought it was earnest and it was authentic. I wasn't trying to be clever or show off in any way. I was just being honest.[1003]

Dreamtime was a stepping stone. The mixture of rock power with the deconstruct of the underground and esoteric showed that the band had maintained their post-punk roots. Their next step would seem them assimilate the two into a potent whole. That moment arrived with the development of a new riff created by Billy Duffy.

> The big thing for us during the spring of '85 was 'She Sells Sanctuary'. That changed everything. Ian wasn't as keen on it initially as I was, but I thought we had something. We had a very good relationship, though, and he would try singing on anything I came up with. I remember writing the music, and he was, 'Oh, it's a bit like Big Country.' Maybe I'd copped a bit of Stuart Adamson of The Skids and Big Country, but it had our dance/rock thing that we liked and a bit extra, and he got it.[1004]

With its iconic chiming eastern scale riff and surging vocal, 'She Sells Sanctuary' saw the band break out worldwide. The band's second album, 1985's *Love,* sold nearly three million copies, and the pair of them were now in their songwriting stride. The

---

1001 Billy Duffy to John Robb.

1002 The groundbreaking and powerful 1970 book by American writer Dee Brown told the history of the USA in the late 19th century, from the Native American point of view.

1003 Ian Astbury to John Robb.

1004 Billy Duffy to John Robb.

album was produced by Steve Brown[1005] who hounded the band for the job. At first, they were hesitant as he came from a more pop background, but when they agreed, he delivered the perfect dance/rock/pop crossover, which remained as layered and nuanced as before. Plus, his stroke of genius made 'She Sells Sanctuary' the iconic hit.

> The song used to start with a snare hit and come in with the riff. Steve's the guy who took out the middle section and said, 'Why don't you play that at the beginning as an intro?' And it made the song. Before 'Sanctuary' became the big hit, we were under much pressure to perform. I remember our publisher, Jeff Chegwin[1006], who worked for Warner Chappell, had suggested us doing a cover. I remember being a bit of a dick in the meeting and going, 'Why the fuck would we do an Iggy Pop song as a cover? Iggy Pop can't have a hit with an Iggy Pop song, so how the fuck would we?'

> So, we toddled off, and we did the *Love* album with basically a license to do whatever the fuck we wanted. I dragged the wah-wahs out, and we ended up with Mark Brzezicki from Big Country sitting in on the drums because we had to fire our drummer because he'd got a little into drugs; Mark came in with his technique dumbed down and mixed with our music created this weird, unusual thing.

> The two heavy songs on there also helped us get attention in the United States. Because they were crying out for a British indie band that actually rocked. American kids didn't have the same tribalistic point of view as us. They'd grown up listening to FM rock radio. So as much as they were into punk, they'd heard Led Zeppelin and Black Sabbath - like Ian had.[1007]

The *Love* album period of The Cult was a combination of musical and sartorial brilliance that underlined the opposing poles of the band that really made them work.

> I was wearing an iron cross, totally copied from the Asheton brothers off The Stooges' first album. I got a Triumph motorcycle belt, skin-tight black leather pants, plus some hippy beads. I was like, well, if Ian's going to become this hippy thing, which he kind of unveiled with the long hair, and he was pissing people off because of the way he looked – I was like, if he's gonna be that I'd better, kinda like, man up, so I went for that kind of bleached white, freaky-deaky, acid rock biker look. Without wanting to parachute into cliché land: we were the yin and the yang of the band, the cowboy and the Indian – you don't have to be a genius to realise those things are assets if used correctly.'[1008]

Whilst the UK music scene was toying with new pop or a post-punk austerity, The Cult were moving in the opposite direction. They were gloriously out of sync with the musical fashions of the time, but they had the songs and the charisma to pull it off. While Billy Duffy was working his guitar God aesthetic to perfection, Ian

---

1005 From the same class in school as Steve Lillywhite, Steve Brown had worked with many bands including Boomtown Rats, Wham and ABC adding the kind of melodic sheen that The Cult were not initially looking for in their quest for the Big Rock.

1006 Brother of the late Keith Chegwin and Janice Long - Jeff is currently a record plugger and remains a popular figure in music circles.

1007 Billy Duffy to John Robb

1008 Billy Duffy to John Robb.

Astbury had turned into rock star classic with long mystic interviews, mixing a down-to-earth realism with the staring black eyes of a seer. Years later, Ian Astbury ponders the move into the esoteric and rockier version of the band and how it could be so easily misinterpreted:

It's interesting now that we have gone away from punk rock, and people can be really objective about that period. I also had that love affair with The Doors and Jim Morrison and what people did in that period with ingesting psychedelics and exploring inward emotive space. They were trying to get to the meaning of it all, and it was earnest, of course. Then, of course, Spinal Tap comes along, and they put up Stonehenge on stage, and everyone has a really good laugh. I was probably the only person who, when Spinal Tap came along, said, 'you know what – we are fucked!' [laughs] because that film was funny, but at the same token, everybody is just going to look at the superficial elements of rock n roll, and that's just going to be it. It's just going to be a big joke, and sadly it's not a safe place anymore to talk about those things that made rock music more interesting and textured, layered and deeper.[1009]

Flushed with the confidence of success, the band fully embraced big rock for 1987's *Electric*. Any vestiges of the UK underground or proto-gothic shadows were banished as they embraced AC/DC and Led Zeppelin entirely on an album built around riffs. Somehow in the middle of the anti-rock 1980s, they had created a powerful rock record that celebrated the form and deified its clichés to a crunching perfection.

It was perfectly complimented by the masterstroke of bringing Rick Rubin on board to produce the record. Rubin was fresh from bringing the rock to hip hop with the Beastie Boys and Run DMC's groundbreaking albums by adding rock riffs and dynamics to the street energy of rap. *Electric* created a template The Cult would stick to for 1989's Bob Rock-produced *Sonic Temple*. This sound would continue throughout the decade's following albums, with occasional diversions such as Ian Astbury's dream job of being Jim Morrison in Ray Manzarek and Robby Krieger Doors' reformed tours.

His stint with The Doors caused a few raised eyebrows, but it was bringing the journey back almost full circle. Jim Morrison had left a massive pair of snakeskin boots to fill, and it took someone with much self-belief to step up to the mic.

Whatever anyone may think about it, working with Ray and Robby on The Doors project, I learned a lot. We had some magnificent moments, and it was done for the right reasons, but it's easy to throw stones at it. Those guys constantly worked in that space, and because they had Morrison, a wounded kid, they could go into the most magnificent places, and it's evident in their body of work. That's why the work is so good to this day. They were fearless in that way. You communicate through playing. It's an emotive thing. Your head turns off, and you start to feel what's going on, and you start to pick up on rhythms and melodies and tempos, and it comes from this space, and they were just the masters at this.

Ray was like the master of the ship. He could guide the energy to wherever he wanted it to go. I can get an idea of the Morrison that people talk about, of

---

1009 Ian Astbury to John Robb.

Morrison being out there on the frontier, on the boundary, on the barricade and going beyond that. Still, the music took him there because of Ray.

These guys were heads. They knew exactly what they were doing. They were working in a psychedelic space. I was talking to a friend about the difference between bands driven by organics and psychedelics, who, for me, were better than bands driven by alcohol and powders, which is a very materialistic, narcissistic thing. The Doors were in that conversation, of course.[1010]

The Cult have continued to release albums to a lesser impact than their heyday, but they remain a big live draw still with an edge that remains from their idealistic post-punk years. Billy Duffy's distinctive guitar and Ian Astbury's unwavering big voice and yearning for the deeper side have become part of rock lore. It's an enduring relationship.

The Cult have been criticised for being a bit overproduced and grandiose at times, but I think we're brave enough to go into those areas and try them out. Sometimes Billy's driving something, and the guitars will be the dominant instrument and I'm always the one who drags it back down to getting down to basics.

It's not always easy. I'm working with a Mancunian for a start! So, you can imagine what that's like! [laughs] But that's his thing, and he's honest about that. He's never had any airs or graces about working with anything else. He's a working guitar player, and in that way, he's very much from that Mick Ronson school of playing, and that's his mentor and also Steve Jones from the Pistols. They are working-class guys who picked up Les Pauls and had an incredible natural gift for playing. Billy is very much a stoic bricklayer blue-collar guy. The guy who goes to football. The guy who likes to wash his car on Sundays, whereas I'm more likely to be happy in the Himalayas, but you put the two things together, and it works.[1011]

Billy Duffy continues to celebrate their relationship to this day:

We have much more in common than we have in differences. When you get down to the minutiae, it works. I've known Ian for longer than most of my family! 40-odd years!

Ian's always been sort of a unique character. The legend is that we hated each other and were at each other's throats. At worst, it was like the Cold War, but that happens with many bands. I think with me and him, though, we genuinely care about each other. These days, we know what works after we've tried to do different stuff. Ian had a few solo albums, and he did The Doors, and I think – the grass isn't any greener. I think by doing all of that, he's come back around to embrace The Cult.[1012]

1010 Ian Astbury to John Robb.

1011 Ian Astbury to John Robb.

1012 Billy Duffy to John Robb.

Chapter 28

WANTED DEAD OR ALIVE

How Liverpool Opened the Doors to a New (North) West Coast Sound

Towering over the city, Liverpool's imposing Gothic revival[1013] cathedral frames the skyline rising above a metropolis of characters and musical misfits. With an ebullient, flamboyant and brilliantly dressed cast of local faces like Pete Burns, Jayne Casey, and future Frankie Goes To Hollywood members Holly Johnson and Paul Rutherford, post-punk Liverpool was a unique micro scene in the clubs like Eric's surrounded by the city's decaying Victorian grandeur.

Post-punk in Liverpool had a dark psychedelic edge; the brooding edifice of Jim Morrison and The Doors lurked in the shadows as the city created its own West Coast sound part inspired by the California dreaming on the other side of the planet. Sieved through post-punk and with a hefty dose of Bowie, Liverpool's post-punk droogs were outrageous characters whose catwalk cacophony was the link between Seditionaries and goth. Nina Antonia is a prolific rock'n'roll writer and was living in Liverpool during the post-punk period. She was on hand to watch the musical culture shift from punk to post-punk to goth, as she notes. 'Nothing exists independently; goth was a kind of fever. It just seemed to seep in on a tide of black lace and black leather.'[1014]

Far more colourful than its deliberately dour Mancunian neighbour, Liverpool's post-punk fraternity had its own distinct flavour. Doreen Allen has been central to the city's culture for decades from seeing The Beatles play to help run the legendary Eric's before setting up her own club, Planet X - the key goth club in town.

> Liverpool was full of characters. My theory is that it had a lot to do with the wacky hairdressers that opened in the 70s where Pete Burns and Jayne Casey worked. They were ahead of the game and even London hairdressers were behind the Liverpool style in the '70s. I remember going to London with Pete Burns, walking past hairdressing saloons and staff coming out to look at our crimped hair. Liverpool was the capital of crimpers, and the clothes would go with the look, which was also to piss the many scallies off.'[1015]

The second city of the Empire and once the biggest port in the world, Liverpool had musically sparked in the 1960s with The Beatles. The Fab Four had left the city for the lure of London, yet football and music remained at the city's beating heart.

The economic decline of the 1970s saw the city fall apart. The boarded-up Victorian mansions of Toxteth and the riots of 1981 left the area nicknamed 'Beirut' and were

---

1013 The 8th biggest church in the world, it was meant to be proper, full on Gothic in its original design.

1014 Nina Antonia to John Robb.

1015 Doreen Allen to John Robb.

both symbolic of the fall of the once great city. Like Manchester, though, a new wave of bands re-inspired the city with a surge of musical self-belief.

At the epicentre of this post-punk culture was Eric's, a club that opened on the cusp of punk in October 1976, hosting The Stranglers on the first night and then Sex Pistols a week later. The club was operated by Roger Eagle – the highly influential Oxford-born promoter who was one of nature's music fanatics. Eagle had spent time in Manchester in the early 1960s, which had seen him build a reputation as a quality DJ. His playlists of the finest black music heard at the Twisted Wheel club helped build this lasting reputation as a soul evangelist. A falling out over demands to play faster records for the amphetamined-up mods paved the way for what would soon be termed 'northern soul'.[1016]

Between 1970 and 1975, Eagle was putting on gigs at Liverpool Stadium before he moved his operations to Eric's. Here, he singularly cajoled and inspired a new generation of bands into action, and a scene coalesced in the club.

Another focal point for new subcultures was Probe Records. Established by Geoff Davies on Clarence Street in 1970, it was founded on the fundamental premise that Davies was selling records that he personally liked. The pioneering shop quickly became a popular hangout spot, a space for like-minded alternatives to mingle and spark. In 1976 the shop moved to Button Street in the city centre. It was here, on the front steps, that the proud peacock parade of punks and proto-goths would display their sartorial feathers in full public view and would sit and mingle on Saturday afternoons, dressed in all their finery.

The shop, wedged in an old warehouse, was full of the stale smell of joss sticks and tobacco as the local youth would flick through and buy new releases championed by John Peel. Such releases would be furtively purchased, though, as one would have to run the gauntlet of the fearsome Pete Burns, who, by now, was a shop fixture behind the counter, armed with his acidic put-downs and lipstick sneer. His acid tongue and switchblade sarcasm made buying records and fanzines a terrifying experience. Each purchase came with a cutting quip. Many talk of the walk of terror to the counter. The experience soon became a punk rock rite of passage, clutching a couple of seven-inch singles awaiting the inevitable putdown from Burns. It was one barb after another, 'God gerrl, worravya gorra dead cat on yer 'ed for?' , 'what you buying that for…its shiite' he would snarl endlessly at his victims, testing their mettle with a machine gun attack of insults.

The small scene coalesced around the shop and club as renowned local music photographer Francesco Mellina, remembers:

> You went to Eric's for a great night out, and then you went to Probe to buy the music you'd heard there. This was in the Button Street days – the two worked

---

1016 The term comes from an article by London-based music writer, Dave Godin, who wrote a piece on the post-Roger Eagle Twisted Wheel noting a different sound - a 'Northern soul'.

together. Hanging around outside the shop, you'd see early goths. It was where everyone went to meet.[1017]

For many like scene veteran, Doreen Allen the Liverpool post-punk scene was the flowering of years of pop culture simmering in the city. Doreen was a prime witness having been, literally, at the front row in Liverpool since rock'n'roll had started.

> My first big show was Cliff Richard at the Liverpool Empire in 1961 when I was 13. After that I was a big fan of Billy Fury who I saw him many times at Liverpool Empire. Once John Lennon and Paul McCartney were sitting directly in front of me watching Billy, and I also saw The Beatles play there later on.
> In 1969/71 I hired a room above O'Connor's Tavern in Liverpool and put on bands like U.F.O, Judas Priest, Stack Waddy once a week. It was here where I first met Roger Eagle and went to work for him at Liverpool Stadium in 1972, where he promoted many bands like David Bowie – who told my parents that I would own my own club one day. From 1976 – 1980 I was the public face of Eric's. I ran to the office and did the door. It was there that I made friendships with many of the key faces from post-punk Liverpool like Ian McCulloch, Pete Wylie, Paul Rutherford, Ian Broudie, Wayne Hussey, and Pete Burns. It was a very special place and time and you could really feel something happening around these unique people'[1018]

Doreen saw this new Liverpool flower right in front of her with the awkward charisma of a young Ian McCulloch, Julian Cope, the fast-talking Pete Wylie, and the geeky Ian Broudie emerging. There were many others circling the scene, including a young Ian Astbury but no one better encapsulated this sense of the exotic, post-punk Liverpool than the aforementioned Pete Burns. His outrageous blur of images changed quickly from week to week from punk rock pirate to a blur of dreads, to full face of makeup with tinted contact lenses and stacks of jewellery to painted yellow and dressed in some kind of nappy and then the next week appearing in full Native American tribal wear.

One thing was for sure; Pete Burns would never be boring.

Before punk arrived, he had spent 1976 hanging out in London's Beaufort Market on the King's Road, immersing himself in the freshly forming scene. Further down the road, he would visit the eponymous Sex shop, where the late Jordan remembers him invariably taking interest in their early designs. He was a genuine pioneer whose meticulous and flamboyant appearance was much copied in the caustic style parade of the early 1980s. Liverpool cultural commentator and promoter Marc Jones celebrates his wide-ranging influence:

> Pete Burns bestrode Liverpool like a colossus! One moment dressed like Davy Crockett or the next like Vivienne Westwood! Then it would be Sitting Bull or some nightmarish android! He was magnificent and he was intimidating. Probe Records was our very own 'Championship Vinyl' out of the book and film, *High Fidelity*. Most of the staff were a bit miserable and played on it, but Pete Burns

---

1017 Francesco Mellina to John Robb.
1018 Doreen Allen to John Robb.

400

was just a skitter, particularly if you were buying picture discs, coloured vinyl or, worst of all, shaped vinyl.'[1019]

Acidic, eccentric and beautifully wild, Pete Jozzeppi Burns was born in 1959. He was created to rule the *Top of the Pops* catwalk as one of the brightest stars of the post-punk fallout.

Marc Almond, whose own dark-tinted music in Soft Cell would see him as one of the biggest-selling pop stars in the world in 1983, grew up in Southport, a genteel seaside town near Liverpool and remembers, 'Pete Burns was always a creation. I knew him a bit and I knew people who knew him. I remember him being around. How could you not!? I would play Dead or Alive a lot when I DJ'ed at the Warehouse in Leeds.'[1020]

Julian Cope, whose own career was taking off in the psych-pop genius of The Teardrop Explodes, remembers visiting Pete Burns in his unlikely Wirral hometown of Port Sunlight:[1021]

> When I was living in Liverpool, I was surrounded by these wonderful exotic people. The most exotic was Pete Burns. These people made me feel such a square! But I got to know Pete quite well, and we became friends of sorts. I even visited his house in Port Sunlight, of all places, for tea once and met his mother and father. His mother was this amazing flamboyant woman[1022], and his father was sat there with a tie and cardigan, quietly reading the paper.'[1023]

As ever, it was these suffocating suburbs that were the birthplace of the maverick revolution. Ian Astbury knew. He was one of the many travelling into the city centre looking for some kind of meaning.

> Fuck, man, Pete Burns! I've heard some amazing stories about him. I saw his original band Nightmares in Wax in Eric's in Liverpool when I was living in Birkenhead in the late '70s. He was such an icon. He was incredibly well-dressed. I always thought he had a wicked wardrobe. He was pre-Boy George. Pre-everybody. He had an incredible sense of style. That guy lived his life in a completely individual direction. He really embraced his inner demon and went for it. I remember going to Probe Records in Liverpool, where he worked behind the counter, and I remember him wearing Seditionaries head to toe. He was one of the first guys I saw with the tribal look as well. That was definitely a big influence on me, no doubt. Yes, he was terrifying, but then after a while, I got talking to him, and he was very sweet, a really cool guy.
> It's amazing that he is from Port Sunlight – just outside Liverpool. Saying that, though, most of the punk kids were from the suburbs. It took someone like Malcolm McLaren – who was an art student and who was educated to have a cultivated eye that saw the shifts in the culture. He was smart enough to define it

---

1019 Marc Jones to John Robb.

1020 Marc Almond to John Robb.

1021 Port Sunlight was the 1930s new town of perfect suburbia built to make soap in Cheshire. It has never been a hotbed of youth culture.

1022 Evelina Maria Bettina Quittner Von Hudec (1913–1987) was born in Heidelberg, Germany. Because her father was Jewish, she had fled to Vienna to escape the anti-Semitic laws of the Nazis.

1023 Julian Cope to John Robb.

somehow and then guide it or chorale it in the way these wild animals running around needed. Punk was this shift in the energy, a shift in the culture. It was not like he tamed it, but he harnessed it. He gave it an identity, and he corralled it and finessed it, and that became post-punk across the UK.'[1024]

Burns' first band was the left-field, Nightmares in Wax,[1025] who released the great 'Black Leather' single and played a clutch of gigs including a support tour with The Cramps. The band soon morphed into Dead or Alive and honed down their dirty disco interpretation of The Doors' baroque trips. Morrison's baritone croon echoed around the band and the city, an influence that created a new kind of gothic and was a key influence on the Bunnymen, The Teardrop Explodes and Pete Burns. Dead or Alive would morph into a dark matter dance band with songs like the classic 'Misty Circles', capturing Liverpool's post-punk love of swooping, swooning vocals with an added electro and disco mix. It was also imbued with a melancholic melodrama, driven by Burns's powerful charisma and voluminous voice.

One of the children of the glam revolution, the late Pete Burns' ever-changing image was like a dystopian Bowie played out on the mean streets of Liverpool. It took nerves of steel and a razor-sharp wit to survive the brickbats hurled in his direction, yet Burns was more interested in the artful process of repeatedly morphing and melting his own public image that cross pollinated with Adam Ant, Boy George and Ian Astbury.

Pete Burns, in turn, was influenced by The Cramps and their long-lost guitar player Bryan Gregory and his homemade bone accessories, and The Cramps' early show in Liverpool was a touchstone for the freak wardrobes. 'I remember getting a coach with Pete and his wife Lynne to see The Cramps play, ' smiles Nina Antonia, 'Pete was in full regalia, looking like a crimped Hiawatha in a fringed jacket, more eye makeup than Dusty Springfield and decked out in bone jewellery. No one else on the coach would sit near us. I think Pete had started throwing sweets at people.'[1026]

Fashion aside, Burns' own rattling corpse jewellery sometimes interfered with his vocal delivery in the recording process. During an early session at Cargo, a post-punk-centric studio in Rochdale[1027], the engineer would spend all night trying to decipher what the rattling sound was. It was past midnight when he discovered that it was the singer's own myriad of bangles and bones clattering together. It took another hour to remove them all from the mix.

Pete Burns was built for pop though. The early 1980s were his moment, and he grabbed it with perfectly manicured hands. Following their work with Divine and Hazell Dean, Stock, Aitkin and Waterman were brought in to produce. The resulting

---

1024 Ian Astbury to John Robb.

1025 In the band scramble of 1977, Pete Burns was initially a member of the ad hoc The Mystery Girls with contemporaries Julian Cope, Pete Wylie, and Phil Hurst. The band only played one gig, bizarrely opening for Sham 69 at Eric's In November 1977. Nightmares in Wax' original name was another typical Liverpool poetic moniker, 'Rainbows Over Nagasaki'. However, they only released one single – 1980's three-track 7" EP entitled *Birth of a Nation* featuring the disco punk 'Black Leather', which halfway through turned into K.C & the Sunshine Band's 'That's the Way (I Like It)', a cover later revived by Dead or Alive.

1026 Nina Antonia to John Robb.

1027 Arguably the key post-punk studio with the likes of Joy Division, OMD, Durutti Column, Section 25 & Nico recording there.

Hi-NRG pop rush of 'You Spin Me Round (Like a Record)' was one of the biggest hits of that year, and Dead Or Alive was their first number one. It was pristine pop, but you could still hear the vocal disdain that once echoed around Probe records. This acerbic wit resurfaced in mainstream consciousness when Burns appeared on there *Big Brother* TV show in 2006. His cutting comments were still as razor-sharp as those from years before when fired at geeky punk rock youth.

Fellow travellers, Big in Japan may never have broken out of the underground, but their legacy is inescapable. Their twitching post Slits, no wave, proto-goth music was groundbreaking in its manic possibilities. Fronted by Jayne Casey with her striking alien-esque look with a shaved head and eyebrows, they were the supergroup whose 'members became super after the band split up', at least according to the Liverpool Echo.[1028]

Much like Burns, Jayne Casey was a flesh canvas art project who self-created many styles and her band were undeniably ahead of their time. After Big In Japan inevitably fell apart, she re-emerged first in Pink Military and then Pink Industry, whose post-punk, synth-driven songs still dripped that disconcerting mystery that matched the surrounding city.

Pete Burns and Jayne Casey were the King and Queen of Liverpool's post-punk, subcultural warzone. Defying convention and catcalls, they paraded through Liverpool city centre together. Like many in those long-lost times, they were walking, talking works of art. Every detail was honed to perfection as though they were self-made sculptures. Liverpool was unique and music writer, Phil Newall was one of the many who flocked to this exotic new scene and noted the cultural tides changing:

> The Bowie/Roxy thing was key; Planet X was rooted in that, as was Jayne Casey and all the Big In Japan stuff. Once Eric's closed, many punters headed to the gay clubs and absorbed the emerging Hi-NRG – I certainly did, listening to the likes of Bobby O, who wrote all the early Divine stuff, followed by pre-Dead or Alive, Nightmares in Wax. Lots of this, I think, opened people up to the early EBM post-industrial scene, which nestled with early goth due to the use of drum machines.

New Romantic was now in town with and having an unlikely effect on Liverpool's alternative fashion. The later day Bowie / Roxy Music scene picked up on the big flouncy white shirts, kilts, shawls & brooches which spilled out into The State and The System clubs. The latter was the haunt of local DJ Steve Proctor, who watched the developing wild dress code with interest:

> Why did Liverpool dress up? The big mystery! But we did. I guess I was inspired by the likes of Pete Burns, Jayne, and Holly. I was 13/14 when I first saw them. They unknowingly set the tone. In Liverpool, the clothes went with the music. The scallies were easily identifiable and often refused entry, ensuring safety for the punters. Aside from Public Disgrace, Liverpool didn't produce a punk band in the 'traditional' studs, mohawks, boots style. Liverpool bands were more open to

---

1028 The likes of Holly Johnson would later front Frankie Goes to Hollywood, Bill Drummond would front KLF, Ian Broudie would found The Lightning Seeds and Budgie would spend time with Siouxsie and the Banshees. All served time in Big In Japan.

Bowie, Doors, and Zappa, so that clearly influenced our clothes which we bought from X-tremes in town.

Jayne Casey remains one of the key cultural driving forces in the city with her bands, the post-punk scene, Cream and now the Baltic Quarter. She was one of the Bowie kids who had moved on to change the world.

I had already done Ziggy in the early '70s at the first clubs that I went to as a 14/15 year old. By '76 /'77, for us, it was more about The Velvets /Lou Reed/ William Burroughs/Warhol/ – the things that Bowie had introduced us to – that, at the time, we were a bit young to fully understand, so in 1975/76 we delved back. We were also into New York Disco in a big way, so it was all New York for us. Many people went to see shows at the Stadium, but none of our lot did. Because of the way we looked, we couldn't get into most clubs or local gigs so we hung around gay clubs or the art /poetry scene that was still booming in the city. The Liverpool poets had a building called the Academy, and we used to go there a lot to cause chaos. We would make up shit poems and demand to perform them! And we would go to the DADA meeting every week and do the same.[1029]

It was this Liverpool of overlapping scenes that mixed pop culture and art that future Banshees drummer, Budgie, who was from St Helens just out of town in woolly back country remembers from just before he left to move to London.

In Liverpool, there was a heavy cross-fertilisation going on. I remember going to Manchester, and the art crowd were doing fine art and were far more separate. In Liverpool, it all crossed over with the clubs and the Everyman Theatre. You were on the same street. Many people came to Liverpool because they were interested in doing things not expected within fine art.

Wayne Hussey had moved to Liverpool from Bristol to join a local band, Walkie Talkies. Within weeks he was snapped up to play the guitar by Pete Burns. It was a very different world from the one he had grown up in. For Hussey, the flamboyant Liverpool differed so greatly from his small town southern roots.

I never had a further education apart from going to Liverpool and hanging out with a bunch of wild people. I went to Liverpool primarily to escape Bristol. I supported Liverpool FC and was a huge Beatles fan, so Liverpool seemed a natural choice to me. I was working in a Co-op at the time, and the first six months were pretty miserable in a cold flat, living on and off the dole but I felt more alive than I had ever done. I went to Eric's on the first band night and started meeting people in bands like Ian McCulloch, Julian Cope, and Pete Burns. It was Pete Wylie who I first met, of course. I was a quiet, shy and timid West Country boy. I was brought up as a Mormon. I was not a drinker at all. I kept seeing people going to the toilets in pairs and wondering what they were doing. I was so naive! 'they are doing speed?' really! … what's speed!

I remember the first openly gay person I met was Holly Johnson on one of those Thursday nights at Eric's. For a naive, innocent West Country boy, it was very eye-opening. It was a really exciting time. I was in an art punk band, Walkie Talkies who were more like Deaf School[1030] than punk. We started playing shows

1029 Jayne Casey to John Robb.

1030 Key mid-1970s Roxy Music-styled art school band from Liverpool.

and gigs at Eric's. Joy Division played with us a couple of times before *Unknown Pleasures* was released. It was around the time that they did the Tony Wilson TV thing. The dressing room was the size of my toilet, and the two bands were in there, but there was not an awful lot of socialising going on. I remember Ian Curtis sat in the corner drinking a pint, smoking a cigarette and watching the others messing about, with Hooky being the most trouble.'[1031]

Now part of the Liverpool fabric, Wayne Hussey played on a few sessions for The Invisible Girls, the new project for former Penetration singer Pauline Murray. The sessions were recorded with the legendary producer Martin Hannett who slept under a table most of the time. A week later, Hussey got called up to join Dead or Alive; it was an intimidating prospect.

I knew them from around town. I was going to Probe and was always scared that Pete might serve me. He was an intimidating character. Pete has the quickest and cruellest wit of anyone I have ever met. Being in a band with him for a couple of years was extreme! He was hugely talented, which is sadly overlooked because of his style. After I joined, Dead or Alive evolved into what Pete wanted. There was a time when it was all guitars and tribal drums from Joey Musker. It was exciting to be in. I just added the chiming guitars before I had a synthesiser. I then found out that if I put my guitar through the synth it sounded great. I took that into the band, and then everything had to go through it, and that's when it evolved into - the techno Dead or Alive, and I was almost superfluous! When you're a hot shot young guitar player, and all your lines are reduced to a synthesiser, then you know it's time to go.'[1032]

His flatmate, Nina Antonia, was his witness.

I watched Wayne's journey from playing in Dead or Alive to The Sisters of Mercy to the inception of The Mission. When he was not gigging, he'd hole up in his room, alternately listening to Led Zeppelin and Siouxsie and the Banshees. I remember when he decided to leave Dead or Alive, he said he'd heard enough about leather G-strings, and it was time to move on! By the time he had The Mission, we were no longer sharing a house, but he got back in touch to tell me that he would write a song about my daughter, Severina and whether it was okay to use her name. Wayne had always been the best babysitter and a staunch pal, so of course, I said yes. The Mission album *God's Own Medicine* is largely based on his experiences of living in Liverpool, sharing a house, and scraping by on nothing but dreams and rock'n'roll. [1033]

Liverpool was changing. The post-punk bands were breaking through to the charts. Echo & The Bunnymen, The Teardrop Explodes, Dead or Alive and Wah Heat were no longer local secrets. Eric's closed in March 1980. The scene moved to Brady's, which was the same club, just with a new name but none of the cultural impact.

What was incredible was that Bradys had so many great bands playing there like D.A.F., A Flock of Seagulls, Crass, Gang of Four, Au Pairs, Modettes, Bauhaus,

---

1031 Wayne Hussey to John Robb.

1032 Wayne Hussey to John Robb.

1033 Nina Antonia to John Robb.

Play Dead, Janet and The Icebergs (pseudonym for a secret show from Siouxsie and Banshees), The Professionals, Theatre of Hate, UK Decay!

The most popular band on the scene was the pre-fame Adam and the Ants who were booked into play Brady's but then went out into the stratosphere when the *Kings of the Wild Frontier* album broke big. In Liverpool, the bands now included Ellery Bop, Ponderosa Glee Boys and my favourites, Blue Poland and, of course, Jayne Casey's new band, Pink Military.

One of the most underrated clubs was The Warehouse on Wood St. Here, I grew up, and my life changed forever. In two years [from] 1982 to 1983, I saw Sex Gang Children, Theatre of Hate, Birthday Party, Wah Heat, The Fall and Membranes, Cabaret Voltaire (with their giant strobe), Southern Death Cult, Dead Kennedys and The Sisters of Mercy. Doreen from Planet X worked the till, but our paths had not crossed yet.

Stylistically, by 1980, it was either the Joy Division look of long overcoats, shirts & ties, black jeans and winklepickers or the fringe flopping over one eye or the army style that was very Teardrop Explodes and a bit Echo & the Bunnymen. These were the camo-wearing youth with t-shirts, netting scarves and bullet belts and Italian army jackets with stars on.[1034]

It was in this confusion of clubs and styles that Liverpool's goth scene coalesced.

In Liverpool, Eric's had been small, and the scene heads had all gone on to be in bands whilst we now stood in their places like black peacocks! It was at this time that the classic post-punk or positive punk look that later became goth emerged. This was the shaved side of the head, bleached hair, biker boots, ripped jeans, t-shirts with cut off at sleeves and everyone chicken dancing style. I loved this young savage look!

There were the annual pilgrimages to festivals like Futurama 3, and then 4, held at Deeside. All my favourites played there, like The Birthday Party, Southern Death Cult and Killing Joke at their most evil. At Liverpool University in October 1982, Southern Death Cult were brilliantly tribal. They came on to *Carmina Burana*. Every boy in the room wanted to be Ian Astbury, who was at the height of his cool. Bauhaus, at the time, were also at the height of their powers and at their darkest, theatrical best.

There was a definitive homespun music scene with the brooding indie of Echo & The Bunnymen crossing over into many goth record collections as well as the lesser-known Rosetta Stone, who were formed in the Wirral breaking out into the national goth scene in 1988, releasing their debut album *An Eye for the Main Chance*, in 1991 and even scoring a top 40 hit with their cover version of The Rattles' 1970 hit *The Witch*.

Like many people at the time, I had started following bands on the road with my kitbag. I was going to gigs up and down the country and being on the road with the bands. *The Tube* was at its height on TV and was really crucial in getting the music and the message out there.

When Planet X opened in Liverpool in 1983, that was our Batcave. Our spiritual home. Leeds might have been the epicentre of the culture, and Liverpool had a great scene, but people forget that Manchester and the Haçienda was the go to place for all the best gigs. For years I went there, often on the famous Planet

---

1034 Liverpool scene face Marc Jones to John Robb.

X coach. It was here that I saw the likes of Xmal Deutschland, Nick Cave and Cavemen, Einstürzende Neubauten, The Cult, Spear of Destiny, The Gun Club and The Cramps.'[1035]

The whole scene finally coalesced at Planet X. The club was the goth epicentre in Liverpool and the city's dark hub and focal point for the 'black peacocks'. Opened in 1983 by Doreen Allen, the club is legendary:

> Busy times! I had the job as manageress of Eric's/Inevitable Records. I also managed Dead or Alive and Ponderosa Glee Boys and worked on the door at the Warehouse Club.
>
> In 1980, Eric's closed, and I started Planet X in 1983. It was one night a week at Macmillan's. It started after my 34th birthday party and over 500 people came, and Dead or Alive and Frankie Goes to Hollywood played. During the eight months when we were at Macmillan's, Wayne Hussey DJ'd and bands who played included Specimen, Lords Of The New Church, Alien Sex Fiend and The Meteors. Even John Lydon came to the club once.
>
> We based Planet X on The Batcave, but when The Batcave tour did our club, they took many of our ideas away. After eight months, we moved to Brady's for bands on Thursdays, with Play Dead, Balaam and the Angel and Getting the Fear.
>
> I also run a bus for out of town shows like to see gigs like The Cramps at the Haçienda. In 1986, I bought a five year lease for my own premises. I opened the club there, booking bands like The Mission, Into A Circle, Rosetta Stone, Christian Death, Johnny Thunders, Danielle Dax, Gaye Bykers On Acid, Scream – who had the pre-Nirvana David Grohl, and also Sex Gang Children.'[1036]

Planet X quickly became the fulcrum of the Liverpool freak scene.

> In one stroke, Doreen changed the city. All of Liverpool's underbelly of people came out to Planet X! The early days in 1983/84 were undoubtedly the most exotic and fantastic! Inside this club, everybody looked amazing! Post-punks mixed with the new gothier types, but New Romantic was still a considerable influence, and the Bow Wow Wow/Vivienne Westwood look was massive! Skinheads mixed with punks and the '50s scene was also huge with Teds, rockabillies and p. Not just quiffs, tattoos and creepers but really sharp suits, bootlace ties and beautiful puffed-out dresses.
>
> I think, for a year, this was Liverpool's alternative night time culture at its greatest. Never have I been in a club with so many stunning people – male and female. Haircuts were outrageous; spikes, back combs, colours all stuck up with an ozone damaging amount of hairspray and superbly decorated leather jackets adorned with your favourite bands. It was a gathering of the clans, the tribes of Liverpool, in a brilliant club run by Queen Doreen, the high priestess of 50's B movies and all things Cramps & B-52's.
>
> 1985 was the pivotal year. It was the year the whole goth thing blew up. The Cult broke through with *Love*; there was also the Sisters of Mercy *First and Last & Always*, Killing Joke's *Night Time*, The Damned with *Phantasmagoria*, and The Cure's, *Head on the Door*. It really did cross over into the mainstream, but it also went very '60s & rock-influenced. It was becoming far less interesting. Paisley

---

1035 Marc Jones to John Robb.

1036 Doreen Allen to John Robb.

shirts were being worn, and goth was becoming a disease, a social leprosy rather than de rigueur! It all seemed overblown and flowery! Don't get me wrong, I was promoting, and I was going to plenty of goth gigs with the likes of Ghost Dance, Fields of the Nephilim, Psycho Surgeons and All About Eve, but I was now getting turned on by the new DIY sounds of hardcore and post-punk America.'[1037]

Dressing up in Liverpool may have been part of the DNA of Planet X, but the rest of the city was not so accommodating. The realities of travelling home would kick in fast after exiting the club.

Liverpool in the '80s could be an ugly place. It was not the lively, fairly cosmopolitan place it is these days. Having funny hair and black clothes meant, on the nicer side, being skit at by *The End* fanzine.[1038] But in reality, trying to get back to Birkenhead on a tunnel bus at 2.30am when marauding scallies were trying to end your life was different and no laughing matter. However, you did survive, and unluckily there was always a poor sod who got it worse. Sometimes the fighting was so bad that the bus driver wouldn't stop and just drove off straight into the tunnel. The idea of the Planet X coach to the Wirral had not arrived yet, which was one of Doreen's most fantastic ideas.[1039]

As one of the city's famous sons once sang, all things must pass. Liverpool's gothic heyday would soon step back to become another black stitch in the city's fabric. Many of the key players in the city's post-punk scene have grown to become pop culture icons, and the goth diaspora has stretched across the world. Even Liverpool itself has changed since those days, and even the dreaded night bus back to Wirral seems far less dicey.

1037 Marc Jones to John Robb.

1038 The End was the pioneering football/pop culture crossover fanzine edited by Peter Hooton, the singer from The Farm.

1039 Marc Jones to John Robb.

Chapter 29

DO YOU BELIEVE IN THE WESTWORLD?

Theatre of Hate

With those stunning operatic vocals, that sense of drama, the pounding, almost tribal rhythms, the dark intensity and the driving bass lines, Theatre of Hate sound like a shoo-in for goth. Yet the band were never part of the inner core of the scene and created their own unique world that still saw their songs as goth club staples. At the time, there was a whole scene of 'Generation Next' youth who grew out of The Clash and took their flat tops to Theatre of Hate bleaching them like Kirk Brandon's and going for the whole Johnson's King's Road style that the band had.

Theatre of Hate not only sounded great, but they also looked great, and in clothes-conscious UK, these things matter. Like The Clash, their threads matched their music. Style was of the essence, and the band's mix of 1950s retrobilly saw them a gang dressed in a mixture of Johnson's[1040] and King's Road clothing. Together, they moved as a mass of Dr Martens shoes, white socks, fringed jackets, retro army surplus, bleached flat tops and blue denim with perfect turn-ups.

Formed by Kirk Brandon from the ashes of his first band, The Pack, they were inspired by punk but were now on their own trajectory and bringing in many ad hoc influences to create a unique whole that was embraced by many on the alternative and goth scenes. For a brief flicker of time, they were perceived as being a new Clash and where produced by that band's Mick Jones.

There was a moment in time when Theatre of Hate were the coolest band in the UK. It was 1982, and the band had a distinctive sound and the best clobber. Frontman Kirk Brandon had the best voice, the best hair, the best jackets and their gigs were wild riots.

Their 'Do You Believe in the Westworld' single of February 1982 was a top 20 hit. They appeared on *Top of the Pops* looking impossibly cool and youthful, resembling a gang of renegade ragamuffins. Arriving in the time of post-punk flux, the band made a quick impression; their sound was powerful and filled with operatic drama, tribal power, and the angular thrashes of post-punk. Johnny Marr remembers just how profound their impact was:

> Theatre of Hate were like the younger brothers of The Clash. They had an aesthetic that was hard to define and stood alone. A lot of people who are in their fifties now look back at their youth as being dressed like The Smiths at our early gigs, but what they were really dressed like was Theatre of Hate which is where the look came from. Me and my friends were very into them and when

---

1040 The King's Road shop of Lloyd Johnson that was the astute driver of many of the sharp tribal looks of the period, from mod to rocker, with 12 different lines, each reflecting a different facet of the art of rock dress. La Rocka! was catalysed by rockabilly, Beat-Beat beatnik and Mex-Tex, an interpretation of really extravagant cowboy clothing.

my best friend, Billy Duffy, joined them that was really cool. Musically and style-wise, you didn't know what Kirk was drawing from. It could be post-punk or Ennio Morricone or opera, which was unusual, to say the least.[1041]

Manchester, in particular, loved the band. Gary 'Mani' Mounfield – the future Stone Roses bassist – was a keen follower of the burgeoning post-punk scene, especially Theatre of Hate.

> I first saw them at a Futurama Festival in the early '80s. I was very taken with their flat tops, music, and, particularly, Kirk Brandon's unique vocalising. I subsequently followed them right through their career via Spear of Destiny and have made a friend in their bassist Stan Stammers. I am still as much a fan today as I always was. Britain will always produce great music like this. It's in our gene pool![1042]

Their debut album, 1982's *Do You Believe in The Westworld,* was a bold and original statement. It may have had its roots in punk, but it was in a hurry to go somewhere else. The album entwined film soundtrack, twanging guitars, 1950s crooners and epic melodies, all combined with its eerie soundscapes and pounding bass-driven rhythms.

Building up to the album, their run of early singles such as 1980's 'Original Sin', 'Rebel Without a Brain' and 'Nero' were heartfelt anthems that had a lyrical idiosyncratic take on the world. These were powerful, rhythmic pieces existing on the fringes of established genres. Alongside Brandon's distinctive vocals, the songs hung onto Stan Stammers' swooping melodic bass lines and John Lennard's oozing saxophone, combining to create a truly distinctive sound.

Kirk Brandon's quasi-operatic vocals were scoured with a Lydon-esque howl but soared with the warmth of a crooner. The resulting songs were impassioned, dripping with emotion and always came with fascinating lyrics that added a genuine political and emotional depth.

Their gigs were intense affairs, and a thousand flat-top hairstyles preened to perfection would flood the shows. The atmosphere was electric, tense, crowded, and so very hot. The crowds would gather with a simmering edge of expectancy, a sense instigated by the emotional power, suffocating claustrophobia and unexpected grandeur of their music.

Quickly, Theatre of Hate were a scene of their own.

They had opened an escape route from punk orthodoxy.

The band had their roots in the squat land of late 1970s London. The period immediately after punk was home to a complex breakdown of pop culture, whereby newly established micro scenes and bands were fighting for attention. It was a time of wild energy and reinvention but also a time when every band seemed to matter. However, the period is also very misunderstood.

1041 Johnny Marr to John Robb.

1042 Gary 'Mani' Mounfield to John Robb.

It's one of the most neglected bits of the whole period. Punk rock is very well documented by filmmakers etc. There is even footage of The Clash filmed for their first gig at the Roxy; you can see the Pistols hanging about in the early days and, after that, hardly anything. It's like a forgotten period.[1043]

Brandon himself was born in London, where his upbringing would be crucial to his later sound. The twin-powerful influences of the blues and his father's love of opera were to have a profound effect and would help him to explain the range of styles incorporated into his music.

> I was born in Westminster in 1956. My dad was a real opera nut. He was a working-class bloke from North Upminster, and he taught himself phonetically to sing opera. It was amazing. He had a great voice. He had all these amazing 78s from the likes of Caruso, and he used to play them all the time. He had an extensive collection of that old stuff, and that must have soaked in because the first music thing I bought was, unbelievably, Robert Johnson. Before that, I was given this album of recordings from a chain gang, and then I got into blues music. I was only twelve when I went to see John Mayall![1044]

The young Kirk Brandon moved to Devon with his parents as they tried to find a better home than the rough streets around London's Elephant and Castle where they were living. However, Brandon's school days were difficult. While in Devon, he was struck with arthritis and was unable to walk for a year. Here, music played its role as his salvation, and he was able to steep himself in the blues rock and fringe prog of the period:

> The '70s music I was into was Zeppelin, Free, Groundhogs, Black Sabbath, and, weirdly, Van Der Graaf Generator because my mate introduced them to me, and they blew my head off – Peter Hammill is a fantastic singer. I don't think that many people liked them at the time, but they were really innovative – that stuff was so bizarre with the arrangements and the tonalities.[1045]

After six years in Devon, he moved back to London and bounced around the burgeoning squat scene of the capital:

> I came back on my own. I was hanging about and living in squats with a stupid lifestyle with the hanger-about-ers in London. There were lots of buildings bombed out from the war, places like you see in films – it was actually like that, like in science fiction films. You go back to these streets now, and it's rich people living their beautiful lives, but then it was a drifting population. I was getting by and writing songs – I have always written songs from the start – even if initially they were pretty silly ones.[1046]

1043 Kirk Brandon to John Robb.

1044 Kirk Brandon to John Robb.

1045 Kirk Brandon to John Robb.

1046 Kirk Brandon to John Robb.

The bombsite culture wars of London was the perfect backdrop to the newly arrived explosive culture of the punk scene, which had captivated Brandon from the first time he heard Sex Pistols.

> I was in a record shop and asked them to play something by the Pistols. I heard it with my mates, and I said, 'that's it! It's a revelation! that is it!' and my mates were going, 'dunno about that'. I stood there and said that this was the way for me. I loved the angry sound and Rotten's singing. It just changed lives. You didn't have to play stadiums with countless guitarists and bring all your gear in articulated trucks; you could play stupid music with silly chords and shout your head off. I saw The Clash very early on, and it was fantastic. Things were really changing then. I tell my girlfriend about it now, and she looks at me like I'm talking Arabic or trying to decode the runes on the side of a sarcophagus, and I tell her it did exist; it really did.[1047]

Inspired by the energy and possibilities of punk, Brandon formed The Pack in 1977. Despite having the limited capabilities of a young band in their primacy, from the off, they had the sense of urgency, adventure, power, drama and off-kilter brilliance that would come to full fruition in Theatre of Hate. Their sense of ambition was empowering and short lived.

> The Pack was doing interesting things musically and was way ahead, but the band imploded with personality issues. Songs like the singles, 'King of Kings' and 'Heathen' were not regular timing. I was more interested in doing something musical as well, and not just shouting my head off and going mental and sticking your Marshall on ten like punk was becoming. I was moving it on in my own way. I remember having a conversation with Captain Sensible and saying that by mid-way of 1978, the whole punk thing was over. He said it had come and gone already. It had changed into something else. I remember seeing the Banshees at the Music Machine in 1978 and thinking there was something really fascinating in their rhythms and the minor chords on their guitars, which were much more interesting than what else was going on. I was now writing a whole bunch of new songs and things to play in a very different way from their arrangements and drum patterns. Songs that shouldn't make sense but did in their own strange way.[1048]

In typical post-punk pioneer style, Brandon knew what he wanted his new band to be. More importantly, he knew what he didn't want them to be. Theatre of Hate immediately pursued a strong musical and stylistic aesthetic; even the band's name was a statement of their artful intent, taken from Antonin Artaud's concept of the Theatre of Cruelty in his book, Theatre and Its Double[1049] with its profound and dangerous ideas of inciting emotional reactions, Brandon harnessed such themes in his hypnotic performances.

The kind of chord progressions I was using could only be used in a certain kind of way. I needed to play with people who wanted to do something original. The

---

1047 Kirk Brandon to John Robb.

1048 Kirk Brandon to John Robb.

1049 Artaud's Theatre of Cruelty had a profound effect on many performers such as Jim Morrison who loved the idea of breaking from traditional Western theatre and creating a performance in which artists assault the senses of the audience.

bass player, Stanley,[1050] was key, and we both had the same idea about getting a sax involved, like in Roxy Music. So, we got a really off-the-wall player, John Lennard, and it gave us a totally unique sound.

I was trying to move myself on. Push myself a bit to make things more interesting and write testing lyrics. I had a conversation recently about the lyrics, and someone said, 'you are using lyrics that sound like they were from years ago' because no one was using words like that anymore. I got my admiration for the English language from my dad. On my tenth birthday, he gave me a dictionary, and he said, look, son, learn this. That way, no one will be able to take the piss out of you, and along with learning Shakespeare at school, it gave me an interest in language.[1051]

Brandon had also picked up a political edge from his upbringing. The protest politics of squat culture and the rebel idealism of punk only helped to fan the flames.

What I had was more of a social-political edge. My dad was political, and my granddad was a card-carrying communist. He became disillusioned when he realised that Stalin was no better than Hitler. In fact, if you play the numbers game, Stalin was actually a lot worse. That put many people off communism, so socialism was the more acceptable side of it.[1052]

After setting the stall with their early singles, Theatre of Hate went into the studio to record their debut album with a different producer.

Mick Jones had come along to one of the shows and loved it. He volunteered to produce the singles and the album, which we were delighted with. He actually plays on the 'Do You Believe in the West World' single. I put the initial guitar line down, and everyone said, 'let's get Mick to play it as well.' He didn't want to do it at first but was persuaded to do it by our then-manager, Terry Razor, who was a bit of a character and also used to do the merchandise with The Clash. So, Mick came in a couple of days later with his Les Paul and doubled up the guitar line, and it sounded great.[1053]

In early 1982, after the album was released, the band hit the road with a new guitar player – Billy Duffy, who had moved to London from Wythenshawe, in Manchester, looking for a gig and was spotted in a club by Kirk Brandon.

I said I'm looking for a guitar player, and someone pointed at Billy and said he's really good. We were introduced, and I said come down to the Elephant on Sunday, and we rehearsed, and he was great. He had been playing with a pre-Smiths Morrissey and said, 'sorry Moz, I'm off – have my best mate Johnny to play with you instead,' and that's how Johnny ended up playing with Morrissey.[1054]

Billy Duffy had moved down to London to follow the rock'n'roll dream. Obsessed with style and music, he had ended up working in Johnson's clothes shop on the

---

1050 Stan Stammers, who had completed his punk apprenticeships in The Straps and The Epileptics, was the key lieutenant in the band. His great bass lines had been a melodic spine to so many of the songs and his bleached flat top a foil to Brandon's.

1051 Kirk Brandon to John Robb.

1052 Kirk Brandon to John Robb.

1053 Kirk Brandon to John Robb.

1054 Kirk Brandon to John Robb.

King's Road. The shop was a mecca for those in love with 1950s style and the retro rocker look and had become a big part of the band's look, as Stan Stammers explains:

We wore a little bit of Johnson's mainly 'coz Billy Duffy worked there, and we grabbed as much stuff at cost before he quit! We were primarily American Classics guys, though. They would call us when the new bails would come in from the States, and we would go down to the basement and sort through them to see what we liked! During that phase, we also got our military stuff from Flak in Kensington Market.[1055] In the right place at the right time, Billy Duffy was now a long way from his roots of growing up on Europe's largest council estate. He found himself in the heart of King's Road and immersed himself in the look which, in turn, was an influence on his young mate, Johnny Marr. What he wanted though was to bring his guitar to a band.

> It wasn't horrible to be a Johnson's employee in 1980 and ‹81, working in the King's Road in Kensington. I had a lot of dough. It was just great. Life was good, but I was still hustling, trying to get the right band. I'd been in several bands and gained some experience. I had got through my drug phase and kind of realised, you know, heroin wasn't for me, and finally – this sounds like really, really, really pretentious and stupid – but Boy George used to work round the corner from Johnson's, he was a DJ at that time. He had a bit of a crush on me – it's in his book. We were at a club called Dial 9 for Dolphin – cos I was out clubbing every night like you do when you're twenty – and he said, 'There's a guy over there, you look like you should be in his band, you're a guitarist aren't you? Go and talk to him; his name's Kirk.'
> So I went up to Kirk. We were dressed the same way, in that kind of pseudo-rockabilly/Clash look that was going around London in 1981. Y'know, a bit of a quiff but with some military clothes, with Levis and white socks and Dr Marten's shoes – I worked in Johnson's, so I presume I dressed pretty well!
> Kirk looked at me and was like, 'Yeah…' so I auditioned for Theatre of Hate and literally within a week, I was playing Stafford Bingley Hall at the Futurama Festival. Within two weeks of that meeting, I played in Berlin, Sweden and Holland. So that was like the moment when I made that decision to leave my cushy job at Johnson's and spend all my money buying a Gretsch White Falcon.[1056]

Within a year, right at the top of their game, with the album flying, a new guitarist, and a big reputation, the wheels started to come off the band. They had run aground on the rocks and aggressive management – the latter being highly effective in the hurly-burly of the early 1980s pop machine was not easy to maintain.

> Terry used to do marketing for Stiff Records – he came up with the famous 'If It Ain't Stiff, It Ain't Worth a Fuck' t-shirt. He was an abrasive character to deal with. He would be sitting there with a Colt 45 stuffed down his waist. People get frightened. That's not good, and things got funny! But not good.

Added to this was that, after twelve months, Billy Duffy was fired, and the band began to unravel:

1055 Stan Stammers to John Robb.
1056 Billy Duffy to John Robb.

What was funny – and this is an absolutely true story – was that I got fired on a tour in Scotland called 'The Holiday in Scotland Tour' in 1982. We'd been on the road so much the idea was that we don't do holidays, so we're gonna play in Scotland. We played in Aviemore and Fort William and all these little places. They told us to get off at one place because they wanted to do the bingo! This actually really happened. Southern Death Cult had come up to play with us as they had already opened for us on the Westworld Tour, and I became friends with their singer, Ian Astbury. I'd been fired on the way to the big gig in Glasgow but still went to it because they didn't send me home. They made me go home with them in the van after the gig, despite having been fired from the band! I had to endure a van ride back down to London with the band that had just fired me![1057]

The journey, unsurprisingly, was painfully awkward.

A bit awkward? A bit very awkward! At the gig in Glasgow, I met Southern Death Cult, and they went, 'Hey Billy, what's up?' and I went, 'I've been fucking fired!' and they went, 'Fuck OFF! Blah blah blah blah….' I said, 'Go and have a look on stage. Can you see my amp?' and my amp wasn't there, and they went, 'Are you fucking kidding me?' I said, 'No, I got the boot. I guess Kirk made the decision, and they let me go, and…y'know…I've got to stick around.' So, I was in their dressing room. But the little moment of sweetness came where Kirk had to ask me how to play the guitar to 'The Hop' because I wrote the riffs, and he had to come to their dressing room, knock on the door and ask me how to play the riff. It was his song, but I wrote the guitar parts, and that was the current single on that tour, so he had to play the song which he was very capable of. The band was better with two guitar players, but he was very capable of playing and singing.

After I got kicked out of Theatre of Hate, Ian left Southern Death Cult. He came to London and found me living in Brixton in that little scene that was going on there, with Sex Gang Children and a few different faces. It was the kind of a gothic scene that was emerging at the time. It was then that we put what was to become Death Cult together in March of '83, and away we went.[1058]

Despite his sacking from the band, Billy Duffy looks back fondly on his baptism of fire:

Theatre of Hate was an amazing band, but it was run on very post-punk, weird, punky, kind of aggressive hatred lines. There was a lot of tough love in it. There was a lot of methodology. I was on forty quid a week, which was way less than I was making at Johnson's. I couldn't really sign on with Theatre of Hate for very long because we were on *Top of the Pops*. Kirk was getting dissatisfied with the band, and I think, in retrospect, he might have fired the wrong person. I think I might have been more of an asset than a liability to Kirk, but I think I was a bit gobby. I read an interview in the *NME* from the time that was with Kirk and me, and looking back on it now, I'm horrified because I'm the guest guitar player in Kirk's band, and I'm gobbing off.[1059]

1057 Billy Duffy to John Robb.

1058 Billy Duffy to John Robb.

1059 Billy Duffy to John Robb.

Theatre of Hate soldiered on until 1983, when the band finally called it a day. It had been short, fierce and bright – a fast turnaround that suited the band's intensity.

We went from living in squats in poverty to playing sold out tours. Obviously, the money from that never found its way to us. That's your education! There was also the spectre of heroin hanging around the band, and it had got its claws into some people. It was everywhere.

I remember a really mad night when Johnny Thunders was playing a gig, and everyone was laughing their heads off, and I said, 'why is everyone laughing?' And this bloke points to the side of the stage, and Johnny is lying there smacked out of his head. I thought it was so sad.

One of our original drummers, Nigel Preston, had joined Billy and Ian's new band, The Cult, and his swansong was their biggest hit, 'She Sells Sanctuary', and then he died of a heroin overdose. That was tragic. He was a great guy.[1060]

Kirk Brandon quickly reconvened the band as Spear of Destiny. Refining the power of Theatre of Hate, he combined their dark operatics with a stadium rock power that was parallel to emerging groups such as U2 and Big Country, playing what was termed 'The Big Music'. These bands were a part of a new scene which were moving away from the claustrophobia of post-punk and into the big soundscapes and large vistas of the new 1980s rock.

Initially, the band had started recording again as Theatre of Hate with me, Stanley and John. Billy was now doing his own thing with Ian, and they were putting together Death Cult after Ian had left Southern Death Cult.

It was a funny period between the end of Theatre before Spear got going. I was just playing music with Stanley, which became Spear. Maybe we should have taken a year off with Theatre of Hate and reconvened, but I was 25 and fucking clueless, mix that in with the Scottish gangster management, and it was kind of obvious where it was going – nowhere! I wish I was clever, but I'm not![1061]

Spear of Destiny had the same essential core of musicians but with grander soundscapes. This new music had more patience and space whilst retaining the hallmarks that made Theatre of Hate so compulsive – the voice, the melodic lead bass lines and the haunting sax but also a chance to stretch and create something very different:

I felt the whole post-punk thing in 1980 was coming to the end of its thing. People were going in different ways. You could see that rock was coming back, and the residue of the post-punk thing was dying quick. We signed with CBS, which was enormous. It's the same label as Springsteen and Bob Dylan. It was my first experience with major labels, which is never a thrilling experience at the best of times. We still had Terry Razor as manager, and I guess it was an odd mixture of people – Terry Razor and CBS! I suppose, in his defence, he had never worked with a major company.[1062]

1060 Kirk Brandon to John Robb.

1061 Kirk Brandon to John Robb.

1062 Kirk Brandon to John Robb.

It was into this strange, strained atmosphere that Spear's first album, *Grapes Of Wrath,* emerged.

> I think the first Spear album was experimental and trying to find our direction. There were all kinds of things on it, from the blues influence to a tiny bit of soul on it and post-punk. I think the recording of it was diabolical. It sounds trite to my ear. It should have basically been indie rock but sounding a bit harder, thicker, and more bombastic, but it was more bash-bang-wallop, and I'm not a fan of it.[1063]

Spear of Destiny's grand ambition and big music was perfect for the time. They had a run of four near-hit albums, all top forty, but they had to watch as the other 'big new rock bands' like U2, and Simple Minds became the biggest acts of the 1980s. Despite their attempts at 'big new sound', there was still something quirky about Kirk Brandon, a whiff of the punk rock about him.

> Spear didn't fulfil its potential – some of it was kind of good, but the actual recordings were not right. It felt like the label were trying to sanitise us. CBS wanted a pretty-boy-singer pop band, and they didn't like what I was serving up. In that case, you have a breakdown of communications. It was like, 'here he is, not doing what it says on the box'. They thought they had a pretty boy singer [laughs]. Look at me now! It never meshed. I dare say I'm not unique in this. It happens to every artist to this day.[1064]

It was these pressures and contradictions that ultimately finished Spear of Destiny.

> The band's first incarnation that recorded the debut still had Stanley and his brilliant bass lines. The second incarnation lasted for two albums with *One Eyed Jacks* and *World Service* which everyone quotes as their favourite album – which is funny for me!
> There were a lot of factions in the band, and they didn't really get on. Put Terry Razor in the pot, and his abrasive character didn't help either. Ultimately, it's not Terry's fault at all. People were going off in different directions, and it lost focus.[1065]

Inevitably, the band fizzled out. Years later, Kirk Brandon reconvenes both Spear of Destiny and Theatre of Hate and also tours a spellbinding acoustic tour with a cello player, alongside being a key part of the Dead Men Walking tours. He still records and is content with his endless touring, delivering impassioned live shows with his unique and haunting voice that has defied the decades using music and words to connect with the emotions: to wake up the nerves and the heart as Artaud would have wanted.

1063 Kirk Brandon to John Robb.

1064 Kirk Brandon to John Robb.

1065 Kirk Brandon to John Robb.

Chapter 30

A NEW FORM OF BEAUTY: VIRGIN PRUNES, DUBLIN

How Lypton Village Changed a Nation

Back in the late '70s, Dublin was a claustrophobic conservative village – a place where despite sparks of culture, creativity felt suppressed, and a stiff religion without a warm spirituality was in control. The powers that be felt that the Irish nation was the last bulwark of an old school Christianity standing against the tide of filth of the western world, with the likes of the Archbishop of Cashel and Emly, Dr Morris, describing the nation in 1961 as 'a Christian country surrounded by paganism.'

The Thin Lizzies and the even thinner hippies had left their mark, but things were moving slowly until the shock troops of glam sieved through punk appeared. The maverick souls in the radical Dublin undergrowth of the mid-to-late 1970s who had part coalesced around the godhead ziggy of Bowie and that dystopian arthouse vision of glam were now inspired into action by the DIY ethos of punk. Virgin Prunes added their own dark theatricality, surrealism, fringe pop culture and a yearning for an esoteric twist on Christian spirituality - a philosophy that was a fascinating addition to their glam take on post-punk, their penchant for shock tactics, and a freakish wardrobe.

It took this ragamuffin gang of freaks to short-circuit the sleepwalking city and drag it into the 20th century. By creating a danceable work of art with a side order of beautiful outrage and a twist of their own innate spirituality, Virgin Prunes pushed the boundaries of music and appearance and helped to kick down the cultural doors of their stuffy home country and helped to create a pathway from the wreckage of punk and the dying embers of glam into an artful end of goth.

> We knew exactly what we were doing. We were following our animal instincts. We were trying to make a new music to try to get somewhere different. In our heads, we thought we were changing the world.[1066]

Gavin Friday was one of the driving forces behind Virgin Prunes. One of the three singers, alongside Guggi[1067] and Dave-id Busaras[1068], he was curating a provocative and artful freak show. Friday and the band's performance art and wonderfully weird, dislocated music was an eclectic electric shock. They were like the Diamond Dogs from Bowie's mid-'70s sci-fi dystopia running amok in the post-punk playground of a late '70s Dublin, defying its claustrophobic and repressed atmosphere that they would be the key catalyst in changing.

1066 Gavin Friday to John Robb.

1067 born Derek Rowen in 1959.

1068 Real name David Watson, a founding member of Virgin Prunes and one of only two members, along with Strongman, to remain with the group for its entire existence.

Dublin was very repressed. There was lots of unemployment. The Troubles were only just up the road in Belfast. There were bombs going off. It was repressed by the church, poverty, unemployment and very conservative. It was a pretty fucked-up country but Bowie and glam were the beacon of light.[1069]

After the glam rock shock of Bowie, Gavin became immersed in a small clutch of cultural outsiders, a very local Ludd gang[1070]. A 'youthful gang' of fellow mavericks that also included pre-U2 members and other fertile demiurgic souls who created their own imaginary community, a surrealistic street gang which they called Lypton Village.

The conceptual village came together in the mid-1970s at their Mount Temple School in Clontarf, North Dublin and was an imaginary and mythical place of escape steeped in many esoteric ideas and provocative interests. This theoretical village was a safe space where the small clutch of outsider droogs could seek and develop their own interests outside of their country's deadening reality.

Lypton Village was akin to Dublin's own Bromley Contingent. They were a similar loose collective of young, artistic minds bristling with reinvention, unconvention and creativity. Forward-facing and desiring to create something new, many of the group found solace and inspiration in their country's own past, a mystical tradition built into the rocks of the island nation. Perhaps Lypton Village was simply another contemporary interpretation of Ireland's romanticised past, as journalist Brian Boyd explained:

> Lypton Village was a little-known area in Ballymun, Dublin. It only ever existed for a few years during the 1970s. Its residents included Fionan Hanvey, David Evans, Paul Hewson and Derek Rowen. You could never find it on a map because it was a virtual village – a psychological place of escape for its inhabitants. Lypton Village had its own laws: art, music and weirdness were good, but everything else was bad. It had its own language, and its members were christened with new names.[1071]

The loose collective turned nicknames into an art form, creating new identities for one another. Derek Rowen became Guggi, and his brother Trevor became Strongman.[1072] In turn, Guggi renamed Fionan Hanvey 'Gavin Friday', their neighbour in Ballum and best friend Paul Hewson was renamed Bono Vox[1073] , and David Watson became Dave-id Busaras. It was a process that saw every member receiving a futuristic takeover and a passport to create whilst providing an escape from their dreary and predictable Dublin lives, offering a chance to be anything they wanted.

When punk arrived in the imaginary commune, its residents had formed what would become their bands – U2 and Virgin Prunes. These were two deliberately

---

1069 Gavin Friday to John Robb.

1070 reference to the great song by The Fall 'Ludd Gang' in which Smith makes a stand against tastelessness, maybe.

1071 Brian Boyd to the *Irish Times*, October 2009.

1072 Real name, Trevor Rowen, brother of vocalist Derek Rowen and elder brother to Peter Rowen, the child who appears on the debut U2 album – now a famous photographer in his own right.

1073 Name taken from 'Bonavox›, a hearing aid shop on Talbot Street in Dublin's City Centre.

different outfits, showcasing the opposing sides of mythical village life. Yet, both groups had morphed out of the same post-punk immaculate conception, even sharing the odd song title before following somewhat different artistic paths.

Forming the bands had been an attempt to reinterpret the new energy of punk, and whilst U2 were aimed at the mainstream jugular, Virgin Prunes added a sense of wild-eyed Celtic art terrorism to the melting pot. The band's differing identities were unavoidable, but this did not affect the village's closeness.

> The U2 connections were very strong because I grew up with Bono. He lived a few doors down from me. As kids, we used to be bored. We didn't use to go out much. When Bono went and formed U2, what they were expressing was totally different to what we were expressing when Virgin Prunes formed, but there was still this closeness, but it was in friendship rather than attitudes and ideas. As the two bands developed, we came to our own identities.[1074]

Musically, Virgin Prunes integrated primal, tribal rhythms, a mutoid disco and an embrace of dissonance and discord with captivating vocals from the singers. If U2 would go on to become the biggest band in the world later in that decade, it was, arguably, the confrontational art of Virgin Prunes that would have an equal yet far different effect on their hometown than the huge successes of their close friends.

Once Virgin Prunes started playing in Dublin in 1978, the band challenged every convention of overbearing Ireland. This confrontation was conducted most potently through their outrageous live shows. These performances often involved blood, theatrical stage fucking, suggested genderless sex, makeup, pigs' heads and a brilliant deconstructed music. Shock values aside, their sound was parallel to the eccentric howling genius of early PiL to make their music eminently danceable and exotically melodic. There was something about Virgin Prunes' beautiful madness that sparked a whole creative new world.

They were the perfect gang of blood-stained diamond droogs who escaped after Bowie had opened the floodgates of pop culture lunacy in the mid-1970s. Dublin needed this jean genie to escape from its bottle because the city in which Virgin Prunes originated was not the modern fun house of the trendy Temple Bar, ubiquitous cultural events, and the capital of a young, forward-thinking nation.

> We were like a Third World country. If you go back to parts of the Eastern bloc of Europe now, that's what Dublin was like in the '60s and '70s. Grey, dull, mass unemployment and complete poverty. Music became a lifeline to escape for kids. Punk gave you a license to form a band with just an attitude. I turned sixteen when punk kicked in, and I had plenty of attitude. I was ready, and for me, punk looked like the abortion that Ziggy had.
> Johnny Lydon said anyone could do it, form a band and scream. This licence was given to us, and it was beautiful. That was the real godsend of punk. I took the DIY thing very seriously. Also, the idea was don't try and ape anyone. We just formed a band in 1977, and all the influences were coming out before we made it our own. You don't know what you are doing at that age. You are just making it

---

1074 Gavin Friday to the Au2 website.

up as you go along. We were hitting out against a lot of things, like the way that Ireland was very repressed sexually and politically. We were messing with all that androgynous shit as well – getting stuff out. Spitting it out.[1075]

Punk already had its champions in Dublin. The motored-up, tough R&B of local bands was easily assimilated by the new nihilistic rush of punk rock. However, these local bands were not going far enough.

> There was a scene of bands in Dublin like The Radiators from Space, with the late Philip Chevron, who would go on to play with The Pogues. I saw them in 1976, and to my mind, they were brilliant. They had signed to Chiswick Records and released the album *TV Tube Heart* in 1977. Their first single, 'Television Screen,' was the first and only punk record to make the Irish Top 20. That was punk to me. I was actually at the Belfield Punk Festival in the summer of 1977 when they played with The Undertones. I remember that it took two hours to walk to that gig. It was also where the first stabbing at a gig in the British Isles and Ireland occurred. That wasn't very good. The violence at gigs in Ireland was pretty intense at the time.[1076]

The Boomtown Rats was the biggest band in town in 1976, just about to break out. Their supercharged take on the pre-punk zeitgeist of Springsteen and Dr Feelgood was armed with an outrageously charismatic frontman which Gavin Friday observed from a distance.

> The Boomtown Rats were still around in town at the time. I have much respect for Bob Geldof, but he had flares and a moustache, and they were doing Dr Feelgood covers before they went punk. I thought they were a show band. They felt different to what we wanted to do.[1077]

Even when punk arrived in Ireland, Virgin Prunes were still outsiders. Too artful for the linear thrashing of established rock, too outrageous for the new puritans, too out there for punk. Gavin Friday liked what he heard but felt separate from it:

> We landed on that scene, and there were a few bands around, but most of them took on an almost power pop feel. The northern bands from Belfast, like The Outcasts, were like the beginning of Oi! really. Stiff Little Fingers were around – 'Alternative Ulster' is a genius pop song – and The Undertones' 'Teenage Kicks' is brilliant as well, but we didn't fit in with any of it. We were dealing one minute with improvisation and performance art, and we were big into German music like Kraftwerk, Can and Neu! I was mad into Public Image Limited, and the darker, more industrial side would become more interesting, but at the same time, I loved in your face punk and pop and Jacques Brel; the band was almost schizophrenic because of this.[1078]

The Irish music scene was a small affair with the post-punk community like a remote colony, clinging together in cultural isolation. Everyone knew everyone else, and the must-have purchases were always a long ferry journey away.

1075 Gavin Friday to John Robb.

1076 Gavin Friday to John Robb.

1077 Gavin Friday to John Robb.

1078 Gavin Friday to John Robb.

There was one shop called Advance Records, off Grafton Street, near the Dandelion Market, which would get imports in for you and another shop called No Romance, which the sisters of Boomtown Rats keyboard player Johnny Fingers ran.[1079] A lot of the time, I would get the ferry over to Liverpool and buy records. I'd say, 'How many people want Cabaret Voltaire's 'Nag, Nag, Nag' single?' and I would go over to Probe Records, where Pete Burns from Dead or Alive would famously work and get 15 copies, and 15 copies of the latest Pere Ubu release. I would make these shopping trips for singles. It really pisses me off today, people moaning about getting hold of stuff: then it was the quest! The weekend on the car ferry![1080]

In the pre-internet days of vinyl currency, a record was like a missive from an imaginary world, a portal to a new culture. Records were invaluable and micro manifestos.

There was a great sense of adventure in travelling to buy the singles. You would have your copy of *Datapanik in the Year Zero* by Pere Ubu, and no one else would have it in the whole country. That felt great! In a weird way, there was a bit of a trainspotting thing goin' on. That was the mentality.[1081]

The anarchic nature of punk and its micro scenes meant that this was no mass movement. The inhabitants of Lypton Village were just a tiny clutch of free thinkers, and there were similar pockets across the UK and Ireland.

I think punk was the last scream of rock'n'roll. It was amazing, with all the energy and excitement. Ten years later, there was the dance scene, and that was an energy as well, [but] punk was ten years after the 1967 summer of love, and this was the summer of hate. The *NME* was the Bible to me as a kid, and then punk came along but, for me, the period just after, from 1978 to 1982, has been very ignored. We were much more related to that era. You can actually trace a lot of that music from the Bowie fans who got into punk – bands like Joy Division, The Slits, The Pop Group, Cabaret Voltaire, and Public Image, who went that way. It was the geezers from the suburbs of Manchester and Sheffield, the grey-coat brigade with the eyeliner – that was what was going on, and we attracted that crowd. I remember going to Futurama Festival in 1980 to see PiL and Joy Division, which was unbelievable, wasn't it? We played the second one, and I remember Lydon had his back to the audience, telling them to 'fuck off, you cunts'.[1082]

That crowd were the early stirrings of the goth scene, and Virgin Prunes were very much part of this post-punk landscape, creating their own distinctive howl.

The name 'Virgin Prunes' had been hanging around for a while. We'd had it since the early '70s. You'd see old people walking around, and we'd call them prunes. That's where it came from. Virgin Prunes were quite innocent, and we always said if we ever had a band, we'd be called that. The name was there; now we had a lineup, and we each had a key role. I was a big, big music fan, and Guggi was also

---

1079 Susan and Regine Moylett, a singer, and subsequent long-time PR person with U2.

1080 Gavin Friday to John Robb.

1081 Gavin Friday to John Robb.

1082 Gavin Friday to John Robb.

a visuals person. When punk happened, it was a godsend. It was like we and U2 were two bands just waiting to pick up an instrument.[1083]

Their second gig in 1978 set the template for their provocative and delicious performance, as Friday fondly recalls:

At first, there was just me and Guggi, with U2 as our backing band, when they were still called The Hype. I worked in a slaughterhouse and got a load of white coats and mesh, which we used to cover up with. We did a 20-minute version of '(I Can't Get No) Satisfaction' slowed right down so that it would take a minute and a half to get one sentence out. It was totally provocative. After that gig, Dik Evans, who was Edge's older brother, left The Hype and came to work with us.[1084]

Another gig soon followed. The ad hoc lineup supported The Clash in 1978, which saw them venturing further into the obscure. In these early performances, they were testing the sensibilities of even the self-styled broadminded punk rock nation. Gavin Friday still relishes the confrontation:

The gig took place at the Top Hat in Dun Laoghaire in October 1978. When we came on, Guggi was wearing a tiny skirt, and I had a plastic suit made out of raincoats, no jocks underneath, and a pair of Docs. We had only played two little gigs before that. Steve Averill from The Radiators from Space played synthesiser with us that night. When we started, the crowd just went apeshit. They thought Guggi was a chick. The adrenaline of all these people pogoing kicked in, and I started jumping around; the next thing, this plastic suit that my ma had made me split completely. I was standing there totally bollock-naked, except for a pair of Dr. Martens. I turned around, and Guggi's skirt had come off, and you could see that he was a bloke. All hell broke loose, bottles were flying, and they were setting the curtains on fire. We were thrown off the stage by The Clash's tour manager and fucked off out the door. We had no money and had to walk home with all our gear from Dun Laoghaire to Ballymun.[1085]

By late 1978, instead of being trapped by the newly buckled straitjacket of punk, the Dublin contingent embraced an 'anything goes' philosophy and pioneered a post-punk artfulness. Their wilful and evocative provocation saw them as the city's interpretation of such dark and artful bands as Public Image Limited, Einstürzende Neubauten, The Fall and The Birthday Party. Their boundary-pushing warped music, avant-garde performance and theatrics soon gained them a local cult audience. They were fiercely loved by few but ridiculed by the culturally conservative community of their homeland. This was their success. Their aim. It was part of their blood.

Ireland was different then. I remember someone rang me to say Johnny Rotten was in town having a pint and that he'd been arrested. That's what it was like. He ended up in Mountjoy Prison. He was supposed to go to court, but he legged it. Lydon had Irish blood, Morrissey had Irish blood, the Gallaghers are fucking Irish – the whole attitude is like that.

1083 Gavin Friday to John Robb.

1084 Gavin Friday to In The State website.

1085 Gavin Friday to state.ie

While Gavin Friday and Guggi's manic vocal interplay had served them well, they had quickly added a third vocalist into the fray. Dave-id Busaras fitted well into the group, with his early performances involving the consumption of a ketchup-smothered chicken as a musical accompaniment. Busaras also began writing songs and performing them live. It proved to be a cathartic outlet for the previously introverted soul who'd experienced a childhood battle against meningitis and had lost his mother at a young age. He became an integral part of Virgin Prunes in the studio, contributing tracks to all of their albums. The wide range of musical styles covered by Dave-id's songwriting reflected his eclectic taste in music; his voice, capable of expressing both a wild rage and soul-melting sorrow, made him a truly unique artist in a truly unique band.

The Prunes' multi-frontman format also saw a solid band behind them. Hot on the heels of guitarist Dik Evans came The Hype's bassist, Strongman,[1086] and drummer Pod,[1087] who was eventually by replaced Haa-Lacka Binttii.[1088] With Binttii on drums, tape loops and keyboards, Virgin Prunes surprised even themselves when they signed with Rough Trade records. They released a brace of singles, including their January 1981 debut, 'Twenty Tens', on their own Baby Records label. A driving, manic song, wild with ideas and sounding so fresh today that it could have been released last week, the single was a shot of maverick energy that could still sit easily in a set by new bucks from Dublin like Murder Capital or Fontaines DC.

They followed it with a second single, the gloriously eccentric 'Moments and Mine (Despite Straight Lines)' that June. Like a perfect Prune Yin to U2's Yang, the bands were running parallel and opposite careers. U2 had begun their ascent into a worldwide success, which; although they were utilising the same source material as Virgin Prunes, was moulded into a new kind of rock music that would fill stadiums. Virgin Prunes resolutely went in the opposite direction, into an art underground with smaller gigs involving innovative music. Not shying from their love of provocation and artful dislocation, these shows would often feature raw meat thrown around a leaf strewn stage, amongst other dark theatrics.

> People have always brought comparisons between the bands musically. But we've never really gone together on musical terms. If I see Bono, I won't talk to him about music. I'd talk about other things. We hate it when people bring it up 'cos they say, 'Hey, you're in Virgin Prunes. Well, tell us all about U2.' We get that a lot, so we hate the U2 connections! It just gets to be a pain in the arse.[1089]

1982 saw the band creating a larger impression with their impassioned and left-field live performances. Their dark theatricality was a definite precursor to what would become goth, and their artful provocation brought an intense coterie of fans. They were obsessed with dark themes and artful confrontation, which continued to feed

---

1086

1087 Real name Anthony Murphy.

1088 Real name Daniel Figgis, now a composer and multimedia producer and curator.

1089 Gavin Friday to John Robb.

into their recorded work. Their music remained hypnotically off-kilter, even during an attempt to become more commercial with 1982's excellent 'Pagan Love Song' and 'Baby Turns Blue' singles, both would become goth club staples with their anthemic choruses and dance floor rhythms.

Their debut 1982 album, ...If I Die, I Die, is, for many followers, their grand statement. It was a release that somehow managed to confine their creative madness into recognisable, near-song structures that ring with a primal, pagan originality. The album wildly swung between emotional extremes and makes for unsettling listening. Besides the tense drama and unique guitar chiming of 'Ulakanakulot' sat the band's closest attempt at a breakthrough song; the electro-drenched hysteria of 'Baby Turns Blue'. As expected from the obtuse band, it was an album full of twists, turns and curious imagination – a complex and brilliant work.

Maintaining their love of the conceptual and artful, the Prunes also released their 1983 A New Form of Beauty compilation album that collected parts 1 through 4 of the A New Form of Beauty project. Of course, though, a volatile band like Virgin Prunes was always going to have an inbuilt obsolescence. They were not built to last.

The group were created to break barriers and then break up.

By 1984, both Guggi and Dik Evans, unhappy with the music business, left the band. Guggi, despite a few years in prison, is now a respected artist whose work has continued to explore the depiction of common everyday objects whilst making magic from the mundane.[1090]

Despite these changes, initially, Virgin Prunes regrouped, with drummer D'Nellon switching to guitar and Pod returning as the band's drummer. The reconstituted lineup started to record their unreleased second album, Sons Find Devils, but it wasn't until 1986 that they finally released a version of the album. As a four-piece, the following year, they released The Moon Looked Down and Laughed, which was produced by Soft Cell's David Ball. Rejecting a consistent sound, the album is full of unique, nursery rhyme-style ballads.

Shortly afterwards, Gavin Friday left to pursue a solo career and to write soundtracks. The band continued as the Prunes, but the moment had passed. Despite never reaching mainstream success, they had opened up a small tear in the fabric of Dublin. To this day, when visiting the city, you see a different vista – more eccentric, more artful, and more off-kilter.

Freer.

Virgin Prunes have left their mark not only musically and sartorially but also culturally and politically. Once Dublin realised that it could nurture something extraordinary, then there was space for similar creatives, the lid was off, and the beautiful madness started in earnest.

> We didn't have a fucking clue. One of the few things I was good at was art. We were always called pretentious pricks simply because we were into the avant-garde. I remember when we were sixteen, when it was a big deal to come into town and

---

1090 With a focus on repetition and abstraction, Guggi is celebrated and exhibited worldwide.

hang out at McDonald's. One day we walked in and saw the performance artist Nigel Wolf naked with paint all over him and a huge stream coming off his mickey, pulling these rocks. We were going, 'What the fuck was that? We just continued from there…[1091]

Virgin Prunes had the same reaction. They were post-punk provocateurs, tapping into the artistic confrontation of punk's inner psyche, duty bound to terrify the mainstream. The band's closest bedfellows were the punk experimenters, musicians tearing rock apart, searching for new angles and ideas to mine, as Gavin Friday explains:

We freaked out the radio stations. The whole 78/82 scene of Gang of Four, Joy Division, the Banshees – was where we fitted in, but our music was also very forward-looking. Some of our stuff could have been made in New York in the 21st century, and I'm surprised that no one ever followed what we tried to do, even with the visual aspect and the performance art end of it. When you travel, you meet a Paddy everywhere you go. Look to America! look west! With his punk interpretation of Irish music, Shane MacGowan hit a chord there in a way that we never could.

Looking back, Friday understands his importance in the cultivation of the proto-goth scene:

That confused us so much. We were sort of instigators in that whole movement. We were the band that wore makeup, then The Cure, Bauhaus, Banshees, and other people picked up on the androgyny.

Post Virgin Prunes, there have been all manner of projects and art exercises. These are creative people, and, in many ways, being in a band was just one part of their art war. Somehow, almost by accident, maybe even by a grand instinctive design, they managed to make some great music that echoes through the decades, sounding barely dated.

We knew exactly what we were doing – following our animal instincts. We were trying to make a new music to try to get somewhere different. In our heads, we thought we were changing the world. There was a scream for identity. Our country was changing. We were the first generation to kick back and say, 'Fuck off and fuck religion – we're getting out of this – fuck your repression.

This common theme of music culture kicking against the suffocating pricks of mainstream consensus was played out over and over again across Europe. Playing with styles, symbols, sound, and even pop culture itself can go a long way in changing your corner of the world, just like the next group on our journey have done.

1091 Gavin Friday to state.ie

Chapter 31

'GOOD POETRY CAN STILL RESONATE LOUDER THAN A THOUSAND GUNS'

Rammstein for GrownUps: Laibach

'Why is our new project based in Iran? Firstly, because the story originates in Persia; secondly, because Iran is an ancient civilisation where music, poetry, politics and philosophy have always been of great importance; and thirdly, because we believe that cultural and political differences in these difficult times must be overcome through a profoundly open cooperation, against all odds. For example, if we were to make an opera about Boris Johnson or Donald Trump, we would want to present this project in the UK or America in every way and without any prejudice.'z[1092]

Turning mystery into an art form and near situationist pranking into perfectly primed musical missives, Laibach have been pushing musical and political boundaries since their formation in 1980. The Slovenian band have been creating a mixture of industrial, martial and neo-classical music that can veer from a musical concrete to classical to folk to even a high camp pop with the contrast between Mina Spiller's beautiful, almost operatic vocals and Milan Fras's ever-present bass growl helping to define their ever-changing muse.

Meanwhile, Laibach create thought-provoking projects that point the finger at the many modern ills of totalitarianism, hypocrisy and 'the ways things are' whilst utilising the aesthetic and exaggerating its pompous stupidity. Their decades of eccentric, brilliantly conceptual and artful releases have encompassed and embraced a bewildering variety of musical styles and ideas. Their industrial roots and dark energy playfulness initially attracted the art goths as they presented a dangerous and highly effective mirror at a world gone mad. Their modus operandi was best summed up by journalist Richard Wolfson, who wrote of the group:

> Laibach's method is extremely simple, effective and horribly open to misinterpretation. First of all, they absorb the mannerisms of the enemy, adopting all the seductive trappings and symbols of state power, and then they exaggerate everything to the edge of parody. Next, they turned their focus to highly charged issues — the West's fear of immigrants from Eastern Europe, the power games of the EU, and the analogies between Western democracy and totalitarianism.[1093]

Laibach were birthed in so-called industrial music with the initial sound collage of their early days. Their later musical journey took them through pop deconstruction,

---

1092 Laibach to John Robb.
1093 Richard Wolfson.

glacial electronica, neo-Euro pop, and classical and then to their 2016 reworking of *The Sound of Music* soundtrack. More than a band, they were even part of their own art movement, the NSK, to further explore the complicated relationship between Germany and what was then their home country of Yugoslavia. Their playful symbolism and ideologies create thought-provoking narratives asking questions that play serious games with pop culture but with a sly and dark sense of humour.

They deal in concepts and confusion with a sound and vision that has been embraced by art-goths and avant-garde fiends alike. Laibach does not operate like a normal band. They are an art collective. Their interviews are conducted as a singular entity, and some band members do not appear on stage. There is a mystery to the group that shape-shifts at will and whose latest project with an orchestra in Iran, like their previous project in North Korea, begs the question of whether the band is deliberately working through the USA's so-called 'axis of evil' countries.

> Oh yes, we do have America on our list as well! Honestly, it's harder for a band to play music in the USA with the prohibitive cost of visas now than go to Iran.[1094]

Laibach are not a 'normal band' but a coalition of machiavellian and brilliant individuals who create a culture war. The wide-ranging and conceptual brilliance of the band parallels the abrasive intellect of the underground industrial scene and has somehow found its way into the mainstream fringe.

They are sonic situationists who have covered whole Beatles albums, deconstructed Queen songs, subtly reinterpreted national anthems, and released an album of pure Europop that questioned the continent's future. They have operated beyond the natural laws of pop culture and made accomplished music of all styles, remaining artfully confrontational and ideologically restless. Like the German playwright Bertolt Brecht, they seem to believe that: 'art is not a mirror held up to reality, but a hammer with which to shape it'.

Laibach formed in 1980 when their homeland of Slovenia was still a province of Yugoslavia – a nation that was then a loose confederation of awkward Balkan states bound together since the war by strongman President Tito. By 1979 Yugoslavia little more than a convenient coalition and about to unravel.

Formed in the small industrial Slovenian mining town of Trbovjle, Laibach has been blurring the edges and artfully desecrating reality for decades. Their hometown was something of a smoke-filled belch in the former Yugoslavia. The discovery of coal in the days of the Austro-Hungarian Empire had turned what was once a beautiful valley and a place for the dukes and local aristocracy to hunt into an Eastern European industrial powerhouse known as the 'the Red District' due to its proletarian, communist population. Their industrial roots were initially reflected in their music as they created soundscapes from metal, old machinery and a pointed sound collage in the shadow of the decline of their hometown.

1094 Laibach to John Robb.

Initially, the system seemed to work, but things started to degrade and fall apart. They started closing everything down, but at its peak, Trbovlje had coal production, machine and cement factories, power plants and so on. Power plants produced a lot of dirt and smoke in the Trbovlje Valley, so they came to the idea of building a higher chimney. Now you can see this chimney all around the area from the mountains; it is the biggest chimney in Europe – in fact, at the time, the highest self-standing structure on the continent.

Some of our fathers were working in Trbovlje's factories, [so] we were industrial Socialist children. We ourselves worked in different factories as kids occasionally, so we could earn some money and understand what was happening in the factories. Our grandparents worked in the mines. Trbovlje is now quite a different city, there's a company there now producing software for NASA. But I think it will take a while before Trbovlje gets rid of its industrial feel.[1095]

Much of the music in this book is forged in this post-industrial decline. It was the same post-war post-industrial story played out across Europe with the same collapsing old buildings and declining industries, leaving dark shadows and a perfect backdrop for the new post-industrial gothic. Iggy Pop similarly describes the mid-west industry's end days as a key part of The Stooges' sound. Black Sabbath invented heavy metal from the clank and grind of the tail end of Birmingham's manufacturing powerhouse, while Factory Records and Joy Division's Manchester was played out to a backdrop of post-industrial decline.

Laibach's choice of a name already showed their keen nose for subversion and for the stirring up of historical baggage. Using the German name of the then state capital Ljubljana,[1096] they deliberately provoked listeners with the rekindling of wartime memories. This, combined with their military uniforms and post-war imagery, was designed to confront and disturb. Their unsettling iconography was already lampooning nationalism at its ugly endpoint. It had the required effect, and the band was at the centre of much controversy.

Their early days of deliberate provocation saw them jolt and jar Yugoslavia. It worked, and the band were public enemy number one after an early national TV appearance. The misunderstanding media soon threw accusations of being Nazi's at the band, mistaking their Yugoslavian military outfits and authoritarian costumes for something far darker. Of course, they would reply in a typically obtuse Laibach way, 'We are fascists as much as Hitler was a painter.'

In the early 1980s, Laibach were operating out of the Slovenian art scene, seeing the group collaborating with art groups like Irwin (painting) and Rdeči Pilot (theatre). They saw artistic subversion as necessary and their narrative important in the national debate:

Laibach was always very useful material for public debate regarding freedom of artistic expression and speech. To a certain degree, we knew that we had to

1095 Laibach to The Quietus website.

1096 The German name for the city, Laibach, had been in sporadic use in the city for centuries.

produce problems so that people like Slavoj Žižek,[1097] the Ljubljana School of Psychoanalysis, and others could debate it. There was a kind of symbiosis between us and other alternative movements in the early '80s.[1098]

Laibach formed in interesting, if troubled, times only three weeks after the death of President Tito, which was the starting point of the gradual collapse of Yugoslavia.

> At the beginning of the '80s, lots of things started to happen. After Tito's death in May 1980, chaos entered Yugoslavian politics. Nobody knew what was going to happen, and the situation was very tense. In Slovenia, we already had the punk movement, which was very important, still anarchic and had a strong political appeal.
>
> Around punk, there were all these alternative political groups and movements who were trying to establish themselves as the opposition to the dying Communist system. We covered streets and entire areas with our posters, with the black Laibach cross, which we chose as our symbol.

The Laibach black cross was taken from Malevich[1099], the Russian modernist painter whose artwork sought pure expression over the natural form. The powerful and simplistic symbolism in his black cross appealed to Laibach, who also revelled in how easily it could be misconstrued and with the painter's complex relationship with the revolution. Laibach enjoyed playing with iconography. They mixed provocative symbols like the black cross with symbols from their mining background, such as the Triglav mountain, deer horns and traditional outfits. They combined these motifs with stern haircuts and their, military-style uniforms and the Malevich cross to create a perfectly misunderstood whole. Somewhat brilliantly, the band countered any barbs aimed at them for dressing in totalitarian military outfits by claiming their look was just like the uniforms that pop bands like The Monkees wore.

> Military service was an obligation in communist Yugoslavia. We all went to serve in the army. Of course, we had uniforms, and as a soldier, you could occasionally go out in them. It was quite a ritual – soldiers were walking up and down in city centres in uniform, trying to talk to girls and getting drunk and fighting with local boys. Most members of Laibach were serving military service in other parts of Yugoslavia than Slovenia, like Serbia, Macedonia, Montenegro, Croatia, Kosovo or Bosnia. A member of Laibach who served his military service in Belgrade would occasionally escape from the barracks dressed as a soldier, only with an added Laibach cross – a badge on the uniform. He was going to punk and other alternative and cultural events or concerts. People thought that this uniform was his regular 'punkish' outfit.
>
> In the Yugoslav army, there were musicians who had to play music in the officers' clubs and so on. Bands were dressed in military uniforms, performing either jazz or rock standards and then mixing them with military songs. Other armies had (and still have) such bands.

1097 Controversial Slovenian philosopher, often referred to as the 'Elvis of cultural theory'.

1098 Laibach to Luke Turner from The Quietus website.

1099 Malevich was a Russian avant-garde artist and art theorist, whose pioneering work and writing had a profound influence on the development of abstract art in the 20th century.

So, the idea to use uniforms was there at the very beginning. When one of the members left the army, he had a chance to take with him a few military uniforms stolen from the magazine. He took them directly to the Laibach concert in Belgrade and dressed the band in these new outfits for the show. It was in the tradition of The Monkees and groups like The Beatles and The Rolling Stones – all these groups had a sort of official uniform at their beginnings.

So, as a Yugoslav rock band, we started to wear authentic Yugoslav military uniforms. Our only addition was the Laibach badge with the cross on it – that was it. A new uniform was born in a different context, and it worked horrifically well.[1100]

The army background was also useful for their then-rudimentary stage show. The addition of stinking smoke bombs 'borrowed' from the armed forces would not only choke everyone in the room but would also start the process of the band's ambitious modern live productions.

We smuggled out some smoke bombs. At the beginning of the '80s, it was hard to get stage hazer or smoke as an additional effect to the show. So, we simply used these camouflage smoke bombs. They were not very pleasant for the eyes, but they looked great; you could see nothing for a while. The first time we used them was in Belgrade, which actually was the ex-army officers' club turned into a student cultural centre. It was a disaster because of the eye pain and tears, but the band insisted on continuing to play onstage. Unfortunately, the audience was not so fanatic and escaped from the venue. It was all very funny and heroic at the same time.[1101]

The band also had a clear idea of what they were and what they were not, which was encased and enshrined in their 1982 manifesto:

First of all, the idea of the 'stage', 'main stage', and audience in the modern culture and society (where everybody is a 'star' – at least for 15 minutes) is very confusing and debatable. In principle, everybody is onstage all the time… Although the 'original' Laibach members might not appear onstage anymore – actually, they do appear occasionally – they are still connected to the group and work with it as much as when they are needed. Laibach 'refuses' the concept of originality and understands the notion of 'original members' as obsolete.

A group is, first of all, a collective mechanism where members have to leave their individual projections and frustrations aside. They have to submit or, even better, 'exclude' individuality in order to accept the functionality and complexity of the 'higher' system. In such a mechanism, every particle is important, but it is also interchangeable. Laibach was and still is an organism whose life and means of activity are higher – in strength and duration – than the goals, lives and means of the individuals which comprise it. It self-reproduces itself as an idea and constantly mutates organically as a progressive virus.[1102]

With individuals absorbed into the group, Laibach were now ready to confront their public. Their first appearance was planned as part of a multimedia project called

1100 Laibach to Luke Turner from *The Quietus* website.

1101 Laibach to The Quietus.

1102 From the Laibach manifesto.

'Rdeči revirji' ('Red District'), which aimed to provoke the political stalemate in their hometown. Their use of iconography, name and image saw them banned before the show, causing a level of notoriety that they would only work to amplify over the years.

The banning of the first gig had set the agenda for the band. Their artful controversy was a big national story, and the misconceptions and confusion they generated were quite deliberate and would soon become the core of their art.

They finally managed to play their first show proper, 'Žrtve letalske nesreče',[1103] in January 1982 at the Ljubljana club FV, which was followed up by performances in Belgrade and Zagreb. The band's aesthetic was to lead to further, even more direct repercussions. At the Novi Rock Festival in Ljubljana in 1982, their then-singer Tomaž Hostnik was hit by a bottle in the face, causing a large bleeding cut that is clearly visible in iconic photos of the gig.

Months after this incident, he committed suicide by hanging himself from one of the most powerful Slovenian national symbols – the kozolec (a wooden hay rack) near his hometown, Medvode. The frontman had been a key part of the band and even co-wrote their manifesto, but Laibach disapproved of his act of suicide and posthumously expelled Hostnik from the group, an act which they claimed returned him to his private identity. Despite this, the group often refer to him and have dedicated various projects to him.

Now describing themselves as 'an avant-garde experimental, industrial and multimedia group, with music being the central tool of expression', Laibach were now entwining their metal percussion textures with gramophones, radio devices and electronic instruments constructed by the band themselves.

Courting controversy, they collided with promoters and the authorities on many occasions, like the night in 1983 at the 'We Are Forging the Future' performance at the 12th Zagreb Music Biennial in Zagreb:

> The Zagreb Biennial was a really great festival. All the important composers of the '60s and '70s performed there – Cage, Stockhausen – everybody doing their experimental classical or acoustic and electronic performances. It was a very serious festival, and we said, 'This is a nice context for Laibach. We are doing a kind of experimental, classical thing as well – let's try to get on the programme.' We invited fellow British groups, 23 Skidoo and Last Few Days, and played this all-night concert. During our heavy industrial concert, we projected historic 35mm film footage of Yugoslavia's economic and political history, and then on top of it, we had Super 8 projections of some selected porno loops. Of course, this was an immense problem because the film was about this happy country of Yugoslavia, socialism and Communism, workers, factories, political rallies – and then you had these brutal porno scenes projected on top.
> In the context of the festival's 'youth' event, this was a bit too much for everybody and the organisers wanted to kick us off. We were pulled off the stage in the end by the army and the police in the middle of the night. The man who is now

---

1103 Slovenian for 'Victims of an Air Accident'.

the president of Croatia[1104] is a composer and musicologist. He was watching the show, and recently he described it as the most radical and provocative sonic performance he has ever seen.

The Croatian Communists were very angry after the show, demanding to their fellow communists in Slovenia that somebody had to do something about Laibach; the party stated that this was simply too much: 'Laibach have desecrated the holy and stepped over the line.[1105]

The band's full on Bill Grundy moment finally arrived in June 1983 on the national current affairs programme *TV Tednik*.[1106] Wearing military fatigues and white armbands bearing the black cross, Laibach were interviewed in front of graphic images of large political rallies that were reminiscent of those in Nuremberg, then the band recited their 'Documents of Oppression'. Their controversial imagery once again revealed the uncomfortable similarities between Fascist and Socialist Realist iconography, and their extremely provocative appearance on the program prompted the show's host to brand them 'enemies of the people', appealing to respectable citizens everywhere to intervene and destroy this dangerous group.

The scandal ended up with this TV interview. This was a plan, a political strategy: 'How to get rid of Laibach, how to do it elegantly.' Let's expose them publicly on the main TV programme. After they appeared, they will cease to exist because the angry reaction of the entire nation will force them to withdraw. And yes, we came to the interview dressed in our military uniforms, which on the mainly black and white TV monitors of that time looked . . . black and white. It was hard to see that these are, in fact, Yugoslav army uniforms.

We said, 'OK, let's do a performance, let's not move at all in front of the camera. We are just going to give our answers in a kind of political, manifest way.' It was pretty shocking to watch that on the TV, although nothing that we said was really problematic, everything was basically a straight manifest, and we even quoted Yugoslav politicians in an elegant and positive manner. The interviewer additionally edited the interview and, in the end, literally called for a public lynching, which was, of course, soon recognised as an over the top abuse of the media. Nevertheless, Laibach was officially forbidden for the next five years, and an administrative/political ban on public appearances and the use of the name Laibach followed.[1107]

There was now no option but to take the project out of the country:

Therefore, we decided to 'export' ourselves to a wider Europe. November and December 1983 saw the first European tour, which we titled the 'Occupied Europe Tour'. The 17-date tour covered 16 cities in 8 countries in Eastern and Western Europe, with the final concert in London's Diorama, after which we signed with Cherry Red Records. Still forbidden in Yugoslavia, we performed around Europe, but we also played rare underground shows anonymously back

---

1104 Ivo Josipović - president of Croatia from 2010 - 2015.

1105 Laibach to The Quietus.

1106 Translated as TV Weekly.

1107 Laibach to Luke Turner of The Quietus website.

home. In 1984, we also co-founded the NSK guerrilla art collective[1108] – a union of several artistic groups that were all inspired by Laibach but worked extensively in different media.[1109]

Misunderstood by the mainstream and banned in their home country, Laibach had formed strong alliances across underground art scenes throughout Europe, creating a a multimedia NSK was a platform for their operation via their own art collective NSK. NSK was envisioned as an independent fictional nation, a fully realised Lypton village complete with its own passport.

> Since Laibach was officially forbidden between 1983 and 1987, this was the perfect situation to establish something that would become bigger than Laibach and would practice the same methods in diverse media, only under a different name. Many people wanted to work with us. Either within the theatre or films or art. So that's how the NSK was established in 1984. It took Laibach's motifs and ideas and implanted them in diverse media groups.
> This really functioned successfully in the '80s. We did some great events together, mixing our skills and knowledge. We did a big theatre project called 'Baptism Under Triglav' and some big exhibitions, and also this very important poster campaign, which kind of started the beginning of the end of Yugoslavia and produced a huge political scandal.[1110]

The band now made their debut tour in the USA, which was never an easy place to play,[1111] but even harder for a strange industrial band from Eastern Europe.

> The first time we went to the USA, it was a culture shock. People from Sonic Youth were at the show we had in New York. The audience was obviously told we were the scariest band in the world, maybe even Nazis. Being in uniforms and coming from Eastern Europe, which the Americans didn't know much about (never mind where Slovenia is or Yugoslavia was), they mixed everything up. They thought we were Germans or Russians or something like that. Doing covers of songs like 'One Vision' had a heavy effect on them. There were all kinds of accusations. It was a mixed reaction – some people even had…fun?[1112]

Laibach had, by now, turned confrontation into an art form. Their whole operation was designed to confound and confuse, fashioning their art and music into brilliantly nuanced attack.

> That is a complex question that can probably be answered only by a thorough analysis, but in Laibach, there is always silence or scandal. This is our state of mind, our natural behaviour. We like conflicting situations, but we never provoked for the sake of provocation itself; we did it out of necessity because, by definition, a work of art is no good if it doesn't provoke – and that is a vital rule, valid in any political system anywhere. Judging by the reactions we get today, we provoke only

---

1108 NSK: Neue Slowenische Kunst or New Slovenian Art was started as a Dadaist take on totalitarian art and ideas. It posed awkward questions about art with a situationist glee that turned clichés back on the accusers.

1109 Laibach to John Robb.

1110 Laibach to Luke Turner from The Quietus website.

1111 Problems could arise due to the extortionate cost of American work visas for European bands, as opposed to the small cost for American bands touring in Europe.

1112 Laibach to The Quietus.

by simply still existing. For instance, even after several sold out shows in Paris, we still have difficulties performing in France. Recently in 2017, we also received a ban from performing in Moscow and St Petersburg, where the Orthodox church attacked us (through the Christian Human Rights Centre) for allegedly being Satan's worshipers – due to the fact that we have recorded and performed The Rolling Stones 'Sympathy for the Devil' – and even the promoter in Kassel (in Germany) was advised not to host Laibach's show for God knows what reasons. So, in reality, nothing has really changed. And if it has, it has changed [for the] worse.[1113]

Their debut album, *Laibach*, was finally released in April 1985 and was an astonishing work, part of a fascinating patchwork of culture and heavy machinery collage and a pioneering album in the new industrial genre. A pivotal moment on the album was the song 'Panorama', which cuts up a speech by a Yugoslavian president, and re-arranges it as a nonsensical narrative. The band's imagery of being clothed in traditional Alpine outfits and employment of the anti-Nazi art of Jon Heartfield toyed with people's expectations, leading many to make the mistake of confusing the imagery and coming to the wrong conclusion. The album, though, saw them get recognition from underground scenes, and they moved to London, where they worked with choreographer Michael Clarke and recorded three John Peel sessions. On returning home they had to perform under secret names because of the controversy they had caused.

By 1987, the band was changing. They were children of the 1960s and could remember The Beatles and The Stones profound musical and cultural effect. They were enthralled by pop culture but also fascinated by the many different and contradictory threads inherent in its power and were now keen to deconstruct them. Returning to tour the UK, they found a new label and the perfect home for their adventures.

> Laibach was one of the bands we booked at the Boardwalk in Manchester in June 1986. I helped them all day long to set up – these antlers, the flag, they had a projector. I worked hard to make the show work. I could see this was going to be great. After the gig, they asked if I wanted to be their manager, so I took them to Daniel Miller, got them signed to Mute, and left it there.[1114]

Once signed to Mute, the band decided to do something that was a bit more 'communicative, not some totally heavy industrial thing'. Their debut release on the label was their third studio album, *Opus Dei*, which was released in 1987, and saw a shift in the band's sound. It also explored their interest in mainstream culture. *Opus Dei* would see them cover Queen's 'One Vision' and Opus's 'Live Is Life' unzipping the songs. Following this, there would be further similar projects that would see them cover The Beatles' *Let It Be* album and numerous versions of The Rolling Stones 'Sympathy for the Devil', which they recorded with a practised deadpan effect that somehow opened the songs up to multiple re-interpretations.

1113 Laibach to John Robb.

1114 Nathan McGough, later the manager of the Happy Mondays, promoter of the Boardwalk gig.

The collective had turned pop culture inside out finding new meanings in the music. They sought to create a darker, more enthralling take on a catalogue of 'vintage classics' with an artful twist on mainstream pop culture iconography.

Singer Milan Fras, who had joined in 1983, could now be heard delivering his defining guttural bass vocal, which would become a motif of the band's sound over the powerful drum loops and disconcerting horns. The German metal giants, Rammstein, were about to take these albums and create a stadium-filling career from their template, with added heavy guitars. Not that Laibach seemed to care.

> Laibach does not believe in originality. . . therefore, Rammstein could not 'steal' much from us. They simply let themselves get inspired by our work, which is absolutely a legitimate process. We are glad that they made it. In a way, they have proven once again that a good 'copy' can make more money on the market than the 'original'. Anyhow, today we share the territory: Rammstein seem to be a kind of Laibach for adolescents, and Laibach are Rammstein for grown-ups.[1115]

For Laibach, the covers they recorded were their attempt at creating a pop music. They wanted to embrace pop but believed they lacked the requisite skills to create it. Subsequently, it was legitimate to take existing pop songs and remould them, slowing them down and changing their atmospheres and textures. *Opus Dei* trod a fine line between hilarity and nightmare, or as they themselves have stated,' We always understood that all songs we covered were historic material which we could use innovatively (making) something completely new out of them. This was our method.'[1116]

Hitting their stride, the band released thought-provoking concepts like 1994's *NATO*, a selection of cover versions on the theme of war, including covers of Edwin Starr's 'War' and Europe's 'The Final Countdown'. Two years later, Laibach followed that with *Jesus Christ Superstars*, a collection of cover versions and originals on the theme of religion. Further concept albums included 2004's self-explanatory great 'hits' called *Anthems*, and 2006's *Volk*, a collection of thirteen songs inspired by national or pan-national anthems, which included 'NSK', the anthem of the virtual state to which Laibach claimed to belong.

Most outsider groups who continue for decades do not necessarily become part of the establishment but are embraced in time after the media furore of their early work is lost to the public mind. Playing 2010's Kunst Exhibition back in Trbovlje, the band shared a stage with the former president of the newly independent Slovenia.

> We invited the ex-President of Slovenia to open our exhibition in Trbovlje in 2010. He was also in power as the head of Slovenian communists at the time when Laibach were forbidden in the '80s. The exhibition was the same exhibition as our forbidden one in the 1980s, except that it was now a significant cultural event, opened by the ex-president of the State. He is not in power anymore, he is now a pensioner, but he came and gave a brilliant opening speech. He told me later that Slobodan Milošević was calling him in the mid-80s because of Laibach and NSK, being very pissed [off and] demanding him to do something about us

---

1115 From the Laibach website.

1116 Laibach to Luke Turner from The Quietus website.

and to stop us somehow. This was back in '87. He also told me that it was a very hot situation, with lots of pressure on him, but he didn't quite know what to do with us. He wasn't exactly following, listening or understanding Laibach, but he understood we were masters of creating problems, and we did some in Milošević's Serbia as well. Although it was a very tricky situation at the time of the poster affair, he refused to put us in jail, for which we are, of course, deeply grateful.[1117]

Over the decades, Laibach have changed their approach several times. Concurrently, their home country has also changed beyond all recognition. Yugoslavia is no more, and the Balkans is now a collection of smaller states. The years of war in the region made Laibach's somehow more perceptive and potent but in peacetime, the tensions remain. Laibach still play with political theatre as on their 2014 *Spectre* album, their most direct pop and yet, most obviously political record yet, a 'state of the times' album addressing an increasingly fractious Europe. They smile and add, 'It really is hard to be poetic in these banal and cynical times that we live in, but we believe that good poetry can still resonate louder than a thousand guns. The best would, of course, be a combination of the two.'

When asked if *Spectre* was also the closest Laibach have come to flirting with pure pop, they replied, 'No. We were already much closer in the past, especially with remakes like 'Across the Universe',[1118] 'Life is Live', and 'Final Countdown'.[1119]

Always capable of making a gig into a big event, Laibach's theatrical roots, sense of space, and occasion came to the fore when they took the album on a world tour, including a big theatrical one-off event in the cavernous and iconic Turbine Hall at London's Tate Modern in 2012 for their big theatrical one-off event.

In 2015 Laibach delivered their most bizarre and brilliant project to date when they somehow managed to get themselves invited to North Korea to play a cover of the whole of the *Sound of Music* musical. The project was instigated by Norwegian film director Morten Traavik, who filmed the cultural confusion around the concert and created a brilliant documentary, *Liberation Day*.

The Sound of Music was one of the few western films known in the closed nation because it was Kim Il-sung's favourite film. When the band played the songs, the looks of confusion of the 5000-strong audience were profound. The *Sound of Music* project saw a complete cover of the iconic musical, drawing out its subtle anti-totalitarian themes initially in front of one of the most totalitarian governments in the world - art as mirror and hammer!

Laibach took their new *Sound Of Music* set on tour around Europe, and large audiences watched the band do their typical Laibach industrial pop take on well-worn and much-loved songs. The brilliant visuals and the band's twisted version of the familiar drew out the film's themes, making for an enticing and mind-boggling

---

1117 Laibach to Luke Turner from The Quietus website.

1118 The troublesome Beatles song that the Fab Four could never record to their satisfaction.

1119 Laibach to John Robb.

spectacle; a perfect post-modern prank that saw Laibach finally become a trans-continental group.

The world in which Laibach exist in now is a very different one to the abrasive post-industrial, post-punk period of their birth. Today, popular music is everywhere in the mainstream, and the internet is the new medium for the narrative. Laibach, however, have learned the art of pop music well and continue to operate as a masterclass in subverting the mainstream. This has resulted in them becoming popular by stealth whilst seeming ever more subtly dangerous.

> It's much more difficult now than in the '80s to do what we do. Back then, it was a Dadaist adventure which we took with a lot of humour, but nowadays, things within pop culture and cultural politics and the economy are getting extremely difficult. Especially after the breaking down of the Wall, the establishment of the internet and with capitalism polluting the area, it's a state of war. Independent labels practically vanished, record sales are going down, there's a big battle for survival on the market, and it is difficult to do what we do and as we do it. It's a jungle out there, and we are all fighting for our place. History? Nobody cares. It's only an ongoing battle of survival of the fittest . . .[1120]

Despite this, their ideas are still mesmerising, and the breadth of their music is exhausting. Perhaps they are more of the mirror than the hammer these days, but their art remains as compulsively fascinating as ever.

1120 Laibach to Luke Turner.

Chapter 32

AT THE GATES OF SILENT MEMORY

Fields of the Nephilim

Like the race of giant biblical angel-human hybrids that they are named after, Fields of the Nephilim own the stage. Emerging out of the haze of dry ice and the stark blue lighting, the band are dressed in their regulation Wild West outrider outfits, looking like pale rider ghosts from a spectral frontier film that is yet to be made.

Appearing out of the mystical landscape they deliver stunning sets that are full of grinding, heavy yet atmospheric music of dark nuance, texture and tension. In the swirling dry ice few bands have such a strong identity, and their shadowy silhouette with trademark wide-brimmed hats, mirrored sunglasses, long duster coats and cowboy boots add a funeral shroud of mystery to the mystic interzone.

Fields of the Nephilim deliver a fully immersive sound that shimmers and create a visual experience to match. Live, it's an exploration of their reference points from dark literature to spaghetti westerns, underlined by their own brooding version of Ennio Morricone's 'Man with A Harmonica', which rings out as a clarion call to their intensely loyal fan base, who promptly begin constructing human pyramids and cranking the anticipation.

The band then deliver their dark sonic with baritone vocals, lead bass lines and textured guitar in a powerful hypnotic whole. Few groups dare to get better as the years roll by, yet their bleak soundscapes, interspersed by Spaghetti Western guitar lines and atmospherics, put the heavy metal disco into dystopia[1121] and create the perfect soundscape for singer Carl McCoy's songs of religion, the occult and the Victorian underworld and a post- apocalyptic world to match the music's brooding sense of gothic unease.

Often looked on as goth outriders, which of course is no bad thing, their closest relatives are also perhaps the post-apocalyptic, post-rock bands like Godspeed! You Black Emperor, Swans and Ulver – bands who work outside verse/chorus/middle eight of rock and stretch out over a very dark canvas of film score.

The band's shapeshifting lineups have all left their contribution to this unique sound but it's the singer's autodictat vision that defines them. Immersed in the dark stuff from Aleister Crowley to horror films to the darkest passages of the darkest book of them all - the Bible - it's a reaction to his own religious upbringing.

It's this sense of faith and devotion twisted and turned into a walk on the dark side that creates this intense fervour for the band from their black t-shirt flock who are entranced in a secret world of ritual and release with arms aloft and heads nodding to the grinding groove. They are lost in the transcendental darkness of the clear,

---

1121 'disco-topia' - dark music that you can dance to.

powerful and concise sound that gives a Panzer platform for the dark songs that smoulder with their perfectly realised dynamics that hold the tension before those climactic endings.

These huge soundscapes, like those skylines in the American Wild West and that stark, vast, sky of sound that glowers with a melancholic pulse, are key.

Fields of the Nephilim were always destined to create dark, heavy, esoteric music. Formed in the concrete London overspill new towns of Hitchin and Stevenage, just after the first wave of goth in 1984, they would transcend their small town roots, and late arrival, to become one of the biggest bands in the loose catch-all. They created their own dark magic in the most unlikely of backdrops, Hertfordshire, typical of the anonymous goth heartlands.

> My first memories were in South London where I was born, so I guess Brixton and Stockwell were like small towns to me. When we moved to Stevenage, it was a new town and a melting pot of people from all over the UK in the 70s / 80s and who all came from somewhere else and all felt that we were going nowhere. It was a kind of cultural wasteland.[1122]

It was in this small town England that in the '70s future Fields of the Nephilim singer, Carl McCoy, was left to immerse himself in all manner of left-field, esoteric and darker cultures that would eventually help his band develop a genuine depth and authenticity to their muse. When these ideas were added to the music it was a potent witches brew, and the word was out about these new, dark outriders arriving on the scene.

If the initial wave of goth was, by then, moving on, splitting up, slowing down, or going pop, then Fields of the Nephilim arrived at just the right time. They reinvigorated the scene with their combination of heavy rock, dark psychic psychedelia and the panoramic possibilities of film score with an added cimmerian twist and a gothic drama.

> Gothic, that's the term I prefer. Also, I admire Ennio Morricone. He was the master of film scores and especially the Sergio Leone movies. There has probably been some kind of influence and honour to him somewhere in our musical journey.
> I love to approach and create music that I can submerge into. Music that lures me into the unknown, like soundtracks for my dreams and nightmares and the exploration and the unfolding journey of the soul with the cold comfort and the sense of isolation but always unformatted and boundless.[1123]

With these expansive influences, Fields of the Nephilim had their own take on the form with an added strong visual aesthetic that embraced their filmic sound. Famous for their dust and death image, they added flour to their outrider look to achieve that spaghetti western style. They took to the stage looking as though they had stepped

---

1122 Carl McCoy to John Robb.
1123 Carl McCoy to John Robb.

straight from a Sergio Leone[1124] movie. Their saddle-worn look became their most visible early trademark and talking point. This image has seen them freeze-framed in the popular goth narrative as high-decibel, dark, wild west outriders building a world from spectral spaghetti westerns. Meanwhile, the band themselves are fully immersed in their own space and have little interest in the bemused media and their reaction to their distinctive style. They are one of the rare bands who don't flinch at the 'goth' label.

> That's the terminology that the press generally labels the fans with, they put them in categories without them knowing, and the goths are generally the people who come to our gigs, and they don't take the normal path, and without them, we couldn't do what we do. So yeah, if they're called goths, then I don't care. What's wrong with that? And it's grown; it's a huge scene. It's all integrated into the metal scene as well, and that's quite a healthy thing, isn't it? It crosses over, and there's nothing wrong with that. It's not just this narrow clique that the British press used to point at and take the piss; it's actually outgrown them. A lot of it became suppressed and underground, but then you go into Europe, and they do festivals where they take a whole town over for a week; the whole city like Leipzig is dedicated to those kinds of people and that's fantastic! [1125]

Added to this is Carl McCoy's apocalyptic vision and an underlying fascination with chaos magick and a mysticism stemming from the darkest passages of bible. Ironically, the heaviest imagery used in goth music and by related subcultures frequently finds its roots within 'the good book'. The faith and devotion and the damnation and redemption have been prime targets for reinterpretation by disillusioned teens and young adults, breaking free of their own often imposed background beliefs or being intrigued by the darker side of belief systems. It's fascinating to see how many people who are actively involved in gothic music and culture are from intensely religious backgrounds.

> It's just kind of the way I was brought up. That symbolism, and studying when I was a child, right through a religious upbringing, it just goes hand in hand with the person I am. So it's all integrated into my whole thought chain. I've used it because that's what I know. It speaks to me. I don't really do it for art's sake – you know, 'that's a nice symbol'. There's always a method, and a lot of it can be personal, it doesn't need explaining. But I think integrating the words, the music... you can't take one away from the other. But there's a real personal, deep level to that. I am pretty serious about that side of it.[1126]

This inherent mysticism is key to the band's work. The flickering otherworldly interests of the frontman infuse their music with an added esoteric depth. This interest saw the use of chaos magick sigils on the band's album covers, a fascination

---

1124 Sergio Leone's films were far more artful than anticipated, with Leone's use of atmosphere and space reflected in Ennio Morricone's soundtracks. These vistas of sound perfectly capture the aching emptiness of the landscape and flashpoint of danger that sat at the core of the films. Ennio Morricone, who died in 2020, was one of the most iconic film soundtrack composers. His soundscapes for spaghetti westerns had a profound effect on the film genre and also upon the later post-punk period. Bands such as The Clash, Adam and the Ants, and Fields of the Nephilim all took inspiration from his compositional skills, his sense of space, epic drama and dark humour.

1125 Carl McCoy to Ben Graham of The Quietus.

1126 Carl McCoy to Ben Graham of The Quietus.

with the 'other' and the yearning for a darker yet more authentic spiritual journey. This serious pursuit of mysticism is also seen in the lives of many contemporaries.

> Occult and mysticism kind of found me really. It was extremely hard to conform and stomach the strict religious teachings that I had to endure as a youth with their hypocritical zealous fanatical belief in the light but fear of the dark. I felt I had some kind of affinity with the works of Austin Osman Spare, Crowley, John Dee, to name a few. They all followed their own individual path and pushed the boundaries to evaluate their own existence. They were truly inspired. So I guess it gave me some kind of comfort and belonging. Not literally the written words but the symbology and rituals which I found evoked inspiration and voice. I also became aware of the Watchers and Nephilim from religious studies and references when I was very young. It became the name I associated to the entity, spirits and influence that surrounded me.[1127]

Chaos Magick is an ever-present but unsung quality in some alternative bands of the 1980s. The system itself is a modern magical practice with pragmatic elements. Chaos Magick's belief systems wildly vary and are highly individualistic. The practice encompasses diverse theories and roots found in areas such as science fiction, scientific theories, traditional ceremonial magic, neo-shamanism, eastern philosophy, and world religions all via individual experimentation.

> For me it was a natural evolution I guess. It's always been there within the works of Austin Osman Spare just modified, modernised for our times and given a new title and not traditional but more experimental, symbolic and sigil based. There are no boundaries. No instructions on the box. All great things come from Chaos.[1128]

Chaos magicians or chaotes use an assortment of gods and ideas to achieve their goals. Conversely, practitioners can regard themselves as religious or atheist or may employ the use of psychedelic drugs or online resources to achieve their magical objectives.

Magick is a philosophy, but the spiritual side of it is more practised, and the ritual side of it comes in many ways, doesn't it? I mean, you could look at a live performance as ritualistic, and I do feel that; I go on stage and pretty much empty my mind. If you had asked me one of my lyrics before I walked on stage, I wouldn't be able to tell you, I've always felt like I'm kind of channelling. I don't know what you'd say that is, but that's how it works for me; it's the only way I can do what I do. It's not something I have to practise.[1129]

The well-read McCoy's songs and lyrics were also steeped in references to writers such as Aleister Crowley, Edgar Allan Poe and H.P. Lovecraft's Cthulhu Mythos

---

1127 Carl McCoy to John Robb.
1128 Carl McCoy to John Robb.
1129 Carl McCoy to John Robb.

mythology. He also drew inspiration from the Sumerian religion,[1130] which layered its ancient imagery into the melting pot of Nephilim ideas and lyricism. These images and ideas were immersed in their brooding powerful sound and catapulted them to the top of the goth pile.

Like many bands from small town England, Fields of the Nephilim had to graft to escape the clutches of their socio-economic and geographical background. Constant gigging, endless support slots and self-released singles and EPs saw them build their own fervent following from the dying embers of goth's first wave.

> We were pretty ambitious and pretty rebellious and opinionated about everything, especially musically. We had the drive, a reason for being out there. There was a big void for the kind of sound we were making together. I think the sound came about as a chemical reaction between our various influences and who we were. It wasn't like an effort.[1131]

Their debut EP, *Burning the Fields*, was released in 1985 by Situation Two records.[1132] The release may not have been as dense or heavy as later works, but it already had many of their hallmarks: the melodic driving bass lines, chiming guitars and powerful drumming, which provided a foundation for McCoy's mysterious deep vocals. By the time of their second release, another EP, 1986's *Returning to Gehenna*, they had the rudiments of their sound in place and had written some particularly deep, moving and mystical songs like 'The Tower'.

After the initial cult success of their early releases, the band released classic goth club floor-filling singles like 'Preacher Man' and 'Power' that saw them begin to make headway with an added surge of The Sisters of Mercy fans as that band's lineup was then falling apart.

> The Sisters were never a threat to us; there was no competition. We were a very uncompetitive band; we weren't competing with anybody and never have been. So long as people like what we do, we're quite happy. [1133]

Their 1987 album debut, *Dawnrazor*, further explored their occult influences and their spaghetti metal hybrid. The album itself covered more rudimentary subject matter compared to future releases, but there were enough mystical references at play to curate their own visual and musical aesthetic. The success of *Dawnrazor* gave the band the confidence to explore their fascination with the edges of sanity and death on their second album, 1988's *The Nephilim*. For the first time, McCoy references his deeper interests in Sumer[1134] and Cthulhu mythologies in an album that builds to create its own vision. It also gave the band their first big track with 'Moonchild',

---

1130 The Sumerians lived in Mesopotamia in 4000 BCE. They believed that the gods had formed order from chaos and the individual's role in life was to labour as a co-worker with the gods in order to ensure that chaos would not return. The gods themselves, however, would later reverse their own work, returning the world to chaos when humanity's noise and trouble became too great to bear.

1131 Carl McCoy to Nick Holmes at Louder Than War.

1132 Situation Two was an imprint of the bigger Beggars Banquet label.

1133 Carl McCoy to Ben Graham of The Quietus.

1134 McCoy registers a deeper interest in Sumer.

named after the Aleister Crowley novel. The band added a new sense of beauty and melancholy to their sound, all whilst finding space in the dense grind.

> I think *The Nephilim* album was kind of when we really found our feet. It was the first album where we concentrated on crafting our sound and creating an album with a constant theme running through it. The first album was an accumulation of loads of songs we'd been playing live for a couple of years that we bunged onto an album so there was no real flow. But the second album, I think, was quite an important marker for us. I have good memories of that time, of what we were feeling and doing in the studio and live. That was an important era, I think, for me, and I think the other band members would probably agree.[1135]

'Psychonaut', released in May 1989, was a ten-minute musical epic with a title inspired by a magical grimoire[1136] by chaos magician Peter Carroll.[1137] Combining their own distinctive sonic aesthetic with the possibilities of the dance floor, the single was a world to get lost in. The track nodded at the surrounding trance and dance culture that was dominating late 1980s music discourse, seeing it merge the 'blissed out' with a dark grind.

A dark bliss?

The artwork for the sleeve included a quotation by the visionary William Blake, 'Of Behemoth he saith he is chief of the ways of God/of Leviathan he saith he is king over all the children of pride' that reiterated the band's interest in the darker and more malevolent aspects of Christian religious doctrine. The single was a top 40 hit despite almost zero radio play and came complete with a mind-altering, grainy video which featured a Sioux Sun Dance ritual in which the candidate is hurled up into the air by claw hooks and bones affixed to his bare chest.

The 1990 third album *Elizium* saw a band confident enough to explore even deeper themes, embracing the biblical energy of the Watchers and Nephilim, musically acknowledging them as the gods and demons of a mountain-like heaven, towering above the Fertile Crescent on which the civilisations of Sumer and Babylon evolved. Two highly evocative tracks, 'For her light' and 'Sumerland', appeared as singles and the album was the culmination of their first phase.

> People change, your attitudes change and to develop...I don't like to be held back on creativity by being restricted with what you've got. If everyone's not seeing eye-to-eye then you've got to something about it, change it. I think that's what came about the first time. But we had other things causing typical problems like every other band does. Management, record labels and all that toss! I think I was also a bit afraid of us getting kind of too popular and mainstream. [1138]

McCoy quit frontman duties in 1991, whilst the rest of the group carried on briefly as Rubicon, before remerging in 1996 with the Zoon album under the flag of

---

1135 Carl McCoy to Ben Graham of The Quietus.

1136 A grimoire is a textbook of magic, typically including instructions on how to create magical objects like talismans and amulets.

1137 Peter Carroll is an English occultist, writer, and physics graduate. He is one of the originators of chaos magic theory and a co-founder of the Illuminates of Thanateros.

1138 Carl McCoy to Ben Graham of The Quietus.

The Nefilim. The album saw an added industrial clank and grind to his music. There were reformations in 2000, solely built around McCoy, and then 2005's acclaimed *Mourning Sun* album. It was to be the first official Fields of the Nephilim studio LP for fourteen years which picked up where they had left off with the different lineup. Since then, the band have been slipping in and out of view with spellbinding gigs and festivals.

They remain intangible, mysterious, the ultimate cult band. The Nephilim exist on their own terms and their dark-hearted music that was built around atmospherics, power and passion inspires an almost religious, shamanic fervour and belief, especially around their intense live shows.

It's that powerful.

Chapter 33

DARKLANDS

How The Dark Energy Infected Indie

In those crazy end of the world '80s, it seemed as though nothing was impervious to the all-pervading, attractive darkness. The new caliginous was infusing popular culture and music, and just beyond the classic goth hinterland, there were a whole host of bands who had an art to their darkness, like Echo & The Bunnymen, The Smiths, The Chameleons, The Jesus and Mary Chain, The Sound, Cocteau Twins, Strawberry Switchblade, Scars and many others.

These bands shared the same brooding sensitivity, poetic spirit and romantic vision as their goth relatives without being in the dark zone of scene central. They also straddled a common soundtrack in alternative clubs, record collections and often shared live bills. The Smiths' guitarist Johnny Marr felt a keen affinity with the darker, parallel culture, citing their common roots:

> We were never interested in the terms like indie or goth. With The Smiths, we never thought we were 'indie'. In fact, the first band I ever heard called 'indie' was us. It was when Rough Trade boss Geoff Travis came into the *Top of the Pops* dressing room when we were on with 'What Difference Does It Make' and said it was the first 'indie' record on the high street and in WH Smiths, and for him, this was the moment that indie had become a big thing.
>
> There was a shared DNA with the goth crowd. There was a deep love for Bowie, Bolan, glam rock, New York Dolls and the extremities of rock n roll like the Velvets and The Stooges. As a fledgling musician at the time, I couldn't ignore the giants of the underground – figures like Siouxsie Sioux, John Lydon and Adam Ant – because they were pop stars, but you knew there was something good at work. You understood how Adam Ant happened with this image, but he also had this really exciting, glammy, clever record, which was obviously Bolan, Bowie, Elvis Presley, and all of this edgy stuff like goth in it as well.[1139]

While The Smiths themselves were never a goth band per se, many goths liked the band, enjoying their literate intelligence and darker shadows. The music's poetic nuances, inbuilt melancholia and stylish delivery was embraced by listeners across the subculture. There were many common strands in the DNA and a shared fascination with the darker side of post-punk entwining the melancholy with a sense of mischief and humour.

Arguably, closer to the swooning heart of goth were Echo & The Bunnymen, who had a certain atramentous grandeur to their muse. Like The Doors, the Bunnymen constructed pop songs with a distinct baroque, onyx psychedelic twist. However, unlike The Doors' sunshine state glamour, the Bunnymen added a rainy-day,

---

1139 Johnny Marr to John Robb.

northern snark to proceedings. A classic band of the period, they released a series of glorious records that perfectly captured Bowie's sense of drama, Jim Morrison's luxurious baritone, the Velvets' street hassle, a billowing ambition and their own dark romantic beauty.

The band was built around an excellent rhythm section that supported guitarist Will Sergeant's brilliantly tripped-out guitar lines. Iconic frontman Ian McCulloch was armed with a laconic sex appeal, perfectly dishevelled hair and a darkly amusing arrogance. Thankfully, he also possessed a phenomenal voice. One reviewer perfectly captured Mac's fascinating conundrum, 'Ian McCulloch has one of the voices of his generation, but the problem is that he knows it.' Mac, in turn, modestly described himself as 'the Michelangelo of songwriters.'

Throughout the 1980s, the Bunnymen would release a series of great albums that combined their dark, sonorous windswept sound with great music. They could have been bigger than U2 – they had the songs and the star power, but that innate Liverpool unwillingness to join the showbiz circus meant that they were never willing to play the game.

The Bunnymen had songs as darkly lush and perfect as 'The Killing Moon' and 'The Cutter', that dripped emotion and imagination. They combined a sense of euphoria and melancholy with perfect chord changes and melodic brush strokes. Indeed, there were songs so good that would even make the aforementioned self-styled musical Michelangelo blush. Perhaps this was not idle bragging, however much Ian McCulloch liked to talk big:

> We just wanted to write beautiful songs, make beautiful sounds, and not sound like the other oafs. A song like 'The Killing Moon' is an example of this. It was striving for beauty. We didn't want to be average.[1140]

With a romantic dark heart, a black leather cool and a classic songwriting nous, The Jesus and Mary Chain moulded pop art into sensual sonic noise, delivering a crystalline pop perfection whilst riding a wave of feedback and classic chords. They tapped into the hallowed turf of the Velvets, Stooges, Ramones and Suicide while adding a melodic death song melancholy from the likes of girl groups like The Shangri-Las. They also straddled the noisenik UK underground, the primetime sex glam of T. Rex, Einstürzende Neubauten and the soon-to-arrive American post-hardcore scene of Swans/Sonic Youth and Big Black, not to mention the audible influence of punk rock. It was all served up with a rock'n'roll poetry that dealt with nihilism and romance in equal measures. Their classic three chord rock'n'roll was drenched with honey-sweet melody and the ugly skreegh of feedback, and somehow, they still made it into the charts.

Few bands have been this capable of moments of great beauty while sounding primed to combust at any second. Few could be this blissful and antagonistic. It was

---

1140 Ian McCulloch to John Robb.

this light, shade and barely concealed violence that made The Jesus and Mary Chain so damn attractive.

Their debut seven-inch single, 'Upside Down', released by Creation Records, caused an incendiary riot on the indie scene. There was a sulky, awkward ruckus when the band, now dressed in black leather, played their first big London show at North London Poly in March 1985. The gig and its reaction caused a press sensation with their manager Alan McGee – a brilliant, maverick one-man riot himself – issuing a statement, 'the audience were not smashing up the hall, they were smashing up pop music', and going on to say, 'This is truly art as terrorism.'

In 2020, Chris Packham is a national treasure and TV icon whose nature shows attract millions of viewers. In 1985, he was a young punk looking for something with the same kind of edge.

> The first time I saw Mary Chain was in 1985. It was one of their classic 15-minute tiny bar gigs. They believed that the short set was the perfect statement which people didn't understand. Every time you went to see them in that period, there was always a notice written on paper with a biro on the door that said the Mary Chain don't do encores.[1141]

Luckily, the band had the songs to back their initial confrontation. Perfect heavenly '60s melodies were semi-sung and semi-whispered by Jim Reid over his brother William's mixture of classic three-chord trick guitar and howling feedback. All was underpinned by Douglas Hart's throbbing Jah Wobble style bass rumble.

Their 1985 debut *Psychocandy* album was recorded in the tiny Southern Studios in London, where Bauhaus had also recorded their debut a few of years before. The album was a perfect distillation of their sound, melding their feedback and noise with a classic melody. It also placed them at the new psych-noise frontline with scene newcomers like Sonic Youth. They were the perfect band of their moment with a sultry, sexy sound that dealt beauty and ugliness in equal measure, and the album was a daring and thrilling landmark of sullen, switchblade, dangerous rock'n'roll.

Instead of crashing and burning after making their musical statement, the Mary Chain were in for the long haul, and the riots were dropped for ice-cool stage shows. In the spring of 1987, they released 'April Skies', their first top ten hit and the first track from their upcoming *Darklands,* an album that saw a tempering of their initial noisier approach but with an added aching sadness. The band's third studio album, *Automatic,* was released two years later and utilised further electronics, giving them a colder darkwave edge with the cranked bass like on the extended mix of Sidewalking, giving them a The Sisters of Mercy style neo-goth groove. Later albums, like the return to abrasion of 1992's *Honey's Dead,* 1994's *Stoned & Dethroned* and 1997's *Munki* saw the band isolated and yet still brilliant. The indie mainstream may have gone rave but they defiantly became entombed in their introverted, feedback-drenched world.

1141 Chris Packham to John Robb.

Empowered by the success of The Jesus and Mary Chain's 'Upside Down' debut single, Creation Records became one of the leading indie labels of the late 1980s and 1990s. They signed a whole stable of pop/noise bands, including My Bloody Valentine.

Formed in Dublin in the early eighties and fascinated by The Birthday Party's oral skreegh and The Cramps' twitching psychodrama, as well as the output of their own hometown's Virgin Prunes, My Bloody Valentine initially created their own dark goth death rattle. It was this fascination that saw them move to Berlin like The Birthday Party before them, before moving back to London. There were lineup shuffles that saw them eventually create their own definitive style, which was lazily titled 'shoegazing', but was so much more with guitars that melted audibly with the whammy bar-controlled noise that sewed the seeds for an oncoming wave of bands. From post-goth to 'shoegaze' to dark ambient and drone, many genres were soaked with the band's distinctive shimmering noise and glissando beauty.

Their November 1988 *Isn't Anything* debut album, and its 1991 *Loveless* follow-up broke through established genres. Their drones, submerged gossamer morning after vocals, and the exotic beautiful guitar sounds created a new soundscape in a groundbreaking album that changed guitar music and blurred all genre edges. The band's key creative force, guitarist and vocalist, Kevin Shields, seemed almost baffled by his own brilliance:

> We seem to be doing things the wrong way around. Most bands start off wild and mellow out, but we started off quiet and got harder as time went on. We've tried to make up unmelodic songs, but we just can't do it! We can't make so-called unmelodic music. Your limitations give you your identity, I suppose.[1142]

Fellow dark creatives, Spacemen 3 had been honing down this sound since 1983. They formed in the backwater town of Rugby, spending years chiselling their sound down to the brooding, controlled and stripped-down tension of their fourth and final 1991 *Recurring* album. The album itself was a veritable melting pot of MC5, Stooges, Velvets and late '60s garage, updated, remoulded and given a very contemporary feel by the about to implode band.

Formed in London in 1986 by Robert Hampson and his then-girlfriend Becky Stewart on drums, Loop were initially running parallel to My Bloody Valentine and Spacemen 3. They took the psychedelic purple haze of the more 'out there' tracks of The Stooges and created tripped-out drones that preceded the current love of the form by decades.

> I don't think that even back in the day, we were influenced directly by psychedelia. I don't think we ever wore that on our sleeves. We were also influenced by Wire and Rhys Chatham and krautrock and it all gelled – a combination of different ideas and styles.[1143]

1142 Kevin Shields to John Robb (in his first interview in Sounds 1988).

1143 Robert Hampson to John Robb.

The vibrant post-punk Glasgow scene had already nurtured several cult bands like The Wake, who featured a pre-Primal Scream, Bobby Gillespie. Formed in 1981, their debut single, 'On Our Honeymoon' has a sense of the same brisk, lo-fi, captivating cold pop that The Cure had pioneered. Their debut album got them noticed by Rob Gretton, the manager of Joy Division/New Order, who signed them to Factory Records and released their debut, *Harmony*, album in 1982.

Glasgow also birthed Strawberry Switchblade, who were two perfect-looking self-creations with a striking style of polka dot dresses, hair strewn with ribbons and stark makeup that was like a baroque, flamenco, art goth explosion. In the UK, they had a brush with pop stardom in 1985, whilst in Japan, they became a sensation. To this day, they are still quoted as a key style influence on the myriad of post-goth scenesters who hang around hip Tokyo markets on Saturday afternoons, dressed in increasingly daring versions of the look the pair sparked into place.

Marketed as a Saturday morning TV pop band, Strawberry Switchblade were anything but. Their music had a darker undertow which led one half of the duo, Rose McDowall to her adventures in the industrial underground.

> I was never just a popette. I have got too much in my head to do one thing in a lifetime. I was a punk even before I heard Ramones, who I loved. I was into music since I was a baby. My dad had a great record collection and taught me to jive at 18 months. I always wanted to be a singer, and punk made it easy. It was my road to freedom from the expectations of what a young girl should be – that was never my path.
> I loved flamenco dancers, fairies, witches, and magic. I was never a normal child. I freaked my mum out when I made things burst into flames usually through the energy of anger. Not on purpose. It just happened. I just wanted to do what I wanted. I had no problem with what others thought. I had learned to deal with bullies at a young age. The first band I was in, The Poems, were not a pop band. I played the drums and did some singing. My then husband, Drew McDowall who went on to play with Coil, was the frontman. [1144]

Rose McDowall's adventures in the stark and emotional territory explored by the industrial underground saw her initially work with David Tibet and others on a myriad of projects. Her haunting high-cheekboned face, captivating voice, mystical air, rubber outfits and witchy pointy hat combined with her innate talent and leant an exotic presence on that scene. Whilst fellow Strawberry Switchblade singer Jill Bryson went back to her art roots, Rose McDowall occasionally appears to this day with her dark and emotive folk songs:

> There was no big plan. I am not a black, white or green witch. I am a psychedelic witch. I like discord and when you sing you find the right note that resonates with a room. It reaches parts of you. It resonates through you. [1145]

It wasn't just Glasgow that was singing from the darker hymn sheet. Edinburgh had Fast records, one of the key indie labels of the time that signed left-field and brilliant

---

1144 Rose McDowall to John Robb.

1145 Rose McDowall to John Robb.

bands like The Fire Engines, Gang of Four and early The Human League, whilst thinking of them all in terms of a bold new pop music that became a partially self-fulfilling prophecy. The label also signed Scars, an Edinburgh band who were one of the greatest of the period and a lost band whose debut 'Adultery/Horrorshow' cuts through the decades with its dark almost goth brilliance.

With their bebop guitars turned onto deluxe and a dislocated sense of songwriting, the single's two songs are full of dread, brilliance, space, dynamics and a tangible power and atmosphere. They were the goth classics that never got fully embraced. Their debut album still has moments of the single's genius but was suffocated by their major label's desire for pop success. Sadly, the band's effective raw edge had been removed and replaced with a more smothering polish. However, the album's demos are a different matter and worth seeking out.

Just next to Edinburgh, in the industrial belt of Grangemouth and Falkirk, a band full of mystery and magic emerged from the shadows of post-punk. Initially, Cocteau Twins were in thrall to The Birthday Party and started attempting to make their own explosive, angular noise, but ended up creating something quite different. With spectral otherworldly melodies, ethereal arrangements, an all-pervading feeling of darkness and distinctive, chiming guitars, they alchemised a myriad of textures for Liz Fraser's captivating voice. Her unique singing delivered mysterious lyrics and sounds that seemed to reinvent words into entwining new shapes that perfectly articulated all emotions without always verbalising them in magical sonic spells.

Guitarist Robin Guthrie was DJing the local punk nights, which is where he met Liz, a Siouxsie and the Banshees fan, with a tattoo of the iconic singer on her arm. He told her about his youthful band, which he had formed with bassist Will Heggie playing Stooges covers. Once Liz joined, they morphed into the magical and recorded a demo which was sent to John Peel, who instantly booked them for a session and Ivo Watts-Russell, head of 4AD, who rang back the Falkirk call box Robin Guthrie was using as his ad hoc office and offered them a deal.

Their 1982 debut, *Garlands*, was full of ghostly dream pop serenades that drip emotion and glistening DIY post-Banshees gothic shadows. The monochromatic rhythms from the fluttering Roland 808 drum machine and the textured guitars created epic and intangible textures for Liz Fraser's vocals and the gripping atmosphere, which can be heard beautifully on 'The Hollow Men' and 'Wax and Wane', contributing to their overarching, shivering wall of sound.

Touring extensively with 4AD label mates The Birthday Party and Modern English, they made an unlikely impact with their introverted yet all-consuming sound and Fraser's unique, untrained and stunning voice. Alan Rankine of The Associates[1146] was brought in to produce their second single, 'Peppermint Pig', and although the single was consistently praised and was only held off the independent charts' number

---

1146 Rankine's own indie-pop was full of the drama and melody of opera with late frontman Billy McKenzie's operatic voice full of passion and beauty which can be heard on The Associates' biggest hit 'Party Fears Two'.

one spot by New Order's 'Blue Monday' it was not the sound that Robin Guthrie wanted for the band.

Their first true masterpiece was 1983's *Head Over Heels* which was recorded as a duo after the departure of Will Heggie. The album upped the levels of production with a much more atmospheric and textured sound. It further explored the voice as an instrument in the beguiling songs. From the opening track 'When Mama Was Moth' onwards, it was a tour de force and a highly original work of emotional and mystery-laced dark wave which captures unique atmospheres and a beguiling claustrophobia and became a template record for generations of bands.

With new bassist Simon Raymonde in the lineup for 1984's 'Spangle Maker' EP, they went on to record several albums, adding layers of sophistication and haunting melody to their sound and subsequently became one of the key alternative bands of the period without losing any of their mystery, gothic tapestry and spectral slices of sonic beauty and originality.

Hated by the band yet standing the test of time, the *Treasure* album was released in 1984 yet captured their ephemeral magic, whilst 1986's *Victorialand* saw them revert back to an album of icy washes and magic spell vocals that was their first top 10. A couple of years later, they released the immersive and often overlooked *Blue Bell Knoll,* which some consider a taming of their wild imaginations but still pulls you into its matrix.

By the time they recorded their 1990 panoramic masterpiece, *Heaven or Las Vegas,* the versatility of Liz Fraser's voice was in full flow. From the operatic singing to the heavens to deeply personal hushed tones - no one has ever managed to create a vocal palette of such dexterity. 1993's *Four-Calendar Cafe* was a swing towards a more pop-oriented take on their sound, with the lyrics easier to make out whilst their final *Milk And Kisses,* album - released in 1996 was overshadowed by the couple splitting in 1993 and recorded for contractual reasons and was understandably less focused. Liz Fraser left a year later and has worked with Massive Attack on tracks like the iconic 'Teardrop' and her current Sun's Signature project releasing work as beguiling as ever. Robin Guthrie tours with his band, The Robin Guthrie Trio and is a producer, whilst Simon Raymonde is the boss of the groundbreaking and successful indie label, Bella Union.

Cocteau Twins were also part of the core of one of the 4AD label's more fascinating projects - This Mortal Coil – a loose collective of label musicians originally conceived as a project to rerecord one of Modern English's overlooked singles. Underlining the label's love of ideas and collaboration, This Mortal Coil released a series of three albums that saw a deconstruction and ambient take on forgotten gems utilising European folk, neo-classical and art rock into a new whole gothic melancholia and haunting beauty.

A less high profile 4AD signing, Modern English, would, initially, be the label's biggest American success. The band's post-Cure dark pop captivated American new wave audiences with their 1981 album, *After the Snow.* The album went on to sell 500,000 copies in the USA after the classic 'I Melt with You' single became a huge radio hit. Their melancholic new wave pop hinted at possibilities for future stadium goth bands and the possibilities of brisk dark indie.

4AD themselves were a key label in the post-punk hinterland with dark artful records in beautiful sleeves designed by the late Vaughn Oliver. There were lesser know releases on the label like the gothic art of Dance Chapter, whose songs like 'Anonymity' hinted at a Banshees-esque taut and terse guitar tension or In Camera's debut 'Die Laughing' single serving notice on their dark matter before they fell apart.

In the early 1990s, London four-piece Lush were one of 4AD's next wave of signings. They were embraced in the then indie meets grunge battlefields of Reading Festival and Lollapazoola for their gothic-tinged indie pop rushes. The band's core was built around two teenage friends, Miki Berenyi and Emma Anderson, who had been fixtures at goth and the noisier Death To Trad Rock London gigs before falling into their own band and managing to eclipse nearly all their heroes with their own success.

> We would go to everything from The Smiths to Echo & The Bunnymen to The Sisters of Mercy, who we loved especially because they had that theatre to it with the dry ice. It always felt like a real event. Unlike blokey indie gigs where everyone was stomping up and down, there wasn't any unpleasantness at goth gigs. An Echo & The Bunnymen gig was very male, but the Sisters had a different vibe. It was really amazing that we eventually supported them. I remember going on stage so excited and saying I've just seen Andrew Eldritch backstage eating cake, and he must have overheard me because when he came on to play, and the atmosphere was very serious with the dry ice and lights, he announced, 'actually I have not eaten any cake...' [1147]

The key nationally distributed magazine on the goth scene in the early 1980s was the reconstituted ZigZag. Founded in the late 1960s as a counterculture Bible, the magazine had been a portal into a deranged underground world before folding. It was later resurrected in the early 1980s under the editorship of Kris Needs and Mick Mercer and became early goth's key chronicler with writers like Antonella Gambotto-Burke, Richard North and Julianne Regan.

With her classic voice and own vision of folk-tinged modern music, Julianne Regan was never going to remain a music writer, and after a short lived stint in The Swarm with Manuela Zwingmann of Xmal Deutschland, she formed All About Eve. [1148] Their 1985 debut single, 'D for Desire', had a whiff of The Banshees' 'The Staircase (Mystery)' to it but with its own playground twist. It was a tumbling, arpeggio-driven song that stood out from the dissipated mundanity of many bands in the mid-1980s malaise and was driven by her warm vocals. Now with a drum machine, the band reconvened as a three-piece for an exploration of their ethereal sound for early singles before they were signed to Phonogram and released their 1988 self-titled album with its patchouli whiff of white magic and faerie tales.

1147 Miki Berenyi to John Robb.

1148 The band was so-named after the brilliantly dark and unnerving 1950 film starring Bette Davis.

Like Fleetwood Mac with a twist of Kate Bush and a romantic twist of the gothic shackled to a rockier chassis, they found their own successful space. The 'Marthas Harbour' single saw the album hit the top 10, as did their second album, *Scarlet and Other Stories,* which was written under the duress of the band's inner core of Julianne and guitarist Tim Bricheno splitting up, resulting in Bricheno leaving the band to re-emerge in The Sisters of Mercy for the *Vision Thing* period.

Whilst never staking out a claim for a gothic space, PJ Harvey emerged on the music scene in 1990 and was instantly lauded. Since then, she has released a series of stark and literate emotionally-charged records - some driven by personal demons, some by poetic genius and some by conceptual narratives that have certainly touched on many dramatic goth themes of sex, love, lust, war and death in a series of deeply intelligent, emotionally captivating, shapeshifting albums.

Being hard to place is, of course, a positive quality in music, and as soon as PJ Harvey is pinned down to one style, she is quick to morph into another. Whatever she sets her hand to, she quickly makes her own, whether it be stark post-punk, gothic balladeering, English folk, post grunge or dark blues. PJ Harvey never repeats herself, and yet consistently, she has had a darker twist in her music that draws you in from her debut *Dry* album to its stark minimalistic Steve Albini recorded follow-up, 1993's *Rid Of Me* - an album that was full of the bare bones and emotional wreckage of a breakup. Its visceral sound matches the songs ripped from her soul. 1995's *To Bring Me Your Love* was an album of love, longing and lust built around a dark, stripped-down blues chassis and full of haunting drama. This was also around the period when she was in a relationship with Nick Cave – a dark-clad high priest and priestess of high-end gothic-tinged art, culture and music in matching outfits and their break up saw Cave write three of his greatest love songs, Into My Arms, West Country Girl and Black Hair and her own *Is This Desire* (1998) album.

Her 2000 *Stories from the City, Stories from the Sea* was inspired by New York and was a life-affirming reaffirmation and the second major commercial success of her recording career, meanwhile, 2004's *Uh Huh Her* was a raw lo-fi step away, whilst 2007's *White Chalk* was piano-driven gothic melodrama. 2011's *Let England Shake* followed this clutch of more experimental works and looked at the heartbreak of war with a very personable emotional response to the futility of bloodshed and was an album full of traditional instruments like the zither and hurdy-gurdy and a collection of dark and captivating songs on an award-winning release. Her most recent album, 2016's *The Hope Six Demolition Project,* was a storytelling album that attempted to understand a broken world. Matching her powerful and restless music journey PJ Harvey has also played with her image, embracing darker twists and turns in her style, seeing her become a later-day goth influence without ever becoming embroiled in the scene.

Back up north, Manchester itself may not have been the trad goth epicentre like Leeds, but it delivered Joy Division and many of the fringe bands of the genre. The Chameleons were hometown stars in the 1980s and were agonisingly close to breaking big worldwide. Yet somehow, they fell apart just as the starting pistol was

THE ART OF DARKNESS

fired. The enigmatic group played dark and powerful music, a missing link between the post-punk Liverpool psych of The Teardrop Explodes and the sombre melancholy of Joy Division.

Songs like 1982's 'In Shreds' were scene classics; huge, heartfelt and anthemic with a melancholic beauty, an all-enveloping visceral power and an emotional landslide. Their endearing legacy remains untarnished, and their intense, loyal following is hooked into their powerful intimacy. There was a whole micro genre of leather jackets with The Chameleons artwork painted on them running around town and on the outer fringes of the goth scene.

The original lineup was full of tension between members that would eventually cause them to finally implode in 1987, leaving a reconstituted version revolving around singer Mark Burgess and guitarist Reg Smithies touring to this day sounding as great as ever. They released three essential albums – the first of which was 1983's influential *Script of the Bridge*. From its television samples introducing "Don't Fall" to the defining dual-guitar mesh of 'Up the Down Escalator', this is an album that is one of the classics of the form. Followed up by 1985's *What Does Anything Mean? Basically* and 1986's *Strange Times,* The Chameleons delivered a post-punk psychedelia tinged with the overcast darkness of gothic climes.

> When we put The Chameleons together, it was important to create something of our own. We had to have our own sound. For the Peel session, Dave Fielding[1149] was already using his flanger on the guitar. No one else was doing that at the time. As we started to evolve, he started to use his Roland chorus space echo as well. There was a psychedelic edge to what we were doing. I think that in itself was a very Manchester thing which removed it from punk. This was coupled with the kind of drugs you were doing then, which made you a bit paranoid. I did a lot of whizz, which was really rooted in the punk thing, but we were also doing mushrooms at the rehearsals, which affected our sound. My girlfriend would put the mushrooms in a big newspaper wrap and take the maggots out whilst we were playing![1150]

In the wake of Joy Division, Manchester's Factory Records had embraced a whole plethora of dark-tinged bands. From the doom funk of A Certain Ratio, whose early recordings, like the 1980 cassette-only *The Graveyard and the Ballroom*[1151], were a perfect synthesis of the new dark and the nod to the dance floor. Their stripped-down funk underpinned a brilliant collection of songs which were even darker than Joy Division. Label mates Stockholm Monsters and early James (with their then-twisted folk) were also emerging from the powerful shadow of Joy Division. Still, perhaps the closest in the dark spirit were Ian Curtis's favourite fellow band of the period, Section 25.

Section 25 might have come from the tatty seaside town of Blackpool – which was more associated with candy floss and tourist guff – but their music was equal to Joy

---

1149 Dave Fielding original guitar player, along with Reg Smithies.

1150 Mark Burgess to John Robb.

1151 One of Martin Hannett's great productions.

Division. Their debut album, *Always Now*, is a record as striking and timeless as their Mancunian label mates. The band was named after the plight of a local eccentric, the late Fes Parker,[1152] and they were dealing with the dark matter from the off. Their songs concerned strange trips, spirituality and the outer limits of the human psyche and were intoned over a clutch of bass-driven spectral songs. They then added elements of new electronic dance to their sound when bassist Larry Cassady's wife, Jenny, joined them. The resulting sublime 'Looking From A Hill Top' single should have been huge with its synthesis of the new electronic music added to their dark magus workouts. Both Jenny and Larry are now sadly dead, but the band continue with younger brother and drummer Vincent Cassidy at the helm.

Perhaps the quintessential dark band who had their own orbit beyond any scene were the aptly named The Psychedelic Furs. Their innovative music caught the sense of adventure of the late 1960s, the decadence of the mid-1970s and the urgency of post-punk into a drawling drone whole. They would become a substantial and undoubted key influence on goth without joining in.

Formed in London in February 1977 and built around the core of singer Richard Butler and his brother Tim on bass and Jon Ashton's influential guitar work, their dark, downbeat sound explored the post-punk terrain with an atmosphere closer to Bowie's urban disco-topia but built around atmospheric drones. They came armed with the deliciously gravelly voice of their frontman, giving the band a distinctive, powerful sound and identity. His voice had shades of John Lydon's acidic, acerbic punk sneer and Bowie's sense of grandeur, placing them on the outside of the post-punk melange.

Their caustic Venus in Furs chemical drones and knack of entwining melody into the mire made their eponymous 1980 top 20 debut album a highly influential work in the still-forming alternative scene. They were particularly beloved by Andrew Eldritch, who tried to form a Psychedelic Furs-style band during his pre-Sisters year at Oxford University. Many others on the scene were also enthralled by the band's command of glowering, introspective darkness. Decades later, their 2020 album *Made Of Rain* sees the band still at the top of their game and sounding as edgy and compulsive as ever – a darker band who found longevity a gift.

Another band that didn't fit the narrative of the punk and post-punk period were Japan, who maintained a brilliant creative edge that fed into the mix. Formed in Catford in South London in 1974 they were initially in thrall to New York Dolls and the Bowie school of rock'n'roll theatrical.

Their early albums, like 1978 debut *Adolescent Sex,* saw a band with shaggy NY Dolls' hair and makeup playing glam riffs that added to an already burgeoning interest in electronics. Whilst their earlier glam phase had won them a hard-earned cult following, it saw them sit awkwardly to the side of the punk scene, as a watching Johnny Marr notes:

1152 Sectioned under Section 25 of the Mental Health Act.

Everything about them was very impressive – working with Giorgio Moroder was a big taste marker. The big millstone around their neck for some people was the makeup. People of my world thought that was a good thing though – me and my mates wore a lot of makeup, but that lent itself to aggravation if you were walking around the Arndale in Manchester.[1153]

By 1981, Japan had morphed into something quite astonishing on their *Tin Drum* album. Their singer, David Sylvian, with his kabuki-styled androgynous pop star styling, was dubbed 'the most beautiful man in the world' by the media and on the album, he sang over sparse, haunting and rhythmic songs that featured Mick Karn's distinctive fretless bass 'boings', scattered over the minimalist soundscapes that were quite unlike anything else. It saw the band as true heirs to that artful, pseudo, prog pop that had been a large part of Roxy Music's 1970s appeal. The album is a classic work, an astonishingly original delicate piece with songs that seemed to flutter like butterflies with a melancholic and mystical atmosphere. They broke into the top five with the *Ghosts* single but tension saw them split as if constant mainstream success was not meant for their artful souls. David Sylvian went on to a career of subtle art pop, and Mick Karn[1154] worked on Peter Murphy's first post-Bauhaus project, Dali's Car, before moving on to many other projects.

Formed in South London in 1979, The Sound were dealing swooping, dramatic songs that were perfect for the period. Built around the late Adrian Borland, who tragically committed suicide in 1999, the band's first release was the *Physical World* EP in 1979. It instantly scored them the support of John Peel and the music press. They were signed to Korova records, who already had the Bunnymen on their books and released their debut 1980 *Jeopardy* album and the 1981 follow-up *From the Lions Mouth* to critical acclaim. Despite wide-eyed devotion from the people that know, the band have remained a cult item. A similar fate befell their 1981 tour buddies, Sheffield's Comsat Angels, who were also fated to remain in the cult underground despite having the brooding ammunition to make a bigger mark at the time. Named after a J.G. Ballard short story and formed in 1978, their bleak heartbreak songs were perfect for the post-punk period. They found recognition in Holland, but despite their distinctive sound, they remained trapped in cult status. However, they became an influence on a slew of future dark indie bands, such as Editors and Interpol.

Sheffield was full of these striking bands with an innate futuristic sci-fi darkness. Artery somehow entwined swirls of melancholia into their post-punk indie aesthetic. Their confrontational live shows are legendary in their home city, where they profoundly influenced a young Jarvis Cocker and other bands in the post-punk community. Early The Human League were a stark and bold manifesto for a future world, whilst bands like Clock DVA, Chakk, and Hula were melding machines to dark funk to create a new soundtrack that was adopted into many fringe goth clubs. I'm So Hollow flickered briefly with their haunting and brilliant 1979 'Dreams to

---

1153 Johnny Marr to John Robb.

1154 The bassist died from cancer in 2011.

Fill the Vacuum' single, and were another reflection of the Sheffield embrace of sci-fi glam futurism, curated within its concrete city centre and the iconic surrounding hilltop flats. That Ballardian architecture provided a stark backdrop for the neon glamour, Dadaism and futuristic sound that would hold a mirror to the surrounding city whilst attempting to escape it. All over the UK in the early 1980s, isolated towns seemed to have their own ambassadors of new noise.

On the 5 Sept 1981 at Manchester Rafters, a very young-looking band, dressed in white, were playing three keyboards on stage whilst their singer was doing a pop star wiggle to about 40 people. Depeche Mode looked fresh and clean and very pop.

In the audience that night was a pre-Smiths Morrissey, who slated the band in his review for *Record Mirror*. He was more interested in writing about the support band, Ludus, who were fronted by the enigmatic Linder Sterling. Ludus were playing a thrilling, dark, weird and uncompromising lounge jazz. Linder, herself, was also an influential artist who had turned down Factory Records when they were looking for a designer and recommended her Manchester Art College fellow student Peter Saville for the job instead. She went on to design sleeves for Buzzcocks and Magazine, and her artwork remains a powerful influence on all who see it.

That night, Depeche Mode were quite different from the stadium beast they would become. Like young foals staggering on their wobbly legs, they looked and sounded impossibly clean-cut. Somehow within ten years, they managed to morph into prime purveyors of dark, perverted goth-pop with an industrial influence that made them one of the key bands in breaking darker musics into the mainstream, taking the culture into the shopping malls of Big America.

Their sonic trajectory has been quite startling but one that makes perfect sense when you consider that they were signed to Mute records. The label was the key for so much dark experimental music and the eventual home of Nick Cave and Einstürzende Neubauten and had already released the brilliant Fad Gadget, whose two debut singles, 1979's 'Back to Nature' and 1980's 'Ricky's Hand' were key signposts in darker synth pop. Mute was also the home of The Normal, the occasional band of label boss Daniel Miller, whose only single, T.V.O.D/Warm Leatherette, was a stripped-down slice of raw electronic and a nod to JG Ballard and is one of the great releases of the period.

Depeche Mode's move to the dark side was sparked when their key songwriter Vince Clarke left in 1981 to form Yazoo and then Erasure. His departure should have seen the band fold, but they rallied and started writing their own music under, initially, the guidance of band member Martin Gore on 1982's *A Broken Frame*. This is an album which still remains pop but with a slightly darker hue that was explored deeper when Alan Wilder, who had been added to the lineup, brought his own dark energy into the mix. Like some sort of diseased animal, Depeche Mode combined going their new influences with becoming a stadium juggernaut that experimented with industrial textures. This was further explored after Martin Gore saw Einstürzende Neubauten live. They then added elements of this industrial sound for 1983's *Construction Time Again,* which came with a sleeve that looked like a Laibach outtake.

This was a process that they continued with on a run of albums, including 1996's goth classic *Black Celebration,* that synthesised their darker muse with a continued knack for pop. The final worldwide breakthrough came in 1990 with *Violator.* Here, they added guitars into the mix, especially with the classic breakout 'Personal Jesus' single seeing them formulate the right balance of shivering spook and stadium guitar riffs. Depeche Mode had created an electronic, future machine pop that hit the mainstream with songs that examined sex, life, death and religion with darkly atmospheric lyrics and musical soundscapes, with the vital elixir being David Gahan's icy lounge-lizard electro-croon.

Violator sold a million copies in the USA and was dark subversive pop at its best and a goth entry album for a new generation. The follow-up, 1993's *Songs of Faith and Devotion,* saw them influenced by the grunge scene, and they recorded a more aggressive, darker, rock-oriented record than before, yet it was an album that still sat well in their lineage.

The grunge lifestyle also impinged on the band, with Dave Gahan suffering a cocaine and heroin overdose, in which he was actually dead for two minutes. After Gahan somehow survived, Alan Wilder quit shortly afterwards. Somehow, the band survived these ructions and maintained their dark creativity and knack for filling stadiums with a steady flow of dark and melancholy records with their poetic, off-kilter lyrics, until the recent death of founder member Andrew Fletcher in 2022 reduced them to a core duo for the future.

At the same time as Depeche Mode were adjusting to the stadiums, other post-punk outliers were making the same kind of move up. Glasgow-based Simple Minds were named after one of the lyrics of David Bowie's iconic 'Jean Genie' single and had grown out of local punk band Johnny And The Self Abusers. While their debut *Life In A Day* album may have been a bit too polished, their second album *Reel to Real Cacophony,* saw the band stretch into their own direction after being exposed to Joy Division and Magazine. The post-Bowie keyboard-coated post-punk on their third album, 1980's *Empires and Dance,* was a cornerstone record with nods to Eno, Kraftwerk, Can and Neu! Built around a futuristic, nihilistic soundtrack of a trip around Europe, the band created a hugely effective paranoid setting for Kerr to dramatise what he saw in a brittle, caustic way. *Sons And Fascination/Sister Feelings Call* saw them crank their rhythm section in a perfect double album of proto cold wave that saw them break out whilst 1982's *New Gold Dream* saw them go 'all U2'; after that, it was a full on stadium from the band. These early albums, though, were part of the myriad of influences on some strands of future goth, with Simple Minds creating a crafted new wave dark pop that was bold, ambitious, and experimental.

Once they had left the Lypton Village, U2 ended up being the biggest band of the decade. Like many other post-punk bands, they had given the nod towards the darker underground and had even gone as far as getting Martin Hannett into producing their 1980 '11 O'clock Tick Tock' single. This was arguably an attempt to create some Joy Division magic, hoping it would rub off on their impassioned, bright, post-punk anthems. Forging out of punk, the Dublin band had created a new sound by taking some of the intrinsic elements of the new alternative underground and applying them to their own muse and Bono's big stadium-filling voice. There were echoes of Keith Levene's chiming acerbic style but it was the Banshees' John McKay's brilliant glass guitar, Severin's driving bass lines, and then John McGeoch's reinvention of the six string that, added to the gothic melodrama of Joy Division, provided the base to their sound.

Not every band with a big sound managed to make the leap into the popular imagination. The Bolshoi were mid-1980s outsiders from Trowbridge, Wiltshire. Starting with early gigs supporting the likes of The Cult, The March Violets and The Lords of the New Church, they also fitted neatly beside the stadium indie of Simple Minds, having a big shiny new sound but retaining a certain gothic swirl to their muse that never quite broke out of the goth cult status.

Arriving in the middle of the baggy Madchester period, Manic Street Preachers were an outlier. The band initially were a DIY home-made Clash from South Wales with big songs that combined the metallic power of Guns N' Roses with the Westway Wonders. The band's third album, 1994's *The Holy Bible*, though, is an intense, introverted and darkly poetic affair and arguably their 'goth' album. They certainly had the smudged mascara and leopardskin but were now going in so much deeper. By now, the band's iconic guitar player Richey Edwards was in a fragile mental state with the dark clouds gathering over his head. His intensity and darkness affected the music, and his often obtuse and impassioned lyrics and worldview hung over the album. Hardcore fans consider *The Holy Bible* to be the band's best effort, and its shadows and intensity are equal to Joy Division and full of gothic shivers. The songs drip with a melancholy that matches the obtuse lyrical shards and snippets from the young guitar player/lyricist who was about to disappear.[1155]

Pop culture has always been about reinvention, and the young Gary Webb, born in 1958 recast himself in the late 1970s as Gary Numan, becoming another maverick to be part embraced by the goth scene. He first took to the stage in 1976 in the punkish band Mean Streets, who had appeared on the *Live at The Vortex* punk compilation album and were a minor footnote in the punk explosion. When the band ground to a halt, he put together Tubeway Army in 1978. Signed to Beggars Banquet, they initially released a more guitar-driven clutch of singles. Their debut album added small flourishes of Minimoog and an added apocalyptic sci-fi lyrical twist, giving a nod to Philip K. Dick.

When Numan finally got his sound right, his dislocated keyboard-driven pop was perfect, with a melancholia that matched his convincing alien aura. He hit pop pay dirt with a great run of albums, starting with 1979's *Replicas*. The album was an immersion in new technology with further dystopian sci-fi lyrical nods. This

---

1155 On 1 February 1995, Richey disappeared and is presumed to have taken his own life. His car was found close to the Severn Bridge.

combination gave the band a futuristic sense that broke into the mainstream with the classic 'Are Friends Electric?' single, a huge hit that launched him as an early 1980s pop star.

Numan really was the man who fell to earth from just around the corner. Taking his new stage name from a dip into the Yellow Pages with a corruption of a local plumber's Neumann moniker, the young singer was all at once freakishly out there and yet perfectly normal. This duality has remained a crucial part of his appeal. His dislocated, detached alien presence was perpetually dressed in black, yet Numan was a David Bowie from the local estate. His new music gave him a sense of remoteness but conversely came with an emotional overlay that was threaded throughout.

His career has had its ups and downs. He was never truly press-friendly, possibly due to his Aspergers Syndrome and his initial notably awkward presence. Subsequently, his dark pop was largely ignored by the media. Despite this, he experienced huge successes in the 1980s. His recent comeback, powered by a hands-on DIY approach and a close rapport with his loyal fans, has allowed him to reinvent himself in the last decade as the master and servant of his acolytes.

Recast now as some kind of post steampunk post-goth overlord, Numan uses music to deal with his melancholic side, creating a playground of musical nightmares. In recent years, he has pulled off this remarkable late-period revival, embraced by the many bands and musicians like Nine Inch Nails and Marilyn Manson, who had previously been inspired by him.

He, in turn, used their energy to make new albums like 2013's *Splinter (Songs from a Broken Mind)* and 2017's *Savage (Songs from a Broken World)*, which sound contemporary and relaunched him into the frontline of pop culture.

> I don't think it's possible to be a big fan of something without some of it rubbing off. I know Trent Reznor from Nine Inch Nails has talked very eloquently on many occasions about how I was an influence on him. It indeed flows both ways. I'm a great admirer of Trent and what he does on many levels. He sets a very high standard.[1156]

In the new millennium, Numan delivers a music of powerful inherent darkness.

> The songs are quite heavy and about dark experiences (as they usually are with me). In much the same way as someone would talk to a therapist or a very close friend, music is a very useful way of getting those negative emotions out. I find that writing about such things helps to empty my head of all the negative things that lurk inside. With *Splinter*, many of the songs are my way of dealing with the after effects of depression, and I genuinely feel that because I could do that, I've come out of it unscarred, and arguably as a nicer person than I was before.[1157]

Delightfully challenging to categorise and with a music that ranges from pre-punk experimental to psychedelic pop to weird pop to neo-industrial noise, Danielle Dax is another highly original performer embraced by the alternative scene. Southend

1156 Gary Numan to Louder Than War.

1157 Gary Numan to Louder Than War.

born Dax she has created a tantalising catalogue of music with a stunning visual creation full of immaculate yet untamed hair, Day-Glo clothes and a wild and exotic image that reflected her propulsive creativity. It was a creativity that emerged with underground releases and blurred photos in the late 1970s *Zigzag* magazine, appearing like a tree spirit running amok in the music scene.

Raised by her grandparents, who encouraged the love of the arts, nature and the occult, creating a true free spirit, at the age of eight, she played the flute at Benjamin Britten's *Noye's Fludde* at the Royal Albert Hall. A few years later, she designed posters and programmes for Opera East and studied classical flute at school. In 1979, it was partly her striking and mystical photograph with an interview in a local paper that sparked her musical career. Another Reading local, Karl Blake, got in touch with her at her next arts group meeting and said he was looking for an artist to join Lemon Kittens. Intrigued, she painted the artwork for the left-field project's first EP, 'Spoonfed and Writhing', before being asked to join the band as a musician.

The Lemon Kittens' complex and brilliant music was an extreme collision between Zappa, Beefheart and The Pop Group with Blake's manic vocals, interspersed with Danielle's cut glass voice flowing over a shattered background of restless rhythms. Their unique sound is best heard on the 1980 album; We *Buy a Hammer for Daddy* and its 1982 follow-up, *Those That Bite, the Hand That Feeds Them Sooner or Later Must Meet... The Big Dentist*. The band perfectly complimented their creation by performing while covered in body paint, creating a striking and brilliantly challenging stage presence. In 1983, Lemon Kittens took an extended rest before Karl Blake re-emerged with the dark, growling post-punk of Shock Headed Peters, continuing his vision of the prog experimental. Their dislocated grinding power fitted neatly into the 'Death to Trad Rock' underground of the mid-1980s and is well worth investigating.

Meanwhile, Danielle Dax embarked on a solo career. Her first album, 1983's *Pop Eyes,* is a multifaceted work that embraces numerous styles, including classical, blues, electronica, Indian, rock, African, psychedelic and medieval. It was a shimmering quixotic release where she played all the instruments herself. The follow-up, 1984's humorously titled *Jesus Egg That Wept*, is a brilliant mini album and established her as one of the groundbreaking musicians on the underground scene. The album strikes the perfect balance between experimental and warped pop and made quite an impression on the underground. This was consolidated by her appearance in *The Company of Wolves*[1158] film where her semi-naked Wild-Eyed stage personality was captured in celluloid for one of the big cult films of the year.

Dax started to move towards the mainstream with 1987's *Inky Bloaters*, a transitional album with added guitars and a sense of song structure. This was further explored on the Stephen Street-produced *Blast the Human Flower* (1990), which saw her hit the apex of her pop ambition, spearheaded by a tripped-out cover of The Beatles'

1158 1984 gothic fantasy horror film directed by Neil Jordan and starring Angela Lansbury, David Warner where Dax plays the part of a she-wolf from the world beneath who arrives at the village.

'Tomorrow Never Knows'. After this, she left music to appear regularly on BBC interior design show before lying low as one of pop culture's great 'what ifs'.

The goth club dance floors could be very accommodating places, often embracing updated rockers in the swirling new gloom. By the mid-'80s, former Generation X singer, Billy Idol had transformed himself into a gonzoid '80s pop star full of G-strings and spike-haired snarls like a genuine Elvis from purgatory. His songs were anthemic and, whilst never goth, were certainly crossing over into that world.

He may have appeared as mainstream pop, but Billy Idol had goth creds that are currently reflected in *Buffy the Vampire Slayer's* Spike character, a goth pin-up and TV icon who would humorously claim in the series that Billy Idol stole his look back in the 1970s.

Emerging from the ashes of punk originals Generation X, solo Billy Idol was a far more astute player of the codes of pop than he was letting on. He ditched his artful side, looked in the mirror and used his chiselled features and good looks to create the ultimate rock n roll star that lived up to his name. Moving to America, he became one of the first MTV rock stars with his sneer and bleached quiff perfectly in place for the tele-visual age. With an image that was a combination of sci-fi biker with beads and leather, Idol stole America's heart and became one of the biggest stars of the period. With enough snarl to keep his place in the alternative soundtrack, his music was a perfect synthesis between the electronic pulse of disco and the slash and burn of rock'n'roll. It was a combination that hit pay dirt and he was now living the runaway life of sex n drugs n rock'n'roll; a sneering, real wild child who was fast-tracking himself for the sort of ugly rock'n'roll demise of his heroes like Jim Morrison.

> The more I did things, the more things opened up for me like taking crack, heroin, cocaine [laughs], and you then realise that you're not doing one – you're doing them all! You're drinking a lot more, and your art is getting a lot more prostituted and there's girls and it's all fantastic fun, but in the end, you know that one day you're going to be in a big pile up. And that's what happened to me in the '90s when it suddenly went bing bong bang, and I'm literally bouncing off the tarmac, and I realised I couldn't stay that way, or I could kill myself or get locked away for a very long time. So, you get back into the music, and that's the best drug of them all.[1159]

Meanwhile, in the mid '80s, his former Generation X partner in crime, Tony James, had also been busy constructing an astonishing guerrilla raid on pop's gilded towers with his new band, Sigue Sigue Sputnik. The band's audacious bid for success saw them take a huge advance from the majors and create a Pistolian press storm under the guiding hand of James. With their over the top image of pineapple hair, dystopian sci-fi outfits and face masks, they looked like the ultimate droogs from the imaginary Moscow street gang which they were named after. Their singer Martin Degville was once described by Boy George as, 'one of the most outrageous people

---

1159 Billy Idol to John Robb.

I've ever met…he looked like an Alsatian from outer space.'[1160] and for a few brief moments, they looked like they had pulled it off,, with their debut 'Love Missile F1-11' single becoming a big hit. Tony James' astutely played the pop game and media, but they quickly lost their allure. The group's demise was a true shame as their Suicide-meets-Eddie Cochrane space-age pop was thrillingly effective, especially on their demo album.

Another outsider finding a home in the post-punk confusion was, initially, an actress.

Toyah Willcox had put a band together in the punk wars, and after a year of grafting at club level, she had picked up a firebrand punk and crossover audience for her flamboyant take on the form. Her new spectacular image saw her recast as some kind of punk warrior queen – a yodelling Boudica that was briefly running parallel with Adam Ant for another unlikely Derek Jarman cult-turned-big star. With her wild hair and wilder songs, she was now partly embraced by the emerging goth scene. Her music, co-written with Joel Bogen, was a weird mixture of punk energy, fidgety pop and a prog aesthetic which was honed down on her first two releases, 1987's mini album *Sheep Farming In Barnet* and 1980's *The Blue Meaning*.

1981's *Anthem* was the breakthrough, though, driven by her hit singles 'It's a Mystery' and 'I Want to Be Free'. By the time of her *Changeling* album the following year, she was dealing in the darker side, making a breakup album with lingering shadows of darkness.

> I like *Changeling* more and more. I couldn't listen to it for years because it was a personal album. I was in a bad place when we made it. It was a tough album to make, to be quite honest but it's one of my albums, and I now perform it a lot. Thank God we had the friction, and we have pulled something out of that and made something very gothic.[1161]

An aspiring actress growing up in mid-1970s Birmingham, Toyah was inspired and fired by punk after seeing an early Sex Pistols show in her hometown on 20 October 1976. Moving down to London, she became an actress. Her big break came with Derek Jarman and his *Jubilee* film that also starred Adam Ant and Jordan.

> Derek was totally in love with Jordan. It was like the closest a homosexual man could love a woman. He just let you almost improvise around the idea. In one scene, he said, 'you go where you want, say what you want and do what you want as long as you start here and end up in bed with Carl Johnson.'
> I was terribly nervous, and my heart was racing. Derek was just gorgeous, and he said, 'don't worry, we will do it again if we have to!' Part of my OTT performance is my nerves and the bravado kicking in. We got right through the whole scene to the point where I jumped into the bed, and I pulled back the bedclothes and completely froze, and Derek said, 'what's the matter?', and I said, 'I've never seen a naked man before!' and the whole set burst into laughter – and that was a kind of innocence which Derek enjoyed.

1160 *Boy George's 1970s: Save Me From Suburbia* (2016).

1161 Toyah to John Robb.

That was very much part of punk as well – I think the naivety for me was just as attractive as the power of The Clash's politics. Punk just scooped all these lost souls up and said, 'you have a voice; you have a place,'
I felt that I wanted to represent a side of women not represented in my life when I grew up, where I was surrounded by Victorian ideals of femininity like Florence Nightingale. I researched all this and embraced these powerful women like Boudica who was more me! Or Mata Hari – the spy executed by the firing squad. I grew up with all these images of being a strong woman, yet I wasn't allowed to be a strong woman even when I finally used my voice. I wanted it to be Boudica battling in war to save her daughters.[1162]

Kate Bush's 1978 debut single 'Wuthering Heights', released when she was just 19, stayed at the top of the UK charts for four weeks. The song's high gothic melodrama positively embraced a romantic poetic atmosphere. It was full of love, lust and romance gone wrong, while her ethereal femininity and unique originality ensnared many ardent fans like John Lydon. Kate Bush was also a big Killing Joke and Stranglers fan, even hanging out with the men in black in 78/79. Her experimental mystical pop, with its literate lyrics and off-kilter vocals, remains forever popular in the goth scene as well as the mainstream, underlined by her recent out of the blue number one hit with 'Running Up That Hill (A Deal with God)' which h had been featured on the gothic flavoured *Stranger Things* TV box set series. Proof that the gothic-tinged world that she created transcended generations. Another huge pop hit that was drenched in delicious goth possibilities was Shakespears Sister and their 1992 number one, 'Stay With me'.

Hovering under the banner of alternative music, dark indie was another reaction to the apocalyptic vibe of the times. Running parallel and sometimes crossing over with goth for a period from post-punk to acid house, dark and sombre styles combined to create a music culture that is still influential to this day.

1162 Toyah to John Robb.

Chapter 34

'WE SING TO THE GODS TO BE FREE'

American Gothic and the Dark Art of the American Dream[1163]

The 1930 Grant Wood painting *American Gothic* is an iconic classic.

The depiction of a stern-faced father with his defiant pitchfork standing next to his even sterner looking daughter seems to depict the fire and brimstone intransigence of rural Middle America a thousand miles away from the Gotham city future goth bubbles and dark culture epicentres of 'those big cities'. Named after the architectural style of the building in the background, the painting captures 'in the flat field' America and its pitchfork values that many future goths were escaping from to create their own quite different take on American Gothic.

Maybe it was the Southern Gothic fiction genre that was closer to the art of darkness with its American take on the Victorian fascination with death and decay. Its love of romantic and emotionally drenched storylines with flawed characters in decayed settings and dark, grotesque situations with an undertow of violence and crime was an American dream gone nightmare. The themes in the literature are closer to the death, and night, and blood at the heart and soul of goth, whilst the *American Gothic* painting was an iconic and subtle tribute to the simple, yet suffocating values ascribed to the American heartland.

By the '80s, 'American Gothic' was getting a new coat of black paint and a new meaning from the children of the dark revolution

Typically for a country obsessed with religion, America had long enjoyed a dance with the Devil. Rock n roll had always dabbled with diablo, and Elvis had been the Devil incarnate for Middle America whilst Little Richard and Jerry Lee Lewis were grappling with their own demons. Dressed in black leather, Link Wray delivered his fuzzed-out guitar lines from hell that would create the sonic chassis so beloved by The Cramps. Meanwhile, the 1960s and 1970s had brought long hair, new drugs and a godless culture out to play. The new electric music was wrestling with America's soul, and culture was where you saw the battle lines.

The Doors' funereal waltzes had soundtracked the dark underbelly of American youth, mirroring the inevitable pop culture mood change. Similarly, The Stooges and Velvets pioneered a more intense and nebulous style of rock music that would crisscross both sides of the Atlantic. The Vietnam war had brought a real Apocalypse Now whilst framing the burgeoning dark subculture with a life and death dread and a potent moral issue.

The flip-side was cartoon America and the ever-present kooky shadow of Halloween, which has long been an American institution and has become a deeply

---

1163 Phrase coined by James Truslow Adams in 1931.

embedded caricature in the national psyche. Borrowing its Halloween customs from Scotland and Ireland via Canada, America turned All Hallows' Eve into a Disney caper with mountains of spooky tack and exported them back. From pumpkins and trick-or-treat to elaborate costumes of witches and draped cobwebs, it all fed into a shadowy background for a new world goth.

American punk and post-punk music culture lacked the same national galvanising effect as in the UK. America is vast and, pre-internet, things moved slowly. However, when the woodwork squeaked, the post-punk freaks finally came out to play, and their energy would be fired up in many localised micro scenes. These would wildly vary in style, from the dark aggression of Black Flag to the deathrock of Christian Death, the horror punk of Misfits to the brooding psychedelia of Swans to Lydia Lunch's harsh words and iconic style. There was Type O Negative and their metallic KO take on trad goth, Big Black's stark drum machine-driven clatter and small town outsiders like the late Mark Lanegan and his soul-seeking baritone or Jesus Lizard, who brought a dark twist to the late 1980s grunge scene to Wax Trax! Records[1164] embrace of the no man's land between industrial and rock.

America's fascination for the dark side was deeply embedded in its popular culture, with Hollywood dealing key films such as George A. Romero's 1968 *Night of the Living Dead*, John Russo's *Return of the Living Dead* (turned into a film by Dan O'Bannon), as well as the all-pervading 1950s horror-themed TV shows such as *The Munsters, The Twilight Zone* and *Dark Shadows,* were all introducing a delicious shiver to the suburbs. There was also the iconic 1950s TV presenter Vampira and her spook wardrobe, not to mention her 1980s equivalent, the horror hostess Elvira with her gothic styles and cleavage-exposing gowns. Both characters proved to be enormously influential in cultivating the female goth/vamp aesthetic. Similarly, there were local DJs and 'horror hosts' like John Zacherle, who broadcast in 1960s Philadelphia and New York and influenced the burgeoning scene and Ghoulardi, a Cleveland DJ, whose kooky vamping substantially influenced a young Lux Interior of The Cramps.

If pop culture had started in the 1960s on a wave of utopian bliss, these bands, movers and shakers helped to reshape it. There was now a dystopian edge to pop's never never land with Nixon, Altamont, bad acid, bankrupt cities like the lower east side of New York in the 1970s and its Batman backdrop of a broken Gotham city impinging on the pop culture hangover and the end of the hippie dream. The joyful Beatlemania screams were becoming much darker, and a general unease and disillusionment filled the air.

It was getting dark out there.

Despite this, Middle America had been sleepwalking into suburban comfort despite the lingering miasma of the Vietnam War or the horror show of the 1968

1164 The Chicago based Waxtrax label created a playground full of pulverising scrap metal riffs, heavily treated guitars, hi-energy fist fuck beats and a confrontational attitude that saw the new industrial rock from Revolting Cocks and Ministry, which laid the foundations for Nine Inch Nails and Marilyn Manson, who would take an American darkness to the top of the charts.

Manson Family murders[1165]. The latter having punctured the Hollywood dream with their savage and creepy-crawly nihilism. The suburbs were daydreaming, but New York's decay saw a rat run full of broken streets, boarded-up shops and empty spaces, providing a perfect backdrop to the throbbing danger of the eternally futuristic outsider art and music of Suicide. Yet suburban America in the seventies was still in a dopamine picket fence bliss, and punk made little impact beyond intense local scenes with different levels of intensity, as pioneer punk warlord Henry Rollins explains:

> I think there was, at least in some parts of the punk scene, a lack of seriousness. A lot of people just wanted to have a good time for a change and not be so worried about getting all the notes right every time, etc. Much good music came from that, but at the same time, there were a lot of very talented people in punk scenes all over the world for whom music became a very serious pursuit. They were giving everything they had to it. I don't think you can throw yourself into something with the full velocity of your life, ambition, fear of failure and desire to fully realise what you can put forth and not have it pick up some seriousness. I'm not saying that as an insult. When you're trying to do something musically, it becomes more complex and more devoted. This is where much of the goth and post-punk music gets its greatness. These people were still around, looking to make music after the party was over.[1166]

Inspired by the new punk rock culture, Rollins enjoyed darker realms of creativity whilst fronting LA-based band Black Flag, who took The Doors' nihilistic trip to a pulverising endpoint. As Jim Morrison had crooned, this truly was The End[1167]. He was also fascinated by other fellow creatives who were finding space for their own adventures in a broad post-punk church of noise, especially those who were truly operating in the heart of darkness and who he firmly places at the forefront of the dark arts:

> I was amazed by Diamanda Galás. As soon as I heard her *The Litanies of Satan* record in 1984. I wrote her a letter, and she wrote me back. We have been pals ever since. What Diamanda was doing, along with The Birthday Party, The Gun Club and Einstürzende Neubauten, all of which I could see live, had a huge impact on me.[1168]

Born in San Diego in 1955 of Greek and Egyptian stock, Galas is like nothing else. Her unnerving, almost operatic, sonorous vocals can be genuinely terrifying. Her brooding, sparse and eclectic music comes laden with political and social themes of AIDS, death, dark literature and the dislocation of the ideas of the likes of the Marquis de Sade and Artaud. Her exploration of the far boundaries of life, dark sensuality and music to match, is compulsive, as she explains:

1165 Charles Manson has been a hovering influence on goth, not least through the very name of Marilyn Manson. The horrific Manson murders and his dark manifesto delivered in the subsequent trial were to provide fascination for would be dark rockers for generations.

1166 Henry Rollins to John Robb.

1167 Perhaps the most classic of all the songs by The Doors.

1168 Henry Rollins to John Robb.

I am very fortunate to have many mediums to create with. Life can be very painful, and without the ability to create, it would be unbearable. We need to feel joy, and we need to be able to deal with pain when it hits. Being able to exorcise, to extrovert, to throw off the little knife wounds is a talent developed over the years.[1169]

Pulling on the beautiful darkness of her Greek background, Galas had several realms from which to draw inspiration. She considered Byzantine chants, traditional haunting ballads and a sense of longing found within the Greek folk blues of Rebetiko[1170]. Similarly, the pain of folk memories fed into her music, adding to her immersive powerful blues and creating something unique and personal.

Someone once told me that the Greek racial group and diaspora is the purple race, and I laughed. But our dromoi (scales, roads) are peculiar to our particular sensibilities; our 'amanes'[1171] are our prayers and our salvation. We sing to the gods to be free. We must sing loudly even when we whisper, or they will not hear us. You are a spear, and you must go far to the next village. You must travel, and you must arrive at a new village every time. It means you must develop power because if you don't, you can't travel. There are too many hard rocks in your way, and you must be able to fly over them.[1172]

Henry Rollins sees post-punk as more of a clutch of bands creating their own narratives and less about umbrella 'scenes'.

I was used to bands never liking Black Flag, I saw Jeffrey Lee Pierce at one of our shows once in 1983, but I left him alone but he was then talking to Dukowski,[1173] so I walked up to the two of them, and Jeffrey was really cool. We remained pals until he passed away. I think he was the best songwriter from that whole LA scene. The Cramps were incredible, and I got to see them many times. I think they were on their own. I'm still playing their records. For me, most of the truly great bands came right after the initial bang of punk. Joy Division, The Ruts, The Fall, Cabaret Voltaire, Wire, Gang of Four, PiL. All the bands from punk that endured, you will notice that they almost all immediately distanced themselves from being 'punk'. Bands like Buzzcocks, The Adverts and others were trying to do their thing. Punk rock became a prison yard with a high wall for many of them to break out.[1174]

It was Los Angeles that saw the founding fathers of American goth emerge. In 1979 Christian Death were formed by Ross Williams, and their taste for the dark side of glam, the theatricality of David Bowie and Roxy Music and the shock tactics of Throbbing Gristle saw them start a decades long culture war against religion and conventional normality that was to have a profound effect on American goth, industrial and metal bands of the future. The band's dark cabaret and its confrontational lyrics

---

1169 Diamanda Galas to John Robb.

1170 The haunting Greek urban folk music with its melancholic chiming bouzouki-driven songs.

1171 The singing lament.

1172 Diamanda Galas to John Robb.

1173 Chuck Dukowski, Black Flag's bass player.

1174 Henry Rollins to John Robb.

of blasphemy, morbidity, drug use, and sexual perversity created what they termed deathrock out of a glam dystopia.

The LA punk scene itself always had a glam element driven by Rodney Bingenheimer's English Disco club. Bingenheimer would later DJ on KROQ radio, and his *Rodney on the ROQ* show would also prove key in the LA punk scene. The glam influence had lingered on into punk through bands like The Germs, The Weirdos and The Nuns. Now christened 'deathrock' by Rozz Williams to describe his band and a loose cabal of dark dissidents like 45 Grave, Kommunity FK, Flesh Eaters and Super Heroines. Built around the Anti Club on Melrose, LA would go on to have the biggest goth and deathrock scene in the USA.

Deathrock was a term initially bandied about in the 1950s to describe the eerie, darker, spooked rock'n'roll records infused with morbid romantic tales of love, dead teenagers and murder. These records came drenched in cadaver heartache, reverb and spookily brilliant sci-fi sound effects. Such melancholic love songs are best exemplified by the Shangri-La's 1964 hit 'Leader of the Pack', Jody Reynolds 1958 hits, 'Endless Sleep' and 'Fire of Love'[1175] or the even more comical, yet endlessly engaging, classic Bobby 'Boris' Pickett and the Crypt-Kickers 'Monster Mash' (1962). This trend arguably ended in 1964 with J. Frank Wilson's 'Last Kiss'.

The term would reemerge in the late '70s as a loose catch-all for a new American Gothic and was first reappropriated either by the late underground film-maker Mick Zedd in 1979 for his *They Eat Scum*, a film which typically featured a fictional cannibalistic "death rock" punk band called 'Suzy Putrid and the Mental Deficients' or in real life by Rozz Williams himself.

Rebelling against a strict Christian upbringing, Williams was sparked by his love of the 1970s schlock of Alice Cooper and Kiss and the possibilities of punk and of local crash and burn punk band The Germs and formed a band called The Upsetters in late 1979 before morphing into Christian Death.

Their spooked take on the new punk scene added ghoulish melodic lines and dark themes borrowed from horror movies, film noir, surrealism and established religious imagery. The band pushed deeper into the emerging goth aesthetic that was now arriving from across the Atlantic and was soon the driving force in the USA.

Their 1982 debut album *Only Theatre of Pain*, was a dark snapshot of the shadowy LA underbelly. Within its flickering graveyard shadows, you can hear hints of early PiL and Virgin Prunes hanging over its inherent darkness, and the album was an early signifier of the more American take on the post-punk goth scene. Christian Death would famously conduct theatrical live shows, wearing wedding dresses and sporting a life-size crucifix, creating a gothic spectacle that Marilyn Manson and many other future freak shows must have noted. Their follow up 1984 album, *Catastrophe Ballet,* saw Rozz Williams pull together a new lineup amid band infighting and drug abuse with guitar player and future band leader Valor Kand from local deathrock band, Pompei 99. The release cranked up the surrealism with synths and an added

---

1175 Covered brilliantly by The Gun Club.

magic mushroom intake that gave the beautifully goth-crooned songs a Dada edge. His voice had gained a Lou Reed street hassle and a shivering Bowie delivery that conveyed a deeper, more nuanced lyrical take on an artful dark beauty than the occult and outrage that had dominated their debut.

Williams quit in 1985, and Kand took over the reins and fronts Christian Death to this day with a more intellectual, political, and metal-oriented direction. Post split, inevitably the two became mired in a dispute over ownership of the Christian Death name, whilst the charismatic Williams then pursued his solo career of different projects until his mysterious suicide in 1998.

Preceding Christian Death were 45 Grave, fronted by a familiar face on the LA scene, Dinah Cancer. The band fell together from the remnants of the debris of local bands, with local faces like Pat Smear[1176] and Paul Roessler – the brother of Black Flag late period bassist Kira – thrown together in the punk rock period of 1979. Their ghoulish keyboard-driven horror pop had an infamous added camp-horror streak and a combination of genres that made them sound like a dysfunctional 60s beach party but rumbled with shadowy garage-band darkness. This darkness was twisted with a nostalgic sense of novelty, again harkening to the spectral records of the 1950s, as much as the surrounding punk rock and hardcore scenes.

In the 1980s, the death rock scene continued to grow, with bands such as Super Heroines, Voodoo Church, Burning Image, Ex-Voto, Radio Werewolf and Screams for Tina being key names. As the scene spread across the rest of America, other deathrock bands emerged, like Theatre of Ice, Your Funeral and Mighty Sphincter from Nevada, Colorado and Phoenix, respectively, and it became a catch-all term for modern dark.

Newly arrived in New York in 1975 from Cleveland, The Cramps had reacted to the Big Apple by inventing psychobilly; meanwhile, Misfits were New York locals who would pick up on comic book horror and add a punk wall of sound and run with it. Since then, their horror punk aesthetic has created a worldwide industry of ghoul merchandise and their clearly defined image and artwork have become undeniably ubiquitous.

Initially, Misfits were a footnote in punk rock lore. They lingered in a handful of grimy photos in the music press, a couple of support shows with The Damned on their first US visit and a hard-to-find clutch of releases. They were low-key players on the local scene, with members Jerry Only and his younger brother Doyle driving Sid Vicious around on the day he was released from prison in 1978. They cooked pasta for him on the night of his 'get out of jail party', hours before he overdosed and died.

Over the years, their horror punk made them stand out. A mix of bodybuilding, B Movies, and horror movie makeup that matched singer Glen Danzig's darkly crooned monster movie songs has made them one of the pillars of American punk. The band's distinctive homemade image was literally welded in their family's New

---

1176 Pat Smear also played in the highly influential LA punk band The Germs, who crashed and burned after the death of their charismatic singer Derby Crash. Smear currently plays in the Foo Fighters.

Jersey machine shop, with the brothers and singer Glenn Danzig forming the band's core. Their deep love of George Romero's movies and their dark arts DIY take on Kiss (with their readily marketable toy doll imagery) was a key influence on their zombie image. Over the years, the band's own creation of 'devilock' hair and a homemade theatricality have become stylistically influential. Their catchy rushes of buzzsaw punk rock with Glen Danzig's baritone would spark off the separate world of horror punk. Post-Misfits, Glen Danzig would form the dark metal band Samhain in 1983 before creating Danzig. Johnny Cash covered his song 'Thirteen' with much acclaim on his *American Recordings* album, and to this day, Misfits merch is almost as visible as a Ramones t-shirt.

Parallel to this psychotic reaction was the much-acknowledged late seventies No Wave scene - New York's thrilling and nihilistic reaction to the new wave. Taking the energy of punk but moving away from the rock, this was frenetic music with a twitching groove or a minimalistic dark noise with a blowtorch attitude in which many goth pioneers found influence.

In 1978 it was a loosely linked scene of firebrand names attempting to create a new kind of post-rock. This was a rejection of the trad rock core of punk rock and the so-called new wave and a multi-genre space for experimental, non-rock music that toyed with noise, dissonance and atonality with scratchy and propulsive energy. Critical bands on the scene included James Chance and the Contortions, Teenage Jesus and the Jerks, Mars, DNA, Theoretical Girls and Rhys Chatham, whilst later on, fringe outfits like Swans and Sonic Youth would be sucked into its orbit.

The initial jagged assaults were driven by punk's kinetic energy but with very different rhythms that nodded at free jazz and disco. The scene would eventually split, with part of it morphing into a more dance-oriented direction with bands such as Liquid Liquid, coalescing at venues like Club 57 and the Mudd Club. The other half, including Swans and Sonic Youth, continued the explorations into noise and atonality. The style and attitude also seeped into cinema with Jim Jarmusch and the art world with graffiti artists such as the legendary Jean-Michel Basquiat, Keith Haring and Michael Holman. No Wave saw all kinds of maverick spirits running amok and using rock's own instruments against itself. Musician, author and daring provocateur Lydia Lunch was one of the iconic faces of the scene and beyond. With her jet black clothes and hair, she looked fierce, her art was fierce. And she talked fierce:

> The whole fucking country was nihilistic. What did we come out of? The lie of the summer of love into Charles Manson and the Vietnam War. Where is the positivity?' [1177]

Lydia Lunch was a goth icon before such a thing even existed. Acidly original, she has always actively avoided being labelled as a 'post-punk' singer. She saw her role

1177 Lydia Lunch to Mute Records website.

as doing something much more confrontational, like an unpinned culture grenade bouncing around a soporific music and arts scene.

> People just don't like to be uncomfortable, but it is my job. . . . What I do is a calling, it's a duty. When I was in my 20s, I said I would be the oldest living woman of rage.[1178]

Born Lydia Anne Koch[1179] in 1959, she moved to New York City from nearby Rochester, driven by her twin teenage passions of authors like Henry Miller, Hubert Selby Jr, Jean Genet and the wilder new music emerging from the city.

> I moved to New York because of the New York Dolls. I felt like a man trapped in a woman's body, and here were men trapped in women's clothing.[1180]

Within weeks of arriving, she was immersed in the exotic art underground of the Big Apple but already looking for more. '...Patti Smith's Piss Factory, Television, New York Dolls — that was all great when you're 13, 14, but when you're 17, it doesn't push it far enough.'[1181]

In the post-punk New York micro scene, she befriended Alan Vega and Martin Rev of Suicide at Max's Kansas City. Then, with James Chance,[1182] she put together the legendary Teenage Jesus and the Jerks, where her disdain for the limitations of punk rock were encapsulated in what would be the ultimate No Wave band.

Since then, she has stamped her highly articulate, intelligent and confrontationally open personality onto a myriad of art forms and collaborations that read like a 'who's who' of underground art and music. Lydia Lunch has been true to her own vision for decades. Still touring and delivering her acetylene muse through spoken word, books, film and music, it's a muse that never falters and continues to inspire anyone who believes in the power of true art.

The noisier wing emerging from No Wave, such as Sonic Youth and Swans, was building a new kind of rock language. Initially inspired by pioneers like Glenn Branca,[1183] they were known for their use of volume drones, repetition and alternative guitar tunings. Similarly, Rhys Chatham and his guitar orchestra created a dissonant and beautiful noise that melded into the post-rock landscape.

Swans were driven by the vision of the 1954 LA-born Michael Gira, who had relocated to New York City in 1979, aged 26, with a headful of ideas for making rock music that would go against the grain. His adventures would go on to capture the dark post-punk atmosphere of the city unintentionally. Like Black Flag, he decided

---

1178 Lydia Lunch to the New York Times.

1179 She obtained her nickname from musician Willy DeVille, who was best known for his 'Spanish Stroll' hit of 1977, because she stole food for her friends.

1180 Lydia Lunch to the New York Times.

1181 Lydia Lunch to the New York Times.

1182 James White AKA James Chance was the sax playing, free jazz leader of the Contortions with a fiery persona that often led to fist fights with the audience.

1183 Branca created a dissonant, guitar-based music, sometimes with his guitar orchestra. He would not only become a key figure on the No Wave scene but provided the basis for much of Sonic Youth's early music. Thurston Moore played with him before Sonic Youth and his record label Neutral Records, released early records from Sonic Youth and Swans.

to slow the music down just as everyone else was speeding up punk rock style. Early Swans music explored space and a heavy, relentless primal groove, creating a captivating new sound. This intense music saw Howling Wolf, and James Brown grooves slowed down to a pulverising grind and dislocated moaning vocals. The lyrics detailed primal love, sex, disgust and physicality. Rehearsing in a converted shop in the then rubble of downtown Manhattan, Gira was creating a new kind of rock. With high volume and a suffocating intensity, they filled venues with an enveloping slab of intoxicating sound. It was a tough and heavy music but never 'noise'.[1184]

Gira had been on this trip from the beginning. He was hip to the dark side of the summer of love; as a teenager in Los Angeles, where his doors of perception were opened.

> The Doors were part of my whole inner psyche. I grew up in southern California, and I guess I was 13 when their first album came out in '67. I was right there. I was taking LSD and listening to it. I have listened to the first three Doors albums so many times that I could recite them in my mind. I didn't think of them as American blues. It was just its own sonic world, you know. They grated very much against mainstream America at the time, which was so different then that it's hard even to describe now. The power music could have in the culture was much more profound then than it is these days.
>
> I gravitated towards punk when it happened. I was too young for the hippies and too old for the punks [laughs] at those early punk shows in LA in '77/'78, but, for me, it was the whole of that musical kind of cataclysm that happened in the 60s to the late 70s that was pretty phenomenal.[1185]

When he moved to New York in 1979, he was soon intrigued by the No Wave scene:

> Fuck the three chords! The No Wave thing was liberating. It was not about the usual three-chords thing of punk. The scene had pretty much died out when I got there, but I planned to make something, for lack of a better word, happen in the space. New York was an incredibly different place then compared to now. The city was in decay and decline. There was lots of violence and hardship. In a way, that was a productive element because it weeded out the weaklings. You had to be brutal to get any kind of thing going and any pretension to being relentless. Many younger musicians in New York now see music as a career option. It certainly was not like that then. I worked in construction, and I took over a derelict 900-square-foot storefront. It was a shabby space when I moved in, but I did much building on it. When I moved in, it was 100 dollars a month to rent, but with much hard work, I made it into a space to work, and that's where I put Swans together.[1186]

Like other concurrent groups moving deep into the primal possibilities of rock, and darker than the darkest heart of goth – The Birthday Party and Einstürzende Neubauten - Swans were tearing the artifice away from rock and returning it to its core. They would take one riff and play it repeatedly to a hypnotic effect. With pounding drums, pile-driving bass and bituminous and minimalistic lyrics inspired

---

1184 Michael Gira hates the term noise as he explained to John Robb 'I don't like the use of the word 'noise'. It's sound. Noise, to me, implies an annoying fly in your ear sound.'

1185 Michael Gira to John Robb.

1186 Michael Gira to John Robb.

by Jean Genet and the Marquis de Sade, they created a whole new musical world captured in their early albums, such as 1983's *Filth* and 1984's *Cop*.

Swans signed to Blast First records in the UK and managed to expand their extreme, dark and relentless music to a worldwide stage. Their concerts were renowned for their sheer primal volume and the enormous repetitive riffs. It was a dark and heavy, utterly transcendental experience, and the band released a series of records exploring all the nuances of this sound.

However, the thaw in their songwriting came when they hooked up with a remarkable singer and keyboard player who had started writing to Gira in 1985, shortly before moving to New York to join the band. Jarboe La Salle Devereaux's contributions sparked a new tangent in the band's music that started with 1986's *Greed* album. Here, she brought her jazz, choral vocal skills and musicality into the mix, which now added a drum machine and grand piano to some pieces.

Jarboe's influence on the band is quite fascinating. Instead of being drowned out by the band's musical juggernaut, she became part of their core sound. Her vocals and songwriting allowed Gira the perfect opportunity for the band's music to grow organically in unexpected directions. This saw an exploration of the nuances and subtleties that were always there. The same year saw the *Holy Money* album that further turned Swans into a more complex, intriguing beast.

The following years' efforts were a balancing act between Gira's intense vision and the demands of survival. There would be albums where they hinted at an almost poppier concept veering from a gothic industrial to a proto-neofolk like on 1989's *The Burning World*, produced by Bill Laswell. This saw Swans at their most tuneful and was released in the wake of their unexpected cover of Joy Division's 'Love Will Tear Us Apart'. Taking such an ambitious project on the road was particularly difficult, yet Gira was always true to his vision, which is never easy in the conservative world of rock, and the band hit a dead end.

Out of the blue in 2010, he reformed Swans without Jarboe (who had been carving out her own idiosyncratic career with several collaborations and musical styles). He released a stunning run of albums that reinvented the band. Starting their first album in 14 years, *My Father Will Guide Me Up a Rope to the Sky*, he created a very different music that saw songs pulled out to over ten minutes of hypnotic power. The new Swans created a brooding drama and intensity that would be further explored in their later releases.

2012's *The Seer* was an astonishing and mesmerising work. The music stretched over the double album with some tracks lasting up to over thirty minutes in length, and even longer live. The albums *To Be Kind*, *The Glowing Man* and *Leaving Meaning* continued these adventures with a new sound and lineup. Dominated by powerful dynamics and a heavy, distinctive groove, these were intense, beautifully crafted heavy trips over a dark lysergic groove.

Also emerging out of the New York No Wave aesthetic were Sonic Youth, who, for many decades, was the personification of New York cool. Their breakout single was 'Death Valley 69', featuring a spooked duet between guitarist Thurston Moore and Lydia Lunch. 'Death Valley 69' was a shivering, claustrophobic account of the Manson murders, with an added creepy-crawly guitar line. The song set the template for the band's subsequent musical adventures and was the track that took Sonic Youth to the full beam after operating in the shadows for so long.

They impacted and defined underground music with their multi-tuned guitars and twin vocals from Moore and bassist Kim Gordon. Catching them live on their first UK tour, they were a band that was genuinely breaking new ground with pounding tripped-out sets of dark-hued modern psychedelia. It was a sound that crossed them over into post-hardcore and gothic scenes. Whilst never a goth band per se, Sonic Youth indeed were prevalent in those worlds, and early gigs saw a ragbag collection of paisley-shirted acolytes, refugees from goth central and the usual array of fierce noiseniks with sawn-off haircuts. The band split up in 2011, leaving behind an influential musical legacy.

Now living in New York, Jim Thirlwell's long career has seen him on an astonishing musical journey, trading under many aliases. He created a stunning and varied series of albums and musical projects throughout his sojourn. These projects piqued other artists' interests, such as Lydia Lunch, who stated: 'The unending, thrilling genius that is JG Thirlwell. Gorgeous, frightening, funny, surreal, sexy, death-defying and beautiful. Both the man and his music. My hero.'

In 1981, Thirlwell had moved to London from Australia, where his production capabilities created powerful noise records released under several aliases like Foetus, Wiseblood, Scraping Foetus Off the Wheel, The Foetus Symphony Orchestra and many more. He added space and dynamic to sounds, lacing songs with a frantic, dark humour which he then performed solo. Armed with his biker-from-hell persona, he was a tall beanpole figure with aviator shades, topped by a collapsing blonde quiff, stickman legs and cowboy boots that saw him embraced by the art goth scene.

Thirlwell's music slotted in somewhere near the so-called industrial melange of Neubauten. From the first album onwards, elements of noise and a skewed, big band swing would be further explored. Throughout his work, he would incorporate elements of 20th-century classical music, noise, Americana, jazz, punk rock, African and Cuban percussion, and epic/horror film soundtracks.

His artwork also had a powerful aesthetic, with every sleeve image being red and black with a dash of yellow and every album title being four letters long. This was the work of a strict art maverick who played all the instruments himself on his recordings, as well as playing the studio itself as a self-styled 'Quincy Jones of the avant-garde'. A Quincy with lyrics drenched in neurotic genius and a fantastic madness with themes including destruction, persecution, anxiety, abuse, incest, masochism, angst, self-destruction, self-abuse, lust, prejudice, murder, failure and machismo whilst using American colloquialism and black humour.

In New York, he became part of the short-lived 'sick cabaret' of the Immaculate Consumptives with Lydia Lunch, Nick Cave and Marc Almond, and he still lives in Manhattan to this day, and his music has expanded into TV and film soundtracks, giving full reign to his powerful musical imagination and command of atmospherics.

America, with its big skylines and bigger everything, was always more about the power and volume of metal music than the UK, which saw its post-punk scenes grow out of the subtle nuance of Bowie and the multi-layers of glam rock. Epitomising this crossover were Type O Negative, formed in 1989 and whose early 1990s albums forged a crossover between goth and metal with a dark brand of gothic eroticism.

Fronted by the late Peter Steele – a six foot eight hulking presence with a dark, self- deprecating sense of humour, and voice to match with an unlikely sensuality and emotional depth – the band set their template with their 1991 debut album, *Slow, Deep, And Hard,* which combined Black Sabbath doom-mongering with industrial and goth overtones. They defined their sound with 1993's *Bloody Kisses,* where the singer's dextrous and sensuous vocals and the band's dynamic range were fully explored. They developed their heavy, yet hooky Beatles-inspired experimental psychedelic melodies with a cranked goth/metal crossover in further albums of gloomy epics, with Steele seductively crooning about sex, heartbreak and death before the singer/bassist died in 2010 at the age of 48, due to an aortic aneurysm. The band he created and left behind had a glowering presence. Steele's legendary voice – that could switch from the shivering baritone of Andrew Eldritch to the blow torch power of metal – remains celebrated long after his death.

Outside New York, punk had already been mangled into hardcore which was still morphing into different shapes. Some bands like TSOL were merging their hardcore with a gothic twist, picked up from The Damned, whilst San Francisco's Dead Kennedys delivered insane surf-tinged garage punk that was armed with a political manifesto and a gothic bounce.

It was Black Flag, though, that truly set sail into the art of darkness. Progressive, dark music doesn't come more brazen and intense than this. The band was led by groundbreaking guitarist Greg Ginn, whose style was honed by his relentless work ethic and tour schedule. After a more 'party band' start, they had taken The Doors' LA Gothic mantle and cranked it up with a tonnage of intensity and dark, feral power. Part of the early 1980s US punk scene, Black Flag, were now being fronted by their fourth singer, the then shaven headed ball of confusion – the intense 20-year-old Henry Rollins.

Rollins joining had seen the band add darker, slower and more intense songs to their debut *Damaged* album. His then threatening muscular masculinity was underlined by the album cover that saw him stare into a smashed mirror. This shot of Rollins would prove to be one of the defining images of the new hardcore scene.

He had literally jumped into the band's van after a show in his Washington DC, hometown, and the off-kilter band were now ratcheting up the intensity with the 1000-yard stare of the new singer:

> I can only speak for myself directly, but I honestly don't think that it ever occurred to anyone in Black Flag that we were intense. It's really just how we were and, therefore, how the music was. Greg Ginn and bassist Chuck Dukowski are some of the most full on people on or off the stage. Everything they did was intense. Our environment was intense, and so we were just existing and reporting from that.

Really, there was never a discussion of things having to be intense. I remember once, right when I joined the band, one of them; I forget which one, told me that the band was a very extreme thing.

I think it was a warning to prepare myself. No matter how much I tried to be ready, it was only doing it that got me there. Soon enough, I didn't understand things any other way. So, what I'm trying to say is that intensity was never a thing that we tried to achieve; it came with the territory. We always strove for perfection in the live setting - like King Crimson dragged through hell. We practised for hours a day, five plus days a week. We sometimes ran the entire set at soundcheck. This being our value set, with the audience we had, with America being where it was at that time, there was often too much intensity.[1187]

Rollins moved to LA before jumping headfirst into one of many soon-legendary challenging Black Flag tours. These were long campaigns where the band burned up the road miles, taking punk rock into the American heartland to often extreme reactions. With his now tattooed skin a sketch pad from this new post-punk frontier, Rollins' had curated a striking look with Einstürzende Neubauten and Misfits logos, Charlie Manson memos, and the infamous search and destroy back piece becoming a powerful image of walking art at a time when tattoos were far from commonplace.

Rollins was one of the great, dark iconic frontmen of the period. He is a missing link between the hardcore underground and new high-decibel poets like Nick Cave and Blixa Bargeld. With his fascination with the dark underbelly of American counterculture, he was immersed in the counter-cultural darkness, holding Charlie Manson as a certain anti-guru. With his hair now grown into a Jim Morrison style mane and his near-naked stage presence, Rollins had the air of a manic, supercharged 1980s lizard king, cranked through the intensity and danger of the new decade. Black Flag are often placed as vanguards of American hardcore. In reality, they were an American equivalent of The Birthday Party/Neubauten musical adventure. However, Rollins refutes such a comparison:

Every band will tell you that they are their own thing, not part of a genre, etc. I get it. For better or for worse, that's how I always felt. To a great degree, I found punk rockers and all their rules of 'how to be' lightweight. Black Flag had friendships with other bands, like the ones on SST Records and a few here and there, but for the most part, we stayed to ourselves. I never felt part of some punk scene, really. As far as bands like The Birthday Party and Einstürzende Neubauten, I was a fan of both, then and now, but never felt any fealty with them or any other band. We weren't looking for adventure or danger. It came looking for us, found us and did its thing with us. Drummer, Bill Stevenson was one of the only nice people in Black Flag. The rest of us? We were not your friends.[1188]

Black Flag escaped the punk straitjacket with sludgy and powerful songs, the roots of which were first seen on the band's debut album. They developed this into a newer, darker, slower sound that confronted audiences who were only familiar with punk's

---

1187 Henry Rollins to John Robb.

1188 Henry Rollins to John Robb.

speed trials. This new music incited a cultural confrontation and audience violence that Rollins documented in his excellent *Get in The Van* book.

Their relentless touring and heavy sound may have been confrontational, but it also created a circuit of clubs and floors on which to sleep across the continent. This circuit eventually became the backbone of the new American rock. Bands like Sonic Youth and Big Black, followed by Nirvana and Nine Inch Nails, would finally break through and create a glowering and heavy culture framework.

A 1984 Black Flag show inspired the whole of the Seattle musical community and a young pre-Nirvana Kurt Cobain who were fired by the then sludgy, heavy and dark music of the band. The relentless grind of early Killing Joke can also be heard, and that stark heaviness is evident in Nirvana's output and, decades later, can still be heard echoing through the sparse dark blues of the brilliant Earth; the band put together by Cobain's best friend, Dylan Carson. It can also be heard in former Screaming Trees singer Mark Lanegan's brooding dark clouds and elixir voice in his acclaimed solo career. The three of them had once shared a house, and their fascination with an outré lifestyle and dark and heavy music would affect each of them in very different ways. For Lanegan himself, these hints of a darker, post-punk culture were drip fed through furtive trips to a Seattle record store:

> I used to take the Greyhound bus to Seattle, and it took about five hours because they stopped everywhere. When I would get there, I'd walk around the record stores buying music by the cover art. That's how I discovered Joy Division. I had no idea of what it was. I just loved the artwork. That's how I found The Gun Club. The Smiths I heard playing in a record store, and I went up and asked what it was, same with The Cure, so I bought those. In Ellensburg, where I came from, I had no place to listen to that stuff and nobody to tell me what it was. I had Joy Division's *Closer* record on cassette, and that got stuck in the car player. It was a freezing winter, foggy. It spoke to me, and I love that record to this day. It's one of the most outstanding records ever made. It saved my life, and I was lucky to come across it. The songwriting of Jeffrey Lee Pierce and Ian Curtis was personal to me but also exotic. Jeff was making something I'd never heard before, and it went straight to me. Those records are the reason I began thinking about writing myself. They were the soundtrack to my existence for a really long time.[1189]

Meanwhile, in Chicago in 1982, perhaps the period's darkest and most thrilling outfit began around a super-intelligent college student, Steve Albini. His abrasive journalism on the local scene had made an impact, but it would be nothing like as powerful as his band, Big Black.

Like Andrew Eldritch, Steve Albini was the aggrieved high IQ super nerd turned gonzoid commentator looking for raw nerve edges to press musically and lyrically and the drum machine and bass-driven clank and grind of The Sisters of Mercy was an influence. To this, he added the minimalistic pulse of Suicide and the new, noisier UK 'Death To Trad Rock' bands. Digging deep into the underbelly of America, he created songs with a taboo-breaking lyrical assault. He wrote stark lyrics about rape,

---

1189 Mark Lanegan to John Robb.

murder, arson, child abuse and misogyny, exposing America's dark heart. This, with an unrelenting, infernal, vision, and delivered with a calculating, clever, academic, and journalistic eye. Musically, the band's two classic albums, 1986's *Atomiser* and 1987's *Songs About Fucking* were driven by a heavy tuff gnarl bass and the twin guitars of Albini and the late Dave Riley, who died in 2019.

During Big Black, he honed his recording techniques, arguably becoming the world's best recording engineer. His visceral studio sound is stamped onto hundreds of releases, including Nirvana's *In Utero* album. His current project, Shellac, have released an intermittent and brilliant series of records that have taken the dislocation of the mid-1980s 'Death To Trad Rock' bands and reinterpreted it to perfection.

Also in Chicago, the Waxtrax label created a playground full of heavily treated guitars, hi-energy fist fuck beats and a confrontational attitude that saw the new industrial morph into releases from Revolting Cocks and Ministry, which laid the foundations for Nine Inch Nails and Marilyn Manson, who would take the new American Dark to the top of the charts. Marilyn Manson himself would become a much debated goth icon of sorts until one scandal too many knocked him from his perch. His exact role in the goth lineage was fiercely argued, but his fusion of rock, industrial and goth had been a dark and potent affair which had seen him regularly top the album charts worldwide in a twenty-year career. His image and fascination with the goth themes of sex and death and the macabre undertow of modern life had seen him lurk very successfully for years. His 1996 breakthrough album, *Antichrist Superstar,* was a fascinating and deeply ugly, squalid affair riddled with dark humour, a compulsive intelligence and the wish fulfilment of someone who understood the machinations of the music business. He was to become the ultimate dark lord rock star in a run of musically intense, but captivating, albums, before his downfall.

All great music thrives on magic and mystery; perhaps the perfect musical distillation of dark, modern unease is found in Montreal's Godspeed You! Black Emperor. The band operate within the realms of post-rock but bring in a billowing cloud of melancholy and epic beauty to their music. This is a sound primarily driven by their string section, with which they make captivating albums. Named after a 1976 Japanese biker documentary[1190] by director Mitsuo Yanagimachi, their mysterious influence can be found all over modern music like in Mogwai's spectral electricity and Clint Mansell's brilliant film soundtracks.

America's dark journey had been very different from the UK's.

Like punk, it took a decade for goth culture to embed itself across the vast nation. By that time, it would crisscross with industrial rock, metal and post-hardcore, creating a stadium-filling dark energy and an underground of new generation bands. It would also flavour the look of Emo and many other micro scenes that emerged in its wake. Emo was the bastard offspring of goth and had emerged from the 'emotional hardcore' of post Discord bands in early 1980s Washington DC and, over the years, had become more immersed in a skinny jeans and eyeliner take on

---

1190 The film followed the biker gang 'The Black Emperors'.

goth style. If emo was to become goth's younger cousin, goth itself is now part of the cultural music core of the USA, and its style has become a staple in music, film and literature, providing another texture to call up in the showbusiness machine and a 2022 re-imagination of the classic American Gothic painting would see the father and daughter covered in tattoos, piercings and dyed hair.

Chapter 35

TRANS EUROPE EXPRESS

Get on board! Kraftwerk's 1977 *Trans Europe Express* album had seen a celebration of the joys of European train travel across a continent in a state of creative flux. The groundbreaking group were vital in this new narrative that found a way to demonstrate pride in their German identity without the wartime baggage and with an added 'hurrah' for the new Europe and its inherent culture.

They had created a futuristic existence that was optimistic and technologically progressive. Their new European music drew from the continent's traditions whilst swerving the Anglo-American axis that had been the driving force of post-war pop culture for decades. Kraftwerk were pioneers. What was taboo was now totem. Whilst listening to Anglo-American music was once seen as a form of cultural de-Nazification, it was now time to celebrate a new post-war Europe.

Once on board the Kraftwerk Express, they underlined that being German was being European. There was no clash; Germany was now a place of cooperation, not coercion, and Europe was a cultural powerhouse. It was a bold and powerful statement and a pivotal moment in the awakening of the continent's own musical culture that flowered in the post-punk period. This was a new, genuinely autonomous and modern, digital, ethnic type of music that had many goth moments and was needed to reveal a new European identity. And post-Kraftwerk, it was everywhere across the continent.

Late '70s Europe was brimming with its own scenes and influences. There was Berlin's creative surge, Yugoslavia's brilliant, intense, yet unknown scene, East Europe's cold and melancholic underground obscurities, the French post-punk scene with its mixture of drum machine driven post-punk skreegh and electronic experimentation, Belgium's idiosyncratic new beat and even Norway's emerging early '80s black metal scene that took part of its influence from the darker and denser end of goth.

There were different bands and new sounds that drew from a European cauldron and tradition as much as rock's fixation on American blues. It was a new palette that cultural commentator Rachel Veloria Rose celebrates: 'For me, Pink Turns Blue, Malaria, Leitmotiv, The Last Days of Jesus, Lucie Cries, Miguel (from Poland) and the Living Dead (sadly no more!) and Los Carniceros del Norte, Gaznevada from Italy, and Neon – there is so much out there now...'[1191]

Across Europe, a line was being drawn in the pop culture sand. In Germany, The Neue Deutsche Welle announced a generation gap in the musical lineage whilst also underlining a Germanic take on the new music with a loose cabal of new German bands who were linked by their post-punk adventures like Abwarts, DAF, Einsturzende Neubauten, Die Krupps, Liaisons Dangereuses, Malaria! Mania

---

1191 Rachel Veloria Rose to John Robb.

D, Mittagspause, Der Moderne Man, Palais Schaumburg, Der Plan, Die Todliche Doris, Xmal Deutschland and many others.

One of the main bands, and Dusseldorf's key post-punk contribution, was Deutsch Amerikanische Freundschaft, or D.A.F., with their astonishing, stripped-down, pumping sex beat. Their name is a neat nod to the international relations between Germany and America in the post-war period – a friendship that had its pros and cons.

Their music was built for the dance floor with pumped EBM industrial electropunk anthems chewing on words and pulverising sequenced bass lines like their classic 'Der Mussolini' – a thrilling exploration of their marriage of the digital to the flesh, in one perfect whole. It was built around breathless phrases delivered over a strident backbeat with the voice and drums cranked with a propulsive modern technology.

Meeting at the influential Ratfinger Hof club, where so much of the Neue Deutsche Welle coalesced, in Dusseldorf in 1978, the late singer Gabi Delgado and multi-instrumentalist drummer Robert Görl were tap dancing on the musical boundaries. Combining a perfect heavy drum driven groove with the frantic vocals, their minimalist pounding songs were performed with homoerotic muscled, oiled torsos resplendent in tight, black leather and SM regalia, making DAF instant club favourites. Robert Görl described the sound on their 1981 big hit *Alles Is Gut* album in Melody Maker as 'We want to bring together this high technique with body power, so you have the past time mixed with the future,' whilst Gabi Delgado described his idiosyncratic vocal style as looking for a new Germanic vernacular:

> The singing isn't like rock 'n' roll or pop singing. It's sometimes like in a Hitler speech, not as a Nazi thing, but in the German character, that crack! crack! crack! way of speaking. From the beginning, DAF didn't want to imitate American pop, rock or whatever. We think there is a powerful American influence everywhere in culture, television, and music already, so in the beginning, one of our primary concerns was to refuse to imitate rock n roll and to refuse to sing in English. We have our own identity. Our identity is not American.

Formed in Hamburg in 1980, Xmal Deutschland's driving and dark music briefly flourished. Their 1982 release 'Incubus Succubus' would become a scene classic with its brooding intensity that aligned perfectly with the band's striking image. A British tour opening for Cocteau Twins resulted in the deal with 4AD, and their well received debut album, *Fetisch*, released in 1983, saw them break through to a significant cult status. Their home city had its own post-war narrative and its own radical post-punk and DIY scene built around Ripood Records and Albert Hilsberg's Zickzack label that had released Einsturzende Neubauten's debut, *Kollaps*, which former singer Anje Huwe celebrates.

> Berlin was the walled city which I didn't like because this wall character was like a prison to me. It had that narrative of David Bowie and Iggy Pop living there, but Hamburg had a pretty big underground scene. We are very much like the northern people in the UK in how we talk, which is very tough, and we are very different compared to Berlin. Berlin musicians were frightened by how tough people here were. There was no in-between, but it was also a very open city as well

when I grew up here. I lived in the St Pauli area – the Reeperbahn of the squats where I had moved from my parent's place. When I moved to London, I kept my apartment here. I was always going to move back.[1192]

It was in this dynamic post-punk environment that the band coalesced.

In the beginning, I shared a huge apartment with Einsturzende Neubauten and Christiane F, who were in town at the time because they worked on a big theatre play – they made the music for it. We were very much part of the arts scene in Hamburg, and we formed in 1980 and started from not knowing about music to soon playing live. Our first gig was with Palais Schaumburg at a New Year's Eve art party. I didn't even think I would be on stage, but there I was.

When the band started, we didn't fit in. People always said, 'you sound so British and not German, ' which was bizarre. People said 'why don't you go to Britain and work there?' Because the German sound at that time used different drum and guitar sounds and presented itself differently. I guess that's the reason we signed to a British label. Ironically in the UK, they said we were very Teutonic and German-sounding! All my life, there has been a situation where I didn't fit in.[1193]

Moving to the UK, they signed to 4AD, where the label's roster and aura of cool invincibility added to the band's artful darkness.

The perception of our dark music was maybe part of our background being signed by 4AD. We liked this music and were friends with Cocteau Twins after touring with them. We didn't get taken as seriously, though. I can't explain it - maybe because we were girls and we were good-looking. Then they came up with the gothic thing. We said that's not us either! We don't want to be part of it. When we were in London, The Batcave always invited us, but we never went there. We had our own idea of what we wanted to sound like. We were reading Baudelaire anyway because that interested us at the time.[1194]

Ironically for a band perceived as being English-sounding in Germany, they sang their lyrics in German, which was rare in the early '80s.

People had just started working in the German language in pop music. I used the language like an instrument, though. The words were important, but people listened to the sound more. I tried to use different ways of expressing this, but people always thought, 'she's on drugs! she has a problem!' but they were love songs – not heavy and not political. These days in Germany, we have a lot of German bands singing in German, and it's great how they use the language – totally different. Back then, singing in German stopped us from getting bigger, but it was important to have no compromise.

After a while, you get into a structure of making music – the first album was more us, and then when we were signed by a bigger label, the producers expected us to work more formerly on verses and choruses and that kind of stuff, and then the way of writing is different – using words – softer words. When writing, I was influenced by the sound of the band. I was the last to come up with my part. I never saw myself as a singer. I was a performer. The singing I liked in the end, and the last songs we wrote, I enjoyed singing because my voice had developed.

1192 Anje Huwe to John Robb.

1193 Anje Huwe to John Robb.

1194 Anje Huwe to John Robb.

Xmal Deutschland were big on the nascent goth scene. They looked the part – dressed in black with great exploding hair and an air of icy cool with an artful approach to their pounding, darkly atmospheric music. However, increasing internal tensions and an unforgiving music business ended the band. Anje Huwe went on to present a techno show on German TV and is now a well-respected artist creating captivating Day-Glo pieces.

> After the band, I went back to my art. I decided at some point to concentrate on that instead, and I started selling it. I found colour more interesting than the music. I always say I paint music, and I hear colour. My work is a synaesthetic translation of sounds and tones whilst my paintings can be heard with the eyes. It was always that way, even in the band I would remember songs as colours – like, this is the red song, or this is the blue song.
> I was not interested in music at all for many years. There were lots of offers, but I turned them all down. Recently I worked in the studio on various songs that were pretty doomy, and it was interesting as an exercise to see how electronic music works.[1195]

Already one of the key pillars of the scene, with their groundbreaking albums like *Stahlwerksynfonie,* Die Krupps were key figures in German post-punk. Their stripped-down post-Public Image grooves with metal percussion were pioneering in the form, and they were rivals with Einsturzende Neubauten for the post-punk experimental crown in Germany. One of the offsprings of the band were the glacial pop trio of Propaganda, who found their chart success in the mid-'80s after being signed to leading post-punk music journalist Paul Morley's ZTT records. Formed in 1982 by Die Krupps member Ralf Dörper with artist Andreas Thein and vocalist Susanne Freytag, it was the inclusion of classically trained musician and composer Michael Mertens and singer Claudia Brücken that saw the band become the next project for the label after the huge success of Frankie Goes To Hollywood.

One of the pioneers of EBM or electronic body music, Liaisons Dangereuses, were formed by Einsturzende Neubauten founder member Beate Bartel (after her stint in Mania D), Chrislo Haas (from the original DAF) together with vocalist Krishna Goineau in 1981. They were part of the European shift away from trad instrumentation and the embracing of technology, which opened up a new raft of sounds captured on their eponymous Conny Plank-produced debut album. From Dortmund, Phillip Boa and Voodoo Club dealt a doom pop that initially came with great tribal voodoo beats that added to his melancholic melodies. His series of top ten albums in Germany has made him an articulate, intelligent icon for decades, whilst with more goth shadows, Pink Turns Blue dealt a post-Cure twilight post-punk

Phillip Boa was once asked by Rammstein to produce their first album, but the East Berlin band forged their own behemoth path. Perhaps the biggest industrial metal band in the world, their hard-driving music is like a gothic post-industrial metal danse macabre with a dark sense of humour. The group now tour stadiums

1195 Anje Huwe to John Robb.

with a combustible sense of the theatrical; a panto-glycerine live show of porno pyrotechnics cranked to the max in a sense-destroying blast of huge flames, angel's wings, juggernaut props and a macabre sense of humour. The band thread gonzoid riffs and strands of Grimms' Fairy Tales with a playful gothic darkness. Toying with the same sort of totalitarian imagery as Laibach, Rammstein enjoyed the confusion that they created, yet their exaggerating of the clichés of Germanic imagery into a gross whole and throwing them back at the audience was a parody of the clichés and has helped to see them become Germany's biggest band. In 2022, it also resulted in them having the best-selling album in Germany with current album *Zeit*.

Rammstein were not the first big homegrown stars in Germany. The nation already had its own post-punk superstar in the gothic form of Nina Hagen. Born in East Berlin, she had started her career as an actress with her mother, Eva-Maria Hagen, before joining the band Automobil. After moving to Hamburg, she formed Nina Hagen Band and was signed to CBS. Her eponymous debut album was full of the exotic madness of the singer's 'million ideas all at once' music that sounded like someone running amok in the playpen of musical possibilities like The Slits' wild-eyed older sister. It sold a quarter of a million copies in her home country, where she remains an icon, powered by her flamboyant goth style and wild presence that was reflected in her music.

Formed in 1981, Clan Of Xymox were the key Dutch band that John Peel once described as 'darkwave' with their dark electronic landscapes and pulsating death disco. Formed in 1981 in Nijmegen, the band was built around Ronny Moorings and Anka Wolbert, who then moved to the Dutch capital and released their debut dark electro mini album, *Subsequent Pleasures*, in 1983. Its pulsating keyboard-driven mystery found a perfect home on the ever vital 4AD records, where they released their third album, 1989's *Twist of Shadows*, and the follow-up 1991's *Phoenix*, which saw them break out on a cult level in the USA, building on this platform for their big breakthrough *Twist of Shadows* with production from the legendary Tony Visconti.

Deconstructing the trad rock of the Anglo-American axis, The Young Gods came out of Fribourg in Switzerland in the mid-'80s. They were fascinated by the possibilities of Einsturzende Neubauten, Kraftwerk and the stripped-down new world of sample driven creativity of early hip hop and the dark grind of dance floor goth. They briefly peered into the future and created a great post-industrial landscape of sample rock that combined the dark side with slashes of sampled guitar, keyboards and drums. Frontman Franz Treichler would deliver his Jim Morrison style croons over the top, somehow managing to influence musicians way beyond the band's fierce cult status. This included a wide-eyed David Bowie, who pointed out that the band were his introduction to this man-and-machine combination before Nine Inch Nails. 'The band that I was quite taken with was three guys from Switzerland called The Young Gods…' Bowie once explained, being in touch with the future yet again, adding, 'I'd been aware of them previously to knowing about Nine Inch Nails.'

For a brief period, The Young Gods were this future, and the likes of Pitchshifter, Mike Patton, Sepultura, The Edge, Devin Townsend, Ithak, Econoline Crush and many others were quoted in their admiration for the group. The power and intensity of their music was extraordinary, considering it was produced mainly by samples and loops. Something was enthralling about watching a band create the dynamics of a rock show with a keyboard, a drummer and a vocalist delivering precision minimalist samples with the intensity of a metal band.

France had been a prime mover in early punk with its 1975 and 1976 Mont De Marsen festivals attended by the youthful Ian Curtis. At one point, it was considered the prime contender for the European punk explosion before the UK took over. Still, it never lost its cutting edge, which went underground with Metal Urbain, who were signed to Rough Trade as a drum machine driven French Sex Pistols.

The band themselves, though, had their own agenda, and their clattering rushes were perfectly futuristic, like a noisier version of New York's Suicide. Metal Urbain's techno primitivism sounds compelling to this day - songs like 'Panik' are full of punk noise and drum machine flutters, whilst 'Paris Maquis' is still the long-lost post-punk classic.

Their influence resounds through the tech side of goth and perhaps to The Sisters of Mercy and the French love of the drum machine in their post-punk journey. Tanit released a couple of singles with a chiming darkness added to their drum machine shenanigans and a moody atmosphere that still sounds so fresh decades later. The fascinating and diverse French post-punk bands like Marquis de Sade, Norma Loy and Warum Joe have been termed coldwave for their detached machine-like rhythm sections and dark introspection. This fascinating melange of styles - the click-clack of the cheap drum machines and the treated guitars on top defines one of the great undiscovered localised scenes in the period. They also recalled the historical left-bank artistic staples of Futurism, Symbolism, Constructivism, Dadaism, and Socialist Realism. This was pushed through the DIY principles of punk rock with a nod to French New Wave and German expressionist filmmakers in feel and style and the latest advanced technologies that took the rock out of the roll and gave it a brave new sheen.

With its inherent natural inclement gloom, Scandinavia would always have a significant stake in all things gothic, and Sweden had a head start. Indeed any country with a city called Gothenburg would be a player! With Leather Nun, whose garage rock swerved into industrial and proto-goth and was released by Genesis P-Orridge on Industrial Records, they lived up to their home city's name, and a fervent goth scene of bands exists in the country to this day including the ever-inventive and popular Opted who have become synonymous with the advent of goth-metal. Next door in Norway, the black metal scene was birthed in the eighties. The movement mixed the new wave of British heavy metal bands like Newcastle's Venom with the dark, heavy end of goth with bands influenced by The Cure's *Pornography* as well as some of the artier, intense end of that scene like Einsturzende Neubauten and The Birthday Party. Additionally, one particularly famous Diamanda Galas concert in Norway became particularly influential, being more intense than anything the local black metal scene had conjured up.

One of the more critical European post-punk scenes was in the former Yugoslavia, which was a hotbed of darker post-punk. Laibach's already documented activities played host to alternative groups and artists like the grinding, heavy groove of Trobecove Krušne Peći.

Many youths were already under the influence of Joy Division and listened to their music over ripped cassettes. The first scent of goth music in the former Yugoslavia was Siouxsie and the Banshees in Ljubljana on June 18, 1981, with Pankrti in support. The first darker bands were Paraf from Croatia, and the dark dance pop project/bend Trotakt, formed in 1980, also Boa and Dorian Gray, whose art rock had a strong dark attitude.

As far as Slovenia was concerned, even after that Siouxsie and the Banshees concert, and then Virgin Prunes on February 14 1983, goth culture itself still didn't become as popular as expected, despite leaving a strong impression on the audience. There were a few outliers, such as the punk band Otroci Socializma, whose bass-driven songs were close to Joy Division. And, of course, Laibach who were forging ahead in their distinctive direction. There were also some garage bands that often used industrial elements, probably under the influence of *The Black Album* by The Damned, *Faith* by The Cure and the first two Bauhaus albums.

There was also the collective, Borghesia, who were initially more concerned with video production, but later went through a body/industrial dance floor phase that was to become very influential on the EBM dance movement.

The most important band in the former Yugoslavia came from Skopje in Macedonia – Mizar. They were a truly unique group that combined dark new wave with ancient Slavic poems, Macedonian and Byzantine tradition and folklore. Mizar were the first band to break big in that small country, singing in the national language and mixing their music with post-punk, darkwave and gothic rock. They displayed clear influences with Joy Division but with a twist, adding elements of traditional Macedonian folklore and Byzantine music. [1196]

All over the continent and to wherever the Trans Europe Express travelled, each country was now on the right side of the tracks and reacting to post-punk in its own idiosyncratic style. Whether it was juxtaposing the Mediterranean love of sensuality, romance and dark clothes with northern Europe's inclement melancholy, after the synthesising of goth in the UK, the scene would take root across Europe and thrive there until this day.

1196 Gregor Bauman, a leading music writer in Slovenia recalls the famous Yugoslav post-punk scene to John Robb.

Chapter 36

IN THE FLAT FIELD. SUBURBS & SATELLITE TOWNS

The Second Coming of Goth

In this green and ghostly land or this sceptred isle,[1197] goth was an exotic culture in mundane towns and their ambassadors of the new noise. Another musical and sartorial stitch in the British style wars. The music was born out of the very soil of the country, outside of the suffocating hipness of the big city cliques. This was a non-metropolitan narrative driven by outsiders, and a newly developing genre untainted by mainstream big city cool and the perfect misinterpretation of pop culture in secondary cities, old market towns, concrete satellite towns near London, northern mill towns and post-industrial rust belts. In places such as these, there was space and time to develop your own individual aesthetic, despite and/or because of the bleak backdrop.

In these backgrounds of frustration and melancholia, goth took root. London may have had a pull, as pop culture guru Jon Savage notes, 'The capital seemed even more alluring when seen from a short but significant distance away.'[1198] Yet so many key drivers made something in their own splendid isolation.

Pre-punk Throbbing Gristle had coalesced in early '70s Hull at the same time Cabaret Voltaire were making their unique music in Sheffield. In post-punk, Bauhaus had gathered together in the slumbering market town of Northampton whilst Bradford watched a micro scene build around New Model Army and Southern Death Cult. The London commuter belt saw The Cure develop in sleepy Crawley, while UK Decay formed in Luton, the suburbs had birthed the Banshees, and Macclesfield gave us Ian Curtis.

Goth's next chapter continued this process. Play Dead was formed in Banbury in 1980. Formed from the remnants of local punk bands, their anthemic, bass-driven songs with the flanged guitar eked out the melodies that had a rolling thunder thanks to powerful drumming that would switch from pounding to tribal. The spirit of the music was captured in their yearning, soaring vocals which combined a palpable sense of despair and elation. The band's four albums were cult successes in the post first wave goth landscape and attracted a fervent fan base. Their fourth album, 1985's *Company of Justice*, was produced by Conny Plank at his legendary Hansa studio and was released on their own label, Tanz. The legendary producer added electronics into the melee and helped to find space in the density of their sound. He also pushed the vocals into new areas and registers and a powerful clarity in the rhythm section,

---

1197 'This royal throne of kings, this sceptred isle': is part of the famous speech from Richard II, William Shakespeare's 1590s history play.

1198 Jon Savage to John Robb.

creating a very listenable, bright space without losing any of the band's billowing darkness and euphoric choruses.

In the post-punk period, the Midlands town of Redditch, where the mighty John Bonham had grown up before joining Led Zeppelin, was the home town of The Cravats, who formed after seeing The Stranglers play in 1977, extrapolating that band's bass driven template and creating their own darker, scratchier version with an added freeform sax they were beloved by John Peel. The band morphed into The Very Things in 1985, whose horror film take on their ghoulish post-punk saw them hover on the fringes of the goth scene.

29 miles to the south of Redditch, in nearby Evesham with its perpendicular gothic bell tower, were another eccentric outfit that in the early 1980s had a brief but equally compelling micro career. The Dancing Did crossed English gothic folk and a linear post-punk with a minimalist and highly original style that created songs that were like vignettes to a rural world and were heavily embraced by the goth magazine Bible, ZigZag and the more esoteric fans of the form but left them marooned as a cult band.

Fifty-two miles to the east of Evesham, Watford, with its gothic revival St Marys church, may have been a semi-forgotten appendage of London but had already gifted the world Wire. From the same city, just below the radar of the music press and fashionable cliques, were the dark psychedelics of the early 1980s band Sad Lovers and Giants. Their potpourri of skewed post-punk, atmospheric keyboards and psychedelia retained a compelling, melancholic glow, loved by John Peel and an unlikely yet key influence on many goth bands.

Perched on the edge of London, on the outside looking in, Harrow is primarily famous for its public school. It was also the home of Ritual. Formed in 1979 and with their songs driven by the thundering tom beats of future Cult drummer Ray Mondo, their twanging lead bass and added sax gave the whole sound its own flavour. Sessioned by John Peel in 1981, Ritual became the support band of choice on the London circuit, playing with the likes of Sex Gang Children and many more. Sitting 80 miles south of Harrow is Brighton which even has an 1822 building called Gothic House. In the post-punk era, the town was far from the hipster paradise of the 21st century, but it had a micro goth scene with Bone Orchard, who were fronted by the powerfully voiced Chrissie McGee. Between 1983 and 1986, they were dealing the finger-clicking swing that the Tracy Pew period of The Birthday Party had perfected. However, McGee's confident and multi-textured voice cut through it all, retaining the band's strong sense of originality and dynamics in their sound.

Bone Orchard were signed to Jungle records in 1983, shortly after their John Peel session. They quickly released their debut EP, 'Stuffed to the Gills' in November 1983 and their debut album, *Jack,* a year later. There was much potential in the group, but unfortunately, there was never enough time to explore it, and their 1985 mini album *Penthouse Poultry* was their final release.

Brighton, in the 1980s, was an epicentre for squat culture. This post anarcho-punk world was already mixed up with English folk traditions, the likes of which appealed to fans of New Model Army and primed to embrace the raggle-taggle end of goth. This combination of modern music and a more grassroots culture was sound-tracked by a local band called Levellers.

Forming in 1987, they would crisscross into different musical genres, becoming a huge band in their own right. Combining the rock 'n' roll folk of the Waterboys with the firebrand punk rock of The Clash and the idealism of their Crass underground, Levellers played free gigs and quickly built up a following of squatters, punks and many emigres from the goth scene who were all drawn to their poetic, punk-fused folk anthems. These were anthems driven by passion, honesty, a punk rock attitude and counterculture idealism, making them arguably the ultimate festival band. In recent years, the band have also promoted their own festival, a celebration of the culture that surrounds them, called 'Beautiful Days'.

This is a place where Levellers and their fans can explore their love of their English folk heritage, punk rock, goth and associated cultures. It's a place where the original festival spirit – lost over the years to corporate sponsorship, 'festival fashions', and celebrity backstage antics – can be celebrated. It is also a safe space where eclectic music packs out the stages. It's a place where Roy Harper is an icon, New Model Army get the respect they deserve and new bands, rave culture, and old school folk share the countryside air, and Joe Strummer smiles down from rock n roll heaven at what would have been his ideal festival.

With his dreads, colourful artistic eye and creative lyricism, Jeremy Cunningham is Levellers' iconic bass player. He epitomises the band and their beloved culture.

> By default, we became the spokes-band for the so-called crusty scene, which wasn't our plan. We spent our whole time saying we were not, and that there is no movement; the people you are talking about, don't have spokespeople. We didn't want anything to do with that role. We were completely out of place, out of the loop. We were not the NME critics' kind of band. If rock music is meant to be anti-establishment, then the NME and all those papers are the musical establishment, and we were quite happy to be on the outside of it all.[1199]

Their second album, 1991's *Levelling the Land*, had already set their punky folk party template. With songs that sung earnestly about their lives, their sound was a shotgun marriage of rousing English folk music and Clash-style punk anthems. Their uplifting songs and sense of community led them to deliver the message of the outsider and the free thinker without hectoring. Later albums continued in the creation of this endearing mixture of poetic and social-political reportage, cementing their status as the voice of the silenced.

85 miles to the northeast of Brighton lies another seaside town, Southend, which has a forgotten Victorian Gothic Revival cathedral called St. Erkenwald's Church. While not an obvious hotbed of creativity, it had already enjoyed a brief moment in the spotlight after giving the world Dr Feelgood who had coalesced on nearby Canvey Island. In the mid-1980s, Southend produced the short-lived Anorexic Dread. The

---

1199 Jeremy Cunningham to John Robb.

band may not have been entirely serious, but their 'Tracey's Burning' single was a brave stab at the late The Birthday Party sound as Nick Cave's droogs continued to have a profound influence on the scene with every poetic madman hoping to marry psychosis, poetry and blues rock. The single was released by the Reading based Criminal Damage label who were an epicentre of much of this new goth action and associated pop/noise, including Stunt Kites, Twisted Nerve, the Membranes, and their biggest band, Ausgang - the Birmingham based goths with towering hair whose frantic early Adam and the Ants chopping sex beat sounds gloriously impatient and thrillingly eccentric decades later.

Another similar, intense moment of creative intensity came from Turkey Bones and the Wild Dogs; a London-based group of wild-haired Scottish renegades who had drifted to the city in the aftermath of punk and had collided Captain Beefheart jazz blues with a wild dark intensity and the claustrophobia of punk to create a temporary explosive live spectacle.

100 miles to the north lies Northampton, with its gothic Guild Hall. The city was already on the post-punk map, thanks to Bauhaus. However, there were other bands struggling to be heard. The Tempest made chiming, classic, early goth, indie-rock rushes. They were fronted by Alex Novak with Mark Refoy on guitar, the latter of who went on to be in Spiritualised and The Pet Shop Boys' backing band! Seventy six miles to the east of Northampton is Haverhill, which had given the world the wild-eyed impresario Stevo Pearce who in 1981 had formed Some Bizzare records, which launched with the release of the *Some Bizzare Album,* a 'futurist' compilation of then unsigned bands including Depeche Mode, Soft Cell, Blancmange and also The The. He released many of the groups in the sprawling post-punk and goth story, such as Soft Cell, Einsturzende Neubauten, Cabaret Voltaire, Coil, Depeche Mode, Foetus and Swans, making Some Bizzare Records one of the key propagators of the form. They also signed B-Movie and released their classic, melancholic 'Remembrance Day' single - a perfect example of the curious culture soup created between post-punk, suburban new romantic and proto-goth, hovering under the banner of alternative music. Always unpredictable and with a good measure of wild-eyed belief, Stevo and the label dealt in chaos and creativity in equal measure and delivered a method to their madness with a brilliant roster of bands. From the same town, the 13th Chime emerged, a band whose long-lost catalogue now fetches a fortune on the collector's market. The band existed in the early 1980s, and their descending, bass-driven, lo-fi releases featured coffins and screaming witches in both their content and imagery.

A hefty 244 miles away in Porthcawl, South Wales, Gene Loves Jezebel were formed and fronted by the identical twins, Michael and Jay Aston. The larger-than-life characters filled the stage with their colourful peacock images and towering presence. Like most bands, they were never happy with the goth tag, which was something of a paradox as 1983's *Promise* and 1985's *Immigrant* were latter-day scene favourites. The pair moved to London in the early '80s and made a mark on the flowering post-punk mish-mash of art and music in the city at the time. The sheer power of the twin focal image, their chiselled looks, and their 'tarantula tops' spectacular hair made them stand out, and the band, briefly with Julianne Regan in the lineup, made an immediate impact. Their debut *Promise,* with its dark twists, gloomy romantic flavours, and intertwined twin vocals, caught the scene's attention.

By the time they had released their third album *Discover*, the band were on the verge of a big breakthrough. The record was quite a musical departure from their assumed goth rock roots yet possessed just enough of a quirky edge to categorise their sound as alternative rock-pop. By 1987, Gene Loves Jezebel had ditched their alternative musical edge in favour of full on pop rock. However, they maintained an alternative image for their fourth album, 1987's *House of Dolls*. At one point, it seemed as though the band were destined for global stardom, but unfortunately, it wasn't to be.

The lookalike twins were going in opposite directions. They were very different people with very different visions. Despite the band beginning to break America, Michael Aston left the band, and they continued without him and had a minor success with the 1990 single 'Jealous' from the album *Kiss of Life*. Unfortunately, they had lost the dynamic and off-kilter appeal of having the striking twins upfront.

In 1993, Michael and Jay joined forces again and formed a new band, toured and wrote new material together. Things turned sour, and they split again. Confusingly, there are currently two versions of the band. Whilst Jay's version consists of the more well-known members, Michael Aston's version of Gene Loves Jezebel have released three albums, and the fallout between the pair remains unresolved.

Early 1980s, Stafford saw a charismatic elfin boy with carefully dishevelled hair hanging out at the local college. Mark Morris, along with his two brothers from Cannock, had moved down from Motherwell and formed a band called Balaam and the Angel.

> We were all very much fans of what was going on, but from a 'musical influence' point of view, we were somewhat different. Our major influences were the likes of Patti Smith and The Doors. We were individually inspired by the punk movement and very much so by the post-punk movement like Joy Division, Magazine, Gang of Four, Killing Joke and so on.
>
> When we set out to promote our brand of music, we actually made a point of wearing white or colourful clothing to embellish our flavour of music – brighter and uplifting as opposed to the darker moods of that time. We wanted the image to complement the style of our music. The music journos back then had the greatest difficulty in finding a pigeonhole to put us in. The whole concept and mystery was totally our own individual evolution, and we were very proud of it. So, I guess we are saying that in some quarters, we were viewed negatively and quite possibly unjustly.[1200]

The recently reformed band produced a series of self-released EPs were the first releases on the Chapter 22 label set up by manager Craig Jennings which has become a key label in its own right. Their angelic-voiced take on goth and alternative saw

---

1200 Des Morris, guitarist with Balaam and the Angel to The Quietus.

them as one of the nearly bands of the period, and their debut album, *The Greatest Story Ever Told,* peaked at No.67 on the UK Albums Chart in August 1986.

Further up north, there were bands slowly morphing out of punk into decidedly darker sounds. Blitz had started as a second wave skin band from New Mills, Derbyshire, and by the time they had recorded their second album, *Second Empire Justice,* the profound effect of Joy Division was evident. Paranoia, from Stoke-on-Trent, was another punk band whose *Shattered Glass* album captures a group in a state of flux. While some songs lean towards punk and others, have a darker sound.

From the northeast of England, Punishment of Luxury had been operating in isolation since punk's heyday and were twisting the form into their own new shapes. Formed in Newcastle in December 1976, they took their name from an 1891 painting by Giovanni Segantini[1201]. Their 1979, *The Laughing Academy* album was a jagged take on the punk sound and they played gigs with a theatre troupe on stage. No one could work out where they fitted into the fractured fallout, and they are a delightful anomaly straddling the hinterland between punk and post-punk.

116 miles south of Newcastle, Bradford had already provided the world with Southern Death Cult and New Model Army, yet there was another important, lesser-known band in their midst. With their pounding sound and incessant grinding power, 1919 would seem like a dead cert for a big league breakthrough. However, the gods were not smiling on the band, and they would have to content themselves with eternal cult status.

> My only regret is that 1919 were never credited with having the most monumental quiffs, post-Billy Fury and pre-Stray cats. The name came from the caved-in head of Mrs Fanny Sellins, Trade Union organiser, killed by Steel Trust gunmen in West Natrona, Pennsylvania, on 26 August 1919, which started my obsession with that year. After that, it appeared at an alarming rate; everywhere I looked...1919.
>
> It was a year of massive change and desperate rebellion. The murder of Rosa Luxembourg, the mutiny of the French fleet in the Black Sea, the Churchill/Trotsky dual, general strikes in Belfast, Glasgow and other cities, and the great red scare in America.
>
> The best 1919 image was Michael Biro's famous worker poster of a naked giant of a man about to administer the most monumental hammer blow ever. Budapest; May Day, 1919. Things were getting rather Fortean, so it became the only contender for the band name. None of the other band members would get in the ring with it, so that's how we came by the name.[1202]

1919 were inspired by the thrill of punk and had seen a Sex Pistols gig at the unlikely location of the Knickers Club in Keighley[1203]. They also attended other important early gigs by the likes of The Clash in Leeds, The Slits, early Adam and the Ants with Matthew Ashman on guitar, Siouxsie and the Banshees at Huddersfield Poly, and

---

1201 Italian painter known for his large pastoral landscapes of the Alps.

1202 1919 to John Robb.

1203 19th December 1977.

Throbbing Gristle at Wakefield. It was a veritable roll call of cutting edge post-punk experiences in faraway towns.

These live shows informed the aesthetic of Ian Tilleard – the original singer and guitarist Mark Tighe. They combined this vision with a northern 'otherness' and a raw power, adding the grime and grit of their surrounding city into the mix. By late 1980, the band had created a powerful, rhythmic post-punk with an enticing northern bleakness. Driven by a dark melody and heavy intensity, the band possessed an imagination that saw them twist their music inside out. Their debut album, *Repulsion*, was sent to John Peel and marked with a 'take it or leave it' message. Of course, the legendary DJ travelled to Shipley Bradford and asked the band to do a session.

Post-session, the follow-up *Machine* LP was heavily inspired by Joseph Conrad's classic novel, *Heart of Darkness*. In August 2015, after a decades-long break, 1919 reformed again. The tragic death of Mark Tighe from cancer threatened to pull the final curtain on proceedings, but at his insistence, they carried on in tribute with an astonishing power still intact.

Sometimes, these satellite towns and communities were not merely close to bigger cities but actually inside them. In the early 1980s, Hulme on the edge of city centre Manchester, was a vast, decaying council estate of brutalist modern architecture full of squats and a sizeable alternative and goth community, many of whom had dropped out of the nearby university or drifted into the area, attracted by its freeform lifestyle. A concrete island immersed in the city with its own distinctive culture and lifestyle, the district was also full of bands, which were made up of drifters and students with flats turned into rehearsal rooms, studios or rent-free living spaces.

In this cultural cauldron of (what was then) Europe's biggest squatted area, a whole micro-culture of groups appeared. These included bands such as indie noiseniks Big Flame, who were much loved by John Peel, and Inca Babies, who took their dislocated Beefheart riffs and wild firebrand blues into the same terror-territory as The Birthday Party. Founding member and guitarist Harry Stafford had moved to Manchester from Derby in the early 1980s, bringing his proto-goth and skewed blues with him:

> At University, I was obsessed with forming a band, having been involved with bands at school. I was in a brilliant Rockabilly band from Derby called Cat Wax Axe Co., but they sacked me for liking Bauhaus too much. When I moved to Hulme, I met Bill Martin in the pub, and we discovered that we both loved The Cramps more than life itself and formed a band there and then. I came up with the name, which was supposed to sound like a '60s garage band.[1204]

From the beginning, Hulme's concrete backdrop and 24/7 squat culture was integral to post-punk creativity.

> Living in Hulme gave us an image. The idea of punks/outlaws in the concrete jungle prepared to live in the counterculture. It gave us the sense that we all

---

1204 Harry Stafford to John Robb.

sounded and felt like we belonged to an exotic scene, like a New York or LA gang – our own Psychedelic Jungle. Our neighbours, A Certain Ratio – had released 'All Night Party' – a brilliant gloomy slab of goth funk if I ever heard one, and the peerless Joy Division had used Hulme as a backdrop, and so did we. We wore black clothes, with pointed boots and backcombed our dyed black hair into ever-unlikely swamp quiffs. Me, Mike and Bill were particularly guilty of this dress code, but I think it certainly persuaded people to check out the band.[1205]

The band's lyrics were glorious, vivid, filmic and full of dystopian brutalist imagery and the broad brush-strokes of classic American beat literature as Harry Stafford expands:

> At the time, I was studying Literature at Manchester Poly, and The American Novel was one of the modules I particularly liked. My songs were full of cut-up images from Burroughs, Kesey, Kerouac, Mailer, Updike et al. as I read everything I could buy or borrow. At the time, I preferred the American Novel as I wanted to escape the stifling domestic topics of British authors. It was also a good time for cinema: Wim Wenders, Nic Roeg, Scorsese, Werner Herzog, John Carpenter and many other visionaries. The idea of going crazy in the wide open spaces with guns, spaceships and Cadillacs seemed to be the only way to express oneself. It all seems a little vacuous now, but I was 21 and had discovered ART![1206]

Inca Babies soon found a home on the northern goth scene but felt more like renegades from a far-flung, exotic Americana of their own imaginations.

> We were discovered by Red Rhino in York, who financed most of our records, and we soon realised that Yorkshire was the home of the Northern scene. We played gigs with Skeletal Family and The Sisters of Mercy and later other bands like Sex Gang Children, Play Dead, Sunglasses After Dark, Bone Orchard, Nick Cave, and Alien Sex Fiend. We didn't see ourselves as goth, because we didn't want to sound British. We felt that bands in the scene sounded very English, Joy Division were a very English band to me, and while we liked them, we didn't want to sound like them. Our heroes were The Birthday Party, The Gun Club, The Cramps and Ramones. What came out of all those influences was thrashy post-punk. In hindsight, I think we also owed a lot to The Fall, Black Sabbath, Wilko Johnson[1207] and punk.[1208]

On the shores of pop culture, there have been endless waves of goth, and they keep coming. The mid-'80s onwards saw the second wave that had a certain linear quality as the new bands took the influence of the key players and operated within the confines. Hailing from Birkenhead, few bands managed to rise above the constraints, like Rosetta Stone, best heard on their *Adrenaline* album, released in 1993 that owned the latter day dance floors and saw the band reach the peak of their popularity. They were who were one of the biggest successes of the period. Their production and vision

---

1205 Harry Stafford to John Robb.

1206 Harry Stafford to John Robb.

1207 Wilko Johnson is the hugely influential guitar player from Dr Feelgood. Arriving on the pub rock circuit in 1975, Dr Feelgood paved the way for punk with their kinetic live shows, driven by Wilko's stage presence and his unique, chopping Fender-Telecaster-guitar style.

1208 Harry Stafford to John Robb.

were way ahead of most of the pack, sometimes adding spook strings that perfectly couched Porl King's vocals. Embracing the vampire and in love with the goth tag and with a name like Nosferatu, the South London band could be little else than operating within the cherished ideas of the form with their lilting and melancholic melodies best captured on their debut album, *Rise*. Then there a whole host of cult names like BFG, Twisted Nerve or the wonderful And Also the Trees.

Post Fields of the Nephilim, there were a clutch of bands who were immersed in the literate side of the occult, like Garden of Delight, who released a series of seven albums one per year with seven tracks on each[1209] . They sang songs of the omnipresent Aleister Crowley, Lovecraft, magick, mysticism, Sumeria, and the occult. Love Like Blood also took the Lovecraft root and delivered it with the same gravelly gravitas as Carl McCoy, with an added metal edge interspersed with a luxurious twelve-string guitar. Further (in a flat) afield, were The Wake, from Columbus, Ohio - they were the first true American goth band and were the midwest's take on The Sisters of Mercy, their debut *Masked* is their calling card and established them as one of the biggest second wave bands worldwide. Taking their name from a song by The March Violets, Children On Stun were one of the more popular bands of the new chapter, and their Sisters drenched sound underlines just how potent an influence Eldtrich had been on the scene.

Since then, the waves have kept crashing and reinventing the black as goth has become entwined with all forms of culture.

1209 The number 7 had been a magic number from antiquity when it had been the number of known planets and then transferred into 7 gods and 7 heavens.

Chapter 37

APOCALYPSE NOW! GOTH'S END DAYS

In these most dystopian of times, even the darkest imaginations of centuries of Gothic writers and musicians could never have concocted a story or song to mimic the world's current gloomy malaise. Trapped in the claustrophobia of a pandemic followed by the terror of modern life and a runaway planet run by inept leaders, the dark visions of mystics and shamanic creatives would be tested to their outer limits in an attempt to soundtrack contemporary society. Many may ask where the righteous anger of punk has gone, yet melancholia is, equally and ironically, a perfect retreat from the madness of the modern world and its carnage visor news bulletins.

21st-century goth is a dark cultural shade, available for anyone who wants to add a veneer of caliginous content to their schtick. Most pop culture is now in a minor key instead of the major key, and 24-hour rolling news delivers 'end of times' headlines, filled with apocalyptic gothic imagery and the nightmarish images of a J.G. Ballard novel come to life.

It's hard to shake the nagging feeling that Jaz Coleman was right all along.

Modern life is couched in a cinematic backdrop of darkness. Today, the stark images of goth offer a series of easily identifiable tropes, ripe for the mainstream to employ without ever needing to acknowledge their roots. The seeds sewn in that post-punk period have sprouted so much creative DNA that it's almost impossible to gauge who or what fits into the genre now.

The dark energy is everywhere, and it enthrals us, and what was once cult is now mainstream.

The current manifestation is *Wednesday*; the American coming-of-age streaming TV series directed by goth fan Tim Burton is based around the character of Wednesday Addams and full of goth touch points. The supernatural, dark comedy, mystery, and horror TV series comes with a great soundtrack and trad goth clothes; it has put the mainstream focus back on the culture yet again.

Every year, a fashion collection takes to the catwalk dressed in black and is daubed 'goth'. The high fashion usage of the G-word is a cyclical process, returning every few years to remind readers of how to wear black in a heatwave and which gothic look is best suited to the gym. Footballers have long been co-opting the Mohawks that were style staples from the period, and pre-customised leather jackets are available on every high street and designer store. In 2016, Kim Kardashian stepped out in a heavily studded leather jacket painted with band logos that were the mainstay of the punk and deathrock scenes. Kardashian's version was not a self-customised work but a creation of Enfants Riches Déprimé[1210], a brand that charged her thousands for the privilege.

1210 Los Angeles and Paris based luxury fashion brand.

Vogue curates lists of 'The Best Gothic Runway Looks of All Time',[1211] where dark wardrobes become separated from their musical roots, distilled to a series of 'looks' and nothing more. 'How to Get That Glam Goth Look That's All Over the Runways', a Vogue article from 2016, presents questionable answers to fashion conundrums that arise from appropriating the subculture's look:

> So how exactly to wear that Elvira-esque lace dress? Top it off with some pentagram hoops and blue velvet platforms! Want to add a pop of colour to any shadowy ensemble? Some crushed velvet fire engine red creepers allow for the perfect bit of contrast. It turns out that going goth doesn't have to be so dreary after all.[1212]

Mainstream pop loves a goth dabble. In 2013, pop and R&B singer Rihanna adopted a darker look of band t-shirts and black lipstick, tagging herself online as #ghettogoth. Her series of looks and hashtags set the internet ablaze, creating a brief fashion wave of highly 'instagrammable' hip-hop meets-goth aesthetic. She also chose to wear black lipstick for her 2016 *ANTI* album, and in 2018, the singer shared a makeup video for 'goth chic casual' on her Fenty Beauty YouTube channel, following the production of her own black lipstick.

Such articles sent knowing murmurs and grumbles across the subculture, frustrated at the co-opting of their style. Black lipstick, in particular, appears to be one of the enduring markers of 'otherness'; a bold choice, identifying the wearer as committed to their dark aesthetic. Yet, as goth leaves and re-enters the fashion world, what was once repulsive, becomes 'wearable for special occasions.'[1213] 'Pop goth', 'goth lite' and 'black dressers' in mainstream pop and fashion take the surface and non of the depth of the culture.

Emo took goth into a new generation whilst new generation bands like My Chemical Romance, Evanescence or HIM, take a darker turn, going minor key or toying with the melancholic with matching styles. Weeknd, The Killers, Cold Cave and even bands like The 1975 get their goth freak on for an occasional darker song.

After a couple of decades where electronic music dominated the clubs and the goth scene, the older generation yearned for new bands to carry the flag. This sense of need melded with a new generation who were gleaning their information online, and the resulting scene has been a thrilling melting pot of styles. The world is full of newer bands touched by the dark velvet hand of goth like The Soft Moon, whose Cure-meets-Nine Inch Nails influence has marked them as innovative scene leaders. Similarly significant are Florida's Crüxshadows, who sport a poppier sheen, and Germany's: Wumpscut: who deal in electro-industrial. In their wake are many contenders like UK's Strange Bones with their kinetic intensity and electronic energy, post-punk guitar bands like Fontaines DC, Crows, Just Mustard or the gothic post-punk of Freya Beer. In electronic music, there is the spectral electronic music of

1211 *Vogue Online*, Kristin Anderson, 31 October 2015.

1212 *Vogue Online US*, Liana Satenstein, Edited by Anny Choi, 24 February 2016.

1213 Harper's Bazaar, Jenna Rosenstein, 1 October 2018.

Gazelle Twin, Lonelady, and even Aphex Twin at his most bonkers and atmospheric.[1214]

There is Blaqk Audio - the Depeche Mode drenched side project of AFI's Davey Havoc and Jade Puget, the aptly named Dark, the dark post-punk of Nadine Shah or Warmduscher or the death disco of Mango In Euphoria. Then there is The Birthday Massacre and their melding of electronic, goth and industrial metal into a spooky whole as well as Raise the Sky and also Twin Tribes revisiting of eighties coldwave.

There are now goth tinged bands everywhere, Angels of Liberty, Cemetery, Dead Space Chamber Music, Virgin In Veil, One Last Caress, Tragic Black, Miracle Scar, Crimson Scarlet, Roadside Memorial, Deathcharge, 13th Sky, and Moira Scar are just a handful of the many names who are reinventing the dark for a new generation.

Arguments rage over whether bands such as She Wants Revenge are goth or not, although their interface between pop punk and goth is one that AFI had previously enjoyed and with which My Chemical Romance had hit pay dirt. She Past Away are a Turkish darkwave duo who are the culmination of this contemporary dark style. No one expected Turkey to hold the key to modern goth, but here they were in all their gloomy reverbed glory – a clear sign that the form can lay its own roots around the world and maintain the culture. Their mix of post-punk, goth and darkwave captured on their 2012 album *Belirdi Gece* brought a new, distinct voice to the goth conversation.

Audible melancholia was further explored by underground bands like Elend,[1215] whose use of chamber orchestras saw them living up to the German translation of their name. Added to this were Nox Arcana's ambient take on the form, Dead Space Chamber Music's atmospheric and traditional choral reinterpretations, Dark Sanctuary's ethereal colouring, Sopor Aeternus & The Ensemble of Shadows' gothic metal, Les Secrets de Morphée's operatic vocals or, in the case of Milan's Camerata Mediolanense, madrigal-esque vocals. Autunna et sa Rose use chamber music vocals together with a spoken dramatic monologue to significant effect. Let's not forget the captivating genius of Wardruna and their Viking folk music about nature and forest lore or Dead Skeletons - the Icelandic band with their mystery occult laced drone dark psychedelia - gothedelics! And taking things even further was Jozef van Wissem and his dark droning gothic lute playing.

The combination of gothicism and neoclassical can also be traced through many Black metal bands' escape routes from the strictures of rock, as with Opeth, Ulver or Sunn O)))'s guitar drone. Glasgow band Mogwai became leaders of the post-rock scene but were always happy to embrace The Cure, Bauhaus or The Sisters Of Mercy as key influences.

Goth's musical roots have extended everywhere. Bristol's Massive Attack wear their post-punk influences on their sleeve. Their combination of melancholia and the groove of black music, such as hip-hop, has helped to pioneer the trip-hop subgenre

---

1214 They are not actual twins…

1215 Elend translates as 'misery'.

alongside bands like Portishead, which, in turn, influenced many later-day goth bands who utilised the same beats. Their *Mezzanine* album is a tremendous latter-day brooding goth masterpiece in all but name. Their live cover of Bauhaus's 'Bela Lugosi's Dead' is a perfect reading of the song, toying with its dark dub undertow and razor-sharp tension. Placebo continue to fill stadiums with their goth tinged melodies about sexuality, drugs and late-night neon-lit adventures. Straddling that space between Sonic Youth's post-rock, detuned rushes and the dark stuff made them a pointy shoe in for later goth enthused generations. Suede also gave their dark indie a gothic sensibility with their songs and music that was driven by suburban sex, dark backdrops, and esoteric visions.

Savages burst on the scene in 2011 like a reinvented Bauhaus for the 21st century. They reimagined that most classic of goth bands, and their everyone playing lead into new shapes and styles with the same tribal darkness and intensity. The further twist was that they were four women breaking the trad mould of male-dominated bands, creating new and inspirational templates for what has always been an audience built on equality. Savages released two albums that have reinvented the past into the future, and their incendiary live shows were full of razor-edge dynamics, sex and danger. Currently, singer Jehnny Beth has struck out on a solo career that explores the hinterland between goth's love of sex and death and casts a shadow over an industrial backdrop with her charismatic and powerful music.

In rock music, the future is female, and what was once a rarity is now standard. In the 21st century, most contemporary groundbreaking music is made by women. Anna Von Hausswolff is creating dramatic canyons of atmospheric sound – emotion-fuelled Scandinavian skyline melodies filled with melancholia and joy over the church organ's haunting tones. She makes vast and epic songs that combine drone with glacial vocal lines and the thrill of the melodramatic and dark. Chelsea Wolfe is moving from starker goth industrial roots to a more nuanced Kate Bush dynamic. Zola Jesus took her classically trained voice and applied it to a post-punk neo-gothic industrial series of experimental clatter with synths that she has turned into a dark soundscape.

Even modern pop can sometimes have a gothic hue.

Lorde dressed darker with black lipstick but had a melancholic twist to get goth pop to match, rapper Rico Nasty adds smudgy mascara noise to her hip-hop skreegh, and Doncaster pop youth Yungblud dresses like an outtake from a Tim Burton movie. Grimes makes wonderful mystery-laced electropop with a constantly changing elfin wardrobe and an innate gothic darkness, whilst Billy Eilish dominates the charts with her inventive goth pop and her connection with green issues and darker stylings.

Meanwhile, Hans Zimmer's brooding soundtracks sculpt the goth atmosphere for the *Batman* films, whilst former Pop Will Eat Itself member, Clint Mansell, has written brilliant film soundtracks that have the ambition of classical within a cinematic context, all with the added goth tinge from his teenage musical loves. His soundtracks for *Moon, The Fountain, Black Swan*[1216] and many others match the sparse beauty of melancholic classical music with post-rock.

> The thought of toying with goth's dark freak show remains irresistible and I also grew up watching many films with my dad at home, and I was always affected by film music, which can bring you into contact with many genres. It was how I first heard Pachelbel's Canon, which, when you are 13 or 14, you think, oh hell, what's this?[1217]

The Art Of Darkness is everywhere you look. Films are steeped in dark matter, matching the dysphoric zeitgeist. The latest film in the Batman saga, 2022's *The Batman*, is mired in gothic gloom. 2019's *The Joker*'s gothic visuals and the uber-brooding dystopian atmosphere was enhanced by the fantastic, desolate beauty of the soundtrack from Icelandic composer Hildur Guðnadóttir. Her gothic cello drone soundscapes painted desolate, sonic, gothic images.

Films were arguably the biggest co-opters of the goth aesthetic. Lydia Deetz in Tim Burton's defining 1988 *Beetlejuice*, 1992's *Bram Stoker's Dracula,* and 1999's *The Matrix* are all stylistic landmarks. Guillermo Del Toro's *Pan's Labyrinth* (2006), is filled with the lingering images of goth culture and uses gothic horror to demonstrate the monstrosities of fascism and underline the importance of revolt and resistance against state oppression.

Virtually all of Tim Burton's filmography, like *Corpse Bride, Dark Shadows, Wednesday* – and even his Batman films – are a mixture of Gothic macabre, ghoulish horror, manic lead characters and creepy scores with an added playfulness. His *Batman* films saw Gotham city live up to its name under the tutelage of the goth-loving director, with the comic book superhero finally getting in touch with his melancholic side. Tim Burton has made a career as *the* post-gothic director and the filmmaker who grew up with goth and wears his influences with pride with his 'gothic suburbia' that uses claymation, stop motion, and shadows to perfect this aesthetic.

Recent films have seen Batman stray further from the rubber closet, adding vast amounts of goth and fetish wear into his wardrobe as the films' backdrops become ever darker and more woebegone. Burton had arguably already made the seminal modern goth film with 1990's *Edward Scissorhands*. It was the ultimate vehicle of Gothic otherness with great hair and a latter-day fairy tale film with actor Johnny Depp as a gothic-haired creation, much like a cross between Robert Smith and Peter Murphy. Burton's *Ed Wood* is similarly relevant. It is a funny yet moving tribute, not only to Wood but to Bela Lugosi too, sensitively depicting their friendship and Lugosi's tragic demise into heroin addiction as a dying Hollywood star.

Film, of course, was always a perfect medium for Gothic adventures. The new form arrived at the turn of the century and was an even more suitable medium for the flickering shadows of fear than the printed word. The history of cinema has undoubtedly helped to create a celluloid backdrop to goth culture. From Dracula

---

1216 Darren Aronofsky's dark ballet classic is full of an emotive goth sensibility.

1217 Clint Mansell to John Robb.

films to other early horrors, the gothic and macabre were intertwined with film from its earliest days. Many early examples of gothic media were short films, long-lost to time. However, some early examples survive intact or have been collated from various surviving prints, as with the iconic *Nosferatu* film of 1922.[1218]

Nosferatu and *The Cabinet of Dr Caligari* are, aside from gothic staples, the epitome of German Expressionist Cinema. It was a movement of great cultural importance, characterised by particular German aesthetics and anxieties. It succeeded in portraying the fear and disorientation experienced by the people of the Weimar Republic as a result of the end of WWI. Similarly, it seeks to represent unseen and uncontrolled forces at play, such as the Versailles Treaty and political uncertainty, not necessarily supernatural beings.

Most importantly, Expressionist Cinema sought to represent the fragmented psychological states of the country through manipulated visual means. At the heart of this visual language is the importance of Gothic architecture and literature, acting as a catalyst for the filmmaker's intent.

More recently, these influences are seen in *Suspiria* (1977), *Near Dark* (1987), *The Orphanage* (2007) and *Crimson Peak* (2015).

Hammer Film Productions made a whole series of gothic horror films on UK shores. More 'Carry On Goth' than the high ideals of German Expressionism, many of these films are actually more atmospheric and creepy due to their low-key approach. While there are many stand out releases – *Twins of Evil* (1971), for instance – many films were made as vehicles for Peter Cushing, Vincent Price, Christopher Lee, and Polish Jewish emigre Ingrid Pitt (Countess Dracula), who survived the Nazi concentration camps.

The controversial film director Roman Polanski also escaped the Nazis but lost his parents to the Holocaust. The psychological trauma appears to emerge in some of his greatest gothic horror works; *Repulsion, Rosemary's Baby* and *The Tenant*. The Holocaust also haunts Maud in Hal Ashby's *Harold and Maud,* which has gothic elements in the pair's fascination with funerals and Harold's obsession with suicide. Further explorations of gothic anxieties are seen in Ken Russell's *The Devils.*

As in literature, the landscape of a gothic protagonist is essential, particularly in psychological interpretations of their homes. Norman Bates' house and motel in *Psycho* are hugely important to the narrative; the house visually dominates the motel, just as 'mother' dominates Norman. Hitchcock spent some of his formative years in the Weimar Republic working with Murnau and, to a lesser extent, Fritz Lang. In films such as *Psycho*, it is clear to see these experiences with German Expressionism layered throughout his work. In Orson Welles' *Citizen Kane*, Kane's 'pleasure dome' of Xanadu is established in the film's opening as a gothic pile reminiscent of Dracula's castle. It is later revealed as an isolating prison for the man who built it.

Kubrick's *The Shining* and Hitchcock's *Rebecca* both make expressive use of architecture-as-character through the Overlook Hotel and Mandalay, respectively. In

---

1218 Dir. F.W. Murnau.

both these films, the oppressive presence of the buildings penetrates the protagonists' psyches.

Perhaps the perfect contemporary gothic film was *Eraserhead*, the unsettling 1977 surrealist debut from David Lynch that tells the story of Henry Spencer, who is left to care for his monstrous child in a desolate industrial landscape. Throughout the film, Spencer experiences dreams or hallucinations featuring his child and the Lady in the Radiator. These domestic hallucinations harken back to Charlotte Perkins Gilman's *The Yellow Wallpaper* (1892), where the mundane fast becomes gothic and threatening. David Lynch's career is full of these inflexions, like his 2001 film *Mulholland Drive* which is similarly filled with the flickers of urban gothic.

Released in 1979, *Apocalypse Now* was a sprawling Vietnam war film that was, in its fuzzy way, intended to be anti-war. However, the film became a psychedelic western, set in the Vietnam war that had defined the 1960s. With its brilliant soundtrack centring on The Doors' quasi-mystical 'The End', the film somehow managed to boost recruitment for the American Army by portraying war as the freakiest LSD trip imaginable. It gave The Doors a considerable revival that sprung them into the heart of the post-punk narrative and helped to synthesise goth.

TV is also drenched in the dark stuff. From box sets to dark comedy to gothy presenters, the culture has seeped in everywhere. Creators of modern culture like Jeremy Dyson, who co-wrote the macabre comedy series *League of Gentlemen*, was once in Leeds neo-goth band Flowers Of Agatha, a band who even played the legendary Le Phono club. Noel Fielding found fame as the 'goth one' from surreal comedy duo The Mighty Boosh and is now about as mainstream as you can get, presenting *The Great British Bake Off*.

Everywhere you look, mainstream film and TV has to have its 'goth character': Lisa in *The Simpsons* briefly morphed into Raven Crow Neversmiles, Eric Draven in *The Crow* became the go to goth pin-up for the suburban youth, Lisbeth Salander in *The Girl with the Dragon Tattoo* was suitably goth-kooky, *South Park* had The Goth Kids, and Nancy Downs in *The Craft* all took the surface aspects of the culture and beamed back a narrowed version of itself to the curious. Even *Harry Potter* has a goth whiff to its castles and mythology, fitting as book author J.K. Rolling was a teenage goth herself.

Television series like *Buffy, the Vampire Slayer* had several vampiric characters dressed like a mid-1980s goth video, the extensive series dripping with sci-fi, goth crossover. The goth aesthetic is also throughout *Dexter* (2006–2013), *Hannibal* (2013–2015), and *Penny Dreadful* (2014–2016). Each series is tinged with a goth aesthetic, from vampires to the fear of the unknown to a simple fascination with darker colours. The latter is also reflected in animation that lends itself perfectly to gothic tropes and concerns, as in *Corpse Bride* (2005), *Coraline* (2009) and *Frankenweenie* (2012).

The revolution in computer gaming is a perfect platform for the dystopian and fantasy visions of goth, with games like 'Alice: Madness Returns' utilising Alice in Wonderland's fantastical, dark visions. Similarly, there are Batman themed games,

'Batman: Arkham Asylum' and 'Batman: Arkham City'. Taking a gothic cue from Little Red Riding Hood, there is 'The Path'.

The importance of vampire-centric games is undeniable, with Vampire: The Masquerade, Bloodlines and Skyrim all proving incredibly popular. Gaming remains a popular pursuit in the goth world, with many other games boasting big goth audiences, such as 'Dawnguard', 'Dream of the Blood Moon' and the 'Resident Evil' Series. Also, there is Castlevania: Symphony Of The Night, Fran Bow, Call Of Cthulu, The Sinking City and Bloodborne, all immersed in shadowy goth graphics and themes.

In the world of literature, modern Gothic writers include Daphne du Maurier, Toni Morrison, Diane Setterfield, Kate Morton, and classics of the contemporary genre include *Mexican Gothic* by Silvia Moreno-Garcia, *Rebecca* by Daphne du Maurier and Sarah Waters *The Little Stranger*, which is an eerie and captivating haunted house story set in the gloom of post-WWII England. It's a gothic tale of class division, deterioration, and ghosts creating an atmosphere of suspense, terror, dark secrets and malevolence.

The bestselling crime novels of Ian Rankin are dotted with references to Joy Division and Throbbing Gristle and ooze a damp melancholic atmosphere. Fellow Edinburgh writer Jenni Fagan writes dark, compelling books about her home city with spectral words and a social realism with a post-punk backdrop. The Cass Neary novels by Elizabeth Hand explore brutal murders and mysterious deaths alongside a landscape of punk, and black metal, whilst Max Porter's surreal *Grief Is A Thing With Feathers* somehow entwines bereavement with a murder of crows and is a captivating read.

21st century goth can still be music. It can still be film. It can still be style.

It can also be Instagram and TikTok influencers with millions of followers, posting endless online photos of goth tinged styles and little to no mention of music. What accelerated goth culture into the 21st century was this social networking. Like so many underground and outsider ideas widely ignored by the mainstream – such as veganism and ecological issues etc – goth found its voice and platform with the fan-driven medium. Initially, goth found its footing on website forums before moving to Netgoth, Myspace, then Facebook, Twitter and now especially Instagram and TikTok.

In the 21st century, for good or bad, you *are* the media.

Goth, with its strong visual, was perfect for the modern age. Prominent goth influencers post images and videos on Instagram, TikTok and YouTube, which are then reposted on hundreds of accounts, all purveying a fabulously over the top image and lifestyle. Through a mixture of images, blogging, videos and opinion pieces, these self-styled influencers can control many of the tides of contemporary goth. Operating as a faster and more open version of the older pin-up/alt website, Suicide Girls, the concept of influencers has blurred the boundaries between audience and celebrity. Contemporary online goth is social networking visual-influencing at its fastest. Online or in the media a raft of iconic women are driving a myriad of styles.

For trad goth, Siouxsie would be my go to example, crossing over from punk into goth. Patricia Morrison's look would be another example. I think it depends on the era though. In contemporary terms, figures like Black Friday have a lot of kudos, with the evolution of YouTube, Web 3.0, and blogging, which have brought style gurus more visibility in the scene as distinct from the music. I also expect everyone would have a different answer to this! I'd also suggest Winona Ryder, Vampira, and overlapping with burlesque, the vintage glamour of figures like Dita von Teese. Certainly in the 1990s, when I was young, *The Craft* was viewed with a bit of scorn, but now Nancy in particular seems to have a cult status. Diamanda Galas would be another icon, I think.[1219]

Beneath the influencer videos and images are a steady stream of hashtags, not limited to #gothstyle, #gothootd (outfit of the day), #witchgoth #tradgoth, #instawitch, #gothgoth[1220] and #gothicstyle, all of which tell their own story. Such tags sum up the themes and priorities that dominate this 21st century's self-documented media, perfect for a form where detail and style were integral. Many social media users' emphasis on image over music has changed much of the focus of the contemporary goth culture, as Kate Cherrell points out:

> I'd say Instagram, TikTok, and YouTube are pretty neck and neck when it comes to driving the visual focus scene at the minute, but perhaps TikTok is a nose ahead. However, the influence of all three, and their emphasis, lands firmly on the image alone.
>
> The bigger 'goth' YouTubers who pursue it as a full or part-time severe revenue stream have their prime source of income via brand sponsorships. Vaguely gothic clothing companies offer a perpetual stream of complimentary items for review and paid sponsorships in exchange for video content, or 'hauls'. These haul videos are broadly more popular than anything else these content creators produce, so they become the blanket theme across the whole platform, partially as a financial necessity.
>
> As much as it may have started for love, it's the image and the clothes that offer the money; clothes become the culture. If you look at prominent gothic social media influencers such as Toxic Tears, Black Friday and Emily Boo with their hundreds of thousands of followers, then you notice that many of them are financially reliant on these sponsorships and advertising revenue. Naturally, on occasion, their other creative projects appear to be pushed to the side by the necessity to cater to trending content. Also, many alternative influencers promote their own merchandise, discount codes, or collaborative handbags as another way of buying into their image.
>
> Through the three main visual platforms, goth is distilled into an image. For the last several years, Black Friday's extreme aesthetic choices have been held up by many young people as not so much the 'pinnacle of extravagance' but the baseline by which all other goths must be judged. This viewpoint has been placed upon her and has never been voiced publicly, making it somewhat of an unwanted burden. Nonetheless, such opinions gain ground, and it seems to be another contribution

---

1219 Prof Claire Nally (Northumbria Uni) to John Robb.

1220 Originated by online influencer 'Toxic Tears' as a means to differentiate goth posts from unrelated images using the 'goth' hashtag.

to the 'that's not goth because…' debate. The more extreme looks we might have saved for the clubs are now promoted as everyday, wearable options.[1221]

Goth is perfect for a visual age. The downside is that the music is often pushed into the background. Modern culture places music as part of the swirl of audio-visual stimulation – no longer the prime driver that it was in the 1970s.

> Music plays very little part on YouTube and even less on Instagram. Occasionally, the once-prolific YouTuber Black Friday mentions a band (such as She Past Away), which piques the interest in the group. Other slightly smaller YouTubers like LilaChris and tattoo artist Spooky do the same. Oyster may showcase their favourite bands or introduce new releases. However, these mentions are few and far between on the platform, and currently, the most significant influences and changes on the scene have arrived solely via visual sources. One of the more prominent creators who stands out as having a genuine vested interest in spreading interest in goth music is Angela Benedict, who has produced several videos about her favourite '90s goth bands.
>
> I doubt that Instagram, TikTok and YouTube have had much measurable influence on the creation of music, however partially due to Black Friday's 'trad goth' look; since around 2016, there's been a noticeable revival of interest in the '80s goth scene; an interest that had already been growing in Germany for some time. There's more interest on the surface, at least, in displaying Bauhaus/ Sisters/45 Grave etc. logos and recreating Siouxsie-style makeup.[1222]

Perhaps reflecting the contradictions of the online world, the strong imagery of goth is perfect for the digital world but is also damaged by it, as Kate Cherrell explains:

> One goth influencer commented that 'people don't actually have to get dressed up and go out to the goth club together… they can do everything online.' Today, many rely on the internet for their goth-related interactions and place more importance on online visual displays rather than in-person interactions.
>
> In recent years, several YouTubers received a certain amount of online backlash for perceiving a weak grasp of the current social scene and relative interest in the musical roots of the culture. In reaction to this, some creators have produced hastily constructed DIY and music-related videos to appease their critics. Many people are uncomfortable with their lack of musical or social involvement in the scene. Still, they would rather feign interest and perceived legitimacy rather than admit their disinterest or find a body of goth music that they personally enjoy.[1223]

Social media's goth influencers frequently play up to and expand upon the established visual clichés of the form, posing dramatically in cemeteries, old factories and damp forests. A fervent underground have joined the gothic dots worldwide, from Moscow to Rio and LA to London, incorporating new styles and sounds along the way. Instagram and TikTok are changing the culture faster than the old print and TV media. Mainstream media may largely ignore the form, aside from its use in celebrity gossip columns. Still, this mainstream has been circumnavigated in the new millennium – just like digital Visigoths pouring into a mainstream Rome.

1221 Kate Cherrell to John Robb.

1222 Kate Cherrell to John Robb.

1223 Kate Cherrell to John Robb.

Like all pop cultures that see its core ideas go mainstream, goth has split into a myriad of micro scenes with a conflict of ideas across the world and subcultures. There are wildly varying interpretations of a genre that many still claim does not exist. Trad goth, darkwave, deathrock, dark ambient, gothic metal, visual kei,[1224] neo-classical, batcave, psychobilly, southern gothic, the list goes on. Modern goth is as much about these musical micro scenes as it is about Hollywood and the lipstick choices of pop stars.

> Obviously, trad goth and the 1980s look are the most iconic. In the popular imagination and popular media outside the subculture, it's still a corset, long Victorian clothes, an obsession with vampires and all black attire with maybe a hint of purple or red. Gothabilly, or 1950s rockabilly style intersecting with goth, is also really popular – swing dresses and skirts, tattooing, vintage hairstyles and accessories, lots of polka dot and cherry prints, but most commonly with a dark palette but goth has evolved now that it's hard to pin it down. Cybergoth still has a lot of currency, and it's often fluorescent not black and has a distinct style – dreads or cyberlocks, breathing masks, glow-sticks and all very futuristic. Similarly, much to the consternation of many in the scene, steampunk has also overlapped into goth, producing, predictably, steamgoth. There is Geisha-Goth – flirting with Japanese culture and looks was something that Siouxsie did, of course, but this has been broadened. Lolita Goth is really huge in Japan, and some of that is visible in the scene over here. Health goth is basically a big advertising joke which has weirdly taken off in hashtags and style – so goths at the gyms will tag photos of themselves #healthgoth. There is a Latino goth scene called chologoth. There are so many subgenres. [1225]

21st-century goth is all-pervading and subdividing. It fractures along countless fault lines as each new incomer brings in their own obsessions in fashion, art, psychology, philosophy, religion and the occult. Even music.

Goth can now also be 'health goth' lycra-clad workouts, ethnogoth's mix n match of world music styles, and the stockpiling of silver-toned Indian and African jewellery. Even the catch-all Nu-Goth is not enough.

> As far as Nu-Goth goes, *Kerrang!* magazine tried to use that term in about 2003/2004 to describe Evanescence, Lacuna Coil and HIM, but the term didn't really catch on beyond a few issues. Nu-Goth, as it is today, is distinctly fashion-based. It applies to the pseudo-witchy style peddled by the likes of the clothing brands Killstar and Disturbia; brands who place emphasis on occult graphics, wide-brimmed 'Lydia' style hats, pop culture (especially films such as *Beetlejuice*, *The Craft* and recent series like *Sabrina and Wednesday*) and being a little big magic'.
>
> It's a kind of 'goth-lite', I suppose, taking primarily contemporary fashion styles, making them black and whacking a graphic on the front. Whether it's a moon,

---

1224 Japanese glam/punk/goth style that is characterised by the use of varying levels of makeup, elaborate hair styles and flamboyant clothing.

1225 Prof Claire Nally (Northumbria University) to John Robb.

a pentagram or a stylised 'F– you', they're clothes designed to be shown online rather than to the workplace. It's very lucrative.[1226]

An example of contemporary, transient gothic style is the subculture's deeper immersion in 'witch' fashion or 'strega fashion'. Both describe the 'modern witch' style, characterised by heavily layered clothing of differing textures and statement jewellery, either woodland-inspired or relating to crystals and runes. It too, has a 'Nu-Goth' flare yet finds its roots in the Dark Mori style, an offshoot of Japanese Mori Kei fashion which celebrates a cutesy, cottage-in-the-woods aesthetic.

Steampunk has taken a vaguely goth industrial look and combined it with anachronistic Victoriana and a nod to sci-fi. Its appeal is primarily visual and social and not so much a musical genre. However, the scene has accumulated loosely affiliated bands like Alice Strange, Victor and the Bully, V2A, Steam Powered Giraffe, Abney Park and The Men That Will Not Be Blamed for Nothing. The latter are a crew of humorous Dickensian ragamuffins who exist on the punk wing of steampunk, describing themselves as 'Crusty punk meets cockney sing-songs meets grindcore in the 1880s.' They took their name from the graffiti that appeared above the blood-stained evidence, discarded by Jack the Ripper after one of his gruesome murders in 1888.

Before the digital age, gothic trends were best viewed through a subscription to one of a handful of gothic magazines. While some magazines, such as *Kaleidoscope* and *Meltdown,* were primarily music-focused, other publications, such as *Gothic Beauty,* pushed the 'goth as a lifestyle' envelope. Articles such as 'The Essential Goth Closet' were less didactic in their narrative, offering vague pointers, rather than a list of branded necessities. In an article from 2005, a columnist suggests that a wardrobe could benefit from:

> Accessories such as stockings, tights, gloves, dog collars and lots of silver jewellery, and, above all else, the essential need is for a good pair of black boots, be they buckled, laced, flat, heeled or pointy.[1227]

The attitude is remarkably relaxed as to brand specificity, which is jarring compared to contemporary 'alternative' advertising methods that push the 'it's us against them' gothic uniform viewpoint. *Gothic Beauty* arguably had its heyday in the early 2000s, where interior decorating tips were featured alongside articles from independent gothic clothing brands, showcasing a variety that much of the modern scene lacks.

The umbrella term of a 'gothic look' now incorporates heavy tattooing, wilder hair, horns (whether fake or implanted), coloured contact lenses, animal bones, skulls, weapons, folk tales, belly dancing and retro-goth t-shirts. These new looks mix ever-provocative images of sex and death with darker clothes, exotic jewellery and direct expressions of sexuality as power. Common looks today incorporate fetish wear, such as black PVC, suspenders, harnesses, enormous stiletto-heeled boots, and

---

1226 Kate Cherrell to John Robb.

1227 Gothic Beauty, Winter 05/05, 'The Essential Goth Closet', Kat Strauss.

exotic piercings, introducing more extreme and taboo images into the club and the everyday street.

Of course, goth itself had no manifesto. It was never set in stone that music had to be central to its core; it always had a style and an aesthetic. Being a retrospective term for something already happening, there were no ten commandments that stretched seductively across the black bricolage. For instance, politically, there may have been a vague embracing of the liberal left attitudes that had been at the heart of its punk cousin but not always. Aside from 2020 Democratic candidate Andrew Yang, who wanted to be the first 'ex-goth president of the USA', few goths have crossed over into the murky world of politics.

> It's certainly the case that many goths espoused the idea of the alternative – perhaps as a reaction (in the North at least) to the Thatcherite era, which makes it implicitly political. I think it depends on where you are though – John Nicholls[1228] has been researching goth and the GDR where being as goth was a highly political statement in '80s East Germany, as they were viewed with such suspicion by the Stasi. Closer to home, goth overlaps with politics but in a more subdued way than perhaps punk did – goths and vegetarianism or veganism, for instance (again, see Siouxsie), or goth and LGBTQ+ (as well as gay identities, and trans culture, I'm thinking polyamory, S&M etc), but it isn't an overt political agenda as such, and you will find goth conservatives (big or small 'c'), goth racists, as well.
>
> For feminism, the 1980s was an interesting time – we had the so-called 'porn wars' (where feminists who were very sex-positive were opposed by those who were very anti-pornography), so I can see a tension in some versions of feminism and the fairly overt sexualisation of the female body in some goth attire. Most of the goth women I know would definitely be feminist in one form or another, but again, I'm really wary of generalisations![1229]

Many modern goths are still ethically and cause-minded, having a natural empathy for veganism, feminism and other 'isms', thanks to their subcultural traditions of sensitivity and intelligence. However, there are also strong scenes of apolitical, nihilistic and right-wing goths. Some may be interested in the satanic side, and others may embrace paganism, but goth truly has no religion. There are Christian goths, Muslim goths, atheist goths, Buddhist goths, and so many more. The same applies to gothic sexuality and gender; there is no defining orientation. There are as many goths who are LGBT+ as heterosexual and as many who are overtly kinky as there are vanilla.

In 2022, the subculture has taken root in small 'only goth in the village' communities worldwide as it proliferates into other countries and cultures. From Japan's permutations of the form to sweltering dark-clad youth in Angola to a huge goth scene in Mexico, unique questions emerge about how to approach the culture clash in countries where the symbolism so beloved by goth takes on different meanings. Sometimes it can cause a string of cultural misunderstandings and unintended controversy. Do you stand alone and defiant in your music and style?

1228 An academic at Hull.

1229 Prof Claire Nally (Northumbria Uni) to John Robb.

Or do you retrieve parts of your own culture and merge them in? Kai Asmaa is from Morocco and has found a great blend between goth and traditional styles:

> It's not easy to be a goth in Morocco. Here we get harassed, and they call us Satanists and some of my friends get physically harassed. We don't get to express our passion for goth through events or anything. Even if I wear black, I still consider my Muslim religion, and I try my best to avoid anything controversial. No verse in our holy book links wearing black or listening to heavy music to Satan or anything like that, so I make sure to keep it clean with my music and my looks. I have been wearing the hijab since I was twelve, before I was introduced to metal and goth culture. I always liked dark stuff and black, so I finally felt like I had found a place where I could fit in. I was fifteen years old then, so I had two choices – either to give up one of those things that I loved so much – goth and being a Muslim. I didn't wear the hijab because my parents made me do it, but because I wanted to, so I decided to wear black and all the other goth styles with my hijab on because that's who I am, and I don't have to give up anything for anyone.[1230]

More than four decades after it coalesced around a group of charismatic individuals and flaming stars, goth is in rude health. The art of darkness is all around us, reacting to the dystopian like it always has. Every generation is still dealing with its blues. Culture blur continues - where it was once easy to stand out in the crowd, provocative clothing has become normalised, and those without tattooed skin are the exception. Piercings fall in and out of fashion and are no longer the signifiers of alternative culture. Black clothes are just another Friday night option, and skulls adorn everything from school bags to cereal packets. The dark side has become cartoon fun instead of a badge of the underground.

Yet beyond the mainstream's meddling and cynical appropriation of the surface of a darkly attractive form, the post-punk alternative's dark matter and energy are everywhere.

Thankfully, the new dark ages still require a fitting soundtrack and the art of darkness is the only modern art that truly defines these dystopian end times.

It's been a long, dark and strange journey into the heart of the darkness– and we wouldn't have it any other way.

1230 Kai Asmaa to John Robb.

INDEX